D1554313

DATE DUE

MR 26 04			

DEMCO 38-296

BROADWAY
SHEET MUSIC

to Charlotte Day State

my first friend in the music business
whose love and friendship, and gifts of music,
encouraged me to accumulate this great
collection of stage music

BROADWAY SHEET MUSIC

A COMPREHENSIVE LISTING OF PUBLISHED MUSIC FROM BROADWAY AND OTHER STAGE SHOWS, 1918–1993

by Donald J. Stubblebine

McFarland & Company, Inc., Publishers
Jefferson, North Carolina, and London

British Library Cataloguing-in-Publication data are available

Library of Congress Cataloguing-in-Publication Data

Stubblebine, Donald J., 1925–
    Broadway sheet music : a comprehensive listing of published music
from Broadway and other stage shows, 1918–1993 / Donald J.
Stubblebine.
      p. cm.
    Includes bibliographical references (p.) and indexes. ∞
    ISBN 0-7864-0047-1 (lib. bdg. : 50# alk. paper)
    1. Musicals — Bibliography.   2. Popular music — Bibliography.
I. Title.
ML128.M78S78   1996
016.7821′4′0263 — dc20
                                                   94-23633
                                                      CIP
                                                      MN

Manufactured in the United States of America

McFarland & Company, Inc., Publishers
 Box 611, Jefferson, North Carolina 28640

Contents

Acknowledgments

Over the years, many people have encouraged me — and supplied me with music. I can mention them only briefly, but each one of them will recognize their contribution.

COLLECTORS: Joe Cantlin, Mike Emmyrs, Bill Engstrom, Joe Friedman, Vi Foerster, Bob Grimes, Phil Haggard, Roger Hankins, Alex Hassan, Fred Hill, Jill Hobbgood, Harold Jacobs, Dave Jasen, Bob Johnson, Miles Kreuger, Sandy Marrone, Abe Samuels, Chuck Sanders, Bill Simon, Steve Suskin, Larry Taylor, Stan White, Howard Wolverton, Saul Zalesch, Larry Zimmerman.

MUSIC PUBLISHERS: Charlotte Day State of Edwin H. Morris and Frank Military of Unichappell.

MUSIC DEALERS: John Aaron, Wayland Bunnell, Shirley Beavers, Carol Birley, Carpenters, Norman Levy, Reba Gartman, Beverly Hamer, Herb Huriwitz, Manny and Frances Kean, Lincoln Music, Joel and Helen Markowitz, Lillian and Dulcina McNeill, Tom Maturo, Tom Norcross, Dean Pappas, Trudy and Howard Clapper, Paul Riseman, Julius Rutin, and John Van Doren.

FRIENDS: Richard Eshelman, Regis Hauber, Dee Halstead, John Leed, Diane Jeral, John Francis Marion plus Allan Behm, Jim and Phoebe Moyer, Dave Refkin, Rose and Buster Snow, Charlotte Day State, Saul Zalesch.

LIBRARIES: Gillian Anderson and the staff of the Library of Congress; Victor T. Cardell and the Archive of Popular American Music at UCLA; the Theatre Collection of the Free Library of Philadelphia and the private collections of Bill Engstrom, Vi Foerster, Joe Friedman, Bob Grimes, Phil Haggard, Roger Hankins, Alex Hassan, Harold Jacobs, Dave Jasen, Bob Johnson, Henry Oakes, Bill Simon.

Special thanks to Dave Jasen for great advice on improving this book — and firm encouragement for its completion.

Preface

Movies can last forever and can be seen in art houses, on television, or on cassette. When a Broadway show closes, it is gone forever. A few shows have been photographed and shown as movies. Many have been adapted as feature films. Quite a few have been photographed for the Lincoln Center Library, but accessibility is highly restricted. Occasionally television variety shows now available on videotape have offered a few scenes from a Broadway play. Otherwise nothing remains of these great old shows except recordings and sheet music.

Before World War I, millions of copies of show songs were sold. These were in the large size and on poor paper. However, a decline in the popularity of show music began after World War II due to the advent of television and the disappearance of the family piano from many homes. Today there are fewer Broadway shows due to the high cost of production, and consequently fewer songs. (Some say a lack of talented composers has contributed to the decrease in Broadway songs.) Recently published sheet music is harder to find because there are now so few specialized music stores.

My first exposure to Broadway music was in 1944 during my first trip to New York City. I managed to see Ethel Merman in "Something for the Boys," Milton Berle in "Ziegfeld Follies," June Havoc in "Mexican Hayride," Gypsy Rose Lee in "Star and Garter," and Gertrude Neisen in "Follow the Girls." Needless to say, I was quite impressed!

I started collecting recordings in 1944 right after traveling to New York. My original intention was to collect one song from each show. However, it was not long until I was collecting everything—large size, movies, shows, bandleaders... Eventually I collected sheet music as well.

There are many books on Broadway shows and songs. Some list all the songs but do not list which ones were published. Some list only the published songs of specific composers. This book lists all published songs from all shows by all composers from 1918 to 1993.

1

I compiled a book titled *Cinema Sheet Music* (and also published by McFarland, in 1991) which covers 75 years of movie music. *Broadway Sheet Music* will make available for the first time a complete record of 75 years of published stage music. Approximately 90 percent of the music is in my collection. The other 10 percent was seen at the Library of Congress and in private collections. If anyone owns any music not listed in this book, it would be appreciated if the information could be passed to me (in care of the publisher) so the book could be made even more complete should it go to a revised edition.

Brief annotations in the entries provide information on such matters as the popular and critical reception of a production, the length of its run, and particular strengths or weaknesses of the production (e.g., a score that was considered particularly good, or acting that was either praised or criticized). This information is included only to provide a fuller picture of the music that was a part of the show and is the focus of this book; it may suggest to the reader opportunities for further research, but is not intended as a thorough study of the stage productions.

In many cases a production was known by at least two different names — sometimes changing, for example, between try-out and opening. In such cases, because separate (sometimes quite different) editions of the sheet music were often published, the production is listed separately under each title, with cross-references to the other applicable titles.

The main purpose of *Broadway Sheet Music* is to provide a complete record for sheet music collectors, musicians, historians and the general public so that it is known what stage music was actually published and is available. For the sheet music collector, this book will provide an essential piece of information — what songs were published with collectible covers. For the musician, this book will aid accessibility to Broadway songs published in any format. For the historian, this book will provide a history of songs, composers, lyricists, and publishers. For the general public, this book enables a greater knowledge of music from stage productions.

How to Use This Book

This book is a listing of live musical stage productions, subarranged by individual song or piece title, showing composers, lyricists, publishers, dates, stars, and brief comments. The following is a sample listing and an explanation (coded by the superscript numbers) of each element of an entry:

[1]**100** [2]**Ari** ([3]Broadway, [4]1971). [5]David Cryer, Constance Towers.

[6]Ari's Promise [PC] / [6]Exodus [PC] / [6]My Galilee [PC] — [7]Leon Uris[w] & [7]Walt Smith[m] [8]*(Chappell)*. [9]A musical based on the hit novel *Exodus* lasting two weeks. [10]COVER: none.

(1) NUMBER: A serial number is assigned to each production. The indexes refer to serial numbers.

(2) PRODUCTION TITLE: This title is exactly as listed on sheet music covers. If a show has an alternate title, the alternate title immediately follows the show title. Alternate titles appear in boldface type inside parentheses. Alternate titles for which there is a corresponding production in this book have a "see also" cross reference.

(3) PRODUCTION TYPE: There are many types of live stage productions. They are broken down into the following categories:

Broadway — Shows that actually opened on Broadway for at least one performance.

Off Broadway — Shows that actually opened for at least one performance.

Closed before Broadway — Shows that were intended for Broadway but folded on the road.

Nightclub — Shows which were staged at such major venues as the Cotton Club and which produced some great songs.

Regional — Important shows that played Chicago and California but not Broadway.

College—College shows such as the "Mask and Wig" productions that generated hit songs and some that produced hit composers such as Sondheim.

Army—Musicals that toured Army camps with songs by Loesser, Rome, and others.

Black—Shows that played black theatres in small and big towns during the era of segregation.

Jewish—These shows from lower Manhattan produced stars like Molly Picon.

Circus—Songs written for lavish production numbers.

Ice—Songs for production numbers by Duke, Styne, and others.

World's Fairs—Songs by famous composers for minimusicals in pavilions.

Opera—Opera produced for Broadway or the opera by Menotti and others.

Concert—One night productions which usually were benefits.

Irish—Touring Irish shows by Ernest Balland Chauncey Alcott.

British—Songs written and published only in England for British shows.

Water—A few songs written for lavish water shows.

(4)   DATE: Year of opening or date of tour.

(5)   PERFORMERS: Two of the leading performers in the production.

(6)   SONG TITLE: Song title with spelling exactly as shown on music. Song titles are listed alphabetically, subarranged by like composer/lyricists due to space requirements. If there are no initials following the title, it is a regular, colored cover. Initials after title show the following:

[PC] Professional copy—black and white, thin paper, no cover.

[BW] Black and white cover—no pictures, titles only.

[VS] These songs were not issued separately but only in a folio. Songs which had their own folio are not selected in special selections index. Songs published in miscellaneous collections are identified here.

[B] British edition. Important songs by big composers not published in the United States.

[ABQ] Advertised but questionable. These songs are listed on cover of music but have never been seen in any collections.

[RC] Rehearsal copy. This category covers songs written for musicals, sometimes cut, that were not published. They are included because they are important songs by famous composers, which collectors and musicians may want to know are available—but only in this format.

(7)   COMPOSER/LYRICIST: Composer is listed as a boldface superscript **m** (for "music") and lyricist as **w** (for "words"). If both worked on a song, their names are marked **w/m**. Music without lyrics is only **m**. Spelling and names appear exactly as shown on sheet music and vary from time to time.

(8)   PUBLISHER: The original publisher of each song. Many companies were bought and sold and songs republished by different companies. In some cases the music was not conventionally published. For example, when the term "Army Script" is used where the publisher's name usually appears, this indicates that the script has been made available by the Army rather than a traditional publisher.

(9) COMMENTS: This brief comment gives an idea of the theme of the play, its success or failure, and some interesting information about the songs and stars of the production.

(10) COVER: This item is included for collectors. It describes what is shown on the cover: namely, stars, authors, directors, and any art or fancy lettering and designs, etc.

Alphabetical Listing of Musical Stage Productions

1 A la Carte (Broadway, 1927). Bobbe Arnst, Harriet Hoctor.

Baby's Blue / The Calinda — Herman Hupfeld[w/m] *(Harms)*; Give Trouble the Air — Leo Robin[w] & Louis Alter[m] *(Harms)*; I'm Stepping Out with Lulu — Henry Creamer[w] & James Johnson[m] *(Harms)*; Sort o' Lonesome — Herman Hupfeld[w/m] *(Harms)*; When the Moon Is High — Harry Steinberg[w] & John McLaughlin[m] *(Witmark)*. A minor revue that lasted one month. COVER: colored designs and lettering.

2 A la Carte (Nightclub, 1949). Gale Robbins, Bill Shirley.

Bella Signora [ABQ] / Face in the Crowd / I Oughta Know More About You / Poker Polka [ABQ] / Sweetheart Semi-Colon / Until Tonight — Edward Heyman[w] & Victor Young[m] *(Morris)*. A revue that became the basis for the musical *Pardon Our French* with Olsen and Johnson. COVER: bright red cover with dancing chefs.

3 Abe Lincoln in Illinois (Off Broadway, 1-21-63). Hal Holbrook, Eileen Fulton.

Abe Lincoln in Illinois Theme — George Fischoff[m] *(Saunders)*. A limited engagement of a Phoenix Theatre show about the early years of Abe Lincoln. COVER: a sketch of Abe Lincoln.

4 Abe Martin (closed before Broadway, 1920). Stars unknown.

The Right Little Girl for You — J.P. Mulgrew[w] & G.C. Mercer[w] & Felix Rice[m] *(Harms)*. COVER: sketch of a man with a shovel and a fishing pole.

5 Abi Gezunt (Jewish, 1949). Molly Picon, Joseph Rumshinsky.

Chai Gelebt — Molly Picon[w] & Joseph Rumshinsky[m] *(Metro)*. COVER: Molly Picon and Joseph Rumshinsky.

6 About Face (Army, 1944). Jules Munshin, Vincente Gomez.

Dogface [VS] / Gee But It's Great to Be in the Army [VS] / PX Parade [VS] / When He Comes Home [VS] — Frank Loesser[w/m] *(Army Script)*; First Class Mary Brown — Frank Loesser[w/m] *(Famous)*; One Little Wac — Frank Loesser[w] & Eddie Dumstedter[m] *(Saunders)*; Why Do They Call a Private a Private? [PC] — Frank Loesser[w/m] & Peter Lind Hayes[w/m] *(Famous)*. A show that travelled around camps for entertainment. COVER: various scenes from military life.

7 Accidentally Yours (closed before Broadway, 1931). Beppie DeVries.

Five Minutes of Spring / My Little Prayer / You Started Something — E.Y. Harburg[w] & Jay Gorney[m] *(Harms)*. COVER: Beppie DeVries and sketch of woman.

8 Ace of Clubs (British, 1950). Graham Payn, Jean Carson.

Chase Me, Charlie [B] / Evening in

Summer [B] / I Like America [B] / In a Boat on a Lake with My Darling [B] / Josephine [B] / My Kind of Man [B] / Nothing Can Last Forever [B] / Sail Away [B] / This Could Be True [B] / Three Juvenile Delinquents [B] / Why Does Love Get in the Way? [B] — Noel Coward$^{w/m}$ *(Chappell)*. A Noel Coward musical, considered very minor, but which did run six months in London. COVER: the ace of clubs and a curtain.

9 The Acquittal (Broadway, 1921). William Harrigan, Chrystal Herne.

Night of Love — Stephen Fuzy$^{w/m}$ & Al Worth$^{w/m}$ & Fred Heltman$^{w/m}$ *(Heltman Music)*. A drama about a murder and the subsequent acquittal presented by Cohan and Harris. COVER: Crystal Herne.

10 The Act *(see also* **In Person**) (Broadway, 1977). Liza Minnelli, Barry Nelson.

Arthur [VS] — Fred Ebb^w & John Kander^m *(Valando)*; City Lights / It's the Strangest Thing / My Own Space / Shine It On — Fred Ebb^w & John Kander^m *(Chappell)*. A minor musical kept going through the talents and popularity of Liza Minnelli. COVER: Liza Minnelli. *Note:* Originally called *In Person*.

11 Adrienne (Broadway, 1923). Richard Carle, Vivienne Segal.

The Hindoo Hop / Just a Pretty Little Home / Love Is All / Sing Sing / Where the Ganges Flows — A. Seymour Brown^w & Albert Von Tilzer^m *(Harms)*. A musical about a jewel robbery and re-incarnation that ran for six months. COVER: sketch of woman and spiritualist.

12 Adrift in New York (Nightclub, 1945). Stars unknown.

Somebody Stole My Moustache Cup — Bernie Williams$^{w/m}$ & Nick Cochrane$^{w/m}$ *(Mills)*. COVER: a gentleman with a large moustache and a beer mug.

13 The Affairs of Vanity Fair (Nightclub, 1947). Stars unknown.

My Young and Foolish Heart —

Charles Tobias$^{w/m}$ & Al Lewis$^{w/m}$ & Ted Murry$^{w/m}$ *(Morris)*; Pineapples — Charles Tobias^w & Ted Murry ^{m} *(Morris)*. COVER: red and black letters and designs.

14 Afgar (Broadway, 1920). Alice Delysia, Lupino Lane.

Be Yourself — Tom Johnstone$^{w/m}$ & Harry Archer$^{w/m}$ *(A H and C)*; Caresses — James Monaco$^{w/m}$ *(Shapiro, Bernstein)*; Dear Lonely Love / Live for Love / Man from Mexico / Rose of Seville / Sunshine Valley / United We Stand / Give the Devil His Due — Douglas Furber^w & Charles Cuvillier^m *(A H and C)*; Eyes of Blue / Why Don't You — Joseph McCarthy^w & Harry Tierney^m *(Feist)*; I Want Love — Leo Wood^w & Irving Bibo^w & Maurice Yvain^m *(Feist)*; Julie-Oolio-Oolio-oo — Leo Wood^w & Irving Bibo^w & Harry Archer^m *(Feist)*. A British musical, featuring Alice Delysia, that ran 20 weeks. COVER: the A H and C covers are black and white; Feist covers show Alice Delysia.

15 Africana *(see also* **Miss Calico**) (Broadway, 1927). Ethel Waters, Billy Mills.

Africana Stomp / Clorinda / Smile — Donald Heywood$^{w/m}$ *(Robbins)*; Chloe — Gus Kahn^w & Neil Moret^m *(Villa Moret)*; Here Comes the Show Boat — Billy Rose^w & Maceo Pinkard^m *(Shapiro, Bernstein)*; I'm Coming Virginia — Will Cook^w & Donald Heywood^m *(Robbins-Engel)*; My Special Friend Is Back in Town — Andy Razaf^w & Bob Schafer^w & J.C. Johnson^m *(Robbins)*. This musical started out as *Miss Calico*, Ethel Waters' first big role. It lasted only ten weeks. COVER: Ethel Waters.

16 Africana (Broadway, 1934). Walter Richardson, Jack Carr.

Africana / Love Me / Stop Beating Those Drums / Yamaboo — Donald Heywood$^{w/m}$ *(Mills)*; Peace in My Soul — Abe Tuvin^w & Donald Heywood^m *(Mills)*. An attempt to re-create the first Africana with authentic native rhythms from Africa. It lasted three performances. COVER: flowers and designs.

17 After the Ball (British, 1954). Graham Payn, Vanessa Lee.

Faraway Land [B] / I Knew That You Would Be My Love [B] / Light Is the Heart [B] / Sweet Day [B] — Noel Coward^(w/m) *(Chappell)*. A Coward musical with a brief run. COVER: black and white cover with titles.

18 After Tomorrow (Broadway, 1931). Donald Meek, Josephine Hull.

After Tomorrow — Arthur Lippmann^w & John Golden^m *(Miller)*. A drama of young love and family problems with a short run. COVER: Donald Meek and a young couple.

19 Afterwhile (Army, 1918). Stars unknown.

Afterwhile — Thomas Bowers^w & Robert Van Alstyne^m *(Remick)*. A victory revue to celebrate the end of World War I. COVER: Military shield and face.

20 Ain't Broadway Grand (Broadway, 1993). Mike Burstyn, Debbie Shapiro.

Ain't Broadway Grand [VS] / Class [VS] / Girls Ahoy [VS] / He's My Guy [VS] / It's Time to Go [VS] / The Man I Married [VS] / Maybe, Maybe Not [VS] / On the Street [VS] / Tall Dames and Low Comedy [VS] / They'll Never Take Me Alive [VS] / Waiting in the Wings [VS] / You're My Star [VS] — Lee Adams^w & Mitch Leigh^m *(Cherry Lane)*. This musical tried out in Philadelphia in 1988 as *Mike*, a musical biography of Mike Todd. After five years and several revisions, it reached Broadway and lasted one month. COVER: Broadway lights and neon signs.

21 Ain't It the Truth (Army, 1921). Edith Thayer.

Baby Blue / Flower of the Orient / Love of My Youth / The Yankee Soldier — Jude Braxton^w & Harry Olsen^m *(Witmark)*. A touring show performed by World War I veterans. COVER: Pink and blue letters and designs.

22 Ain't Love Grand (*see also* **Lovely Lady**) (Broadway, 1927). Edna Leedom, Donald Brian.

Breakfast in Bed / Just Say the Word / Lost Step / Lovely Lady / Make Believe You're Happy — Cyrus Wood^w & Dave Stamper^m & Harold Levey^m *(Shapiro, Bernstein)*. A musical based on a pretense of marriage lasting 21 weeks. The try-out title was *Ain't Love Grand* but it opened as *Lovely Lady*. COVER: Edna Leedom.

23 Ain't Misbehavin' (Broadway, 1978). Nell Carter, Andre DeShields.

Ain't Misbehavin' — Andy Razaf^w & Fats Waller^m & Harry Brooks^m *(Chappell)*; Black and Blue [VS] / Off-Time [VS] — Andy Razaf^w & Fats Waller^m & Harry Brooks^m *(Big Three)*; Cash for Your Trash [VS] — Ed Kirkeby^w & Fats Waller^m *(Big Three)*; Find Out What They Like and How They Like It [VS] / Keepin' Out of Mischief Now [VS] — Andy Razaf^w & Fats Waller^m *(Big Three)*; Handful of Keys [VS] — Richard Maltby^w & Murray Hurwitz^w & Fats Waller^m *(Big Three)*; Honeysuckle Rose — Andy Razaf^w & Fats Waller^m *(Chappell)*; How Ya Baby [VS] — J.C. Johnson^w & Fats Waller^m *(Big Three)*; I Can't Give You Anything But Love [VS] — Dorothy Fields^w & Jimmy McHugh^m *(Big Three)*; I'm Gonna Sit Right Down and Write Myself a Letter [VS] — Joe Young^w & Fred Ahlert^m *(Big Three)*; It's a Sin to Tell a Lie [VS] — Billy Mayhew^(w/m) *(Big Three)*; I've Got a Feeling I'm Falling [VS] — Billy Rose^w & Fats Waller^m & Harry Link^m *(Big Three)*; I've Got My Fingers Crossed [VS] — Ted Koehler^w & Jimmy McHugh^m *(Big Three)*; The Jitterbug Waltz [VS] / Lounging at the Waldorf [VS] — Richard Maltby^w & Fats Waller^m *(Big Three)*; Joint Is Jumpin' [VS] — Andy Razaf^w & J.C. Johnson^w & Fats Waller^m *(Big Three)*; Ladies Who Sing with the Band [VS] / When the Nylons Bloom Again [VS] — George Marion^w & Fats Waller^m *(Big Three)*; Lookin' Good, But Feeling Bad [VS] — Lester Santly^w & Fats Waller^m *(Big Three)*; Mean to Me [VS] — Roy Turk^(w/m) & Fred

Alert[w/m] *(Big Three)*; Spreadin' Rhythm Around [VS] — Ted Koehler[w] & Richard Maltby[w] & Jimmy McHugh[m] *(Big Three)*; Squeeze Me [VS] — Clarence Williams[w] & Fats Waller[m] *(Big Three)*; Tain't Nobody's Biz-ness If I Do [VS] — Porter Grainger[w/m] & Everett Robbins[w/m] *(Big Three)*; That Ain't Right [VS] — Nat King Cole[w/m] *(Big Three)*; Two Sleepy People [VS] — Frank Loesser[w] & Hoagy Carmichael[m] *(Big Three)*; Viper's Drag-Reefer Song [VS] — Fats Waller[m] *(Big Three)*; Yacht Club Swing [VS] — J.C. Johnson[w] & Fats Waller[m] & Herman Autrey[m] *(Big Three)*; Your Feet's Too Big — Ada Benson[w/m] & Fred Fisher[w/m] *(Fisher)*. A well written revue based on Fats Waller songs featuring a wonderful cast. It had a run of four years. COVER: Nell Carter, Andre DeShields, A. McQueen, K. Page, E. Woodard.

24 The Al Chemist Show (closed before Broadway, 1980). Georgia Brown, James Booth.

I Depend on Me — Steve Allen[w/m] *(Meadowlane)*. A musical that folded in Los Angeles. COVER: Georgia Brown.

25 Alabama Bound (Black, 1923). Irvin C. Miller, Ida Brown.

Alabama Bound Blues — Perry Bradford[w/m] *(Bradford)*. COVER: Black and white with title only.

26 Aladdin (British, 1962). Doretta Morrow, Bob Monkhouse.

I Am Loved [B] — Cole Porter[w/m] *(Chappell)*. A limited run stage version in London of the American TV musical. COVER: Oriental letters and sketches.

27 The Alarm Clock (closed before Broadway, 1932). Charlotte Greenwood.

I Don't Know How I Can Do Without You — Raymond Egan[w] & Martin Broones[m] *(Sherman Clay)*. COVER: Charlotte Greenwood.

28 Alice in Wonderland (Broadway, 1933). Josephine Hutchinson, Burgess Meredith.

Beautiful Soup / A Boat Beneath a Sunny Sky — Lewis Carroll[w] & Richard Addinsell[m] *(Chappell)*. Eva LeGallienne was involved in three productions of *Alice*: 1933, 1947, and 1982. All had limited runs. COVER: sketch of Alice and her friends.

29 Alison (closed before Broadway, 1968). Stars unknown.

Curious [PC] / I Want to Run Out from Under My Skin [PC] — Larry Norman[w/m] & Herb Hendler[w/m] *(Beechwood)*; Love on Haight Street [PC] / Mary Jane [PC] / We All [PC] — Larry Norman[w/m] *(Beechwood)*; Wake Up to Me Gently [PC] — Ken Mansfield[w/m] *(Beechwood)*. A rock musical. COVER: none.

30 Alive and Kicking (Broadway, 1950). David Burns, Jack Gilford.

If You Don't Love Me — Paul F. Webster[w] & Ray Golden[w] & Hoagy Carmichael[m] *(Chappell)*; Love, It Hurts So Good — Harold Rome[w/m] *(Chappell)*; One! Two! Three! — Paul F. Webster[w] & Ray Golden[w] & Sonny Burke[m] *(Chappell)*; There's a Building Going Up / A World of Strangers — Paul F. Webster[w] & Ray Golden[w] & Sammy Fain[m] *(Chappell)*. A poor revue that lasted five weeks — remembered for Gwen Verdon's dancing. COVER: sketch of dancing girl.

31 All American (Broadway, 1962). Ray Bolger, Eileen Herlie.

The Fight Song / If I Were You / I'm Fascinating / It's Fun to Think / I've Just Seen Her / Nightlife / Once Upon a Time / Our Children / We Speak the Same Language / What a Country — Lee Adams[w] & Charles Strouse[m] *(Morris)*; Born Too Late [CUT] [VS] — Fred Tobias[w] & Charles Strouse[m] *(Columbia)*. A college musical with a poor book and a few good tunes. The show ran for ten weeks. COVER: sketch of Ray Bolger with suitcase and umbrella.

32 All Clear (British, 1939). Beatrice Lillie, Bobby Howes.

I Went to a Marvelous Party [B] /

I'm So Weary of It All [B] — Noel Coward[w/m] *(Chappell)*. A war revue that was a big hit for Bea Lillie with two of Noel Coward's best songs. COVER: Beatrice Lillie, Bobby Howes, and other stars.

33 All Clear (Army, 1943). Stars unknown.

All Clear — William Hodapp[w] & Mitchell Stanley[m] *(Bowman)*; Da Da Dit — Walter Head[w/m] *(Bowman)*; The People I Meet in My Dreams — William Hodapp[w/m] & Ed Ballantine[w/m] *(Bowman)*; Rainbow Corner — William Hodapp[w] & Walter Reed[m] *(Bowman)*. A show produced at the Bowman Field Air Force Base. COVER: four sketches of military life.

34 All for Love (Broadway, 1949). Grace and Paul Hartman, Bert Wheeler.

All for Love / Dreamer with a Penny / The Humphrey Bogart Rhumba / My Baby's Bored / No Time for Nothin' but You / Oh, How Fortunate Ye Mortals Be [ABQ] / On the Benjamin B. Odell / Run to Me My Love — Allan Roberts[w/m] & Lester Lee[w/m] *(Simon)*; My Heart's in the Middle of July — Allan Roberts[w/m] & Lester Lee[w/m] *(Shapiro, Bernstein)*; Why Can't It Happen Again? — Sammy Gallop[w] & Michel Emer[m] *(Cecille)*. A poor revue kept running for three months by the millionaire Farrell. COVER: Grace and Paul Hartman, with Bert Wheeler.

35 All for You (closed before Broadway, 1925). William Gaxton.

All for You / If You Love Her, Tell Her So / In a Happy Home for Two / In My Little Blue Bonnet / Keeping Out of Trouble / Mr. Cozy Corner Man / When the Day Is Ended — Arthur Freed[w/m] *(Sherman Clay)*. A California musical. COVER: orange and blue designs and lettering.

36 All in Fun (Broadway, 1940). Bill Robinson, Phil Baker.

It's a Big Wide Wonderful World — John Rox[w/m] *(BMI)*; Love and I — Irving Graham[w] & Baldwin Bergersen[m] *(BMI)*; That's Good Enough for Me — Virginia Faulkner[w] & Baldwin Bergersen[m] *(BMI)*. A revue with a lot of talent that lasted three performances. COVER: Imogene Coca, Pert Kelton, Bill Robinson, Phil Baker.

37 All in Love (Off Broadway, 1961). David Atkinson, Gaylea Byrne.

All in Love / Don't Ask Me / I Found Him / I Love a Fool / The Lady Was Made to Be Loved / A More Than an Ordinary Glorious Vocabulary / What Can It Be? — Bruce Geller[w] & Jacques Urbont[m] *(Marks)*. A musical adaptation of *The Rivals*. It was very well done and ran for five months. COVER: sketch of man and woman.

38 All Kinds of Giants (Off Broadway, 1961). Bill Hinnant, Richard Morse.

All Kinds of Giants / Be Yourself / My Star / Paint Me a Rainbow — Tom Whedon[w] & Sam Pottle[m] *(Morris)*. A musical set in medieval times. It ran for two weeks. COVER: cartoon of lady with bow and arrow.

39 All Points West (Concert, 1936). Ray Middleton, Philadelphia Orchestra.

All Points West — Lorenz Hart[w] & Richard Rodgers[m] *(Chappell)*. A symphonic poem to be narrated to music by an orchestra. COVER: black and grey titles.

40 All That Glitters (College, 1949). Ronald Moir, Betty Dissell.

I Love You Etcetera [VS] / I Must Be Dreaming [VS] / I Need Love [VS] / Let's Not Fall in Love [VS] / When I See You [VS] — Stephen Sondheim[w/m] *(BMI)*. Sondheim's second show at Williams College. COVER: black and white titles.

41 All the King's Horses (Broadway, 1934). Guy Robertson, Betty Starbuck.

Charming / Evening Star / I Found a Song / I've Gone Nuts Over You — Fred Herendeen[w] & Edward Horan[m] *(Harms)*. An operetta dealing with a king and his look-alike. Its run was three months. COVER: sketch of horses.

42 Allah Be Praised! (Broadway, 1944). Patricia Morison, Joey Faye.

Let's Go Too Far — George Marion[w] & Don Walker[m] *(Chappell)*; Secret Song — George Marion[w] & Baldwin Bergersen[m] *(Chappell)*. A poor revue lasting only two weeks. COVER: sketch of sultan and dancing girl.

43 Allegro (Broadway, 1947). John Battles, Lisa Kirk.

Allegro — complete vocal score / Come Home / A Fellow Needs a Girl / The Gentleman Is a Dope / Money Isn't Everything / So Far / You Are Never Away — Oscar Hammerstein[w] & Richard Rodgers[m] *(Williamson)*. An original musical about the life of a man — running only nine months. COVER: sketch of wedding couple and dancers.

44 Alley Up! (*see also* **Satires of 1920** *and* **Sunkist**) (Broadway, 1920). Fanchon and Marco.

My Sweetie's Smile — Fanchon & Marco[w/m] *(Remick)*. A revue with a Hollywood theme that toured as *Alley Up* and *Satires of 1920,* but opened as *Sunkist.* COVER: a girl in an evening gown.

45 Allez-oop! (Broadway, 1927). Victor Moore, Charles Butterworth.

All My Life / Blow Hot and Heavy / Pull Yourself Together — Leo Robin[w] & Philip Charig[m] & Richard Myers[m] *(Harms)*. A pleasant revue that ran for three months. COVER 1: black and green designs, states Richard Lambert presents Leand and Mayfield. COVER 2: black and green designs, states Carl Hemmer's revue *Allez-oop.*

46 All's Fair (*see also* **By Jupiter**) (Broadway, 1942). Ray Bolger, Constance Moore.

Careless Rhapsody / Everything I've Got / Here's a Hand / Jupiter Forbid / Nobody's Heart / Wait Till You See Her — Lorenz Hart[w] & Richard Rodgers[m] *(Chappell)*. A fantasy in which women were in control. A wonderful score and cast running for a year and closed only because Bolger left. Try-out title was *All's Fair,* Broadway title was *By Jupiter.* COVER: sketch of Ray Bolger and a Greek warrior.

47 All's Fair (closed before Broadway, 1968). Stars unknown.

All's Fair [VS] / America, America, America [VS] / Berger, Boozer, and Digby [VS] / A Brand New World [VS] / He's My Son [VS] / I Think I'm Going to Faint [VS] / My American [VS] / What's Happened to Love [VS] / You Can't Take a Man Out of Romance [VS] — Dick Stern[w/m] & Lou Carter[w/m] *(Big Three)*. COVER: red lettering and designs.

48 All's Well That Ends Well (Broadway, 1981). Margaret Tyzack, Geoffrey Hastings.

All's Well That Ends Well — Guy Woolfenden[m] *(Ariel)*. A limited run of the Royal Shakespeare Production. COVER: sketch of man and woman dancing.

49 Aloma of the South Sea (Broadway, 1925). Vivienne Osborne, Ben Johnson.

Aloma — Francis DeWitt[w] & Robert Hood Bowers[m] *(Robbins-Engel)*. A hit drama about a native girl and her American lover. COVER: Vivienne Osborne and native.

50 Along Fifth Avenue (Broadway, 1949). Nancy Walker, Jackie Gleason.

The Best Time of Day / If / I Love Love in New York / Skyscraper Blues / Weep No More / With You So Far Away — Tom Adair[w] & Gordon Jenkins[m] *(Supreme)*; Call It Apple Fritters / Santo Dinero — Milton Pascal[w] & Richard Stutz[m] *(Supreme)*; Maybe It's Because — Harry Ruby[w] & Johnnie Scott[m] *(B V and C)*; A Trip Doesn't Care at All — Thomas Howell[w] & Philip Kadison[m] *(Supreme)*. A revue that ran for six months due to the talents of Nancy Walker and Jackie Gleason. COVER: sketch of a New York street sign.

51 Always You (*see also* **Joan of Arkansaw**) (Broadway, 1920). Helen Ford, Walter Scanlon.

Always You / Don't You Remember / Drifting On / I Never Miss / I'll Say So / Misterioso / Pousse Cafe / Same Old Place / Some Big Something

/ A String of Girls / Syncopated Heart / Wonderful War – Oscar Hammerstein[w] & Herbert Stothart[m] *(Remick)*. Hammerstein's first big show running only eight weeks. It was called *Joan of Arkansaw* in try-out. COVER: trees, sky and designs.

52 Amahl and the Night Visitors (Opera, 1952). Chet Allen, Rosemary Kuhlmann.

Amahl and the Night Visitors – complete score – Gian Carlo Menotti[w/m] *(Schirmer)*. An opera written for TV that was also presented at the NY City Center and NY City Opera. COVER: a Nativity scene.

53 The Amazing Adele (closed before Broadway, 1956). Tammy Grimes, Johnny Desmond.

Go and Get Yourself a YoYo / Never Again / Now Is the Time – Albert Selden[w/m] *(Morris)*. A musical dealing with clairvoyance that folded in Boston. COVER: a girl in a bikini.

54 Ambassador (Broadway, 1972). Howard Keel, Danielle Darrieux.

All of My Life / Love Finds the Lonely / Tell Her / Young with Him – Hal Hackady[w] & Don Gehman[m] *(Screen Gems–Columbia)*. A musical based on a Henry James novel which tried out in London and got mixed reviews. After a small summer production in Philadelphia, it was given a lavish production in NY but lasted only two weeks. COVER: sketch of elegant lady and gentleman.

55 The Amber Fluid (closed before Broadway, 1924). Fredda Brindley.

If All My Thoughts Were Stars – Arthur Lamb[w] & Con Conrad[m] *(Marks)*. COVER: Fredda Brindley.

56 Amelia Goes to the Ball (Opera, 1938). Margaret Daum, Conrad Mave.

Amelia Goes to the Ball – complete score – Gian-Carlo Menotti[w/m] *(Schirmer)*; While I Waste These Precious Hours – Gian-Carlo Menotti[w/m] *(Ricordi)*. A Menotti opera performed by the New York City Opera Company. COVER: elegant couple in carriage.

57 American Jubilee (World's Fair, 1940). Ray Middleton, Wynn Murray.

How Can I Ever Be Alone / My Bicycle Girl / Tennessee Fish Fry / We Like It Over Here – Oscar Hammerstein[w] & Arthur Schwartz[m] *(Chappell)*. A patriotic pageant. COVER: titles and designs.

58 The American Way (Broadway, 1939). Fredric March, Florence Eldridge.

The American Way – Buddy Bernier[w/m] & Bob Emmerich[w/m] *(Crawford)*; A Lemon in the Garden of Love – M.R. Rourke[w] & Richard Carle[m] *(Vogel)*. A patriotic play about life in America running for 20 weeks. COVER: titles and designs.

59 Americana (#1) (Broadway, 1926). Lew Brice, Betty Compton.

Blowin' the Blues Away / Sunny Disposish – Ira Gershwin[w] & Philip Charig[m] *(Harms)*; Dreaming – J.P. McEvoy[w] & Henry Souvaine[m] & Con Conrad[m] *(Harms)*; Nobody Wants Me – Morrie Ryskind[w] & Henry Souvaine[m] *(Harms)*; Promise in Your Eyes – B.G. DeSylva[w] & James Hanley[m] *(Harms)*; Swanee River Melody – Al Wilson[w/m] & Charles Weinberg[w/m] *(Harms)*; That Lost Barbershop Chord – Ira Gershwin[w] & George Gerswhin[m] *(Harms)*; Why Do Ya Roll Those Eyes – Morrie Ryskind[w] & Philip Charig[m] *(Harms)*. A revue about topical events with some good songs and talented people – running six months. COVER: titles and designs.

60 Americana (#2) (Broadway, 1928). Rosamund Johnson, Frances Gershwin.

Ameri-Can-Can / He's Mine / Hot Pants / No Place Like Home / Wild Oat Joe / Young Black Joe – Irving Caesar[w] & Roger Wolfe Kahn[m] *(Harms)*; Life as a Twosome – Irving Caesar[w] & Joseph Meyer[m] & Roger Wolfe Kahn[m] *(Harms)*. An attempt to re-create the successful 1926 revue. It lasted two weeks. COVER 1: red, white, blue – states J.P. McEvoy's *American*, 2nd edition book by J.P. McEvoy. COVER 2: red, white, blue –

states *The New Americana*, book by
Bugs Baer and J.P. McEvoy.

61 Americana (#3) (Broadway,
1932). Phil Baker, Lloyd Nolan.

Brother, Can You Spare a Dime—
E.Y. Harburg^w & Jay Gorney^m
(Harms); If I Love Again—J.P. Mur-
ray^w & Ben Oakland^m *(Harms)*;
Satan's Li'l Lamb—E.Y. Harburg^w &
John Mercer^w & Harold Arlen^m
(Harms); Whistling for a Kiss—E.Y.
Harburg^w & John Mercer^w & Richard
Myers^m *(Harms)*; Wouldja for a Big
Red Apple—Henry Souvaine^w/m &
Everett Miller^w/m & John Mercer^w/m
(Harms). The third edition in this series
was a failure of ten weeks but produced
one hit song. COVER: titles and designs.

62 America's Sweetheart (Broadway,
1931). Harriette Lake, Jack Whiting.

How About It / I Want a Man / I've
Got Five Dollars / A Lady Must Live /
There's So Much More / We'll Be the
Same—Lorenz Hart^w & Richard
Rodgers^m *(Harms)*. A musical with a
Hollywood theme starring Harriette
Lake, who left for Hollywood and
became Ann Sothern. This musical had
several good Rodgers and Hart songs
and ran four months. COVER: sketch of
lady surrounded by gentlemen.

63 Among the Girls (closed before
Broadway, 1919). Percival Knight.

I Want to Go Back to the War—
Henry Blossom^w & Percy Knight^w &
Raymond Hubbell^m *(Harms)*; I'm a
Human Pousse Cafe—Harry B.
Smith^w & Raymond Hubbell^m
(Harms); In Dreams Alone / M-O-N-E-Y
/ Tell Me Tonight—Henry Blossom^w
& Raymond Hubbell^m *(Harms)*; Say-
on-ar-a—George Hobart^w & Henry
Blossom^w & Raymond Hubbell^m
(Harms). COVER: a gentleman sur-
rounded by pretty faces.

64 Among the Stars (Broadway,
1937). Stars unknown.

Among the Stars—Charles Chancer^w
& Erno Rapee^m *(words and music)*. A
limited run musical production of
Leonidoff at the Radio City Music
Hall. COVER: stars and designs.

65 The Amorous Flea (Off Broadway, 1964). Lew Parker, Imelda
DeMartin.

Learning Love—Bruce Montgomery^w/m
(Frank); When Time Takes Your
Hand—Jerry Devine^w & Bruce Mont-
gomery^m *(Frank)*. A musical version
of *School for Wives* that ran four
weeks. COVER: sketch of beautiful girl
holding a flea.

66 And the World Goes Round (Off
Broadway, 1991). Bob Cuccioli, Karen
Mason.

And All That Jazz [VS] / Arthur [VS]
/ But the World Goes Round [VS] /
Cabaret [VS] / Class [VS] / Coffee in a
Cardboard Cup [VS] / Colored Lights
[VS] / The Grass Is Always Greener [VS]
/ The Happy Time [VS] / How Lucky
Can You Get [VS] / I Don't Remember
You [VS] / Isn't This Better [VS] / Kiss
of the Spider Woman [VS] / Marry Me
[VS] / Maybe This Time [VS] / Me and
My Baby [VS] / Mr. Cellophane [VS] /
Money, Money [VS] / My Coloring
Book [VS] / New York, New York [VS]
/ Only Love [VS] / Pain [VS] / A Quiet
Thing [VS] / Ring Them Bells [VS] / The
Rink [VS] / Sara Lee [VS] / Sometimes a
Day Goes By [VS] / There Goes the Ball
Game [VS] / We Can Make It [VS] / Yes
[VS]—Fred Ebb^w & John Kander^m
(Valando). A successful revue featuring
the songs of Kander and Ebb with a
long run. COVER: colored designs.

67 And Very Nice Too (closed
before Broadway, 1922). Stars unknown.

And Very Nice Too [ABQ] / Baby /
Love Will Do the Rest [ABQ] / Oh John
[ABQ] / Wedding Anvils [ABQ] / When
I Hear a Syncopated Strain / When
You Come Back to Me / When Your
Sweet Lips Meet Mine—Raymond
Peck^w & Percy Wenrich^m *(Feist)*.
COVER: sketch of boy pursuing girl.

68 Angel (Broadway, 1978). Don
Scardino, Fred Gwynne.

All the Comforts of Home [VS] /
Angel Theme [VS] / Astoria Gloria [VS]
/ A Dime Ain't Worth a Nickel [VS] /
Drifting [VS] / Fatty [VS] / Feelin' Loved

/ Fingers and Toes [VS] / How Do You Say Goodbye [VS] / I Can't Believe It's You [VS] / I Get a Dream to Sleep On [VS] / If I Ever Loved Him [VS] / It's Gotta Be Dixie [VS] / Like the Eagles Fly [VS] / Make a Little Sunshine [VS] / Railbird [VS] / Tomorrow I'm Gonna Be Old [VS] — Peter Udell[w] & Gary Geld[m] *(Geld-Udell)*. A musical version of *Look Homeward Angel* that lasted for five performances. COVER: black and gold titles.

69 Angel Face (Broadway, 1919). Jack Donahue, Howard Johnson.

Call It a Day / Everybody's Crazy Half of the Time / How Do You Get That Way? / I Don't Want to Go Home / I Might Be Your Once in a While / Lullaby / My Idea of Something to Go Home To / Those "Since I Met You" Days / Tip Your Hat to Hattie — Robert Smith[w] & Victor Herbert[m] *(Harms)*. A musical about staying young — lasting seven weeks. COVER: an angel's face.

70 Angel Face (closed before Broadway, 1921). Stars unknown.

At the Mummies Ball / That Haunting Waltz — Maurice Gunsky[w] & Nat Goldstein[m] *(Goldstein)*. COVER: sketch of man and woman taking bows.

71 Angel in the Pawnshop (Broadway, 1951). Eddie Dowling, Joan McCracken.

Angel Mine / The Music Box Gavotte — Jimmy Kennedy[w] & Will Irwin[m] *(Sam Fox)*. A short lived comedy about a pawnshop and its customers. COVER: Eddie Dowling and Joan McCracken.

72 Angel in the Wings (Broadway, 1947). The Hartmans, Elaine Stritch.

Big Brass Band from Brazil / Civilization / If It Were Easy to Do / The Thousand Islands Song — Bob Hilliard[w] & Carl Sigman[m] *(Morris)*. A very entertaining revue with good comedy and Elaine Stritch having a run of nine months. COVER: sketch of angel's hand touching Broadway sign.

73 Angela (*see also* **The Queen's Taste**) (Broadway, 1928). Jeanette MacDonald, Florenz Ames.

I Can't Believe It's True / Love Is Like That / You've Got Me Up a Tree — Mann Holiner[w] & Alberta Nichols[m] *(Shubert)*. A musical dealing with a royal marriage lasting five weeks. The try-out title was *The Queen's Taste*. COVER: lady with crown accepting jewels from page.

74 Animal Crackers (Broadway, 1928). Marx Brothers, Margaret Dumont.

Hooray for Captain Spaulding (plain cover) / Long Island Low Down / Waiting / Watching the Clouds Roll By / Who's Been List'ning to My Heart — Bert Kalmar[w/m] & Harry Ruby[w/m] *(Harms)*. A hit for the Marx Brothers with a robbery on a Long Island estate — running six months. COVER: Marx Brothers.

75 Ankles Aweigh (Broadway, 1955). Kean Sisters, Mark Dawson.

Eleven O'Clock Song (plain cover) / La Festa / Headin' for the Bottom / Here's to Dear Old Us / His and Hers / Kiss Me and Kill Me with Love / Nothing at All / Skip the Build Up — Dan Shapiro[w] & Sammy Fain[m] *(Chappell)*. A real old-fashioned musical comedy with gags, girls, and pleasant songs running six months. COVER: girl in sailor outfit.

76 Anna Ascends (Broadway, 1920). Alice Brady, Rod La Rocque.

Moon Flower — Wilbur Weeks[m] & Alexander Maloof[m] *(Schirmer)*. A drama about a successful immigrant. COVER: Alice Brady.

77 Anne of Green Gables (Broadway, 1971). Gracie Finley, Elizabeth Mawson.

Anne of Green Gables [B] [VS] / Anne of Green Gables — complete score / Ice Cream [B] [VS] / Kindred Spirits [B] [VS] / Summer [B] [VS] / Wond'rin' [B] [VS] — Donald Harron[w] & Elaine Campbell[w] & Norman Campbell[m] *(Chappell)*; Gee, I'm Glad I'm No One Else [B] [VS] — Elaine Campbell[w] & Norman Campbell[m] *(Chappell)*; Learn Ev'rything [B] — Mavor Moore[w] & Norman Campbell[m] *(Chappell)*. A musical hit in Canada and London but only a two week limited engagement in New York. COVER: sketch of a joyous Anne.

78 Annie (*see also* Annie Dear) (Broadway, 1924). Billie Burke, Ernest Truex.

Slither, Slither / Wooing — Clare Kummer^w/m *(Harms)*; Whisper to Me — Clifford Grey^w & Sigmund Romberg^m *(Harms)*. A lavish production by Ziegfeld for Burke with a three month run. Try-out title was *Annie*.

79 Annie (Broadway, 1977). Andrea McArdle, Dorothy Loudon.

Annie [VS] / Easy Street / I Don't Need Anything But You [VS] / I Think I'm Gonna Like It Here [VS] / It's the Hard Knock Life [VS] / Little Girls / Maybe / A New Deal for Christmas / n.y.c. / Something Was Missing [VS] / Tomorrow / We'd Like to Thank You Herbert Hoover [VS] / You Won't Be an Orphan for Long [VS] / You're Never Fully Dressed Without a Smile — Martin Charnin^w & Charles Strouse^m *(Morris)*. A smash hit with pleasant songs, orphans, villains, and a happy ending, running six years. COVER: Annie.

80 Annie Dear (*see also* Annie) (Broadway, 1924). Billie Burke, Ernest Truex.

Annie Dear / I Want to Be Loved / Slither, Slither / Wooing — Clare Kummer^w/m *(Harms)*; Bertie / Whisper to Me — Clifford Grey^w & Sigmund Romberg^m *(Harms)*; Louwanna — Clifford Grey^w & Sigmund Romberg^m & Jean Schwartz^m *(Harms)*; Someone, Someday, Sweetheart — Clifford Grey^w & Rudolf Friml^m *(Harms)*. A lavish production that didn't last. The try-out title was *Annie* and opening title *Annie Dear*. COVER: Billie Burke.

81 Annie Get Your Gun (Broadway, 1946). Ethel Merman, Ray Middleton.

Anything You Can Do / Colonel Buffalo Bill / Doin' What Comes Natur'lly / The Girl That I Marry / I Got Lost in His Arms / I Got the Sun in the Morning / I'll Share It All with You / I'm a Bad, Bad Man / I'm an Indian Too / Moonshine Lullaby / My Defenses Are Down / There's No Business Like Show Business / They Say It's Wonderful / Who Do You Love I Hope / You Can't Get a Man with a Gun — Irving Berlin^w/m *(Berlin)*. Berlin's best score and biggest hit and Ethel Merman's greatest role. The song became the Broadway anthem and the show ran three years. COVER: sketch of Annie, guns and Indians.

82 Annie Get Your Gun (Regional, 1948). Mary Martin, John Raitt.

Anything You Can Do / Doin' What Comes Natur'lly / The Girl That I Marry / I Got Lost in His Arms / I Got the Sun in the Morning / There's No Business Like Show Business / They Say It's Wonderful / You Can't Get a Man with a Gun — Irving Berlin^w/m *(Berlin)*. A successful tour of this big hit. COVER: sketch of Annie on horseback.

83 Annie Get Your Gun (Broadway, 1966). Ethel Merman, Bruce Yarnell.

An Old Fashioned Wedding — Irving Berlin^w/m *(Berlin)*. A successful revival with a new song added. Merman was still in great shape. COVER: sketch of Annie on horseback.

84 Annie Two (closed before Broadway, 1990). Dorothy Loudon, Harve Presnell.

When You Smile / A Younger Man — Martin Charnin^w & Charles Strouse^m *(Belwin)*. This sequel to *Annie* folded in Washington. It played a limited engagement at Goodspeed in the summer of 1990. The next version opened and closed at a theatre in Illinois in 1992. Another version opened Off Broadway in New York in July 1993 to good reviews. COVER: sketch of Annie and Sandy.

85 Annina (*see also* Music Hath Charms) (Broadway, 1934). Maria Jeritza, Allan Jones.

Annina / Love / My Heart Is Yours / My Palace of Dreams / Romance / Sweet Fool — Rowland Leigh^w & John Shubert^w & Rudolf Friml^m *(Schirmer)*. *Annina* was written for opera star Maria Jeritza, with co-star Allan Jones.

The show was not a success in its try-out and they were dismissed. It was revised and opened as *Music Hath Charms* and was a big flop. COVER: Maria Jeritza.

86 Anya *(see also* **I, Anastasia)** (Broadway, 1965). Constance Towers, Lillian Gish.

Anya [PC] / Drawn to You [PC] / Hand in Hand [PC] / Here Tonight Tomorrow Where? [PC] / If This Is Goodbye / Little Hands / Now Is My Moment [PC] / Snowflakes and Sweethearts / This Is My Kind of Love — Robert Wright[w/m] & George Forrest[w/m] & S. Rachmaninoff[w/m] *(Frank)*. A lavish flop whose only claim to fame was being the last show to play the Ziegfeld Theatre, which was demolished when this show folded. Two regional productions, *I Anastasia* and *The Anastasia Game* both folded. COVER: a sketch of Anya.

87 Anyone Can Whistle (Broadway, 1964). Angela Lansbury, Lee Remick.

Anyone Can Whistle / Anyone Can Whistle — complete score / Come Play wiz Me / Everybody Says Don't / I've Got You to Lean On / A Parade in Town / See What It Gets You / There Won't Be Trumpets / With So Little to Be Sure Of — Stephen Sondheim[w/m] *(Burthen)*. An unusual musical that failed with three talented leads and an interesting score. COVER: colored designs.

88 Anything Goes (Broadway, 1934). Ethel Merman, William Gaxton.

All Through the Night / Anything Goes / Anything Goes — complete score / Blow, Gabriel, Blow / Buddie Beware / Gypsy in Me / I Get a Kick Out of You / Kate the Great [CUT] [VS] / Waltz Down the Aisle / You're the Top — Cole Porter[w/m] *(Harms)*. One of Cole Porter's biggest hits about fun and adventure on a ship which ran for over a year. COVER: William Gaxton, Ethel Merman, Victor Moore.

89 Anything Goes (British, 1935). Sydney Howard, Jeanne Aubert.

Lady Fair — B piano selections —

Cole Porter[m] *(Chappell)*. This American musical was a hit in London and ran for nine months. COVER: Sydney Howard, Jeanne Aubert.

90 Anything Goes (Broadway, 1935). George Murphy, Shirley Ross.

All Through the Night / Anything Goes / Blow, Gabriel, Blow / Buddie Beware / Gypsy in Me / I Get a Kick Out of You / You're the Top — Cole Porter[w/m] *(Harms)*. Three new stars take over this hit musical. COVER: George Murphy, Shirley Ross, Hugh O'Connell.

91 Anything Goes (Broadway, 1988). Patti LuPone, Howard McGillin.

All Through the Night [VS] / Anything Goes [VS] / Be Like a Blue Bird [VS] / Blow, Gabriel, Blow [VS] / Buddie Beware [VS] / Easy to Love [VS] / Friendship [VS] / Goodbye Little Dream Goodbye [VS] / Gypsy in Me [VS] / I Get a Kick Out of You [VS] / It's De-Lovely [VS] / Public Enemy #1 [VS] / You're the Top [VS] — Cole Porter[w/m] *(Warner Bros.)*. A revival of this hit musical at Lincoln Center was very successful and toured. COVER: sketch of girl and ship.

92 Aphrodite (Broadway, 1919). Dorothy Dalton, Richard Hale.

Alexandria / Aphrodite — Arthur Penn[w] & Anselm Goetzl[m] *(Witmark)*; Aphrodite Waltz — Anselm Goetzl[m] *(Witmark)*. A musical set in Egypt with pageantry and ballets running four months. COVER: sphynx and Eygptian mummies.

93 Applause (Broadway, 1970). Lauren Bacall, Len Cariou.

Applause / Applause — complete score / Backstage Babble / The Best Night of My Life / But Alive / Fasten Your Seat Belts [VS] / Good Friends [VS] / Hurry Back / It Was Always You / Love Comes First / One of a Kind [VS] / One Halloween [VS] / She's No Longer a Gypsy [VS] / Something Greater / Think How It's Gonna Be / Welcome to the Theatre / Who's That Girl [VS] — Lee Adams[w] & Charles

Strouse[m] *(Morris)*. A musical version of *All About Eve* with a talented cast and serviceable score. It ran two years. COVER 1: Baltimore — actress taking bow and the name of Diane McAfee as Eve. COVER 2: New York — actress taking bow and the name of Penny Fuller as Eve. COVER 3: London and reprints — actress taking bow and name of Angela Richards as Eve.

94 Apple Blossoms (Broadway, 1919). Fred and Adele Astaire.

Apple Blossoms — complete score — William Le Baron[w] & Victor Jacobi[m] & Fritz Kreisler[m] *(Harms)*; Brothers / Little Girls, Goodbye / On the Banks of the Bronx / When the Wedding Bells Are Ringing / You Are Free — William Le Baron[w] & Victor Jacobi[m] *(Harms)*; A Girl, a Man, a Night, a Dance / I'm in Love / Second Violin / Star of Love / Who Can Tell — William Le Baron[w] & Fritz Kreisler[m] *(Harms)*; I'll Be True to You — piano selections — Victor Jacobi[m] *(Harms)*. An operetta with good music, talented people, and lavish sets by Urban. It ran for a year. COVER: pink blossoms.

95 The Apple Tree (Broadway, 1966). Barbara Harris, Larry Blyden.

The Apple Tree / The Apple Tree — complete score / Beautiful, Beautiful World / I'm Lost / I've Got What You Want / Oh, to Be a Movie Star [VS] / Wealth [VS] / What Makes Me Love Him? / You Are Not Real [VS] — Sheldon Harnick[w] & Jerry Bock[m] *(Valando)*. Three interesting one act musicals that kept running for one year by the talents of Barbara Harris. COVER: Three apples with bite marks.

96 Aqua Spectacular (Water, 1962). Stars unknown.

Holiday in Haiti / Let's Start the Show — Richard Hayman[m] *(Mills)*. COVER: A lady diver with clowns.

97 Arabian Nights (Broadway, 1954). Laurita Melchior, Helena Scott.

The Hero of All My Dreams / How Long Has It Been? / It's Great to Be Alive / A Long Ago Love / Marry the One You Love / Teeny Weeny Genie / A Thousand and One Nights / A Whale of a Story — Carmen Lombardo[w/m] & John J. Loeb[w/m] *(Shapiro, Bernstein)*. An original musical performed for two summers at the Jones Beach theatre in New York. COVER: dancing girls, a whale and oriental designs.

98 Archy and Mehitabel (*see also* Shinbone Alley) (Off Broadway, 1957). Cast unknown.

Archy and Mehitabel — finale [VS] / Archy and Mehitabel — opening [VS] / Cheerio, My Deario [VS] / Cheerio, My Deario — Reprise [VS] / Dance of the Cockroach [VS] / I Am Only a Poor Humble Cockroach [VS] / Lightning Bug Song [VS] / Look at the Pretty Kittens [VS] / Mehitabel, the Way She Used to Be [VS] / Mehitabel and Bill Duet [VS] / Mehitabel's Return [VS] / There's a Dance or Two in the Old Girls Yet [VS] — Joe Darion[w] & George Kleinsinger[m] *(Chappell)*. A musical written as a concert piece and later turned into the Broadway musical *Shinbone Alley*. COVER: black and white titles only.

99 Are You with It? (Broadway, 1945). Johnny Downs, Dolores Gray.

Here I Go Again / Just Beyond the Rainbow / Slightly Perfect / This Is My Beloved — Arnold Horwitt[w] & Harry Revel[m] *(Chappell)*. A musical dealing with carnival people in a boarding house lasting almost nine months. COVER: carnival tents, flags, and a barker.

100 Ari (Broadway, 1971). David Cryer, Constance Towers.

Ari's Promise [PC] / Exodus [PC] / My Galilee [PC] — Leon Uris[w] & Walt Smith[m] *(Chappell)*. A poor musical based on the hit novel *Exodus* lasting two weeks. COVER: none.

101 Arms and the Girl (Broadway, 1950). Nanette Fabray, Georges Guetary.

A Cow and a Plough and a Frau / Don't Talk / Nothin' for Nothin' / That's My Fella / There Must Be Something Better Than Love / You Kissed Me — Dorothy Fields[w] & Morton Gould[m] *(Chappell)*. A poor musical, based on *The Pursuit of Happiness*, lasting three months. COVER: a girl holding a gun.

102 Around the World (in Eighty Days) (Broadway, 1946). Orson Welles, Mary Healy.

If You Smile at Me / Look What I Found / Pipe-Dreaming / Should I Tell You I Love You / There He Goes, Mr. Phileas Fogg / Wherever They Fly the Flag of Old England — Cole Porter$^{w/m}$ *(Chappell)*. An over-produced Orson Welles extravaganza with a poor Cole Porter score which lasted two months, however, Mike Todd bought it and turned it into a highly successful movie. COVER: two men, a stranded ship in a cover.

103 Around the World in Eighty Days (Broadway, 1963). David Atkinson, Robert Clary.

His Little World / Once I Wondered — Harold Adamson^w & Sammy Fain^m *(Liza Music)*. A summer spectacle produced by Guy Lombardo at Jones Beach in New York. COVER: colored balloons.

104 Artists and Models (1923 edition) (Broadway, 1923). Frank Fay, Grace Hamilton.

Back in Circulation / Black Rhythm / Golfing Blues / Jackie Coogan — Harold Atteridge^w & Jean Schwartz^m *(Harms)*; Music of Love — Cyrus Wood^w & Alfred Goodman^m *(Harms)*; One in a Million to Me — Jean Schwartz$^{w/m}$ *(Harms)*; Say It with a Ukelele — Art Conrad$^{w/m}$ *(Harms)*; Somehow / Take Me Back to Samoa Some More — Cyrus Wood^w & Jean Schwartz^m *(Harms)*. An attempt by the Shuberts to imitate the Vanities. It had topless girls and ran nine months. COVER: an artist's palette and brushes.

105 Artists and Models (1924 edition) (Broadway, 1924). Frank Gaby, Mabel Withee.

Hula Lou — Jack Yellen^w & Milton Charles^m & Wayne King^m *(A Y and B)*; Riviera Rose — Jean Frederick^w & Horatio Nicholls^m *(Harms)*; Tomorrow's Another Day — Clifford Gray^w & Sam Coslow^w & Sigmund Romberg^m

& Fred Coots^m *(Harms)*. A poor revue with a lot of nudity running eight months. COVER: an artist's palette and brushes.

106 Artists and Models (Paris, 1925 edition) (Broadway, 1925). Walter Woolf, Frances Williams.

Flexatone / Lucita / Oriental Memories / The Promenade Walk / Venetian Wedding Moon — Clifford Grey^w & Al Goodman^m & Maurie Rubens^m & Fred Coots *(Harms)*; Making Believe I'm Glad — Sid Silvers$^{w/m}$ & Phil Baker$^{w/m}$ & Ben Bernie$^{w/m}$ *(Remick)*; Mothers of the World — Clifford Grey^w & Sigmund Romberg^m *(Harms)*; When You See That Aunt of Mine — Irving Bibo^w & Rudolph Nelson^m *(Marks)*. Another cheap revue with lots of dancing and nude girls running one year. COVER: an artist's palette and brushes.

107 Artists and Models (new 1927 edition) (Broadway, 1927). Ted Lewis, Jack Osterman.

Baby Feet Go Pitter Patter — Gus Kahn$^{w/m}$ *(D B and H)*; The Call of Broadway / Is Everybody Happy Now? — Jack Osterman$^{w/m}$ & Ted Lewis$^{w/m}$ & Maurie Rubens *(Shapiro, Bernstein)*; Here Am I — Broken Hearted — B.G. DeSylva$^{w/m}$ & Lew Brown$^{w/m}$ & Ray Henderson$^{w/m}$ *(D B and H)*; The Lobster Crawl / Oh Peggy / The Only One for Me / Snap Out of It / There's Nothing New in Old New York — Benny Davis^w & Harry Akst^m *(Harms)*. This poor revue featured 100 nude girls and ran for 19 weeks. COVER: an artist's palette and brushes.

108 Artists and Models (*see also* **Dear Love**) (Paris-Riviera, 1930 edition) (Broadway, 1930). Aileen Stanley, Phil Baker.

Humming a Love Song — Sid Silvers$^{w/m}$ & Phil Baker$^{w/m}$ *(Feist)*; I'd Like to Find the Guy That Wrote the Stein Song — Johnny Johnson$^{w/m}$ & Harry McDaniel$^{w/m}$ *(Shapiro, Bernstein)*; Je T'aime — Ernie Golden$^{w/m}$ & Powers Gouraud$^{w/m}$ *(Harms)*; My Real Ideal — Samuel Lerner^w & Burton Lane^m

(Harms); Two Perfect Lovers — Haydn Wood^w/m & Joe Tunbridge^w/m & Jack Waller^w/m & B. Lane? *(Harms)*; Who Cares? — Dion Titheradge^w & Haydn Wood^m & Joe Tunbridge^m & Jack Waller^m *(Harms)*. An English musical imported by the Shuberts and toured as *Dear Love*. It was revised and opened in New York as *Artists and Models* but only ran seven weeks. COVER: a girl on the wings of an airplane.

109 Artists and Models (1943 edition) (Broadway, 1943). Jane Froman, Jackie Gleason.

Let's Keep It That Way — Milton Berle^w & Ervin Drake^w & Abner Silver^m *(Crawford)*; Swing Low Sweet Harriet / You Are Romance / You'll Know That It's Me — Dan Shapiro^w/m & Milton Pascal^w/m & Phil Charig^w/m *(Crawford)*. A poor attempt to revive this series lasting three weeks. COVER: an artist's palette with brushes.

110 As the Girls Go (Broadway, 1948). Bobby Clark, Irene Rich.

As the Girls Go / Father's Day / I Got Lucky in the Rain / It Takes a Woman to Take a Man / It's More Fun Than a Picnic / Nobody's Heart but Mine / Rock, Rock, Rock / There's No Getting Away from You / You Say the Nicest Things Baby — Harold Adamson^w & Jimmy McHugh^m *(Sam Fox)*. A musical about a lady president with an excellent score running for one year. COVER 1: Clark and girls with purple letters and orange background. COVER 2: Clark and girls with blue letters and pink background designed by Petty.

111 As Thousands Cheer (Broadway, 1933). Marilyn Miller, Clifton Webb.

Easter Parade / The Funnies / Harlem on My Mind / Heat Wave / How's Chances / Lonely Heart / Not for All the Rice in China / Revolt in Cuba — piano selections / Supper Time — Irving Berlin^w/m *(Berlin)*. Marilyn Miller's last show and a triumph for Ethel Waters, this revue had a run of one year. COVER: sketch of people cheering.

112 As You Were (Broadway, 1920). Sam Bernard, Irene Bordoni.

Follow Mister Watteau / Helen of Troy / If You Could Care / Live for All You're Worth / Ninon Was a Naughty Girl / Two Bits of Greece — Arthur Wimperis^w & Herman Darewski^m *(Remick)*; I Am Cleopatra / If You'll Only Say It with Flowers / Under Grecian Skies / When You're Dancing in Your Nightie on the Lawn — E. Ray Goetz^w/m *(Remick)*; On the Bosom of the Sleepy Nile — E. Ray Goetz^w & Howard Smith^m *(Remick)*; Washington Square — Cole Porter^w & E. Ray Goetz^w & Melville Gideon^m *(Remick)*; Who Ate Napoleons with Josephine — Alfred Bryan^w & E. Ray Goetz^m *(Remick)*. A musical about famous historical beauties which had a four month run. COVER: Sam Bernard and Irene Bordoni.

113 Ask Dad (*see also* **Oh, My Dear!**) (Broadway, 1918). Ivy Sawyer, Joseph Santley.

Boat Song / I Wonder Whether / I'd Ask No More / The Land Where Journeys End / You Never Know — P.G. Wodehouse^w & Louis Hirsch^m *(Harms)*. The last princess show ending when Kern left. This show ran six months, opening as *Oh, My Dear!* but toured as *Ask Dad*. COVER: letters and designs.

114 Aspects of Love (Broadway, 1990). Ann Crumb, Michael Ball.

Anything But Lonely [VS] / Chanson d'Enfance [VS] / Everybody Loves a Hero [VS] / Falling [VS] / The First Man You Remember [VS] / Hand Me the Wine and the Dice [VS] / Journey of a Lifetime [VS] / Leading Lady [VS] / Love Changes Everything [B] / Memory of a Happy Moment [VS] / Mermaid Song [VS] / Other Pleasures [VS] / Parlez-vous Francais? [VS] / Seeing Is Believing [VS] / She'd Be Far Better Off with You [VS] / Stop, Wait, Please [VS] / There Is More to Love [VS] — Don Black^w & Charles Hart^w & Andrew Lloyd Webber^m *(Really Useful)*. A musical about love and its complications. A moderate hit in London but a failure on Broadway.

COVER: a heart and two people kissing.

115 Assassins (Off Broadway, 1991). Terrence Mann, Victor Garber.

Assassins—complete score / The Ballad of Booth [VS] / The Ballad of Guiteau [VS] / The Ballad of Ozolgosz [VS] / Everybody's Got the Right [VS] / Something Just Broke / Unworthy of Your Love [VS]—Stephen Sondheim^w/m *(Warner Bros.)*. An unusual and interesting musical about Presidential assassins produced for a limited run. COVER: white stars on blue background.

116 At Home Abroad (Broadway, 1935). Beatrice Lillie, Ethel Waters.

Farewell My Lovely / Got a Bran' New Suit / The Hottentot Potentate / Love Is a Dancing Thing / O Leo! / That's Not Cricket / Thief in the Night / What a Wonderful World—Howard Dietz^w & Arthur Schwartz^m *(Chappell)*; Get Away from It All (Come Along to Our Show) [VS] / Lady with the Tap-Tap-Tap (Soldier with the Tap-Tap-Tap [VS]—Howard Dietz^w & Arthur Schwartz^m *(USO)*. An excellent revue beautifully staged by Vincent Minnelli with a run of six months. COVER: Ethel Waters, Eleanor Powell, Beatrice Lillie.

117 At the Drop of a Hat (Broadway, 1959). Michael Flanders, Donald Swann.

A-G-NU [VS] / The Elephant [VS] / Have Some Madeira, M'Dear [VS] / Hippopotamus Song / The Rhinoceros [VS] / A Song of the Weather [VS] / Transport of Delight [VS] / Wart Hog Song / The Whale [VS]—Michael Flanders^w/m & Donald Swann^w/m *(Chappell)*; Youth of the Heart—Sydney Carter^w & Donald Swann^m *(Chappell)*. An intimate revue by two British entertainers with a limited run. COVER: Flanders and Swann.

118 At the Drop of Another Hat (Broadway, 1966). Michael Flanders, Donald Swann.

The Gas Man Cometh / Twenty Tons of T.N.T.—Michael Flanders^w/m & Donald Swann^w/m *(Chappell)*. A return engagement of the two Englishmen. COVER: Flanders and Swann.

119 At Your Service (Army, 1943). Soldiers.

I Got the Bird on the Canary Islands—Edward Heyman^w & Paul Baker^m *(Sanders)*; I Wonder How She Is Tonight / Isn't Love a Rainbow? / It's Hot in Chile—Edward Heyman^w & Pat Abernathy^m *(Sanders)*; Spirit of the A.S.C.—J.W. Ehrle^w & Eddie Heyman^w & Michael Cleary^m *(Shapiro, Bernstein)*. COVER: soldiers and planes.

120 Atta Boy (Broadway, 1918). Frank Tinney.

Another Good Man Gone Wrong—Ballard MacDonald^w & Nat Osborne^m *(Shapiro, Bernstein)*; Dad Would Have Been with Us Soon / Father Will Be with Us Soon—H.H. Skerrett^w & Ballard MacDonald^m & Nat Osborne^m *(Shapiro, Bernstein)*; Just to Be a Little Boy Again / Magic in Your Big Blue Eyes / M'sieur Jimmy, Come, and Shake Z Shimmy / On a Little Farm in Normandie / She's Like a Great Big Bouquet / Strolling 'Round the Camp with Mary / Victory Song / With the Rose, I Send This Heart of Mine—Ballard MacDonald^w & Nat Osborne^m *(Shapiro, Bernstein)*. A musical that mocked Army life lasting three weeks. COVER 1: Orange cover with girl waving to silhouette of soldier. COVER 2: Green, brown, orange cover with a soldier and two girls.

121 Away We Go (*see also* **Oklahoma!**) (Broadway, 1943). Alfred Drake, Joan McCracken.

Boys and Girls Like You and Me / Many a New Day / Oh, What a Beautiful Mornin' / People Will Say We're in Love / The Surrey with the Fringe on Top—Oscar Hammerstein^w & Richard Rodgers^m *(Crawford)*. This show was called *Away We Go* for four days in New Haven and two days in Boston and was then changed to *Oklahoma* to match the song. After a struggle to stay afloat during its try-out it went on to become one of Broadway's most celebrated musicals. Sheet music with the title *Away We Go* was sold only during the first week and then probably destroyed. The song *Boys and Girls Like You and Me* is the most rare and was dropped from the show. This show ran for five years on Broadway and had many tours and revivals. COVER: brown and yellow cover with couple in western clothes.

122 Babes in Arms (Broadway, 1937). Alfred Drake, Mitzi Green.

All at Once / All Dark People / Babes in Arms / Babes in Arms — complete score / I Wish I Were in Love Again / Johnny One Note / The Lady Is a Tramp / My Funny Valentine / Way Out West / Where or When — Lorenz Hart[w] & Richard Rodgers[m] *(Chappell)*. One of the best Rodgers and Hart musicals loaded with hit songs and talented youngsters running nine months. COVER: three masks.

123 Babes in the Wood (Off Broadway, 1964). Ruth Buzzi, Danny Carroll.

Babes in the Wood / Helena / I'm Not for You / Little Tear / Love Is Lovely / Lover Waits / Moon Madness / There's a Girl — Rick Besoyan[w/m] *(Cimino)*. Rick Besoyan tried to follow *Mary* with another hit but wound up with a five week failure. COVER: boy chasing girl around a tree.

124 Babes in Toyland (Off Broadway, 1979). Robert Berlott, Georgia McEver.

It's Fun to Feel We're Young [VS] / It's Toyland [VS] / Slumber Song [VS] / Toyland, Toyland [VS] / Toymaker's Song [VS] / Your Heart Is Where You Are [VS] / Zim-Zam-Zumble [VS] — Alice Mathias[w] & Victor Herbert[m] *(Lamb)*; March of the Toys — Victor Herbert[m] *(Lamb)*. A new version of the old classic performed on a limited run. COVER: a little girl and animals.

125 Baby (Broadway, 1983). Beth Fowler, Liz Callaway.

And What If We Had Loved Like That [VS] / At Night She Comes Home to Me [VS] / Baby, Baby, Baby [VS] / Bear, the Tiger, the Hamster, the Mole [CUT] [VS] / Easier to Love [VS] / Fatherhood Blues [VS] / Fathers of Fathers [CUT] [VS] / I Chose Right [VS] / I Want It All / I Wouldn't Go Back [CUT] [VS] / Like a Baby [CUT] [VS] / Patterns [CUT] [VS] / The Story Goes On [VS] / Two People in Love [VS] / With You [VS] — Richard Maltby, Jr.[w] & David Shire[m] *(Fiddleback)*. A very creative musical with good tunes and acting. Being special, it didn't catch on and ran only six months. COVER: red and grey titles and musical notes.

126 Baby Blues (Black, 1919). Ida Brown, Alex Rogers.

Baby Blues / Daddy Noon [ABQ] / Jewel of the Nile [ABQ] / Rain Song [ABQ] / Rock-a-by-Baby Blues [ABQ] / The Wedding [ABQ] — Alex Rogers[w] & C. Lukeyth Roberts[m] *(Manhattan)*. A musical produced by the Quality Amusement Co. to tour their theatres. COVER: titles and designs.

127 Back in My Life (Off Broadway, 1989). Gretchen Cryer, Robin Cryer.

Changing [VS] / Do Whatcha Gotta Do [VS] — Gretchen Cryer[w] & Nancy Ford[m] *(Multimood)*. A limited run revue of Cryer and Ford songs. COVER: Cryer and Ford.

128 Bad (Regional, 1959). Tommy Prisco, Cozy Cole.

Only Once — Steve Allen[w] & De Curtis[m] *(Vernon)*. A concert program of pop stars. COVER: Tommy Prisco.

129 Bad Habits of 1926 (Broadway, 1926). Elise Bonwit, Molly Burnside.

Geisha Girl / Gone Away Blues / Manhattan Transfer / Would-ja? — Arthur Herzog[w] & Manning Sherwin[m] *(Marks)*. A poor revue which lasted two weeks. COVER: showgirl and chorus.

130 Bagels and Yox (Broadway, 1951). Larry Alpert, Lou Saxon.

Chi-ri-bim, Chi-ri-bom / Let's Dance a Frailachs — Sholom Secunda[w/m] & Hy Jacobson[w/m] *(Mills)*. A Jewish revue and a moderate hit of six months. COVER: the Barton Brothers.

131 Bajour (Broadway, 1964). Chita Rivera, Nancy Dussault.

Bajour / Guarantees [VS] / Honest Man [VS] / I Can [VS] / Living Simply / Love Is a Chance / Love-Line / Mean [VS] / Move Over America [VS] / Move Over New York [VS] / Must It Be Love? / Soon [VS] / Where Is the Tribe for Me? [VS] / Words, Words, Words [VS] — Walter Marks^{w/m} *(Morris)*. A musical about gypsies in New York that survived for six months due to Chita Rivera's performance. COVER: a sketch of gypsies.

132 Baker Street (Broadway, 1965). Fritz Weaver, Inga Swenson.

Baker Street March [ABQ] / Finding Words for Spring / I'd Do It Again / Jewelry / A Married Man / A Veritable Work of Art [ABQ] / What a Night This Is Going to Be! — Marian Grudeff^{w/m} & Raymond Jessel^{w/m} *(Marks)*; Buffalo Belle / Cold Clear World / I Shall Miss You Holmes / I'm in London Again — Jerry Bock^{w/m} & Sheldon Harnick^{w/m} *(Marks)*. A lavish and well-acted musical with a poor score and book which lasted nine months. Some of the songs were written by Bock and Harnick but their names do not appear on the sheet music. COVER: sketch of Holmes, Moriarty, and Adler.

133 The Baker's Wife (closed before Broadway, 1976). Patti LuPone, Paul Sorvino.

If I Have to Live Alone [VS] / Meadowlark [VS] / Where Is the Warmth [VS] — Stephen Schwartz^{w/m} *(Warner Bros.)*. A big musical that toured the country with Topol as the star. He was very unhappy with the part and quit in Washington, to be replaced by Sorvino. Two weeks later the show folded. COVER: sketch of bakery.

134 The Bal Tabarin (closed before Broadway, 1923). Stars unknown.

Chiquette / Innocent Eyes / Lady / My Rose — McElbert Moore^{w} & Fred Coots^{m} & Jean Schwartz^{m} *(Harms)*. A gentleman inherits a shady ballroom and trys to make it legitimate. COVER: a ballerina with balloons.

135 Balancing Act (Off Broadway, 1992). Nancy Carroll, Diane Fratantoni.

The Fifth from the Right [VS] / Hollywood 'n' Vinyl [VS] / I Knew the Music [VS] / I Left You There [VS] / Let's Get More Men into Nursing [VS] / Life Is a Balancing Act [VS] / A Long, Long Way [VS] / Play Away the Blues [VS] / That Kid's Gonna Make It [VS] / Welcome, Bienveuneui [VS] / Where Is the Rainbow? [VS] — Dan Goggin^{w/m} *(Warner Bros.)*. A small musical about finding happiness in a well balanced life. COVER: titles with a see-saw.

136 Ball at the Savoy (British, 1933). Maurice Evans, Natalie Hall.

All I Want Is a Home [B] / Ball at the Savoy [B] / A Girl Like Nina [B] / I Always Keep My Girl Out Late [B] / I Live for Love [B] / I'll Show You Off [B] / Oh Why, Oh Why, Oh Why [B] / On the Bosphorus [B] / Up and Down — Oscar Hammerstein^{w} & Paul Abraham^{m} *(Chappell)*; Baby Wait Till It Happens to You [B] piano selections / I Think I'm in Love with My Wife [B] piano selections / Le Marquis de Faublas [B] piano selections / Moon Will Ride Away [B] piano selections — Paul Abraham^{m} *(Chappell)*. A British adaptation of a German musical short run — noted only for Hammerstein's lyrics. COVER: dancing couples in a ballroom with a girl orchestra leader and orchestra.

137 Ballad for a Firing Squad (*see also* Mata Hari) (Off Broadway, 1968). Renata Vaselle, James Hurst.

Maman [PC] — Martin Charnin^{w} & Edward Thomas^{m} *(Morris)*. A revised version of the failure *Mata Hari*. This version lasted one week. COVER: none.

138 Ballad for Bimshire (Off Broadway, 1963). Christine Spencer, Ossie Davis.

Ballad for Bimshire / Chicken's a Popular Bird / Deep in My Heart / 'Fore Day Noon in the Mornin' / Hail Britannia / Have You Got Charm / Lately I've Been Feeling So Strange / My Love Will Come By / My Master Plan / Pardon Me, Sir / Silver Earring

/ We Gon' Jump Up / Yesterday Was Such a Lovely Day — Irving Burgie[w/m] *(Burlington)*. A black musical with a Caribbean setting that lasted only eight weeks. COVER: calypso boy and girl.

139 The Ballad of Baby Doe (Opera, 1958). Beverly Sills, Walter Cassel.

Augusta's Aria / Ballad of Baby Doe — complete score / Farewell Song / Letter Song / Silver Song / Warm as the Autumn Light / Willow Song — John Latouche[w] & Douglas Moore[m] *(Chappell)*. A big hit for the NYC Opera Co. and Beverly Sills about silver mining. COVER: titles and designs.

140 The Ballad of Johnny Pot (Off Broadway, 1971). Betty Buckley, John Perry.

A Carol / Head Down the Road / How Wonderful It Is — Carolyn Richter[w] & Clinton Ballard[m] *(Morris)*. A musical about life in the early '70s and a quick failure of two weeks. COVER: sketch of young man.

141 The Ballad of Magna Carta (Concert, 1940). Stars unknown.

The Ballad of Magna Carta — Maxwell Anderson[w] & Kurt Weill[m] *(Chappell)*. A concert piece to honor the Magna Carta. COVER: old English titles.

142 Ballet Ballads (Broadway, 1948). Richard Harvey, Katherine Litz.

I've Got Me / My Yellow Flower / Ridin' on the Breeze — John Latouche[w] & Jerome Moross[w] *(Chappell)*. Three one act plays with singing and dancing and a run of two months. COVER: titles and designs.

143 Ballroom (Broadway, 1978). Dorothy Loudon, Vincent Gardenia.

Dreams / Fifty Per Cent [VS] / Goodnight Is Not Goodbye [VS] / I Love to Dance / I Wish You a Waltz [VS] / I've Been Waiting All My Life [VS] / More of the Same / One by One [VS] / Somebody Did All Right for Herself [VS] / A Song for Dancin' [VS] / Terrific Band and a Real Nice Crowd [VS] — Alan Bergman[w] & Marilyn Bergman[w] & Billy Goldenberg[m] *(MacMillan)*. A musical version of the TV drama about finding love in a ballroom. It was interesting only for the wonderful Michael Bennett choreography. It lasted three months. COVER: a couple dancing in a ballroom.

144 Ballyhoo (1930) (Broadway, 1930). W.C. Fields, Grace Hayes.

Blow Hot, Blow Cold / How I Could Go for You / If I Were You / That Tired Feeling / Throw It Out the Window — Harry Ruskin[w] & Leighton Brill[w] & Louis Alter[m] *(Harms)*; Cheer Up, Smile, Nerts — Norman Anthony[w] & Misha Portnoff[m] & Wesley Portnoff[m] *(Famous)*; I'm One of God's Children — Oscar Hammerstein[w] & Harry Ruskin[w] & Louis Alter[m] *(Harms)*; No Wonder I'm Blue — Oscar Hammerstein[w] & Louis Alter[m] *(Harms)*. A musical with Fields running a derby to help unemployed actors. The play ran for two months and Fields moved to Hollywood permanently. COVER: three girls gazing at a map.

145 Ballyhoo of '32 (Broadway, 1932). Bob Hope, the Howard Brothers.

Falling off the Wagon — E.Y. Harburg[w] & Johnny Mercer[w] & Lewis Gensler[m] *(Harms)*; How Do You Do It? / Love and Nuts and Noodles / Riddle Me This / Thrill Me — E.Y. Harburg[w] & Lewis Gensler[m] *(Harms)*. A three month revue with great comedy and poor music. COVER: sketches of faces.

146 The Bandwagon (Broadway, 1931). Fred and Adele Astaire.

Beggar's Waltz — published in 1931 in piano selections, and in 1932 as *Is It a Dream* — Arthur Schwartz[m] *(Harms)*; Confession / Dancing in the Dark / High and Low / Hoops / I Love Louisa / Miserable with You / New Sun in the Sky / Sweet Music — Howard Dietz[w] & Arthur Schwartz[m] *(Harms)*. A brilliant revue loaded with hit songs and wonderful talent. The first use of a revolving stage and the last stage appearance of Adele Astaire. It ran for almost nine months. COVER: Fred and Adele Astaire, Frank Morgan, Helen Broderick and others.

147 Banjo Eyes (Broadway, 1941). Eddie Cantor, Audrey Christie.

Banjo Eyes [BW] / Don't Let It Happen Again [BW] / I Always Think of Sally [BW] / I'll Take the City [BW] / My Song Without Words [BW] / Nickel to My Name / Not a Care in the World — John Latouche[w] & Vernon Duke[m] *(Robbins)*; Make with the Feet / We're Having a Baby — Harold Adamson[w] & Vernon Duke[m] *(Robbins)*; We Did It Before — Cliff Friend[w] & Charles Tobias[m] *(Witmark)*; Yanks Are on the March Again [BW] — Harold Adamson[w] & Peter DeRose[m] *(Robbins)*. Eddie Cantor returned to Broadway after 14 years in Hollywood. He could not stand the climate, and returned to Hollywood. The show folded, having run three months. COVER: Eddie Cantor and his big eyes.

148 The Banker's Daughter (Off Broadway, 1962). David Daniels, Helena Scott.

Say No More / The Sun Rises / Unexpectedly — Edward Eliscu[w] & Sol Kaplan[m] *(Chappell)*. A musical about the elegance in New York at the turn of the century which ran two months. COVER: a gentleman and a lady.

149 Bare Facts of 1926 (Broadway, 1926). Rubert Lucas, Mary Doerr.

Nice Girl / Sky Scrapers / Stand Up on Your Feet and Dance / Third from the End — Henry Myers[w] & Charles Schwab[m] *(Marks)*. A poor revue that lasted three months. COVER: a chorus girl.

150 Bare Facts of 1927 (Broadway, 1927). Stars unknown.

Blue Step / Greenwich Village Violet / The Moon, You and I / Ola in Your Little Gondola / Romance in a Dance / Samoa Sam — Love Me Some More / Sh-Sh-Shirley / You Can't Stop the Sun — Marion Gillespie[w] & Menlo Mayfield[w] & John Hagen[m] *(Shapiro, Bernstein)*. Another poor revue with a short life. COVER: sketch of pretty girl.

151 Barefoot Boy with Cheek (Broadway, 1947). Red Buttons, Nancy Walker.

After Graduation Day / I Knew I'd Know / It's Too Nice a Day to Go to School / The Story of Carrot / When You're Eighteen — Sylvia Dee[w] & Sidney Lippman[m] *(Chappell)*. A college musical with an ordinary score. Nancy Walker kept it running for three months. COVER: college boy and girl.

152 Barnum (Broadway, 1980). Jim Dale, Glenn Close.

Bigger Isn't Better [VS] / Black and White [VS] / The Colors of My Life / Come Follow the Band [VS] / I Like Your Style [VS] / Join the Circus [VS] / Love Makes Such Fools of Us All [VS] / Museum Song [VS] / One Brick at a Time [VS] / Out There [VS] / Prince of Humbug [VS] / Thank God I'm Old [VS] / There Is a Sucker Born Ev'ry Minute — Michael Stewart[w] & Cy Coleman[m] *(Notable)*. A circus musical with good music that ran for two years. COVER: a showman.

153 Battling Butler *(see also* **The Dancing Honeymoon***)* (Broadway, 1923). Charles Ruggles, Marie Saxon.

As We Leave the Years Behind — Ballard MacDonald[w] & Joseph Meyer[m] *(Harms)*; Dancing Honeymoon — Douglas Furber[w] & Ballard MacDonald[w] & Philip Braham[m] *(Harms)*; In the Spring — Ballard MacDonald[w] & Adorjan Otvos[m] *(Harms)*; Someday, You Will Marry Me / Two Little Pals / Will You Marry Me? (Someday) — Ballard MacDonald[w] & Walter Rosemond[m] *(Harms)*; Tinkle Tune — Ballard MacDonald[w] & Louis Breau[w] & Adorjan Otvos[m] *(Harms)*. A British musical about prizefighting which was a moderate hit of nine months. Try-out title was *Dancing Honeymoon*. COVER: bandleader and chorus girls.

154 Be Careful Dearie (closed before Broadway, 1922). Stars unknown.

Be Careful Dearie / Garden of Lies / La-Lo-La / Me for Araby / My Night-Light Girl / Something New / Somewhere — Victor Schertzinger[w/m] *(Sherman-Clay)*. COVER: a girl with balloons.

155 Be Happy (Jewish, 1942). Yetta Zwerling, Menasha Skulnik.

Freilach Zol Sein (Be Happy) — Isidore Lillian[w] & Sholom Secunda[m] *(Metro)*; Seit Du Bist Avek Fun Mir — Isidore Lillian[w] & Sholom Secunda[m] *(Kammen)*. COVER: Yetta Zwerling, Menasha Skulnik.

156 Be Yourself (Broadway, 1924). Jack Donahue, Queenie Smith.

Bongo Boo — Owen Murphy[w] & Jay Gorney[w] & Milton Schwarzwald[m] *(Harms)*; The Decent Thing to Do / Little Bit of This / Love and the Rose / My Road — Marc Connelly[w] & George Kaufman[w] & Lewis Gensler[m] *(Harms)*; I Came Here — Marc Connelly[w] & George Kaufman[w] & Ira Gershwin[w] & Lewis Gensler[m] *(Harms)*; Uh-Uh! / Wrong Thing at the Right Time — Marc Connelly[w] & George Kaufman[w] & Ira Gershwin[w] & Milton Schwarzwald[m] *(Harms)*. A musical about a feud in Tennessee lasting three months. COVER: titles and designs.

157 Beachcomber Club Revue of 1946 (Nightclub, 1946). Stars unknown.

Farewell My Lovely / The Girl in the Front Porch Swing / Little Washer Woman Down in Rio — Edward Eager[w] & Fred Coots[m] *(Mills)*. COVER: girl in tropical outfit.

158 Beachcomber Nites (Nightclub, 1942). Stars unknown.

The Gaucho with the Black Mustache / Rio Rhythm / When — Benny Davis[w] & Sam Stept[m] *(Mills)*. COVER: a dancing girl.

159 Beat the Band (Broadway, 1942). Susan Miller, Jack Whiting.

Ev'ry Other Heartbeat / Let's Comb Beaches / Proud of You / The Steam Is on the Beam — George Marion[w] & Johnny Green[m] *(Crawford)*. A very minor musical involving a girl and a bandleader running two months. COVER: a bandleader and chorus girls.

160 The Beauty Part (Broadway, 1962). Bert Lahr, Alice Ghostley.

The Beauty Part — Don Walker[m] *(Frank)*. A comedy with Bert Lahr playing many roles with a short run. COVER: Bert Lahr.

161 The Beauty Prize (British, 1923). Dorothy Dickson, Leslie Henson.

Cottage in Kent [B] [VS] / For the Man I Love [B] [VS] / It's a Long, Long Day [B] / Meet Me Down on Main Street [B] / We Will Take the Road Together [B] [VS] / You Can't Make Love by Wireless [B] — George Grossmith[w] & P.G. Wodehouse[w] & Jerome Kern[m] *(Chappell)*; Honeymoon Isle [B] / I'm a Prize [B] / Joy Bells [B] [VS] / Moon Love [B] / Non-Stop Dancing [B] / When You Take the Road with Me [B] / You'll Find Me Playing Mah-Jongg [B] [VS] — P.G. Wodehouse[w] & Jerome Kern[m] *(Chappell)*. Musical of love among the rich. It was a hit in London with a run of six months. COVER: Leslie Henson, Dorothy Dickson, George Grossmith.

162 Beggar's Holiday (Broadway, 1946). Alfred Drake, Zero Mostel.

Brown Penny [VS] — Duke Ellington[m] *(Mutual)*; I've Got Me [VS] / Maybe I Should Change My Ways [VS] / On the Wrong Side of the Railroad Tracks / Take Love Easy / Tomorrow Mountain / Tooth and Claw [VS] / Wanna Be Bad / When I Walk with You — John Latouche[w] & Duke Ellington[m] *(Mutual)*. This show was *The Beggar's Opera* updated with a good book, but ill-matched music. It was a small show lost in a big Broadway house running three months. COVER: boy and girl embracing on fire escape.

163 The Belle of New York of 1921 (*see also* **The Whirl of New York of 1921**) (Broadway, 1921). J. Harold Murray, Smith & Dale.

Gee, I Wish I Had a Girl Like You — Cliff Friend[w] & Lew Pollack[m] & Al Goodman[m] *(Remick)*; One Last Good Time — Cyrus Wood[w] & Lew Pollack[m] & Al Goodman[m] *(Remick)*. A musical about a girl's life in New York running three months. The tryout title was *Belle of New York of 1921*. COVER: a Salvation Army girl.

164 The Belle of Quakertown (*see also* **No Other Girl** *and* **The Town Clown** (Broadway, 1923). Eddie Buzzell, Helen Ford.

Doing the Town / Honduras / In the Corner of My Mind / No Other Girl — Bert Kalmar$^{w/m}$ & Harry Ruby$^{w/m}$ *(Berlin)*. A musical about building a highway running two months. The tryout title was *Belle of Quakertown* and *The Town Clown.*

165 Belle Starr (British, 1969). Betty Grable, Ray Chiarella.

Belle [B] / Gee, You're Pretty [B] — Steve Allen$^{w/m}$ *(Flying D Music)*. A musical written for Betty Grable by Steve Allen lasting two weeks. COVER: Betty Grable.

166 Bells Are Ringing (Broadway, 1956). Judy Holliday, Sydney Chaplin.

Bells Are Ringing / Bells Are Ringing — complete score / Drop That Name / Hello, Hello, There / I Met a Girl / Independent / Just in Time / Long Before I Knew You / Mu-Cha-Cha / The Party's Over — Betty Comden^w & Adolph Green^w & Jule Styne^m *(Stratford)*. A musical dealing with a telephone answering service. With a good book and a score with hit songs it ran for two and one half years. COVER: Judy Holliday.

167 Le Bellybutton (Off Broadway, 1976). Marilyn Chambers, Alan Scott.

Jenny — Scott Mansfield$^{w/m}$ *(Mansfield)*; Marilyn's Theme — Scott Mansfield^m *(Mansfield)*. A short lived "X-rated" musical. COVER: Marilyn Chambers.

168 The Beloved Bandit (closed before Broadway, 1925). Gerald Griffin.

After the Rain — Gerald Griffin$^{w/m}$ & Roy Barton$^{w/m}$ *(Feist)*; Arizona Rose — Gerald Griffin$^{w/m}$ & Lon Healy$^{w/m}$ *(Feist)*; The Garden of Eden Was in Ireland / I'm Always Reaching for the Moon — Gerald Griffin$^{w/m}$ *(Feist)*; Sunset Hour — Gerald Griffin$^{w/m}$ & Dan Sullivan$^{w/m}$ *(Feist)*. COVER: Gerald Griffin, cowboys and horses.

169 Beloved Rogue (*see also* **Venus in Silk**) (closed before Broadway, 1932). Florenz Ames, Audrey Christie.

Baby, Play with Me / Eyes That Are Smiling / I Ask Not Who You Are — Lester O'Keefe^w & Robert Stolz^m *(Chappell)*. This operetta was produced by the St. Louis Opera Co. as *The Beloved Rogue*. It was revised and toured as *Venus in Silk* but folded in Washington before Broadway. COVER: sketch of a rogue.

170 Ben Franklin in Paris (Broadway, 1964). Robert Preston, Ulla Sallert.

Diane Is [VS] / God Bless the Human Elbow / Half the Battle / Hic Haec Hoc [VS] / How Laughable It Is / I Invented Myself [VS] / I Love the Ladies / Look for Small Pleasures / We Sail the Seas [VS] / Whatever Became of Old Temple? [VS] / When I Dance with the Person I Love / You're in Paris [VS] — Sidney Michaels^w & Mark Sandrich^m *(Morris)*; To Be Alone with You / Too Charming [VS] — Jerry Herman$^{w/m}$ *(Morris)*. A musical about Ben Franklin that was pretty bad and lasted only six months. Two songs were written by Jerry Herman but credited to Michaels and Sandrich. COVER: Franklin and kite.

171 Ben Marden Palais Royal Revue (Nightclub, 1934). Stars unknown.

I Love Gardenias / I'm Full of the Devil / Lost in a Fog / Tell Me / Thank You for a Lovely Evening — Dorothy Fields^w & Jimmy McHugh^m *(Robbins)*. COVER: an elegant couple.

172 Ben Marden Riviera Follies of 1936 (Nightclub, 1936). Stars unknown.

Do the Riviera / Face Behind the Veil / You Foolish Heart — Milton Drake$^{w/m}$ & Harry Stride$^{w/m}$ & Bernard Maltin$^{w/m}$ *(Mills)*. COVER: showgirl and dancers.

173 Ben Marden Riviera Follies of 1937 (Nightclub, 1937). Stars unknown.

I'm Happy Darling Dancing with You / The Image of You / It's the Smile That Gets 'Em / A Whippoorwill in a Willow Tree / You'll Get a Cold in Your Toes — Joe Young^w & Fred

Ahlert[m] *(Feist)*. COVER: an elegant couple.

174 Berlin to Broadway with Kurt Weill (Off Broadway, 1972). Jerry Lanning, Ken Kercheval.

Alabama Song [VS] — Bert Brecht[w] & Kurt Weill[m] *(Leonard)*; The Bilbao Song [VS] / Surabaya Johnny [VS] — Michael Feingold[w] & Bert Brecht[w] & Kurt Weill[m] *(Leonard)*; A Boy Like You / What Good Would the Moon Be [VS] — Langston Hughes[w] & Kurt Weill[m] *(Leonard)*; Green-Up Time [VS] / Here I'll Stay [VS] / Love Song [VS] / Susan's Dream [VS] — Alan Jay Lerner[w] & Kurt Weill[m] *(Leonard)*; It Never Was You [VS] / Little Grey House [VS] / Lost in the Stars [VS] / September Song [VS] / Stay Well [VS] / There's Nowhere to Go but Up [VS] / Trouble Man [VS] — Maxwell Anderson[w] & Kurt Weill[m] *(Leonard)*; Listen to My Song [VS] / Mon Ami, My Friend [VS] — Paul Green[w] & Kurt Weill[m] *(Leonard)*; Mack the Knife [VS] — Marc Blitzstein[w] & Bert Brecht[w] & Kurt Weill[m] *(Leonard)*; My Ship [VS] / The Saga of Jenny / Sing Me Not a Ballad [VS] / This Is New [VS] — Ira Gershwin[w] & Kurt Weill[m] *(Leonard)*; Speak Low [VS] — Ogden Nash[w] & Kurt Weill[m] *(Leonard)*. A tribute to Kurt Weill which ran several months. COVER: silver letters.

175 Best Foot Forward (Broadway, 1941). June Allyson, Nancy Walker.

Buckle Down, Winsocki / Ev'ry Time / I Know You by Heart / Just a Little Joint with a Juke Box / Shady Lady Bird / That's How I Love the Blues / The Three "R's" / What Do You Think I Am? / Wish I May — Hugh Martin[w/m] & Ralph Blane[w/m] *(Chappell)*. A musical about a college and a movie star with the direction of George Abbott and a hit song that ran for ten months. COVER: a building and an envelope.

176 Best Foot Forward (Off Broadway, 1963). Liza Minnelli, Glenn Walken.

A Raving Beauty / You Are for Loving — Hugh Martin[w/m] & Ralph Blane[w/m] *(Feist)*. A revival with Minnelli in her stage debut running six months. COVER: Liza Minnelli.

177 The Best Little Whorehouse in Texas (Broadway, 1978). Delores Hall, Carlin Glynn.

The Aggie Song / Bus from Amarillo / Doatsy Mae / Girl, You're a Woman / Good Old Girl / Hard Candy Christmas / A Li'l Ole Bitty Pissant Country Place / No Lies / The Sidestep / Texas Has a Whorehouse in It / Twenty Fans / Twenty Four Hours of Lovin' / Watch Dog Theme — Carol Hall[w/m] *(M.C.A.)*. A musical dealing with a whorehouse and its problems. It was a hit Off Broadway and moved to Broadway running for four years. COVER: a map of Texas, a TV set, and a pair of legs.

178 Betsy (Broadway, 1926). Belle Baker, Allen Kearns.

Blue Skies — Irving Berlin[w/m] *(Berlin)*; Come and Tell Me / If I Were You / Sing / This Funny World / You're the Mother Type — Lorenz Hart[w] & Richard Rodgers[m] *(Harms)*; Stonewall Moskowitz March — Irving Caesar[w/m] & Lorenz Hart[w/m] & Richard Rodgers *(Harms)*. A musical about a mother and her daughters' suitors. It was produced by Ziegfeld who did not like the show or Rodgers and Hart. He allowed Belle Baker to sing Irving Berlin's *Blue Skies,* which became the hit of the show further annoying Rodgers and Hart. The show lasted only five weeks. COVER: a lady and her suitors.

179 Better 'Ole (Broadway, 1918). Charles Coburn, Edwin Taylor.

Have a Little Regiment of Your Own / When You Take This Trip Across the Rhine — Percival Knight[w/m] *(Feist)*; I Wish I Was in Blighty — W.R. Titterton[w/m] & Herman Darewski[w/m] *(Feist)*; I'm Sick of This 'Ere Blinkin' War — Herman Darewski[w/m] *(Feist)*; It's Our Wedding Day — Grant Stewart[w/m] & Percival Knight[w/m] *(Feist)*; My Word, Ain't We Carrying On — Percival Knight[w/m] & Melville Gideon[w/m] &

James Heard^{w/m} & Herman Darewski^{w/m} *(Feist)*; She's Venus De Milo to Me — Peter Bernard^{w/m} & Oliver DeGerde^{w/m} *(Feist)*; Tommy — James Heard^w & Herman Darewski^m *(Feist)*; When You Look in the Heart of a Rose — Marian Gillespie^w & Florence Methven^m *(Feist)*. A big hit European musical about soldiers and spies with a run of almost a year. Cover: Mr. and Mrs. Charles Coburn.

180 Better Times (Broadway, 1922). Nanette Flack, Robert McLellan.

Better Times / Blowing Bubbles All Day Long / The Grand Opera Ball / My Golden Dream Ship / Peach Blossom Time / The Tale of a Fan / An Up to Date Tune — R.H. Burnside^w & Raymond Hubbell^m *(Harms)*; Peanut Vendor — Marion Sunshine^w & L. Wolfe Gilbert^w & Moises Simons^m *(Marks)*. The last Hippodrome spectacle lasting for one year. Charles Dillingham left after this production. Cover: a map of the United States.

181 Betty Be Good (Broadway, 1920). Frank Crumit, Josephine Whittell.

Betty Behave / By Pango Pango Bay / I'd Like to Take You Away / Just Listen to My Heart Beat / Keep the Love Lamp Burning / Same Old Stars, Same Old Moon / Tell Me, Daisy / 'Tis in Vain That I Try to Forget You / You Must Be Good, Girls — Harry B. Smith^w & Hugo Riesenfeld^m *(Berlin)*. A musical from a French farce dealing with old lovers running for three weeks. Cover: a well dressed lady with dog.

182 Betty Dear (closed before Broadway, 1924). Stars unknown.

Then You Know That You're in Love — Owen Murphy^{w/m} & Harry Richman^{w/m} & Jay Gorney^{w/m} *(Harms)*; Whistle in the Rain — McElbert Moore^w & Fred Coots^m *(Berlin)*. Cover: titles and designs.

183 Betty Lee (Broadway, 1924). Joe E. Brown, Hal Skelly.

Arabian Dream / Betty Lee — Otto Harbach^w & Irving Caesar^w & Louis Hirsch^m *(Harms)*; I Am Thinking of You — Irving Caesar^w & Louis Hirsch^m *(Harms)*; I'm Going to Dance at Your Wedding — Irving Caesar^w & Con Conrad^m *(Harms)*; Let's Kiss Goodbye — Otto Harbach^w & Irving Caesar^w & Louis Hirsch^m & Con Conrad^m *(Harms)*. A musical about racing that was kept going for three months only by the antics of Joe E. Brown. Cover: a building and trees.

184 Between the Devil (Broadway, 1937). Jack Buchanan, Evelyn Laye.

By Myself / Don't Go Away Monsieur / I Believe in You [PC] / I See Your Face Before Me / Triplets [BW] / Why Did You Do It? / You Have Everything — Howard Dietz^w & Arthur Schwartz^m *(Crawford)*; The Uniform (dance, revised form) [VS] — Howard Dietz^w & Arthur Schwartz^m *(USO)*. A story of one man with two wives running three months. It had some hit songs but was the end of Dietz and Schwartz as a songwriting team. Cover: the devil and ladies faces.

185 Biff! Bing! Bang! (Broadway, 1921). Al Plunkett, Ross Hamilton.

Down Texas Way — Fred Godfrey^{w/m} & A.J. Mills^{w/m} & Bennett Scott^{w/m} *(Feist)*; I Know Where the Flies Go — Sam Mayo^{w/m} & John Harrington^{w/m} *(Feist)*. A limited run on Broadway for this touring Canadian soldier show. Cover: Albert Plunkett.

186 Big as Life (College, 1948). Stars unknown.

Everybody Loses / Great Wisconsin / Stairway Lullaby / Why Sing a Love Song? — Jack Royce^w & Jerry Bock^m *(BMI)*. A college show which was Bock's first show. His name was listed as Jerrold Bock. Cover: lumber man with an axe.

187 Big Boy (Broadway, 1925). Al Jolson, Nancy Carroll.

As Long as I've Got My Mammy / Born and Bred in Old Kentucky / The Dance from Down Under / Hello Tucky / Lackawanna / Who Was Chasing Paul Revere? — B.G. DeSylva^w & Joseph Meyer^m & James Hanley^m

(Harms); If You Knew Susie — B.G. DeSylva[w/m] *(Shapiro, Bernstein)*; I'm Tellin' the Birds, Tellin' the Bees — Lew Brown[w/m] & Cliff Friends[w/m] *(Berlin)*; It All Depends on You — B.G. DeSylva[w/m] & Lew Brown[w/m] & Ray Henderson[w/m] *(D B and H)*; Keep Smiling at Trouble — Al Jolson[w] & B.G. DeSylva[w] & Lewis Gensler[m] *(Harms)*; Miami / Nobody but Fanny — Al Jolson[w/m] & B.G. DeSylva[w/m] & Con Conrad[w/m] *(Harms)*; On the Z-R-3 — Sam Lewis[w] & Joe Young[w] & Walter Donaldson[m] *(W B and S)*; One O'Clock Baby — B.G. DeSylva[w] & Lew Brown[w] & Al Jolson[m] *(D B and H)*. A musical about horse racing which appeared to be in for a long run but was cut short due to Jolson's illness. Jolson returned after several months and the show ran on plus a tour. COVER: Al Jolson.

188 The Big Mogul (Broadway, 1925). Fiske O'Hara, Charlotte Kent.

Heart o' Mine / Mother Asthore / Mrs. Donegan — Eddie Dowling[w/m] *(Harms)*. A comedy with some songs about a plumber and his inheritance. COVER: Fiske O'Hara.

189 Big River (Broadway, 1985). Daniel Jenkins, Ron Richardson.

Arkansas/How Blest We Are [VS] / The Boys [VS] / The Crossing [VS] / Do Ya Wanna Go to Heaven? [VS] / Free at Last [VS] / Guv'ment [VS] / Hand for the Hog [VS] / I, Huckleberry, Me [VS] / Leavin's Not the Only Way to Go [VS] / Muddy Water / River in the Rain / The Royal Nonesuch [VS] / Waitin' for the Light to Shine / When the Sun Goes Down in the South [VS] / Worlds Apart / You Oughta Be Here with Me [VS] — Roger Miller[w/m] *(Leonard)*. A musical version of *Huckleberry Finn* that ran for two years. It was not that great but there was a lean period on Broadway. COVER: Huck and Jim on a raft on the Big River.

190 The Big Show (Nightclub, 1939). Stars unknown.

Hello, Mr. Love / I Still Can Hear Your Sighs / So Close to Heaven / Tahiti / We May Not Get Another Chance / You're an Eyeful — George Brown[w/m] & Irving Actman[w/m] *(Mills)*. COVER: a naked girl dancing.

191 Bill Miller's Riviera (Nightclub, 1951). Stars unknown.

Bless All the Beautiful Girls / You've Got Me Singin' — Benny Davis[w/m] *(B V and C)*. COVER: a beautiful show girl.

192 Billie (Broadway, 1928). Polly Walker, Joseph Wagstaff.

Billie / Come to St. Thomas's / Every Boy in Town's My Sweetheart / Go Home Ev'ry Once in a While / Happy / I'm a One Girl Man / Personality / Say It Some More / They Fall in Love / Those Wonderful Friends / The Two of Us / Where Were You — Where Was I? — George M. Cohan[w/m] *(Witmark)*. A musical about a chewing gum factory and a secretary. It was Cohan's last Broadway show and is remembered only for its excellent dancing. It ran three months. COVER: Polly Walker.

193 Billion Dollar Baby (Broadway, 1945). David Burns, Helen Gallagher.

Bad Timing / I Got a One Track Mind / I'm Sure of Your Love — Betty Comden[w] & Adolph Green[w] & Morton Gould[m] *(Chappell)*. A "roaring twenties" musical with golddiggers and gangsters. It was very ordinary with a run of six months. COVER: a dollar sign and lady with champagne.

194 Billy Barnes L.A. (Regional, 1962). Joyce Jameson, Ken Berry.

Does Anybody Here Love Me? / L.A. Is / Where Was the Music? — Billy Barnes[w/m] *(Tylerson)*. A West Coast edition of the Broadway hit with some new songs. COVER: titles and designs.

195 Billy Barnes Revue (Broadway, 1959). Joyce Jameson, Bert Convy.

Foolin' Ourselves / Too Long at the Fair — Billy Barnes[w/m] *(Tyler)*. A revue from California that lasted six months and produced one hit song. COVER: Joyce Jameson and the cast.

196 Billy Rose Aquacade (Great Lakes Exposition) (Regional, 1937). Johnny Weissmuller, Eleanor Holm Jarrett.

The Camera Doesn't Lie—Edgar Leslie[w] & Joe Burke[m] *(Santly Bros.-Joy)*; Happy Birthday to Love—Billy Rose[w/m] & Stanley Joseloff[w/m] & Dana Suesse[w/m] & Rudolph Bertram[w/m] & Fenyes Szabolcs[w/m] *(Crawford)*; It Can't Happen Here—Billy Rose[w] & Stanley Joseloff[w] & Dana Suesse[m] *(Crawford)*; It Happened in Miami— Billy Rose[w] & Dana Suesse[m] *(Crawford)*; Strangers in the Dark—Billy Rose[w] & Stanley Adams[w] & Belle Fenstock[m] *(Crawford)*. COVER: Weissmuller and Jarrett; bathing beauty and buildings.

197 Billy Rose Aquacade (New York World's Fair) (Regional, 1939). Eleanor Holm, Johnny Weissmuller.

Roller Skating on a Rainbow—Billy Rose[w/m] & Irving Kahal[w/m] & Harry Warren[w/m] *(B V and C)*; Yours for a Song— Billy Rose[w] & Ted Fetter[w] & Dana Suesse[m] *(Robbins)*. COVER: Eleanor Holm; World's Fair buildings.

198 Billy Rose Aquacade (Golden Gate International Exposition) (Regional, 1940). Stars unknown.

Yours for a Song—Billy Rose[w] & Ted Fetter[w] & Dana Suesse[m] *(Robbins)*. COVER: the main tower and buildings.

199 Billy Rose Aquacade (New York World's Fair) (Regional, 1940). Eleanor Holm.

Eleanor, I Adore You / There's a New Gang on the Way / When the Spirit Moves Me / You Think of Everything—Joseph McCarthy[w] & Billy Rose[w] & Jimmy Van Heusen[m] *(Robbins)*; You're Too Good to Be True— Billy Rose[w] & Dana Suesse[m] *(Robbins)*. COVER: Eleanor Holm and buildings.

200 Billy Rose Casa Manana (Fort Worth) (Regional, 1936). Paul Whiteman, Sally Rand.

Another Mile—Billy Rose[w] & Irving Kahal[w] & Dana Suesse[m] *(Words and Music)*; It Happened in Chicago / Lone Star / The Night Is Young / You're Like a Toy Balloon—Billy Rose[w] & Irving Kahal[w] & Dana Suesse[m] *(Chappell)*. COVER: girl riding a bronco.

201 Billy Rose Casa Manana (Fort Worth) (Regional, 1937). Stars unknown.

The Devil Dance / Gone with the Dawn / It Can't Happen Here—Billy Rose[w] & Stanley Joseloff[w] & Dana Suesse[m] *(Words and Music)*. COVER: cowgirl and buildings; the Statue of Liberty.

202 Billy Rose Casa Manana (New York) (Nightclub, 1938). Morton Downey, Wini Shaw.

At a Perfume Counter—Edgar Leslie[w] & Joe Burke[m] *(Donaldson)*; The Sun Will Shine Tonight—Billy Rose[w] & Ted Fetter[w] & Ned Lehac[m] *(Miller)*. COVER: Morton Downey, Wini Shaw, Oscar Shaw, Abe Lyman, Sally Rand.

203 Billy Rose Casino de Paree Revue (#1) (Nightclub, 1934). Stars unknown.

Frosted Chocolate—Billy Rose[w] & Paul F. Webster[w] & John Loeb[m] *(Harms)*; Got the Jitters—Billy Rose[w] & Paul F. Webster[w] & John Loeb[m] *(Keit-Engel)*; I Wanna Be Loved—Billy Rose[w] & Edward Heyman[w] & John Green[m] *(Famous)*. COVER: frosted soda with face; red, white and blue girls dancing.

204 Billy Rose Casino de Paree Revue (#2) (Nightclub, 1934). Stars unknown.

Have a Little Dream on Me—Billy Rose[w] & John Murray[w] & Phil Baxter[m] *(Harms)*; You're Sensational— Paul F. Webster[w/m] & John Loeb[w/m] *(Harms)*. COVER: sketch of castle and tree.

205 Billy Rose Crazy Quilt (Broadway, 1931). Phil Baker, Fanny Brice.

Crazy Quilt—Bud Green[w] & Harry Warren[m] *(D B and H)*; Have a Little Drinkee—Edward Eliscu[w] & Ned Lehac[m] *(D B and H)*; I Found a Million Dollar Baby—Billy Rose[w] & Mort Dixon[w] & Harry Warren[m] *(Remick)*; In the Merry Month of Maybe—Ira Gershwin[w] & Billy Rose[w] & Harry Warren[m] *(Harms)*; It's in the Air—E.Y. Harburg[w] & Billy Rose[w] & Lou Alter[m] *(D B and H)*; Sing a Little

Jingle—Mort Dixon[w] & Harry Warren[m] *(D B and H)*; To Think That Once We Were Sweethearts—Edgar Leslie[w] & Billy Rose[w] & James Monaco[m] *(D B and H)*. A revised edition of the revue called *Sweet and Low/Corned Beef and Roses*. It ran for only two months but produced one hit song. COVER: silhouette of man and woman.

206 Billy Rose Crazy Quilt of 1933 (Broadway, 1933). Anita Page.

I Wanna Be Loved—Billy Rose[w] & Edward Heyman[w] & John Green[m] *(Famous)*; It's Only a Paper Moon—Billy Rose[w] & E.Y. Harburg[w] & Harold Arlen[m] *(Harms)*. This revised edition had a short run and short tour. It is notable for the first publication of the song *Paper Moon* which had been written for an earlier Billy Rose show. COVER: couple under tree; Anita Page.

207 Billy Rose Diamond Horseshoe (Nightclub, 1939). Stars unknown.

Let's Dream Again—Billy Rose[w/m] & James Hanley[w/m] & Jean Herbert[w/m] *(B V and C)*. COVER: a diamond horseshoe.

208 Billy Rose Music Hall Revue (Nightclub, 1934). Stars unknown.

Beautiful Face Have a Heart—Billy Rose[w] & Ballard MacDonald[w] & Leo Edwards[m] *(Donaldson)*. COVER: Phil Harris, singer and bandleader.

209 Birth of a Nation (Down South Prologue) (Broadway, 1930). Stars unknown.

Close in Your Arms / I've Got You to Thank for That / Steamboat Song—Irving Bibo[w/m] & Albert Von Tilzer[w/m] *(Sherman Clay)*. A minimusical performed between showings of the classic film *Birth of a Nation*, 1930 revival. COVER: titles and designs.

210 Bits and Pieces (closed before Broadway, 1920). Joseph Santley, Ivy Sawyer.

Some Pretty Day—Sam Lewis[w] & Joe Young[w] & Fred Ahlert[m] *(Berlin)*. COVER: Joseph Santley, Ivy Sawyer.

211 Bittersweet (Broadway, 1929). Evelyn Laye, Peggy Wood.

Bittersweet—complete score / The Call of Life / Dear Little Cafe / Green Carnations / If Love Were All / If You Could Only Come with Me / I'll See You Again / Kiss Me / Ladies of the Town / Tokay / What Is Love? / Zigeuner—Noel Coward[w/m] *(Harms)*. A lavish Ziegfeld production of a big London hit that ran for only 20 weeks in New York, despite some lovely Noel Coward songs and Evelyn Laye. COVER: framed picture of a lady and piano.

212 Bittersweet Blues (Broadway, 1928). Stars unknown.

Bittersweet Blues—James Dietrich[w/m] & Bobby Lewis[w/m] *(Famous)*. A mini musical performed in between showings of Paramount films in large theatres. COVER: trees, clouds, and the sky.

213 Bizarrities (Nightclub, 1933). George Jessel.

I Can Sew a Button / Moody and Blue / My International Girl / Once in a While / Till Doomsday—Sammy Lerner[w] & Gerald Marks[m] *(Witmark)*. COVER: girl with top hat.

214 Black and Blue (Broadway, 1990). Lavern Baker, Linda Hopkins.

After You've Gone [VS]—Henry Creamer[w/m] & Turner Layton[w/m] *(Belwin)*; Am I Blue [VS]—Grant Clarke[w] & Harry Akst[m] *(Belwin)*; Black and Blue [VS]—Fats Waller[w/m] & Harry Brooks[w/m] *(Belwin)*; Black and Tan Fantasy [VS]—Duke Ellington[m] & Bud Miley[m] *(Belwin)*; Body and Soul [VS]—Edward Heyman[w] & Robert Sour[w] & Frank Eyton[w] & John Green[m] *(Belwin)*; Call It Stormy Monday [VS]—Aron T. Walker[w/m] *(Belwin)*; I Can't Give You Anything But Love [VS]—Dorothy Fields[w] & Jimmy McHugh[m] *(Belwin)*; I Gotta Right to Sing the Blues [VS]—Ted Koehler[w] & Harold Arlen[m] *(Belwin)*; If I Can't Sell It, I'll Keep Sittin' on It [VS]—Alex Hill[w/m] & Andy Razaf[w/m] *(Belwin)*; I'm a Woman [VS]—Cora Taylor[w/m] & Elias McDaniel[w/m] *(Belwin)*; I'm Gettin' 'long Alright [VS]—Bobby Sharp[w/m] & Charles Singleton[w/m] *(Belwin)*; In a

Sentimental Mood [VS] — Duke Ellington^m *(Belwin)*; Royal Garden Blues [VS] — Clarence Williams^{w/m} & Spencer Williams^{w/m} *(Belwin)*; St. Louis Blues [VS] — W.C. Handy^{w/m} *(Belwin)*; Stompin' at the Savoy [VS] — Benny Goodman^{w/m} & Chick Webb^{w/m} & Edgar Sampson^m *(Belwin)*; Tain't Nobody's Bis-ness If I Do [VS] — Porter Grainger^{w/m} & Everett Robbins^{w/m} *(Belwin)*. A big hit revue featuring famous blues and other songs running for two years. COVER: two volumes of songs — one with black titles and one with blue titles.

215 Black and White Revue (Broadway, 1935). Stars unknown.

I Gotta Take My Hat Off to You — Albert Silverman^w & Kay Swift^m *(Miller)*. A revue at Radio City Music Hall by Russell Market. COVER: sketch of elegant lady.

216 Black Berries of 1930 (Nightclub, 1930). Stars unknown.

Bumpty Bump / Come Along, Mandy / Cotton Club Stomp / Doin' the Crazy Walk — Irving Mills^w & Duke Ellington^m *(Mills)*; Swanee River Rhapsody — Clarence Gaskill^{w/m} & Irving Mills^{w/m} & Duke Ellington^{w/m} *(Mills)*; You're the Reason Why I Fell in Love — Irving Mills^w & Duke Ellington^m *(Mills)*. One of a series of annual shows done at the Cotton Club. COVER: black girl dancing.

217 Black Berries of 1932 (Broadway, 1932). Mantan Moreland, Moms Mabley.

The Answer Is No / Blackberries / Brown Sugar / First Thing in the Morning / Harlem Mania — Donald Heywood^{w/m} *(Remick)*; Love Me More — Love Me Less — Ben Bernard^w & Tom Peluso^m *(Shapiro, Bernstein)*. A poor imitation of the Blackbirds that lasted only three weeks. COVER: colored lettering and designs.

218 Black Bottom (Black, 1927). Stars unknown.

All That I Had Is Gone / Hydrant Love / It's Right Here for You / Original Black Bottom Dance / We'll

Meet Again — Perry Bradford^{w/m} *(Bradford)*; Wasn't It Nice — Mike Jackson^{w/m} & Gus Horsley^{w/m} *(Bradford)*. COVER: boy and girl dancing.

219 Black Rhythm (Broadway, 1936). Avon Long, Joe Byrd.

Bow Down Sinners / Emaline / Here 'Tis / I Bring You Orchids / The Todle-lo / Trucker's Ball — Donald Heywood^{w/m} *(Mills)*. Another black show by Donald Heywood that failed after one week. COVER: musicians, dancers, buildings.

220 Blackbirds of 1928 (Broadway, 1928). Adelaide Mall, Bill Robinson.

Baby / Bandanna Babies / Digga Digga Do / Dixie / Doin' the New Lowdown / Here Comes My Blackbird / I Can't Give You Anything But Love / I Must Have That Man / Magnolia's Wedding Day / Porgy / Shuffle Your Feet — Dorothy Fields^w & Jimmy McHugh^m *(Jack Mills)*; St. Louis Blues — W.C. Handy^{w/m} *(Handy)*. A smash hit all black revue that contained many hit songs. COVER: blackbirds on a tree branch.

221 Blackbirds of 1930 (Broadway, 1930). Ethel Waters, Flournoy Miller.

Baby Mine / Blackbirds on Parade / Doin' the Mozambique / Memories of You / My Handy Man Ain't Handy No More / Roll Jordan / That Lindy Hop / Wakin' Up the Folks Downstairs / You're Lucky to Me — Andy Razaf^w & Eubie Blake^m *(Shapiro, Bernstein)*; Green Pastures — Will Morrissey^w & Andy Razaf^w & Eubie Blake^m *(Shapiro, Bernstein)*; Just a Crazy Song — Spencer Williams^{w/m} & C. Smith^{w/m} *(Williams)*; Papa De Da Da — Clarence Todd^{w/m} & Spencer Williams^{w/m} & Clarence Williams^{w/m} *(Williams)*. An elaborate revue with some good songs which had only a short run. COVER: a row of blackbirds.

222 Blackbirds of 1934 (Broadway, 1934). Bill Robinson, Edith Wilson.

Concentrate a Little on Love — Alberta Nichols^{w/m} & Mann Holiner^{w/m} *(Robbins)*; Do the Shim-Sham / A Hundred Years from Today / Let Me

Be Born Again / Tappin' the Barrel—Joseph Young^w & Ned Washington^w & Victor Young^m *(Robbins)*; I Just Couldn't Take It Baby / I'm Walkin' the Chalk Line / Your Mother's Son-in-Law—Mann Holiner^w & Alberta Nichols^m *(Robbins)*. Lew Leslie put on *Blackbirds of 1933* which was a complete failure. He revised it and called it *Blackbirds of 1934* but it didn't do any better. COVER: dancing girl with blackbirds.

223 Blackbirds of 1936 (British, 1936). Florence Mills, Lavaida Carter.

Arabella's Wedding Day [B] / Be Happy [B] / Do the Black Bottom with Me [B] / HottenTrot [B] / Levee Gang [B] / Silver Rose [B] / Smilin' Joe [B]—George W. Meyer^w/m *(A H and C)*; Dixie Isn't Dixie Anymore [B] / I Knew [B] / Jo-Jo the Cannibal Kid [B] / Keep a Twinkle in Your Eye [B] / The Swing Is the Thing [B] / Your Heart and Mine [B]—Johnny Mercer^w & Rube Bloom^m *(Sun Music)*. Having failed on Broadway with the last versions of Blackbirds, Lew Leslie produced a version with Charles Cochran which ran for three months. COVER: Florence Mills and fancy designs and lettering.

224 Blackbirds of 1939 (Broadway, 1939). Lena Horne, Bobby Evans.

Dixie Isn't Dixie Anymore / Jo-Jo, the Cannibal Kid—Johnny Mercer^w & Rube Bloom^m *(Robbins)*; Name It and It's Yours—Mitchell Parish^w/m & Sammy Fain^w/m & Abner Silver^w/m *(Robbins)*; Thursday—Dorothy Sachs^w & Irvin Graham^w & Louis Haber^m *(Robbins)*; You're So Indiff'rent—Mitchell Parish^w & Sammy Fain^m *(Robbins)*. Lew Leslie's last attempt on a Blackbird revue using most of the songs from the 1936 London version. It lasted one week. COVER: colored cover with two blackbirds.

225 Blackouts of 1942 (Nightclub, 1942). Marie Wilson, Ken Murray.

Say When—Harry Carroll^w/m & Pauline Carroll^w/m *(Carroll)*. COVER: Marie Wilson and Ken Murray.

226 Blackstone (Broadway, 1980). Blackstone and Magic Acts.

Oriental Magic—Michael Valenti^m *(Assoc. Music)*. Blackstone took his magic show to Broadway for a three month run. COVER: Blackstone.

227 The Blarney Stone (Irish, 1923). Walter Scanlon.

A Bit o' Pink and White / Kitty / Wait for a Warm, Sunny Day / When I Kissed the Blarney Stone—Walter Scanlan^w/m *(Berlin)*; Mother in Ireland—Gerald Griffen^w/m & Herman Kahn^w/m & Tommy Lyman^w/m *(Berlin)*. COVER: Walter Scanlan.

228 Bless You All (Broadway, 1950). Pearl Bailey, Jules Munshin.

I Can Hear It Now / Little Things / Love Letter to Manhattan / A Rose Is a Rose / Summer Dresses / Take Off the Coat / You Never Know What Hit You (When It's Love)—Harold Rome^w/m *(Crawford)*. A short run revue with talented comedians and dancers. COVER: dancing girls and theatre curtain.

229 The Blonde Sinner (Broadway, 1926). Enid Markey, Marjorie Gateson.

Bye Bye Babe / Don't You Cheat / Lips / The Whispering Song—Leon De Costa^w/m *(Harms)*. A comedy with music about a boarding house and its characters which ran six months. COVER: designs and lettering.

230 Blood Brothers (Broadway, 1993). Stephanie Lawrence, Con O'Neill.

Bright New Day [B] [VS] / Easy Terms [B] [VS] / I'm Not Saying a Word [B] [VS] / Kids Game [B] [VS] / Light Romance [B] [VS] / Long Sunday Afternoon [B] [VS] / Madman [B] [VS] / Marilyn Monroe [B] [VS] / My Child [B] [VS] / My Friend [B] [VS] / Shoes Upon the Table [B] [VS] / Take a Letter, Miss Jones [B] [VS] / That Guy [B] [VS]—Willy Russell^w/m *(Wise)*; Tell Me It's Not True [B]—Willy Russell^w/m *(Russell Music)*. A long running British hit moved to Broadway but not received as well. COVER: a girl and two boys.

231 Blood Red Roses (Broadway, 1970). Philip Bruns, Jeanie Carson.

Blood Red Roses / The Fair Dissenter

Lass — John Lewin[w] & Michael Valenti[m] *(Remsen)*. An anti-war musical that lasted for one performance. COVER: a toy soldier.

232 Bloomer Girl (Broadway, 1944). Celeste Holm, David Brooks.

The Eagle and Me / Evelina / I Got a Song / Right as the Rain / T'morra', T'morra' / When the Boys Come Home — E.Y. Harburg[w] & Harold Arlen[m] *(Crawford)*; Promise Me Not to Love Me (1976) — Harburg[w] & Arlen[m] *(Belwin)*. A moderate hit with a Civil War theme and several good Arlen songs. COVER: man and woman in costumes of the Civil War period.

233 Blossom Time (Broadway, 1921). Olga Cook, Bertram Peacock.

Intermezzo Serenade — Sigmund Romberg[m] *(Feist)*; Keep It Dark / Let Me Awake / Love Is a Riddle / My Springtime Thou Art / Only One Love Ever Fills the Heart / Peace to My Lonely Heart / Serenade / Song of Love / Tell Me Daisy / There Is an Old Vienna Town / Three Little Maids — Dorothy Donnelly[w] & Sigmund Romberg[m] *(Feist)*. An operetta based on Schubert melodies that became a huge hit. It was revived many times on Broadway and toured the country for years. COVER: pink blossoms.

234 Blossom Time (Broadway, 1938). Everett Marshall, Mary McCoy.

Keep It Dark / Let Me Awake / Love Is a Riddle / My Springtime Thou Art / Only One Love Ever Fills My Heart / Peace to My Lonely Heart / Serenade / Song of Love / Tell Me Daisy / There Is an Old Vienna Town / Three Little Maids — Dorothy Donnelly[w] & Sigmund Romberg[m] *(Feist)*. This edition had a long run on Broadway with a touring edition. COVER: pink flowers on square background.

235 Blue Bird Revue (Broadway, 1931). Yascha Yushny.

The Huntman's Song of Love / Nichevo Means Yes — Leo Robin[w] & N. Gogotzky[m] *(Harms)*; On a Little Journey in Springtime with You — Lee Robin[w] & Walter Jurman[m] *(Harms)*.

A Russian and international revue imported by S. Hurok. COVER: boy and girl dancing.

236 Blue Eyes (Broadway, 1921). Lew Fields, Mollie King.

Blue Eyes / Just Suppose / Take Me to Heaven / When Grammercy Park Was Uptown / Without a Girl Like You — Z. Myers[w] & I.B. Kornblum[m] *(Harms)*. With a tired plot and ordinary music this musical was gone after a month. COVER: These songs were published with two different covers. One set depicted a smiling Lew Fields and Mollie King and the other plain black and blue designs.

237 Blue Eyes (British, 1928). Evelyn Laye, Edward O'Bryen.

Back to the Heather [B] / Blue Eyes [B] / Blue Eyes — complete score [B] / Bow Belles [B] / Do I Do Wrong? [B] / Henry [B] / In Love [B] / No One Else but You [B] — Graham John[w] & Jerome Kern[m] *(Harms)*. A moderate Jerome Kern hit in London which never made it to the States. COVER: lettering and designs.

238 The Blue Flame (Broadway, 1920). Theda Bara, Alan Dinehart.

The Blue Flame Theme Song — W.F. Peters[m] *(Harms)*. A melodrama about a scientist dreaming he can restore life to the dead. COVER: Theda Bara.

239 The Blue Kitten (Broadway, 1922). Lillian Lorraine, Robert Woolsey.

The Best I Ever Get Is the Worst of It / A Twelve O'Clock Girl in a Nine O'Clock Town / Where the Honeymoon Alone Can See — William Duncan[w] & Rudolf Friml[m] *(Harms)*; Blue Kitten Blues / Cutie / Daddy / I Found a Bud Among the Roses / Madeleine / Smoke Rings / When I Waltz with You — Otto Harbach[w] & Rudolf Friml[m] *(Harms)*. An old fashioned operetta type musical by Friml with a tired story about an inheritance which lasted only a couple of months. COVER: Blue designs and lettering.

240 Blue Skies (British, 1927). Stars unknown.

When I Discover My Man [B] — Alice

D. Miller[w] & Jerome Kern[m] *(Harms)*. A revue that used an old Jerome Kern song from *The Charm School*. COVER: designs.

241 The Blue Widow (Broadway, 1933). Queenie Smith, Helen Flint.

You're Everywhere — Stanley Adams[w] & Manning Sherwin[m] *(Harms)*. A comedy about a supposedly bereaved widow looking for a new love. COVER: Queenie Smith.

242 Blueberries Are a Way of Life (closed before Broadway, 1972). Stars unknown.

Here I Am — Walker Daniels[w/m] *(Hansen)*. COVER: a hippie.

243 The Blushing Bride (Broadway, 1922). Cecil Lean, Cleo Mayfield.

Bad Little Boy and Good Little Girl / Good-bye / Just a Regular Girl / Love's Highway / Mr. and Mrs. / Rosy-Posy / Springtime Is the Time for Loving — Cyrus Wood[w] & Sigmund Romberg[m] *(Witmark)*. A moderately successful Romberg musical about a hat check girl and public chaperon and their courtship. COVER: This show comes with two complete sets of covers. One depicts Cecil Lean and Cleo Mayfield as bride and groom and the other plain grey-brown lettering.

244 The Boardwalk (Nightclub, 1922). Stars unknown.

Boardwalk Blues / Boardwalk Strut / If You Don't Think So You're Crazy — Roy Turk[w/m] & J. Russel Robinson *(Berlin)*. A musical at Lew Leslie's Boardwalk-Midnight Frolic. COVER: bathing beauty and beach scene.

245 Bobby Heath Revue (closed before Broadway, 1925). Stars unknown.

Roll 'em Girls — Bobby Heath[w/m] & Micky Marr[w/m] & Archie Fletcher[w/m] *(Joe Morris)*. COVER: chorus girls.

246 The Body Beautiful (Broadway, 1957). Steve Forrest, Mindy Carson.

All of These and More / Hidden in My Heart / Just My Luck / Leave Well Enough Alone / Uh-Huh, Oh Yeah — Sheldon Harnick[w] & Jerry Bock[m] *(Valando)*. The first pairing of Bock and Harnick which was a quick failure, but

they soon went on to much greater things. COVER: boxer and lady with gloves.

247 The Body in the Seine (closed before Broadway, 1954). Alice Pearce, Barbara Ashley.

But Wonderful / Chacun a Son Gout / Where Do I Go from Here? / Why Can't You Be You? — David Lippincott[w/m] *(General)*. A musical written for Broadway and recorded by a full cast. COVER: sketch of French street.

248 La Boheme (Broadway, 1952). Stars unknown.

I Go My Way / It's the End of My Life — Howard Dietz[w] & G. Puccini[m] *(Schirmer)*. An updated version of *La Boheme* performed at the Met. COVER: sketches and lettering.

249 Bombo (Broadway, 1921). Al Jolson, Janet Adair.

Ain't Love Grand — B.G. DeSylva[w/m] & Walter Donaldson[w/m] & Con Conrad *(Von Tilzer)*; Any Place Will Do with You / In the Way Off There / Jazzadadadoo / Oh, Oh, Columbus / The Very Next Girl I See / Wetona — Harold Atteridge[w] & Sigmund Romberg[m] *(Harms)*; April Showers — B.G. DeSylva[w] & Louis Silvers[m] *(Harms)*; Arcady — Al Jolson[w/m] & B.G. DeSylva[w/m] *(Feist)*; A Bundle of Love / Coo-Coo Song — Al Jolson[w/m] & B.G. DeSylva[w/m] *(Harms)*; Barefoot Days — Al Wilson[w/m] & James Brennan[w/m] *(Marks)*; California, Here I Come — Al Jolson[w/m] & B.G. DeSylva[w/m] & Joseph Meyer[w/m] *(Witmark)*; Carolina Mammy — Billy James[w/m] *(Feist)*; Dirty Hands, Dirty Face — Grante Clarke[w] & Edgar Leslie[w] & Al Jolson[w] & James Monaco[m] *(C and L)*; Don't Cry Swanee / Morning Will Come — Al Jolson[w/m] & B.G. DeSylva[w/m] & Con Conrad[w/m] *(Harms)*; Don't Send Your Wife to the Country — B.G. DeSylva[w] & Harold Atteridge[w] & Con Conrad[m] *(Harms)*; Down South / Give Me My Mammy — B.G. DeSylva[w] & Walter Donaldson[m] *(Harms)*; How D'ya Like to Be a Kid Again — Jimmy McHugh[w/m] & Bennett Sisters[w/m] & Billy Colligan[w/m] *(Mills)*; I'm Goin' South —

Abner Silvers^{w/m} & Harry Woods^{w/m} *(Witmark)*; In Old Grenada—Harold Atteridge^w & Sigmund Romberg^m & Al Jolson^m *(Harms)*; It's You—Benny Davis^w & Con Conrad^m *(Harms)*; Koo-Kee-Koo—King Zany^w & Nacio Herb Brown^m *(Feist)*; Last Night on the Back Porch—Lew Brown^{w/m} & Carl Schraubstader^{w/m} *(Shapiro, Bernstein)*; Old Fashioned Girl—Al Jolson^{w/m} *(Richmond-Robbins)*; Tallahassee—B.G. DeSylva^{w/m} & Luckieth Roberts^{w/m} *(Harms)*; Tell Me with Smiles—Cliff Friend^{w/m} & Walter Hirsch^{w/m} *(Richmond-Robbins)*; That Barber in Seville—Harold Atteridge^w & Con Conrad^m *(Harms)*; Toot, Toot, Tootsie—Gus Kahn^{w/m} & Ernie Erdman^{w/m} & Dan Russo^{w/m} *(Feist)*; Who Cares?—Jack Yellen^w & Milton Ager^m *(A Y and B)*; Yoo-Hoo—B.G. DeSylva^w & Al Jolson^m *(Remick)*. An ordinary Jolson musical kept going by Jolson and all his hit songs. COVER: Al Jolson.

250 Bomboola (also known as Bamboola) (Broadway, 1929). Isabell Washington, Percy Winters.

Africa Whoopee / Dixie Vagabond / Rub-a-dub Your Rabbit's Foot / Somebody Like Me / Tampico Tune / The Way to Do Bomboola—Frank Marcus^{w/m} & Bernard Maltin^{w/m} *(D B and H)*. A short run black musical with great dancing that was accused of imitating white shows. COVER: Isabell Washington.

251 Bonanza Bound (closed before Broadway, 1948). Allyn Ann McLerie, Adolph Green.

Bonanza / Fill 'er Up / I Know It's True / Tell Me Why / Up in Smoke—Betty Comden^w & Adolph Green^w & Saul Chaplin^m *(Crawford)*. A musical about the gold rush in Alaska that folded after a one week try-out in Philadelphia. COVER: people heading for the gold rush.

252 The Bone Room (Off Broadway, 1975). Ray Stewart, Susan Watson.

Postcards [VS] / A Wonderful Way to Die [VS]—Tom Jones^w & Harvey Schmidt^m *(Leonard)*. An experimental musical in a limited run. This was a workshop production. COVER: Jones and Schmidt.

253 Bonita *(see also* **The Love Call** *and* **My Golden West**) (Broadway, 1927). Berna Dean, John Barker.

Eyes That Love / Good Pals / I Live, I Die for You! / Rangers Song / 'Tis Love—Harry B. Smith^w & Sigmund Romberg^m *(Harms)*. This show started its pre-Broadway tour as *Bonita* and then *My Golden West* before arriving on Broadway as *Love Call*. This was a short lived musical about rangers and Indians that was bad in every respect. COVER: cowgirl riding a horse.

254 Boom Boom (Broadway, 1929). Jeanette MacDonald, Stanley Riggs.

Blow the Blues Away / Shake High, Shake Low / What a Girl / What Could I Do—Mann Holiner^w & J. Keirn Brennan^w & Werner Janssen^m *(Shubert)*. Another quick flop in the early career of Jeanette MacDonald about a shipboard romance. COVER: boy and girl ballet dancers.

255 Bottomland (Broadway, 1927). Sara Martin, Clarence Williams.

Anytime—Joe Jordan^w & Clarence Williams^m *(Williams)*; Bottomland—Joe Trent^w & Clarence Williams^m *(Williams)*; Come On Home—Donald Heyword^{w/m} *(Williams)*; Dancing Girl—Spencer Williams^{w/m} & Clarence Williams^{w/m} *(Williams)*; I'm Gonna Take My Bimbo Back to the Bamboo Isle / Steamboat Days—Clarence Williams^{w/m} *(Williams)*; Shootin' the Pistol—Chris Smith^w & Clarence Williams^m *(Williams)*; When I March in April with May—Gerald Williams^{w/m} & Spencer Williams^{w/m} *(Williams)*; You're the Only One That I Love—Clarence Williams^w & Len Gray^m *(Williams)*. A black musical which lasted for three weeks about tough life in Harlem. COVER: black man walking on railroad tracks back to his home.

256 Bow Bells (British, 1932). Stars unknown.

Mona Lisa—Desmond Carter^w & Louis Henneve^w & Henry Sullivan^m

(Chappell); You're Blase — Bruce Sievier[w] & Ord Hamilton[m] *(Harms)*. A revue of the 30s that produced a hit song in the U.S. COVER: a lady's face.

257 The Bow-Wows (British, 1927). Elsie Gregory, Georges Metaxa.

For Goodness Sake [B] — James Dyrenforth[w] & Vernon Duke[m] *(Chappell)*. A forgettable revue. COVER: designs and lettering.

258 The Box Party (closed before Broadway, 1922). Stars unknown.

Just a Little Love Song — Joe Young[w] & Sam Lewis[w] & Joe Cooper[m] *(Berlin)*. COVER: bird bath with birds.

259 The Boy Friend (Broadway, 1954). Julie Andrews, John Hewer.

The Boy Friend — complete score / Fancy Forgetting / I Could Be Happy with You / It's Never Too Late to Fall in Love / A Room in Bloomsbury — Sandy Wilson[w/m] *(Chappell)*. A wonderful musical about flappers and the jazz age which gave us Julie Andrews. COVER: a flapper.

260 The Boy Friend (Broadway, 1970). Judy Carne, Sandy Duncan.

Fancy Forgetting / I Could Be Happy with You / It's Never Too Late to Fall in Love / Poor Little Pierrette [VS] / A Room in Bloomsbury / Sur le Plage [VS] / Won't You Charleston with Me? — Sandy Wilson[w/m] *(Chappell)*. An unsuccessful revival of the hit musical that made Julie Andrews. COVER: a flapper.

261 Boy Meets Boy (Off Broadway, 1975). Joe Barrett, Bobby Bowers.

Boy Meets Boy / Does Anybody Love You? / Giving It Up for Love / It's a Boy's Life / It's a Dolly / Just My Luck / Let's / Marry an American / Me / What Do I Care / You're Beautiful — Bill Solly[w/m] *(Oublietta)*. An Off Broadway hit that ran for one year. COVER: designs and lettering.

262 Boys and Girls Together (Broadway, 1940). Ed Wynn, Dell Parker.

I Want to Live / The Latin in Me / Sun'll Be Up in the Morning / Times Square Dance — Jack Yellen[w] & Sammy Fain[m] *(Crawford)*; Such Stuff as Dreams Are Made Of / You Can't Put Ketchup on the Moon — Irving Kahal[w] & Sammy Fain[m] *(Crawford)*. Ed Wynn kept this minor revue running for six months. COVER: Ed Wynn.

263 The Boys from Syracuse (Broadway, 1938). Eddie Albert, Jimmy Savo.

The Boys from Syracuse — complete score / Falling in Love with Love / Oh, Diogenes! / The Shortest Day of the Year / Sing for Your Supper / This Can't Be Love / You Have Cast Your Shadow on the Sea — Lorenz Hart[w] & Richard Rodgers[m] *(Chappell)*. A very entertaining musical with an excellent score by Rodgers and Hart based on Shakespeare's *Comedy of Errors*. COVER: silhouettes of Greek ladies and men.

264 The Boys from Syracuse (Off Broadway, 1963). Karen Morrow, Ellen Hanley.

Falling in Love with Love / Oh, Diogenes! / Shortest Day of the Year / Sing for Your Supper / This Can't Be Love / You Have Cast Your Shadow on the Sea — Lorenz Hart[w] & Richard Rodgers[m] *(Chappell)*. An excellent Off Broadway revival of a great musical which ran much longer than the original. COVER: a Hirschfeld sketch of twins.

265 Brainchild (closed before Broadway, 1974). Tovah Feldshuh, Dorian Harewood.

The First Time I Heard a Bluebird [PC] — Hal David[w] & Michel Legrand[m] *(Chappell)*. A strange musical taking place in a girl's mind. Closed after two weeks in Philadelphia. COVER: none.

266 Bravo Giovanni (Broadway, 1962). Michele Lee, David Opatoshu.

Ah! Camminare / If I Were the Man / I'm All I Got / The Kangaroo / Miranda / One Little World Apart / Rome / Steady, Steady — Ronny Graham[w] & Milton Schafer[m] *(Morris)*. A poor musical about competition between two restaurants running two months. COVER: couple on scooter before a row of houses.

267 Brevities (closed before Broadway, 1924). George Griffin.

If the Orange Grew in Ireland — Ralph

Larsen[w] & William McCarthy[w] & Bart Grady[m] *(Waterson)*; Mamie – Harry B. Smith[w] & Jack Shilkret[m] *(W B and S)*. COVER: George Griffin and lady.

268 Brigadoon (Broadway, 1947). Marion Bell, David Brooks.

Almost Like Being in Love / Brigadoon / Brigadoon – complete score / Come to Me, Bend to Me / Down on MacConnachy Square / From This Day On / The Heather on the Hill / I'll Go Home with Bonnie Jean / Jeannie's Packin' Up [VS] / The Love of My Life / My Mother's Weddin' Day / There But for You Go I / Waitin' for My Dearie – Alan Jay Lerner[w] & Frederick Loewe[m] *(Sam Fox)*; Brigadoon – piano selections (Sword Dance; Once in the Highlands; Ballet Music) – Frederick Loewe[m] *(Sam Fox)*. A romantic musical with lovely tunes about a lost village in Scotland which was a big hit. COVER: a boy and girl dancer.

269 The Brigand (Broadway, 1927). Leo Carrillo.

Magic Voices of the Night – Al Dubin[w] & Meyer Gusman[m] *(Berlin)*. This show was billed as a drama and presented by Harry Cort. COVER: Leo Carillo.

270 Bright Lights (Broadway, 1943). James Barton, Buddy Clark.

Don't Forget the Girl from Punxsutawney / Thoughtless – Mack David[w] & Jerry Livingston[m] *(Chappell)*. A terrible revue which lasted for four performances. COVER: chorus girls.

271 Bring Back Birdie (Broadway, 1981). Donald O'Connor, Chita Rivera.

Middle Age Blues [VS] / Young [VS] – Lee Adams[w] & Charles Strouse[m] *(Columbia)*. An unsuccessful attempt to do a sequel to the smash hit *Bye Bye Birdie*. COVER: Charles Strouse.

272 Bring On the Girls (closed before Broadway, 1934). Jack Benny, Porter Hall.

Down on the Old-Time Farm – Morrie Ryskind[w] & Arthur Schwartz[m] *(Harms)*. A Kaufman satire that did not work and closed in Washington. COVER: Jack Benny.

273 Bringing Up Father (Broadway, 1925). Stars unknown.

Bringing Up Father – selections – Paul Smith[w] & R. Carroll[w] & Seymour Furth[m] & Leo Edwards[m] *(Rossiter)*. One of a series of musicals based on the popular comic strip. This version was a failure. COVER: cartoon of father.

274 Bringing Up Father in Gay New York (Broadway, 1930). Emma Weston, Johnnie Jess.

Bringing Up Father in Gay New York – selections – Leo Edwards[w] & Seymour Furth[m] *(Rossiter)*. Another short run musical based on the cartoon series. COVER: cartoon of "father" staring at beautiful girl.

275 Bringing Up Father in Society (Broadway, 1919). Lillian Goldsmith.

Sunshine Girl of Mine – C.W. Wood[w] & Charles Maynard[m] *(Meyer Cohen)*. One of the early stage versions of the cartoon character. COVER: Lillian Goldsmith.

276 Broadway Brevities (1st edition) (Broadway, 1920). Eddie Cantor, Bert Williams.

Anna in Indiana – Billy Gorman[w/m] & Eddie Gorman[w/m] & Harry Rose[w/m] *(Broadway)*; Beautiful Faces – Irving Berlin[w/m] *(Berlin)*; But Where? / Love, Honor and Oh, Baby! / Stolen Sweets / That Means Home to Me – Blair Treynor[w] & Archie Gottler[m] *(Harms)*; Cruel and Brutal – W. Deleon[w/m] & Will Vodery[w/m] *(Harms)*; He Always Goes Farther Than Father – Blanche Franklyn[w/m] *(Milly)*; I Makes Mine Myself / Moon Shines on the Moonshine – Francis DeWitt[w] & Robert Hood Bowers[m] *(Shapiro, Bernstein)*; I Want to Know Where Tosti Went – Chris Smith[w/m] *(Shapiro, Bernstein)*; I've Got the Blues for My Kentucky Home / Kentucky Blues – Clarence Gaskill[w/m] *(Witmark)*; I Wish That I'd Been Born in Borneo – Grant Clarke[w] & Walter Donaldson[m] *(Berlin)*; Lu Lu / Snowflakes – Arthur Jackson[w] & George Gershwin[m] *(Harms)*; Rainy Afternoons / Santa Monterey – Con Conrad[w/m] *(Berlin)*; Rose of Old

Seville — J. Russel Robinson[w/m] & Con Conrad[w/m] *(Berlin)*; Somebody Else — Not Me — Ballard MacDonald[w] & James Hanley[m] *(Shapiro, Bernstein)*; Spanish Love — Irving Caesar[w] & George Gershwin[m] *(Harms)*; Springtime — Gus Kahn[w] & Anatol Friedland[m] *(Remick)*; Stage Door Blues — Bert Kalmer[w/m] & Harry Ruby[w/m] *(Berlin)*. An ordinary revue featuring Cantor and Williams. COVER: various covers — Eddie Cantor, Bert Williams, show girls, Bettie Parker.

277 Broadway Brevities (2nd edition) (Broadway, 1920). Dorothy Jardon, Bert Williams.

But Where? / In a Doll's House / A Little Tent for Two / Stolen Sweets / That Means Home to Me — Blair Treynor[w] & Archie Gottler[m] *(Harms)*; Cruel and Brutal — William DeLeon[w/m] & Will Vodery[w/m] *(Harms)*; Daddy — Stanley Dunkerley[w] & Nat Osborne[m] *(Harms)*; In Cherry Blossom Time with You — Blair Treynor[w] & Dorothy Jardon[m] & Joseph Daly[m] *(Harms)*; My Only One — George Moriarty[w] & Dorothy Jardon[m] & Joseph Daly[m] *(Harms)*; Stage Door Blues — Bert Kalmar[w/m] & Harry Ruby[w/m] *(Berlin)*. A revised but still ordinary edition of this revue with Williams but without Cantor. COVER: Dorothy Jardon and chorus girl.

278 Broadway Brevities (3rd edition) (Broadway, 1921). Bert Williams.

Eve Cost Adam Just One Bone — Charles Bayha[w/m] *(Skidmore)*; Save a Little Dream for Me / You'll Never Need a Doctor No More — Chris Smith[w/m] *(Skidmore)*. Another revised edition of this revue with Bert Williams. This was his last New York stage appearance. He died shortly thereafter. COVER: Bert Williams.

279 Broadway for Peace (Broadway, 1968). Barbra Streisand, Leonard Bernstein.

So Pretty — Betty Comden[w] & Adolph Green[w] & Leonard Bernstein[m] *(Schirmer)*. A special concert at Philharmonic Hall, New York in the interests of peace. COVER: lettering and designs.

280 Broadway Gaieties (Black, 1926). Billy Pierce.

Black Bottom Dance — Gus Horsle[w/m] & Perry Bradford[w/m] *(Bradford)*. COVER: lady looking over nightclub poster of herself.

281 A Broadway Musical (Broadway, 1978). Anne Francine, Tiger Haynes.

The 1934 Hot Chocolate Jazz Babies Revue [VS] — Lee Adams[w] & Charles Strouse[m] *(Columbia)*. A musical about producing a musical which lasted for one performance. COVER: Charles Strouse.

282 Broadway Nights (Broadway, 1929). Frank Gaby, Odette Myrtil.

Baby Doll Dance — J. Keirn Brennan[w] & Moe Jaffe[w] & Maury Rubens[m] & Philip Svigals[m] *(Shubert)*; The Right Man / Why Don't We? / Your Broadway and Mine — Moe Jaffe[w] & Sammy Timberg[m] & Maury Rubens[m] *(Shubert)*. A short lived revue staged by Busby Berkeley with nothing to remember. COVER: designs and lettering.

283 Broadway Rastus (Black, 1919). Flo Brown, Irvin C. Miller.

Beale Street Blues / Lonesome / Love Is a Funny Proposition / Madura Isle / Ostrich Stroll / Sweet Child — Irving Miller[w] & Dormer Brown[m] *(Pace and Handy)*; Dancing Deacon / Mauvolyene Waltz — Dormer Brown[m] *(Pace and Handy)*; Oh, Death, Where Is Thy Sting — Clarence Stout[w/m] *(Pace and Handy)*. COVER: black couple in elegant clothes.

284 Broadway Sho-Window (Broadway, 1936). Joe Cook, Ruth Ambrose.

Poverty Row or Luxury Lane — Howard Johnson[w] & Gus Edwards[m] *(Paramount)*. A poor revue by Gus Edwards. COVER: black and white cover with Paramount Pictures logo.

285 Broadway Whirl (Broadway, 1921). Blanche Ring, Charles Winninger.

All Girls Are Like the Rainbow / Babe Ruth / Broadway Whirl / Oh! Dearie (You Must Come Over) — Joseph McCarthy[w] & Harry Tierney[m] *(Feist)*; Black-eyed Susans / Caring for No One But You / Toddle-top — John

Mears^w & Earnest Golden^m *(Feist)*; Stand Up and Sing for Your Father – Henry Burr$^{w/m}$ & Ray Perkins$^{w/m}$ *(Witmark)*; There's a Typical Tipperary Over Here – Alex Gerber^w & Abner Silver^m *(Witmark)*. An ordinary revue which lasted for ten weeks due to the talents of Ring and Winninger. COVER: Blanche Ring, Charles Winninger, and other cast members.

286 Broke! (*see also* **A Lucky Break**) (Broadway, 1925). George Mac-Farlane, Lucille Sears.

Hurdy Gurdy / Nora Dear I Am Longing for You / Rainbow / With You Beside Me – Zelda Sears^w & Harold Levey^m *(Harms)*. A failure about a poor man who makes good. The pre–Broadway title was *Broke* and it arrived on Broadway as *A Lucky Break*. COVER: George MacFarlane.

287 The Broken Wing (Broadway, 1920). George Abbott, Mary Worth.

Adelai – George Abbott^w & Joseph Spurin^m *(Harms)*; To-Morrow – Harry B. Smith^w & Otto Motzan^m & M.K. Jerome^m *(Berlin)*. A drama of a Mexican girl in love with an American pilot. COVER: man and woman with a dog.

288 Bronx Express (Broadway, 1922). Charles Coburn, Mrs. Charles Coburn.

Bronx Express – Henry Creamer$^{w/m}$ & Turner Layton$^{w/m}$ *(Shapiro, Bernstein)*. A comedy drama about a father and his problems with his daughter's choice of a suitor. COVER: Mr. and Mrs. Coburn on the Bronx Express.

289 Brown Buddies (Broadway, 1930). Ada Brown, Bill Robinson.

Betty Lou – Rosamond Johnson$^{w/m}$ & Joe Jordan$^{w/m}$ *(Harms)*; Dancin' 'Way Your Sin – James Johnson$^{w/m}$ *(Mills)*; Darky Rhythm – Peter Tinturin^w & Victor Young^m *(Mills)*; Don't Leave Your Little Blackbird Blue – Joe Jordan$^{w/m}$ & Porter Grainger$^{w/m}$ & Shelton Brooks$^{w/m}$ *(Harms)*; Excuse My Dust – Ray Klages$^{w/m}$ & Jesse Greer$^{w/m}$ *(Mills)*; Give Me a Man Like That – George Little$^{w/m}$ & Art Sizemore$^{w/m}$ *(Mills)*; Happy – Nat Reed$^{w/m}$ & Bob Jaffe$^{w/m}$ *(Mills)*; Just a Crazy Song – A. Smith$^{w/m}$ & Spencer Williams$^{w/m}$ *(Williams)*; Missouri – Nat Reed$^{w/m}$ *(Harms)*; When a Black Man's Blue – George Little$^{w/m}$ & Art Sizemore$^{w/m}$ & Ed Nelson$^{w/m}$ *(Feist)*. A black musical with little book but good singing and dancing. COVER: Ada Brown and dancers with piano player.

290 Brown Derby (closed before Broadway, 1925). Bert Wheeler, Betty Wheeler.

Meaning You – Clifford Grey$^{w/m}$ & Ray Perkins$^{w/m}$ & Paul Lannin$^{w/m}$ *(Harms)*; One Little Smile / The Woofus Bird – Clifford Grey^w & Ray Perkins^m *(Harms)*; Sari – Clifford Grey^w & Ray Perkins^w & Ray Perkins^m & Paul Lannin^m *(Harms)*; That Wonderful Day – Clifford Grey^w & Paul Lannin^m *(Harms)*. COVER: a brown derby and designs.

291 Brown Skin Models (Black, 1924). Irvin Miller.

Everybody Mess Around / I Ain't Gonna Play Second Fiddle [ABQ] / Just Met a Friend from My Home Town [ABQ] / So's Your Old Man [ABQ] / Wasn't It Nice [ABQ] / We'll Meet Again, Bye and Bye – Irvin Miller^w & Perry Bradford^m *(Bradford)*. COVER: black and white with titles only.

292 Brown Skin Revue (Black, 1925). Irvin C. Miller, Lily Yuen.

Ain't You My Baby / Charleston Ball / Hula Lou / Mary Ann – Donald Heywood$^{w/m}$ *(Marks)*. COVER: gentleman and lady dancer.

293 Brown Sugar (Black Berries of 1932) (Nightclub, 1930). Duke Ellington.

Linda / Song of the Gigolo – Ted Koehler^w & Harold Arlen^m *(Remick)*. COVER: sketch of man and woman.

294 Brownbilt Footlites (closed before Broadway, 1930). William Wirges.

Upside Down in Love – W.A. Phelps^w & Anne Phelps^m *(Phelps Music)*. COVER: large red heart with man chasing woman.

295 B.S. Moss Varieties (closed before Broadway, 1931). Stars unknown.

If I Could Live My Life All Over –

Mack Gordon[w] & Harry Revel[m] *(Miller)*. COVER: four dancers in silhouette.

296 Bubbles (closed before Broadway, 1919). Stars unknown.

Bubble Land — Arthur Anderson[w/m] *(Witmark)*. COVER: bubbles in the air, the stars and the moon.

297 Bubbles (Broadway, 1928). Stars unknown.

Bubbles — Ben Black[w] & Gene Lucas[m] *(Famous)*. A Publix stage production performed in between showings of new Paramount films. COVER: a large bunch of colored bubbles.

298 Bubbling Brown Sugar (Broadway, 1975). Josephine Premice, Avon Long.

Bubbling Brown Sugar — Danny Holgate[w/m] & Lillian Lopez[w/m] & Emme Kemp[w/m] *(Chappell)*. A black revue using some great old tunes and recalling the days of Bert Williams and Bill Robinson and the like. A hit running for almost two years. COVER: dancer and musician.

299 Bubbling Over (closed before Broadway, 1926). Cecil Lean, Cleo Mayfield.

Breezin' Along / Bubbling Over / Cradle Snatcher / I'm a One Man Girl / It's Alright with Me / Say It with a Uke / Shake Me and Wake Me / Snap Out of the Blues / True to Two — Leo Robin[w] & Richard Myers[m] *(Harms)*. COVER: Lean and Mayfield with bubbles and girls.

300 Bubbling Over (closed before Broadway, 1927). Stars unknown.

Anything to Make You Happy — Buddy Valentine[w/m] *(B B and L)*. COVER: boy and girl in romantic pose.

301 Bublitchki (Jewish, 1938). Molly Picon.

Dance Baby Dance / Old Gypsy / Sascha / Sashinka / Where Is My Luck? / You've Got It — Dailey Paskman[w] & A. Ellstein[m] *(Marks)*. COVER: Molly Picon and Jan Pearce with sketch of costumed lady.

302 Buddies (Broadway, 1919). Peggy Wood, Donald Brian.

After Awhile / Weaver of Dreams — Melville Gideon[w/m] *(Feist)*; Altogether Too Fond of You — Melville Gideon[w/m] & James Heard[w/m] & Cole Porter *(Feist)*; Darling I / Fairy Tales / The Homes They Hold So Dear / Hullo Home / My Buddies / My Indispensable Girl / Oh, Tell Me Where My Buddie Is / Please Learn to Love / To Be Together Is the Thing / Twilight Song — B.C. Hilliam[w/m] *(Witmark)*; I Never Realized — Melville Gideon[w/m] & Cole Porter[w/m] *(Feist)*; Washington Square — Cole Porter[w] & Ray Goetz[w] & Melville Gideon[m] *(Remick)*. A moderate hit taking place in France after the Armistice. It was made interesting by the talents of Brian and Wood. COVER 1: a cartoon of two soldiers and a nurse; COVER 2: a rectangular picture of Peggy Wood and Donald Brian; COVER 3: a rectangular picture of Donald Brian, Peggy Wood, Wallace Eddinger; COVER 4: a pink cover with oval pictures of Wood, Brian, and Eddinger.

303 Buddy (Broadway, 1990). Paul Hipp, Philip Anthony.

Chantilly Lace [B] [VS] — J.P. Richardson[w/m] *(Wise)*; Everyday [B] [VS] / Listen to Me [B] [VS] / Maybe Baby [B] [VS] / Not Fade Away [B] [VS] — Charles Hardin[w/m] & Norman Petty[w/m] *(Wise)*; I'm Looking for Someone to Love [B] [VS] / It's So Easy [B] [VS] / True Love Ways [B] [VS] — Buddy Holly[w/m] & Norman Petty[w/m] *(Wise)*; Oh Boy [B] [VS] / Rave On [B] [VS] — Sunny West[w/m] & Bill Tilghman[w/m] & Norman Petty[w/m] *(Wise)*; Peggy Sue [B] [VS] / That'll Be the Day / Well All Right — Jerry Allison[w/m] & Norman Petty[w/m] & Buddy Holly[w/m] *(Wise)*; Peggy Sue Got Married [B] [VS] / Words of Love [B] [VS] — Buddy Holly[w/m] *(Wise)*. A British hit with a modern U.S. run consisting of Buddy Holly songs and story. COVER: Buddy Holly.

304 The Bunch and Judy (Broadway, 1922). Fred Astaire, Adele Astaire.

Every Day in Every Way / Have You

Forgotten Me Blues / Hot Dog / How Do You Do, Katinka? / Morning Glory / The Pale Venetian Moon / Peach Girl — Anne Caldwell[w] & Jerome Kern[m] *(Harms)*; Lovin' Sam — Jack Yellen[w] & Milton Ager[m] *(A Y and B)*. A musical written for the young Astaires running only six weeks due to a poor book and rather ordinary Kern songs. COVER: two ladies draping a mirror.

305 Bunk of 1926 (Broadway, 1926). Carol Joyce, Gene Lockhart.

Chatter / Modest Little Thing / The Way to Your Heart — Eugene Lockhart[w/m] *(Harms)*; Cuddle Up — Percy Waxman[w] & Robert Armbruster[m] *(Harms)*; Milky Way — Percy Waxman[w] & Eugene Lockhart[m] *(Harms)*. A modest little revue written, produced, and directed by the star, Gene Lockhart. COVER: plain blue lettering.

306 Burlesque (Broadway, 1927). Barbara Stanwyck, Oscar Levant.

Either You Do or You Don't / I'm Wonderin' Who — Jo Trent[w] & Ed Grant[w] & Albert Von Tilzer[m] & Peter DeRose[m] *(Shapiro, Bernstein)*; Just an Hour of Love — Jo Trent[w] & Albert Von Tilzer[m] & Peter DeRose[m] *(Shapiro, Bernstein)*. A hit comedy that ran for almost a year. COVER: two men kissing a lady's hands.

307 Butterflies Are Free (Broadway, 1969). Keir Dullea, Eileen Heckart.

Butterflies Are Free — Steve Schwartz[w/m] *(Sunbury)*. A comedy about a boy, girl and mother that was a big hit. COVER: young couple and large butterfly.

308 Buttrio Square (Broadway, 1952). Billy Gilbert, Susan Johnson.

I Keep Telling Myself / There's No Place Like the Country — Gen Genovese[w] & Arthur Jones[m] *(Chappell)*; Love Swept Like a Storm / More and More — Gen Genovese[w] & Fred Stamer[m] *(Chappell)*. A musical about American soldiers in Italy and called the worst of the season which ran one week. COVER: a soldier chasing a girl through a square.

309 Buzzin' Around (Broadway, 1920). Elizabeth Brice, Will Morrissey.

Buzzin' Around / Ching-a-Ling / Good-night Dear / I'll Be Just the Same / Poor Winter Garden Girl — Edward Madden[w/m] & Will Morrissey[w/m] *(Remick)*. A terrible revue with magic acts, jugglers, etc. that lasted three weeks. COVER: beautiful girl surrounded by seven gentlemen angels.

310 By Hex (Off Broadway, 1956). Ken Cantril, Wynne Miller.

Something New / What Is Love — Howard Blankman[w/m] *(Chappell)*. A short run musical about the Amish in Lancaster, Pennsylvania. COVER: rural road and woods.

311 By Hex (Regional, 1967). Marianne Weicksel, Fred Vanderpoel.

Laugh a Little / Something New / You Don't Know Me at All — Howard Blankman[w/m] *(Chappell)*. A summer theatre production of the Off Broadway play of 1956. COVER: hex signs.

312 By Jupiter *(see also* **All's Fair***)* (Broadway, 1942). Ray Bolger, Constance Moore.

Careless Rhapsody / Ev'rything I've Got / Here's a Hand / Jupiter Forbid / Nobody's Heart / Wait Till You See Her — Lorenz Hart[w] & Richard Rodgers[m] *(Chappell)*. One of the best Rodgers and Hart featuring an outstanding Ray Bolger and taking place in early Greece. It was called *All's Fair* in try-out. COVER: Ray Bolger and Greek soldier.

313 By Jupiter (Off Broadway, 1967). Bob Dishy, Sheila Sullivan.

Careless Rhapsody [vs] / Ev'rything I've Got [vs] / Here's a Hand [vs] / Jupiter Forbid [vs] / Nobody's Heart [vs] / Wait Till You See Her [vs] — Lorenz Hart[w] & Richard Rodgers[m] *(Chappell)*. A well-done revival of the 1942 musical. The music was republished and a first time recording of the great score. COVER: a Greek warrior.

314 By the Beautiful Sea (Broadway, 1954). Shirley Booth, Wilbur Evans.

Alone Too Long / Hang Up! / Happy Habit / More Love Than Your Love / The Sea Song — Dorothy Fields[w] & Arthur Schwartz[m] *(Morris)*. A very entertaining period piece with pleasant tunes and a great performance by Booth. COVER: large balloon with lady in the basket.

315 By the Way (Broadway, 1925). Jack Hulbert, Cicely Courtneidge.

Bargain Basement Blues [B] — Vivian Ellis[w/m] & A. Parsons[w/m] *(Chappell)*; Gather Roses While You May / London Bank Clerk Blues / There's Nothing New Under the Sun / What Can They See in Dancing — Graham John[w] & Vivian Ellis[m] *(Feist)*; High Street Africa — Cumberland Clark[w/m] & Huntley Trevor[w/m] & Everett Lynton[w/m] *(Harms)*; Hum a Little Tune — John Long[w] & Vivian Ellis[m] *(Feist)*; I've Found a Bluebird / Looking Around — Leo Robin[w] & Richard Myers[m] *(Harms)*; My Castle in Spain — Isham Jones[w/m] *(Feist)*; No One's Ever Kissed Me — Donald Jeans[w] & Philip Braham[m] *(Feist)*; Oh, How I've Waited for You — Harry Carlton[w] & Nat Ayer[m] *(Harms)*. A minor hit revue imported from England with the talents of Hulbert and Courtneidge. COVER: Jack Hulbert.

316 Bye Bye Barbara (Broadway, 1924). John Hazzard, Janet Velie.

Bo-Beep Waltz / Bye Bye Barbara / Gee, I Must Be in Love / Kiss Invention / Let's Pretend / One in the World for Me / Quaint Little House — Monte Carlo[w/m] & Alma Sanders[w/m] *(Marks)*. A short lived flop about a balloonist running away from his ex-wife. COVER: a house on the bay.

317 Bye Bye Birdie (Broadway, 1960). Dick Van Dyke, Chita Rivera.

Baby, Talk to Me / Bye Bye Birdie [PC] / Bye Bye Birdie — complete vocal score / Honestly Sincere [PC] / How Lovely to Be a Woman / Hymn for a Sunday Evening [PC] / Kids! / A Lot of Livin' to Do / One Boy (One Girl) / One Guy [PC] / One Last Kiss / Put On a Happy Face / Rosie / Telephone Hour [PC] — Lee Adams[w] & Charles Strouse[m] *(Morris)*. A rock 'n' roll star is drafted and causes problems for his agent, the agent's girlfriend, the agent's mother, and a whole town of parents and teenagers. Very entertaining with great songs and dancing. COVER: a hand waving goodbye.

318 Bye Bye, Bonnie (Broadway, 1927). William Frawley, Georgie Hale.

Anyone Who Do's That / September Night — Seymour Brown[w] & Albert Von Tilzer[m] *(Harms)*; Just Cross the River from Queens — Neville Fleeson[w] *(Harms)*; Love Is Like a Blushing Rose / Tampico Tap / You and I Love You and Me — Neville Fleeson[w] & Albert Von Tilzer[m] *(Harms)*. A four month run of an average musical about a secretary and her boss and their problems. COVER: fancy designs and lettering.

319 Ca C'est Paris! (At the Moulin Rouge) (Nightclub, 1955). Stars unknown.

Evening in Paris / Heavenly Holiday / Such Loveliness as You — Pony Sherrell[w/m] & Phil Moody[w/m] *(American Academy)*. COVER: the Eiffel Tower and can-can girls.

320 Cabaret (Broadway, 1966). Joel Grey, Lotte Lenya.

Cabaret / Cabaret — complete vocal score / Don't Tell Mama [VS] / I Don't Care Much / If You Could See Her [VS] / It Couldn't Please Me More [VS] / Married / Meeskite / Perfectly Marvelous [VS] / So What? [VS] / Tomorrow Belongs to Me / What Would You Do [VS] / Why Should I Wake Up? / Wilkommen — Fred Ebb[w] & John Kander[m] *(Valando)*. A hit musical running almost three years dealing with a sleazy nightclub in Nazi Germany. A stunning performance by Joel Grey as the M.C. and also Lotte Lenya as the landlady of a boarding house. It was staged brilliantly by Harold Prince. COVER: sketch of nighclub scene with girl orchestra and patrons.

321 The Cabaret Girl (British, 1922). Dorothy Dickson, George Grossmith.

The Cabaret Girl—complete vocal score [B]—George grossmith[W] & P.G. Wodehouse[W] & Jerome Kern[m] *(Chappell)*; Dancing Time [B] / Oriental Dreams [B]—George Grossmith[W] & Jerome Kern[m] *(Chappell)*; First Rose of Summer [B]—P.G. Wodehouse[W] & Anne Caldwell[W] & Jerome Kern[m] *(Chappell)*; Journey's End [B] / Looking All Over for You [B] / Shimmy with Me [B]—P.G. Wodehouse[W] & Jerome Kern[m] *(Chappell)*; Ka-Lu-A—Anne Caldwell[W] & Jerome Kern[m] *(Chappell)*. A follow-up in London to the Kern hit *Sally* with almost all the same authors, stars, and plot about a poor working girl looking for love, wealth and fame. COVER: designs and lettering.

322 The Cabaret Girls (Nightclub, 1920). Leona Fox.

Lulu—Ben Holmes[W] & Joseph Loudis[m] *(Holmes and Loudis)*. COVER: Leona Fox.

323 Cabin in the Sky (Broadway, 1940). Ethel Waters, Todd Duncan.

Cabin in the Sky / Do What You Wanna Do / Honey in the Honeycomb / In My Old Virginia Home / Love Me Tomorrow / Love Turned the Light Out / Savannah—John Latouche[W] & Vernon Duke[m] *(Miller)*; Taking a Chance on Love—John Latouche[W] & Ted Fetter[W] & Vernon Duke[m] *(Miller)*. A beautiful production with Vernon Duke's best score and Ethel Waters' best performance. A fantasy about a woman trying to save her husband from sin. COVER: a cabin in the sky.

324 Cabin in the Sky (Off Broadway, 1964). Rosetta LeNoire, Ketty Lester.

Cabin in the Sky—John Latouche[W] & Vernon Duke[m] *(Miller)*; Livin' It Up—Vernon Duke[w/m] *(Miller)*; Taking a Chance on Love—John Latouche[W] & Ted Fetter[W] & Vernon Duke[m] *(Miller)*. A not too successful revival with one new song by Duke. COVER: a cabin in the sky.

325 Cafe Crown (Broadway, 1964). Alan Alda, Theodore Bikel.

I'm Gonna Move / A Lifetime Love / Make the Most of Spring / A Man Must Have Something to Live For / Someone's Waiting—Marty Brill[W] & Albert Hague[m] *(Harms)*. An instant flop of a busboy dreaming of backing a Broadway show. COVER: Theatre marquee and street lamp.

326 La Cage aux Folles (Broadway, 1983). George Hearn, Gene Barry.

The Best of Times / La Cage aux Folles / I Am What I Am / A Little More Mascara [VS] / Look Over There / Masculinity [VS] / Song of the Sand / We Are What We Are [VS] / With You On My Arm [VS]—Jerry Herman[w/m] *(Morris)*. A hit musical from a hit movie that was very entertaining, but that's all. COVER: a girl in furs.

327 Calamity Jane (British, 1962). Stars unknown.

Calamity Jane—complete score [B]—Paul F. Webster[W] & Sammy Fain[m] *(Chappell)*. A short run stage version of the old movie musical. COVER: lettering only.

328 Call Me Madam (Broadway, 1950). Ethel Merman, Paul Lukas.

The Best Thing for You / Call Me Madam—complete vocal score / For the Very First Time [CUT] [BW] / Free / The Hostess with the Mostes' on the Ball / It's a Lovely Day Today / Marrying for Love / The Ocarina / Once Upon a Time Today / Something to Dance About / They Like Ike / Washington Square Dance / You're Just in Love—Irving Berlin[w/m] *(Berlin)*. A big hit for Irving Berlin with Merman portraying a lady minister to Lichtenburg (a la Pearl Mesta and Luxembourg). COVER: Peter Arno sketch of Ethel Merman.

329 Call Me Mister (Broadway, 1946). Betty Garrett, Jules Munshin.

Along with Me / Call Me Mister / The Drugstore Song / The Face on the Dime / Going Home Train / His Old Man / Little Surplus Me / Love Remains the Same / Military Life (The Jerk Song) / Red Ball Express / South America, Take It Away / When We Meet Again—Harold Rome[w/m] *(Witmark)*. A hit musical about Army life and its aftermath with a big song, *South America, Take It Away*. It ran almost two years. COVER: titles and designs.

330 Calling All Stars (Broadway, 1934). Gertrude Niesen, Phil Baker.

He Just Beats a Tom Tom / I Don't Want to Be President / I'd Like to Dunk You in My Coffee / If It's Love / I've Nothing to Offer / Just Ask for Joe / Just Mention Joe / Stepping Out of the Picture / Straw Hat in the Rain — Lew Brown^w & Harry Akst^m *(Witmark)*. A short lived revue with poor jokes and music. COVER: Gertrude Niesen, Phil Baker, Jack Whiting, Mitzi Mayfair and other stars.

331 Camelot (Broadway, 1960). Richard Burton, Julie Andrews.

Camelot / Camelot — complete score / Fie on Goodness [PC] / Follow Me / How to Handle a Woman / I Loved You Once in Silence / If Ever I Would Leave You / The Lusty Month of May / The Seven Deadly Virtues [PC] / The Simple Joys of Maidenhood / What Do the Simple Folk Do? — Alan Jay Lerner^w & Frederick Loewe^m *(Chappell)*. A musical based on the King Arthur story. Even with poor notices, it ran two years due to the lavish production, Burton and the title songs, and Julie Andrews. COVER: titles and designs.

332 Can-Can (Broadway, 1953). Lilo, Peter Cookson.

Allez-vous-en, Go Away / Can-Can / Can-Can — complete score / C'est Magnifique / Come Along with Me / I Am in Love / I Love Paris / If You Loved Me Truly / It's All Right with Me / Live and Let Live / Montmart' / Never Give Anything Away / To Think That This Could Happen to Me [CUT] [VS] / When Love Comes to Call [CUT] [VS] / Who Said Gay Paree [CUT] [VS] — Cole Porter$^{w/m}$ *(Chappell)*. A musical set in Paris which received poor notices but ran for two years due to the peppy songs of Cole Porter and the dancing of Gwen Verdon and the girls. COVER: a can-can dancer.

333 The Canary (Broadway, 1918). Julia Sanderson, Joseph Cawthorn.

Ding-Dong / I Have Just One Heart for Just One Boy / I Wouldn't Give That for the Man Who Couldn't Dance / It's the Little Bit of Irish / You're So Beautiful — Irving Berlin$^{w/m}$ *(Berlin)*; The Hunting Honeymoon / Julie and Her Johnnies / That's What Men Are For / Thousands of Years Ago — P.G. Wodehouse^w & Ivan Caryll^m *(Harms)*; The Jazz Marimba Melody / Oh, Doctor — Anne Caldwell^w & Harry Tierney^m *(Harms)*; Love Me in the Spring — Richard Fechheimer^w & William Kernell^m *(Harms)*; Oh Promise Me You'll Write to Him Today — Harry Clarke^w & Jerome Kern^m *(Harms)*; Only in Dreams — Harry B. Smith^w & Ivan Caryll^m *(Harms)*; Take a Chance — Harry B. Smith^w & Jerome Kern *(Harms)*; That Little German Band — Benjamin Burt^w & Ivan Caryll^m *(Harms)*; This Is the Time — Clifton Crawford$^{w/m}$ *(Harms)*. A musical involving a swallowed diamond and its results. It ran for 20 weeks. COVER: Julia Sanderson, Joseph Cawthorn.

334 Candide (Broadway, 1956). Max Adrian, Barbara Cook.

The Ballad of El Dorado [VS] — Lillian Hellman^w & Leonard Bernstein^m *(Boosey, Hawkes)*; The Best of All Possible Worlds [VS] / Make Our Garden Grow [VS] / Oh, Happy We / VS / Glitter and Be Gay (long version) [VS] — Richard Wilbur^w & Leonard Bernstein^m *(Boosey, Hawkes)*; Bon-Voyage [VS] — Richard Wilbur^w & Leonard Bernstein$^{w/m}$ *(Boosey, Hawkes)*; Buenos Aires — Leonard Bernstein$^{w/m}$ *(Schirmer)*; Candide — complete score — John Latouche$^{w/m}$ & Lillian Hellman$^{w/m}$ & Richard Wilbur$^{w/m}$ & Leonard Bernstein$^{w/m}$ *(Schirmer)*; Glitter and Be Gay [BW] / It Must Be Me / What's the Use — Richard Wilbur^w & Leonard Bernstein$^{w/m}$ *(Schirmer)*; I Am Easily Assimilated [VS] — Leonard Bernstein$^{w/m}$ *(Boosey, Hawkes)*; My Love

[VS] / You Were Dead, You Know [VS] — John Latouche[w] & Richard Wilbur[w] & Leonard Bernstein[m] *(Boosey, Hawkes)*. A musical based on the classic story that lasted two months. A beautiful production with a marvellous score and talented cast but a poor mixed-up book. COVER: marching people with banners.

335 Candide (Broadway, 1974). Lewis J. Stadlen, Maureen Brennan.

The Best of All Possible Worlds [VS] — John Latouche[w] & Leonard Bernstein[m] *(Schirmer)*; Bon Voyage [VS] / It Must Be So [VS]/ Make Our Garden Grow [VS] / Oh Happy We [VS] — Richard Wilbur[w] & Leonard Bernstein[m] *(Schirmer)*; Candide's Lament [VS] / Life Is Happiness Indeed [VS] — Stephen Sondheim[w] & Leonard Bernstein[m] *(Schirmer)*; I Am Easily Assimilated [VS] — Leonard Bernstein[w/m] *(Schirmer)*; My Love [VS] — John Latouche[w] & Richard Wilbur[w] & Leonard Bernstein[m] *(Schirmer)*. A revised edition produced in Brooklyn and moved to Broadway and directed by Harold Prince. This version ran for two years and still lost money. It did bring attention to the great music and opera companies all over the world were soon performing it, thus making in into a classic. COVER: a sketch of Candide.

336 Candle-Light (Broadway, 1929). Gertrude Lawrence, Reginald Owen.

Candle-Light — Robert Sour[w] & Edward Heyman[w] & John Green[m] *(Harms)*. A comedy dealing with impersonations. COVER: Gertrude Lawrence.

337 Canterbury Tales (Broadway, 1969). George Rose, Hermione Baddeley.

Canterbury Tales Theme [VS] — Richard Hill[m] & Jack Hawkins[m] *(Frank)*; Come On and Marry Me, Honey [B] [VS] / Darling, Let Me Teach You How to Kiss [VS] / I Am All A-Blaze [VS] / I Have a Noble Chick [B] [VS] / If She Has Never Loved Before [VS] / Love Will Conquer All [VS] / Where Are the Girls of Yesterday [VS] / The Wife of Bath [VS] — Nevill Coghill[w] & Richard Hill[m] & Jack Hawkins[m] *(Frank)*. A musical based on the famous story. A big hit in London but a three month failure in New York. COVER: a couple in an embrace.

338 Cape Cod Follies (Broadway, 1929). Lloyd Nolan, Dorothy Llewellyn.

Clutching at Shadows / That's the Time When I Miss You — Seymour Morris[w] & Alexander Fogarty[m] *(Shubert)*; That's Why We Misbehave — Edith Lois[w] & Urana Clarke[w] & Alexander Fogarty[m] *(Shubert)*; Wondering Who — George Fitch[w] & Alexander Forgarty[m] *(Shubert)*. A summer revue from Cape Cod lasting three weeks. COVER: a girl, a whale, a ship and the ocean.

339 Capitol Revue, the Demi-Tasse (Broadway, 1919). Paul Frawley, Muriel DeForrest.

Arizona — James Heard[w] & Melville Gideon[m] *(Feist)*; Come to the Moon — Ned Wayburn[w] & Lou Paley[w] & George Gershwin[m] *(Harms)*; How Can You Tell? — Ned Wayburn[w] & Harold Orlob[m] *(Feist)*; Swanee — Irving Caesar[w] & George Gershwin[m] *(Harms)*; You're the Finest of Them All — Rennold Wolf[w] & Dave Stamper[m] *(Harms)*. A small vaudeville revue in celebration of the opening of the Capitol Theatre on Broadway. COVER: a well-dressed man and woman.

340 Caprice (Broadway, 1928). Lynn Fontanne.

Ilsa — Philip Moeller[w/m] *(Harms)*. A drama about a wealthy man and his mistresses. COVER: Lynn Fontanne.

341 Captain Jinks (Broadway, 1925). Joe E. Brown, Louise Brown.

Ain't Life Wonderful — B.G. DeSylva[w] & Stephen Jones[m] *(Harms)*; Fond of You / I Do / Kiki / New Love / The Only One for Me / Sea Legs / You Must Come Over Blues — B.G. DeSylva[w] & Lewis Gensler[m] *(Harms)*. A musical dealing with the romance of the military and a dancer. Only the clowning of Joe E. Brown kept it going for 20 weeks. COVER: a man in a military uniform.

342 Caravan (Broadway, 1928). Virginia Pemberton, Katherine Clinton.

My Caravan — Jay Gorney^{w/m} *(Harms)*. A short lived drama about gypsy life. COVER: a gypsy wagon.

343 Carefree Heart *(see also* **The Love Doctor)** (closed before Broadway, 1955). Jack Carter, Allen Case.

The Carefree Heart / I Would Love You Still / Promised / Rich Man, Poor Man / Who Is? You Are! / Would I Were — Robert Wright^{w/m} & George Forrest^{w/m} *(Frank)*. A musical based on a classic, with an original score by Wright and Forrest. It folded after four weeks on the road. These two writers seem to do better adapting than writing original songs. COVER: sketch of doctor and ladies.

344 Carib Song (Broadway, 1945). Katherine Dunham, Avon Long.

Sleep Baby, Don't Cry / A Woman Is a Rascal — William Archibald^w & Baldwin Bergersen^m *(Chappell)*. A musical about love and revenge in the tropics which ran for one month. COVER: Caribbean dancers.

345 Carmelina (Broadway, 1979). Georgia Brown, Cesare Siepi.

It's Time for a Love Song / One More Walk Around the Garden / Why Him? (black and white) — Alan Jay Lerner^w & Burton Lane^m *(Chappell)*. A romance between an American soldier and an Italian girl during the war running two weeks. COVER: flower and a soldier's helmet.

346 Carmen Jones (Broadway, 1943). Muriel Smith, Luther Saxon.

Beat Out That Rhythm on a Drum [BW] / Dat's Love / Dere's a Cafe on de Corner [VS] / Dis Flower [VS] / My Joe / Stan' Up an' Fight / You Talk Just Like Maw [VS] — Oscar Hammerstein^w & Georges Bizet^m *(Chappell)*. A hit musical based on the opera, kept going for 15 months by Billy Rose's creative publicity. COVER: Carmen.

347 Carnival (Broadway, 1961). Anna Maria Alberghetti, Kaye Ballard.

Beautiful Candy / Carnival Theme / Direct from Vienna (Piano Selections) / Fairyland (Puppet Song) [VS] / Golden Delicious Fish (Puppet Song) [VS] / Grand Imperial Cirque de Paris / Her Face / It Was Always You / Love Makes the World Go Round / Mira / The Rich (Puppet Song) [VS] / She's My Love / Yes, My Heart / Yum, Ticky, Ticky, Tum, Tum (Puppet Song) [VS] — Robert Merrill^{w/m} *(Robbins)*. A hit musical based on the great movie *Lili*. It ran for two years. COVER: girl with balloons and circus tent.

348 Carnival in Flanders (Broadway, 1953). Dolores Gray, John Raitt.

For a Moment of Your Love / Here's That Rainy Day / How Far Can a Lady Go? [BW] / I'm One of Your Admirers / It's a Fine Old Institution [BW] / It's an Old Spanish Custom / Ring the Bell [BW] / A Seventeen Gun Salute [BW] / Small Things [BW] / The Stronger Sex [BW] / The Sudden Thrill / Take the Word of a Gentleman [BW] / Unaccustomed as I Am [BW] / The Very Necessary You / You're Dead [BW] — Johnny Burke^w & James Van Heusen^m *(B and V H)*. A musical set in 17th Century Flanders that was a one week flop with one lovely song, *Rainy Day*. COVER: carnival people and a castle.

349 Caroline (Broadway, 1921). Tessa Kosta, Harold Murray.

Argentine / Land of Romance — Harry B. Smith^w & Eduard Kunneke^m & Al Goodman^m *(Harms)*; I'm Only a Pilgrim / Man in the Moon / Pay the Piper / Shoulder Arms / Sweetheart / Will-o'-the-Wisp / Your Fortune — Harry B. Smith^w & Eduard Kunneke^m *(Harms)*; Some Day — Adrian Ross^w & Ralph Benatzky^m *(Harms)*; Way Down South — Harry B. Smith^w & Al Goodman^m *(Harms)*. A musical about the Civil War taking place in Virginia, running 20 weeks. Romberg's biography lists Romberg as composer of *Man in the Moon, Will o' the Wisp, Sweetheart and Shoulder Arms,* but the sheet music says Eduard Kunneke. COVER: lettering and designs.

350 Carousel (Broadway, 1945). John Raitt, Jan Clayton.

Carousel — complete vocal score / If I Loved You / June Is Bustin' Out All Over / Mister Snow / A Real Nice Clambake / Soliloquy / What's the Use of Wond'rin' / When the Children Are Asleep / You'll Never Walk Alone — Oscar Hammerstein[w] & Richard Rodgers[m] *(Williamson)*; Carousel Waltz [BW] — Richard Rodgers[m] *(Williamson)*. The best Rodgers-Hammerstein musical of all. Running for two years it had superb singing, dancing and acting. COVER: a carousel.

351 Carry Nation (Opera, 1968). Stars unknown.

I Lie Awake and Listen — William Jayme[w] & Douglas Moore[m] *(Galaxy)*. This production was written for the New York City Opera about the great prohibitionist after the Civil War. COVER: cameo of man and woman.

352 Carry On *(see also* **Sons o' Guns)** (Broadway, 1929). Lily Damita, Jack Donahue.

The Can-Canola / It's You I Love / Let's Merge / May I Say I Love You / Over Here / Red Hot and Blue Rhythm / Sentimental Melody / There's a Rainbow on the Way / When Two Hearts Are True Hearts / Why — Arthur Swanstrom[w/m] & Benny Davis[w/m] & Fred Coots[w/m] *(D C and L)*. A wartime musical set in France, with lush Joseph Urban sets, pleasant tunes, and chorus girls. It was called *Carry On* before Broadway where it became *Sons o' Guns*. COVER: Jack Donahue, Lily Damita and chorus girls.

353 Carter DeHaven's Fancies (Regional, 1926). Stars unknown.

African / Gates of Love / Somehow / Which Is Which and Who Is Who — Richard Coburn[w] & Nacio Herb Brown[m] *(Sherman Clay)*; Doll Dance — Nacio Herb Brown[m] *(Sherman Clay)*. A California musical that never made it to Broadway. COVER: lettering and designs.

354 Casino de Paree (Gosse de Paris) (Nightclub, 1934). Mistinguette.

I've a Feeling You'll Say Yes Today — Joe Young[w/m] & Rene Sylvano[w/m] *(Harms)*. A revue featuring the famous French star. COVER: Mistinguette.

355 Casino de Paree (Nightclub, 1935). Mitzi Mayfair, Jack Whiting.

I Don't Love You — Not Much / I'd Rather Be with You / Lost My Rhythm, Lost My Music, Lost My Man / Then You Walked into the Room / You're Waltzing on My Heart — Lew Brown[w/m] & Elsa Maxwell[w/m] & Harry Akst[w/m] *(Harms)*. An elaborate show featuring many stars. COVER: Mitzi Mayfair.

356 Casino Varieties (Nightclub, 1933). Stars unknown.

Cuh-razy for Love / My Carolina Hide-a-way — Arthur Swanstrom[w] & Fred Coots[m] *(Harms)*; I'm All In / Rain in My Heart — Arthur Swanstrom[w] & Louis Alter[m] *(Harms)*. COVER: girl and a large circle with designs.

357 Castles in the Air *(see also* **Land of Romance)** (Broadway, 1926). Vivienne Segal, Harold Murray.

Baby / The First Kiss of Love / Girls and the Gimmies / I Would Like to Fondle You / Land of Romance / My Lips, My Love, My Soul / Other Fellow's Girl / The Rainbow of Your Smile — Raymond Peck[w] & Percy Wenrich[m] *(Feist)*; Lantern of Love — Raymond Peck[w/m] & Edward Locke[w/m] & Percy Wenrich[w/m] *(Feist)*. A musical about romance, a prince, and a castle. A moderate show with a run of five months. The pre-Broadway title was *Land of Romance*. COVER: troubadour serenading lady in window.

358 The Cat and the Canary (Broadway, 1922). Florence Eldridge, Henry Hull.

The Cat and the Canary — Dorothy Dare[w] & Theodore Bendix[m] *(Harms)*. A melodrama about a will and the heirs involved. COVER: a black cat.

359 The Cat and the Fiddle (Broadway, 1931). Odette Myrtil, George Meader.

The Cat and the Fiddle — complete vocal score / Don't Ask Me Not to Sing / I Watch the Love Parade / A New Love Is Old / The Night Was Made for Love / One Moment Alone / Poor Pierrot / She Didn't Say Yes / Try to Forget — Otto Harbach[w] & Jerome Kern[m] *(Harms)*. A musical about two composers trying to make it. Loaded with beautiful Jerome Kern songs, it had a run of almost one year. COVER: a boy and girl dancing while a clown watches.

360 Catch a Star (Broadway, 1955). David Burns, Pat Carroll.

Twist My Arm [PC] — Paul F. Webster[w] & Sammy Fain[m] *(Chappell)*. A very short-lived revue remembered only for the Neil Simon sketches.

361 Cats (Broadway, 1982). Betty Buckley, Terrence Mann.

The Ad-dressing of Cats [VS] / The Ballad of Billy M'Caw [VS] / Bustopher Jones: The Cat About Town [VS] / Grizabella: The Glamour Cat [VS] / Growltiger's Last Stand [VS] / Gus: The Theatre Cat [VS] / The Journey to the Heavyside Layer [VS] / Macavity: The Mystery Cat [VS] / Mr. Mistoffelees [VS] / Mungojerrie and Rumpleteazer [VS] / The Naming of Cats [VS] / Old Deuteronomy [VS] / The Old Gumbie Cat [VS] / The Rum-Tum Tugger [VS] / Skimbleshanks: The Railway Cat [VS] / The Song of the Jellicles [VS] — T.S. Eliot[w] & Andrew Lloyd Webber[m] *(Leonard)*; Cats — overture [VS] — Andrew Lloyd Webber[m] *(Leonard)*; Jellicle Songs for Jellicle Cats — T. Nunn[w] & R. Stilgoe[w] & T.S. Eliot[w] & A.L. Webber[m] *(Leonard)*; Memory — Trevor Nunn[w] & T.S. Eliot[w] & Andrew Lloyd Webber[m] *(Leonard)*. A musical based on Eliot's poems, *Cats* became one of the longest running musicals in Broadway history mostly due to the song *Memory*. It was basically a big Halloween show. COVER: the eyes of a cat.

362 Cavalcade (British, 1931). John Mills, Binnie Barnes.

Cavalcade — incidental music [B] — Noel Coward[m] *(Chappell)*; Lover of My Dreams [B] / Twentieth Century Blues [B] — Noel Coward[w/m] *(Chappell)*. One of Noel Coward's greatest triumphs which has never been produced since the original production. A British family and their lives from 1899 to 1930 including the Boer War, Queen Victoria, and World War I. The British critics hailed this as a magnificent play. COVER: fancy lettering.

363 Caviar (Broadway, 1934). Nanette Guilford, George Houston.

My Heart's an Open Book / Nothing Was Ever Like This / The Ocean Will Never Run Dry / Silver Sails / You're One in a Million — Edward Heyman[w] & Harden Church[m] *(Harms)*. A love story of an opera singer and a prince which was a failure. COVER: fancy lettering and designs.

364 Celebration (Broadway, 1969). Keith Charles, Susan Watson.

Celebration / Celebration — complete vocal score / I'm Glad to See You Got What You Want / It's You Who Makes Me Young [VS] / Love Song / My Garden / Somebody [VS] / Under the Tree — Tom Jones[w] & Harvey Schmidt[m] *(Chappell)*. An experimental type musical about an orphan seeking his garden. It was a battle between good and evil and a failure. COVER: designs and lettering.

365 Central Park (*see also* **Up in Central Park**) (Broadway, 1944). Wilbur Evans, Betty Bruce.

April Snow / Close as Pages in a Book / The Fireman's Bride / It Doesn't Cost Anything to Dream — Dorothy Fields[w] & Sigmund Romberg[m] *(Williamson)*. This show was a big hit even though it was an old-fashioned operetta dealing with New York politicians and their families. It featured pleasant Romberg melodies and a lovely ballet. The try-out title was *Central Park,* but the opening title on Broadway was *Up in Central Park*. COVER: horses and carriages in Central Park.

366 Century Grove Revue (Broadway, 1918). Stars unknown.

Bolsheviki Glide / Campanile / Love

Me in the Candlelight / You Don't Know What I Know About You – Alfred Bryan[w] & Harry Tierney[m] *(Remick)*; Wouldn't You Like to Have Me Tell Your Fortune – John Mears[w] & Harry Tierney[m] *(Remick)*. COVER: girl and a large clock.

367 Century Midnight Whirl (Broadway, 1919). Blanche Ring, Dorothy Dickson.

If They Ever Take the Sun Out of Sunday – William Jerome[w] & Harry Von Tilzer[m] *(Von Tilzer)*; Milady's Perfume / Society's Shimmying Now / Witches – Joseph McCarthy[w] & John Mears[w] & Harry Tierney[m] *(M and F)*; Peggy – Harry Williams[w] & Neil Moret[m] *(Feist)*; Your Baby for All the Time – Will Smith[w] & Jesse Greer[m] *(Remick)*. A limited run revue staged on the roof of the Century Theatre. COVER: man in top hat with chorus girl; also Blanche Ring and Dorothy Dickson.

368 Century Revue and the Midnight Rounders (Broadway, 1920). Jack Strouse.

Let Me Whisper in Your Ear / A Mouthful of Kisses / My Lady of the Cameo / O, You Heavenly Body / Shimmy-Nods from Chaminade / Wild Romantic Blues / William Tell Me – Alfred Bryan[w] & Jean Schwartz[m] *(Remick)*; O-H-I-O – Jack Yellen[w] & Abe Olman[m] *(Forster)*; You're the Only Girl That Made Me Cry – Fred Fisher[w/m] *(Fisher)*. One of the many revues staged on the Century Theatre roof. COVER: theatre curtains, birds and a fountain.

369 C'est la Vie (Nightclub, 1955). Stars unknown.

Far Away from Everybody [PC] / Moon Must Have Followed Me Home – Bob Hilliard[w] & Milton Delugg[m] *(Morris)*. COVER: Tim Kirby, singer.

370 Champagne, Sec (Broadway, 1933). Helen Ford, Peggy Wood.

Any Woman Except His Wife [VS] / Brother Dear [VS] / Csardas [VS] / Just for To-night [VS] / Never Fear [VS] / Oh My Dear Marquis [VS] – Robert

Simon[w] & Johann Strauss[m] *(Harms)*. A short run for a new version of the opera *Fledermaus*. COVER: lettering and designs.

371 Chance Vought Varieties of 1944 (Army, 1944). Stars unknown.

Let's Keep the Corsairs Flying High – John Fico[w/m] & Lewis Faust[w/m] *(Hi-Tone)*. COVER: defense workers watching a pair of Air Force planes.

372 Change Your Luck (Broadway, 1930). Nina Mae McKinney.

Be Careful with Those Eyes / Tailspin – Maceo Pinkard[w/m] *(Austin)*. COVER: chorus girls on airplane's wings.

373 Chapeau (closed before Broadway, 1977). Brooks Baldwin, Daniel Corcoran.

Surprises – Alfred Uhry[w] & Robert Waldman[m] *(MacMillan)*. COVER: a horse chewing on a hat.

374 Charlot's Revue of 1924 (British, 1924). Gertrude Lawrence, Beatrice Lillie.

Love Life and Laughter [B] / Parisian Pierrot [B] / 'Specially for You [B] – Noel Coward[w/m] *(Keith Prowse)*; That Forgotten Melody [B] – Douglas Furber[w] & Vincent Youmans[m] *(Harms)*. One of the first Charlot Revues done in England and later imported to the U.S. COVER: titles and designs.

375 Charlot's Revue of 1924 (Broadway, 1924). Gertrude Lawrence, Beatrice Lillie.

I Don't Know / I Might – Ronald Jeans[w] & Philip Braham[m] *(Harms)*; I'm in Love with You – Arthur Wimperis[w] & Max Darewski[m] *(Harms)*; Limehouse Blues – Douglas Furber[w] & Philip Braham[m] *(Harms)*; March with Me – Douglas Furber[w] & Ivor Novello[m] *(Harms)*; Night May Have Its Sadness – Collie Knox[w] & Ivor Novello[m] *(Harms)*; Oldest Game in the World – Ronald Jeans[w] & Ivor Novello[m] *(Harms)*; Parisian Pierrot – Noel Coward[w/m] *(Harms)*; You Were Meant for Me – Eubie Blake[w/m] & Noble Sissle[w/m] *(Harms)*. A smash hit revue imported from London which gave the U.S. Buchanan, Lillie and Lawrence. COVER: colored designs and lettering.

376 Charlot's Revue of 1926 (Broadway, 1926). Gertrude Lawrence, Beatrice Lillie.

Carrie / Poor Little Rich Girl / Russian Blues — Noel Coward[w/m] *(Harms)*; Cup of Coffee, a Sandwich, and You — Billy Rose[w] & Al Dubin[w] & Joseph Meyer[m] *(Harms)*; Gigolette — Irving Caesar[w] & Franz Lehar[m] *(Harms)*; I Don't Know — Ronald Jeans[w] & Philip Braham[m] *(Harms)*; Mender of Broken Dreams — John Bratton[w/m] *(Harms)*; Mouse! Mouse! — Hilda Brighten[w] & Muriel Lillie[m] *(Harms)*; Susannah's Squeaking Shoes — Arthur Weigall[w] & Muriel Lillie[m] *(Harms)*. A revised edition of the 1924 revue still with its three bright stars, but not lasting quite as long. COVER: colored designs and lettering.

377 Charlotte Sweet (Off Broadway, 1982). Mara Beckerman, Timothy Landfield.

A-weaving [VS] / At the Music Hall [VS] / Bubbles in Me Bonnet [VS] / Forever [VS] / It Could Only Happen in the Theatre [VS] / Keep It Low [VS] / Liverpool Sunset [VS] / Lonely Canary [VS] / My Baby and Me [VS] / Vegetable Reggie [VS] — Michael Colby[w] & Gerald Markoe[m] *(Leonard)*. A pleasant little musical set in Victorian Music Hall days with an innocent girl, a villain, and a happy ending. It ran for a couple of months. COVER: a group of people and theatre curtain.

378 The Charm School (Broadway, 1920). James Gleason, Sam Hardy.

When I Discover My Man — Alice D. Miller[w] & Jerome Kern[m] *(Harms)*. A comedy about a young man who inherits a girls' school and tries to make changes. It had a short run. COVER: two little children.

379 The Charmer (*see also* **Chopin** *and* **White Lilacs**) (Broadway, 1928). DeWolf Hopper, Odette Myrtil.

Don't Go Too Far Girls / Far Away and Long Ago / Give Me a Chance / Love's a Sunbeam / My Dream Comes True / A Vision Haunts Me / Vive l'Amour — Harry B. Smith[w] & Karl Hajos[m] *(Harms)*. The Shuberts were trying to create another *Blossom Time* and imported this European operetta. Harry B. Smith did the book and lyrics about the lives of Chopin and George Sand. It was called *Chopin* and *The Charmer* on the road but reached Broadway as *White Lilacs,* where it stayed for only a few months. COVER: A house, a tree and blossoms.

380 Chatter Box Revue (closed before Broadway, 1925). Stars unknown.

Chatterbox Girl / Cinderella Dreams / Keep Sakes / My Empty Arms / Rose of Tenement Row / Susan / Treasure Island / Wanda — Raymond Egan[w] & Richard Whiting[m] *(Shapiro, Bernstein)*. COVER: A beautiful girl with flowers.

381 Chauve Souris (Broadway, 1922). Nikita Balieff, Dianina Fechner.

The Chinese Bilikens / The Night Idyl / The Volga Boat Song — Dailey Paskman[w] & Alexei Archangelsky[m] *(Harms)*; Dark Eyes / Two Guitars — AvrahmYarmolinsky[w] & A. Salama[m] *(Harms)*; Dear Nightingale — Dailey Paskman[w] & A. Aliabieff[m] *(Harms)*; Grief — Dailey Paskman[w] & Frederick Chopin[m] *(Harms)*; Katinka — Fizchok Czarovich[w] & Alexei Archangelsky[m] *(Harms)*; The Passing Regiment — Fred Leigh[w] & Oscar Straus[m] *(Harms)*; Pierrot's Moonlight Serenade — Dailey Paskman[w] & anonymous[m] *(Harms)*; Porcelaine de Saxe — Frank Waller[w/m] *(Harms)*; The Parade of the Wooden Soldiers — Victor Olivier[w/m] & Leon Jessel[w/m] *(Marks)*; Sparkling Wine / The Three Huntsmen — Dailey Paskman[w/m] *(Harms)*; Twas in the Month of May — Brian Hooker[w] & W. Kollo[m] *(Harms)*; The Volga Boatman's Song — Alex Archangelsky[m] *(Marks)*. A pleasant revue of songs and pantomime imported from Paris and performed by actors from the Moscow Art Theatre. It was revived and revised many times. COVER: These songs come with two sets of covers. One is the bat cover and the other shows a couple enjoying their music in front of their home.

382 Chauve Souris (Broadway, 1925). Nikita Balieff.

Anuschka — Dailey Paskman^w & Oskar Steiner^m & Oskar Virag^m *(Harms)*; I Miss My Swiss — L. Wolfe Gilbert^w & Abel Baer^m *(Feist)*; Love in the Ranks — Leo Wood^w & Alexis Archangelsky^m *(Feist)*; O, Katharina! — L. Wolfe Gilbert^w & Richard Fall^m *(Feist)*. A revised edition of the successful Russian revue. COVER: Balieff and cast members.

383 Chauve Souris (Broadway, 1927). Stars unknown.

Where Is My Meyer? — L. Wolfe Gilbert^w & Anton Profes^m *(Feist)*. Another edition of the Russian revue. COVER: cartoon character with helmet and spike shoes heading for the Himalayas.

384 Chauve Souris (Broadway, 1929). Mmes. Alexandrova Guerman.

Baby Save Your Tears — L. Wolfe Gilbert^w & Robert Stolz^m *(Marks)*; In a Little French Cafe — Mitchell Parish^w & Sammy Fain^m *(Gotham)*. A later edition of the Russian revue. COVER: Balieff and a pretty girl.

385 Chee-Chee (Broadway, 1928). Helen Ford, Betty Starbuck.

Better Be Good to Me / Dear, Oh Dear! / I Must Love You / Moon of My Delight / Singing a Love Song / The Tartar Song — Lorenz Hart^w & Richard Rodgers^m *(Harms)*. A Rodgers and Hart failure in an oriental setting dealing with the subject of castration. COVER: oriental designs and flowers.

386 Cherries Are Ripe (closed before Broadway, 1931). Vilma Banky, Rod La Rocque.

Cherries Are Ripe — Ben Gordon^w & Allen Taub^w & Lou Herscher^m *(Marks)*. COVER: Banky and LaRocque.

387 Cherry (Off Broadway, 1969). Stars unknown. Something to Believe

In [PC] — Ron Miller^w/m & Tom Baird^w/m *(Miller-Baird)*. A musical based on the hit play *Bus Stop;* advertised to open Off Broadway but never did. COVER: None.

388 Cherry Blossom (closed before Broadway, 1926). Stars unknown.

Ask Me Some Other Time [VS] / Forget [VS] / The Iris [VS] / Pink Cherry Blossom [VS] / Temple Bells [VS] / When Love Is True Love [VS] — Edward Paulton^w & Bernard Hamblen^m *(Feist)*; China Loo [VS] — Bernard Hamblen^w/m *(Feist)*. COVER: three oriental ladies, lanterns, and blossoms.

389 Cherry Blossoms (*see also* **Yo-San**) (Broadway, 1927). Desiree Ellinger, Howard Marsh.

I've Waited for You / My Own Willow Tree / Some Day / Tell Me Cigarette / Wait and See — Harry B. Smith^w & Sigmund Romberg^m *(Harms)*; 'Neath the Cherry Blossom Moon — J. Keirn Brennan^w & William Ortmann^m *(Harms)*. A poor imitation of *Madame Butterfly* that didn't last. It was called *Yo-San* before Broadway. COVER: oriental designs and lettering.

390 Cherry Pie Revue (closed before Broadway, 1926). Stars unknown.

Some Baby — Edward Wever^w & Eugene Berton^m *(Harms)*; Wicked Little Pair of Eyes — Carroll Carroll^w & Edward Wever^w & Eugene Berton^m *(Harms)*. COVER: a group of people in various costumes.

391 Chess (Broadway, 1988). David Carroll, Judy Kuhn.

American and Florence/Nobody's Side [VS] / Anthem [VS] / Bangkok [VS] / Chess [VS] / Embassy Lament [VS] / Heaven Help My Heart [VS] / Merano [VS] / Mountain Duet [VS] / One Night in Bangkok / Pity the Child [VS] / Quartet of a Model of Decorum and Tranquility [VS] / Where I Want to Be [VS] / You and I [VS] — Benny Anderson^w/m & Tim Rice^w/m & Bjorn Ulvaeus^w/m *(M.C.A.)*; I Know Him So Well [B] — Benny Anderson^w/m & Tim Rice^w/m & Bjorn Ulvaeus^w/m *(Music*

Sales). One of the most under-rated shows in recent Broadway history. It had some very good songs and very good singing, but a poor book about a chess match between a Russian and an American intermingled with a love story. It failed on Broadway and on tour. COVER: a chess board.

392 Chez Paree (Nightclub, 1942). Kay Allen, Lou Breese.

In the Blue of Evening—Tom Adair[w] & D'Artega[m] *(Shapiro, Bernstein)*. COVER: bandleader Sammy Kaye.

393 Chic (Off Broadway, 1959). Eileen Rodgers, Virginia de Luce.

Chic / Julie Is Mine—Lester Judson[w] & Raymond Taylor[m] *(Claridge)*; Tallahassee Lassie—Frank Slay[w/m] & Bob Crewe[w/m] & Fred Piscariello[w/m] *(Conley)*. A revue about being chic, which it wasn't. It had six performances. COVER: a man's hand reaching to a lady's hand.

394 Chicago (Broadway, 1975). Gwen Verdon, Chita Rivera.

All I Care About [VS] / And All That Jazz / Class [VS] / Funny Honey [VS] / I Can Do It Alone [VS] / A Little Bit of Good [VS] / Me and My Baby [VS] / Mr. Cellophane [VS] / My Own Best Friend / Nowadays [VS] / Razzle Dazzle [VS] / Roxie / When You're Good to Mama [VS]—Fred Ebb[w] & John Kander[m] *(Chappell)*. A hit musical due to the direction and choreography of Bob Fosse and the dancing of Gwen Verdon and Chita Rivera. No hit songs in this tale of murderesses in Chicago. COVER: sketch of chorus girls, orchestra, and audience.

395 Chickens (*see also* Glory and Lily Dale) (Broadway, 1921). Helen Groody, Jack Clifford.

Friendly Eyes / The Kindly Little Things We Do / Let's Show You to the Girls / The Little White House with Green Blinds / Mother's Wedding Dress / Nine O'Clock Bell / Post Office, Parlor Games / Saw Mill River Road / The Tenor Married the Soprano / Three Little Peas in a Pod / Underneath the Lantern Glow / We've Got to Build—Joseph McCarthy[w] & Harry Tierney[m] *(Feist)*. A quick failure about a girl who goes from rags to riches. This musical was known as *Chickens* and then *Lily Dale* before arriving on Broadway as *Glory*. COVER: A little white house and chickens.

396 The Chiffon Girl (Broadway, 1924). Eleanor Painter, Joseph Lertora.

Cuddle Me Up / Did You Come Back? / Just One Rose / Mia Cara / My Tonita / The Raindrop and the Rose / Till the End of Time / We're Sweethearts / When the Sun Goes Down—Monte Carlo[w/m] & Alma Sanders[w/m] *(Remick)*. A short run musical about a girl who becomes a prima donna and marries a bootlegger. COVER: Eleanor Painter.

397 Children of Eden (British, 1991). Ken Page, Martin Smith.

Ain't It Good [B] [VS] / Children of Eden [B] / The Hardest Part of Love [B] [VS] / In the Beginning [B] [VS] / In Whatever Time We Have [B] [VS] / Lost in the Wilderness [B] [VS] / The Spark of Creation [B] [VS] / Stranger to the Rain [B] [VS] / A World Without You [B] [VS]—Stephen Schwartz[w/m] *(Faber)*. Lavish sets and costumes could not make this biblical musical. It failed due to the book. COVER: designs and lettering.

398 Children Without a Name (Jewish, 1943). Anna Winters, Flora Freiman.

Feigele un Chanele / Kinder on a Heim—Isidore Lillian[w] & Ilia Trilling[m] *(Metro)*. COVER: Ilia Trilling and scenes from the play.

399 Chin Toy (Broadway, 1920). Joseph Howard.

Garden of Memory / My Chin Toy—Joseph Howard[w/m] & I.B. Kornblum[w/m] & Z. Myers[w/m] *(Stern)*; A Kiss from You—Joseph Howard[w/m] & I.B. Kornblum[w/m] & Z. Myers[w/m] *(Remick)*; Sweet Little Mary Ann—Garfield Kilgour[w] & Joseph Howard[m] & Jack King[m] *(Berlin)*; Whistle a Song—Z.

Myers[w] & Joseph Howard[m] & I.B. Kornblum[m] *(Stern)*; The World Is Mine — Z. Myers[w] & I.B. Kornblum[m] *(Stern)*. COVER: a Chinese family.

400 The China Blue Plate (closed before Broadway, 1923). Stars unknown.

Underneath a Chinese Moon — Jack Arnold[w] & Baldwin Sloane[m] *(Witmark)*. COVER: a blue plate with oriental designs.

401 China Rose (Broadway, 1925). Harold Murray, Olga Steck.

China Bogie Man / China Rose / Home / I'm All Alone / We'll Build a Brand New Bamboo Bungalow / Who Am I Thinking Of — Harry Cort[w] & George Stoddard[w] & Baldwin Sloane[m] *(Witmark)*. A musical about love and marriage in ancient China. It is known only for its lavish settings and Chinese dances. It was Sloane's last Broadway score. COVER: Chinese lady by a bridge.

402 Chinese Love (closed before Broadway, 1921). Stars unknown.

Golden Love / See How It Sparkles — Clare Kummer[w/m] *(Marks)*. COVER: sketch of Chinese man and woman.

403 Chinese Nights in San Francisco (Broadway, 1928). Stars unknown.

In the Heart of Chinatown — Phil Boutelje[w/m] *(Berlin)*. A stage show presented during intermission at the showing of a new Paramount film. COVER: oriental designs.

404 Ching-A-Ling (closed before Broadway, ?). Stars unknown.

Basket of Oriental Flowers / Castilian Dreams / Cherry Blossom Maid / Chop-stick Blues / Dan Sing / Draggin' the Dragon Drag / For Ching-A-Ling and Me / Java / My Oriental Home / Poor Little Doll from Japan — Roy Turk[w] & Arthur Johnston[m] *(Berlin)*. COVER: oriental designs and lettering.

405 Chocolate Brown (*see also* **Put and Take**) (Black, 1921). Andrew Tribble, Mildred Smallwood.

At the Tik Tak Ball / Chocolate Brown / Dance Your Cares Away / I Can't Forget the Old Folks at Home / June Love / Land of Creole Girls / The Meanest Man in the World / Shoulder / Snag 'em Blues — Spencer Williams[w/m] *(Irvin Miller)*. According to the song titles and authors, this appears to be an earlier version of the musical *Put and Take* which opened sometime later in 1921. COVER: colored designs and lettering.

406 Chocolate Dandies (*see also* **In Bamville**) (Broadway, 1924). Josephine Baker, Elisabeth Welch.

All the Wrongs You've Done to Me — Lew Payton[w/m] & Chris Smith[w/m] & Edgar Dowell[w/m] *(Williams)*; Dixie Moon / Jassamine Lane / Manda / There's a Million Little Cupids / There's No Place as Grand / Thinking of Me / You Ought to Know — Noble Sissle[w/m] & Eubie Blake[w/m] *(Harms)*; The Slave of Love — Noble Sissle[w] & Eubie Blake[m] *(Harms)*. This black musical about horse racing did not receive good notices. The critics said it was over-produced and "too white." It ran for only three months. This show toured as *In Bamville* and then opened on Broadway as *The Chocolate Dandies*. COVER: colored lettering and designs.

407 Chocolate Drops of 1930 (Nightclub, 1930). Stars unknown.

Ain't Got No Worry / Buffalo / The Golliwogs Parade / I Ain't Blue No More / I've Lost My Head — Spencer Williams[w/m] *(Mills)*. COVER: Singing stars Hortense Ragland, Marcella Shields, Helene Handin.

408 Chocolate Kiddies (Black, 1925). Stars unknown.

Jig Walk / Jim Dandy / With You — Jo Trent[w] & Duke Ellington[m] *(Robbins-Engel)*. COVER: three black dancers.

409 Chopin (*see also* **The Charmer** *and* **White Lilacs**) (Broadway, 1928). DeWolf Hopper, Odette Myrtil.

Don't Go Too Far Girls / Far Away and Long Ago / Give Me a Chance / I Love You and I Adore You / Love's a

Sunbeam / My Dream Comes True / Vive L'Amour — Harry B. Smith[w] & Karl Hajos[m] *(Harms)*. An imitation of *Blossom Time* imported from Europe; about Chopin and George Sand. It was called *Chopin* and *The Charmer* on the road and reached Broadway as *White Lilacs*. It was a quick failure. COVER: a house, a tree, and blossoms.

410 A Chorus Line (Broadway, 1975). Donna McKechnie, Priscilla Lopez.

A Chorus Line — complete vocal score / At the Ballet [VS] / Dance: Ten; Looks: Three / Hello Twelve, Hello Thirteen, Hello Love [VS] / I Can Do That / I Hope I Get It [VS] / The Music and the Mirror / Nothing! [VS] / One / Sing! [VS] / What I Did for Love / Who Am I Anyway [CUT] [PC] — Edward Kleban[w] & Marvin Hamlisch[m] *(Morris)*. Broadway's longest running musical, conceived and directed by Michael Bennett with brilliant performers and the song *What I Did for Love*. COVER: a chorus line.

411 Christine (Broadway, 1960). Maureen O'Hara, Morley Meredith.

Christine / Happy Is the Word / I Never Meant to Fall in Love / I'm Just a Little Sparrow / My Little Lost Girl — Paul F. Webster[w] & Sammy Fain[m] *(Harms)*. A poor imitation of *The King and I* that starred the lovely Maureen O'Hara. An inferior score from Sammy Fain and a terrible book by Pearl Buck. The show lasted only two weeks. COVER: Maureen O'Hara.

412 Chu Chem (closed before Broadway, 1966). Molly Picon, Menasha Skulnik.

Chu-Chem [RC] / Empty Yourself [RC] / I Once Believed in Nothing but Beliefs [RC] / I'll Talk to You [RC] / It's Not the Truth [RC] / It's Possible [RC] / Love Is [RC] / A Lovely Place [RC] / My Only Love [RC] / One at a Time [RC] / Our Kind of War [RC] / We Dwell in Our Hearts [RC] / What Happened, What? [RC] — Jim Haines[w] & Jack Wohl[w] & Mitch Leigh[m] *(Scott)*. A Chinese-Yiddish musical that lasted four days in Philadelphia. A later Off

Broadway revival was also a failure. COVER: none.

413 Cinderella (British, 1959). Tommy Steele, Jimmy Edwards.

Cinderella — complete score / Do I Love You? [B] / In My Own Little Corner [B] / A Lovely Night [B] / Marriage Type Love [B] / Ten Minutes Ago [B] / A Waltz for a Ball [B] — Oscar Hammerstein[w] & Richard Rodgers[m] *(Williamson)*; You and Me [B] — Tommy Steele[w/m] *(Williamson)*. A lavish holiday version of the Rodgers TV musical. COVER: Tommy Steele, Jimmy Edwards.

414 Cinderella on Broadway (Broadway, 1920). Flo Burt, John Murray.

Any Little Melody / Cindy / Just Like the House That Jack Built / The Land Beyond the Candlelight / The Last Waltz I Had with You / Phantom Loves / Primrose Ways / Whistle and I'll Come to Meet You / Why Don't You Get a Sweetie — Harold Atteridge[w] & Bert Grant[m] *(Berlin)*; Naughty Eyes — Cliff Friend[w/m] & Harry Richman[w/m] *(Berlin)*. A Winter Garden production which started out as the *Passing Show of 1920*, then became *Rip Van Winkle,* before becoming *Cinderella*. It had a poor score and bad sketches but managed to run for four months. COVER: the prince and Cinderella.

415 Cinders (Broadway, 1923). Queenie Smith, George Bancroft.

Cinders — Anne Caldwell[w] & Edward Clark[w] & Rudolf Friml[m] *(Harms)*; On Hawaiian Shores / One Good Turn / Wedding Bells / You and I — Edward Clark[w] & Rudolf Friml[m] *(Harms)*. The same old rags to riches Cinderella story which lasted almost a month. COVER: a poor sad girl sitting on a trash can.

416 Cindy (Off Broadway, 1964). Johnny Harmon, Thelma Oliver.

Cindy / Who Am I? — Johnny Brandon[w/m] *(Wemar)*. Another Cinderella story where a kitchen girl makes it to the Plaza. With young performers and a pleasant score, this musical ran for almost a year. COVER: Johnny Harmon, Thelma Oliver, and dancers.

417 The Circus Princess (Broadway, 1927). Guy Robertson, Desiree Tabor.

Dear Eyes That Haunt Me / I Dream of Your Eyes / Like You / We Two Shall Meet Again / Who Cares / You Are Mine Evermore — Harry B. Smith[w] & Emmerich Kalman[m] *(Harms)*; What D'ya Say — Raymond Klages[w] & Jesse Greer[m] *(Harms)*. An imported operetta about a prince who loses his fortune and joins a circus. The operetta ran for several months. COVER: a girl in a very elaborate costume.

418 The City Chap (Broadway, 1925). Irene Dunne, George Raft.

He Is the Type / No One Knows / Sympathetic Someone / Walking Home with Josie / When I Fell in Love with You — Anne Caldwell[w] & Jerome Kern[m] *(Harms)*; I'm Head and Heels in Love — Irving Caesar[w] & Leo Edwards[m] *(Harms)*; Journey's End — P.G. Wodehouse[w] & Jerome Kern[m] *(Harms)*. A musical about a fortune hunter turning good. A poor book and minor Kern score. The musical had a short run. COVER: a city chap beside a country home.

419 City of Angels (Broadway, 1989). James Naughton, Gregg Edelman.

Alaura's Theme [VS] / City of Angels — complete score / City of Angels — theme [VS] / Everybody's Gotta Be Somewhere [VS] / Funny / L.A. Blue [VS] / Lost and Found / Stay with Me [VS] / The Tennis Song [VS] / What You Don't Know About Women [VS] / With Every Breath I Take / You Can Always Count on Me / You're Nothing Without Me [VS] — David Zippel[w] & Cy Coleman[m] *(Warner Bros.)*. A very original musical with Gelbart's book, Zippel's lyrics, and Coleman's music. Add a talented cast and you have a hit musical running for almost two years. The story dealt with a second rate detective, a movie scriptwriter, and other assorted types. COVER: a beautiful girl.

420 Clair de Lune (Broadway, 1921). Ethel Barrymore, John Barrymore.

An Air from India / Chanson de Dea / Claire de Lune Waltz — Michael Strange[w/m] *(Marks)*. Two entertainers in the palace get involved in royal family marriage plans with dire consequences. Based on V. Hugo's *The Man Who Laughed*. COVER: Ethel and John Barrymore.

421 The Clinging Vine (Broadway, 1922). Irene Dunne, Peggy Wood.

The Clinging Vine / Home Made Happiness / Love Needs No Single Words / Omar Khayyam Was Right / Once Upon a Time / Pathway to Paradise / Roumania — Zelda Sears[w] & Harold Levey[m] *(Harms)*. A business woman outsmarts her high brow suitors in a real estate deal and retires to the country to marry her poor schoolboy lover. An ordinary musical which ran six months. COVER: a vine growing on a trellis.

422 Closer Than Ever (Off Broadway, 1989). Brent Barrett, Sally Mayes.

Back on Base [VS] / Closer Than Ever / Closer than Ever — complete score / If I Sing [VS] / Life Story [VS] / Miss Byrd [VS] / One of the Good Guys [VS] — Richard Maltby, Jr.[w] & David Shire[m] *(Fiddleback)*. A collection of excellent songs by Maltby and Shire that had a moderate run. COVER: a page of music notes.

423 Clothes for a Summer Hotel (Broadway, 1980). Geraldine Page, David Canary.

Ghosts / Zelda — Michael Valenti[m] *(Assoc. Music)*. A Tennessee Williams drama about Zelda in a mental hospital. COVER: black and gray lettering.

424 Club Alabam Fantasies at the Black Narcissus (Nightclub, 1925). Helen Stokes, Henry Myres.

Black Bottom / Dixie Dreamland / Narcisse Noir — Francis Weldon[w] & Dave Dreyer[m] *(Club Alabam)*. COVER: showgirl in beautiful costume and a nude lady in large perfume bottle.

425 Club Savannah (Fall Revue) (Nightclub, 1951). The Glamourettes.

Mardi Gras in New Orleans / Sweet Lady of the Perfume / Zanzibar — Dave Oppenheim[w/m] *(Top Notch)*. COVER: the Glamourettes singing group.

426 Cochran's Revue of 1926 (British, 1926). Billy Bradford, Marion Hamilton.

I'm Crazy 'bout the Charleston [B] — Donovan Parsons[w] & Richard Rodgers[m] *(Chappell)*; Tahiti [B] — Eubie Blake[w/m] & Noble Sissle[w/m] *(Chappell)*. One of Cochran's many revues at the London Pavilion; this one ran five months. COVER: lettering and designs.

427 Cochran's Revue of 1930 (British, 1930). Douglas Byng, Maisie Gay.

The Wind in the Willows — Desmond Carter[w] & Vivian Ellis[m] *(Harms)*. Another Cochran revue; it ran for almost eight months. COVER: a willow tree and a lake.

428 Cochran's Revue of 1931 (British, 1931). Ada May, John Mills.

Any Little Fish [B] / Bright Young People [B] / City [B] / Half-caste Woman [B] — Noel Coward[w/m] *(Chappell)*; The Peanut Vendor [B] — Marion Sunshine[w] & L. Wolfe Gilbert[w] & Moises Simons[m] *(Wright)*. A Cochran revue at the London Pavillion with only a four week run. COVER: Noel Coward, Ada May.

429 Cockles and Champagne (British, 1953). Stars unknown.

Darling, They're Playing Our Song — Sam Coslow[w/m] *(Chappell)*. A minor revue at the Saville Theatre in London. COVER: chorus girl with large bottle of champagne.

430 Coco (Broadway, 1969). Katharine Hepburn, George Rose.

Always Mademoiselle / A Brand New Dress / But That's the Way You Are / Coco / Let's Go Home / Money Rolls Out Like Freedom / Someone on Your Side — Alan Jay Lerner[w] & Andre Previn[m] *(Chappell)*; Gabrielle — Andre Previn[m] *(Chappell)*. Nothing great but Hepburn kept it running for a year. COVER: caricature of Hepburn.

431 Cocoanuts (1925 edition) (Broadway, 1925). Marx Brothers, Margaret Dumont.

Always [CUT] [BW] / Five O'Clock Tea / Florida by the Sea / A Little Bungalow / Lucky Boy / Monkey Doodle-Doo / Tango Melody / Too Many Sweethearts / We Should Care (#1) / We Should Care (#2) / With a Family Reputation — Irving Berlin[w/m] *(Berlin)*. A big hit for the Marx Brothers. The show deals with real estate in Florida. The Berlin songs were average. COVER: coconut tree and hut.

432 Cocoanuts (1926 summer edition) (Broadway, 1926). Marx Brothers, Margaret Dumont.

Everyone in the World Is Doing the Charleston [PC] / Five O'Clock Tea / Florida by the Sea / Gentlemen Prefer Blondes [PC] / Lucky Boy / Monkey Doodle-doo / Tango Melody / Ting-a-ling, the Bells'll Ring / Why Do You Want to Know Why — Irving Berlin[w/m] *(Berlin)*. A revised edition of the 1925 hit with some new songs. COVER: coconut trees, a hut and the words *New Summer Edition.*

433 Colette (Off Broadway, 1970). Zoe Caldwell, Mildred Dunnock.

Earthly Paradise — TomJones[w] & Harvey Schmidt[m] *(Chappell)*. A play based on the works of Colette. COVER: sketch of Colette.

434 Colette (Off Broadway, 1983). Joanne Beretta, Susan Baum.

The Room Is Filled with You [VS] — Tom Jones[w] & Harvey Schmidt[m] *(Leonard)*. A lavish production of *Colette* folded in Seattle in 1982. This was a small version derived from that failure that played for a limited run. COVER: Jones and Schmidt.

435 Collette (*see also* **The Daring Duchess**) (closed before Broadway, 1926). Stars unknown.

Dream of the Future / I Don't Believe in Anyone but You / I Want You for My Own / I've So Many Sweethearts / Just One You / Lordy Me — We're too Free / Necking / Out in the West / Pick Up Your Feet / Spend

Your Time in Loving Me / There Will Come a Time / There's Just One You / When I'm Furious, I'm Very, Very Mad / Why Do They Steal You Away—Joseph Garren^{w/m} *(Feist)*. This musical toured as *Collette* and *The Daring Duchess*. COVER: man and woman in an embrace.

436 Come Along (Broadway, 1919). Harry Tighe, Allen Kearns.

Big Drum, Little Drum / Doughnuts / Gas Mask / Rollin' de Bones at Coblenz on de Rhine—Bide Dudley^w & John Nelson^m *(Witmark)*; Hunting the Huns with Hoover / It's a Long Long Time Before Pay Day Comes 'Round / Kitchen Police / Little Wooden Cross / Mother Dear / Thoughts / When Cupid Flies / When You Are Happy—John Nelson^{w/m} *(Witmark)*; Poilu Pal—John Clifford^w & John Nelson^m *(Witmark)*; She's Salvation Sal—Bide Dudley^w & Fred Watson^m *(Meyer Cohen)*; Sonora—Bide Dudley^{w/m} *(Witmark)*. A tired war musical about soldiers and nurses; the musical had a short run. COVER: a girl in a soldier's uniform.

437 Come Along, Mandy (Black, 1924). Salem Whitney, Homer Tutt.

Brown Sugar / Come Along, Mandy / I Want Something / A Lark on a Shark After Dark / My Gal with the Polka Dot Hose / Tenement Moon / Where Are the Pals of Yesterday? / Wiggle-de-Dee—Arthur Lamb^w & Leon De Costa^m *(Remick)*. COVER: titles and designs.

438 Come Along, Mary (closed before Broadway, 1920). Stars unknown.

Come Along, Mary / Hawaiian Moon / In Honolulu Town / Sometime If Dreams Come True—Louis Weslyn^{w/m} & Edward Paulton^{w/m} *(Stern)*. COVER: a pretty girl with a fan.

439 Come of Age (Broadway, 1934). Judith Anderson, John Austin.

The Golden Peribanou / I Came to Your Room / I Come Out of a Dream / I'm Afraid of the Dark / The River Song / Too Much Work—Clemence

Dane^w & Richard Addinsell^m *(Miller)*. A fantasy about a suicide victim who returns to earth to right his wrongs. It folded after one month. COVER: a burning candle.

440 Come On Strong (Broadway, 1962). Carroll Baker, Van Johnson.

Come On Strong—Sammy Cahn^w & Jimmy Van Heusen^m *(Melrose)*. A comedy about young love; the show lasted for a month. COVER: sketch of man and woman.

441 Come Seven (Broadway, 1920). Arthur Aylsworth, Earle Foxe.

Read 'em and Weep—Al Bernard^w & Walter Haenschen^m *(Triangle)*. A comedy in black face about borrowed money and big business deals. It had a short run. COVER: Aylsworth and Foxe.

442 Come Summer (Broadway, 1968). Ray Bolger, David Cryer.

Come Summer / Feather in My Shoe / How Far Is Far Away / So Much World / Think Spring—Will Holt^w & David Baker^m *(Morris)*. A musical about a traveling peddler which lasted one week. COVER: Ray Bolger.

443 Comedy (*see also* **Smile, Smile, Smile**)(closed before Broadway, 1972). Joseph Bova, George Irving.

Open Your Heart [PC] / Smile, Smile, Smile [PC]—Hugo Peretti^{w/m} & Luigi Creatore^{w/m} & George D. Weiss^{w/m} *(Screen Gems-Columbia)*. A poor musical that folded in Boston but was revised as *Smile, Smile, Smile*. It toured the summer circuit, opened Off Broadway, and lasted one performance. COVER: none.

444 Comic Supplement (closed before Broadway, 1925). W.C. Fields, Betty Compton.

By the Side of the Road / Dreaming—J.P. McEvoy^w & Henry Souvaine^m *(Harms)*; Kissing—J.P. McEvoy^w & Con Conrad^m *(Harms)*. A big Ziegfeld production that folded on the road. The material and W.C. Fields were sent back to New York where they were incorporated into the current Follies. COVER: titles and designs.

445 Common Flesh (closed before Broadway, 1935). Stars unknown.

Today Is Tomorrow — Harry Tobias[w] & Phil Boutelje[m] *(Famous)*. This drama toured the West Coast and folded. The language was considered too risque for Broadway. It is rumored that it was written by Mae West. COVER: a girl, a tree, and the moon.

446 Company (Broadway, 1970). Dean Jones, Elaine Stritch.

Another Hundred People / Barcelona [B] [VS] / Being Alive / Company / Company — complete score / Getting Married Today [PC] / Happily Ever After [VS] [CUT] / The Ladies Who Lunch / The Little Things You Do Together / Marry Me a Little [VS] [CUT] / Side by Side by Side / Someone Is Waiting / Sorry-Grateful / What Would We Do Without You [B] [VS] / You Could Drive a Person Crazy — Stephen Sondheim[w/m] *(Valando)*. A hit musical about a bachelor and his married friends with a great score that ran almost two years. COVER: titles and designs.

447 Compulsion (Broadway, 1958). Roddy McDowall, Dean Stockwell.

Compulsion Rag [VS] / A Couple of Hot Shots [VS] / Java Bounce [VS] / Roddy's Dance [VS] — Cy Coleman[m] *(Melrose)*. A drama based on the Leopold-Loeb case. COVER: two men and a book.

448 Congress of Beauty (World's Fair, 1939). Jean Anthony, Axie Dunlap.

Does Anybody Want a Baby? / Get Hot with Red White and Blue Rhythm / Give This Little Girl a Great Big Hand / Is It Just an Illusion? / You're the Fairest of the Fair — Dave Oppenheim[w/m] & Harry Brent[w/m] & Henry Tobias[w/m] *(Mills)*; Hello, Sucker, Hello — Dave Oppenheim[w/m] & Harry Brent[w/m] *(Mills)*. A revue featuring beautiful girls presented by (NTG) Nils Thor Granlund. COVER: the World's Fair Perisphere and trylon with dancing girls.

449 Congress Revue (Nightclub, 1935). Frank Parish, Charlie Davis.

Beautiful Girl — Billy Dawson[w/m] & Lionel Shapiro[w/m] *(Mills)*; A Cavalcade of Blues — Billy Dawson[w/m] *(Shapiro, Bernstein)*. COVER: Frank Parish.

450 A Connecticut Yankee (Broadway, 1927). William Gaxton, Constance Carpenter.

I Blush / I Feel at Home with You / My Heart Stood Still / On a Desert Island with Thee / Someone Should Tell Them / Thou Swell — Lorenz Hart[w] & Richard Rodgers[m] *(Harms)*; Knight's Opening (piano selections) / Nothing Wrong — piano selections — Richard Rodgers[m] *(Harms)*. A bachelor dreams he is in King Arthur's court. A hit musical with a great score that ran for a year. COVER: a medieval castle.

451 A Connecticut Yankee (Broadway, 1943). Vivienne Segal, Dick Foran.

Can't You Do a Friend a Favor / I Feel at Home with You / My Heart Stood Still / On a Desert Island with Thee / Thou Swell / To Keep My Love Alive / You Always Love the Same Girl — Lorenz Hart[w] & Richard Rodgers[m] *(Harms)*. An unsuccessful revival with new Rodgers and Hart songs. Hart died five days after the opening. COVER: a knight and a lady in a jeep.

452 The Conquering Hero (Broadway, 1961). John McMartin, Lionel Stander.

Hail, the Conquering Hero / Must Be Given to You / Only Rainbows / Past the Age of Innocence — Norman Gimbel[w] & Moose Charlap[m] *(Chappell)*. A poor musical based on a hit movie. The story of a mistaken hero that lasted one week. COVER: confused hero and crowd.

453 The Consul (Broadway, 1950). Patricia Neway, Marie Powers.

Consul — complete score / The Empty-Handed Traveler / Lullaby / To This We've Come — Gian-Carlo Menotti[w/m] *(Schirmer)*. An opera performed on Broadway for eight months which dealt with a family's efforts to flee an iron curtain country. COVER: three sad people.

454 Continental Varieties of 1934 (Broadway, 1934). Lucienne Boyer, Carmita.

Dancing with My Darling / Hands Across the Table / Speak to Me with Your Eyes — Mitchell Parish[w] & Jean Delettre[m] *(Mills)*; I Need New Words — E.Y. Harburd[w] & Jean Delettre[m] *(Harms)*; Is It the Singer or the Song — Annette Mills[w/m] *(Mills)*; See Peteet — Mitchell Parish[w] & Gaston Claret[m] *(Mills)*; Speak to Me of Love — Bruce Siever[w] & Jean Lenoir[m] *(Harms)*. An imported revue featuring the singer Lucienne Boyer and a series of vaudeville acts. COVER: Lucienne Boyer.

455 Continental Varieties of 1936 (Broadway, 1936). Lucienne Boyer, Helen Gray.

I Found a Bit of Paris in the Heart of Old New York / It's a Thrill All Over Again — Stella Unger[w] & Jean Delettre[m] *(Mills)*; That's How Little Dreams Are Born / This Is the Kiss of Romance — Mitchell Parish[w] & Jean Delettre[m] *(Mills)*. A new edition of the 1934 revue with Lucienne Boyer; it lasted only one week. COVER: Lucienne Boyer.

456 Conversation Piece (Broadway, 1934). Yvonne Printemps, George Sanders.

Coversation Piece — complete vocal score — Noel Coward[w/m] *(Chappell)*; I'll Follow My Secret Heart / Nevermore / Regency Rakes / There's Always Something Fishy About the French — Noel Coward[w/m] *(Harms)*. A British hit which was a failure in the states. The story of a guardian, who loved his ward, containing some of Noel Coward's loveliest melodies. COVER: a very elegant lady.

457 Cool Off (closed before Broadway, 1964). Stanley Holloway, Hermione Baddeley.

A Dream Ago / For the Life of Me / Only Wonderful / Warm Up —

Howard Blankman[w/m] *(Chappell)*. A musical about a bored woman who sells her soul to the devil for a better life. COVER: lettering and designs.

458 Co-optimists of 1922 (British, 1922). Stars unknown.

Down with the Whole Darn Lot! [B] — Noel Coward[w] & Melville Gideon[m] *(F D and H)*. An annual revue in London such as the scandals and vanities. COVER: the cast of the show.

459 Co-optimists of 1923 (British, 1923). Phyllis Monkman, Austin Melford.

You're Such a Lot [B] — Austin Melford[w] & Fred Astaire[m] *(F D and H)*. The third of this series with a song by Fred Astaire. COVER: Monkman and Melford.

460 Co-optimists of 1924 (British, 1924). Stars unknown.

There May Be Days [B] — Noel Coward[w] & Melville Gideon[m] *(F D and H)*. The fourth edition of these revues. COVER: the cast of the show.

461 Co-optimists of 1930 (British, 1930). Stanley Holloway, Cyril Ritchard.

The Moment I Saw You [B] — Howard Dietz[w] & Greatrex Newman[w] & Arthur Schwartz[m] *(Chappell)*; Steeplejack [B] / Sunday Afternoon [B] — Greatrex Newman[w] & Arthur Schwartz[m] *(Chappell)*. The sixth edition of this series with some songs by Arthur Schwartz. COVER: the cast of the show being watched by an elegant couple.

462 Copacabana Revue (Nightclub, 1942). Connie Russell, Joe E. Lewis.

Are Ya Kiddin' Bud? [VS] / Brazilian Boogie Woogie [VS] / Let It Be Gay [VS] / No Hard Feelings [VS] / This Is New York [VS] / You Just Can't Copa with a Copacabana Baby [VS] — Benny Davis[w/m] & Ted Murray[w/m] *(Robbins)*. COVER: beautiful girl with tropical turban.

463 Copacabana Revue (Nightclub, 1944). Joe E. Lewis, Sophie Tucker.

April Can't Do This to Me / La Pintada / The Sky Ran Out of Stars /

Who's Got a Match? — Eddie De-Lange[w] & Irving Actman[m] *(Leeds)*. COVER: girl in turban.

464 Copacabana Revue (Nightclub, 1944). Joe E. Lewis.

Bahia / I Can Still Remember / The Loveliness You Are / Poco Loco — Eddie DeLange[w] & Sam Stept[m] *(Mayfair)*. COVER: a dancing girl.

465 Copacabana Revue (Nightclub, 1944). Stars unknown.

A Touch of You / The Way That I Want You — Eddie DeLange[w] & Josef Myrow[m] *(Mills)*. COVER: dancing girl.

466 Copacabana Revue (Nightclub, 1945). Stars unknown.

No Can Do — Charlie Tobias[w] & Nat Simon[m] *(Robbins)*. COVER: girl in turban.

467 Copacabana Revue (Nightclub, 1946). Stars unknown.

The Coffee Song — Bob Hilliard[w/m] & Dick Miles[w/m] *(Valiant)*; Deevil, Devil, Divil — Bob Russell[w/m] & Carl Sigman[w/m] & Lee Kaydan[w/m] *(Loft-Marmor)*. COVER: Frank Sinatra.

468 Copacabana Revue (Nightclub, 1947). Stars unknown.

It Began in Havana — Barclay Allen[w/m] & Roc Hillman[w/m] & Bob McLaughlin[w/m] *(Martin)*. COVER: musical instruments.

469 Copacabana Revue (Nightclub, 1950). Stars unknown.

An Arm with a Bow in Its Hand — Bob Hilliard[w/m] & Carl Sigman[w/m] *(Morris)*; Dearie — Bob Hilliard[w/m] & Dave Mann[w/m] *(Laurel)*. COVER: singer Evelyn Knight.

470 Copacabana Revue (Nightclub, 1952). Stars unknown.

Heart of Stone — Heart of Wood — Joan Edwards[w/m] & Lyn Duddy[w/m] *(Morris)* COVER: singer Toni Arden.

471 Copacabana Revue (Nightclub, 1953). Georgia Gibbs.

Somebody Bad Stole De Wedding Bell — Bob Hilliard[w/m] & Dave Mann[w/m] *(Morris)*. COVER: Georgia Gibbs.

472 Copacabana Revue (Nightclub, 1955). Stars unknown.

The Center of Attraction / Manhattan Has a Million Cinderellas / Once Upon a Dream / Saturday Night at the Taj Mahal — Michael Durso[w/m] & Mel Mitchell[w/m] & Marvin Kahn[w/m] *(Wood)*. COVER: chorus girls.

473 Copper and Brass (Broadway, 1957). Nancy Walker, Joan Blondell.

Baby's Baby / Don't Look Now / Me and Love / Sweet William / You Walked Out — David Craig[w] & David Baker[m] *(Chappell)*. Nancy Walker as a policewoman in a musical with poor material and plain score; it ran only one week. COVER: Nancy Walker.

474 Corned Beef and Roses (*see also* **Sweet and Low**)(Broadway, 1930). Fannie Brice, George Jessel.

Cheerful Little Earful — Ira Gershwin[w] & Billy Rose[w] & Harry Warren[m] *(Remick)*; Overnight — Billy Rose[w] & Charlotte Kent[w] & Louis Alter[m] *(Robbins)*. This revue toured as *Corned Beef and Roses* but opened in New York as *Sweet and Low*. Some of *Sweet and Low* was absorbed into *Billy Rose's Crazy Quilt*. It contained a few good songs and the comedy of Fannie Brice and ran for half a year. COVER: three cartoon characters.

475 Cotton Club (*see also* **Rhythmania)** (Spring) (Nightclub, 1931). Cab Calloway.

I Love a Parade — Ted Koehler[w] & Harold Arlen[m] *(Harms)*. The first of the famous Cotton Club revues; also known as *Rhythmania*. COVER: a drum major.

476 Cotton Club (Fall) (Nightclub, 1931). Cab Calloway.

Minnie, the Moocher [PC] — Cab Calloway[w/m] & Irving Mills[w/m] & Clarence Gaskill[w/m] *(Mills)*. COVER: none.

477 Cotton Club (Spring) (Nightclub, 1932). Cab Calloway.

In the Silence of the Night / Minnie the Moocher's Wedding Day / New Kind of Rhythm / You Gave Me Ev'rything But Love — Ted Koehler[w] & Harold Arlen[m] *(Mills)*. COVER: dancing girl.

478 Cotton Club (Fall) (#21) (Nightclub, 1932). Aida Ward, Cab Calloway.

Harlem Holiday / I've Got the World on a String / That's What I Hate About Love / The Wail of the Reefer Man — Ted Koehler[w] & Harold Arlen[m] *(Mills)*. Another Arlen score which produced the standard *I've Got the World on a String*. COVER: a man and a woman dancing; a man playing a saxophone.

479 Cotton Club (Spring) (#22) (Nightclub, 1933). Ethel Waters, Duke Ellington.

Calico Days / Get Yourself a New Broom / Happy as the Day Is Long / Muggin' Lightly / Raisin' the Rent / Stormy Weather — Ted Koehler[w] & Harold Arlen[m] *(Mills)*. One of the best editions with Ethel Waters singing *Stormy Weather*. COVER: silhouette of a girl and two men.

480 Cotton Club (Fall) (#23) (Nightclub, 1933). Aida Ward, Cab Calloway.

Can This Be the End of Love? — Milton Drake[w] & Harry Stride[m] *(D D and G)*; Chiquita, Say "No!" — Jules Loman[w] & Allan Roberts[w] & Francis Shuman[m] *(Broadway)*; Got a Need for You — Jeanne Burns[w/m] *(Handy)*; Harlem Fan Tan — Cab Calloway[w/m] *(Exclusive)*; Harlem Hospitality — Jimmy Van Heusen[w] & Jerry Arlen[m] *(Exclusive)*; The Jumpin' Jive — Cab Calloway[w/m] & Frank Froeba[w/m] & Jack Palmer[w/m] *(Marks)*; Keep Tempo — Jack Stanley[w/m] & George Little[w/m] *(Broadway)*; Lady with the Fan — Cab Calloway[w/m] & Jeanne Burns[w/m] & Al Brackman[w/m] *(Exclusive)*; Little Town Gal — Jeanne Burns[w/m] *(Exclusive)*; On a Steamer Coming Over — Joe Goodwin[w] & Henry Bergman[w] & Lou Handman[m] *(Broadway)*; Way Up North in Southland — George Whiting[w] & Nat Schwartz[w] & J.C. Johnson[m] *(Broadway)*. COVER: chorus girl, Cab Calloway, Aida Ward.

481 Cotton Club (Spring) (#24) (Nightclub, 1934). Adelaide Hall,

Jimmy Lunceford.

As Long as I Live / Breakfast Ball / Here Goes / Ill Wind / Primitive Prima Donna — Ted Koehler[w] & Harold Arlen[m] *(Mills)*; Jazznochracy [PC] — Will Hudson[m] *(Exclusive)*. COVER: a large girl's face smoking a cigarette.

482 Cotton Club (Fall) (#25) (Nightclub, 1934). Stars unknown.

Dixie After Dark / I'm a Hundred Per Cent for You / Jingle of the Jungle / Like a Bolt from the Blue / Ridin' High / Sidewalks of Cuba — Ben Oakland[w/m] & Mitchell Parish[w/m] & Irving Mills[w/m] *(Mills)*. COVER: a dancing girl.

483 Cotton Club (#26) (Nightclub, 1935). Nina Mae McKinney, Claude Hopkins.

Cotton / Dinah Lou / Good for Nothin' Joe / Rhythm River / Truckin' / Waiting in the Garden — Ted Koehler[w] & Rube Bloom[m] *(Mills)*. COVER: a dancing couple.

484 Cotton Club (#27) (Nightclub, 1936). Bill Robinson, Cab Calloway.

Alabama Barbecue / Copper Colored Gal / Doin' the Suzi-Q / Frisco Flo / Hi-De-Ho Miracle Man / I'm at the Mercy of Love / That's What You Mean to Me / There's Love in My Heart / Weddin' of Mister and Missus Swing — Benny Davis[w/m] & Fred Coots[w/m] *(Mills)*. COVER: a piece of cotton with various black characters inside each petal.

485 Cotton Club (#28) (Nightclub, 1937). Ethel Waters, Duke Ellington.

Cantcha Kinda Go for Me / Headin' for Heaven / Old Plantation / Where Is the Sun? — John Redmond[w/m] & Lee David[w/m] *(Mills)*; Chile / The Tap Is Tops — Andy Razaf[w] & Reginald Forsythe[m] *(Mills)*; Don't Know If I'm Comin' or Goin' — Lee Wainer[w/m] & Lupin Fien[w/m] *(Mills)*; The Music Makin' Man — Haven Gillespie[w] & Fred Coots[m] *(Mills)*. Another edition with the return of the great Ethel Waters. This edition appears to be the last edition performed at the old Cotton Club in Harlem. Sometime around this period, Herman Stark took over the name *Cotton Club*. He opened his version at Broadway and 48th Street. According to sheet music, the next edition is "3rd" which indicates there could have been a "1st" and "2nd" edition by Stark. COVER: silhouettes of dancers.

486 Cotton Club (3rd edition) (Nightclub, 1937). Bill Robinson, Cab Calloway.

The Bill Robinson Walk / Go South, Young Man / Harlem Bolero / Hi-De-Ho Romeo / I'm Always in the Mood for You / Night Fall in Louisiana / Savage Rhythm / She's Tall, She's Tan, She's Terrific — Benny Davis[w/m] & Fred Coots[w/m] *(Mills)*. COVER: Robinson and Calloway.

487 Cotton Club (4th edition) (Nightclub, 1938). Duke Ellington, Peg-leg Bates.

Braggin' in Brass / Carnival in Caroline / I Let a Song Go Out of My Heart / If You Were in My Place / I'm Slappin' Seventh Avenue / Lesson in "C" / Skrontch / Swingtime in Honolulu — Irving Mills[w] & Henry Nemo[w] & Duke Ellington[m] *(Mills)*. An interesting score by Duke Ellington including the hit song *I Let a Song Go Out of My Heart.* COVER: Duke Ellington and his orchestra.

488 Cotton Club (5th edition) (Nightclub, 1938). Cab Calloway, Nicholas Brothers.

The Boogie Woogie / The Congo Conga / The Highland Swing / I'm Madly in Love with You / Jive / Miss Hallelujah Brown / Picketing the Old Plantation / Style / There's a Sunny Side to Everything — Benny Davis[w] & Fred Coots[m] *(Mills)*. COVER: Cab Calloway.

489 Cotton Club (6th edition) (Nightclub, 1939). Stars unknown.

It's My Turn Now — Sammy Cahn[w/m] & Saul Chaplin[w/m] *(Harms)*; Love's Got Me Down Again / You're a No Account — Sammy Cahn[w/m] & Saul Chaplin[w/m] *(Remick)*; You're a Lucky Guy — Sammy Cahn[w/m] & Saul Chaplin[w/m] *(Witmark)*. COVER: three dancers

in silhouette.

490 Cotton Club (World's Fair edition) (Nightclub, 1939). Bill Robinson, Cab Calloway.

Don't Worry 'Bout Me / Floogie Walk / The Ghost of Smoky Joe / Got No Time / If I Were Sure of You / Jitterbug Jamboree / The Mayor of Harlem / What Goes Up Must Come Down — Ted Koehler[w] & Rube Bloom[m] *(Mills)*. This edition was billed as the World's Fair edition, with the big fair going on in New York. It produced one hit song, *Don't Worry 'Bout Me,* by Rube Bloom. COVER: the World's Fair symbols of the Perisphere and the Trylon.

491 Cotton Club (1956 edition) (Nightclub, 1956). Stars unknown.

Doin' the Town / Evalina / Life / Rock 'n' Roll Romeo — Benny Davis[w/m] *(Mills)*. COVER: dancers.

492 Cotton Club (1958 edition) (Nightclub, 1958). Cab Calloway, Four Step Brothers.

The Beginnin' of Sinnin' / Big Town Blues / Sinful / Sweeter Than Sweet / Tzatskela, My Darling — Benny Davis[w/m] & Clay Boland[w/m] *(Mills)*; Born to Be Happy / Never Had It So Good — Benny Davis[w/m] *(Mills)*. This last edition of the famous Cotton Club revues featured Cab Calloway, who had appeared in the first edition in the early thirties. COVER: a group of dancers.

493 Count Me In (Broadway, 1942). Charles Butterworth, Luella Gear.

On Leave for Love / Someone in the Know / Ticketyboo / The Women of the Year / You've Got It All — Ann Ronell[w/m] *(Chappell)*. A short-lived revue dealing with the war and spies. COVER: a map of the U.S. and stars and stripes.

494 Countess Maritza (Broadway, 1926). Walter Woolf, Yvonne D'Arle.

The Call of Love — Harry B. Smith[w] & Alfred Goodman[m] *(Harms)*; Dear Home of Mine, Goodbye / I'll Keep On Dreaming / The One I'm Looking For / Play Gypsies, Dance Gypsies / Say

Yes, Sweetheart, Say Yes / Sister Mine — Harry B. Smith[w] & Emmerich Kalman[m] *(Harms)*; Love Has Found My Heart — Harry B. Smith[w] & Alfred Goodman[m] & Emmerich Kalman[m] *(Harms)*. An imported operetta with Kalman's greatest music. The songs and the talented singers kept this musical going for almost a year despite the poor book and lyrics of Smith. COVER: lettering and designs.

495 The Courtesan (*see also* Topics of 1923) (Broadway, 1923). Donald Brian, Nancy Carroll.

In the Cottage of My Heart / Love in a Haystack / When You Love / Yankee Doodle Oo-La-La — Harold Atteridge[w] & Jean Schwartz[m] *(Harms)*. This show toured as *The Courtesan* and opened on Broadway as *Topics of 1923*. It was written for Alice Delysia, a European singer, but it was a failure. COVER: lettering and designs.

496 Courtin' Time (Broadway, 1951). Joe E. Brown, Billie Worth.

Fixin' for a Long Cold Winter / Goodbye! Dear Friend! Goodbye! / Heart in Hand / I Do! He Doesn't / A Man Never Marries a Wife / The Sensible Thing to Do / The Wishbone Song — Jack Lawrence[w/m] & Don Walker[w/m] *(Harms)*. This musical opened in Philadelphia with Lloyd Nolan as the lead. He had voice problems and left the show. It opened in New York with Joe E. Brown in the lead. The story deals with a farmer courting his housekeeper. It was a quick failure. The sheet music for this show comes with two sets of covers: one states Lloyd Nolan in *Courtin' Time* and the other states Joe E. Brown in *Courtin' Time*. The Joe E. Brown cover is unusual because his name, on a thin strip of paper, is pasted over Lloyd Nolan's name. COVER: people going on a hay ride.

497 Coward at Las Vegas (Nightclub, 1955). Noel Coward.

Louisa [VS] / Why Must the Show Go On [VS] — Noel Coward[w/m] *(Chappell)*. This was another chance to make money, this time $40,000 per week in Las Vegas. COVER: Noel Coward.

498 Coward at the Cafe de Paris (Nightclub, 1952). Noel Coward.

There Are Bad Times Just Around the Corner [VS] — Noel Coward[w/m] *(Chappell)*. Coward had financial problems and took to the nightclub circuits to make money, in some cases writing new songs for his appearances. COVER: Noel Coward.

499 Cowboy in Israel (Jewish, 1962). Leo Fuchs, Miriam Kressyn.

I'm Beginning to Like It — Jacob Jacobs[w] & Sholom Secunda[m] *(Mills)*. COVER: Fuchs and Kressyn.

500 The Cradle Will Rock (Broadway, 1937). Will Geer, Howard Da Silva.

The Cradle Will Rock / Croon-Spoon / Doctor and Ella / Drugstore Scene / The Freedom of the Press / Gus and Sadie Love Song / Honolulu / Joe Worker / Leaflets — Art for Art's Sake / Nickel Under the Foot / The Rich — Marc Blitzstein[w/m] *(Chappell)*. An unusual musical in the Kurt Weill style first produced by the WPA Theatre Projects under John Houseman and Orson Welles. After seeing the first preview, the government agency shut down the theatre. A temporary theatre was found until Welles' Mercury Theatre took over the production. Not for all music lovers but it ran four months. COVER: lettering and designs.

501 Cranks (Broadway, 1956). Anthony Newley, Annie Ross.

Don't Let Him Know You — piano selections / Gloves — piano selections / Lullaby — piano selections / Please Come Soon — piano selections / Valse Angleterre — piano selections / Who Is It Always? / Who's Who — piano selections / Would You Let Me Know? — John Cranko[w] & John Addison[m] *(Chappell)*. A revue from London that was too stylish for New York and left after five weeks. COVER: one girl and three boys in a doorway.

502 Crazy for You (Broadway, 1992). Harry Groener, Jodi Benson.

Bidin' My Time [VS] / But Not for Me [VS] / Could You Use Me? [VS] / Embraceable You / I Can't Be Bothered Now [VS] / I Got Rhythm [VS] / K-ra-zy for You [VS] / Nice Work If You Can Get It [VS] / The Real American Folk Song [VS] / Shall We Dance? [VS] / Slap That Bass [VS] / Stiff Upper Lip [VS] / They Can't Take That Away from Me [VS] / Things Are Looking Up [VS] / Tonight's the Night [VS] / What Causes That? [VS] — Ira Gershwin[w] & George Gershwin[m] *(Warner Bros.)*; Naughty Baby [VS] — Ira Gershwin[w] & Desmond Carter[w] & George Gershwin[m] *(Warner Bros.)*. A smash hit revised production of *Girl Crazy* with all of the *Girl Crazy* hit songs plus a few unknown stage songs and some wonderful movie songs with a talented cast and some unusual choreography. COVER: cartoon of boy and girl on musical fence under the moon.

503 Crazy with the Heat (Broadway, 1941). Luella Gear, Willie Howard.

Crazy with the Heat — Walter Nones[w] & Carl Kent[w] & Rudi Revil[m] *(BMI)*; The Time of Your Life — Peter Smith[w] & William Provost[m] *(BMI)*; Wine from My Slipper / With a Twist of the Wrist / You Should Be Set to Music — Irvin Graham[w/m] *(BMI)*; Yes, My Darling Daughter — Jack Lawrence[w/m] *(Feist)*. Despite poor material, a revue that lasted for a few months due to Ed Sullivan's plugs. COVER: chorus girl.

504 Criss-Cross (Broadway, 1926). Dorothy Stone, Fred Stone.

Bread and Butter / Cinderella Girl / In Araby with You / Kiss a Four Leaf Clover / You Will Won't You? — Anne Caldwell[w] & Otto Harbach[w] & Jerome Kern[m] *(Harms)*; Suzie — Anne Caldwell[w] & Jerome Kern[m] *(Harms)*; That Little Something — Bert Kalmar[w] & Harry Ruby[w] & Jerome Kern[m] *(Harms)*. A vehicle for Fred Stone and his acrobatic antics, along with his daughter, Dorothy. Pleasant Kern tunes in a musical about an aviator and

a fortune hunter; it ran six months. COVER: lettering and designs.

505 Cross My Heart (Broadway, 1928). Edgar Fairchild, Mary Lawlor.

Come Along, Sunshine / Dream Sweetheart / Hot Sands / Lady Whippoorwill / Right Out of Heaven / Salaaming the Rajah / We'll Have Our Good Days — Joseph McCarthy[w] & Harry Tierney[m] *(Harms)*. A mother searches for a rich lover for her daughter who loves a poor man. A quick failure and the last McCarthy-Tierney score for Broadway. COVER: silhouette of a couple embracing before a large red heart.

506 Cry for Us All (Broadway, 1970). Robert Weede, Joan Diener.

Cry for Us All / That Slavery Is Love / The Verandah Waltz — William Alfred[w] & Phyllis Robinson[w] & Mitch Leigh[m] *(Scott)*. A musical with a political theme; based on *Hogan's Goat*. It lasted one week. COVER: sketch of lady and man.

507 The Crystal Heart (Off Broadway, 1960). Mildred Dunnock, John Stewart.

How Strange the Silence [B] / I Wanted to See the World [B] — William Archibald[w] & Baldwin Bergersen[m] *(Chappell)*. A musical fantasy which ran for one week. COVER: Gladys Cooper.

508 Cuckoo (closed before Broadway, 1920). Stars unknown.

Come On and Cuckoo / My Romance, My Love, My Ideal / You're Such a Flatterer / You're the Only One — Felix Adler[w/m] & Herman Kahn[w/m] *(Berlin)*. COVER: a cuckoo clock.

509 Cuddle Up (closed before Broadway, 1923). Doris C. James.

Caroline [VS] / Cuddle Up [VS] / Going Back to New York Town [VS] / Kissing Isn't All [VS] — John James[w/m] *(Paramount)*. COVER: Doris C. James.

510 Curley McDimple (Broadway, 1968). Butterfly McQueen, Bernadette Peters.

Are There Any More Rosie O'Gradys? [VS] / At the Playland Jamboree [VS] / Curley McDimple / Dancing in the Rain [VS] / I Try [VS] / I've Got a Little Secret / Love Is the Loveliest Love Song [VS] / The Meanest Man in Town [VS] / Swing-a-Ding-a-Ling [VS] — Robert Dahdah^w/m *(Morris)*. A hit musical about child film stars; it ran for two and one half years. COVER: Curley McDimple.

511 Curtain Going Up (closed before Broadway, 1952). Marilyn Cantor, Larry Storch.

I Love You, I Love You, I Love You / Lizzie Borden / Swamp Boy (Swamp Girl) — Michael Brown^w/m *(Hill and Range)*. The stage debut of Larry Storch and Eddie Cantor's daughter Marilyn could not save this slight revue which lasted for two weeks in Philadelphia. COVER: plain red and green covers showing a bunch of clouds.

512 Cynthia (*see also* **Miss Happiness**) (closed before Broadway, 1926). William Gaxton, Peggy Hope.

I Want to Be a Liberty Belle / Let's Make Believe / Open Your Arms / That's Happiness — George Stoddard^w & Jay Gorney^m *(Shapiro, Bernstein)*. A musical which toured first as *Cynthia,* then as *Miss Happiness.* COVER: a girl's face.

513 Cyrano (Broadway, 1973). Christopher Plummer, Leigh Beery.

Amorous Moron [VS] / Autumn Carol [VS] / From Now Till Forever [VS] / Love Is Not Love [VS] / You Have Made Me Love — Anthony Burgess^w & Michael Lewis^m *(Almo)*. Despite a superb performance by Plummer, this show had a weak score and lasted only a couple of weeks. COVER: a sketch of Cyrano.

514 Cyrano de Bergerac (Regional, 1959). Dick Cavett, Carrie Nye.

Autumn [VS] — Richard Maltby, Jr.^w & David Shire^m *(Fiddleback)*. A college show and the first song written by Maltby and Shire as a team. COVER: lettering and designs.

515 Daddies (Broadway, 1918). George Abbott, Jeanne Eagels.

Daddies — Abel Green^w/m & Sam Coslow^w/m *(Harris)*. A comedy about family life that ran for almost a year. COVER: two daddies with their children.

516 Daffy Dill (Broadway, 1922). Guy Robertson, Marion Sunshine.

Doctor! — Kenneth Klein^w & Herbert Stothart^m *(Harms)*; I'll Build a Bungalow / My Boy Friend / One Flower That Blooms for You / Prince Charming / Tartar / Two Little Ruby Rings / You Can't Lose Me — Oscar Hammerstein^w & Herbert Stothart^m *(Harms)*. A Cinderella story featuring vaudeville star Frank Tinney, who kept it running for nine weeks in spite of its weak score and book. COVER: lettering and designs.

517 The Dagger and the Rose (closed before Broadway, 1928). Stars unknown.

The Dagger and the Rose / Hear Me / The Key to My Heart / Little Woman at My Elbow / You Alone — Edward Eliscu^w & Eugene Berton^m *(Harms)*. This musical which closed on the road was based on *The Firebrand.* The director was George Cukor. COVER: a man and woman embracing.

518 Dakota (Nightclub, 1952). Stars unknown.

Clothes Make the Man / Dakota / Doncha Know / He's All That I Want in a Guy / I'd Rather Be in Love / I'll Take a Raincheck / In a Barn / In Every Cowboy Song / Indian Lament / It's Springtime / My Love Song / Runaway Blues / Young Romance — Frances Ziffer^w/m & Hardy Wieder^w/m & Horty Belson^w/m *(Mills)*. COVER: cartoon of gentleman with mustache.

519 Dames at Sea (Off Broadway, 1969). Bernadette Peters, Steve Elmore.

The Beguine [VS] / Dames at Sea / It's You [VS] / Let's Have a Simple Wedding [VS] / Raining in My Heart / Star Tar [VS] / There's Something About You [VS] / Wall Street [VS] — George Haimsohn^w & Robin Miller^w & Jim Wise^m *(Hastings)*; Broadway Baby

[VS] / Choo-Choo Honeymoon [VS] / The Echo Waltz [VS] / Good Times Are Here to Stay [VS] / The Sailor of My Dreams [VS] / Singapore Sue [VS] — George Haimsohn[w] & Jim Wise[m] *(Hastings)*. A spoof of the Ruby Keeler–Dick Powell musicals in which the chorus girl goes on at the last minute and becomes a star which is what happened to Bernadette Peters after this show. A big hit which ran for a year and a half. COVER: cartoon of girl in sailor outfit.

520 Damn Yankees (Broadway, 1955). Gwen Verdon, Ray Walston.

Damn Yankees — complete vocal score / Goodbye, Old Girl / Heart / A Man Doesn't Know / Near to You / Shoeless Joe from Hannibal, Mo. / Two Lost Souls / Whatever Lola Wants / Who's Got the Pain — Richard Adler[w/m] & Jerry Ross[w/m] *(Frank)*. A smash hit musical about an old baseball player's deal with the devil to be young again. With the talents of Gwen Verdon, the choreography of Bob Fosse, the direction of George Abbott, and the songs of Adler and Ross, this musical ran almost three years. It was the last musical for Jerry Ross who died soon after it opened, after writing three hit musicals with Adler. COVER: a devil's pitchfork and a baseball hat.

521 Dance a Little Closer (Broadway, 1983). Len Cariou, Liz Robertson.

Another Life / Dance a Little Closer / I Never Want to See You Again / There's Always One You Can't Forget / There's Never Been Anything Like Us [VS] — Alan Jay Lerner[w] & Charles Strouse[m] *(Columbia)*. A musical based on the old play *Idiot's Delight*; it closed after one performance. COVER: a couple dancing on a world globe.

522 Dance Me a Song (Broadway, 1950). Bob Fosse, Joan McCracken.

I'm the Girl / Lilac Wine / Matilda / Strange New Look — James Shelton[w/m] *(Chappell)*; My Little Dog Has Ego — Herman Hupfeld[w/m] *(Chappell)*. A poor revue with some great

dancing by Fosse; the revue lasted four weeks. COVER: sketches of dancing girls.

523 Dancing Diana (closed before Broadway, 1924). Bothwell Browne.

Dancing Diana / My Lady of Diamonds / Rainbow / South Sea Moon / Sweetheart — Bothwell Browne[w/m] *(Marks)*. A musical produced by, directed by, and starring Bothwell Browne, who was a female impersonator. COVER: Bothwell Browne in chorus girl outfit.

524 The Dancing Girl (Broadway, 1923). Marie Dressler, Jack Pearl.

Cuddle Me as We Dance / Romance / Why? — Harold Atteridge[w] & Sigmund Romberg[m] *(Harms)*; I Find 'Em, I Fool 'Em, Fondle and Forget 'Em — Alex Gerber[w] & Eddie Buzzell[w] & Jean Schwartz[m] *(Berlin)*; I've Been Wanting You — Harold Atteridge[w] & Jay Gorney[m] & Alfred Goodman[m] *(Harms)*; That American Boy of Mine — Irving Caesar[w] & George Gershwin[m] *(Harms)*; Way in Pago Pago — Harold Atteridge[w] & Carley Mills[m] & Sigmund Romberg[m] *(Harms)*. A shipboard romance between a rich boy and a poor Spanish dancer. Basically a series of revue numbers with a run of three months. COVER: lettering and designs.

525 The Dancing Honeymoon *(see also **Battling Butler**)* (Broadway, 1922). Charles Ruggles, William Kent.

As We Leave the Years Behind — Ballard MacDonald[w] & Joseph Meyer[m] *(Harms)*; Dancing Honeymoon — Ballard MacDonald[w] & Philip Braham[m] *(Harms)*; Tinkle Tune — Ballard MacDonald[w] & Louis Breau[m] & Adorjan Otvos[m] *(Harms)*; Two Little Pals / Will You Marry Me? — Ballard MacDonald[w] & Walter Rosemont[m] *(Harms)*. An English musical on prizefighting which was a moderate hit. Toured as *The Dancing Honeymoon* but opened on Broadway as *Battling Butler*. COVER: a sketch of the moon as a performing cartoon character.

526 Dancing in the Streets (closed before Broadway, 1943). Mary Martin, Ernest Cossart.

Dancing in the Streets / Got a Bran' New Daddy / Indefinable Charm / Irresistible You — Howard Dietz[w] & Vernon Duke[m] *(Chappell)*. A war-time musical set in Washington dealing with the housing situation. Everything in it was so bad that it opened and closed in Boston after a two week run. It was sad that Mary Martin turned down the lead in *Oklahoma* for this show! COVER: cartoon of an admiral and dancing girls before the Capitol dome.

527 The Dancing Widow (closed before Broadway, 1919). Stars unknown.

A Girl Should Know a Little Bit of Everything / Have a Dance with Me / He's Some Boy, Believe Me / I Must Love Someone / O' You Dancing Widow / There Are All Kinds of Girls / When the Honeymoon Is Over / When the Right Man Comes Along — Charles Horwitz[w] & George Rosey[m] *(Stern)*. COVER: beautiful widow in black with male admirers.

528 A Dangerous Maid (closed before Broadway, 1921). Vivienne Segal, Vinton Freedley.

Boy Wanted [IG] / Dancing Shoes [IG] / Just to Know You Are Mine [IG] / The Simple Life [IG] / Some Rain Must Fall [IG] — Arthur Francis[w] & George Gershwin[m] *(Harms)*. This quick failure in Atlantic City was the first complete score of the Gershwin brothers. COVER: a pretty girl.

529 The Daring Duchess (*see also* **Collette**) (closed before Broadway, 1926). Stars unknown.

Dream of the Future / I Don't Believe in Anyone but You / I Want You for My Own / I've So Many Sweethearts / Just One You / Lordy Me, We're Too Free / Necking / Out in the West / Pick Up Your Feet / Spend Your Time in Loving Me / There Will Come a Time / There's No Place Like Somewhere Else / When I'm Furious, I'm Very, Very Mad / Why Do They

Steal Away? — Joseph Garren[w/m] *(Feist)*. This musical was based on a Robert Stolz operetta and toured as *The Daring Duchess* and *Collette*. COVER: man and a woman on stage embracing.

530 Dark Rosaleen (Broadway, 1919). Eileen Huban.

Dark Rosaleen — Alfred Bryan[w] & Abbey Greene[m] *(Remick)*. A short-run comedy about Irish family life. COVER: Eileen Huban.

531 Darling of the Day (*see also* **Married Alive**) (Broadway, 1968). Vincent Price, Patricia Routledge.

It's Enough to Make a Lady Fall in Love / I've Got a Rainbow Working for Me / Let's See What Happens / Not on Your Nellie / Under the Sunset Tree — E.Y. Harburg[w] & Jule Styne[m] *(Chappell)*. A short run musical with a pleasant score by Styne and Harburg and a good performance by Patricia Routledge but with a bad book (uncredited) and a dull performance by Vincent Price. It was called *Married Alive* when trying out in Boston. COVER: a just married couple in a carriage.

532 Daughter of Rosie O'Grady (Irish, 1925). Marion Brent, Pat Rooney.

Homeward Bound / I Want a Girl Like Mother Was / I'll Follow You / Irish Moon / The Two Best Girls I Love / Wherever You Go — Cliff Hess[w] & Joseph Santley[m] *(Remick)*. COVER: Pat Rooney, Marion Brent.

533 Daughter of Silence (Broadway, 1961). Rip Torn, Janet Margolin.

Daughter of Silence — Carl Sigman[w/m] *(Chappell)*. A poor drama based on the Morris West novel. The drama was a quick failure. COVER: lettering and designs.

534 David and Esther (Jewish, 1938). Ola Lillith, Chaim Tauber.

David and Esther — Chaim Tauber[w] & Illia Trilling[m] *(Metro)*. COVER: Ola Lillith and Chaim Tauber, Julius Nathanson, Illia Trilling.

535 The Day Before Spring (Broadway, 1945). Bill Johnson, Irene Manning.

The Day Before Spring / God's Green World / I Love You This Morning / A Jug of Wine / My Love Is a Married Man / This Is My Holiday / You Haven't Changed at All — Alan Jay Lerner[w] & Frederick Loewe[m] *(Feist)*. A romantic fantasy told in song and dance with an interesting score, a first rate cast, but a tedious book. It lasted four months. COVER: silhouette of a man and a woman with a book and a tree branch.

536 A Day in Hollywood, a Night in the Ukraine (Broadway, 1980). Priscilla Lopez, David Garrison.

Again [VS] / Famous Feet [VS] / It All Comes Out of the Piano / Just Like That [VS] / Natasha [VS] / A Night in the Ukraine [VS] / Samovar the Lawyer [VS] — Richard Vosburgh[w] & Frank Lazarus[m] *(Regent)*; The Best in the World — Jerry Herman[w/m] *(Jewel)*; Doin' the Production Code [VS] — Richard Vosburgh[w] *(Regent)*; I Love a Film Cliche [VS] — Richard Vosburgh[w] & Trevor Lyttleton[m] *(Regent)*; Just Go to the Movies / Nelson — Jerry Herman[w/m] *(Regent)*. A hit musical revue imported from England, directed and choreographed by Tommy Tune. The first half is a take-off on old Hollywood musicals and its stars, and the second part is a loose musicalization of Chekhov's *The Bear* as done by the Marx Brothers and Margaret Dumont. With the touch of Tommy Tune, the show ran for over a year. COVER: a cartoon sketch of the Marx Brothers.

537 A Day in the Life of Just About Everyone (Off Broadway, 1971). Earl Wilson, Jr., June Gable.

Goin' Home [PC] / If I Could Live My Life Again [PC] / The Man I Could Have Been [PC] / When I Was a Child [PC] — Earl Wilson, Jr.[w/m] *(Damila)*. A musical failure of one week about a man's daily life. COVER: none.

538 Dear Love (*see also* **Artists and Models** [1930 edition] (Broadway, 1930). Aileen Stanley, Phil Baker.

Two Perfect Lovers / Who Cares? — Haydn Wood[w/m] & Joseph Tunbridge[w/m] & Jack Waller[w/m] *(Chappell)*. This musical was imported from London and toured as *Dear Love*. It was so bad that it never would have made it on Broadway. Rather than waste the lavish sets and costumes, the Shuberts re-vamped it into a revue called *Artists and Models 1930* Riviera Revue. It still became a failure. COVER: boy and girl staring at castle.

539 Dear Me (Broadway, 1921). Grace LaRue, Hale Hamilton.

Dear Me — Grace LaRue[w] & John Golden[m] *(Harms)*; Flowers, Who'll Buy? — Lucille DeMert[w/m] *(Harms)*; The Gypsy's Prophecy / Only a Little Moss Rose / Only a Little Moss Rose — Ethel Mumford[w] & Ward Stephens[m] *(H and D)*; Someone's in Love with You — Robert Harty[w] & S.J. Stocco[m] *(Remick)*; There's a Voice in the Night Calling Me — Will Cobb[w] & Leo Edwards[m] *(Witmark)*; When I Think of the Sweethearts I Might Have Had — Joseph McCarthy[w] & Harry Carroll[m] *(Fred Fisher)*. A poor lady becomes a musical comedy star and marries her mentor. This was a moderate hit of four months. COVER: Grace LaRue.

540 Dear Sir (Broadway, 1924). Walter Catlett, Oscar Shaw.

All Lanes Must Reach a Turning / Gypsy Caravan / I Want to Be There / If You Think It's Love You're Right / Weeping Willow Tree — Howard Dietz[w] & Jerome Kern[m] *(Harms)*. A failure about love in high society with early Dietz lyrics and so-so Kern music. Add a poor book and you have a two week failure. COVER: plain lettering.

541 Dear World (Broadway, 1969). Angela Lansbury, Jane Connell.

And I Was Beautiful / Dear World / Dickie [VS] / Each Tomorrow Morning [VS] / I Don't Want to Know / I Like Me [CUT] [RC] / I Never Said I Love You / Kiss Her Now / Memories [VS] / One Person / Pearls [VS] / The Spring of Next Year [VS] / Thoughts

[VS] / Through the Bottom of the Glass [CUT] [PC] / Voices [VS] — Jerry Herman^w/m *(Morris)*; Garbage — Jerry Herman^m *(Morris)*. A musical based on *The Mad Woman of Chaillot*. When it opened in Boston, there were some good things in it; however, due to personnel changes, cuts, and additions it arrived in New York as a disaster. COVER: face and gloves of the Countess.

542 Dearest Enemy (Broadway, 1925). Helen Ford, Charles Purcell.

Bye and Bye / Cheerio! / Here in My Arms / Here's a Kiss / Sweet Peter — Lorenz Hart^w & Richard Rodgers^m *(Harms)*. A charming musical with the song *Here in My Arms*. It was all about a lady's efforts to help the Americans win the Revolutionary War. A hit with a run of nine months. COVER: lettering and designs with a girl's face.

543 Dearie (closed before Broadway, 1920). Stars unknown.

After You're Married Awhile / Dearie, My Dearie / Derby Day / Following the Hounds / I Think So Much of All the Boys / In Days of Long Ago / Johnny from London Town / My New Kentucky Home / Take a Little Tip from Me / That Linger Longer Look — John Wilson^w & Malvin Franklin^m *(Witmark)*; My Easy Ridin' Man — Malvin Franklin^w/m *(Witmark)*; Southern Nights — John Wilson^w & Malvin Franklin^m & Billie Griffith^m *(Witmark)*. COVER: a girl and her horse.

544 Death of a Salesman (Broadway, 1949). Mildred Dunnock, Arthur Kennedy.

Ben's Theme / Grandfather's Theme / Linda's Theme / Willy Loman's Theme — Alex North^m *(Mills)*. A highly praised drama about a has-been salesman and his sons with incidental music by North. COVER: lettering and designs.

545 The Decameron (Off Broadway, 1961). Jan Miner, Bob Roman.

Deceive Me / I Know, I Know — Yvonne Tarr^w & Edward Earle^m *(Shayne)*. A failure based on Boccac-

cio's *Decameron*. It lasted one month. COVER: lettering and designs.

546 The Deep Blue Sea (Broadway, 1952). Margaret Sullavan, James Hanley.

The Deep Blue Sea — John Latouche^w & Ulpio Minucci^m *(Sherwin)*. An imported British drama which was a good start for Margaret Sullavan. COVER: a woman's face.

547 Deep River (Broadway, 1926). Jules Bledsoe, Rose McClendon.

Ashes and Fire [VS] / Cherokee Rose [VS] / De Old Clay Road [VS] / Dis Is de Day [VS] / Love Lasts a Day [VS] / Po' Li'l Black Chile [VS] / Serenade Creole [VS] / Soft as de Moonlight [VS] / Two Little Stars [VS] — Laurence Stallings^w & Frank Harling^m *(Feist)*. A musical taking place in pre-Civil War New Orleans with beautiful music. Billed as a native opera, it was ahead of its time and a quick failure. COVER: man and woman in a very elegant garden with marble, vases, flowers.

548 Delilah (*see also* **The Vamp**) (Broadway, 1955). Carol Channing, David Atkinson.

Have You Met Delilah? / I've Always Loved You / Ragtime Romeo / Why Does It Have to Be You — John Latouche^w & James Mundy^m *(Robbins-Wise)*. A quick failure with Carol Channing as the queen of the silent screen. It was called *Delilah* while previewing, but changed to *The Vamp* for the opening. All four songs are published as *The Vamp* and as *Delilah*. COVER: Carol Channing.

549 Demi-Dozen (Nightclub, 1958). Jane Connell, Gordon Connell.

Sunday in New York — Portia Nelson^w/m *(Mayfair)*; You Fascinate Me So — Carolyn Leigh^w & Cy Coleman^m *(Mayfair)*. One of Julius Monk's revues which started many famous composers and lyricists. COVER: an actress and a theatre curtain in pieces.

550 Dere Mable (closed before Broadway, 1920). Sam Ash, George Cukor.

Before Me Lies the World — Edward

Streeter[w/m] & John Hodges[w/m] & Rosamond Hodges[w/m] *(Harms)*; Island of Do as You Please — Edward Streeter[w] & John Hodges[w] & Rosamond Hodges[m] *(Harms)*; Madamuzzelle Bon Nuit — John Hodges[w/m] & Rosamond Hodges[w/m] *(Harms)*; One Little Girl I Prize / When Love Comes Knocking at Your Heart / Why Must We Say Goodbye — Sam Ash[w/m] & J. Keirn Brennan[w/m] & Bert Rule[w/m] *(Witmark)*; We're Pals / Yankee [CUT] — Irving Caesar[w] & George Gershwin[m] *(Harms)*. COVER: a soldier writing a letter.

551 Desert Inn Revue (Nightclub, 1956). Stars unknown.

Small Town [PC] — Pony Sherrell[w/m] & Phil Moody[w/m] *(American Academy)*. COVER: none.

552 The Desert Song (*see also* Lady Fair) (Broadway, 1926). Robert Halliday, Vivienne Segal.

The Desert Song / The Desert Song — complete vocal score / "It" / Let's Have a Love Affair / Love's Dear Yearning / One Alone / One Flower Grows Alone in Your Garden / The Riff Song / Romance — Otto Harbach[w] & Oscar Hammerstein[w] & Sigmund Romberg[m] *(Harms)*; Desert Song Valse [B] — Sigmund Romberg[m] *(Chappell)*. A big hit in the old fashioned operetta style with some wonderful Romberg songs. The story was based on current incidents dealing with the Arab revolt against the French. It was called *Lady Fair* during its try-out period. COVER: an Arab and a girl in a desert.

553 Destry Rides Again (Broadway, 1959). Dolores Gray, Andy Griffith.

Anyone Would Love You / Are You Ready, Gyp Watson? / Every Once in a While / Fair Warning / Hoop de Dingle / I Know Your Kind / I Say Hello / Once Knew a Fella / Ring on Her Finger / Rose Lovejoy of Paradise Alley — Harold Rome[w/m] *(Chappell)*. A musical based on the Dietrich movie *Destry,* with an ordinary score by Rome but great performances by Griffith and Gray with exceptional choreography from M. Kidd. It ran one year. COVER: a gun and a rose.

554 The Devil and Daniel Webster (Opera, 1943). Walter Cassel, Norman Kelley.

I've Got a Ram — Stephen V. Benet[w] & Douglas Moore[m] *(Boosey, Hawkes)*. Commissioned for the New York City Center. COVER: lettering and designs.

555 Dew Drop Inn (*see also* In the Moonlight) (Broadway, 1923). James Barton, Lee Kelso.

Goodbye / If There Were Not Any Men — Cyrus Wood[w] & Alfred Goodman[m] *(Harms)*; Lady — McElbert Moore[w] & Jean Schwartz[m] & Fred Coots[m] *(Harms)*; M.T. Pocket Blues — Eli Dawson[w/m] & Lewis Michelson[w/m] & Victor Olivier[w/m] *(Fisher)*; That's a Lot of Bunk — Al Wilson[w/m] & James Brennan[w/m] & Mack Henshaw[w/m] *(Marks)*; Waitin' for the Evenin' Mail — Billy Baskette[w/m] *(Berlin)*; We Two — Cyrus Wood[w] & Rudolf Friml[m] *(Harms)*. A flop with almost no plot and Barton's famous drunk scene. It toured as *In the Moonlight* before reaching Broadway as *Dew Drop Inn.* COVER: James Barton.

556 Diamond Lil (closed before Broadway, 1929). Mae West.

Diamond Lil — Robert Sterling[w/m] *(Marks)*; Easy Rider — Shelton Brooks[w/m] *(Rossiter)*. A touring production of Mae West which played the West Coast and Chicago. A new version in 1949 finally made it to Broadway. COVER: Mae West.

557 Diana Comes to Town (*see also* The Naughty Diana) (closed before Broadway, 1923). Stars unknown.

Dreams / Good Night, the Sun Is Shining / I've Found Love at Last — Cyrus Wood[w] & Will Ortmann[m] *(Harms)*. Toured as *Diana Comes to Town* and as *The Naughty Diana.* COVER: lettering and designs.

558 Didn't You Hear That Thunder? (*see also* Raisin) (Broadway, 1973). Virginia Capers, Deborah Allen.

He Come Down This Morning [RC] / It's a Deal [RC] / Measure the Valleys [RC] / Sweet Time [RC] / A Whole Lotta Sunlight [RC] — Robert Brittan[w] & Judd Woldin[m] *(Blackwood)*. A hit musical about a poor black family trying to get ahead. A competent score and good acting. It was called *Didn't You Hear That Thunder?* while seeking financing. COVER: none.

559 Dilly Dally (closed before Broadway, 1932). Stars unknown.

Glory Bound / Gotham Has Got 'Em / In a Quaint Little English Town / Plink Plonk / We'll Dilly Dally Along — Tom Connell[w/m] & Will Heagney[w/m] *(Mills)*. COVER: beautiful show girl with gentleman suitor.

560 Dinah (Black, 1923). Irvin C. Miller, Will Cook.

Ghost of the Blues — Tim Brymn[w/m] & Sidney Bechet[w/m] *(Williams)*. A musical dealing with the theft of an inheritance. COVER: lettering and designs.

561 The Dish-Washer (Jewish, 1934). Herman Yablokoff.

The Dishwasher — Herman Yablokoff[w/m] *(Kammell)*. COVER: Herman Yablokoff.

562 Divine Moment (Broadway, 1934). Peggy Fears.

I Can't Forgive Myself — John Moroney[w/m] *(D B and H)*. A drama of an unhappily married woman who has a moment of romance with another man. COVER: Peggy Fears.

563 Divorce for Chrystabel (British, 1943). Frances Day.

All the Things You Are — Oscar Hammerstein[w] & Jerome Kern[m] *(Chappell)*. A drama which included this Jerome Kern song. COVER: Frances Day.

564 Dixie Jubilee, a Sepia Swing Show (Black, 1937). Stars unknown.

Someday, You'll Belong to Me — Donald Heywood[w/m] & L. Marx[w/m] *(Harms)*. COVER: sketch of Major Bowes.

565 Dixie to Broadway (*see also* **Plantation Follies**) (Broadway, 1924). Florence Mills, Shelton Brooks.

Dixie Dreams / I'm a Little Blackbird Looking for a Bluebird / Jazz Time Came from the South / Jungletown Has Moved to Dixieland / Mandy Make Up Your Mind — Grant Clarke[w] & Roy Turk[w] & George Meyer[m] & Arthur Johnston[m] *(Berlin)*. A black revue kept going by its great dancing and the singing of Florence Mills who died shortly thereafter. It was called *Plantation Follies* before Broadway. COVER: black men singing and dancing along the river.

566 Do I Hear a Waltz? (Broadway, 1965). Elizabeth Allen, Sergio Franchi.

Do I Hear a Waltz? / Do I Hear a Waltz? — complete vocal score / Here We Are Again / Moon in My Window / Perhaps / Someone Like You / Stay / Take the Moment / Thank You So Much / Two by Two — Stephen Sondheim[w] & Richard Rodgers[m] *(Williamson)*. A musical about a lonely woman and a gigolo in Italy. A charming score by Rodgers and Sondheim. The dreary book by Laurents made it a failure which ran for six months. COVER: boy, girl, and gondola.

567 Do Re Mi (Broadway, 1960). Phil Silvers, Nancy Walker.

All You Need Is a Quarter / Asking for You / Cry Like the Wind / Do Re Mi — complete vocal score / Fireworks / I Know About Love [PC] / Make Someone Happy / What's New at the Zoo — Betty Comden[w] & Adolf Green[w] & Jule Styne[m] *(Chappell)*. A very entertaining musical with the clowning of Silvers and Walker and a nice score by Jule Styne. Even though it ran one year, it lost money. COVER: this music was published with two sets of covers; one set shows a large juke box with lettering and the other is a caricature of Silvers with dancing girls.

568 Dr. Willy Nilly (Off Broadway, 1959). Howard Da Silva, Ann Thomas.

Jacqueline — Edward Eager[w] & Pembroke Davenport[m] *(Saunders)*. COVER: doctor chasing young girl.

569 A Doll's Life (Broadway, 1982). George Hearn, Barbara Lang.

A Doll's Life [VS] / Learn to Be Lovely [VS] / No More Tomorrows [VS] / Power [VS] / Rare Wines [VS] / Stay with Me, Nora [VS] / You Interest Me [VS] — Betty Comden^w & Adolph Green^w & Larry Grossman^m *(Fiddleback)*. A terrible musical based on Ibsen's Nora. COVER: sketch of people dancing and a woman's eyes.

570 Donnybrook! (Broadway, 1961). Art Lund, Susan Johnson.

The Day the Snow Is Meltin' / Deelightful Is the Word / Donnybrook / Ellen Roe / For My Own / He Makes Me Feel I'm Lovely / I Have My Own Way / I Wouldn't Bet One Penny / If It Isn't Everything / Sad Was the Day / Sez I / A Toast to the Bride — Johnny Burke^{w/m} *(Harms)*. An unsuccessful musical based on *The Quiet Man*. *Donnybrook* was quickly forgotten. COVER: man and woman embracing.

571 Don't Bother Me, I Can't Cope (Broadway, 1972). Micki Grant, Bobby Hill.

Don't Bother Me, I Can't Cope [VS] / Fighting for Pharaoh [VS] / I Gotta Keep Movin' [VS] / It Takes a Whole Lot of Human Feeling / Questions [VS] / So Little Time [VS] / Thank Heaven for You — Micki Grant^{w/m} *(Fiddleback)*. A long running black revue stating blacks' attitudes toward a world they don't own. COVER: silhouette of a group of singers.

572 Don't Worry (Jewish, 1951). Miriam Kressyn, Leo Fuchs.

I Wanna I Wanna I Wanna — Jacob Jacobs^w & Abe Ellstein^m *(Metro)*. COVER: Kressyn and Fuchs.

573 Double Dublin (Broadway, 1963). Noel Sheridan, John Molloy.

Dublin Saunter — Leo Maguire^{w/m} *(Boston)*; I Have a Bonnet Trimmed with Blue / I Was Strolling / I'll Tell Me Ma / Irish Jig / The Little Skillet Pot — Baldwin Bergersen^{w/m} *(Boston)*. A small Irish revue which lasted four performances. COVER: lettering and designs.

574 Double Entry (Off Broadway, 1961). Jane Connell, Rosetta LeNoire.

Kinda Sorta Doing Nothing / Miss Lucy Long / Same Old Summer — Jay Thompson^{w/m} *(Morris)*. Two one act musicals that failed. COVER: sketch of a girl's face.

575 Down in the Valley (Regional, 1948). Marion Bell, James Welch.

Down in the Valley — complete vocal score / The Lonesome Dove — Arnold Sundgaard^w & Kurt Weill^m *(Schirmer)*. A folk opera first performed at the University of Indiana. COVER: a peaceful valley with little white houses.

576 Down Limerick Way (Irish, 1919). Fiske O'Hara.

Dear Little Angel from Heaven — N.H. Jefferson^{w/m} *(Feist)*; Down Limerick Way — George Gartlan^{w/m} *(Feist)*; If They'd Only Give Old Ireland to the Irish — Queenie Hewlett^w & Ben Jerome^m *(Feist)*. COVER: Fiske O'Hara.

577 Drat the Cat (Philadelphia version) (Broadway, 1965). Elliott Gould, Eddie Foy, Jr.

Deep in Your Heart / I Like Him / Let's Go / Today Is a Day for a Band to Play — Ira Levin^w & Milton Schafer^m *(Morris)*; Drat! The Cat! Samba — Ira Levin^m & Milton Schafer^m *(Morris)*. A musical about a crooked heiress and a policeman. While in Philadelphia, Eddie Foy Jr. was featured but wisely left. The early sheet music features his name. COVER: beautiful girl in cat costume with the note "Also starring Eddie Foy, Jr." with a gold cover.

578 Drat the Cat (New York version) (Broadway, 1965). Elliott Gould, Lesley Ann Warren.

Dancing with Alice [VS] / Holmes and Watson [VS] / I Like Him / It's Your Fault [VS] / She Touched Me / She's Roses [VS] / Wild and Reckless [VS] — Ira Levin^w & Milton Schafer^m *(Morris)*; Drat! The Cat! Samba — Ira Levin^m & Milton Schafer^m *(Morris)*. This poor musical about a cat burglar and a cop lasted one week. It did produce one song which has become a standard, *She Touched Me* thanks to

Mrs. Gould. COVER: a yellow cover with girl in cat costume and no mention of Eddie Foy, Jr.

579 The Dream Girl (Broadway, 1924). Fay Bainter, George LeMaire.

All Year Round / At the Rainbow's End / The Broad Highway / Bubble Song / The Dream Girl / Gypsy Life—piano selections / If Someone Only Would Find Me / My Dream Girl / My Hero—Rida J. Young[w] & Victor Herbert[m] *(Harms)*; Stop! Look! Listen!—piano selections—Victor Herbert[m] *(Harms)*. Herbert's last operetta—about reincarnation—with pleasant songs. It ran four months and toured. COVER: girl's head in a bunch of clouds.

580 The Dream Weaver (Jewish, 1934). Maximilien Rosenblatt, Gertrude Bullman.

Give Me Your Heart—S.H. Cohen[w] & Harry Lubin[m] *(Kammen)*. COVER: Harry Lubin.

581 Dream with Music (Broadway, 1944). Ronald Graham, Vera Zorina.

Baby, Don't Count on Me / I'm Afraid I'm in Love / Love at Second Sight—Edward Eager[w] & Clay Warnick[m] *(Chappell)*. A musical with an Arabian Nights theme which lasted three weeks. COVER: sketch of musicians and dancers.

582 Dreamgirls (Broadway, 1981). Jennifer Holliday, Loretta Devine.

Ain't No Party [VS] / And I Am Telling You I'm Not Going [VS] / Cadillac Car [VS] / Dreamgirls [VS] / Fake Your Way to the Top [VS] / Family [VS] / Hard to Say Goodbye, My Love [VS] / I Am Changing [VS] / Move [VS] / One Night Only [VS] / Steppin' to the Bad Side [VS] / When I First Saw You [VS]—Tom Eyen[w] & Henry Krieger[m] *(Warner Bros.)*. A hit musical running almost four years loosely based on the story of the Supremes. Its long run was due to the talented cast and the direction of Michael Bennett. COVER: three girls on stage with mikes.

583 Die Dreigroschenoper (*see also* **The Threepenny Opera**) (Broadway,

1993). Steffi Duna, Marjorie Dille.

Alabama Song [BW] / Barbara Song [BW] / Seerauberjenny [BW]—Bert Brecht[w] & Kurt Weill[m] *(Universal)*; Moritat [BW]—Kurt Weill[m] *(Harms)*. The first American performance of this musical lasted less than two weeks. COVER: lettering and designs.

584 The Drunkard (Nightclub, 1934). Stars unknown.

The Drunkard Song—Rudy Vallee[w/m] *(Shapiro, Bernstein)*; There Is a Tavern in the Town—Ted Fiorito[w/m] *(Robbins)*. A production of the American Music Hall in New York City. COVER: a scene from the play.

585 The Drunkard (Nightclub, 1937). Stars unknown.

Pork and Beans—Albert Von Tilzer[w/m] & Harry Tobias[w/m] *(Von Tilzer)*. A production of this old play as done at the Theatre Mart in Hollywood. COVER: a scene from the play.

586 The Dubarry (Broadway, 1932). Grace Moore, Pert Kelton.

The Dubarry / Happy Little Jean / I Give My Heart / If I Am Dreaming / Without Your Love—Rowland Leigh[w] & Carl Millocker[m] *(Chappell)*. A German operetta revived for ten weeks as a vehicle for Grace Moore. COVER: Grace Moore.

587 DuBarry Was a Lady (Broadway, 1939). Ethel Merman, Bert Lahr.

But in the Morning, No! / Come On In / Do I Love You? / Ev'ry Day Is a Holiday / Friendship / Give Him the Oo La La / It Ain't Etiquette [VS] / It Was Written in the Stars / Katie Went to Haiti / Well, Did You Evah? / When Love Beckoned—Cole Porter[w/m] *(Chappell)*. A washroom attendant dreams he is Louis XV wooing Madame DuBarry. Some great Cole Porter songs with the clowning of Bert Lahr and the singing of Ethel Merman made this show a hit running well over one year. COVER: Merman and Lahr.

588 The Duchess Misbehaves (Broadway, 1946). Audrey Christie, Joey Faye.

Couldn't Be More in Love / You Are My Only Romance — Gladys Shelley[w] & Frank Black[m] (Chappell). A musical that lasted five days about a man who dreams he is Goya pursuing the Duchess of Alba. COVER: lettering and designs.

589 Duchess of Chicago (closed before Broadway, 1929). Walter Woolf, Arthur Treacher.

Hands Across the Sea / Having My Own Sweet Way / In Chicago / Song of Vienna — Edward Eliscu[w] & Emmerich Kalman[m] (Harms); Look in My Eyes / On the Up and Up — Edward Eliscu[w] & Maurie Rubens[m] (Harms). COVER: a duchess staring at skyscrapers.

590 Dude (Broadway, 1972). William Redfield, Rae Allen.

Baby Breath [PC] / Boo Boo [PC] / Goodbyes, Living a Life at Home [PC] / I Know Your Name [PC] / No One [PC] / So Long, Dude [PC] / There's Only a Few More Years [PC] — Gerome Ragni[w] & Galt MacDermott[m] (M and R). A rock musical about a man's search of the universe. The theatre was totally re-constructed inside and the actors roamed to every corner. The authors hoped this would be another Hair but it failed after two weeks. COVER: none.

591 The Dutch Girl (closed before Broadway, 1925). Irene Dunne, Frank Gardiner.

By the Silver Sea / The Dreamland Lover — Harry Graham[w] & Emmerich Kalman[m] (Chappell). Another imported operetta. COVER: lettering and designs.

592 Earl Carroll — Broadway to Hollywood (Nightclub, 1939). Beryl Wallace and 60 Beauties.

By Candlelight — Ray Noble[w/m] (Harms); A Face in the Crowd — Paul F. Webster[w] & Louis Alter[m] (Wolfe-Gilbert). The first Carroll production at his theatre-restaurant in Hollywood. Bankrupt in New York, Carroll fled to Hollywood where he managed to open this huge nightclub. It was a sensation for several years and was the major hang-out for most of the Hollywood stars. COVER: showgirls.

593 Earl Carroll — Palm Island Revue (Nightclub, 1936). Stars unknown.

By the Candlelight / Charms, Beautiful Charms — Ray Noble[w/m] (Harms); Hot Spell / I'm in Love / Juba — Joe Myrow[w/m] & Irving Mills[w/m] (Exclusive); Ringside Table for Two — Dave Oppenheim[w/m] & Michael Cleary[w/m] (Exclusive). Another Earl Carroll revue that appears to have been presented around the time of the Sketchbook of 1935, in New York. COVER: palm trees.

594 Earl Carroll — Riviera Revue (Nightclub, 1935). Stars unknown.

I Want to Report a Fire — Ned Wever[w/m] & Muriel Pollock[w/m] & Edward Heyman[w/m] (Harms); I'm Living in the Past — Milton Berle[w] & David Oppenheim[w] & Abner Silver[m] (Mills). This Earl Carroll revue must have been presented in New York during the period Carroll was going bankrupt before he fled to Hollywood. COVER: show girl, flames.

595 Earl Carroll — Sketchbook (Broadway, 1929). William Demarest, Patsy Kelly.

Crashing the Golden Gate — Jay Gorney[w/m] & Phil Cohan[w/m] & Edgar Y. Harburg[w/m] (Robbins); Don't Hang Your Dreams on a Rainbow — Irving Kahal[w] & Arnold Johnson[m] (Robbins); Fascinating You — Benee Russell[w/m] & Charles Tobias[w/m] & Harry Tobias[w/m] & Vincent Rose[w/m] (Robbins); For Someone I Love — Benny Davis[w] & Ted Snyder[m] (Robbins); Kinda Cute / Like Me Less, Love Me More — Edgar Y. Harburg[w] & Jay Gorney[m] (Robbins); Rhythm of the Waves / Song of the Moonbeams — Charles Tobias[w] & Harry Tobias[w] & Vincent Rose[m] (Robbins). With no ideas for a 1929 version of the Vanities, Carroll decided to try a new revue and call it the Sketchbook. It ran for a year with the comedy of Demarest and Kelly, some pleasant songs, and girls.

COVER: four showgirls sitting on large open book.

596 Earl   Carroll — Sketchbook (Broadway, 1935). Ken Murray, Beryl Wallace.

Anna Louise — Norman Zeno^w & Will Irwin^m *(Harms)*; At Last — Charlie Tobias^w & Sam Lewis^w & Henry Tobias^m *(Harms)*; The Day You Were Born — Edward Heyman^w & Dana Suesse^m *(Harms)*; Gringola / Let's Swing It / Moonlight and Violins / Silhouettes Under the Stars / Twenty Four Hours a Day / Young Ideas — Charlie Tobias$^{w/m}$ & Charles Newman$^{w/m}$ & Murray Mencher$^{w/m}$ *(Harms)*; The Man Who Makes the Gun — Raymond Egan^w & Gerald Marks^m *(Harms)*; There's Music in a Kiss — Al Sherman$^{w/m}$ & Al Lewis$^{w/m}$ & Abner Silver$^{w/m}$ *(Harms)*. As the Vanities were losing favor, Carroll called this *Sketchbook*. It ran for six months and depicted American history through the years as seen through the eyes of a chorus girl. COVER: sketch of chorus girls and a large girl's face.

597 Earl   Carroll — Sketchbook (Broadway, 1945). Stars unknown.

Dreamer, Dreamer! — Irving Caesar^w & Oscar Straus^m *(Robbins)*; Just the Way You Are — Earl Carroll^w & Harry Revel^m *(Robbins)*. This revue was produced and directed by Earl Carroll. This was a low time in his career and was the second to last show with his name before he died. COVER: beautiful girls.

598 Earl Carroll — Star Spangled Glamour (Nightclub, 1942). Stars unknown.

I Wanna Foof on a Fife / The Jittarumba / My Favorite Song / Star Spangled Glamour / While We Dance / Wishful Thinking — Sid Kuller$^{w/m}$ & Hal Borne$^{w/m}$ & Earl Carroll$^{w/m}$ *(Mills)*. This was probably the last known revue that Carroll produced at his lavish Hollywood club. COVER: beautiful girls.

599 Earl Carroll — The World's Fairest (Nightclub, 1939). Stars unknown.

Charming / The Lady Has Oomph — Dorcas Cochran^w & Charles Rosoff^m *(Wolfe-Gilbert)*; Face in the Crowd — Paul F. Webster^w & Louis Alter^m *(Wolfe-Gilbert)*. A revue produced at the Hollywood nightclub at the height of its popularity. COVER: a lady's face.

600 Earl Carroll — Vanities (#1) (Broadway, 1923). Joe Cook, Peggy Hopkins Joyce.

The Band Plays Home Sweet Home / My Cretonne Girl / Pretty Peggy — Earl Carroll$^{w/m}$ *(Berlin)*; A Girl Is Like Sunshine — Roy Turk$^{w/m}$ & William Daly$^{w/m}$ *(Berlin)*; Laugh While You're Dancing — Roy Turk$^{w/m}$ & William Daly$^{w/m}$ & Earl Carroll$^{w/m}$ *(Berlin)*. Earl Carroll persuaded an oil man to build a large theatre at 49th Street and 7th Avenue which he called the *Earl Carroll*. It opened with the first edition of the *Vanities*. It ran for six months with nothing going for it except Joe Cook's comedy and nude girls. COVER: beautiful girls in various costumes.

601 Earl Carroll — Vanities (#2) (Broadway, 1924). Sophie Tucker, Joe Cook.

Christmas Night / Counting the Hours / In the South of France / Tiddle-lee-tot — Earl Carroll$^{w/m}$ *(Harms)*; Everybody Loves My Baby — Spencer Williams$^{w/m}$ & Jack Palmer$^{w/m}$ *(Williams)*. The second edition of the *Vanities* ran four months. It had the clowning of Joe Cook, the singing of Sophie Tucker, and even more sensational nudes. COVER: Sophie Tucker; beautiful nude girl.

602 Earl Carroll — Vanities (#3) (Broadway, 1925). Ted Healy, Jessica Dragonette.

Don't Wake Me Up — L. Wolfe Gilbert^w & Albel Baker^m & Mabel Wayne^m *(Feist)*; A Kiss in the Moonlight — Clarence Gaskill$^{w/m}$ *(Harms)*; Pango Pango Maid — Fred Phillips^w & Irving Bibo^m *(Abrahams)*; Ponies on Parade / Thinking of You — Clarence Gaskill$^{w/m}$ *(Remick)*; Sentimental Sally — Billy Rose^w &

Clarence Gaskill[m] *(Remick)*; Somebody's Crazy About You — Jay Gorney[w/m] & Owen Murphy[w/m] *(Shapiro, Bernstein)*. This edition had the most lavish production numbers of any Vanities. With lots of dancing and the comedy of Ted Healy it ran for one year. COVER: beautiful girls.

603 Earl Carroll — Vanities (#4) (Broadway, 1925). Charles Dale, Dorothy Knapp.

Dorothy / Gate of Roses / Love in the Shadows — Clarence Gaskill[w/m] *(Feist)*; Rhythm of the Day — Owen Murphy[w] & Donald Lindley[m] *(Marks)*. This fourth edition of the Vanities was a revised version of the third edition. Adding some new people and some new songs, it ran for four months. COVER: beautiful girls, Dorothy Knapp.

604 Earl Carroll — Vanities (#5) (Broadway, 1926). Smith and Dale, Dorothy Knapp.

Adorable — Tom Ford[w] & Ray Wynburn[m] *(Feist)*; Alabama Stomp — Henry Creamer[w] & Jimmy Johnson[m] *(Robbins-Engel)*; Climbing Up the Ladder of Love — Raymond Klages[w] & Jesse Greer[m] *(Robbins-Engel)*; Cool 'em Off / Gates of Madrid / True to the Girl I Love / Twilight / Vanity — Grace Henry[w] & Morris Hamilton[m] *(Feist)*; Don't Wait Too Long — Irving Berlin[w/m] *(Berlin)*; Excuse My Dust — A. Wells[w] & A. Spencer[m] *(Feist)*; The Hanging Gardens of Babylon — Monte Carlo[w/m] & Alma Sanders[w/m] *(Feist)*; Hugs and Kisses — Raymond Klages[w] & Lou Alter[m] *(Robbins-Engel)*; Natacha — Berton Braley[w/m] & M. deJari[w/m] & Alex James[w/m] *(Feist)*; Red Nichols Jazz Breaks — Red Nichols[m] *(Alfred)*; Who Do You Love — Ray Klages[w/m] & Hugo Frey[w/m] & Fred Rich[w/m] *(Robbins-Engel)*. The nudes kept this edition going for eight months, not the entertainment or the music. COVER: girl in Spanish outfit; a little courtyard beside building.

605 Earl Carroll — Vanities (#6) (Broadway, 1927). Charles Mack, Jessie Matthews.

Alabama Stomp — piano selections — Jimmy Johnson[m] *(Robbins)*; Climbing Up the Ladder of Love — piano selections — Jesse Greer[m] *(Robbins)*; Hugs and Kisses — piano selections — Lou Alter[m] *(Robbins)*; Who Do You Love — piano selections — Hugo Frey[m] *(Robbins)*. This edition was an extension of the fifth edition with material from the *Charlot's Revue of 1926* plus the cast. It ran four more months. COVER: black and white letters.

606 Earl Carroll — Vanities (#7) (Broadway, 1928). W.C. Fields, Lillian Roth.

Blue Shadows — Raymond Klages[w] & Louis Alter[m] *(Robbins)*; Bob White / I'm Flyin' High — Abner Silver[w/m] & Jack LeSoir[w/m] & Ray Doll[w/m] *(Berlin)*; My Arms Are Open — Ned Washington[w] & Ed Lowry[w] & Michael Cleary[m] *(A Y and B)*; O! What a Night to Love — Jean Herbert[w] & Al Koppel[w] & Seger Ellis[m] *(Robbins)*; Once in a Lifetime — Raymond Klages[w] & Jesse Greer[m] *(Robbins)*; Raquel — George Whiting[w] & Joe Burke[m] *(Robbins)*; Vaniteaser — Paul Jones[w] & Michael Cleary[m] *(Shapiro, Bernstein)*; Watch My Baby Walk — Jo Trent[w] & Peter De Rose[m] *(Berlin)*; You Alone — Jean Herbert[w] & Bernard Maltin[m] *(Spier and Coslow)*. The public did not pay attention to the comedy of W.C. Fields or the singing of Lillian Roth in this edition. They paid to see the lavish production numbers with nude girls for six months. COVER: show girls in costumes.

607 Earl Carroll — Vanities (#8) (Broadway, 1930). Jack Benny, Patsy Kelly.

Contagious Rhythm / Hittin' the Bottle / The March of Time / One Love / Out of a Clear Blue Sky — Ted Koehler[w] & Harold Arlen[m] *(Remick)*; I Came to Life / Ring Out the Blues — E.Y. Harburg[w] & Jay Gorney[m] *(Remick)*; Rumba Rhythm — Stella Unger[w] & Jimmie Johnson[m] *(Remick)*. Earl Carroll lost the Earl Carroll

Theatre to creditors and Ziegfeld took it over. Carroll had to rent Ziegfeld's New Amsterdam Theatre for this edition. The excessive nudity in this version was classed by the police as obscenity and the show was raided with many arrests. Due to the notoriety, this very ordinary edition lasted for six months. The five Arlen songs were undistinguished. COVER: a nude show girl and faces.

608 Earl Carroll – Vanities (#9) (Broadway, 1931). Will Mahoney, William Demarest.

Goin' to Town / Have a Heart / Love Came Into My Heart – Harold Adamson^w & Burton Lane^m (Robbins); Good Night Sweetheart – Ray Noble$^{w/m}$ & Jimmy Campbell$^{w/m}$ & Reg Connelly$^{w/m}$ (Robbins); I'm Back in Circulation – Max Liaf^w & Nat Lief^w & Michael Cleary^m (Robbins); It's Great to Be in Love – Cliff Friend$^{w/m}$ (Robbins); Let's Think About the Weather – Charlotte Kent$^{w/m}$ (Robbins); Tonight or Never – Raymond Klages^w & Jack Meskill^w & Vincent Rose^m (Robbins). Earl Carroll had his millionaire friend tear down the first Earl Carroll Theatre and build a new and larger one on the same site. This edition was the first show in this new spectacular theatre. The theatre and the nudes kept it running for seven months. COVER: silhouettes of chorus girls.

609 Earl Carroll – Vanities (#10) (Broadway, 1932). Milton Berle, Helen Broderick.

Along Came Love – Charles Tobias^w & Haven Gillespie^w & Henry Tobias^m (Harms); Forsaken Again / My Darling – Edward Heyman^w & Richard Myers^m (Harms); I Gotta Right to Sing the Blues / Rockin' in Rhythm – Ted Koehler^w & Harold Arlen^m (Harms); Love, You Are My Inspiration – Ted Koehler^w & Andre Renaud^m (Harms); Take Me Away – Sidney Clare^w & Charles Tobias^w & Peter Tinturin^m (Harms). One of the best editions with one of the shortest

runs of ten weeks. It had some great comedy by Milton Berle, an outstanding song by Arlen – *I Gotta Right to Sing the Blues* – and some imaginative staging by Vincent Minnelli. It was the last full-scale edition of the Vanities. There were three feeble imitations later. COVER: silhouettes of men in top hats with several ladies.

610 Earl Carroll – Vanities (#11) (Broadway, 1934). Stars unknown.

I Saw Stars – Maurice Sigler$^{w/m}$ & Al Goodhart$^{w/m}$ & Al Hoffman$^{w/m}$ (Robbins); Two Cigarettes in the Dark / Water Under the Bridge – Paul F. Webster^w & Lew Pollack^m (Crawford). COVER: beautiful show girl.

611 Earl Carroll – Vanities (#12) (Broadway, 1940). Jerry Lester, Beryl Wallace.

Angel / The Starlit Hour – Mitchell Parish^w & Peter De Rose^m (Robbins); I Want My Mama – Al Stillman^w & A. Jararaca^m & Vicente Paiva^m (Robbins). Earl Carroll was operating his nightclub in Hollywood and decided to bring some of the talent to New York as a new edition of the Vanities. It lasted three weeks and he and the cast headed back for California. For this production, Earl Carroll had his singers equipped with microphones and thus started a trend which has gone on since. COVER: a beautiful girl.

612 Earl Carroll – Vanities (#13) (Broadway, 1947). Stars unknown.

Bagpipes on Parade / Rolling Along – Earl Carroll^w & Harry Von Tilzer^m (Von Tilzer); A Beautiful Girl – Earl Carroll^w & Peter De Rose^m (Robbins); You, Wonderful You – Earl Carroll^w & Harry Revel^m (Von Tilzer). This must have been the last work of Earl Carroll as he was killed in a plane crash in early 1948 with his girlfriend, Beryl Wallace. COVER: beautiful girl; drum majorette and bagpipe player.

613 Early to Bed (Broadway, 1943). Jane Kean, John Lund.

The Ladies Who Sing with a Band / Slightly Less Than Wonderful / There's a Man in My Life / This Is So

Nice / When the Nylons Bloom Again [PC] — George Marion[w] & Fats Waller[m] *(Advanced)*. A musical about a bawdy house and some innocent people who get involved. The scenery was supposedly the biggest hit of the show. The score was ordinary, but it ran nine months. COVER: a canopied bed.

614 East Is West (Broadway, 1918). Fay Bainter, Hassard Short.

Chinese Lullaby — Robert Hood Bowers[w/m] *(Schirmer)*; East Is West — Hassard Short[w] & Silvio Hein[m] *(Harms)*; Sing-Song Girl — E.B. Thiele[m] & M. David[m] *(Belwin)*. A comedy with an oriental setting. COVER: Fay Bainter.

615 East Is West (closed before Broadway, 1928). Marilyn Miller.

In the Mandarin's Orchid Garden — Ira Gershwin[w] & George Gershwin[m] *(Harms)*. This was a show Ziegfeld wanted to do for Marilyn Miller; however, he lost interest when the idea of *Show Girl* came along. Two of the melodies written for this show became *Embraceable You* and *Blah Blah Blah*. COVER: fancy designs.

616 East of Suez (Broadway, 1922). Florence Reed, John Halliday.

Chinese Flower — Francis DeWitt[w] & Robert Hood Bowers[m] *(Harms)*. Another drama with an oriental story. COVER: Florence Reed.

617 East Wind (Broadway, 1931). Harold Murray, Charlotte Lansing.

Are You Love? / East Wind / I'd Be a Fool / It's a Wonderful World / When You Are Young / You Are My Woman / Young Man in Love — Oscar Hammerstein[w] & Sigmund Romberg[m] *(Harms)*. A romance in Saigon with a poor score, it lasted three weeks. COVER: lady and Chinese boat.

618 Easy for Zee Zee (Regional, 1929). Stars unknown.

Zee-Zee — Sidney Goldtree[w] & Bill Montgomery[m] *(Goldtree)*. A long running sex-drama on the West Coast that never made it to Broadway. COVER: a man and a woman in an embrace.

619 Easy Virtue (closed before Broadway, 1939). Constance Bennett.

I Travel Alone — Noel Coward[w/m] *(Harms)*. Constance Bennett made her stage debut in this Noel Coward play which closed in Chicago. COVER: Constance Bennett.

620 Echoes of Broadway (closed before Broadway, 1922). Henry Stremel.

Whispering Pines — Paul Cunningham[w/m] & Irving Weill[w/m] *(Witmark)*. COVER: Henry Stremel.

621 The Eclipse (British, 1919). Nancy Gibbs, Pope Stamper.

I Never Realized [B] — Cole Porter[w] & Melville Gideon[m] *(Chappell)*; In Chelsea Somewhere [B] — Cole Porter[w] & James Heard[w] & Melville Gideon[m] *(Chappell)*. A comedy with songs which had a moderate run in London. COVER: lettering and designs.

622 The Ed Wynn Carnival (Broadway, 1920). Lillian Fitzgerald, Ed Wynn.

Can You Tell — Alex Sullivan[w/m] & Ray Miller[w/m] & Louis Handman[w/m] *(Remick)*; Come Along / My Log Fire Girl / Sphinx of the Desert / Thumbs Down — Ed Wynn[w/m] *(Remick)*; Down in Honeymoon Town — Alex Sullivan[w/m] & Ray Miller[w/m] & Clarence Seena[w/m] *(Berlin)*; Goodbye Sunshine, Hello Moon — Gene Buck[w] & William Eckstein[m] *(Harms)*; I Love the Land of Old Black Joe / My Sahara Rose / Rather Than See You Once in a While — Grant Clarke[w] & Walter Donaldson[m] *(Berlin)*; In Old Japan — Alfred Bryan[w/m] & Ed Wynn[w/m] *(Remick)*; In the Springtime — Jack Maloy[w/m] *(Remick)*; It Must Be You — Bobby Jones[w] & Con Conrad[m] *(Remick)*; Molly — Ray Miller[w/m] & Ring Hager[w/m] *(Rega)*; Oo, How I Love to Be Loved by You — Lou Paley[w] & George Gershwin[m] *(Harms)*; Rose of Spain — Tom Brown[w/m] & Billy Frazioli[w/m] & Ray Miller[w/m] *(Fisher)*; Underneath the Dixie Moon — Ray Miller[w/m] & Billy Fazioli[w/m] & Ray Klages[w/m] *(Rossiter)*. A poor show that ran for four months due to Ed Wynn.

COVER: Ed Wynn and other cast members.

623 The Education of H*Y*M*A*N K*A*P*L*A*N (Broadway, 1968). Tom Bosley, Hal Linden.

All American [ABQ] / Anything Is Possible [ABQ] / I Never Felt Better in My Life [ABQ] / Love Will Come [ABQ] / Loving You [ABQ] / Spring in the City [ABQ] / When Will I Learn — Paul Nassau^{w/m} & Oscar Brand^{w/m} *(T R O)*. A musical about Jewish life on the Lower East Side after World War II. It lasted four weeks. COVER: blackboard with letters.

624 Elsie (Broadway, 1923). Luella Gear, Vinton Freedley.

Baby Bunting / Everybody's Struttin' Now / I'd Like to Walk with a Pal Like You / Jazzing Thunder Storming Dance / Jingle Step / Lovin' Chile / My Crinoline Girl / A Regular Guy / Sand Flowers / Two Hearts in Tune / With You — Noble Sissle^{w/m} & Eubie Blake^{w/m} *(Witmark)*; Clouds of Love / Elsie / Glow Worm / Honeymoon Home / I'll Find the Key to Your Heart / One Day in May / Pretty Little Firefly / Two Lips Are Roses — Monte Carlo^{w/m} & Alma Sanders^{w/m} *(Remick)*. A musical romance between a gentleman and actress. With ordinary music, it had a run of one month. COVER: titles and designs.

625 Elsie Janis and Her Gang (Broadway, 1919). Elsie Janis, Eva LaGallienne.

Ah, Oui! / Gee, But It's Great! / In the Latin Quarter / Just a Little Touch of Paris / Let's Go / Somewhere in America — Richard Fechheimer^w & William Kernell^m *(Harms)*. Elsie Janis could well have been the Bob Hope of World War 1. She toured all the war fronts with musical shows. This military war type show ran on Broadway for seven months. COVER: Elsie Janis and soldiers.

626 Elsie Janis and Her Gang (Broadway, 1922). Elsie Janis, Florence Courtney.

After the War! — B.C. Hilliam^{w/m} *(Witmark)*; All the World Is Wonderful — Elsie Janis^w & Seymour Simons^m *(Berlin)*; The Bonus Blues — Elsie Janis^w & Carey Morgan^m & Arthur Swanstrom^m *(Berlin)*; I've Got the Red White and Blues / I've Waited All My Life / Why All This Fuss About Spain / Will You Remember? — Elsie Janis^{w/m} *(Berlin)*; Just a Little After Taps — Richard Fechheimer^w & William Kernell^m *(Chappell)*; Love in the Springtime — Elsie Janis^w & George Hirst^m *(Berlin)*; Nuthin' — Seymour Simons^{w/m} *(Berlin)*. A revue with a war theme that had good reviews but a run of only two months. COVER: Elsie Janis.

627 The Elusive Lady (closed before Broadway, 1922). Julian Eltinge.

Fascination / I Break the Hearts of Men / A Tune Like You / The Violin and Cello — Glen MacDonough^w & Raymond Hubbell^m *(Harms)*. A show with the female impersonator Julian Eltinge. COVER: Julian Eltinge.

628 Enchanted Isle (Broadway, 1927). Kathryn Reece, Basil Ruysdael.

Abandon / California Tango / Close in Your Arms / Could I Forget? / Down to the Sea / Dream Boat / Dream Girl / Enchanted Isle / Forgotten / Julianne / Longing / Voice of the High Sierras — Ida Hoyt Chamberlain^{w/m} *(Marks)*. A love affair between a society matron and a forest ranger; it ran four weeks. COVER: a garden.

629 Erlich Is Scwerlich (Jewish, 1945). Pesach Burstein.

Eingepakt — L. Markowitz^w & Sholom Secunda^m *(Karmen)*. COVER: P. Burstein.

630 Erminie (Broadway, 1920). Francis Wilson, DeWolf Hopper.

Darkest the Hour — Harry Paulton^w & E. Jakobowski^m *(Harms)*; Lullaby / A Soldier's Life / What the Dickybirds Say / When Love Is Young — Claxson Bellamy^w & Harry Paulton^w & E. Jakobowski^m *(Harms)*. A limited-run revival of an 1886 operetta. COVER: Francis Wilson, DeWolf Hopper.

631 Ernest in Love (Off Broadway, 1960). Leila Martin, John Irving.

A Handbag Is Not a Proper Mother / Lost / My Very First Impression / Perfection / A Wicked Man / You Can't Make Love—Anne Croswell[w] & Lee Pockriss[m] *(Morris)*. A musical from an Oscar Wilde story which received good reviews but lasted only two months. COVER: a gentleman holding a cupid.

632 Escapade (closed before Broadway, 1929). Stars unknown.

Ah, Love Believe—Lawrence Eyre[w] & Mortimer Browning[m] *(Harms)*. COVER: a man dangling three women on puppet strings.

633 The Eternal Road (Broadway, 1937). Sam Jaffe, Kurt Kasznar.

The Dance of the Golden Calf [VS] / David's Psalm [VS] / March to Zion [VS] / Promise [VS] / Song of Miriam [VS] / Song of Ruth [VS]—Franz Werfel[w] & Kurt Weill[m] *(Chappell)*. A biblical spectacle presented at the Metropolitan Opera House for five months. COVER: sketch of the Eternal Road.

634 Eubie! (Broadway, 1978). Gregory Hines, Maurice Hines.

Daddy Won't You Please Come Home [VS] / Dixie Moon [VS] / If You've Never Been Vamped by a Brownskin [VS] / I'm Just Wild About Harry [VS] / In Honeysuckle Time [VS] / Low Down Blues [VS] / Shuffle Along [VS]—Noble Sissle[w/m] & Eubie Blake[w/m] *(Warner Bros.)*; Gee, I Wish I Had Someone to Rock Me in the Cradle of Love [VS]—Noble Sissle[w] & Eubie Blake[m] *(Warner Bros.)*; I'm a Great Big Baby [VS] / Memories of You [VS] / My Handy Man Ain't Handy No More [VS] / Roll, Jordan [VS] / Weary [VS]—Andy Razaf[w] & Eubie Blake[m] *(Warner Bros.)*; I'm Craving for That Kind of Love [VS]—Noble Sissle[m] & Eubie Blake[m] *(Warner Bros.)*; You Got to Git the Gittin' While the Gittin's Good [VS]—F. Miller[w] & Eubie Blake[m] *(Warner Bros.)*. A revue based on Eubie Blake songs. With a very talented cast, the revue ran for over a year. COVER: dancer and piano player.

635 Evergreen (British, 1930). Jessie Matthews, Sonnie Hale.

The Colour of Her Eyes [PC] / Dancing on the Ceiling / Dear! Dear! [B] / Harlemania [PC] / If I Give In to You [B] / In the Cool of Evening [B] / No Place but Home [B]—Lorenz Hart[w] & Richard Rodgers[m] *(Chappell)*; When the Old World Was New—piano selections [B]—Richard Rodgers[m] *(Chappell)*. A hit in London for Rodgers and Hart with the talented Jessie Matthews and the song *Dancing on the Ceiling*. COVER: lettering and designs.

636 Everybody's Welcome (Broadway, 1931). Frances Williams, Harriette Lake.

As Time Goes By—Herman Hupfeld[w/m] *(Harms)*; Even as You and I / Is Rhythm Necessary / That's Good That's Bad / You've Got a Lease on My Heart—Irving Kahal[w] & Sammy Fain[m] *(Harms)*; Nature Played an Awful Trick on You—Arthur Lippman[w] & Milton Pascal[w] & Manning Sherwin[m] *(Harms)*. A short-lived musical about a struggling young couple in Greenwich Village with ordinary Sammy Fain songs, a concert by the Dorsey Brothers, and the birth of *As Time Goes By*. COVER: lady's face.

637 Everything (Broadway, 1918). Tom Brown, DeWolf Hopper.

The Circus Is Coming to Town / Come Along to Toy Town—Irving Berlin[w/m] *(Berlin)*; Every Girl Is Doing Her Bit—Clifford Harris[w] & James Tate[m] *(Harms)*; Everything Is Hunky Dory Down in Honky Tonky Town—Joseph McCarthy[w] & Harry Tierney[m] *(M and F)*; Follow the Flag—R.H. Burnside[w] & Raymond Hubbell[m] *(Harms)*; I Like New York / The Land of Romance—John Golden[w] & James Tate[m] *(Harms)*; Roll Along / You're the Very Girl I've Looked For—John Golden[w] & William Daly[m] *(Harms)*; Sunshine Alley—R.H. Burnside[w] & John Golden[w] & R.P. Weston[m] & Bert Lee[m] *(Harms)*. A Hippodrome spectacle which included a full circus. It ran for over a year. COVER: sketch of pretty girl and various vaudeville characters.

638 Everything Will Be All Right (closed before Broadway, 1924). Harry Carroll, Linda.

Elsie / Faded Rose / Mamie McGee — Harry Carroll^w/m *(Jack Mills)*. COVER: Carroll and Linda.

639 Evita (Broadway, 1979). Bob Gunton, Patti LuPone.

And the Money Kept Rolling In [VS] / Another Suitcase in Another Hall / Buenos Aires [VS] / Don't Cry for Me Argentina / Eva, Beware of the City [VS] / High Flying, Adored [VS] / I'd Be Surprisingly Good for You [VS] / On This Night of a Thousand Stars / Rainbow High [VS] / She Is a Diamond [VS] / Waltz for Eva and Che [VS] — Tim Rice^w & Andrew Lloyd Webber^m *(Leeds)*. Based on the career of Eva Peron, this musical ran for four years thanks to the staging of Harold Prince, the singing of Patti LuPone, and an interesting score by Webber. COVER: Evita.

640 Excess Baggage (Broadway, 1927). Morton Downey, Miriam Hopkins.

For Old Time's Sake — B.G. DeSylva^w/m & Lew Brown^w/m & Ray Henderson^w/m *(D B and H)*; Let a Smile Be Your Umbrella — Irving Kahal^w & Francis Wheeler^w & Sammy Fain^m *(Berlin)*. A moderate hit drama about a vaudeville juggler who becomes a movie star. COVER: a small orchestra.

641 Expressing Willie (Broadway, 1924). Richard Sterling, Alan Brooks.

Express Yourself! — Rachel Crothers^w & John Eagen^m *(Berlin)*. A drama about a rich boy going wrong until his sweetheart saves him. COVER: vases and flowers.

642 Fables of 1924 (closed before Broadway, 1924). Stars unknown.

Alabam' Banjo Man — Art Conrad^w/m & Frank Gillen^w/m *(Marks)*. COVER: black banjo player.

643 Face the Music (Broadway, 1932). Mary Boland, Harold Murray.

I Say It's Spinach / Let's Have Another Cup o' Coffee / Manhattan Madness / On a Roof in Manhattan / Soft Lights and Sweet Music — Irving Berlin^w/m *(Berlin)*. A Broadway show is backed by a crooked cop in Moss Hart's book. This musical had some good Berlin songs but only a moderate run. COVER: sketch of dancing girls.

644 Fade Out Fade In (Broadway, 1964). Carol Burnett, Jack Cassidy.

Call Me Savage [VS] / Fade Out — Fade In / Fear [RC] / Go Home, Train! [VS] / I'm with You / It's Good to Be Back Home [VS] / Lila Tremaine [RC] / The Usher from the Mezzanine [VS] / You Mustn't Feel Discouraged — Betty Comden^w & Adolph Green^w & Jule Styne^m *(Chappell)*. Carol Burnett was very funny as the usher who became a movie star in this problematic musical. She was not happy with the show and quit, incidentally starting a hit series on CBS shortly thereafter. The show was closed temporarily and re-opened with a series of new leading ladies, including Betty Hutton, but it failed. COVER: Carol Burnett.

645 Fair Enough (College, 1939). Stars unknown.

From Me to You / Home Made Heaven — Alan Jay Lerner^w/m *(Mills)*; I Dream of You / I Just Gotta Make Love — Sherwood Rollins^w/m *(Mills)*. A Harvard show remembered only for the first songs of Lerner. COVER: World's Fair trademark, the Perisphere and the Trylon.

646 Fair Helen (closed before Broadway, 1919). Stars unknown.

Apple Song / Cabaret Song / Fair Helen / Fair Helen Waltz / Oh Love Divine — Charles Towne^w & J. Offenbach^m *(Remick)*. COVER: silhouette of man and woman.

647 Falsettoland (Broadway, 1990). Michael Rupert, Stephen Bogardus.

The Baseball Game [VS] / A Day in Falsettoland [VS] / Everyone Hates His Parents [VS] / Holding to the Ground [VS] / Something Bad Is Happening [VS] / Unlikely Lovers [VS] / What

More Can I Say? [VS] / What Would I Do [VS] / You Gotta Die Sometime [VS] — William Finn^{w/m} *(Warner Bros.)*. William Finn's third play about the bi-sexual Marvin, his family and friends. The music and lyrics were clever in this one hour musical which also dealt with AIDS. COVER: the cast of the show.

648 Falsettos (Broadway, 1993). Mandy Patinkin, Chip Zien.

Baseball Game [VS] / A Day in Falsettoland [VS] / Everyone Hates His Parents [VS] / Father to Son [VS] / Four Jews in a Room Bitching [VS] / The Games I Play [VS] / Holding to the Ground [VS] / I Never Wanted to Love You [VS] / I'm Breaking Down [VS] / Making a Home [VS] / March of the Falsettos [VS] / Marriage Proposal [VS] / Something Bad Is Happening [VS] / Unlikely Lovers [VS] / What More Can I Say? [VS] / What Would I Do [VS] / You Gotta Die Sometime [VS] — William Finn^{w/m} *(Warner Bros)*. A combination of *March of the Falsettos* and *Falsettoland* performed in one evening. COVER: the cast of the show.

649 Falstaff (Broadway, 1928). Mr. and Mrs. Charles Coburn.

Beside Your Window / A Memory — Brian Hooker^w & Porter Steele^m *(Harms)*. An adaptation of the Shakespeare play that ran only two weeks. COVER: sketches of characters from the play.

650 A Family Affair (Broadway, 1962). Eileen Heckart, Larry Kert.

Beautiful / A Family Affair / Harmony / Mamie in the Afternoon / There's a Room in My House — John Kander^{w/m} & James Goldman^{w/m} & William Goldman^{w/m} *(Valando)*. A musical about a Jewish family and its marital problems; it ran for eight weeks. It was forgettable except for the fact it was John Kander's first show and Prince's first directing job. COVER: a totem pole of faces and people.

651 Fanchon and Marco Ideas (Regional, 1928). Stars unknown.

Anna in Indiana — Billy Gorman^{w/m} & Eddie Gorman^{w/m} & Harry Rose^{w/m} *(Broadway)*; Happy — Larry Yoell^w & Neil Moret^m *(Moret)*; O-H-I-O — Jack Yellen^w & Abe Olman^m *(Forster)*; Ready for the River — Gus Kahn^w & Neil Moret^m *(Moret)*. A West Coast revue that never made it to New York. COVER: a chorus girl.

652 Fanchon and Marco Little Club (Nightclub, 1922). Stars unknown.

My Girl Is Like a Rainbow — Fanchon and Marco^{w/m} & Lester Stevens^{w/m} *(Sherman Clay)*. COVER: a girl in evening gown.

653 Fanny (Broadway, 1954). Ezio Pinza, Walter Slezak.

Be Kind to Your Parents / Fanny / Fanny — complete vocal score / I Have to Tell You / I Like You / Love Is a Very Light Thing / Never Too Late for Love / Octopus / Restless Heart / To My Wife / Welcome Home / Why Be Afraid to Dance — Harold Rome^{w/m} *(Chappell)*. A musical based on Pagnol's movie trilogy; *Fanny* marked Merrick's directorial debut. It was a two year hit with Rome's wonderful score and the talented cast. COVER: sketch of boy and girl kissing.

654 Fanshastics (*see also* **Merry Wives of Gotham**) (Broadway, 1924). Grace George, Laura Hope Crews.

Heart o' Mine — Laurence Eyre^w & Victor Herbert^m *(Harms)*. A comedy about two Irish orphans who meet in New York. The music was also published as from *Merry Wives of Gotham*. COVER: black lettering.

655 The Fantasticks (Off Broadway, 1960). Kenneth Nelson, Jerry Orbach.

The Fantasticks — complete vocal score / I Can See It [VS] / Much More [VS] / Never Say No [VS] / Plant a Radish [VS] / Soon It's Gonna Rain / They Were You / Try to Remember — Tom Jones^w & Harvey Schmidt^m *(Chappell)*. The longest running show in New York history with a run of over thirty years. It was based on a French play dealing with the romance of a boy and girl. The story and music are both charming. COVER: fancy lettering.

656 Fashion (Off Broadway, 1974). Mary Jo Catlett, Ty McConnell.

A Life Without Her—Steve Brown[w] & Don Pippin[m] *(Morris)*. A musical dealing with a rich family preserving early American dreams; *Fashion* had a ten week run. Cover: a girl's face, long fingernails, and a rose.

657 The Fashion Girl (Off Broadway, 1923). Tom Martelle.

The Fashion Girl / An Old Fashion Girl—Tom Martelle[w/m] *(Century)*. A female impersonator show. Cover: Tom Martelle.

658 Fashions of 1924 (Broadway, 1924). Arnold Daly, Jimmy Hussey.

A Little Bit of Love / One More Waltz—Harry B. Smith[w] & Ted Snyder[m] *(Berlin)*; Oh! Joe—Harry De Costa[w] & Ted Snyder[m] *(Berlin)*. An elaborate fashion show that lasted two weeks. Cover: girl in high fashion dress.

659 Fast and Furious (Broadway, 1931). Dusty Fletcher, Moms Mabley.

Shadows on the Wall / Walking on Air—Mack Gordon[w] & Harry Revel[m] *(Miller)*; So Lonesome—Rosamond Johnson[w/m] & Joe Jordan[w/m] *(Miller)*; Where's My Happy Ending?—Mack Gordon[w/m] & Harold Adamson[w/m] & Harry Revel[w/m] *(Miller)*. An all black revue that lasted one week. Cover: silhouettes of three dancing girls.

660 Feeling No Pain (closed before Broadway, 1973). Stars unknown.

Hello, Los Angeles—Leslie Bricusse[w/m] *(Stage and Screen)*. This was billed as a new musical from Bricusse. Cover: singer Steve Lawrence.

661 Festivities of 1927 (closed before Broadway, 1927). George LeMaire, Joe Sullivan.

If I Can Take You from Someone—Joseph Howard[w/m] *(Harris)*. Cover: Joseph Howard.

662 Fiddler on the Roof (Broadway, 1964). Zero Mostel, Beatrice Arthur.

Far from the Home I Love [VS] / Fiddler on the Roof / Fiddler on the Roof—complete vocal score / If I Were a Rich Man / Matchmaker / Miracle of Miracles [VS] / Now I Have Everything / Sabbath Prayer [PC] / Sunrise, Sunset / To Life [VS] / Tradition [PC]—Sheldon Harnick[w] & Jerry Bock[m] *(Valando)*. One of the best and one of the longest running musicals in Broadway history. This show benefited from a good book, the direction of Jerome Robbins, fine score, and talented actors. Cover: sketch of a fiddler.

663 Fiddlers Three (Broadway, 1918). Louise Groody, Hal Skelly.

All on Account of Nipper / As the Flitting Swallows Fly / Can It Be Love at Last? / Don't You Think You'll Miss Me? / Fiddlers Three—complete vocal score / For Love / (My) Love of a Day / One Hour, Sweetheart, with You / When the Fiddle Bows Begin to Fly—William Duncan[w] & Alexander Johnstone[m] *(Witmark)*. An old-fashioned operetta about violin makers in Italy; it folded quickly. Cover: a fiddle.

664 The Fifth Avenue Follies (Nightclub, 1926). Constance Carpenter, Betty Compton.

Maybe It's Me / Where's That Little Girl—Lorenz Hart[w] & Richard Rodgers[m] *(Harms)*. Billy Rose's first nightclub venture which was a failure with minor Rodgers and Hart songs. Cover: lettering and designs.

665 Fifty-Fifty (closed before Broadway, 1920). Stars unknown.

Entirely Surrounded by Girls / If It Wasn't for the Wife / Moonshine of Kentucky / Move into My Heart / A Rose, a Child, a Butterfly—Harold Atteridge[w] & Harry Carroll[m] *(Berlin)*. Cover: little nymphs with musical instruments and a theatre mask.

666 Fifty-Fifty (closed before Broadway, 1920). Herbert Corthell.

Any Kind of a Daddy Will Do / Argentines, the Portuguese, and the Greeks / Home Is Never Home Sweet Home / I'll Be Lonesome After You Go / I'll Fifty-Fifty with You / I'm a Jazz Vampire / The Land Where Lovers Go / My Sweet Little Bumble-Bee / Our Little Love Affair / Safe in

Your Arms / Settle Down in New York Town / You're Too Pretty to Be Lonesome — Art Swanstrom[w] & Carey Morgan[m] *(Stern)*. COVER: Herbert Corthell.

667 Fifty-Fifty Ltd. (Broadway, 1919). Herbert Corthell, Gertrude Vanderbilt.

Every Little Girlie Has a Way of Her Own / The Gimmies / The Girl or the Gown / Honey Bunch / The Magic Place / My Might Have Been / Nanette / Silence of Love / Spooky Nights / A Teeny Bit of Jazz / Won't You Cuddle Up a Little Closer? — Leon De Costa[w/m] *(Remick)*. This production, about a private home rented to a musical comedy cast, failed after one month. COVER: flowers and trees.

668 Fifty Million Frenchmen (Broadway, 1929). Helen Broderick, William Gaxton.

Find Me a Primitive Man / The Happy Heaven of Harlem / I Worship You / I'm in Love / I'm Unlucky at Gambling / Let's Step Out / Paree, What Did You Do to Me? / Please Don't Make Me Be Good / The Queen of Terre Haute / Tale of the Oyster [VS] / Why Don't We Try Staying Home? [VS] / You Do Something to Me / You Don't Know Paree / You've Got That Thing — Cole Porter[w/m] *(Harms)*. A smash hit with funny characters, excellent songs, stunning sets, and love in Paris. COVER: outdoor cafe scene.

669 The Fig Leaves Are Falling (Broadway, 1969). Barry Nelson, Dorothy Loudon.

All of My Laughter / Did I Ever Really Live? / The Fig Leaves Are Falling / For the Rest of My Life / Juggling / Light One Candle / Like Yours / My Aunt Minnie — plain cover / Today I Saw a Rose / We — Allan Sherman[w] & Albert Hague[m] *(Fox)*. Marital problems in a dismal musical that lasted for four performances. COVER: two pairs of naked legs protruding from tree.

670 Fine and Dandy (Broadway, 1930). Joe Cook, Eleanor Powell.

Can This Be Love? / Fine and Dandy / The Jig Hop / Let's Go Eat Worms in the Garden / Nobody Breaks My Heart / Rich or Poor / Starting at the Bottom — Paul James[w] & Kay Swift[m] *(Harms)*. The clowning of Joe Cook as a worker trying to get ahead, the tap dancing of Eleanor Powell, and a good score by Swift made this musical a hit. COVER: sketch of two dancing girls.

671 Finian's Rainbow (Broadway, 1946). Donald Richards, David Wayne.

The Begat / Finian's Rainbow — complete vocal score / How Are Things in Glocca Morra? / If This Isn't Love / Look to the Rainbow / Necessity / Old Devil Moon / Something Sort of Grandish / That Great Come-and-Get-It Day / When I'm Not Near the Girl I Love / When the Idle Poor Become the Idle Rich — E.Y. Harburg[w] & Burton Lane[m] *(Crawford)*. A smash hit involving an Irish immigrant, a leprechaun, and a stolen pot of gold. A social message about racism, and an excellent score and cast added to this shows success. The sheet music for this show is published with two slightly different sets of covers. One set states "Robert Fryer and Lawrence Carr Present" and the other set states "Lee Sabinson and William Katzell Present." COVER: assorted characters and a pot of gold.

672 Fiorello! (Broadway, 1959). Tom Bosley, Howard Da Silva.

Gentleman Jimmy / Home Again [PC] / I Love a Cop [VS] / Little Tin Box / Politics and Poker / 'Til Tomorrow / The Very Next Man / When Did I Fall in Love? / Where Do I Go from Here? — Sheldon Harnick[w] & Jerry Bock[m] *(Valando)*. A hit musical based on the career of La Guardia with a well written book, a good score and a great performance from Tom Bosley. COVER: sketch of Fiorello and New York skyline.

673 Fioretta (Broadway, 1929). Fanny Brice, Leon Errol.

Alone with You — Grace Henry[w] & Jo Trent[w] & G. Romilli[m] *(Robbins)*;

Blade of Mine — Grace Henry[w] & George Bagby[m] *(Robbins)*; Carissima — Grace Henry[w] & G. Romilli[m] *(Robbins)*; Dream Boat — Grace Henry[w] & Jo Trent[w] & George Bagby[m] *(Robbins)*; Fioretta / My Heart Belongs to You / Roses of Red — G. Romilli[w/m] *(Robbins)*. A lavish spectacle set in old Italy with the clowning of Leon Errol and Fanny Brice, and loaded with girls in all types of costumes. The show nevertheless enjoyed only a three month run. COVER: sketch of girl in lavish gown.

674 The Firebrand (Broadway, 1924). Joseph Schildkraut, Frank Morgan.

The Voice of Love — Ira Gershwin[w] & Russell Bennett[m] & Maurice Nitke[m] *(Harms)*. A medieval story which was a show-case for Schildkraut. COVER: Joseph Schildkraut.

675 The Firebrand of Florence (*see also* **Much Ado About Love**) (Broadway, 1945). Melville Cooper, Lotte Lenya.

Allesandro the Wise [RC] / Come to Florence [RC] / Come to Paris [RC] / Finale of Act I (Firebrand) [RC] / Life, Love and Laughter / The Little Naked Boy [RC] / A Rhyme for Angela / Sing Me Not a Ballad / Song of the Hangman [RC] / When the Duchess Is Away [RC] / World Is Full of Villains [RC] / You Have to Do What You Do Do [RC] / You're Far Too Near Me — Ira Gershwin[w] & Kurt Weill[m] *(Chappell)*. A musical about an Italian conspiracy with a lavish production and a run of five weeks. COVER: titles and designs.

676 The Fireman's Flame (Broadway, 1937). Philip Bourneuf, Ben Cutler.

Do My Eyes Deceive Me? / Doin' the Waltz [VS] / Fire Belles Gallop [VS] / The Fireman's Flame [VS] / Hose Boys [VS] / I Like the Nose on Your Face / It's a Lovely Night on the Hudson River / Mother Isn't Getting Any Younger [VS] / We're Off [VS] — Ted Fetter[w] & Richard Lewine[m] *(Chap-*

pell). A musical melodrama on rivalry between two fire companies done in an exaggerated style; it was a moderate hit of six months. COVER: flames.

677 The First (Broadway, 1981). David Huddleston, Lonette McKee.

The First / There Are Days and There Are Days / Will We Ever Know Each Other — Martin Charnin[w] & Bob Brush[m] *(Leonard)*. A baseball musical based on the Jackie Robinson story; the musical lasted four weeks. COVER: silhouette of baseball player.

678 First Impressions (Broadway, 1959). Polly Bergen, Farley Granger.

As Long as There's a Mother / The Heart Has Won the Game / I Feel Sorry for the Girl / Love Will Find Out the Way / Not Like Me — Robert Goldman[w/m] & Glenn Paxton[w/m] & George Weiss[w/m] *(Chappell)*. A musical version of *Pride and Prejudice* which ran for only twelve weeks. COVER: sketch of man and two ladies.

679 Five Guys Named Moe (Broadway, 1992). Jerry Dixon, Glenn Turner.

Cal'donia [VS] — Claude Moine[w/m] & Fleecy Moore[w/m] *(Wise)*; Choo Choo Ch' Boogie [VS] — Vaughn Horton[w/m] & Denver Darling[w/m] & Milton Gabler[w/m] *(Wise)*; Don't Let the Sun Catch You Crying [VS] — Joe Greene[w/m] *(Wise)*; Five Guys Named Moe [VS] — Larry Wynn[w/m] & Jerry Bresler[w/m] *(Wise)*; I Like 'em Fat Like That [VS] — Claude Demetrius[w/m] & Louis Jordan[w/m] & Mayo Williams[w/m] *(Wise)*; Is You Is or Is You Ain't [VS] — Billy Austin[w/m] & Louis Jordan[w/m] *(Wise)*; Life Is So Peculiar [VS] — Johnny Burke[w] & Jimmy Van Heusen[m] *(Wise)*; Messy Bessy [VS] — Jimmy Smith[w/m] *(Wise)*; Push Ka Pi Shee Pie [VS] — J. Willoughby[w/m] & Louis Jordan[w/m] & W. Merrick[w/m] *(Wise)*; Safe, Sane and Single [VS] — Johnny Lange[w/m] & Hy Heath[w/m] & Louis Jordan[w/m] *(Wise)*; There Ain't Nobody Here But Us Chickens [VS] — Joan Witney[w/m] & Alex Kramer[w/m] *(Wise)*; What's the Use of Gettin' Sober [VS] — Busbey Meyers[w/m] *(Wise)*. A British revue of five guys performing the music of Louis Jordan and his hits. COVER: sketch of "five guys."

680 The Five O'Clock Girl (Broadway, 1927). Mary Eaton, Oscar Shaw.

Happy Go Lucky / Happy Go Lucky Bird / Thinking of You / Up in the Clouds / Who Did—You Did!—Bert Kalmar^w & Harry Ruby^m *(Harms)*. A poor girl and a rich boy make up this pleasant musical which ran for six months. It produced one hit song, *Thinking of You*. COVER: Eaton and Shaw.

681 Flahooley (*see also* **Jollyanna**) (Broadway, 1951). Barbara Cook, Jerome Courtland.

Come Back Little Genie [VS] / Flahooley / Here's to Your Illusions / He's Only Wonderful / Spirit of Capsulanti [RC] / The Springtime Cometh / Who Says There Ain't No Santa Claus [BW] / The World Is Your Balloon—E.Y. Harburg^w & Sammy Fain^m *(Chappell)*. A charming musical that never made it. It had a nice score by Sammy Fain and the singing of Barbara Cook; however, the book which dealt with the toy business ruined it all. A revised edition called *Jollyanna* was presented by the Los Angeles Civic Opera in 1952. COVER: a genie with his toys.

682 Flashes of the Great White Way (closed before Broadway, 1925). Stars unknown.

Hey, Hey, Fever / I'm a Little Jail Bird—Mack Gordon^w & Anton Scibilia^w & George Wiest^m & Edgar Dowell^m *(Marks)*; Snap Your Fingers—Mack Gordon^w & Anton Scibilia^w & George Wiest^m *(Marks)*. COVER: chorus girl.

683 Flatbush Follies (Regional, 1944). Stars unknown.

Brooklyn Polka—Zeke Manners$^{w/m}$ *(Shapiro, Bernstein)*. COVER: sketch of pilgrim, Indian, and Brooklyn bridge.

684 Fledermaus (Opera, 1950). Lily Pons.

Fledermaus Fantasy—George Toupin^w & Johann Strauss^m *(Fischer)*. COVER: Lily Pons.

685 Fledermaus (Opera, 1950). Brenda Lewis, William Horne.

Fledermaus—complete vocal score / The Girl with Yellow Hair / Look Me Over Once / P's and Q's / Some Days You Are Lonely / You and I—Howard Dietz^w & Johann Strauss^m *(Boosey, Hawkes)*. A new edition of *Fledermaus*. With lyrics by Howard Dietz, the opera became a big hit for the Met. COVER: man and woman waltzing.

686 The Fleet's Lit Up (British, 1938). Stanley Lupino, Frances Day.

It's Delovely [B]—Cole Porter$^{w/m}$ *(Chappell)*. A musical—of six months' duration—about a cruise. COVER: a dancing couple.

687 The Flirting Flapper (closed before Broadway, 1925). Howard Blair.

The Flirting Flapper / The Waltz of Love—Howard Blair$^{w/m}$ *(Century)*. A female impersonator show. COVER: Howard Blair.

688 A Flood of Sunshine (closed before Broadway, 1920). Richard Carle, Milton Dawson.

Dashing Matador / Farewell to Love / Hispaniola / Home Again / I Like to Look Around / Idol of the Ring / Land of Make Believe / Love Is Like This Little Wheel of Mine / Loving a la Spain / Marabella Maid / Minnow Men / Something Nice in Lingerie / Sunshine Jazz / Treat 'Em Rough / What's the Idea—William Duncan^w & Alexander Johnstone^m *(Witmark)*. COVER: a smiling sun.

689 Flora, the Red Menace (Broadway, 1965). Liza Minnelli, Bob Dishy.

All I Need / Dear Love / Express Yourself / I Believe You / Knock, Knock / Not Every Day of the Week / A Quiet Thing / Sing Happy—Fred Ebb^w & John Kander^m *(Valando)*. The debut of Kander, Ebb and Minnelli on Broadway in an uneven musical with a social message and a run of only 11 weeks. COVER: sketch of Flora and crowd.

690 Florentine Gardens Revue (Nightclub, 1942). Stars unknown.

Easter Sunday Down in Harlem / I Was Born 'Neath a Lucky Star / Swingin' with the Swing Shift — Dave Oppenheim$^{w/m}$ & Roy Ingraham$^{w/m}$ *(Gilbert)*. COVER: defense worker; pretty girl.

691 Florida Girl (Broadway, 1925). Vivienne Segal, Ritz Brothers.

Daphne — My Wonderful One [ABQ] / It's Trouble — It's Trouble [ABQ] / Lady of My Heart [ABQ] / Oh You! / Skipper [ABQ] / Take a Little Dip [ABQ] / Twice Told Tales [ABQ] / Venetian Skies [ABQ] / Wee-Toy [ABQ] — Paul Porter^w & Benjamin Burt^w & Milton Suskind^m *(Feist)*. Diamond smuggling in Florida was the subject of this musical lavishly produced by Earl Carroll. With the dancing and clowning of the Ritz Brothers, it lasted five weeks. COVER: a villa and beach scene in Florida.

692 Florodora (Revival) (Broadway, 1920). Eleanor Painter, Walter Woolf.

Caramba! — Harry B. Smith^w & Milan Roder^m *(Berlin)*; Love Will Find You — Harry B. Smith^w & P. Tirindelli^m *(Berlin)*. A limited run revival of this old operetta to star Eleanor Painter. COVER: Eleanor Painter.

693 Flossie (Broadway, 1924). Alice Cavanaugh, Doris Duncan.

The First Is the Last / I'm in Wonderland / Now Is the Time / Poogie-Woo / Walla Walla / When Things Go Wrong / You Will Be Mine — Ralph Murphy^w & Armand Robi^m *(Marks)*. A marital mix-up musical that ran three weeks. COVER: a little naked cupid with wings.

694 Flower Drum Song (Boston) (Broadway, 1958). Miyoshi Umeki, Larry Blyden.

Grant Avenue / I Enjoy Being a Girl / Love Look Away / My Best Love / She Is Beautiful / Sunday / You Are Beautiful — Oscar Hammerstein^w & Richard Rodgers^m *(Williamson)*. A musical about Chinese immigrants in San Francisco. The first set of sheet music covers issued did not mention the producers and director; they also included two songs which were dropped and changed, *My Best Love* and *She Is Beautiful*. COVER: Chinese pagoda and people.

695 Flower Drum Song (New York) (Broadway, 1958). Miyoshi Umeki, Larry Blyden.

Don't Marry Me / Flower Drum Song — complete vocal score / Grant Avenue / A Hundred Million Miracles / I Enjoy Being a Girl / Love Look Away / Sunday / You Are Beautiful — Oscar Hammerstein^w & Richard Rodgers^m *(Williamson)*. A musical about Chinese immigrants in San Francisco filled with lovely songs, talented people, and lavish sets and direction by Gene Kelly. This second set of sheet music covers lists the producers, writer, and director plus two new songs. COVER: Chinese pagoda and people.

696 Flowers for Algernon (Broadway, 1980). P.J. Benjamin, Edward Earle.

Charley / I Got a Friend / Midnight Riding / No Surprises / Whatever Time There Is — David Rogers^w & Charles Strouse^m *(Big Three)*. This musical opened in London as *Flowers for Algernon* with Michael Crawford and the sheet music represents this production. It opened in New York as *Charlie and Algernon* with P.J. Benjamin with no music published from this production. It was a failure both places. COVER: Michael Crawford and friends.

697 Fly Blackbird (Off Broadway, 1962). Micki Grant, Robert Guillaume.

Couldn't We? / Fly Blackbird / Natchitoches, Louisiana / Rivers to the South / Wake Up — C. Jackson$^{w/m}$ *(Marks)*; Ev'rything Comes to Those Who Wait — C. Jackson$^{w/m}$ & G. Kingsley$^{w/m}$ *(Marks)*. An Off Broadway musical with a mixed cast and a run of four months. COVER: sketch of dancers.

698 Fly with Me (Broadway, 1920). College students.

Fly with Me — complete score — Lorenz Hart^w & Richard Rodgers^m

(Rodgers). The first Rodgers and Hart show which was performed at Columbia University. This show was done again in 1980 by another Columbia University cast and recorded at that time. COVER: lettering.

699 Flying Colors (Broadway, 1932). Clifton Webb, Charles Butterworth.

Alone Together / Fatal Fascination / Louisiana Hayride / A Rainy Day / A Shine on Your Shoes / Smokin' Reefers — Howard Dietz$^{w/m}$ & Arthur Schwartz$^{w/m}$ *(Harms)*; Mein Kleine Acrobat — piano selections — Arthur Schwartz^m *(Harms)*; Two Faced Woman — Howard Dietz^w & Arthur Schwartz^m *(Harms).* A revue which was rather similar to all the Dietz-Schwartz revues. It featured lavish sets by Bel Geddes, the clowning of Webb and Kelly, and several beautiful songs including *Alone Together.* It ran almost six months. COVER: Webb, Kelly, Geva, and Butterworth with chorus girls.

700 Flying High (Broadway, 1930). Bert Lahr, Oscar Shaw.

Good for You — Bad for Me / Happy Landing / I'll Know Him / I'm Flying High / Red Hot Chicago / Thank Your Father / Wasn't It Beautiful While It Lasted? / Without Love — B.G. DeSylva$^{w/m}$ & Lew Brown$^{w/m}$ & Ray Henderson$^{w/m}$ *(D B and H).* A musical based on the current craze of the day — aviation. Several good songs and the clowning of Bert Lahr kept this show running for four months. COVER: airplanes.

701 Folies Bergere (Broadway, 1923). Stars unknown.

Lovin' Mama — Benny Davis$^{w/m}$ *(Fox)*; Nights in the Woods — Harold DeBozi^m *(Fox).* An imported Folies that played the Broadway theatre. COVER: moonlight in the woods.

702 Folies Bergere at the Casino de Paris) (Nightclub, 1924). Stars unknown.

It's Young and It Doesn't Know — Al Dubin^w & Charles Borel-Clerc^m *(Jack Mills).* COVER: baby reading newspaper.

703 Folies Bergere at the French Casino) (Nightclub, 1937). Betty Bruce, Rolf Holbein.

Terrific! — Sammy Cahn^w & Saul Chaplin^m & Charles Borel-clerc^m *(Chappell).* COVER: chorus girl.

704 The Folies Bergere Revue *(see also* **Hot Rhythm)** (Off Broadway, 1930). Stars unknown.

Green Pastures / Tropical Moon — Will Morrissey^w & Eubie Blake^m *(Shapiro, Bernstein)*; Loving You the Way I Do — Jack Scholl^w & Will Morrissey^w & Eubie Blake^m *(Shapiro, Bernstein).* A small revue in the village which later transferred to Broadway for a short run as *Hot Rhythm.* COVER: show girl with large head dress.

705 Folies Fantastique (Latin Quarter) (Nightclub, 1942). Stars unknown.

We're All in the Same Boat Now — Al Hoffman$^{w/m}$ & Milton Drake$^{w/m}$ & Jerry Livingston$^{w/m}$ *(Mills).* COVER: nude girl.

706 Follies (Broadway, 1971). Alexis Smith, Dorothy Collins.

Ah, Paris! [VS] / All Things Bright and Beautiful [VS] [CUT] / Broadway Baby [BW] / Can That Boy Fox Trot! [VS] / Could I Leave You? [VS] / Follies — Beautiful Girls / Follies — complete vocal score / The God-Why-Don't-You-Love-Me Blues [VS] / I'm Still Here [VS] / In Buddy's Eyes [VS] / Little White House [VS] [CUT] / Losing My Mind / One More Kiss [VS] / Too Many Mornings / Uptown, Downtown [VS] [CUT] / Waiting for the Girls Upstairs [VS] / Who Could Be Blue? [VS] [CUT] / Who's That Woman [VS] — Stephen Sondheim$^{w/m}$ *(Valando).* A stunning musical beautifully staged by Harold Prince and Michael Bennett with a lovely score by Sondheim and a so-so book by Goldman. A classic! COVER: girl's face with a large crack in it.

707 Follies (British, 1987). Diana Rigg, Julia McKenzie.

Ah, But Underneath [B] [VS] / Ah, Paris! [B] [VS] / Beautiful Girls [B] [VS] /

Broadway Baby [B] [VS] / Could I Leave You? [B] [VS] / Country House [B] [VS] / The God-Why-Don't-You-Love-Me Blues [B] [VS] / I'm Still Here [B] [VS] / In Buddy's Eyes [B] [VS] / Losing My Mind [B] [VS] / Loveland [B] [VS] / Make the Most of Your Music [B] [VS] / One More Kiss [B] [VS] / Too Many Mornings [B] [VS] / Waiting for the Girls Upstairs [B] [VS] / Who's That Woman? [B] [VS] — Stephen Sondheim[w/m] *(I.M.P.)*. A revised edition of *Follies* produced in London which got good reviews but was not a smash hit. COVER: a show girl.

708 Follies Bergere (Nightclub, 1921). Bee Palmer.

I'm Looking for a Bluebird — Blanche Merrill[w] & Fred Rich[m] *(Richmond)*. COVER: Bee Palmer.

709 Follies of the Day (closed before Broadway, 1924). Stars unknown.

Tell the Rose — Billy Baskette[w/m] *(Marks)*. COVER: a rose.

710 Follow the Girls (Broadway, 1944). Gertrude Niesen, Jackie Gleason.

Follow the Girls / I Wanna Get Married / I'm Gonna Hang My Hat / Today Will Be Yesterday Tomorrow / Twelve O'Clock and All Is Well / Where You Are / You're Perf — Dan Shapiro[w/m] & Milton Pascal[w/m] & Phil Charig[w/m] *(Robbins)*. A smash hit musical taking place in a serviceman's canteen and bordering on glorified burlesque with Niesen stopping the show with *I Wanna Get Married*. It ran for two years. COVER: two sailors following two girls.

711 Follow the Sun (British, 1936). Claire Luce, Nick Long.

Dangerous You [B] / Nicotina [B] — Desmond Carter[w] & Arthur Schwartz[m] *(Chappell)*; How High Can a Little Bird Fly? [B] / Sleigh Bells [B] — Howard Dietz[w] & Arthur Schwartz[m] *(Chappell)*. A London revue which ran for six months. COVER: lettering and designs.

712 Follow Thru (Broadway, 1929). Jack Haley, Eleanor Powell.

Button Up Your Overcoat / Follow Thru / I Could Give Up Anything But You / I Want to Be Bad / My Lucky Star / No More You / Still I'd Love You / Then I'll Have Time for You / You Wouldn't Fool Me, Would You? — B.G. DeSylva[w/m] & Lew Brown[w/m] & Ray Henderson[w/m] *(D B and H)*. A smash hit musical about the country club set with great songs and lively dancing. It ran for one year. COVER: golf balls.

713 Foolish Father (Jewish, 1928). Joseph Shoengold.

Foolish Father — Isidor Lillian[w] & Abe Ellstein[m] *(Metro)*. COVER: Shoengold and Ellstein.

714 Fools Rush In (#1) (Nightclub, 1934). Stars unknown.

Harlem Barcarolle / Two Get Together — Norman Zeno[w] & Will Irwin[m] *(Harms)*. A nightclub show performed on a boat. COVER: sketch of a goofy blonde.

715 Fools Rush In (#2) (Broadway, 1934). Imogene Coca, Richard Whorf.

I'm So in Love / Love Come Take Me / Rhythm in My Hair / Two Get Together — Norman Zeno[w] & Will Irwin[m] *(Harms)*; Let's Hold Hands — June Sillman[w] & Richard Lewine[m] *(Harms)*. A nightclub revue which transferred to a theatre and failed after two weeks. COVER: chorus girls as angels and as devils.

716 Footlights (Broadway, 1927). Jack Wilson, Hazel Dean.

You Can't Walk Back from an Aeroplane! — Irving Bibo[w/m] & William Friedlander[w/m] *(B B and L)*. A total failure about backing a Broadway musical. COVER: Jack Wilson.

717 For Goodness Sake (*see also* **Stop Flirting**) (Broadway, 1922). Fred and Adele Astaire.

All My Life / Every Day / Oh Gee, Oh Gosh! / Twilight — Arthur Jackson[w] & William Daly[m] *(Harms)*; French Pastry Walk — Arthur Jackson[w] & Arthur Francis (IG)[w] & William Daly[m] & Paul Lannin[m] *(Harms)*; Someone / Tra-La-La — Arthur Francis

(IG)^w & George Gershwin^m *(Harms)*; The Whichness of the Whatness — Arthur Jackson^w & William Daly^m & Paul Lannin^m *(Harms)*. A musical dealing with a jealous husband and wife. An ordinary score and book but it kept going for 14 weeks because of the Astaires. Produced in London as *Stop Flirting*. COVER: flowers and designs.

718 Forbidden Melody (closed before Broadway, 1930). Stars unknown.

Maybe It's You [RC] — Otto Harbach^w & Jerome Kern^m *(Harms)*. A musical that was never produced. COVER: none.

719 Forbidden Melody (Broadway, 1936). Carl Brisson, Lillion Clark.

How Could a Fellow Want More? / Just Hello / Lady in the Window / Moonlight and Violins / No Use Pretending / Shadows That Walk in the Night / You Are All I've Wanted — Otto Harbach^w & Sigmund Romberg^m *(Robbins)*. A musical of royal infidelity or a dated, terrible operetta that closed almost immediately. It has one distinction in that it was the last live musical to play the New Amsterdam on 42nd Street. After this show, it became a seedy movie house. COVER: flowers and designs.

720 Forever Plaid (Off Broadway, 1990). Stan Chandler, David Engel.

Catch a Falling Star — Paul Vance^w/m & Lee Pockriss^w/m *(Warner Bros.)*; Crazy 'Bout Ya, Baby — Pat Barrett^w & Rudi Maugeri^m *(Warner Bros.)*; Cry — Churchill Kohlman^w/m *(Warner Bros.)*; Heart and Soul — Frank Loesser^w & Hoagy Carmichael^m *(Warner Bros.)*; Love Is a Many Splendored Thing — Paul F. Webster^w & Sammy Fain^m *(Warner Bros.)*; Moments to Remember / No, Not Much! — Al Stillman^w & Robert Allen^m *(Warner Bros.)*; Rags to Riches — Richard Adler^w/m & Jerry Ross^w/m *(Warner Bros.)*; Shangri-la — Carl Sigman^w & Matty Malneck^m & Robert Maxwell^m *(Warner Bros.)*; Sixteen Tons — Merle Travis^w/m *(Warner Bros.)*; Three Coins in the Fountain — Sammy Cahn^w & Jule Styne^m *(Warner Bros.)*; Undecided — Sid Robin^w & Charles Shavers^m *(Warner Bros.)*. A charming little musical consisting of pop songs which has been running in New York for years and in many cities around the country. COVER: four boys with microphones.

721 Fortuna (Off Broadway, 1962). Gabriel Dell, Jane Connell.

Angelica / Life Is a Long Winter's Day [BW] / Million Goes to Million [BW] / Speak in Silence / Speech — Arnold Weinstein^w & Francis Thorne^m *(Morris)*. A musical about life in an Italian tenement; the musical ran for five performances. COVER: an alley with tenements and balconies.

722 The Fortune Hunter (Nightclub, 1957). Stars unknown.

Evening in Apple Valley — Gordon Vanderburg^w/m & Ernie Cuba^w/m & Homer Laughlin^w/m *(Souvenir)*. COVER: Jean Robla, singer.

723 Forty-Second Street (Broadway, 1980). Tammy Grimes, Jerry Orbach.

About a Quarter to Nine / Dames [VS] / Forty-Second Street / Go into Your Dance [VS] / The Gold-diggers' Song / I Know Now [VS] / Lullaby of Broadway / Shadow Waltz / Shuffle Off to Buffalo / Young and Healthy [VS] / You're Getting to Be a Habit with Me — Al Dubin^w & Harry Warren^m *(Warner Bros.)*; Getting Out of Town [VS] — Michael Stewart^w & Harry Warren^m *(Warner Bros.)*; There's a Sunny Side to Every Situation [VS] — Johnny Mercer^w & Harry Warren^m *(Warner Bros.)*. A smash hit musical based on the old Warner film of the chorus girl making good. Using the best of Harry Warren songs from several movies, it was blessed with the best choreography ever done by Gower Champion, who died during previews. COVER: pretty chorus girl.

724 Forward March (*see also* Strike Me Pink) (Broadway, 1932). Hugh Herbert, Johnny Downs.

Home to Harlem / I Hate to Think

That You'll Grow Old, Baby / It's Great to Be Alive / Let's Call It a Day / Strike Me Pink—Lew Brown$^{w/m}$ & Ray Henderson$^{w/m}$ *(D B and H)*. This revue called *Forward March* folded in Pittsburgh after getting bad reviews. It was re-written and re-cast with Jimmy Durante and Lupe Velez and opened several months later as *Strike Me Pink,* becoming a moderate hit. COVER: a bunch of chorus girls.

725 Four Below (Nightclub, 1956). Dody Goodman, Murray Grand.

So This Is Paris—Murray Grand$^{w/m}$ *(Almanac)*. COVER: Sylvia Sims, singer.

726 Four Seasons (Nightclub, 1957). Shirley Lynn.

A Heart That I Can't Give Away— George Roncevich^w & Gordon Vanderburg^m *(Souvenir)*. COVER: Shirley Lynn.

727 Fourteen Carat Fool (Nightclub, 1957). Stars unknown.

Hooray for Harry—Ted Mossman$^{w/m}$ & Sammy Ostrow$^{w/m}$ & Gordon Vanderburg$^{w/m}$ *(Souvenir)*. COVER: the three composers.

728 Fourth Avenue North (Off Broadway, 1961). Linda Lavin, Clint Anderson.

So Long as He Loves You [VS]—Bart Howard$^{w/m}$ *(Hampshire)*. A revue that lasted two performances. COVER: Bart Howard.

729 Foxfire (Broadway, 1982). Jessica Tandy, Hume Cronyn.

Dear Lord [VS] / My Feet Took t'Walkin' [VS] / Sweet Talker [VS]— Jonathan Holtzman$^{w/m}$ & Susan Cooper$^{w/m}$ & Hume Cronyn$^{w/m}$ *(Cherry Lane)*. A drama, with some folk songs, about a rural mountain family in Georgia. COVER: a mountain range.

730 Foxy (Broadway, 1964). Bert Lahr, Larry Blyden.

I'm Way Ahead of the Game / My Night to Howl / Run, Run, Run Cinderella / Talk to Me Baby—Johnny Mercer^w & Robert E. Dolan^m *(Commander)*. A short lived musical about

the Klondike gold rush with a pleasant score and the last stage appearance by Bert Lahr. COVER: dance hall girls with bags of gold.

731 Fragments (closed before Broadway, 1921). Horace Rouay.

The Piano My Grandmother Played—F. Stuart Whyte^w & B.C. Hilliam^m *(Witmark)*. COVER: lady at a piano.

732 Frank Fay's Fables (Broadway, 1922). Frank Fay, Bernard Granville.

Fables / It's a Pop, Pop, Popular Song / That Swanee River Melody / Two Are One—Clarence Gaskill$^{w/m}$ *(Harms)*. A dull review that lasted four weeks. COVER: fragments of paper with lettering.

733 Frank Silvers Revue (closed before Broadway, 1925). Stars unknown.

Call of the Great White Way / Icky Wicky Woo—Sam Closlow$^{w/m}$ & Frank Silvers$^{w/m}$ *(Marks)*. COVER: Frank Silvers.

734 Frederica (British, 1930). Joseph Hislop, Lea Seidl.

Oh Maiden, My Maiden / Wayside Rose / Why Did You Kiss My Heart Awake?—Harry Pepper^w & Franz Lehar^m *(Chappell)*. An operetta imported to London from the continent and a failure of three months. These three songs were published in the U.S. from that production in the hopes of a N.Y. version but it didn't happen until 1937. COVER: lettering and designs.

735 Frederika (Broadway, 1937). Dennis King, Helen Gleason.

A Kiss to Remind You / One / Rising Star / Rose in the Heather / Why Did You Kiss My Heart Awake?—Edward Eliscu^w & Franz Lehar^m *(Chappell)*. A lavish production of the Lehar operetta with new lyrics by Eliscu. It was too dated and did not last as long as the London version of 1930. COVER: lettering and designs.

736 Free for All (Broadway, 1931). Jack Haley, Dorothy Knapp.

Not That I Care / Open Your Eyes /

Slumber Song / Tonight / When Your Boy Becomes a Man / You're Only the Girl Next Door — Oscar Hammerstein[w] & Richard Whiting[m] *(Harms)*. A plot similar to *Girl Crazy* and a quick failure of two weeks. COVER: a sketch of two couples.

737 Freedomland (Regional, 1960). Stars unknown.

Johnny Freedom — George Weiss[w] & Jule Styne[m] *(Chappell)*. A song written for the opening of the amusement park. COVER: Johnny Horton, singer.

738 The French Doll (Broadway, 1922). Irene Bordoni, William Williams.

Do It Again — B.G. DeSylva[w] & George Gershwin[m] *(Harms)*; Gee! But I Hate to Go Home Alone — Joe Goodwin[w] & James Hanley[m] *(Shapiro, Bernstein)*; When Eyes Meet Eyes, When Lips Meet Lips — Will Cobb[w] & Gus Edwards[m] *(Harms)*; You Don't Love as I Do! — Paul Rubens[w/m] & Hugh Wright[w/m] & E. Ray Goetz[w/m] *(Harms)*. A comedy with songs produced by Ray Goetz for his wife, Irene Bordoni. It had a short run. COVER: Irene Bordoni.

739 Friars Frolic of 1949 (Regional, 1949). Gene Kelly, Spencer Tracy.

This Is My Night with Trixie — L. Wolfe Gilbert[w] & Joseph Cooper[m] *(Mills)*. A one night benefit show for the Friars with the appearance of many big movie stars. COVER: Spencer Tracy, Gene Kelly, John Wayne, Ray Milland, Gary Cooper, and others.

740 Friendly Enemies (Broadway, 1918). Sam Bernard, Regina Wallace.

Dear Old Pals — Eddie Door[w/m] & Lew Porter[w/m] *(Meyer Cohen)*. A comedy drama about a family and the war. COVER: one scene showing the departure of a soldier and another showing his return.

741 Frivolities of 1920 (Broadway, 1920). Irene Delroy, Henry Lewis.

Adam and Eve / Araby / The Cuddle-uddle / The Farmerettes / In Barcelona / In Peacock Alley / Military Marches / Music / On a Moonlight Night / What Is Love? — William Friedlander[w/m] *(Remick)*; Don't Take Advantage — Howard Rogers[w] & James Monaco[m] *(Shapiro, Bernstein)*; If an Apple Tempted Adam — Alex Gerber[w/m] & Henry Lewis[w/m] & Abner Silver[w/m] *(Witmark)*; Jazz Up Jasper — Harry Auracher[w/m] & Tom Johnstone[w/m] *(Remick)*; Oh How I Love You — Andrew Sterling[w/m] & Henry Lewis[w/m] & Dave Dreyer[w/m] *(Von Tilzer)*; Peachie — Jack Yellen[w] & Albert Gumble[m] *(Remick)*; Pretty Little Cinderella — Blanche Franklin[w] & Nathaniel Vincent[m] *(Jack Mills)*. A terrible revue that lasted less than two months. COVER: designs and lettering.

742 Frogs (Regional, 1974). Larry Blyden, Jerome Dempsey.

Fear No More [VS] / Invocation and Instructions to the Audience [VS] — Stephen Sondheim[w/m] *(Revelation)*. A special musical performed in the swimming pool at Yale for a limited run. COVER: Stephen Sondheim.

743 From Broadway to Paris (Nightclub, 1930). Irving Aaronson and his orchestra.

Country Cousin / Seasick Blues / Sticky Feet — Jo Trent[w/m] & Peter De-Rose[w/m] *(Shapiro, Bernstein)*. COVER: a beautiful girl in a garden.

744 From Time to Time (closed before Broadway, 1985). Stars unknown.

You Got It All — Rupert Holmes[w/m] *(Holmes)*. This song is from a musical announced but never produced. COVER: a singing group called Jets.

745 Fun of the Fayre (British, 1921). Clifton Webb, "June."

Whose Baby Are You? [B] — Anne Caldwell[w] & Jerome Kern[m] *(Chappell)*. A London revue from Cochran with a song by Jerome Kern. COVER: Clifton Webb and "June."

746 The Funniest Man in the World (closed before Broadway, 1966). Stars unknown.

Chaplinesque [RC] / Cliff-Hanger [RC] / My Little Tramp [RC] / Old-timers Melody [RC] — Albert Hague[w/m] *(Chappell)*. A musical about Chaplin which was planned but never produced. COVER: none.

747 Funny Face (Smarty) (Broadway, 1927). Fred and Adele Astaire.

The Babbitt and the Bromide / Dance Alone with You / Funny Face / He Loves and She Loves / High Hat / How Long Has This Been Going On? / In the Swim [VS] / Let's Kiss and Make Up / My One and Only (What Am I Gonna Do) / 'S Wonderful / Tell the Doc [BW] / What Am I Gonna Do / The World Is Mine — Ira Gershwin[w] & George Gershwin[m] *(Harms)*. A musical loaded with Gershwin hits and the Astaires. It ran more than six months on Broadway. It was called *Smarty* in its try-out. COVER: titles and designs.

748 Funny Girl (Broadway, 1964). Barbra Streisand, Sydney Chaplin.

Cornet Man [VS] / Don't Rain on My Parade / Funny Girl [BW] / Funny Girl — complete score / Henry Street [VS] / I Am Woman, You Are Man [VS] / I Want to Be Seen with You [VS] / Music That Makes Me Dance / People / Who Are You Now? / You Are Woman, I Am Man — Bob Merrill[w] & Jule Styne[m] *(Chappell)*. A triumph for Streisand as Fanny Brice. The score was excellent and the show ran three years. COVER: sketch of upside-down girl on roller skates.

749 Funny Side Up (British, 1939). Sally Gray, Bernard Clifton.

Terribly Attractive [B] Dorothy Fields[w] & Arthur Schwartz[m] *(Chappell)*. A hit musical in London that used this American song. COVER: Sally Gray and Bernard Clifton.

750 A Funny Thing Happened on the Way to the Forum (Broadway, 1962). Zero Mostel, Jack Gilford.

Comedy Tonight / Everybody Ought to Have a Maid / A Funny Thing Happened — complete score / I Do Like You / Impossible [VS] / Love I Hear / Love Is in the Air / Lovely / Pretty Little Picture [VS] / That'll Show Him / Your Eyes Are Blue — Stephen Sondheim[w/m] *(Chappell)*. A delightful musical with Zero Mostel as a slave trying to secure his freedom. A good score and a run of two years. COVER: sketch of man carrying girl in front of Roman building.

751 Gaieties of 1919 by the Shuberts (Broadway, 1919). Gilda Gray, George Jessel.

Beale Street Blues — W.C. Handy[w/m] *(Pace and Handy)*; Coat of Mine / Dippy Doodle-Um / This Is the Day — Blanche Merrill[w] & M.K. Jerome[m] *(Berlin)*; Cherry Blossom Lane / Cozy Corner / Freedom of the C's / Heart-Breaker / I've Made Up My Mind to Mind a Maid Made Up Like You / Lamp of Love / Let Us Keep the Shimmie / Little Boy Blue / A Little Bull / Military Decoration Dance / My Beautiful Tiger Girl / On My Private Telephone / Please Don't Take Away the Girls / Rainbow Ball / Somnambula / Valparaiso — Alfred Bryan[w] & Jean Schwartz[m] *(Remick)*; He Went In Like a Lion and Came Out Like a Lamb — Andrew Sterling[w] & Harry Von Tilzer[m] *(Von Tilzer)*; It's Hard to Settle Down — R. Weston[w/m] & Bert Lee[w/m] *(Harms)*; Jazz Babies Ball — Charles Bayha[w] & Maceo Pinkard[m] *(Shapiro, Bernstein)*; You'd Be Surprised — Irving Berlin[w/m] *(Berlin)*; You'll See the Day — Bud Green[w/m] & Charlie Pierce[w/m] & Ted Fiorito[w/m] *(Piantadosi)*. A terrible revue thrown together by the Shuberts to fill an empty theatre. It ran ten weeks. COVER: flowers and designs.

752 The Galician Rabbi (Jewish, 1937). Menashe Skulnik.

Ai-Ai-Ai — Israel Rosenberg[w] & Joseph Rumshinsky[m] *(Metro)*. COVER: Rumshinsky and Skulnik.

753 The Gang's All Here (Broadway, 1931). Hal LeRoy, Ted Healy.

Adorable Julie / Baby Wanna Go Bye-Bye with You / By Special Permission / It Always Takes Two / More Than Ever / Speak Easy / Speaking of You — Owen Murphy[w] & Robert

Simon[w] & Lewis Gensler[m] *(Harms)*. A musical about bootleggers; it lasted for three weeks. COVER: sketch of a large group of people with signs.

754 Garrick Gaieties (Broadway, 1925). Sterling Holloway, Edith Meiser.

April Fool / Do You Love Me? / Guilding the Guild (Opening) [VS] / Manhattan / On with the Dance / Sentimental Me — Lorenz Hart[w] & Richard Rodgers[m] *(Marks)*; The Butcher, the Baker, the Candlestickmaker — Benjamin Kaye[w] & Mana Zucca[m] *(Cassel)*; Old Fashioned Girl — Edith Meiser[w] & Richard Rodgers[m] *(Marks)*. A small intimate revue put on by the Theatre Guild to raise money. It became successful due to the actors and the songs by Rodgers and Hart. Especially noteworthy was the song *Manhattan*. COVER: a dancing girl.

755 Garrick Gaieties (Broadway, 1926). Sterling Holloway, Edith Meiser.

Back to Nature [VS] / Davey Crockett [VS] / It May Rain [VS] / Say It with Flowers [VS] — Lorenz Hart[w] & Richard Rodgers[m] *(USO)*; Keys to Heaven / A Little Souvenir / Mountain Greenery / Queen Elizabeth / Sleepyhead / What's the Use of Talking — Lorenz Hart[w] & Richard Rodgers[m] *(Harms)*. A second edition of the small revue with the same people and some new and good songs by Rodgers and Hart. It also included a miniature musical called *Rose of Arizona* which was a spoof of operettas and a forerunner to *Little Mary Sunshine*. COVER: sketch of boy and girl dancing.

756 Garrick Gaieties (Broadway, 1930). Sterling Holloway, Edith Meiser.

Ankle Up the Altar with Me — Edward Eliscu[w] & Richard Myers[m] *(Harms)*; I Am Only Human After All — Ira Gershwin[w] & E.Y. Harburg[w] & Vernon Duke[m] *(Harms)*; I've Got It Again / Love Is Like That — Allan Boretz[w] & Ned Lehac[m] *(Harms)*; Lazy Levee Loungers — Willard Robison[w/m] *(Berlin)*; Out of Breath — John Mercer[w]

& Everett Miller[m] *(Harms)*; Put It Away Till Spring — Josiah Titzell[w] & Peter Nolan[m] *(Harms)*; Too, Too Divine — E.Y. Harburg[w] & Vernon Duke[m] *(Harms)*; Triple Sec (mini-opera) — Ronald Jeans[w] & Marc Blitzstein[m] *(Harms)*; You Lost Your Opportunity — Charles Schwab[w] & Henry Myers[m] *(Harms)*. The third and final edition of this series; this one was entertaining but no match for the other two. COVER: a sketch of dancers.

757 Gay Divorce (Broadway, 1932). Fred Astaire, Luella Gear.

After You / How's Your Romance? / I've Got You on My Mind / Mister and Missus Fitch [BW] / Night and Day / You're in Love — Cole Porter[w/m] *(Harms)*; I Love You Only [B] / Never Say No [B] / Salt Air [B] — piano selections *(Chappell)*. A Fred Astaire musical without Adele which became a moderate hit due to the song *Night and Day*. It was Fred Astaire's last Broadway show. COVER: lettering and designs.

758 The Gay Life (Broadway, 1961). Walter Chiari, Barbara Cook.

Bloom Is Off the Rose / Come a-Wandering with Me / For the First Time / I'm Glad I'm Single / Magic Moment / Oh Mein Liebchen / Something You Never Had Before / Who Can? You Can! / Why Go Anywhere at All? — Howard Dietz[w/m] & Arthur Schwartz[w/m] *(Harms)*. A musical with a man-about-town in old Vienna starring Italian movie star Walter Chiari. He could not act, sing, dance, or speak English. It had some lovely songs by Dietz and Schwartz. COVER: a very well-dressed lady followed by a gentleman.

759 Gay New Orleans (World's Fair, 1940). Stars unknown.

I Touched a Star / It Wouldn't Be Love — Allan Roberts[w/m] & Buddy Bernier[w/m] & Jerome Brainin[w/m] *(Chappell)*. An attempt by Mike Todd to out-do Billy Rose at the World's Fair with a revue of girls, etc. COVER: sketch of stage with scenery and girls.

760 Gay Paree (#1) (Broadway, 1925). Jack Haley, Winnie Lightner.

Bamboo Babies – Ballard MacDonald^w/m & Joe Meyer^w/m & James Hanley *(Harms)*; Beautiful Girls – Al Goodman^w/m & Fred Coots^w/m & Maurie Rubens^w/m *(Harms)*; Collegiate / Hocus Pocus – James Hanley^w/m & Ballard MacDonald^w/m *(Shapiro, Bernstein)*; Give Me the Rain – Lester Allen^w/m & Henry Creamer^w/m & Maurie Rubens^w/m *(Shapiro, Bernstein)*; Oh Boy, What a Girl – Bud Green^w & Wright Bessinger^m *(Shapiro, Bernstein)*; Sugar Plum – B.G. DeSylva^w & Joseph Meyer^m *(Harms)*; Tilly of Longacre Square – James Hanley^w/m & Harold Atteridge^w/m & Ballard MacDonald^w/m *(Shapiro, Bernstein)*; Venetian Wedding Moon – Al Goodman^w/m & Maurie Rubens^w/m & Fred Coots^w/m *(Harms)*; Wide Pants Willie – James Hanley^w/m & Harold Atteridge^w/m & Henry Creamer^w/m *(Harms)*. A lavish revue that was quite ordinary, but it ran six months. COVER: Winnie Lightner; titles and designs; and pretty girls.

761 Gay Paree (#2) (Broadway, 1926). Chic Sale, Winnie Lightner.

Heart of a Rose – Clifford Grey^w/m & Fred Coots^w/m & Maurie Rubens^w/m *(Harms)*; Je T'aime Means I Love You – Powers Gouraud^w/m *(Harms)*; Kandahar Isle / Sing a Little Tune / There Never Was a Town Like Paris – Mann Holiner^w & Alberta Nichols^m *(Harms)*; Me, Too – Harry Woods^w/m & Charles Tobias^w/m & Al Sherman^w/m *(Shapiro, Bernstein)*. What Did I Tell Ya? – B.G. DeSylva^w & Walter Donaldson^m *(Shapiro, Bernstein)*. Another edition of this ordinary revue that ran for five months. COVER: titles and designs.

762 Gay Paree (#3) (Broadway, 1927). Sophie Tucker, Rita Gould.

America Did It Again – Ted Koehler^w/m & Marty Bloom^w/m *(Weil)*; Baby Feet Go Pitter Patter – Gus Kahn^w/m *(D B and H)*; I Can't Believe That You're in Love with Me – Jimmy McHugh^w/m & Clarence Gaskill^w/m *(Mills)*; I Lost My Heart – Maurie Rubens^w/m & J. Keirn Brennan^w/m *(Harms)*; I'm in Love Again – Cole Porter^w/m *(D B and H)*; Real Estate Papa – Eugene West^w/m & Carl Perillo^w/m *(Weil)*; Tie All Your Troubles to the Tail of a Kite – Billy Rose^w & Jimmy Monaco^m *(Weil)*. The third and final edition of this series which had a very short run. COVER: Rita Gould; Sophie Tucker; Ben Bernie.

763 The Gay Young Bride (closed before Broadway, 1923). Tom Martell.

The Gay Young Bride – Tom Martell^w/m *(Century)*. A female impersonator show. COVER: Tom Martell.

764 Gene Lockhart's Revue (Regional, 1941). Gene Lockhart.

Missus Tommy Atkins – Gene Lockhart^w/m *(Lockhart)*. A Hollywood revue to benefit British War Relief. COVER: titles and designs.

765 Gentlemen Be Seated (Opera, 1963). Dick Shawn, Alice Ghostley.

The Freedom Train [VS] / Have You Seen Her? [VS] / I Can't Remember [VS] – Edward Eager^w & Jerome Moross^m *(Chappell)*. A limited-run musical written for the New York City Opera Co. COVER: Civil War soldiers.

766 Gentlemen Prefer Blondes (Broadway, 1949). Carol Channing, George Irving.

Bye Bye Baby / Coquette [VS] / Diamonds Are a Girl's Best Friend / Gentlemen Prefer Blondes [VS] / Homesick [VS] / I Love What I'm Doing [VS] / I'm Atingle, I'm Aglow [VS] / It's Delightful Down in Chile / It's High Time [VS] / Just a Kiss Apart / Keeping Cool with Coolidge [VS] / A Little Girl from Little Rock / Mamie Is Mimi [VS] / Sunshine / You Say You Care – Leo Robin^w & Jule Styne^m *(Robbins)*. A very entertaining musical loaded with hit songs and comedy. It ran for two years. COVER: two blondes and their suitors.

767 Gentlemen Unafraid (*see also* **Hayfoot Strawfoot**) (closed before Broadway, 1938). Ronald Graham, Vicki Cummings.

Cantabile – A Song Without Words [RC] – Jerome Kern^m *(Chappell).* A musical produced for the St. Louis Opera Co. It was revised as *Hayfoot Strawfoot* but still didn't make it to Broadway. This melody written for *Gentlemen Unafraid* later became *All the Things You Are.* COVER: none.

768 George M! (Broadway, 1967). Joel Grey, Bernadette Peters.

All Aboard for Broadway [VS] / All in the Wearing / All Our Friends / The American Rag Time [ABQ] / Belle of the Barber's Ball [ABQ] / Billie / Dancing My Worries Away [ABQ] / Down by the Erie Canal / Forty-Five Minutes from Broadway / Give My Regards to Broadway / The Great Easter Sunday Parade [VS] / Harrigan / I Want to Hear a Yankee Doodle Tune / The Man Who Owns Broadway [ABQ] / Mary's a Grand Old Name / Musical Comedy Man [VS] / Musical Moon [VS] / My Town / Nellie Kelly I Love You / Oh, You Wonderful Boy [VS] / Over There [VS] / Popularity / Push Me Along in My Pushcart [VS] / Rose / So Long, Mary [VS] / Twentieth Century Love [VS] / The Two of Us [ABQ] / Yankee Doodle Dandy / You Can Tell That I'm Irish [ABQ] / You're a Grand Old Flag – George M. Cohan *(Marks).* A musical based on the life of George M. Cohan with a dynamic performance by Joel Grey. Scores of Cohan songs, along with spirited dancing, kept it going for a year. COVER: red, white and blue dancing legs.

769 George White's Gay White Way (Nightclub, 1941). Stars unknown.

Beau Night in Hotchkiss Corners / The Calypso / The Gay White Way – Herb Magidson^w & Ben Oakland^m *(Berlin).* COVER: chorus girls and Broadway.

770 George White's Music Hall Varieties (#1) (Broadway, 1932). Bert Lahr, Lili Damita.

And So I Married the Girl / Lady, Don't Look at Me Like That – Herb Magidson^w & Sam Stept^m *(Remick);* Fit as a Fiddle – Arthur Freed^w & Al Hoffman^m & Al Goodhart^m *(Feist);* Five Cent Piece – Irving Caesar^{w/m} *(Caesar);* Hold Me Closer – Jack Scholl^{w/m} & Frank Littau^{w/m} & Max Rich^{w/m} *(Caesar);* Let's Put Out the Lights [PC] – Herman Hupfeld^{w/m} *(Harms);* Street of Dreams – Sam Lewis^w & Victor Young^m *(Feist);* Toward the Dawn – Dave Ringle^{w/m} & Jess Jaffey^{w/m} *(Ringle);* Two Feet in Two Four Time – Irving Caesar^w & Harold Arlen^m *(Harms);* Waltz That Brought You Back to Me – Irving Caesar^w & Carmen Lombardo^m *(Caesar).* George White, in deep financial trouble, could not mount his annual *Scandals* so he produced this low budget ordinary revue instead. It ran for a month. COVER: Harry Richman, Bert Lahr, Lili Damita.

771 George White's Music Hall Varieties (#2) (Broadway, 1933). Stars unknown.

A Hundred Years Ago / There'll Never Be Another Girl Like You – Cliff Friend^{w/m} & Herb Magidson^{w/m} *(Harms);* You Get a Lot of Help When You're in Love [BW] – Lew Brown^w & Harry Akst^m *(Witmark).* A revised edition of the first revue which lasted only three weeks. COVER: lettering and designs.

772 George White's Scandals of 1919 (#1) (Broadway, 1919). Ann Pennington, Ona Munson.

At the Old Drug Store – Arthur Jackson^w & Albert Gumble^m *(Remick);* Broadway Belles / Girls Are Like the Weather / Up Above the Stars – Arthur Jackson^w & Herbert Spencer^m *(Remick);* Gimme the Shimme – Sidney Clare^{w/m} & James Morgan^{w/m} & Arthur Jackson^{w/m} *(Remick);* Girls – Alfred Bryan^w & Harry Carroll^m *(Remick);* I Could Be Happy with One

Little Boy / Land of My Heart's Desire / My Little Address Book / Peacock Alley / Picture Framed in My Heart / Shimmee Baby / Step This Way / The Three Mile Limit Cafe — Arthur Jackson[w] & Richard Whiting[m] *(Remick)*. The first edition of this series was not all that great. It had beautiful girls and great dancing but ordinary songs. It ran for only four months. COVER: sketch of a gentleman and a lady.

773 George White's Scandals of 1920 (#2) (Broadway, 1920). Ann Pennington, Lou Holtz.

Idle Dreams / My Lady / On My Mind the Whole Night Long / The Scandal-Walk / The Songs of Long Ago / Tum On and Tiss Me — Arthur Jackson[w] & George Gershwin[m] *(Harms)*; O-H-I-O — Jack Yellen[w] & Abe Olman[m] *(Forster)*; You've Got to Give the Babies a Bottle — Howard Johnson[w/m] & Milton Ager[w/m] *(Feist)*. The second edition's best feature was its dancing. The Gershwin songs were not notable. Like the first one, it ran for only four months. COVER: girl staring at mirror with gentleman peeping.

774 George White's Scandals of 1921 (#3) (Broadway, 1921). Ann Pennington, George White.

Drifting Along with the Tide / I Love You / She's Just a Baby / South Sea Isles / Where East Meets West — Arthur Jackson[w] & George Gershwin[m] *(Harms)*; I Didn't Start In to Love You — Bob Schafer[w] & Sam Coslow[w] & James Durante[m] *(Triangle)*; Mother Eve — Ballard MacDonald[w] & James Hanley[m] *(Shapiro, Bernstein)*; Russian Dance — piano selections — George Gershwin[m] *(Harms)*. Gershwin's second score for the *Scandals* was much etter than the first. Even though this edition had some good comedy and superior dancing, it lasted only three months. COVER: naked girl in garden surrounded by animals.

775 George White's Scandals of 1922 (#4) (Broadway, 1922). W.C. Fields, Winnie Lightner.

Across the Sea / Argentina /

Cinderelatives / Where Is the Man of My Dreams — B.G. DeSylva[w] & Ray Goetz[w] & George Gershwin[m] *(Harms)*; Blue Monday — piano solos [BW] / Lullaby from Blue Monday — solo (plain cover) — George Gershwin[m] *(Warner Bros.)*; Has Anybody Seen My Joe [BW] — George Gershwin[m] *(New World)*; How Ya Gonna Keep Your Mind on Dancing — Lew Brown[w] & James Hanley[m] *(Shapiro, Bernstein)*; I Found a Four Leaf Clover / Oh, What She Hangs Out / She Hangs Out in Our Alley — B.G. DeSylva[w] & George Gershwin[m] *(Harms)*; I'll Build a Stairway to Paradise — B.G. DeSylva[w] & Arthur Francis (IG)[w] & George Gershwin[m] *(Harms)*. This edition, with the Gershwin classic *I'll Build a Stairway to Paradise,* the comedy of W.C. Fields, and some beautiful girls survived for only 11 weeks. COVER: newspaper titles.

776 George White's Scandals of 1923 (Broadway, 1923). Lester Allen, Winnie Lightner.

Cannibola / The Gold-digger — James Hanley[w/m] *(Shapiro, Bernstein)*; Home Lights I Long to See (not published); Let's Be Lonesome Together / There Is Nothing Too Good for You / Throw 'er In High — B.G. DeSylva[w] & Ray Goetz[w] & George Gershwin[m] *(Harms)*; Life of a Rose / Lo-La-Lo / On the Beach at How've-You-Been / Where Is She? — B.G. DeSylva[w] & George Gershwin[m] *(Harms)*; More — Abner Silver[w/m] & Sidney Mitchell[w/m] & Lew Pollack[w/m] *(Witmark)*; San — Lindsay McPhail[w/m] & Walter Michels[w/m] *(Curtis)*; Stingo Stungo / Take a Look at This — Lew Brown[w] & James Hanley[m] *(Shapiro, Bernstein)*; You and I — B.G. DeSylva[w] & George Gershwin[m] & Jack Green[m] *(Harms)*. A rather ordinary edition in this series with some less-than-great Gershwin songs. It did run for 21 weeks, however. COVER: two peacocks and designs.

777 George White's Scandals of 1924 (#6) (Broadway, 1924). Winnie Lightner, Will Mahoney.

I Need a Garden / Kongo Kate / Mah-Jongg / Night Time in Araby / Rose of Madrid / Tune In — To Station J.O.Y. / Year After Year — B.G. DeSylva^w & George Gershwin^m *(Harms)*; In My Pajamas — Sam Gould^w/m & Lew Pollack^w/m & Will Mahoney^w/m & Charlie Winston^w/m *(Jack Mills)*; Nuthin's Gonna Stop Me Now — Willy White^w/m & Bernard Grossman^w/m & Rubey Cowan^w/m *(Stark, Cowan)*; One of These Days — Lew Brown^w & James Hanley^m *(Shapiro, Bernstein)*; Somebody Loves Me — Ballard MacDonald^w & B.G. DeSylva^w & George Gershwin^m *(Harms)*. Gershwin's last score for the *Scandals* produced only one hit, *Somebody Loves Me*. This edition ran longer than any of the others — almost six months — but it was not that good! COVER: The Gershwin music for this edition comes in two sets of covers. One set is orange with photo of a girl and the other set is a bunch of blue and orange swirls.

778 George White's Scandals of 1925 (#7) (Broadway, 1925). Helen Morgan, Tom Patricola.

Beware of a Girl with a Fan / Give Us the Charleston / I Want a Lovable Baby / Rose-Time / The Whosis-Whatsis — B.G. DeSylva^w & Lew Brown^w & Ray Henderson^m *(Harms)*; The Black Black Bottom Blues — George Wintz^w & Baldy Wetzel^m *(Wintz)*; Fly Butterfly / What a World This Would Be — B.G. DeSylva^w & Ray Henderson^m *(Harms)*. An edition with ordinary songs noted only for its girls and great dancing. It ran 20 weeks. COVER: lettering and designs.

779 George White's Scandals of 1926 (#8) (Broadway, 1926). Ann Pennington, Harry Richman.

The Birth of the Blues / Black Bottom / The Girl Is You and the Boy Is Me / Here I Am / It All Depends on You / Lucky Day / Sevilla / Tweet Tweet — B.G. DeSylva^w & Lew Brown^w & Ray Henderson^m *(Harms)*. With good comedy skits, fine dancing, and an excellent score by DeSylva, Brown, and Henderson this edition ran longer than any of the others — over one year. It contained quite a few hit songs! COVER: chorus girl dressed as a clown.

780 George White's Scandals of 1928 (#9) (Broadway, 1928). Ann Pennington, Harry Richman.

Alone with Only Dreams / American Tune / Blue Grass / I'm on the Crest of a Wave / Pickin' Cotton / The Tap Dance / What D'ya Say? / Where Your Name Is Carved with Mine — B.G. DeSylva^w/m & Lew Brown^w/m & Ray Henderson^w/m *(D B and H)*; King for a Day — Sam Lewis^w & Joe Young^w & Ted Fiorito^m *(Remick)*; What a Night for Spooning — Ballard MacDonald^w/m & Dave Dreyer^w/m *(Berlin)*. This show had ordinary songs and poor comedy skits, but the great dancing kept this edition on for six months. COVER: dancing chorus girl.

781 George White's Scandals of 1929 (#10) (Broadway, 1929). Howard Brothers, Frances Williams.

Bigger and Better Than Ever / Bottoms Up / Is Izzy Azzy Woz? / Love Is Free to Every One / Sittin' in the Sun — Cliff Friend^w/m & George White^w/m *(Harms)*; I'm Marching Home to You — Abner Silver^w/m & Al Sherman^w/m & Al Lewis^w/m *(Shapiro, Bernstein)*; Love Birds — Cliff Friend^w/m & Irving Caesar^w/m *(Harms)*; There's Something Spanish in Your Eyes / You Are My Day-dream — Irving Caesar^w & Cliff Friend^m *(Harms)*. A run of 20 weeks for this edition that had nothing good in it. COVER: chorus girl.

782 George White's Scandals of 1931 (#11) (Broadway, 1931). Ethel Merman, Rudy Vallee.

Hummin' to Myself — Herb Magidson^w & Monty Siegel^w & Sammy Fain^m *(D B and H)*; If I Thought I Could Live Without You, I'd Die / I'm in That Mood / Life Is Just a Bowl of Cherries / My Song / That's Love / That's Why Darkies Were Born / This Is the Missus / The Thrill Is Gone / You Didn't Live to Love — Lew Brown^w/m and Ray Henderson^w/m *(D B and H)*; Wipe That

Frown Right Off Your Face – Mack Gordon[w] & Harry Revel[m] *(Miller)*. One of the best editions of the *Scandals* with the singing of Ethel Merman and Rudy Vallee. The dancing of Ray Bolger and the girls, the sets of Joseph Urban, and some pleasant songs including the hit *Life Is Just a Bowl of Cherries* gave it a run of six months. COVER: chorus girls; Ethel Merman.

783 George White's Scandals of 1936 (#12) (Broadway, 1935). Rudy Vallee, Bert Lahr.

Anything Can Happen / Cigarette / I'm the Fellow Who Loves You / I've Got to Get Hot / Life Begins at Sweet Sixteen / May I Have My Gloves? / Pied Piper of Harlem / Tell Her the Truth – Jack Yellen[w] & Ray Henderson[m] *(Harms)*; The Man on the Flying Trapeze – Walter O'Keefe[w/m] *(Robbins)*. George White was having financial troubles and could not produce a *Scandals* for five years. This poor short-lived edition did not improve his situation! COVER: chorus girl.

784 George White's Scandals of 1939–40 (#13) (Broadway, 1939). Ann Miller.

Are You Havin' Any Fun? / Good Night, My Beautiful / Our First Kiss – Jack Yellen[w] & Sammy Fain[m] *(Crawford)*; Mexiconga / Something I Dreamed Last Night – Jack Yellen[w] & Herb Magidson[w] & Sammy Fain[m] *(Crawford)*. The final edition of the *Scandals*. It included a wonderful dancing chorus led by Ann Miller and several very good Sammy Fain songs, however, the day of the annual revues was over and this show failed. COVER: Ann Miller and chorus girls.

785 Georgia Music (Regional, 1940). Stars unknown.

Stop Pretending [PC] – Buddy Johnson[w/m] *(Georgia)*. COVER: none.

786 Georgy (Broadway, 1970). Dilys Watling, Stephen Elliott.

Electric Windows / Fog-Out / Georgy (vocal) / Gettin' Back to Me / Half of Me / Howdjadoo / Just for the Ride / Ol' Pease Puddin' / So What? / Something Special / Sweet Memory / There's a Comin' Together / This Time Tomorrow / Toy Balloon – Carole Bayer[w] & George Fishchoff[m] *(Columbia)*; Georgy (instrumental version) – George Fischoff[m] *(Columbia)*. Adapted from the popular movie, this musical was a disaster and lasted four performances. COVER: Georgy.

787 Gertrude Stein's First Reader (Off Broadway, 1969). Joy Garrett, Sandra Thornton.

Gertrude Stein's First Reader – complete score of 17 songs – Gertrude Stein[w] & Ann Sternberg[m] *(Chappell)*. This revue was based on the writings of Gertrude Stein but lasted only one month. COVER: abstract sketch of the cast.

788 G.I. Almanac (Military, 1945). Soldiers.

Counting the Days – Hy Zaret[w] & Alex Kramer[m] *(Santly Bros.–Joy)*. A show which toured Army bases for entertainment. COVER: military insignias.

789 Gigi (Broadway, 1973). Alfred Drake, Daniel Massey.

The Earth and Other Minor Things [VS] / Gigi [VS] / Gigi – complete vocal score / I Remember It Well [VS] / I'm Glad I'm Not Young Anymore [VS] / In This Wide, Wide World [VS] / Night They Invented Champagne [VS] / Paris Is Paris Again [VS] / She Is Not Thinking of Me / Thank Heaven for Little Girls – Alan Jay Lerner[w] & Frederick Loewe[m] *(Chappell)*. A terrible adaptation of the beautiful movie; it lingered for three months. COVER: sketch of two happy people.

790 Gimme a Thrill (closed before Broadway, 1922). Stars unknown.

Gimme a Thrill / A Rainy Day – Will Johnstone[w] & Tom Johnstone[m] *(Harms)*. COVER: designs and lettering.

791 Ginger (*see also* **Take a Chance**) (Broadway, 1923). Letta Corder, Walter Douglas.

Don't Forget / Teach Me How – H.I. Phillips[w] & Harold Orlob[m]

(Harms). A musical about testing parachutes; it lasted a month. It was called *Take a Chance* in try-out. COVER: flowers.

792 The Ginger Box (Off Broadway, 1922). Stars unknown.

Big Chief Hooch / California Poppy / Canoodle-Oddle-Oo / Come Over / Cottage for Two / Eugene O'Neill / Sister Teams — Paul duPont[w] & Arthur Gutman[m] *(Remick)*. This Off Broadway revue played at the Greenwich Village Theatre. COVER: costumed man and woman embracing.

793 The Gingham Girl (*see also* **Love and Kisses**) (Broadway, 1922). Helen Ford, Eddie Buzzell.

Business Is Bad / Forty-Second Street Strut / The Gingham Girl / Just as Long as You Have Me / Libby / Love and Kisses / Plunk / Tell Her While the Waltz Is Playing / The Twinkle in Your Eye / When My Buddy Steps with Me — Neville Fleeson[w] & Albert Von Tilzer[m] *(Harms)*. A charming little musical about two small-towners making good in New York. The critics liked its sweetness and it ran nine months. It was called *Love and Kisses* in try-out. COVER: This music was published with two sets of covers. One set is a vase filled with flowers and the other shows a boy and a girl holding hands.

794 The Girl Behind the Gun (Broadway, 1918). Wilda Bennett. Donald Brian.

Back to the Dear Old Trenches / The Girl Behind the Man Behind the Gun / Happy Family / I Like It / I've a System / Oh, How Warm It Is Today / Some Day Waiting Will End / There's a Light in Your Eyes / There's Life in the Old Dog Yet / That Ticking Taxi's Waiting at the Door [ABQ] / Women Haven't Any Mercy on a Man — P.G. Wodehouse[w] & Ivan Caryll[m] *(Chappell)*; The Girl Behind the Gun — one step / The Girl Behind the Gun — waltz — Ivan Caryll[m] *(Chappell)*; I'm True to Them All — George M. Cohan[w/m] *(Witmark)*; No Conversa-

tion (fox trot) — Charles Previn[m] *(Chappell)*. This was not a war story, but a story of a husband and wife's jealousy of each other. The critics loved the Wodehouse-Bolton book but turned down the Caryll score. It was a moderate hit at five months. COVER: this show comes with two sets of covers. One is very patriotic with red, white and blue designs and the other shows a soldier-girl shooting at four men behind a target.

795 Girl Crazy (Broadway, 1930). Ginger Rogers, Ethel Merman.

Bidin' My Time / Boy! What Love Has Done to Me! / But Not for Me / Could You Use Me? / Embraceable You / Girl Crazy — complete vocal score / I Got Rhythm / Sam and Delilah — Ira Gershwin[w] & George Gershwin[m] *(Harms)*. A smash musical loaded with hit songs and talented stars. COVER: girl with lasso.

796 The Girl Friend (Broadway, 1926). Eva Puck, Sam White.

The Blue Room / The Girl Friend / Good Fellow Mine / Sleepyhead / Why Do I? — Lorenz Hart[w] & Richard Rodgers[m] *(Harms)*; Look for the Damsel — piano selections / What Is It? — piano selections — Richard Rodgers[m] *(Harms)*. A musical about a bicycle race that turned out to be a nine month hit. The excellent Rodgers and Hart score produced two standards, *Blue Room* and *Girl Friend*. COVER: lettering and designs.

797 The Girl Friend (British, 1927). Clifford Mollison.

The Blue Room [B] / The Girl Friend [B] / Mountain Greenery [B] / What's the Use of Talking? [B] — Lorenz Hart[w] & Richard Rodgers[m] *(Chappell)*. This musical had no relation to the American *Girl Friend* except that it used the two hit songs from the score plus several other Rodgers and Hart songs. This version was a big success in London and ran for over a year. COVER: designs and lettering.

798 The Girl from Child's (closed before Broadway, 1927). Stars unknown.

The House That Jazz Built / Little Miss Nobody / Only a Paper Rose / A Perfect Little Lady — Phil Cook[w] & Tom Johnstone[m] *(Harms)*. COVER: lettering and designs.

799 The Girl from Cook's (British, 1927). Stars unknown.

I'm in Love, It's a Wonderful Feeling / Love Is Not Always Just What It Seems / The Road to Happiness / Stella / You Tell Him — R.H. Burnside[w] & Raymond Hubbell[m] *(Harms)*. Burnside and Hubbell were the principal composers for the spectacles at the Hippodrome in New York. This show was written with New York in mind. They tried it out in London where it failed. The music was published by Harms in New York and Chappell in London. COVER: a pretty girl dreaming of a vacation.

800 The Girl from Home (*see also* The New Dictator) (Broadway, 1920). Frank Craven, Marion Sunshine.

I Miss a Place Called Home / It's a Wonderful Spot / I've Got a Great Idea / Just Say Goodbye / Manana / Marimba / Money / Nine Little Missionaries / Ocean Blues / Sometime / Wireless Heart / You're the Nicest Girl I Ever Met — Frank Craven[w] & Silvio Hein[m] *(Harms)*. An American gets involved with a South American revolution. It was set to music, but a quick failure. It was called *The New Dictator* in its try-out tour. COVER: lettering and designs.

801 The Girl from Nantucket (Broadway, 1945). James Barton, Jane Kean.

From Morning Till Night / That's How I Know That I'm in Love / Your Fatal Fascination — Kay Twomey[w] & Jacques Belasco[m] *(Chappell)*. A painter and his mistaken identity were the basis of this one week failure. COVER: bathing beauty and whale.

802 The Girl from Wyoming (Broadway, 1938). Philip Huston, June Walker.

Boston in the Spring / Dying Cowboy / Finaletto Act II / Hats Off / Kickin' the Corn Around / Lullaby of the Plain / Manuello / Our Home / Ride, Cowboy, Ride / Stay East Young Man — Ted Fetter[w] & Richard Lewine[m] *(Mills)*. A poor take-off on *Girl Crazy* that lasted for ten weeks. COVER: cowgirl with lariat.

803 The Girl in Pink Tights (Broadway, 1954). Jeanmaire, Charles Goldner.

Free to Love / In Paris and in Love / Lost in Loveliness / My Heart Won't Say Goodbye — Leo Robin[w] & Sigmund Romberg[m] *(Chappell)*. A poor musical based on the creation of *The Black Crook* with Romberg's last score. Romberg died three years before this show made it to Broadway. COVER: Jeanmaire.

804 The Girl in the Private Room (*see also* Lulu) (closed before Broadway, 1920). Queenie Smith.

All's Fair in Love and War / And Then Came a Carriage / Dancing the Razza-ma-tazz / Different Days / Goodbye, Take Care of Yourself / I Love My Art / Look for the Rainbow / My Old New Jersey Home / Silver Wedding Day / Some Things Cannot Be Explained / A Table for Two — Edward Clark[w] & Gitz Rice[m] *(Shapiro, Bernstein)*. This musical toured as *Lulu* and *Girl in the Private Room*. COVER: girl surrounded by suitors.

805 The Girl in the Spotlight (Broadway, 1920). Hal Skelly, John Dooley.

Catch 'em Young, Treat 'em Rough, Tell 'em Nothing / I Cannot Sleep Without Dreaming of You / I Love the Ground You Walk On / I'll Be There / It Would Happen Anyway / Marry Me and See [ABQ] / Only You [ABQ] / Somewhere I Know There's a Girl for Me / There's a Tender Look in Your Eyes — Richard Bruce[w] & Victor Herbert[m] *(Harms)*. A failure for Victor Herbert dealing with a budding singer who becomes a star. COVER: dancing girl in spotlight.

806 Girl of My Heart (closed before Broadway, 1920). Dottie Ray Greene.

Dreaming Sweet Dreams of You — Jesse Westover[w/m] *(Lincoln)*; The Girl

I Couldn't Get — D.O. Starnes[w] & Harry Jay[m] *(Lincoln)*; Girl of My Heart — waltzes — Lillian Sarver[m] *(Lincoln)*; If the Girls in This World Were Fishes — Winifred White[w] & Harry Jay[m] *(Lincoln)*; Jennie — Orville Barcus[w/m] *(Lincoln)*. COVER: beautiful girl.

807 The Girl of Yesterday (Jewish, 1922). Molly Picon, Eddie Friedlander.

Di Emese Liebe — Molly Picon[w] & Joseph Rumshinsky[m] *(Trio)*. COVER: Molly Picon.

808 The Girl Who Came to Supper (Broadway, 1963). Jose Ferrer, Florence Henderson.

Here and Now / I'll Remember Her / I've Been Invited to a Party / London / Lonely / This Time It's True Love — Noel Coward[w/m] *(Chappell)*. A dreary Noel Coward musical based on *The Prince and the Show Girl*; it lasted three months. COVER: Prince and show girl.

809 A Girl with a Past (Jewish, 1920). Jennie Goldstein, David Popper.

Just Like a Dream — Harry Lubin[w] & Jennie Goldstein[m] *(Trio)*. COVER: Jennie Goldstein.

810 The Girls Against the Boys (Broadway, 1959). Bert Lahr, Nancy Walker.

Girls and Boys / I Gotta Have You / Where Did We Go? Out. — Arnold Horwitt[w] & Richard Lewine[m] *(Saunders)*. Lahr and Walker were wasted in this un-funny revue with bad songs. It ran two weeks. COVER: girl's legs on man's head.

811 Girls of Summer (Broadway, 1956). Shelley Winters, Pat Hingle.

The Girls of Summer — Stephen Sondheim[w/m] *(Chappell)*. A short lived drama with incidental music by Sondheim. COVER: flowers.

812 Glad to See You (closed before Broadway, 1944). Jane Withers, Eddie Foy, Jr.

Any Fool Can Fall in Love / Guess I'll Hang My Tears Out to Dry / I Don't Love You No More — Sammy Cahn[w] & Jule Styne[m] *(Chappell)*. A musical

about a USO troupe entertaining overseas. With bad reviews in Philadelphia and Boston it folded. It did leave behind one lovely song, *Guess I'll Hang My Tears Out to Dry*. COVER: a girl waving her arm.

813 The Globe Revue (British, 1952). Graham Payn, Dora Bryan.

Give Me the Kingston By-Pass [B] / There Are Bad Times Just Around the Corner [B] — Noel Coward[w/m] *(Chappell)*. A very successful London revue which ran for 30 weeks. COVER: Noel Coward.

814 Glorianna (Broadway, 1918). Eleanor Painter, Alexander Clark.

Chianti / The Dance of the Servants / The Dancing Lesson / Frocks and Frills / Just a Little Laughter / Love! Love! Love! / Nenette and Rintintin / Oriental Song / Rintintin / So Undulating, So Fascinating / Speak for Yourself, John / Tell Me, Crystal Ball / Toodle-oo — Catherine Cushing[w] & Rudolf Friml[m] *(Schirmer)*; I Love You, Dear — Al Kendall[w] & Rudolf Friml[m] *(Schirmer)*. This musical depicted a widow after a legacy. It had a poor book and score, thus folding quickly. COVER: lettering and designs.

815 Glory *(see also* **Chickens** *and* **Lily Dale)** (Broadway, 1922). Jack Clifford, Helen Groody.

The Goodly Little Things We Do / Little White House / The Moon That Was Good Enough for Dad and Mother / Mother's Wedding Dress / Popularity / Post Office / Sawmill River Road / The Upper Crust / We've Got to Build / When the Tenor Married the Soprano — Joseph McCarthy[w] & Harry Tierney[m] *(Feist)*; When the Curfew Rings at Nine — Al Brown[w/m] *(Feist)*. A rags to riches story and a quick failure. This musical toured as *Lily Dale* and *Chickens*. COVER: designs and lettering.

816 Go Easy, Mabel! (Broadway, 1922). Ethel Levey, Margaret Dumont.

Ethel Levey's Smile Song / Go Easy, Mabel / Honey, I Love You / Love Is King — Charles George[w/m] *(Harms)*. A failure of two weeks dealing with extra-marital affairs. COVER: Ethel Levey.

817 Go-Go (Broadway, 1923). Bernard Granville, Josephine Stevens.

Doggone Whippoorwill / Go-Go Bug / Isabel / Mo' Lasses / Rosetime and You / Struttin' the Blues Away / Uno / When You Dance with a Wonderful Girl — Alex Rogers[w] & C. Luckeyth Roberts[m] *(Shapiro, Bernstein)*. A musical about the confusion of twins. Despite a good score by Luckeyth Roberts, the musical lasted only four months. COVER: seven girls dancing around a policeman.

818 Godspell (Off Broadway, 1971). Stephan Nathan, David Haskell.

All for the Best / All Good Gifts / Finale — Long Live God / Learn Your Lessons Well / Light of the World / Save the People / Turn Back, O Man — Stephen Schwartz[w/m] *(Hansen)*; By My Side — Jay Hamburger[w] & Peggy Gordon[m] *(Hansen)*; Day by Day / Godspell — complete vocal score / O Bless the Lord, My Soul / On the Willows / Prepare Ye the Way of the Lord / We Beseech Thee — Stephen Schwartz[w/m] *(Valando)*. A small musical with an updated biblical theme; *Godspell* ran for over six years. COVER: a face with one eye and long hair.

819 Going Greek (British, 1937). Leslie Henson, Louise Browne.

But Me No "Buts"! / Is There Anyone More Wonderful, Than You? / A Little Co-operation from You / Love Came and Swept Me Off My Feet / The Sheep Were in the Meadow / There'll Be the Devil to Pay — Sam Lerner[w/m] & Al Goodhart[w/m] & Al Hoffman[w/m] *(Mills)*. A smash musical written for Leslie Henson by Guy Bolton and others with the score by three American songwriters. The songs were published in the U.S. by Mills Music. COVER: Leslie Henson.

820 The Gold-diggers (Broadway, 1919). Ina Claire, Luella Gear.

What Good Is Alimony on a Lonesome Night — Alex Gerber[w] & Anselm Goetzl[m] *(Witmark)*. A drama about a gold-digger and her redemption. COVER: Ina Claire.

821 Goldele Dem Bekers (Jewish, 1941). Herman Yablokoff.

Zog, Zog, Zog Es Mir — Chaim Tauber[w] & Ilia Trilling[m] *(Metro)*. COVER: Ilia Trilling.

822 The Golden Apple (Broadway, 1954). Priscilla Gillette, Kaye Ballard.

Goona-Goona / It's the Going Home Together / Lazy Afternoon / Store-bought Suit / When We Were Young / Windflowers — John Latouche[w] & Jerome Moross[m] *(Chappell)*. An exquisite musical which was a big hit Off Broadway, but failed when it moved uptown. A re-working of the *Iliad/Odyssey* stories to a small American town. The score was excellent and produced one standard, *Lazy Afternoon*. COVER: a golden apple.

823 Golden Boy (Broadway, 1964). Sammy Davis, Billy Daniels.

Can't You See It? / Colorful [VS] / Don't Forget 127th Street [VS] / Everything's Great [VS] / Gimme Some / Golden Boy / I Want to Be with You / Lorna's Here / Night Song / No More [VS] / Stick Around / This Is the Life / What Became of Me? [VS] / While the City Sleeps — Lee Adams[w] & Charles Strouse[m] *(Morris)*; Golden Boy Theme — piano solo [PC] — Charles Strouse[m] *(Strada)*. The great drama transformed into a musical with the boxer being black to update the story. The score by Strouse, which included such lovely songs as *Night Song*, was very underappreciated. Due to the popularity of Sammy Davis, the show ran for a year and a half. COVER: black arms around blonde white girl.

824 Golden Dawn (Broadway, 1927). Louise Hunter, Archie Leach.

Consolation / Here in the Dark / It's Always the Way / Mulunghu Thabu / My Bwanna / We Two / The Whip — Otto Harbach[w] & Oscar Hammerstein[w] & Emmerich Kalman[m] & Herbert Stothart[m] *(Harms)*; Dawn — Otto Harbach[w] & Oscar Hammerstein[w] &

Robert Stolz[m] & Herbert Stothart[m] *(Harms)*. A musical set in Africa about a tribal village and their gods. An ordinary show that opened the new Hammerstine Theatre. It had a profitable run of six months. COVER: flowers on a trellis.

825 Golden Gate International Exposition of 1939 (Regional, 1939). Stars unknown.

Bells of Treasure Isle / I've Got a Moonlight Date — Paul F. Webster[w] & Frank Churchill[m] *(Paramount)*. COVER: buildings.

826 The Golden Land (Jewish, 1943). Leo Fuchs, Aaron Lebedeff.

Hostu-Bistu-Gistu — F. Kanapoff[w] & J. Jacobs[w] & Alexander Olshanetsky[m] *(Metro)*. COVER: Olshanetsky and Lebedeff.

827 Golden Rainbow (Broadway, 1968). Edie Gorme, Steve Lawrence.

For Once in Your Life [VS] / Golden Rainbow / He Needs Me Now / How Could I Be So Wrong? / It's You Again [VS] / I've Gotta Be Me / Kid [VS] / Life's a Gamble [VS] / Taking Care of You [VS] / We Got Us [VS] — Walter Marks[w/m] *(Damila)*. A vehicle for Gorme and Lawrence with a Las Vegas setting. The appeal of Steve and Edie plus one hit song, *I've Gotta Be Me*, kept the show going for one year. COVER: a golden rainbow.

828 Goldilocks (Broadway, 1958). Don Ameche, Elaine Stritch.

Heart of Stone / I Never Know When / Lady in Waiting / Lazy Moon / The Pussy Foot / Save a Kiss / Shall I Take My Heart and Go — Walter Kerr[w] & Jean Kerr[w] & Joan Ford[w] & Leroy Anderson[m] *(Mills)*. A charming musical about the silent film industry. It had some lovely songs by Anderson, and featured the wonderful Elaine Stritch. It had lavish sets; however, it lasted only for five months. The leading male role was played by Barry Sullivan in the Philadelphia try-out. Since he couldn't sing, he was replaced by Don Ameche. The song *Heart of Stone* was published with Barry Sullivan as the

star. After that, all the sheet music has been published with Don Ameche as the star. COVER: girl dancing with a bear.

829 Gone with the Wind (British, 1972). Harve Presnell, June Ritchie.

Blueberry Eyes [B] / How Often How Often [B] / Little Wonders [B] [VS] / Lonely Stranger [B] / My Soldier [B] [VS] / Scarlett [B] [VS] / Strange and Wonderful [B] / A Time for Love [B] [VS] / Two of a Kind [B] [VS] / We Belong to You [B] [VS] — Harold Rome[w/m] *(Chappell)*. The musical version of *Gone with the Wind* began in Tokyo as *Scarlett*. It was a successful production and then opened in London as *Gone with the Wind* where the spectacle of it kept it going for a year at the Drury Lane. COVER: a sketch of Scarlett and the sun.

830 Gone with the Wind (closed before Broadway, 1973). Pernell Roberts, Lesley Ann Warren.

Gone with the Wind / Lonely Stranger / We Belong to You — Harold Rome[w/m] *(Big Three)*. After playing Tokyo and London, this musical opened in the U.S. for a long national tour. After three months of poor business, it folded. In addition to book problems and ordinary music, the stage version suffered from comparison with the unforgettable movie version with Gable and Leigh. COVER: a sketch of Scarlett.

831 Good Boy (Broadway, 1928). Helen Kane, Charles Butterworth.

After I Hit Broadway — piano selections / Nina and Her Concertina — piano selections — Herbert Stothart[m] & Harry Ruby[m] *(Harms)*; Good Boy / I Wanna Be Loved by You / Manhattan Walk / Some Sweet Someone — Bert Kalmar[w] & Herbert Stothart[m] & Harry Ruby[m] *(Harms)*; You're the One — Otto Harbach[w] & Arthur Schwartz[m] *(Harms)*. Two small town brothers try to make good in New York in this musical. The book was better than the score and the show ran for nine months. COVER: flowers and designs.

832 Good Companions (Broadway, 1931). Valerie Taylor, Hugh Sinclair.

Going Home — Frank Eyton^w & Richard Addinsell^m *(Witmark)*; Slipping Round the Corner — Harry Graham^w & Richard Addinsell^m *(Witmark)*. A comedy with songs about a group of strangers who meet and form a concert party. COVER: lettering and designs.

833 The Good Companions (British, 1974). John Mills, Judi Dench.

All Mucked Up [RC] / And Point Beyond [RC] / The Dance of Life [B] / Darkest Before the Dawn [B] [VS] / Footloose [B] [VS] / Good Companions [B] / Goodbye Dicky Doos [RC] / The Great North Road [RC] / I'll Tell the World [B] [VS] / A Little Travelling Music [B] [VS] / On My Way [RC] / The Pleasure of Your Company [B] / The Pools [RC] / Slippin' Around the Corner [B] [VS] / Stage Struck [B] [VS] / Susie for Everybody [B] [VS] / Ta Luv [B] — Johnny Mercer^w & Andre Previn^m *(Chappell)*. A bunch of strangers meet and form a concert party; from the famous Priestley novel. This musical, by two American songwriters, had a run of seven months in London. The book was poor, the music was uneven, and most of the cast couldn't sing. Its ultimate aim was Broadway, but it never made it. COVER: a group of happy people.

834 Good Luck Sam (Military, 1918). Lorenz Gilbert, Chris Hayes.

Good Luck Sam / Into the Kitchen Boys / It's the Same Old Chow / O Need I Speak / Oh! It's Nice to Get Money from Home / There Once Was a War / There's a Trace of War / Watermelon and a Pair of Dice — Edward Anthony^w & Louis Merrill^m *(Harms)*. A show written by soldiers to tour camps. COVER: a large horseshoe.

835 Good Morning Dearie (Broadway, 1921). Oscar Shaw, Louise Groody.

Blue Danube Blues / Didn't You Believe? / Easy Pickin's / Good Morning Dearie / Good Morning Dearie — complete vocal score / Ka-Lu-A / My Lady's Dress / Niagara Falls / Rose-Marie / Sing-Song Girl / Toddle / Way Down Town — Anne Caldwell^w & Jerome Kern^m *(Harms)*. A musical about young love and a jewel robbery with a good book and a fine score by Kern. It had a run of ten months. COVER: lettering and designs.

836 Good Morning Judge (Broadway, 1919). Mollie King, Charles King.

Dinky Doodle Dicky / Game That Ends with a Kiss — Lionel Monckton$^{w/m}$ & Howard Talbot$^{w/m}$ & Adrian Ross$^{w/m}$ & Percy Greenbank$^{w/m}$ *(Chappell)*; Here Comes the Bride — Ray Goetz^w & George Meyer^m *(Feist)*; I Want to Go Bye-Bye / It's Nothing to Do with You / Little Miss Melody / Make Hay, Little Girl! / O Land of Mine / Oh, That We Two Were Playing / Pansy Day / Sporty Boys — Percy Greenbank^w & Lionel Monckton^m *(Chappell)*; I'm Not Jealous — Harry Pease^w & Ed Nelson^m & Fred Mayo^m *(Stasny)*; I Was So Young — Irving Caesar^w & Al Bryan^w & George Gershwin^m *(Harms)*; I've Got a Pair of Swinging Doors — Sam Lewis^w & Joe Young^w & Bert Grant^m *(Berlin)*; Love Came First When I Saw You / You — Harold Vicars$^{w/m}$ *(Chappell)*; One Night, One Waltz, One Girl — Ivan Reid^w & Shep Camp^m *(Harms)*; Some Quiet Afternoon — Gus Kahn^w & Egbert Van Alstyne^m *(Remick)*; Take Me — Edward Breier^w & Ed Weinstein^m*(Chappell)*; There's More to the Kiss Than the X.X.X. — Irving Caesar^w & George Gershwin^m *(Harms)*. An imported British musical starring the Kings; it ran only a couple of months. COVER: Charlie and Mollie King.

837 Good News (Broadway, 1927). John Sheehan, Inez Courtney.

The Best Things in Life Are Free / A Girl of the Pi Beta Phi / Good News / Good News — complete vocal score / Happy Days / He's a Ladies Man / Just Imagine / Lucky in Love / The Varsity Drag — B.G. DeSylva$^{w/m}$ & Lew Brown$^{w/m}$ & Ray Henderson$^{w/m}$ *(D B and H)*; Just a Little Bit of Driftwood — Benny Davis$^{w/m}$ & Dohl

Davis$^{w/m}$ & Abe Lyman$^{w/m}$ *(Robbins)*. A musical about football and young love in college. It had one of the best scores by this trio with five hit songs. It was loaded with peppy dance numbers and ran for a year and a half. COVER: college girl with newspaper.

838 Good News (Broadway, 1973). Alice Faye, John Payne.

The Best Things in Life Are Free / Button Up Your Overcoat [VS] / The Girl of the Pi Beta Phi [VS] / Good News [VS] / He's a Ladies Man [VS] / I Want to Be Bad [VS] / Just Imagine [VS] / Lucky in Love [VS] / Sunny Side Up [VS] / Together [VS] / The Varsity Drag / You're the Cream in My Coffee [VS] — B.G. DeSylva$^{w/m}$ & Lew Brown$^{w/m}$ & Ray Henderson$^{w/m}$ *(Chappell)*. A dismal revival of the 1927 hit with a poorly updated book and a revised score. This production was a vehicle for Alice Faye and John Payne and had a long national tour before reaching Broadway. It folded after two weeks. COVER: college girl with newspaper.

839 The Good Road (*see also* **Ideas Have Legs**) (Regional, 1947). Stars unknown.

Change for Every Joe — Eleanor Purdy$^{w/m}$ *(Moral Rearmament)*; Come Along / Ideas Have Legs / The Spirit of the West — Cecil Broadhurst$^{w/m}$ *(Moral Rearmament)*; Families Can Be Fun / The Good Road — Alan Thornhill^w & Paul Misraki^m *(Moral Rearmament)*; Heartpower — Dorothy Saul^w & Katharine Miller^m & Marie Sanger^m *(Moral Rearmament)*; Struggle Alley / Sorry Is a Magic Little Word — Cecil Broadhurst^w & Richard Hadden^m *(Moral Rearmament)*; The Third Way — A. Garrett^w & Katharine Miller^m *(Moral Rearmament)*; The Whole World Is My Neighbor — Jessie Allen$^{w/m}$ & Marie Sanger$^{w/m}$ *(Moral Rearmament)*; Whatcha Gonna Do, Mister? — Cecil Broadhurst^w & Svenerik Back^m *(Moral Rearmament)*. A political revue also called *Ideas Have Legs*. COVER: sketches of families and friends.

840 Good Times (Broadway, 1920). Nanette Flack, Joe Jackson.

Cling-Clang / Colorland / Down in the Valley of Dreams / Hands Up / Hello Imagination / Just Like a Rose / The Land I Love / The Wedding of the Dancing Doll / You Can't Beat the Luck of the Irish / You're Just Like a Rose — R.H. Burnside^w & Raymond Hubbell^m *(Harms)*; Youth and Truth — piano selections — Raymond Hubbell^m *(Harms)*. An annual spectacle at the Hippodrome which ran for over one year. COVER: lettering and designs.

841 A Good Woman, Poor Thing (Broadway, 1933). Irene Purcell, Arthur Margetson.

Love Me — Arthur Margetson$^{w/m}$ *(Harms)*. A comedy, with one song, that lasted for one week. COVER: Purcell and Margetson.

842 The Goodbye Girl (Broadway, 1993). Bernadette Peters, Martin Short.

A Beat Behind / Don't Follow in My Footsteps / Good News, Bad News / How Can I Win? / I Can Play This Part / My Rules / No More (#1) / No More (#2) / Paula (An Improvised Love Song) / What a Guy — David Zippel^w & Marvin Hamlisch^m *(Warner Bros.)*. A musical based on the Simon movie with uninspired music by Marvin Hamlisch, a poor book, weird sets, and so-so performances by Peters and Short. COVER: Empire State Building and dancing girl.

843 Goodtime Charley (Broadway, 1974). Joel Grey, Ann Reinking.

Goodtime Charley / I Leave the World / To Make the Boy a Man / Tomorrow's Good Old Days — Hal Hackady^w & Larry Grossman^m *(Dramatis)*. A musical of 15th century France — Joan of Arc and the Dauphin. It lacked a coherent book, a good score, and good performances. It had a run of three months. COVER: Joel Grey as Goodtime Charley.

844 A Goose for the Gander (Broadway, 1944). Gloria Swanson, Conrad Nagel.

How Do You Stay in Love? — Jim

Carhart[w] & Stuart McBane[m] *(Boston).* A one-song comedy which lasted two weeks. COVER: Gloria Swanson.

845 The Gorilla (Broadway, 1925). Clifford Dempsey, Frank McCormack.

Mr. Mulligan and Mr. Garrity — Percy Wenrich[w/m] *(Gorilla Corporation)*; Where the Heck Is Mulligan? — Ralph Spence[w] & Billy Rose[w] & Con Conrad[m] *(Remick).* A comedy about a mystery writer being confronted by a "criminal gorilla" and a "real gorilla." COVER: Dempsey and McCormack.

846 Gowns by Roberta (*see also* **Roberta**) (Broadway, 1933). Bob Hope, Lyda Roberti.

Armful of Trouble / Let's Begin / Smoke Gets in Your Eyes / Something Had to Happen / Touch of Your Hand / Yesterday — Otto Harbach[w] & Jerome Kern[m] *(Harms).* Kern's last big Broadway show dealing with the fashion world in Paris. A wonderful score with many hit songs. The try-out title was *Gowns by Roberta* and the Broadway title was *Roberta.* COVER: model beside curtain.

847 The Grab Bag (Broadway, 1924). Ed Wynn, Marion Fairbanks.

Alabamy Bound — B.G. DeSylva[w/m] & Bud Green[w/m] & Ray Henderson[w/m] *(Shapiro, Bernstein)*; A Chorus Girl's Song / Doodle-doo-doo / Flame of Love / Heart of My Rose / I Had Someone Else Before I Met You / I Want a Home — Ed Wynn[w/m] *(Harms)*; It's Right Here for You — Perry Bradford[w/m] *(Bradford)*; Kentucky's Way of Sayin' Good Mornin' — Gus Kahn[w] & Egbert Van Alstyne[m] *(Harms)*; Let It Rain, Let It Pour — Cliff Friend[w] & Walter Donaldson[m] *(Feist)*; Let Me Linger Longer in Your Arms — Cliff Friend[w] & Abel Baer[m] *(Feist)*; Sometimes You Will — Henry Creamer[w/m] & James Hanley[w/m] *(Harms)*; What Did Annie Laurie Promise — Ed Wynn[w/m] & Ned Wever[w/m] & Al Nathan[w/m] *(Harms)*; When I Was the Dandy and You Were the Belle — Herman Ruby[w] & Lou Handman[m] & Dave Dreyer[m] *(Berlin)*; When My Sugar Walks Down

the Street — Gene Austin[w/m] & Jimmy McHugh[w/m] & Irving Mills[w/m] *(Mills)*; When the One You Love Loves You — Cliff Friend[w] & Paul Whiteman[m] & Abel Baer[m] *(Feist).* A pleasant evening of songs and comedy with Ed Wynn; it lasted six months. COVER: Ed Wynn, Eva Shirley.

848 Graham Crackers (Nightclub, 1963). Bob Kaliban, Bill McCutcheon.

Crossword Puzzle [VS] / The Sound of Muzak [VS] — Richard Maltby, Jr.[w] & David Shire[m] *(Fiddleback).* A little revue at the Upstairs at the Downstairs. COVER: lettering and designs.

849 Grand Hotel (Broadway, 1989). David Carroll, Michael Jeter.

As It Should Be [VS] / Grand Charleston (Happy) [VS] / Grand Foxtrot (Trottin' the Fox; Who Couldn't Dance with You?) [VS] / Grand Tango (Table with a View) [VS] / I Waltz Alone [VS] / Maybe My Baby Loves Me [VS] / Villa on a Hill [VS] / We'll Take a Glass Together [VS] / What You Need [VS] — Robert Wright[w/m] & George Forrest[w/m] *(Leonard)*; At the Grand Hotel [VS] / Bonjour Amour [VS] / Grand Parade / I Want to Go to Hollywood [VS] / Love Can't Happen [VS] / Roses at the Station [VS] — Maury Yeston[w/m] *(Cherry Lane). Grand Hotel* started out in 1958 in Los Angeles with Paul Muni as the star and *At the Grand* as its title; it failed. A new version was produced in 1989. During its try-out, half of the dreary Wright-Forrest score was thrown out and new songs by Yeston were added. It opened in New York and became a big hit — not because of its music, but because of the stupendous staging by Tommy Tune. It ran for a year and a half and toured. Wright and Forrest published their own part of the music with Leonard while Yeston published his part with Cherry Lane. COVER: fancy lettering and designs.

850 Grand Street Follies (#1) (Off Broadway, 1923). Aline MacMahon, Agnes Morgan.

As Far as Thought Can Reach / In

the Beginning — Agnes Morgan[w] & Lily Hyland[m] *(Neighborhood)*. A small revue that attracted attention and lasted for eight editions. COVER: lettering.

851 Grand Street Follies (#2) (Off Broadway, 1924). Albert Carroll, Aline MacMahon.

Home from India / Little Maids in Waiting / National Sport / Oils Well That Ends Swell / Serenade (Player Queen) / Unicorn Waltz — Agnes Morgan[w] & Lily Hyland[m] *(Neighborhood)*. This edition spoofed current plays and players, running five months. COVER: lettering and designs.

852 Grand Street Follies (#3) (Off Broadway, 1925). Albert Carroll, Aline MacMahon.

Glory! Glory! Glory! — Dan Walker[w/m] *(Marks)*. This edition ran twenty weeks with spoofs on Eugene O'Neill's and other current plays. COVER: Dan Walker.

853 Grand Street Follies (#4) (Off Broadway, 1926). Albert Carroll, Agnes Morgan.

If You Know What I Mean — Theodore Goodwin[w] & Albert Carroll[w] & Arthur Schwartz[m] *(Harms)*; Little Igloo for Two / Polar Bear Strut — Agnes Morgan[w] & Arthur Schwartz[m] *(Harms)*; Northern Blues — Robert Simon[w] & Walter Haenschen[m] *(Harms)*. With some songs by Arthur Schwartz, this edition ran for only seven weeks. COVER: a polar bear on top of the world.

854 Grand Street Follies (#5) (Off Broadway, 1927). Albert Carroll, Agnes Morgan.

If You Haven't Got "It" / Oh How I Long to Be Simple / Silver Apron Strings / Three Little Maids from Broadway / Where the Wild Time Grows — Agnes Morgan[w] & Max Ewing[m] *(Marks)*; I'm Not Blue, I'm Mauve — Albert Carroll[w] & Max Ewing[m] *(Marks)*. A moderate run. COVER: dancing girl and peacock.

855 Grand Street Follies (#6) (Broadway, 1928). Vera Allen, James Cagney.

Briny Blues / Someone to Admire — Agnes Morgan[w] & Serge Walter[m] *(Harms)*; Husky Dusky Annabel — Agnes Morgan[w] & Max Ewing[m] *(Harms)*; Just a Little Love — Max Ewing[w/m] *(Harms)*; Tu Sais — Louis Weslyn[w] & Serge Walter[m] & Eddy Ervande[m] *(Sherman Clay)*. This edition opened on Broadway for the first time with some wonderful spoofs and a young dancer named James Cagney. COVER: a dancing cannibal.

856 Grand Street Follies (#7) (Broadway, 1929). James Cagney, Agnes Morgan.

I Love You and I Like You — Max Lief[w] & Nathaniel Lief[w] & Arthur Schwartz[m] *(Harms)*; I Need You So — David Goldberg[w] & Howard Dietz[w] & Arthur Schwartz[m] *(Harms)*; I've Got You on My Mind — Max Ewing[w/m] *(Harms)*; What Did Della Wear — Agnes Morgan[w] & Albert Carroll[w] & Arthur Schwartz[m] *(Harms)*. A short run for the final edition of this series whose welcome was now worn out. COVER: designs and lettering.

857 Grand Terrace Revue (First Edition) (Nightclub, 1937). Stars unknown.

Everyone's Wrong But Me / If You Ever Should Leave / Posin — Sammy Cahn[w] & Saul Chaplin[m] *(Chappell)*. COVER: sketch of dancing chorus girls.

858 Grand Terrace Revue (Third Edition) (Nightclub, 1937). Stars unknown.

Bear Down — Edgar Dowell[w/m] & Lou Fox[w/m] *(Chappell)*; Muddy Shores — Edgar Dowell[w/m] *(Chappell)*. COVER: dancing chorus girls.

859 Grand Terrace Revue (Fifth Edition) (Nightclub, 1938). Stars unknown.

Saving Myself for You / What Do You Hear from the Mob in Scotland — Sammy Cahn[w/m] & Saul Chaplin[w/m] *(Harms)*. COVER: dancing girl with top hat.

860 Grand Terrace Revue (Sixth Edition) (New) (Nightclub, 1939). Stars unknown.

The G.T. Stomp / If It's Good / Kick

It / No More—Walter Hirsch[w] & Gerald Marks[m] *(Robbins)*. COVER: curtains.

861 Grand Terrace Revue (Seventh Edition) (New) (Nightclub, 1939). Stars unknown.

Baby, What Else Can I Do? / It's the Things You Do with Your Feet / Me and Columbus / The Timbuctoo / Waltz in Blue—Walter Hirsch[w] & Gerald Marks[m] *(Mills)*. COVER: silhouette of dancer.

862 Grand Terrace Revue (Eighth Edition) (New) (Nightclub, 1940). Stars unknown.

Dancing Silhouette / I've Got Two Left Feet / Magnolias and Moonbeams / The Man Is Solid / What Could I Do Without You—Walter Hirsch[w] & Gerald Marks[m] *(Mills)*. COVER: a nude girl.

863 The Grand Tour (Broadway, 1979). Joel Gray, Ron Holgate.

For Poland [VS] / I Belong Here [VS] / I Think I Think [VS] / I Want to Live Each Night [PC] [CUT] / I'll Be Here Tomorrow / Marianne / Mazel Tov [VS] / More and More, Less and Less [VS] / Mrs. S.L. Jacobowsky [VS] / One Extraordinary Thing [VS] / We're Almost There [VS] / You I Like—Jerry Herman[w/m] *(Schirmer)*. A poorly written, weakly acted and dreary musical. It lasted less than two months. COVER: a car loaded with suitcases.

864 The Grass Harp (Broadway, 1971). Barbara Cook, Karen Morrow.

Chain of Love [VS] / Floozies [VS] / I Trust the Wrong People / If There's Love Enough / Indian Blues [VS] / The One and Only Person in the World [VS] / Reach Out [VS] / Share My Joy and Love [VS] / What Do I Do Now He's Gone [VS] / Yellow Drum—Kenward Elmslie[w] & Claibe Richardson[m] *(Chappell)*. A beautiful little musical that lasted one week. It was based on the Truman Capote story and the book was poorly written; however, it did have pleasant songs and a wonderful performer in Barbara Cook. COVER: a tree.

865 Grease (Broadway, 1972). Barry Bostwick, Adrienne Barbeau.

All Choked Up [VS] / Alma Mater [VS] / Alone at the Drive-In Movie [VS] / Beauty School Dropout [VS] / Born to Hand Jive [VS] / Freddy, My Love [B] / Grease—complete vocal score / Greased Lightnin' [VS] / It's Raining on Prom Night [VS] / Look at Me, I'm Sandra Dee [VS] / Mooning [VS] / Rock 'n' Roll Party Queen [VS] / Summer Nights / There Are Worse Things I Could Do / Those Magic Changes [B] / We Go Together [VS] — Warren Casey[w/m] & Jim Jacobs[w/m] *(Morris)*. This rock and roll musical started Off Broadway and quickly moved to Broadway where it lasted eight years. It was not that great but it had some charm that attracted customers. COVER: a dancing couple.

866 Great Day (Broadway, 1929). Mayo Methot, Allan Prior.

Great Day / Happy Because I'm in Love / More Than You Know / Open Up Your Heart / Without a Song— William Rose[w] & Edward Eliscu[w] & Vincent Youmans[m] *(Youmans)*. A musical about the old South produced by Youmans himself with plenty of problems. It lasted four weeks but produced three standard songs, *Without a Song, More Than You Know,* and *Great Day!* COVER: sunrise over beautiful trees.

867 Great Lady (Broadway, 1938). Irene Bordoni, Helen Ford.

I Have Room in My Heart / May I Suggest Romance? / There Had to Be the Waltz / Why Can't This Night Last Forever—Earle Crooker[w] & Frederick Loewe[m] *(Chappell)*. The story of a great lady and her various love affairs over a couple of centuries. It was Frederick Loewe's first full Broadway score. It was so bad, it lasted only two weeks. COVER: sketch of a lady with turban.

868 Great Scot (Off Broadway, 1965). Allan Bruce, Charlotte Jones.

He Knows Where to Find Me / I Left a Dream Somewhere / That Special

Day / Where Is That Rainbow — Nancy Leeds[w] & Don McAfee[m] *(Valando)*. An Off Broadway musical about Robert Burns. It lasted four weeks. COVER: boy and girl with dog.

869 The Great Temptations (Broadway, 1926). Jack Benny, Jay Flippen.

Beauty Is Vanity — Clifford Grey[w] & Maurie Rubens[m] *(Harms)*; Love Birds — Clifford Grey[w] & Kenneth Burton[m] *(Harms)*; Temptation Strut — Clifford Grey[w] & Earl Lindsay[m] & Maurie Rubens[m] *(Harms)*; Valencia — Clifford Grey[w] & Jose Padilla[m] *(Harms)*; White Rose — Red Rose — Clifford Grey[w] & R. Moretti[m] *(Harms)*. A dull Shubert revue with poor music and skits. Its run was six months. COVER: flowers and designs.

870 Great to Be Alive! (*see also* **What a Day!**) (Broadway, 1950). Vivienne Segal, Mark Dawson.

Blue Day / Call It Love / Dreams Ago / It's a Long Time Till Tomorrow / What a Day! — Walter Bullock[w] & Abraham Ellstein[m] *(Chappell)*. A hopeless musical about a haunted mansion; it lasted for four weeks. It had a fine cast but no material. It was called *What a Day* during its try-out. COVER: sketch of a house and dancing people.

871 The Great Waltz (Broadway, 1934). Guy Robertson, Marion Claire.

Danube So Blue / For We Love You Still / Love Will Find You / While You Love Me / With All My Heart — Desmond Carter[w] & Johann Strauss[m] *(Harms)*. One of the most spectacular stage productions of the '30s with the music of Johann Strauss and a simple story based on some of his life's events. It was booked for a limited run in New York, toured the country, and returned for an encore. COVER: flowers and designs.

872 The Great Waltz (Regional, 1965). Stars unknown.

An Artist's Life [VS] / The Blue Danube [VS] / The Enchanted Wood [B] [VS] / The Gypsy Told Me [VS] / Music! [VS] / Of Men and Violins [VS] / On the Beautiful Blue Danube [B] [VS] / Philosophy of Life [VS] / Radetzky March [B] [VS] / Teeter-Totter Me [B] [VS] / Two by Two [VS] / A Waltz with Wings [VS] / Where Would I Be? [B] [VS] — Robert Wright[w/m] & George Forrest[w/m] & Johann Strauss[w/m] *(Chappell)*; Love and Gingerbread [VS] — Forman Brown[w] & Johann Strauss[m] *(Chappell)*. A limited run production of the Los Angeles Civic Light Opera that never made it to New York although it did have a short run in London. COVER: a couple waltzing.

873 Greatest Show on Earth (Circus, 1919). Carrie Lowery.

I'm Gonna Jazz My Way Right Thru Paradise — Will Skidmore[w/m] & Marshall Walker[w/m] *(Skidmore)*. A song from an early edition of Ringling Bros. circus. COVER: Carrie Lowery with cartoon characters.

874 Greatest Show on Earth (1948 edition) (Circus, 1948). Stars unknown.

The Circus Ball / Dear Santa Claus — John Murray Anderson[w] & Henry Sullivan[m] *(Chappell)*. COVER: elephant with banjo.

875 Greatest Show on Earth (1949 edition) (Circus, 1949). Stars unknown.

Girl in the Moon [VS] / Glorious Fourth [VS] / Happy Birthday [VS] / San Francisco Forty-nine [VS] / There Was an Old Woman [VS] — John Murray Anderson[w] & Henry Sullivan[m] *(B V and C)*. COVER: three girls riding a team of horses.

876 Greatest Show on Earth (1952 edition) (Circus, 1952). Stars unknown.

Butterfly Lullaby / Gold Dollar Moon / New Orleans, the Mardi Gras and You / Someday Today Will Be the Good Old Times — Ray Goetz[w] & John Ringling North[m] *(Chappell)*. COVER: elephant with banjo.

877 Greatest Show on Earth (1953 edition) (Circus, 1953). Stars unknown.

Americana U.S.A. [VS] / Derby Day Honeymoon [VS] / Gone Are the Days [VS] / Minnehaha [VS] — Ray Goetz[w] & John Ringling North[m] *(Chappell)*. COVER: elephant with banjo.

878 Greatest Show on Earth (1954 edition) (Circus, 1954). Stars unknown.

Dreamland / Fiesta / Rocket to the Moon / U.N. — Ray Goetz[w] & John Ringling North[m] *(Chappell)*. COVER: elephant with banjo.

879 Greatest Show on Earth (1955 edition) (Circus, 1955). Stars unknown.

Impossible / On Honolulu Bay — Irving Caesar[w] & John Ringling North[m] *(Caesar)*. COVER: elephant with banjo.

880 Greatest Show on Earth (1956 edition) (Circus, 1956). Stars unknown.

Baby, It's Cold Outside [VS] / Guys and Dolls [VS] / If I Were a Bell [VS] / Lovelier Than Ever [VS] / On a Slow Boat to China [VS] / Once in Love with Amy [VS] / Thumbelina [VS] / What Do You Do in the Infantry [VS] / A Woman in Love [VS] / Wonderful Copenhagen [VS] — Frank Loesser[w/m] *(Frank)*. COVER: a clown with a daisy.

881 Greatest Show on Earth (1957 edition) (Circus, 1957). Stars unknown.

Clippety Clop / Dreamer / The Lover's Waltz — Tony Velona[w/m] *(Chappell)*; Open the Window Wide — Tony Velona[w] & John Ringling North[m] *(Chappell)*. COVER: elephant with banjo.

882 Greek to You (closed before Broadway, 1937). Stars unknown.

Greek to You [VS] — Cole Porter[w/m] *(Warner Bros.)*. This song was written for a musical to be produced by Vinton Freedley but the project died. COVER: Cole Porter.

883 Green Fruit (*see also* The Madcap) (Broadway, 1928). Arthur Treacher, Mitzi.

Honey Be My Honey Bee / Something to Tell / Stop, Go! — Clifford Grey[w] & Fred Coots[m] & Maurie Rubens[m] *(Harms)*. A French farce of love and marriage which lasted three months and is better forgotten. It was titled *Green Fruit* on its try-out tour and arrived on Broadway as *The Madcap*. COVER: columns and designs.

884 Green Pastures (Broadway, 1930). Richard Harrison, Inez Wilson.

City Called Heaven / Hold On / Jesus, Lay Your Head in de Winder / Way Up in Heaven — Hall Johnson[w/m] *(Robbins)*; Green Pastures — 25 spirituals — Hall Johnson[w/m] *(Fischer)*. A biblical story adapted to Negro life in the old South. COVER: lettering and designs.

885 Green Pond (Off Broadway, 1977). Christine Ebersole, Stephen James.

I Live Alone / On the Ground at Last — Robert Montgomery[w] & Mel Marvin[m] *(Schirmer)*. A limited run musical about the South presented by the Chelsea Theatre Center. COVER: an alligator.

886 Greenwich Village Follies (#1) (*see also* **Greenwich Village Nights**) (Broadway, 1919). Ted Lewis, Frances White.

All That I Need Is a Hallway / Give Me the Sultan's Harem — Alex Gerber[w] & Abner Silver[m] *(Witmark)*; Bo-la-bo — George Fairman[w/m] *(Witmark)*; Critics Blues — Philip Bartholomae[w] & John M. Anderson[w] & A. Baldwin Sloane[m] *(Witmark)*; Ding Toes — Jack Caddigan[w/m] & Chick Story[w/m] *(Broadway)*; Gee, I Wish I Was a Caveman's Kid — Phil Ponce[w] & Earnest Golden[m] *(Remick)*; Gypsy Moon — Leo Camby[w] & Ed Moebus[m] & Robert King[m] *(Shapiro, Bernstein)*; I Know Why — Benny Davis[w] & Ted Lewis[m] & Jimmy Morgan[m] *(Berlin)*; I Want a Daddy Who Will Rock Me to Sleep / I'm Ashamed to Look the Moon in the Face / I'm the Hostess of a Bum Cafe / I've a Sweetheart to Each Star / The Message of the Cameo / My Little Javanese / My Marionette / Red, Red as a Rose — Philip Bartholomae[w] & John M. Anderson[w] & Baldwin Sloane[m] *(Witmark)*; I'd Like to Have a Girl — Seymour Brown[w] & Alex Marr[m] *(F-B and M)*; I'll See You in C-U-B-A — Irving Berlin[w/m] *(Berlin)*; Moonshine — Al Herman[w] & Allen Behr[m] *(Witmark)*; Such a Little Queen — John Mears[w] & Earnest Golden[m] *(Remick)*; True Blue Sal — Al Herman[m] & Alex Gerber[m] & Abner Silver[m] *(Witmark)*; When My Baby Smiles at Me — Andrew Sterling[w] &

Ted Lewis^w & Bill Munro^m *(Von Tilzer)*; The Wimmen Won't Let Me Alone — E.Z. Keough^w & Roy Mack^m *(Van Alstyne and Curtis)*. This new annual musical started in the village as *Greenwich Village Nights* but proved to be so popular that it moved uptown as *Greenwich Village Follies* much to Ziegfeld's annoyance. The music was forgettable but the production numbers and skits were excellent. It ran for eight months. COVER: sketch of people frolicking; Ted Lewis, Frances White, Al Herman.

887 Greenwich Village Follies (#2) (Broadway, 1920). Frank Crumit, Howard Marsh.

At the Krazy Kat's Ball / Come to Bohemia / I'll Be Your Valentine / Just Sweet Sixteen / The Naked Truth / Perfume of Love / Tam, Tam, Tam Tam Tam / Tsin — John M. Anderson^w & Arthur Swanstrom^w & Baldwin Sloane^m *(Witmark)*; I'm a Lonesome Little Raindrop — Joe Goodwin^w & Murray Roth^w & James Hanley^m *(Shapiro, Bernstein)*; Just Snap Your Fingers at Care — B.G. DeSylva^{w/m} *(Harms)*; Madeline — Lew Brown^w & Albert Von Tilzer^m *(Broadway)*; Marimba — Howard Johnson^w & Cliff Hess^w & Johnny Black^m *(Feist)*; O-H-I-O — Jack Yellen^w & Abe Olman^m *(Forster)*; Oh Yeedle Ay — Fred Fisher^w & Irving Maslof^m *(Fisher)*. This edition had opulent sets and costumes with good comedy skits but still with poor music. It ran six months. COVER: beautiful show girl; Frank Crumit.

888 Greenwich Village Follies (#3) (Broadway, 1921). Ted Lewis, Al Herman.

Bang! Bang! Bang! / Bluebeard / The Haunted Violin / I'm Up in the Air Over You / Greenwich Village Girl / Jeckyll and Hyde / The Last Waltz / Mlle. Loose Heels / Oh-Heigh-Ho / Snowflake / Sweet Simplicity / When Dreams Come True — John M. Anderson^w & Arthur Swanstrom^w & Carey Morgan^m *(Feist)*; Down the Old Church

Aisle — Ray Perkins^{w/m} *(Witmark)*; Easin' Along — Irving Bibo^{w/m} & Thomas Morris^{w/m} *(Feist)*; I Want a Picture of You — Percy Wenrich^{w/m} *(Feist)*; I've Got My Habits On — Chris Smith^w & Bob Schafer^w & Jimmie Durante^m *(Goodman, Rose)*; Kill 'em with Kindness — William Tracey^w & Abner Silver^m *(Witmark)*; Maybe — Ted Lewis^{w/m} & Earnest Golden^{w/m} *(Shapiro, Bernstein)*; Sun-Down — Al Dubin^w & Paul Cunningham^w & Charles Edmonds^m *(Witmark)*; That Reminiscent Melody / A Young Man's Fancy — John M. Anderson^w & Jack Yellen^w & Milton Ager^m *(Feist)*; Three O'Clock in the Morning — Dorothy Terriss^w & Julian Robledo^m *(Feist)*; Unlucky Blues — Ted Lewis^{w/m} & J. Russel Robinson^{w/m} *(Berlin)*; Wha Wha — Phil Furman^{w/m} & Lester Stevens^{w/m} *(Feist)*. This version which ran for five months was again not noted for its music but for its brilliant use of lighting and scenery with the production numbers. COVER: dancing chorus girls; Ted Lewis; Al Herman; Donald Kerr.

889 Greenwich Village Follies (#4) (Broadway, 1922). Carl Randall, Julia Silvers.

Cinderella Blues / Did You Mean It? / Nightingale Bring Me a Rose / Sixty Seconds Ev'ry Minute / Sweetheart Lane / You Are My Rain-beau — Irving Caesar^w & John M. Anderson^w & Louis Hirsch^m *(Victoria)*; Fate — Byron Gay^{w/m} *(Witmark)*; Georgette — Lew Brown^w & Ray Henderson^m *(Shapiro, Bernstein)*; Jenny Lind — Irving Caesar^w & Louis Hirsch^m *(Victoria)*. Another edition with poor music but excellent skits and dance numbers; it ran six months. COVER: faces of actors and actresses.

890 Greenwich Village Follies (#5) (Broadway, 1923). Irene Delroy, Tom Howard.

Annabel Lee / Golden Trail / I Am Thinking of You / Kama's Garden — Irving Caesar^w & John M. Anderson^w & Louis Hirsch^m *(Victoria)*; Cock-a-Doodle-Doo / Lovey / Moonlight

Kisses / Raisin' the Roof—Irving Caesar[w] & John M. Anderson[w] & Con Conrad[m] *(Victoria)*; Hot Hindoo—Arthur Francis (IG)[w] & Lewis Gensler[m] *(Victoria)*; If I Should See You Cry—Benton Ley[w] & Lee David[m] *(Witmark)*; The Old Folks at Home—Gus Kahn[w] & Raymond Egan[w] & Richard Whiting[m] *(Remick)*; There's Just a Bit o' Heaven in Your Smile—Benton Ley[w] & Lee David[m] *(Witmark)*. This edition had the shortest run of four months. In addition to its weak score, it had a female impersonator and a couple of lavish dance numbers, Martha Graham included. COVER: lettering and designs; Tom Burke; Karyl Norman.

891 Greenwich Village Follies (#6) (Broadway, 1924). Robert Alton, Vincent Lopez.

Brittany / I'm in Love Again (plain cover / Make Ev'ry Day a Holiday / My Long Ago Girl / Wait for the Moon—Cole Porter[w/m] *(Harms)*; Follow the Swallow—Billy Rose[w] & Mort Dixon[w] & Ray Henderson[m] *(Remick)*; Garden of Used to Be—Owen Murphy[w] & Jay Gorney[m] *(Harms)*; Happy Melody—Irving Caesar[w] & John M. Anderson[w] & Philip Charig[m] & Ben Bernie[m] *(Harms)*; Happy Prince—Irving Caesar[w] & John M. Anderson[w] & Willy Engelberger[m] *(Harms)*; He Sure Can Play the Harmonica—James Kendis[w/m] & Hal Dyson[w/m] *(K.B. Co.)*; On the Radio—Vincent Lopez[w/m] & Owen Murphy[w/m] *(Robbins-Engel)*; Too Tired—Benton Ley[w] & Lee David[m] *(Witmark)*. This edition ran four months and even though Cole Porter contributed some songs the score was still weak. COVER: a girl's face; Vincent Lopez; Brooks and Ross.

892 Greenwich Village Follies (#7) (Broadway, 1925–1926). Florence Moore, Irene Delroy.

Go South—Owen Murphy[w] & Richard Myers[m] *(Harms)*; I Love My Baby—Bud Green[w] & Harry Warren[m] *(Shapiro, Bernstein)*; Lady of the Snow / You Have Me—I Have You—Owen Murphy[w] & Harold Levey[m] *(Harms)*; So Will I—Lew Brown[w/m] & Cliff Friend[w/m] *(Berlin)*; Tinkle-Tot / Wouldn't You—Owen Murphy[w/m] *(Robbins-Engel)*; Whistle Away Your Blues—Leo Robin[w] & Richard Myers[m] *(Harms)*. A poor edition of this series and the signal of the end-to-come. COVER: a girl's face.

893 Greenwich Village Follies (#8) (Broadway, 1928). Blossom Seeley, Benny Fields.

Brooklyn Heights / Get Your Man / The Subway Sun / Who's the Boy?—Max Lief[w] & Nathaniel Lief[w] & Ray Perkins[m] *(Harms)*; King for a Day—Sam Lewis[w] & Joe Young[w] & Ted Fiorito[m] *(Remick)*; What's the Reason?—Harold Atteridge[w] & Maurie Rubens[m] *(Harms)*; Why Should We Be Wasting Time?—Eddie Conrad[w] & Fred Coots[m] & Maurie Rubens[m] *(Harms)*. This was a very poor and the last official edition of the GVF. COVER: a girl's face.

894 Greenwich Village Follies (Broadway, 1934). Stars unknown.

Beautiful You / Kiss the Bride Now / Shadows on the Wall / Walk the Plank / Washington Square / Wedding Waltz—George Bennett[w] & Harry Carroll[m] *(Southern)*. This show was billed as G.V.F. of 1934. COVER: beautiful show girl.

895 Greenwich Village Follies of 1924–1925 (#6a) (Touring Production, 1924–25). Fred Allen, Robert Allen.

Manhattan / On with the Dance / Sentimental Me—Lorenz Hart[w] & Richard Rodgers[m] *(Marks)*. This edition of the GVF went on a national tour. It combined some of the songs and sketches from the 1925 *Garrick Gaieties* and some of the best material from the GVF of 1924 plus songs from other Broadway shows. COVER: dancing chorus girl.

896 Greenwich Village Nights (*see also* **Greenwich Village Follies** [#1]) (Off Broadway, 1919). Ted Lewis, Frances White.

Greenwich Village / I Want a Daddy Who Will Rock Me to Sleep / I'm Ashamed to Look the Moon in the Face / Message of the Cameo / My Little Javanese / Red, Red as a Rose—Philip Bartholomae[w] & John M. Anderson[w] & Baldwin Sloane[m] *(Witmark)*; Tell Me—Will Calahan[w] & Max Kortlander[m] *(Remick)*. This small revue opened Off Broadway as *Greenwich Village Nights,* and was so successful that it was transferred uptown as *Greenwich Village Follies.* It lasted for nine editions. COVER: a bunch of frolicking people.

897 Greenwillow (Broadway, 1959). Tony Perkins, Pert Kelton.

Clang Dang the Bell [VS] / Faraway Boy / Gideon Briggs, I Love You / Greenwillow Christmas (Carol) / The Music of Home / Never Will I Marry / Summertime Love / Walking Away Whistling—Frank Loesser[w/m] *(Frank).* An interesting failure from Frank Loesser about a lonely mixed-up boy. COVER: a large willow tree and a couple.

898 Grind (Broadway, 1985). Ben Vereen, Stubby Kaye.

All Things to One Man [VS] / The Grind [VS] / Katie, My Love [VS] / My Daddy Always Taught Me to Share [VS] / Never Put It in Writing [VS] / A New Man [VS] / A Sweet Thing Like Me [VS] / These Eyes of Mine [VS] / This Must Be the Place [VS] / Who Is He? [VS]—Ellen Fitzhugh[w] & Larry Grossman[m] *(Fiddleback).* A musical on the subject of burlesque with nothing going for it, thus making it a quick failure. COVER: a burlesque dancer.

899 La Grosse Valise (Broadway, 1962). Ronald Fraser, Victor Spinett.

Delilah Done Me Wrong / For You / Slippy Sloppy Shoes / Xanadu—Harold Rome[w] & Gerard Calvi[m] *(Chappell).* An imported revue which lasted one week. COVER: a valise and a group of characters.

900 Gus Edwards Revue (Broadway, 1920). Gus Edwards.

In the Land of School Days / You're There, Little Girl—Al Dubin[w] & Gus Edwards[m] *(Witmark).* COVER: Gus Edwards.

901 Gus Edwards Revue (Broadway, 1921). Connor Twins, Gus Edwards.

Every Mother's Lullaby—B.C. Hilliam[w] & Gus Edwards[m] *(Witmark);* I Must Be Loved by Someone / I Want You Morning Noon and Night / Lend Me a Kiss Until Tomorrow / Let's Mend the Crack in the Liberty Bell / Letters That Lighten Broadway / Little Partner of Mine / Lucky Day That I Found You / Mediterranea / When Old New York Was Young—Will Cobb[w] & Gus Edwards[m] *(Witmark);* When Shall We Meet Again—Raymond Egan[w] & Richard Whiting[m] *(Remick).* COVER: Gus Edwards.

902 Gus Edwards Revue (Broadway, 1922). Gus Edwards.

Wonderful You—Will Cobb[w] & Gus Edwards[m] *(Marks).* COVER: Gus Edwards.

903 Gus Edwards Revue (Broadway, 1923). Gus Edwards.

If My Heart Belonged to Somebody Else—Gus Edwards[w/m] *(Berlin).* COVER: Gus Edwards.

904 Gus Edwards Revue (Broadway, 1924). Gus Edwards, Doris Walker.

Old Familiar Faces—Billy Rose[w] & Gus Edwards[m] *(Berlin).* COVER: Doris Walker, Hazel Johnson.

905 Guys and Dolls (Broadway, 1951). Robert Alda, Vivian Blaine.

Adelaide's Lament / A Bushel and a Peck / Follow the Fold / Fugue for Tinhorns / Guys and Dolls / Guys and Dolls Preamble / If I Were a Bell / I'll Know / I've Never Been in Love Before / Luck Be a Lady / Marry the Man Today / More I Cannot Wish You / My Time of Day / The Oldest Established / Sit Down You're Rockin' the Boat / Sue Me / Sue Me Argument—Frank Loesser[w/m] *(Morris);* Guys and Dolls—complete vocal score / Take Back Your Mink / Three Cornered Tune—Frank Loesser[w/m] *(Frank).*

When this show opened in Philadelphia, the songs were published by Morris. Three songs were listed which were not published. After opening in New York, the songs were published by Frank Music and songs were added, dropped, and changed. The cover remained the same. This is one of the best Broadway musicals and ran for three years with many revivals. COVER: a bunch of guys and dolls.

906 Guys and Dolls (Broadway, 1992). Peter Gallagher, Faith Prince.

Guys and Dolls — vocal selections (12 songs) — Frank Loesser[w/m] *(Leonard)*. A revival of this great show with a wonderful cast and a big hit all over again. COVER: lettering and dice.

907 Gypsy (Broadway, 1959). Ethel Merman, Jack Klugman.

All I Need Is the Girl / Everything's Coming Up Roses / Gypsy — complete vocal score / If Momma Was Married [VS] / Let Me Entertain You / Little Lamb / Mama's Talkin' Soft / Mr. Goldstone / Small World / Some People / Together Wherever We Go / You Gotta Get a Gimmick [VS] / You'll Never Get Away from Me — Stephen Sondheim[w] & Jule Styne[m] *(Williamson)*. Another blockbuster which ran for two years and has had many revivals. This is the story of Gypsy Rose Lee and her domineering mother. A powerful score and cast. COVER: a sketch of backstage behind curtain.

908 Gypsy (Broadway, 1974). Angela Lansbury, Rex Robbins.

Everything's Coming Up Roses [B] / Small World [B] — Stephen Sondheim[w] & Jule Styne[m] *(Chappell)*. A British revival of this great show with Angela Lansbury. It later toured the U.S. and had a limited run on Broadway. COVER: sketch of theatre marquees and backstage.

909 Gypsy (Broadway, 1990). Tyne Daly, Jonathan Hadary.

Gypsy — vocal selections (8 songs) — Stephen Sondheim[w] & Jule Styne[m] *(Leonard)*. A very successful revival of this musical with an excellent performance by Tyne Daly. COVER: Tyne Daly.

910 The Gypsy Baron (Regional, 1940). John Charles Thomas.

Flirtation Intermezzo / Love Can Be Dreamed / Love Deals the Cards Tonight / Open Road, Open Sky / When Lovers Meet / The World Is Wide Open to Me / Your Eyes Shine in My Own — Ann Ronell[w/m] & Johann Strauss[w/m] *(Schirmer)*. A new production of the Strauss operetta by the Los Angeles Civic Opera. The *Gypsy Baron* had a limited run. COVER: This music was published with two sets of covers. One shows a picture of John Charles Thomas and the other, plain designs and lettering.

911 Gypsy Lady (Broadway, 1946). Billy Gilbert, Helena Bliss.

Keepsakes [B&W] / My Treasure [B&W] / Springtide [B&W] — Robert Wright[w] & George Forrest[w] & Victor Herbert[m] *(Witmark)*. An old fashioned operetta set to Herbert melodies and given a lavish production but failing. COVER: plain lettering.

912 Hair (Broadway, 1967). Diane Keaton, Melba Moore.

Ain't Got No [VS] / Air [VS] / Aquarius / Dead End [RC] / Donna [VS] / Easy to Be Hard / Electric Blues [RC] / Exanaplanetouch [RC] / Frank Mills / Good Morning Starshine / Hair / Hair — complete voal score / I Got Life [VS] / Let the Sunshine In / Where Do I Go? — James Rado[w] & Gerome Ragni[w] & Galt MacDermott[m] *(United Artists)*; What a Piece of Work Is Man [VS] — William Shakespeare[w] & James Rado[w] & Gerome Ragni[w] & Galt MacDermott[m] *(United Artists)*. A rock musical that lasted four years. It had very little plot, some nudity, and some very good songs. Its popularity was due to the fact that it captured the spirit of the young at that time. COVER: a young man's face and wild hair-do.

913 Half a Sixpence (Broadway, 1965). Tommy Steele, Polly James.

Flash, Bang, Wallop! / Half a Sixpence / If the Rain's Got to Fall / Long

Ago / Money to Burn / The Party's on the House / She's Too Far Above Me — David Heneker^{w/m} *(Chappell)*. A British revue with Tommy Steele singing and dancing for over a year. COVER: Tommy Steele.

914 Half a Widow (Broadway, 1927). Gertrude Lang, Benny Rubin.

France Will Not Forget — Gordon Johnstone^w & Geoffrey O'Hara^m *(Remick)*; It's Great to Be a Doughboy / Longing for You / Tell Me Again — Frank Dupree^w & Shep Camp^m *(Remick)*; Under the Midsummer Moon — Harry B. Smith^w & Shep Camp^m *(Remick)*. A romance between an American soldier and a French girl. It lasted one week. COVER: a soldier and a country girl.

915 The Half Moon (Broadway, 1920). Joseph Cawthorn, Ivy Sawyer.

The Dancing Band / Days That Used to Be / Deep in Your Eyes / The Girls Along Fifth Avenue / Half Moon / Half Moon — complete vocal score / The Little Book / Serenade / What's the Matter with Women / When You Smile — William Le Baron^w & Victor Jacobi^m *(Harms)*. A dull and boring musical about the rich in Boston; it lasted six weeks. COVER: the moon.

916 Half-Past Wednesday (Off Broadway, 1962). Dom DeLuise, Sean Garrison.

Companionship / The Spinning Song / To Whit — To Whoo / You're the Sweet Beginning — Nita Jones^{w/m} & Robert Colby^{w/m} *(Sam Fox)*; Grandfather / How Lovely, How Lovely — Robert Colby^{w/m} *(Sam Fox)*. A musical based on *Rumpelstiltskin*; the musical lasted two performances. COVER: sketch of little man.

917 Hallelujah, Baby! (Broadway, 1967). Leslie Uggams, Robert Hooks.

Being Good Isn't Good Enough / Hallelujah, Baby! / I Want to Get Arrested [RC] / I Wanted to Change Him [VS] / My Own Morning / Not Mine / Now's the Time [VS] / Talking to Yourself / Ugly, Ugly, Gal [RC] / Watch My Dust [RC] / When the

Weather's Better — Betty Comden^w & Adolph Green^w & Jule Styne^w *(Stratford)*. An unusual musical covering many decades in a girl's life. It had a good score by Styne and an excellent performance by Leslie Uggams to keep it going for nine months. COVER: silhouette of girl with umbrellas and flowers.

918 Halloween (closed before Broadway, 1972). David Wayne, Dick Shawn.

Bazoom [RC] / A Strange Variation of Love [RC] — Joe Darion^w & Mitch Leigh^m *(Scott)*; In the Autumn of the Night [RC] / Love in a Barbershop [RC] — Sidney Michaels^w & Mitch Leigh^m *(Scott)*. A musical whose setting was an asylum. It ran for ten days in New Hope, Pennsylvania, and folded. COVER: none.

919 Hammerstein's Nine O'Clock Revue (Broadway, 1923). Colin Campbell, Irene Olsen.

I Wonder Why the Glow Worm Winks His Eye at Me — Oscar Hammerstein^w & Herbert Stothart^m *(Harms)*; Susannah's Squeaking Shoes — Arthur Weigall^w & Muriel Lillie^m *(Harms)*; That's the Tune — Nelson Keys^w & Graham John^w & Max Darewski^m *(Harms)*. A British revue done on the Century Roof for a few performances before folding. COVER: dancing girl with clock.

920 A Hand Is on the Gate (Broadway, 1966). James Earl Jones, Moses Gunn.

A Hand Is on the Gate [PC] — William Lee^{w/m} & Stuart Scharf^{w/m} *(Chappell)*. An evening of poetry and folk songs; the show folded after two weeks. COVER: none.

921 Hang On to the Good Times (Off Broadway, 1985). Terri Klausner, Don Scardino.

Blackberry Wine [VS] / Do Whatcha Gotta Do [VS] — Gretchen Cryer^{w/m} *(Fiddleback)*; Changing [VS] / Hang On to the Good Times [VS] / Joy [VS] / You Can Never Know My Mind [VS] — Gretchen Cryer^w & Nancy Ford^m *(Fiddleback)*. A limited run musical for the

Manhattan Theatre Club. COVER: Cryer and Ford.

922 Hans Andersen (British, 1974). Tommy Steele, Milo O'Shea.

Anywhere I Wander [B] [VS] / I'm Hans Christian Andersen [B] [VS] / The Inch Worm [B] [VS] / Jenny Kissed Me [B] / The King's New Clothes [B] / No Two People [B] [VS] / Thumbelina [B] [VS] / The Ugly Duckling [B] / Wonderful Copenhagen [B] — Frank Loesser**w/m** *(Frank)*. A stage musical based on the hit movie. It was produced for the Christmas season in London for three seasons. COVER: Tommy Steele.

923 The Happiest Girl in the World (Broadway, 1961). Cyril Ritchard, Janice Rule.

Adrift on a Star / Five Minutes of Spring / The Happiest Girl in the World / Honestly / Never Bedevil the Devil / Shall We Say Farewell — E.Y. Harburg**w** & J. Offenbach**m** *(Edlee Music)*. A dated operetta with great Harburg lyrics, lush orchestrations, and Cyril Ritchard but a flop of three months. COVER: a sexy girl holding a rose.

924 Happily Ever After (Nightclub, 1955). Stars unknown.

Just for the Bride and Groom / Southern Cross — Bob Hilliard**w** & David Mann**m** *(Morris)*. COVER: Leroy Holmes and the Ames Brothers.

925 Happy! (Broadway, 1927). Fred Santley, Madeleine Fairbanks.

Happy / Lorelei / Mad About You / Sunny Side of You / Through the Night — Earle Crooker**w** & McElbert Moore**w** & Frank Grey**m** *(Harms)*. A dull musical about a young man seeking his fortune; the musical lasted ten weeks. COVER: a tree and blossoms.

926 Happy Birthday! (Broadway, 1946). Helen Hayes, Jack Diamond.

I Haven't Got a Worry in the World — Oscar Hammerstein**w** & Richard Rodgers**m** *(Williamson)*. A long running comedy with Helen Hayes on Broadway and Miriam Hopkins on tour. COVER: one cover mentions Helen Hayes as the star; the other, a picture of Miriam Hopkins.

927 The Happy Cavalier (Irish, 1921). Fiske O'Hara.

I'm Always in Love with Someone / Let Me Remember / Little Man — George Graff**w** & Ernest Ball**m** *(Witmark)*; Laddie Buck of Mine — J. Keirn Brennan**w** & Ernest Ball**m** *(Witmark)*. COVER: Fiske O'Hara.

928 Happy Days (*see also* **Here and There**) (Broadway, 1919). Vera Bailey, Arthur Hill.

Don't You Remember Those School Days / Happy Days / I've Found the Girl I've Been Looking For / The Lily and the Rose / Love Is Wonderful / My Beautiful American Rose / My Sing Song Girl / Somewhere There's a Girl — R.H. Burnside**w** & Raymond Hubbell**m** *(Harms)*. An annual spectacle at the Hippodrome featuring vaudeville and production numbers. It was done later in Atlantic City as *Here and There*. COVER: the Hippodrome theatre.

929 Happy Days (closed before Broadway, 1928). Stars unknown.

Let's Pretend / Listen and Your Heart Will Tell You / Tampa / When the Girlie You Love, Loves You — Walter Craig**w** & Leo Flanders**m** *(Sherman Clay)*. This musical closed in San Francisco. COVER: two smiling clowns.

930 Happy End (Broadway, 1977). Meryl Streep, Liz Sheridan.

Bilbao Song — Bert Brecht**w** & Kurt Weill**m** *(Universal)*. A sort of "Guys and Dolls" musical set in Berlin in 1929. This update lasted two months. COVER: black and white with titles.

931 Happy Go Lucky (Broadway, 1926). Taylor Holmes, Jack Squire.

Choose Your Flowers / Happy Melody / How Are You Lady Love / Love Thoughts / Sing a Little Song — Gwynne Denni**w** & Lucien Denni**m** *(Harms)*; When I Make a Million for You — Helene Evans**w** & Lucien Denni**m** *(Harms)*. A musical with a Scrooge-like theme. It lasted two months. COVER: titles and designs.

932 Happy Hunting (Broadway, 1956). Ethel Merman, Fernando Lamas.

The Game of Love / Gee, But It's Good to Be Here / If'n / I'm a Funny Dame / Mr. Livingstone / Mutual Admiration Society / A New-Fangled Tango / She's Just Another Girl / This Is What I Call Love / This Much I Know — Matt Dubey[w] & Harold Karr[m] *(Chappell)*. A musical about a royal wedding; it was kept going for one year by Merman and one hit song. COVER #1: yellow cover with Merman face stating "Ethel Merman in *Happy Hunting.*" COVER #2: yellow cover with Merman face stating "Ethel Merman in *Happy Hunting* with F. Lamas."

933 The Happy Hypocrite (Off Broadway, 1968). Rosemarie Heyer, Howard Girven.

Face of Love — Tony Tanner[w] & James Bredt[m] *(Chappell)*; It's Almost Too Good to Be True — Edward Eager[w] & James Bredt[m] *(Chappell)*. A musical, with an English setting, which lasted two weeks. COVER: sketch of man and woman.

934 The Happy Time (Broadway, 1967). Robert Goulet, David Wayne.

Among My Yesterdays / A Certain Girl / The Happy Time / I Don't Remember You / The Life of the Party / Please Stay [VS] / St. Pierre [VS] / Seeing Things / Tomorrow Morning / Without Me — Fred Ebb[w] & John Kander[m] *(Valando)*. A musical about a boy growing up. This was a poor overblown production that lasted nine months. COVER: two boys with cameras.

935 Hard Job Being God (Broadway, 1972). John Twomey, Tom Martel.

A Psalm of Peace — Tom Martel[w/m] *(Black Mtn. Music)*. A rock musical with a religious theme that lasted for one week. COVER: a bearded man.

936 Hard to Be a Jew (Off Broadway, 1973). Joseph Buloff, David Carey.

Hard to Be a Jew — vocal selections (12 songs) — Yitzchok Perlov[w] & Sholom Secunda[m] *(Ethnic)*. A musical about the harsh life in Russia. It ran for five months. COVER: musical notes.

937 Harlem Hotcha (Nightclub, 1932). Don Redman.

Aintcha Got Music / Harlem Hotcha / I Was So Weak, Love Was So Strong / My Headache / Stop That Dog / Summer Was Made for Lovers / Yours All Yours — Andy Razaf[w] & James Johnson[m] *(Handy)*. A revue at Connie's Inn in Harlem. COVER: dancer with fancy headdress.

938 Harlem Swingcopations at the Plantation Club (Nightclub, 1938). Barrington Guy.

Embrace Me / I Hit the Lucky Number / I Wonder Where My Right Gal's Gone / I'm a High Yella / The Slap Happy — Donald Heywood[w/m] *(Mills)*. COVER: designs and lettering.

939 Harry Carroll's Revue (at the Hollywood Music Box) (Nightclub, 1929). Dottie Wilson.

Blue Step / The Carroll-ina / Japanese Toyland / Out of a Clear Blue Sky / What Do I Care — Raymond Klages[w/m] & Jesse Greer[w/m] & Harry Carroll[w/m] *(Shapiro, Bernstein)*; Hayfoot-Strawfoot Charleston — Ballard MacDonald[w/m] & Harry Carroll[w/m] & Arthur Freed[w/m] *(Sherman Clay)*. COVER: Harry Carroll, Dottie Wilson.

940 Harry Delmar's Revels (Broadway, 1927). Frank Fay, Bert Lahr.

Four Walls — Al Jolson[w/m] & Billy Rose[w/m] & Dave Dreyer[w/m] *(Berlin)*; I Can't Give You Anything But Love — Dorothy Fields[w] & Jimmy McHugh[m] *(Mills)*; I Love a Man in Uniform / Irresistible You / Say It with a Solitaire — Billy Rose[w] & Ballard MacDonald[w] & Jimmie Monaco[m] *(Remick)*; If You Have Troubles Laugh Them Away — Lester Lee[w/m] *(Remick)*; Jig-a-Boo Jig — Billy Rose[w] & Ballard MacDonald[w] & Lester Lee[m] *(Remick)*; My Rainbow — Lester Lee[w/m] & Jeanne Hackett[w/m] *(Remick)*. A revue loaded with comedic talent; the revue lasted 14 weeks. COVER: Frank Fay; face with chorus girls.

941 Harvey (Broadway, 1946). Frank Fay, Josephine Hull.

Harvey! (the rabbit) — Rex Terrell[w]

& J. Russel Robinson[m] *(Producers)*. One of the longest running comedies on Broadway. Joe E. Brown toured with it for several years. COVER: Joe E. Brown and Harvey.

942 Harvey's Greater Minstrels (Regional, 1922). Leland Goldman, R.M. Harvey.

If You Gamble in the Game of Love — Leland Goldman[w/m] *(Harvey's Minstrels)*; My Little Black Lamb — Paul Dunbar[w] & Whitney Viney[m] *(Harvey's Minstrels)*. A minstrel show that toured the Midwest. COVER: Goldman and Harvey.

943 Hassard Short's Ritz Revue (Broadway, 1924). Charlotte Greenwood, Raymond Hitchcock.

Midsummer Night's Dream / Our Crystal Wedding Day / Sun Girl — Anne Caldwell[w] & Frank Tours[m] *(Harms)*; Springtime — Kenneth Webb[w/m] & Roy Webb[w/m] *(Harms)*; Ukin the Uke — Franke Harling[w/m] *(Harms)*; When You and I Were Dancing — Graham John[w] & H.M. Tennent[m] *(Harms)*. A lavish and beautiful production with the great comedy of Charlotte Greenwood. COVER: naked dancer with huge beautiful net done in black and gold.

944 Hats Off to Ice (Ice Show, 1944). Carol Lynne, Jimmy Sisk.

Headin' West / Isle of the Midnight Rainbow — Jimmy Littlefield[w] & Johnny Fortis[m] *(Marks)*; With Ev'ry Star / You've Got What It Takes — Jimmy Littlefield[w/m] *(Marks)*. A lavish ice show at the Center Theatre that ran for two years. COVER: top hat and ice skater.

945 Havana (Broadway, 1928). Stars unknown.

Under Your Skies of Blue — Ev Lyn[w/m] & Alfred Bryan[w/m] & Ted Snyder[w/m] *(Berlin)*. A mini stageshow from Paramount-Publix performed between movies at large theatres. COVER: a Spanish dancer.

946 Having Wonderful Time (Broadway, 1937). John Garfield, Katherine Locke.

Having Wonderful Time — Bill Livingston[w/m] *(Paull-Pioneer)*. A minor hit of romance in a summer camp. COVER: Garfield and Locke.

947 Hayfoot Strawfoot (*see also* **Gentlemen Unafraid**) (closed before Broadway, 1942). Stars unknown.

Abe Lincoln Had Just One — A Country — Oscar Hammerstein[w] & Otto Harbach[w] & Jerome Kern[m] *(Harms)*; When a New Star — Otto Harbach[w] & Jerome Kern[m] *(Harms)*. *Gentlemen Unafraid* was a musical which folded in St. Louis. It was revised in 1942 as *Hayfoot Strawfoot* but never went anywhere. COVER: lady in gown with two soldiers.

948 Hayseed (*see also* **Our Nell**) (Broadway, 1922). Mr. and Mrs. James Barry.

By and By / Walking Home with Angeline — Brian Hooker[w] & George Gershwin[m] *(Harms)*; Innocent Ingenue Baby — Brian Hooker[w] & William Daly[m] & George Gershwin[m] *(Harms)*; Old New England Home — Brian Hooker[w] & William Daly[m] *(Harms)*. A terrible melodrama musical that lasted five weeks. It opened on Broadway as *Our Nell*. COVER: lettering and designs.

949 Hazel Flagg (Broadway, 1953). Helen Gallagher, Jack Whiting.

How Do You Speak to an Angel? / I Feel Like I'm Gonna Live Forever / Salomee / Think How Many People Never Find Love / You're Gonna Dance with Me, Willie — Bob Hilliard[w] & Jule Styne[m] *(Chappell)*. A musical based on the movie *Nothing Sacred* with pleasant Styne songs and Helen Gallagher but which ran for only six months. COVER: a girl and dancers.

950 He Didn't Want to Do It (Broadway, 1918). Helen Shipman, Ned Sparks.

I'm Dying to Dance with Oscar / The Song of the Trees / Song of the World / You're the Only One for Me — George Broadhurst[w] & Silvio Hein[m] *(Harms)*. A musical about fake jewels and insurance. It lasted three weeks. COVER: titles and designs.

951 Head Over Heels (Broadway, 1918). Mitzi, Joe Keno.

All the World Is Swaying / The Big Show / Funny Little Something / Head Over Heels / I Was Lonely / Mitzi's Lullaby / Moments of the Dance — Edgar Woolf[w] & Jerome Kern[m] *(Harms)*; Every Bee Has a Bud — Edgar Woolf[w] & Harold Levey[m] *(Harms)*; Head Over Heels Fox Trot / Spring — piano selections — Jerome Kern[m] *(Harms)*; Let Us Build a Little Nest — Edgar Woolf[w] & Jerome Kern[w] & Jerome Kern[m] *(Harms)*. A circus musical written for Mitzi. It had an ordinary score and book and ran for three months. COVER: Mitzi.

952 Headin' South (closed before Broadway, 1928). Mabel Elaine, June Taylor.

Hot Choc'late / Mister Mississippi — Alfred Bryan[w] & Jean Schwartz[m] *(I.C.L.A.)*; When Sweet Susie Goes Steppin' By — Whitey Kaufman[w/m] & Fred Kelly[w/m] & Irving Bibo[w/m] *(B B and L)*. COVER: banjo player and show boat.

953 Heads Up *(see also* **Me for You)** (Broadway, 1929). Ray Bolger, Victor Moore.

As Though You Were There [BW] / I Can Do Wonders with You / It Must Be Heaven / Me for You! / My Man Is on the Make / A Ship Without a Sail / Sky City / Why Do You Suppose? — Lorenz Hart[w] & Richard Rodgers[m] *(Harms)*; Daughter Grows Older — piano selections — Richard Rodgers[m] *(Harms)*; Knees — piano selections — Richard Rodgers[m] *(Harms)*. A musical about rum-running with some good songs. It ran four months. The try-out title was *Me for You*. COVER: girl and sailor in a boat.

954 Heart o' Mine *(see also* **The Hold-up Man)** (Irish, 1924). Joseph Regan.

Heart o' Mine / I Love a Wee Bit of Irish / Tinkle, Tinkle, Tinkle Bell — Fleta Brown[w] & Herbert Spencer[m] *(Marks)*; Love Will Lead the Way — Joseph Regan[w] & William Goldenburg[m] *(Marks)*; Nearest Place to Heaven — Joseph Regan[w/m] & Frank Magine[w/m] *(Marks)*. This show toured as *Heart o' Mine* and as *The Hold-up Man*. COVER: Joseph Regan.

955 Hearts Delight Follies '69 (closed before Broadway, 1969). Bobby Dimple, Darvana Payne.

American Moon — Bob Crewe[w/m] *(Saturday Music)*. COVER: the moon and an American flag.

956 Hearts of Erin (Irish, 1920). Walter Scanlon.

Daddy Dudeen / Nora / On Sweetheart Shore / There Is One Girl — Garfield Kilgour[w] & Walter Scanlan[m] *(Berlin)*; The Harp That Once Through Tara's Halls — William Jerome[w] & Walter Scanlan[m] *(Von Tilzer)*. COVER: Walter Scanlan.

957 Hearts on Parade (closed before Broadway, 1934). Stars unknown.

Haunting Me — Eddie DeLange[w] & Joe Myrow[m] *(Mills)*. COVER: Ozzie Nelson, bandleader.

958 Heaven on Earth (Broadway, 1948). David Burns, Peter Lind Hayes.

Heaven on Earth / Home / You Are So Near / You're the First Cup of Coffee — Barry Trivers[w] & Jay Gorney[m] *(Chappell)*. A cheap imitation of *Finian's Rainbow* that lasted for one week. COVER: sketch of people in carriages.

959 Heigh Ho (closed before Broadway, 1929). Stars unknown.

Breathin' Heavy / In You, All My Dreams Come True / Lookin' Hot and Keepin' Cool / Lovable Rogue / Love Me — Love My Dog / The Nonchalant / Some Little Girl / You're My Little Theme Song — Dolph Singer[w] & Harry Von Tilzer[m] *(Feist)*. COVER: chorus girls and musicians.

960 The Heiress (Regional, 1961). Julie Harris, Farley Granger.

The Heiress Theme — Robert Corbert[m] *(Marks)*. A touring production of this old hit play. COVER: Julie Harris and Farley Granger.

961 Helen Goes to Troy (Broadway, 1944). Jarmila Novotna, Ernest Truex.

If Helen Only Knew It / The Judgement of Paris / Love at Last / What Will the Future Say — Herbert Baker[w] & Jacques Offenbach[m] *(Chappell)*. A musical comedy adaptation of this operetta with an opera star and a run of three months. COVER: Helen and a horse.

962 Helen of Troy New York (Broadway, 1923). Helen Ford, Queenie Smith.

Cry Baby / Helen of Troy New York / I Like a Big Town, I Like a Small Town / It Was Meant to Be / Little Bit of Jazz / Look for the Happy Ending / My Ideal / Nijigo Novgo / We Must Be Up on Our Toes / What Makes a Business Man Tired / What the Girls Will Wear — Bert Kalmar[w/m] & Harry Ruby[w/m] *(Berlin)*; Keep a Goin' — Byron Gay[w/m] *(Richmond-Robbins)*; Moonlight Lane — Lorenz Hart[w] & Franke Harling[m] *(Berlin)*. Kalmar and Ruby's first Broadway score which was a moderate hit for six months. COVER: a well-dressed Helen.

963 Hello Alexander (Broadway, 1919). Lou Clayton, Gilda Gray.

Cleopatra / Give Me the South All the Time / June My Honeymoon Girl / Mississippi Lullaby / My Chocolate Soldier Sammy / On the Road to Calais / Pretty Up, Pretty Up, Pretty Baby / Shimmying Everywhere / Those Dixie Melodies / Two Lips to Georgia / When Those Mason Dixon Minstrels Hit Town / You're Living Right Next Door to Heaven — Alfred Bryan[w] & Jean Schwartz[m] *(Remick)*; My Isle of Golden Dreams — Gus Kahn[w] & Walter Blaufuss[m] *(Remick)*; That Naughty Waltz — Edwin Stanley[w] & Sol Levy[m] *(Forster)*; Why Are Chickens So High? — Carey Morgan[w/m] *(Remick)*; Why Do They Call 'em Wild Women? — Billy Frisch[w/m] *(Remick)*. A musical which in reality was a big vaudeville show that lasted seven weeks. COVER: titles and designs; Sophie Tucker.

964 Hello America (closed before Broadway, 1918). Sam Lewis, Kitty Glasco.

Follow Me / I'm Lonesome Dear for You / That Broadway Rag / Your Mammy's Goin' to Kiss Your Tears Away — Will Smith[w] & Nat Osborne[m] *(Shapiro, Bernstein)*. COVER: marching soldiers and Kitty Glasco.

965 Hello Beautiful at the International Casino) (Nightclub, 1939). Harry Richman.

To You — Benny Davis[w/m] & Tommy Dorsey[w/m] & Ted Shapiro[w/m] *(Paramount)*. COVER: Harry Richman.

966 Hello Charley (Jewish, 1965). Jacob Jacobs, Miriam Kressyn.

Let's Speak Yiddish — Jacob Jacobs[w] & Maurice Rauch[m] *(Mills)*. COVER: a straw hat, a cane, and a flower.

967 Hello Daddy (Broadway, 1928). Constance Carpenter, Lew Fields.

As Long as You Are in Love / Futuristic Rhythm / In a Great Big Way / Let's Sit and Talk About You / Out Where the Blues Begin / Your Disposition Is Mine — Dorothy Fields[w] & Jimmy McHugh[m] *(Mills)*. A musical about fatherhood and child support with a pleasant score and a six month run. COVER: title and designs.

968 Hello Dolly! (Broadway, 1964). Carol Channing, David Burns.

Before the Parade Passes By — Jerry Herman[w/m] & Charles Strouse[w/m] & Lee Adams[w/m] *(Morris)*; Dancing / Hello Dolly! / I Put My Hand In [VS] / It Only Takes a Moment / It Takes a Woman [VS] / Put On Your Sunday Clothes / Ribbons Down My Back / So Long, Dearie — Jerry Herman[w/m] *(Morris)*; Elegance [VS] / Motherhood March [VS] — Bob Merrill[w/m] *(Morris)*; Hello Dolly! — complete score — Jerry Herman[w/m] & Bob Merrill[w/m] & Charles Strouse[w/m] & Lee Adams[w/m] *(Morris)*. One of Broadway's longest running musicals with good songs, comedy, and dances. It did have trouble in its out-of-town tour and required the help of several other top composers. It ran for seven years with the help of Betty Grable, Ginger Rogers, Dorothy Lamour, Martha Raye, and others. COVER: a girl, a heart, and a bow and arrow.

969 Hello Dolly! (British, 1965). Mary Martin, Loring Smith.

Hello Dolly! / It Only Takes a Moment / It Takes a Woman / Ribbons Down My Back / So Long Dearie — Jerry Herman$^{w/m}$ *(Morris)*. A smash hit in London with a run of one year. Mary Martin was the star. COVER: titles and designs.

970 Hello Dolly! (Broadway, 1968). Pearl Bailey, Cab Calloway.

Hello Dolly! — Jerry Herman$^{w/m}$ *(Morris)*. David Merrick was a shrewd promoter and installed a black cast to keep this show running. COVER: Pearl Bailey and Cab Calloway.

971 Hello Dolly! (Broadway, 1970). Ethel Merman, Jack Goode.

Love, Look in My Window / World, Take Me Back — Jerry Herman$^{w/m}$ *(Morris)*. *Hello Dolly* was written with Ethel Merman in mind. She finally made it in this version and with two new songs. COVER: titles and designs.

972 Hello Everybody (closed before Broadway, 1923). Gertrude Hoffman, Harry Lauder.

I Want to Step / Japanese Willow / Red Riding Hood on Broadway — Fred Coots$^{w/m}$ & McElbert Moore$^{w/m}$ *(Harms)*. COVER: titles and designs.

973 Hello Lola (Broadway, 1926). Jay Flippen, Elisha Cook.

In the Dark / My Baby Talk Lady / Swinging on the Gate — Dorothy Donnelly^w & William Kernell^m *(Harms)*. A musical version of *Seventeen* that lasted six weeks. COVER: a tree and blossoms.

974 Hello Molly (Jewish, 1920). Molly Picon, Rose Greenfield.

My Mama — Molly Picon^w & Joseph Rumshinsky^m *(Lipshitz)*. COVER: Molly Picon and Rose Greenfield.

975 Hello Paris (*see also* **So This Is Paris**) (Broadway, 1930). Polly Walker, Chic Sale.

Every Bit of You / I Stumbled Over You / I'll Admit — Charles Locke^w & Russell Tarbox^m *(Harms)*. A newly rich oil man goes to Paris, where he stays only four weeks. The try-out title

was *So This Is Paris*. COVER: man with suitcase dreaming of Paris.

976 Hello Yourself (Broadway, 1928). Fred Waring, Lucy Monroe.

He-Man / I Want the World to Know / Say That You Love Me / True Blue / You've Got a Way with You — Leo Robin^w & Richard Myers^m *(Harms)*. Another college musical that ran eleven weeks. It was helped only by Fred Waring and the band. COVER: a waving flag.

977 Hellzapoppin (1938 edition) (Broadway, 1938). Olsen and Johnson.

The Cockeyed Mayor of Kaunakakai — Alex Anderson^w & Al Silverman^w & Alex Anderson^m *(Marks)*; Fuddle-Dee-Duddle / It's Time to Say "Aloha" — Charlie Tobias^w & Sammy Fain^m *(Crawford)*; Hellzapoppin — Don George$^{w/m}$ & Teddy Hall$^{w/m}$ *(Crawford)*; No Wonder [BW] — Buddy Bernier$^{w/m}$ & Bob Emmerich$^{w/m}$ *(Crawford)*; When You Look in Your Looking Glass — Sam Lewis^w & Paul Mann^m & Stephan Weiss^m *(Crawford)*. The first edition of a crazy vaudeville entertainment that ran for years. COVER: fireworks, clouds, and lightning.

978 Hellzapoppin (1940 edition) (Broadway, 1940). Olsen and Johnson.

Blow a Balloon Up to the Moon / When McGregor Sings Off Key — Charlie Tobias^w & Sammy Fain^m *(Crawford)*; Boomps-a-daisy — Annette Mills$^{w/m}$ *(D B and H)*; Oh! Gee, Oh! Gosh, Oh! Golly, I'm in Love — Olsen and Johnson^w & Ernest Breuer^m *(Mills)*; We Won't Let It Happen Here — Don George$^{w/m}$ & Teddy Hall$^{w/m}$ *(Crawford)*. COVER: fireworks, clouds, and lightning.

979 Hellzapoppin (1941 edition) (Broadway, 1941). Olsen and Johnson.

Bounce / G'bye Now / Mary Goes Round / My Heart's in America / Window Wiper Song — Olsen and Johnson$^{w/m}$ & Jay (Levison) Livingston$^{w/m}$ & Ray Evans$^{w/m}$ *(BMI)*. The 1941 edition is interesting because it featured songs by two men who were to become two of the biggest Hollywood song-writers. COVER: Olsen and Johnson.

980 Hellzapoppin (1943 edition) (Broadway, 1943). Olsen and Johnson.

Hellzapoppin Polka [PC] — Olsen and Johnson[w/m] & Jay (Levison) Livingston[w/m] & Ray Evans[w/m] *(Peer)*. This was the last edition directly connected with Olsen and Johnson. COVER: none.

981 Hellzapoppin (1967 edition) (closed before Broadway, 1967). Soupy Sales.

Hellzapoppin [RC] / Sunshine [RC] / You Make It All Worthwhile [RC] — Marian Grudeff[w/m] & Raymond Jessel[w/m] *(Sunbeam)*. This version was performed at the Expo '67 in Montreal with the hope of coming to Broadway. COVER: none.

982 Hellzapoppin (1976 edition) (closed before Broadway, 1976). Jerry Lewis, Lynn Redgrave.

Bouncing Back for More [RC] — Carolyn Leigh[w] & Cy Coleman[m] *(Morris)*. This edition was an attempt by Alexander Cohen to revive the old hit but it failed. After touring several cities and having many problems, it folded in Boston. Cohen blamed the failure on his difficulties in dealing with Lewis, but nothing would have helped this show. COVER: none.

983 Help, Help, the Globolinks! (Opera, 1969). Judith Blegen, Richard Best.

Help, Help, the Globolinks! — complete vocal score — Gian Carlo Menotti[w/m] *(Schirmer)*. A show for children performed at the City Center along with *Amahl*. COVER: lettering and designs.

984 Henry, Sweet Henry (Broadway, 1967). Don Ameche, Carol Bruce.

Dearest Darling [PC] / Do You Ever Go to Boston? / Henry, Sweet Henry / Here I Am / I Wonder How It Is to Dance with a Boy / Love of My Life [PC] / My Kind of Person [PC] / Somebody, Someplace [PC] / Weary Near to Dyin' / You Might Get to Like Me [PC] — Bob Merrill[w/m] *(Merrill)*. An

interesting musical but it failed because of its book. It had some good Merrill songs and a couple of wonderful kids. COVER: colored balloons.

985 Her Family Tree (Broadway, 1920). Nora Bayes, Donald Sawyer.

As We Sow, So Shall We Reap / The Gold Diggers / I Love You / In the Land Where Tomorrows Begin / Love Has Come to Me / No Other Girl / Ouija Board / When Cupid Flies Away / Why Worry — Seymour Simons[w/m] *(Remick)*; Remember the Rose — Sidney Mitchell[w] & Seymour Simons[m] *(Remick)*. A dull musical which ran three months about a ouija board game at a party. COVER: silhouette of a lady's head and a tree.

986 Her First Roman (Broadway, 1968). Richard Kiley, Leslie Uggams.

Her First Roman / I Fell In with Evil Companions / In Vino Veritas / Just for Today / Let Me Lead the Way / Rome / The Things We Think We Are / When My Back Is to the Wall / The Wrong Man — Ervin Drake[w/m] *(W-7 Music)*. This musical version of *Caesar and Cleopatra* lasted two weeks. COVER: Caesar and Cleopatra.

987 Her Great Secret (Jewish, 1940). Jennie Goldstine, Simon Wolf.

Ich Bin a Mame — Jennie Goldstein[w] & J. Jaffe[m] *(Trio)*. COVER: Jennie Goldstein.

988 Her Master's Voice (Broadway, 1933). Roland Young, Laura Hope Crews.

Only with You — Clare Kummer[w/m] *(Harms)*. A comedy hit that ran six months. COVER: Roland Young and girl.

989 Here and There (see also Happy Days) (Regional, 1919). Stars unknown.

Don't You Remember Those School Days / My Sing Song Girl / Somewhere There's Some Girl — R.H. Burnside[w] & Raymond Hubbell[m] *(Harms)*. A revised edition of the Hippodrome spectacle *Happy Days* which was presented at the "Auditorium" in Atlantic City. COVER: the ocean, the sun, and a sea gull.

990 Here Comes the Bride (British,

1930). Clifford Mollison, Edmund Gwenn.

High and Low [B] / I'm Like a Sailor [B] — Howard Dietz^w & Desmond Carter^w & Arthur Schwartz^m *(Chappell)*; Hot [B] — Desmond Carter^w & Lew Levinson^w & Arthur Schwartz^m *(Chappell)*; I Love You and I Like You [B] — Max Lief^w & Nathaniel Lief^w & Arthur Schwartz^m *(Chappell)*; I'll Always Remember [B] — Max Lief^w & Nathaniel Lief^w & Desmond Carter^w & Arthur Schwartz^m *(Chappell)*; Rose in Your Hair [B] — Desmond Carter^w & Arthur Schwartz^m *(Chappell)*. A comedy with songs with a run of five months in London. This was Arthur Schwartz's first big show. Cover: bride with two cupids.

991 Here Goes the Bride (Broadway, 1931). Clark and McCullough.

Hello! My Lover, Good-bye / It's My Nature / My Bathing Suit / My Sweetheart 'Tis of Thee / Ohhh! Ahhh! / One Second of Sex / Shake Well Before Using / We Know Reno / Well, You See — Oh You Know / What's the Difference — Oh You Know — Edward Heyman^w & John Green^m *(Famous)*; It Means So Little to You / Music in My Fingers / Remarkable People We — Edward Heyman^w & Richard Myers^m *(Famous)*. A musical in the tradition of *La ronde* which lasted for seven performances. Cover: a couple embracing before an annoyed bride.

992 Here's Howe! (Broadway, 1928). Ben Bernie, William Frawley.

Crazy Rhythm / Imagination / Life as a Twosome / On My Mind a New Love — Irving Caesar^w & Joseph Meyer^m & Roger Kahn^m *(Harms)*. A rags-to-riches-to-rags story with one hit song, *Crazy Rhythm*, and a run of only six weeks. Cover: champagne and balloons.

993 Here's Love (Broadway, 1963). Janis Page, Craig Stevens.

Arm in Arm / The Big Clown Balloons / Dear Mister Santa Claus / Expect Things to Happen / Here's Love / It's Beginning to Look Like Christmas / Love, Come Take Me Again / My State, My Kansas, My Home / My Wish / Pine Cones and Holly Berries / That Man Over There / You Don't Know — Meredith Willson^{w/m} *(Frank)*. This production was *The Miracle on 34th Street* as a musical with a few good songs but nothing else. It ran nine months. Cover: hearts and circles.

994 Here's Where I Belong (Broadway, 1968). Paul Rogers, Nancy Wickwire.

Here Is Where I Belong / No Time Is a Good Good-bye Time / Pulverize the Kaiser [RC] / Soft Is the Sparrow / Waking-Up Sun / We're a Home — Alfred Uhry^w & Robert Waldman^m *(United Artists)*. A musical, based on *East of Eden,* that lasted one performance. Cover: silhouette of boy and girl.

995 Hey Nonny-Nonny! (Broadway, 1932). Frank Morgan, Ann Seymour.

Be a Little Lackadaisical / Let's Go Lovin' / Wouldn't That Be Wonderful — Herman Hupfeld^{w/m} *(Harms)*; For Better or Worse / The Season Ended / Tell Me Something About Yourself — Max Lief^w & Nathaniel Lief^w & Michael Cleary^m *(Harms)*. An off-color musical with a burlesque theme. It ran two weeks. Cover: sketches and lettering.

996 Hey Rookie (Military, 1942). "The Yard Birds."

I Met a Wac / It's a Helluva, Swelluva, Helluva, Life in the Army / It's Great to Be in a Uniform / Take a Chance / There Goes Taps — J.C. Lewis^{w/m} *(Lewcon)*. An Army musical revue which toured bases on the West Coast. Cover: sketch of rookie.

997 Hi Diddle Diddle (British, 1934). Douglas Byng.

Miss Otis Regrets... — Cole Porter^{w/m} *(Harms)*. A campy song by Cole Porter which was used in this revue. Cover: a lady with a dazed look.

998 Hi-There! (closed before Broadway, 1930). Stars unknown.

Do That Hallelujah [ABQ] / I Wish We Were the Siamese Twins [ABQ] / Lullaby in Blues [ABQ] / Say When [ABQ] / That Mr. Brown [ABQ] / Um Pucca Vampucca [ABQ] / Wake Up Sally [ABQ] / Why Worry [ABQ] — authors unknown *(Feist)*; Dream Music — Hamilton Breeze^w & Griff Williams^m *(Feist)*; No One But the Right Man — Max Lief^w & Nathaniel Lief^w & Ralph Rainger^m *(Feist)*; Once in a Million Years — Greg Williamson^w & Jack Wiggin^m *(Feist)*. COVER: musicians, actors, and audience.

999 Hi Ya Gentlemen (closed before Broadway, 1940). Stars unknown.

I Heard You Were Lovely [VS] / Never a Dull Moment [VS] — Harold Adamson^w & Johnny Green^m *(Chappell)*. These two songs are from an unproduced musical. COVER: Johnny Green.

1000 Hi, Yank! (Military, 1944). David Brooks, Joshua Shelley.

Classification Blues [VS] / Little Red Rooftops [VS] / The Most Important Job [VS] / Yank, Yank, Yank [VS] — Frank Loesser^w/m *(Army Script)*; My Gal and I [VS] — Jack Hill^w & Frank Loesser^m *(Army Script)*; Saga of a Sad Sack [VS] — Hy Zaret^w & Frank Loesser^m *(Army Script)*. An Army show that toured the camps. COVER: lettering.

1001 High and Dry (*see also* **It's Up to You**) (Broadway, 1921). Charles King, Betty Pierce.

The Boy Who Bangs the Drum / I'll Always Believe You / I'll Tell the World — E.A. Paulton^w & John McManus^m *(Witmark)*; Dear Ouija — E.A. Paulton^w & Mason Wright^w & John McManus^m *(Witmark)*; Everytime I See You Dear / I Want a Home / I Wish You Would Leave Me Alone / Love Me with Your Lips / Someone Console Me / We Hate to Go In When It Rains — E.A. Paulton^w & Manuel Klein^m *(Witmark)*. A poor rags-to-riches musical that lasted three weeks. This show tried out as *High and Dry,* and after revisions it opened on Broad-

way as *It's Up to You.* COVER: girl with fishing pole and suitors.

1002 High Button Shoes (Broadway, 1947). Phil Silvers, Nanette Fabray.

Can't You Just See Yourself / Get Away for a Day / I Still Get Jealous / On a Sunday by the Sea / Papa, Won't You Dance with Me? / There's Nothing Like a Model "T" / You're My Girl — Sammy Cahn^w & Jule Styne^m *(Morris)*. A conman in a small town was the basis for this smash musical which ran two years. It had a good score, a marvellous ballet, and a great cast. COVER: trolleys, carriages, and other characters.

1003 High Hat (Broadway, 1928). Stars unknown.

Sally's Coming Home — Cliff Hess^w/m & Joseph Santley^w/m *(Famous)*. A Paramount-Publix stage show presented in between motion pictures in large cities. COVER: well dressed lady with trunk.

1004 High Kickers (Broadway, 1941). Sophie Tucker, George Jessel.

Cigarettes / I've Got Somethin' / Panic in Panama / The Time to Sing / Waltzing in the Moonlight / You're on My Mind — Bert Kalmar^w & Harry Ruby^m *(Harms)*. Burlesque and vaudeville were the subjects of this musical. It was the last Broadway score of Kalmar and Ruby's. The material was poor but Jessel and Tucker kept it going for five months. COVER: a high kicking girl.

1005 High-Lo (closed before Broadway, 1928). Stars unknown.

Dancing on the Green / Hudson River / Let's Sing a Love Song / Love Is a Terrible Thing / Lunching with Venus / Spotlight in the Sky / Where the Sky Meets the Ocean — Henry Myers^w & Henry Sullivan^m *(Marks)*. This musical was billed as a "snappy musical revue de luxe." COVER: a girl with jewels, furs, and a rose.

1006 High Spirits (Broadway, 1964). Beatrice Lillie, Tammy Grimes.

Faster Than Sound [PC] / Forever

and a Day / I Know Your Heart / If I Gave You / Something Tells Me / Was She Prettier Than I? / You'd Better Love Me — Hugh Martin^{w/m} & Timothy Gray^{w/m} *(Cromwell).* Noel Coward's *Blithe Spirit* as a musical with Bea Lillie as the dizzy spiritualist. It was very funny and ran for almost a year. COVER: Bea Lillie on a bike.

1007 Higher and Higher (Broadway, 1940). Jack Haley, Shirley Ross.

Disgustingly Rich [VS] / Ev'ry Sunday Afternoon / From Another World / It Never Entered My Mind / It's a Lovely Day for a Murder [VS] / Nothing But You — Lorenz Hart^w & Richard Rodgers^m *(Chappell).* A musical about servants in a mansion and their problems. It was a failure of three months. COVER: sketch of people stepping out.

1008 Himberama (Broadway, 1953). Ray Middleton, Richard Himber.

Love Is Not for Children — Richard Himber^{w/m} *(Chappell).* A one performance revue at Carnegie Hall. COVER: designs and lettering.

1009 Hip Hip Hooray (1920 edition) (Broadway, 1920). Helen McClain.

Love Is a Beautiful Dream — Charles Horwitz^w & Perrin Somers^m *(Somers).* A new touring edition of the 1915 *Hippodrome* revue. COVER: Helen McClain.

1010 Hippodrome (Broadway, 1923). Dorothy Jardon, Paul Nolan.

Down at the Hippodrome — Cliff Friend^w & Walter Donaldson^m *(Berlin).* A theme song for the *Hippodrome* which consisted of a special program of vaudeville. COVER: four girls as clowns, dancers, and musicians.

1011 His and Hers (Broadway, 1953). Celeste Holm, Robert Preston.

His and Hers — Ruth Aarons^w & Albert Selden^m *(Templeton).* A romantic comedy with a moderate run. COVER: Holm and Preston.

1012 History Loves Company (closed before Broadway, 1991). Stars unknown.

New Words — Maury Yeston^{w/m} *(Cherry Lane).* COVER: sketch of historical characters.

1013 Hit the Deck (Broadway, 1927). Charles King, Louise Groody.

An Armful of You / Hallelujah! / The Harbor of My Heart / Join the Navy! / Loo-Loo / Lucky Bird / Nothing Could Be Sweeter / Why, Oh, Why? — Leo Robin^w & Clifford Grey^w & Vincent Youmans^m *(Harms);* Opening of Act II — piano selections — Vincent Youmans^m *(Harms);* Sometimes I'm Happy — Irving Caesar^w & Vincent Youmans^m *(Harms).* This musical about a girl and a sailor in love was a hit and ran for almost a year. It contained some great dancing and some of Youman's best songs. COVER: lettering and designs.

1014 Hitchy Koo of 1918 (Broadway, 1918). Irene Bordoni, Leon Errol.

Christmas Tide / It Took 1,918 Years to Make a Beautiful Girl Like You / Rag Doll / Stop, You're Camouflaging with Me / They'll Be Whistling It All Over Town — Ray Goetz^w & Jean Schwartz^m *(Witmark);* Come Dance with Me / Here Come the Yanks with Tanks / How Can You Tell? / Underneath a Parasol — Ned Wayburn^w & Harold Orlob^m *(Feist);* It'll All End with the Right End Up — Henry Marshall^{w/m} *(Witmark);* Jazz-Mu-Tazz — Ned Wayburn^{w/m} *(Feist);* Oh, What a Beautiful Baby / Twilight Night — Stanley Murphy^w & Harry Tierney^m *(Remick);* San Sebastian's Shores — Harry Carroll^{w/m} *(Remick);* Say Hitchy Koo, That's All — S.D. Mitchell^w & Willy White^m *(Witmark);* Where Do They Come From — Fred Herendeen^w & Harold Orlob^m *(Feist);* You-OO — Just You — Irving Caesar^w & George Gershwin^m *(Remick).* An ordinary revue that ran for only nine weeks. COVER: lettering and designs; Raymond Hitchcock.

1015 Hitchy Koo of 1919 (Broadway, 1919). Raymond Hitchcock, Joe Cook.

Another Sentimental Song / Bring Back My Butterfly / I Introduced / In Hitchy's Garden / I've Got Somebody Waiting / My Cozy Little Corner in the Ritz / Old Fashioned Garden / Peter

Piper — The Sea Is Calling / That Black and White Baby of Mine / When I Had a Uniform On — Cole Porter^{w/m} *(Harms)*. Another edition of Hitchcock's revue with nothing special except Porter's "Old Fashioned Garden." COVER: Raymond Hitchcock and sketch of girl on large bird.

1016 Hitchy Koo of 1920 (Broadway, 1920). Raymond Hitchcock, Julia Sanderson.

Bring 'em Back / Buggy Riding / Chick! Chick! Chick! / Cupid, the Winner / Ding Dong, It's Kissing Time / Girls in the Sea / Moon of Love / The Old Town / The Star of Hitchy-Koo / Sweetie — Anne Caldwell^w & Jerome Kern^m *(Harms)*; Congo Nights — Rubey Cowan^w & Violinsky^m *(Stark, Cowan)*. A two month run for a dull revue with a drab score. COVER: colored flowers.

1017 Hitchy Koo of 1922 (closed before Broadway, 1922). Jack Pearl, Raymond Hitchcock.

The American Punch / The Bandit Band / The Harbor Deep Down in My Heart / Love Letter Words / When My Caravan Comes Home — Cole Porter^{w/m} *(Harms)*. This edition of *Hitchy Koo* was so poor it folded in Philadelphia. COVER: colored flowers.

1018 Hitchy Koo of 1923 (closed before Broadway, 1923). Raymond Hitchcock.

Do You Love As I Love? — Irving Caesar^w & Joseph Meyer^m & Lewis Gensler^m *(Harms)*; Isle of Sweethearts — Irving Caesar^w & Maurice Yvain^m *(Harms)*; Lullaby Lane / Romeo — Irving Caesar^w & Lewis Gensler^m *(Harms)*; Tom Tom — Oscar Hammerstein^w & Lewis Gensler^m *(Harms)*. COVER: Raymond Hitchcock.

1019 Hits and Misses (closed before Broadway, 1929). Stars unknown.

Down by the Sea — Tys Terwey^{w/m} *(Huntzinger)*; My Little Honey — Mary Landis Holden^{w/m} *(Huntzinger)*. COVER: lettering and designs.

1020 Hobokenes (Regional, 1929). Stars unknown.

I Don't Work for a Living — Edward Lee^{w/m} & James Mullan^{w/m} *(Shapiro, Bernstein)*. Theme song of a local revue presented by Will Morrisey in Hoboken. COVER: a hobo.

1021 Hold Everything (Broadway, 1928). Betty Compton, Bert Lahr.

Don't Hold Everything / Heel Beat / Here's One Who Wouldn't / To Know You Is to Love You / Too Good to Be True / You're My Necessity / You're the Cream in My Coffee — B.G. DeSylva^{w/m} & Lew Brown^{w/m} & Ray Henderson^{w/m} *(D B and H)*. A prizefighting musical with some great songs and an excellent performance by Bert Lahr. This was Lahr's first big smash and it ran for a year. COVER: a girl winner in a boxing ring.

1022 Hold It! (Broadway, 1948). Johnny Downs, Red Buttons.

About Face / Always You / Buck in the Bank / Down the Well / Friendly Enemy / Hold It! / It Was So Nice Having You / Nevermore / You Took Possession of Me — Sam Lerner^w & Gerald Marks^m *(Sam Fox)*. Another collegiate musical which was just pleasant and no more. It lasted six weeks. COVER: show girls with camera man and college pennants.

1023 Hold My Hand (British, 1931). Stanley Lupino, Sonnie Hale.

Hold My Hand — Maurice Elwin^{w/m} & Harry Graham^{w/m} & Noel Gay^{w/m} *(Harms)*. This song was published in the U.S. It comes from a hit musical of Stanley Lupino's in London. COVER: flowers and lettering.

1024 Hold On to Your Hats (Broadway, 1940). Al Jolson, Martha Raye.

Don't Let It Get You Down / Swing Your Calico [PC] / There's a Great Day Coming Manana / The World Is in My Arms / Would You Be So Kindly — E.Y. Harburg^w & Burton Lane^m *(Chappell)*. Jolson returned from Hollywood to play a radio cowboy in this musical. The show was a moderate hit, but after 20 weeks, Jolson returned to Hollywood, and the show folded. COVER: a cowboy and a map of New Mexico.

1025 Hold Your Horses (Broadway, 1933). Joe Cook, Harriet Hoctor.

Do You? / High Shoes / Hold Your Horses / I'd Like to Take You Home / Swapping Sweet Nothings with You — Robert Simon^{w/m} & Owen Murphy^{w/m} & Russell Bennett^{w/m} *(Harms)*; Happy Little Week-end / Peanuts and Kisses — Arthur Swanstrom^w & Louis Alter^m *(Harms)*; If I Love Again — J.P. Murray^w & Ben Oakland^m *(Harms)*; Singing to You — Ben Oakland^{w/m} & Robert Simon^{w/m} & Margot Millham^{w/m} *(Harms)*. A musical about a cab driver involved in politics. It was very dull and lasted only 11 weeks. COVER: a parade of people.

1026 The Hold-up Man (*see also* Heart o' Mine) (Irish, 1924). Joseph Regan.

Heart o' Mine / The Song of the Bandit — Fleta Brown^w & Herbert Spencer^m *(Marks)*; Land of Make Believe / Love Will Lead the Way — Joseph Regan^w & William Goldenburg^m *(Marks)*; Nearest Place to Heaven — Joseph Regan^{w/m} & Frank Magine^{w/m} *(Marks)*. This show toured as *The Hold-up Man* and as *Heart o' Mine* but never reached Broadway. COVER: Joseph Regan.

1027 Holiday on Ice of 1949 (Ice Show, 1949). Stars unknown.

It's Wintertime — Letty Barbour^w & Carmen Nappo^m *(BMI)*. COVER: a row of ice skating beauties.

1028 Holka-Polka (*see also* Nobody's Girl *and* Spring in Autumn) (Broadway, 1925). Orville Harrold, Patti Harrold.

Holka-Polka / Home of My Heart / In a Little While / Spring in Autumn / When Love Is Near — Gus Kahn^w & Ray Egan^w & Will Ortmann^m *(Harms)*. This quick flop toured the country as *Nobody's Girl* and *Spring in Autumn* before reaching Broadway as *Holka-Polka*. COVER: colored flowers.

1029 Holly Golightly (aka Breakfast at Tiffany's) (Broadway, 1966). Richard Chamberlain, Mary Tyler Moore.

Breakfast at Tiffany's [PC] / Ciao, Compare [PC] / Holly Golightly [PC] / I've Got a Penny [PC] / Travellin' [PC] / You've Never Kissed Her [PC] — Bob Merrill^{w/m} *(Treetop)*. This show opened in Philadelphia as *Holly Golightly* and previewed in New York as *Breakfast at Tiffany's*. It was terrible from the beginning and re-writes on the road by Edward Albee made it worse. It had several previews on Broadway but wisely closed before opening. COVER: none.

1030 Hollywood Follies (closed before Broadway, 1922). Stars unknown.

California Sunshine / My Dream Girl of the Screen / Show Me the Way to Your Heart / Three Musketeers of the Screen — Will Morrissey^{w/m} *(Forster)*. COVER: black and white letters.

1031 Hollywood Hilarities of 1938 (Nightclub, 1938). Stars unknown.

Glamorous Lady / Love Is International / On the Silver Sands at Waikiki / Sounds in the Night — Abner Silver^{w/m} & Dorothy Gulman^{w/m} *(Hollywood)*. COVER: chorus girl.

1032 Hollywood Holiday (closed before Broadway, 1935). Bebe Daniels, Ben Lyons.

Dream Shadows / Hollywood Holiday — Mitchell Parish^{w/m} & Haven Gillespie^{w/m} & Fred Coots^{w/m} *(Mills)*. COVER: Gallagher, Daniels, Lyons.

1033 Hollywood Music Box Revue (1927 edition) (Nightclub, 1927). Stars unknown.

African / Gates of Love / Somehow / Which Is Which and Who Is Who — Richard Coburn^w & Nacio Herb Brown^m *(Sherman Clay)*; The Doll Dance — Nacio Herb Brown^m *(Sherman Clay)*. COVER: stars and designs.

1034 Hollywood Music Box Revue (1927 Spring Edition) (Nightclub, 1927). Fanny Brice.

All Alone Monday — Bert Kalmar^w & Harry Ruby^m *(Harms)*; Hold Me in Your Arms Again — Arthur Freed^{w/m} *(Harms)*; You Smiled at Me — Bert Kalmar^{w/m} & Harry Ruby^{w/m} *(Harms)*. COVER: chorus girl with bird.

1035 Hollywood Music Box Revue (1929 edition) (Nightclub, 1929). Lupino Lane.

Dance of the Marionettes / Memories of Picardy / My Pierrot — Carlton Kelsey^{w/m} & Lupino Lane^{w/m} & Val Burton^{w/m} *(Harms)*. COVER: lettering and designs.

1036 Hollywood Music Box Revue (1934 edition) (Nightclub, 1934). Stars unknown.

Panama — Edward Lambert^{w/m} & Gerald Dolin^{w/m} *(Shapiro, Bernstein)*. COVER: Jack Denny.

1037 Hollywood Nine O'Clock Revue (Nightclub, 1931). Eddie Lambert, Al Herman.

The Day I Met You / When We're Alone — Will Jason^{w/m} & Val Burton^{w/m} *(Famous)*. COVER: a clock showing nine.

1038 Hollywood Restaurant Revels (Nightclub, 1933). Rudy Vallee, Rita White.

By a River in Spain / Dolly Dimples Holiday / Lenox Avenue — Dave Oppenheim^{w/m} & Michael Cleary^{w/m} *(Shapiro, Bernstein)*. COVER: Ethel Shutta; a group of pretty girls.

1039 Hollywood Revels of 1935 (Nightclub, 1935). Rudy Vallee.

The Lady from Broadway — Dave Oppenheim^{w/m} & Max Rich^{w/m} *(Sherman Clay)*; I'm Taking Care of Myself / Mississippi Show Boat / Music Puts Me in the Strangest Mood / Never Too Tired for Love / Out of a Clear Blue Sky / We Fell in Love While Dancing — Dave Oppenheim^w & Michael Cleary^m *(Southern)*. COVER: Rudy Vallee and chorus girls.

1040 Hollywood Revels of 1936 (Nightclub, 1936). Stars unknown.

Born to Be Bored / The International / It's a Lot of Idle Gossip / The Topic of the Tropics / When April Comes Again — Al Neiburg^{w/m} & Marty Symes^{w/m} & Jerry Levinson^{w/m} *(Mills)*; It's About Time — Al Neiburg^{w/m} & Marty Symes^{w/m} & Jerry Levinson^{w/m} *(Feist)*. COVER: a chorus girl.

1041 Hollywood Revels of 1937 (Nightclub, 1937). Harry Richman.

Kisses from My Violin to You / Vanessa — Al Bryan^w & Doris Fisher^m *(Berlin)*; Struttin' to Sutton Place — Dave Oppenheimer^{w/m} & Jacques Krakeur^{w/m} *(Popular)*. COVER: a struttin' gentleman.

1042 Hollywood Revels of Spring 1937 (Nightclub, 1937). Stars unknown.

The Pigmy Dance / Say It with Your Eyes / There's Something About the Weather / When We Met in Paris — Dave Oppenheim^{w/m} & Henry Tobias^{w/m} *(Mills)*. COVER: chorus girl and dancers.

1043 Hollywood Revue (On Broadway 1938–39) (Nightclub, 1938). Stars unknown.

The Flea Hop / Let's Go Broadway / Love, I'd Give My Life for You / Oriental Magic / Sockin' the Cymbal / Swingin' the Nursery Rhymes / We Always Get Our Man / Wiggly Walk — Dave Oppenheim^{w/m} & Jack Palmer^{w/m} & Al Jacobs^{w/m} *(Stasny)*. COVER: chorus girl and balloons.

1044 Honey Girl (*see also* **What's the Odds**) (Broadway, 1920). Lynne Overman, Edna Bates.

Close to Your Heart / I Love to Fox-Trot / I'm Losing My Heart to Someone / I'm Trying / It's a Very Simple Matter / Mytyl and Tyltyl / Racing Blues / Small Town Girl / What Do You Think of That? / You're Just the Boy for Me — Neville Fleeson^w & Albert Von Tilzer^m *(Broadway)*. A musical dealing with horse racing. It had a melodic score, a good book, and a lavish production. However, it didn't catch on and lasted only four months. It started out on the road as *What's the Odds* but arrived on Broadway as *Honey Girl*. COVER: flowers and designs.

1045 Honeydew (Broadway, 1920). Sam Ash, Dorothy Follis.

Believe Me, Beloved / The Bug Song / A Cup of Tea / Drop Me a Line / The Eyes of the Girl I Love / Marry for Wealth / Morals of a Sailor-Man /

Morning Glory / My Husband's Dearest Friend / Oh, How I Long for Someone / The Sound of Sound / Sunshine of Love / When I Led the Amazon Army / Your Second Wife — Joseph Herbert[w] & Efrem Zimbalist[m] *(Remick)*. A musical dealing with bugs and exterminators. With pleasant music by Zimbalist, it ran six months. COVER: tree branches with blossoms.

1046 Honeymoon Cruise (*see also* **The Maiden Voyage**) (closed before Broadway, 1925). Stars unknown.

A Honeymoon Cruise / Hot Patootie Land [ABQ] / I Am Angling for You [ABQ] / I Want You / Just One More Waltz with You [ABQ] / Oui! Oui! Oui! [ABQ] / Pango Moon / Persian Skies [ABQ] / Pompadour [ABQ] / Rain! Rain! Rain! / The Whole World's Doing It Now [ABQ] — Arthur Swanstrom[w] & Carey Morgan[m] *(Feist)*. This show toured as *Honeymoon Cruise* and *The Maiden Voyage* but never reached Broadway. COVER: a group of people boarding a yacht.

1047 Honeymoon House (Broadway, 1923). Jack Norworth.

If Winter Comes — Clifford Grey[w] & Melville Gideon[m] *(Feist)*. A comedy with one song. COVER: Jack Norworth.

1048 Honeymoon Lane (Broadway, 1926). Eddie Dowling, Johnny Marvin.

Chorus Pickin' Time / Gee, But I'd Like to Be Bad / Halloween / Head Over Heels in Love / The Little White House / Marching On to Hollywood / Waddya Say — We Steal Away — Eddie Dowling[w/m] & James Hanley[w/m] *(Shapiro, Bernstein)*; Dreams for Sale — Herbert Reynolds[w] & James Hanley[m] *(Shapiro, Bernstein)*; Half a Moon — Herbert Reynolds[w/m] & Eddie Dowling[w/m] & James Hanley[w/m] *(Shapiro, Bernstein)*; Jersey Walk / Mary Dear — Henry Creamer[w/m] & Eddie Dowling[w/m] & James Hanley[w/m] *(Shapiro, Bernstein)*. A rags-to-riches story which had some decent songs and ran nine months. COVER: Eddie Dowling and little white house.

1049 Honeymoon Town (closed before Broadway, 1919). Bernard Granville, Helen Bolton.

Cleopatra Had a Little Song / Now I Lay Me / Poor Mr. Keeley / Snuggle, Snuggle, Snuggle / There's Everything Waiting for You / What Was Adam Doing / Wonderful Night with You — Will Hough[w] & Byron Gay[m] *(Harms)*; Come Along to Honeymoon Town — Will Hough[w] & Felix Rice[m] *(Harms)*; Tip Toe — Will Hough[w] & Milton Schwarzwald[m] *(Harms)*. COVER: a little town with beautiful trees and houses.

1050 Honky Tonky Nights (Broadway, 1986). Joe Morton, Ira Hawkins.

Honky Tonk Nights [VS] / Hot and Bothered [VS] / I Took My Time [VS] / Man of Many Parts [VS] / Promised Land [VS] / Sparrow [VS] / Stomp the Blues Away [VS] — Ralph Allen[w] & David Campbell[w] & Michael Valenti[m] *(McHugh)*. A musical about black vaudeville which was very dreary and had a short run. COVER: a banjo player and a stage.

1051 Hooray for What (Broadway, 1938). Jack Whiting, Ed Wynn.

Buds Won't Bud / Down with Love / God's Country / I've Gone Romantic on You / In the Shade of the New Apple Tree / Life's a Dance / Moanin' in the Mornin' — E.Y. Harburg[w] & Harold Arlen[m] *(Chappell)*; Hooray for What (Hooray for Us) — E.Y. Harburg[w] & Harold Arlen[m] *(USO)*. A musical with an anti-war theme. Thanks to Ed Wynn, the musical became a moderate hit. There were some fine songs from Arlen. COVER: people, guns, flags, etc.

1052 The Hostage (Broadway, 1960). Victor Spinetti, Avis Bunnage.

The Bells of Hell — Brendan Behan[w/m] *(Chappell)*. A famous Irish play which had a moderate run. COVER: lettering and designs.

1053 Hot Chocolates (1929 edition) (Broadway, 1929). Eddie Green, Edith Wilson.

Ain't Misbehavin' / Black and Blue / Can't We Get Together / Dixie

Cinderella / Goddess of Rain / Off Time / Say It with Your Feet / Sweet Savannah Sue / That Jungle Jamboree / That Rhythm Man / That Snake Hip Dance / Waltz Divine—Andy Razaf[w] & Thomas Waller[m] & Harry Brooks[m] *(Mills)*; Darkies Have Music in Their Soul—Sammy Cahn[w/m] & Saul Chaplin[w/m] *(Mills)*. A black nightclub revue revised for Broadway with great talent and great music; it lasted for six months. It produced the hit song *Ain't Misbehavin'*. COVER: chorus girls and musician.

1054 Hot Chocolates (1935 edition) (Nightclub, 1935). Stars unknown.

Lovely Liza Lee / Machinery / The Only Time You're Out of Luck / Please Take My Heart / That Rhythm Parade—Andy Razaf[w/m] & Paul Denniker[w/m] *(Mills)*; What Harlem Is to Me—Andy Razaf[w/m] & Russell Wooding[w/m] & Paul Denniker[w/m] *(Mills)*. This edition of *Hot Chocolates* was done at Connie's Inn. COVER: chorus girls.

1055 Hot Chocolates (1936 edition) (Nightclub, 1936). Stars unknown.

Blue Notes / Nature and I—Sammy Cahn[w] & Saul Chaplin[m] & Nat Gardner[m] *(Mills)*; Do the Truck / Drum Brigade / Fourscore and Seven Years Ago / I'm Just a Slave to Your Crave / The King of Swing Is Havin' a Dream / Rhythm Holiday / Rhythm Makes the World Go Round / Shoe Shine Boy / The Spirit of the Tom-Tom / Three Foot Two of Rhythm / What's on Your Mind—Sammy Cahn[w] & Saul Chaplin[m] *(Mills)*. COVER: chorus girls.

1056 Hot Mikado (Broadway, 1939). Bill Robinson, Rose Brown.

The Flowers That Bloom in the Spring / "I" the Living "I" / I've Got 'em on the List / Let the Punishment Fit the Crime / Three Little Maids from School Are We / Tit-Willow / A Wand'ring Minstrel, I—W.S. Gilbert[w] & Arthur Sullivan[m] & Charles Cooke[m] *(Robbins)*. This black version of *The Mikado* played on Broadway for ten weeks and then moved to the New York

World's Fair before a long tour. COVER: Bill Robinson.

1057 Hot Rhythm *(see also* **The Folies Bergere Revue**) (Broadway, 1930). Edith Wilson, Arthur Bryson.

Believe Me, I'm Blue / Hungry for Love / I'll Get Even with You / Just Say the Word—Donald Heywood[w/m] *(Shapiro, Bernstein)*; For the First Time / Will You Be Hating Me Tomorrow?—Jean Herbert[w/m] & Al Koppell[w/m] & Irving Actman[w/m] *(Popular)*; Loving You the Way I Do—Jack Scholl[w] & Will Morrissey[w] & Eubie Blake[m] *(Shapiro, Bernstein)*; Penalty of Love—Heba Jamath[m] & Donald Heywood[w/m] *(Shapiro, Bernstein)*. A black revue which lasted eight weeks on Broadway. The title *Folies Bergere Revue* turned into *Hot Rhythm* on Broadway. COVER: girl with large head-dress.

1058 Hot September (closed before Broadway, 1965). Marlyn Mason, John Stewart.

Golden Moment [PC] / Goodbye Girls [VS] / Hot September [VS] / I Got It Made [VS] / Show Me Where the Good Times Are [VS] / Somethin' More [VS] / Tell Her [VS] / What Do You Do? [VS] / You [VS]—Rhoda Roberts[w] & Kenneth Jacobson[m] *(Valando)*. A musical based on the hit play *Picnic*. The musical played three weeks in Boston and folded. COVER: boy running to girl under a hot sun.

1059 Hot Spot (Broadway, 1963). Judy Holliday, Joseph Campanella.

Big Meeting Tonight / Gabie / Hey, Love / I Think the World of You / Little Trouble Goes a Long, Long Way / Live In / Nebraska / That's Good, That's Bad / Welcome to Our Country—Martin Charnin[w] & Mary Rodgers[m] *(Morris)*; Don't Laugh [PC]—Mary Rodgers[w/m] & Martin Charnin[w/m] & Stephen Sondheim[w/m] *(Morris)*. A musical about the Peace Corps. It had nothing going for it and closed in one month. COVER: Judy Holliday.

1060 Hot-Cha (Broadway, 1932). Bert Lahr, Lupe Velez.

Hot-Cha / It's Great to Be Alive / Say / There I Go Dreaming Again / There's Nothing the Matter with Me / You Can Make My Life a Bed of Roses — Lew Brown[w/m] & Ray Henderson[w/m] *(D B and H)*. A musical with a Mexican setting and Bert Lahr which ran for only four months. COVER: a bullfighter and a bull.

1061 The Hotel Mouse (*see also* Little Miss Raffles) (Broadway, 1922). Taylor Holmes, Frances White.

I'll Dream of You / Mauricette — Clifford Grey[w] & Armand Vecsey[m] *(Chappell)*; Little Mother / Manana / Romance — Clifford Grey[w] & Ivan Caryll[m] & Armand Vecsey[m] *(Chappell)*; Santiago — Clifford Grey[w] & Ivan Caryll[m] *(Chappell)*. A musical about robbery. It ran ten weeks before failing and was called *Little Miss Raffles* on its try-out tour. COVER: designs and lettering.

1062 The House Beautiful (Broadway, 1931). Mary Phillips, James Bell.

House Beautiful — Paula Anderson[w] & Betty Laidlaw[m] *(Marks)*. A love story which had a moderate run. COVER: a young couple dreaming they are a knight and his lady.

1063 House of Flowers (Broadway, 1954). Pearl Bailey, Diahann Carroll.

Albertina's Beautiful Hair [RC] [CUT] / Can I Leave Off Wearin' My Shoes? [VS] / Don't Like Goodbyes [VS] / House of Flowers / I Never Has Seen Snow / One Man Ain' Quite Enough [VS] / A Sleepin' Bee / Smellin' of Vanilla / Two Ladies in de Shade of de Banana Tree — Truman Capote[w] & Harold Arlen[w] & Harold Arlen[m] *(Morris)*. An exquisite musical that failed. It had beautiful sets and a wonderful Harold Arlen score. It also had a poor book and backstage troubles with the star. COVER: girl in hammock.

1064 House of Flowers (Off Broadway, 1968). Thelma Oliver, Josephine Premice.

Don't Like Goodbyes [VS] / House of Flowers [VS] / I Never Has Seen Snow [VS] / Madame Tango's Particular Tango [VS] / A Sleepin' Bee [VS] / Smellin' of Vanilla [VS] / Somethin' Cold to Drink [VS] / Two Ladies in de Shade of de Banana Tree [VS] / Waitin' [VS] / What Is a Friend For? [VS] / Wife Never Understan' [VS] — Truman Capote[w] & Harold Arlen[w] & Harold Arlen[m] *(Morris)*; Jump de Broom [VS] — Truman Capote[w] & Harold Arlen[m] *(Morris)*. A failed revival of a beautiful show. COVER: flowers.

1065 The House That Jack Built (British, 1929). Cicely Courtneidge, Jack Hulbert.

She's Such a Comfort to Me [B] — Douglas Furber[w] & Donovan Parsons[w] & Arthur Schwartz[m] *(Chappell)*. A successful revue. COVER: Courtneidge and Hulbert.

1066 The House-Boat on the Styx (Broadway, 1928). Blanche Ring, Jack Hazzard.

The House-Boat on the Styx / My Heaven / Red River / Soul Mates / You've Got to Know Just How to Make Love — Monte Carlo[w] & Alma Sanders[m] *(Harms)*. A houseboat in "hell" where notorious parties are held by famous historical characters. COVER: Blanche Ring, a book and some sketches.

1067 Houses of Sand (Broadway, 1925). Paul Kelly, Vivienne Osborne.

Rose of Japan — Marion Burton[w] & William Kernell[m] *(Feist)*. A love affair between an American and a Japanese girl. COVER: Vivienne Osborne.

1068 How Come? (Broadway, 1923). Alice Brown, Eddie Hunter.

The Cut-Out / E-Gypsy-Ann / Gingerena / Jazz / Love Will Bring You Happiness / Pickaninny Vamp / Sweetheart Farewell / Syncopated Strain / When I'm Blue — Ben Harris[w/m] & Henry Creamer[w/m] & Will Vodery[w/m] *(Goodman, Rose)*. A black musical that dealt with embezzlement and lasted one month. COVER: flowers and designs.

1069 How Do You Do I Love You (closed before Broadway, 1967). Phyllis Newman, Carole Cook.

One Step [VS] — Richard Maltby, Jr.[w] & David Shire[m] *(Chappell)*. A musical from the summer circuit. COVER: lettering and designs.

1070 How Now Dow Jones (Broadway, 1967). Brenda Vaccaro, Anthony Roberts.

A.B.C. [VS] / Big Trouble [VS] / Finale of How Now Dow Jones [VS] / Gawk, Tousle and Shucks [VS] / He's Here [VS] / Just for the Moment [VS] / Little Investigation [VS] / Live a Little / The Pleasure's About to Be Mine [VS] / Rich Is Better [VS] / Shakespeare Lied [VS] / Step to the Rear / They Don't Make 'em Like That Any More [VS] / Touch and Go [VS] / Walk Away / Where You Are — Carolyn Leigh[w] & Elmer Bernstein[m] *(Morris)*. COVER: girl with headdress of ticker-tapes. There are two sets of covers. One set says "Directed by Arthur Penn" and one set says "Directed by George Abbott."

1071 How to Be a Jewish Mother (Broadway, 1967). Molly Picon, Godfrey Cambridge.

Child You Are, Man You'll Be / Since That Time We Met — Herbert Martin[w] & Michael Leonard[m] *(Morris)*. A comedy with music about a "Jewish mother" who befriends a black man. It lasted one week. COVER: mother hen and chicks.

1072 How to Steal an Election (Off Broadway, 1968). Bill McCutcheon, Clifton Davis.

Comes the Right Man [PC] / Mr. Might've Been [PC] / More of the Same [PC] / Nobody's Listening [PC] — Oscar Brand[w/m] *(T R O)*. A musical about politics. It lasted for ten weeks. COVER: none.

1073 How to Succeed in Business Without Really Trying (Broadway, 1961). Robert Morse, Rudy Vallee.

Brotherhood of Man / Cinderella, Darling [VS] / Coffee Break [VS] / The Company Way [VS] / Grand Old Ivy / Happy to Keep His Dinner Warm / How to Succeed / How to Succeed — complete vocal score / I Believe in You / Love from a Heart of Gold / Paris Original / Rosemary [VS] / A Secretary Is Not a Toy [VS] — Frank Loesser[w/m] *(Frank)*. A super-hit on making it in big business. It had everything including a perfect book and score and Robert Morse's turning in the best performance of his lifetime. COVER: an office chair, a man's arm, and a girl's legs.

1074 How's the King (closed before Broadway, 1925). Joe Cook, Virginia O'Brien.

The Girl That's Most Chased After / Gypsy Rose / How's the King / I'll Save All My Evenings for You / Lady, You Don't Know Me / One Wonderful Night / Twilight / When the Right Boy Meets the Right Girl — Owen Murphy[w] & Jay Gorney[m] *(Feist)*. COVER: Joe Cook.

1075 Hoyt's Musical Revue (Regional, 1920). Allie Bagley.

Ev'ry Girl in Town Likes My Boy — William Loveday[w/m] *(Brewster)*; Fan Tan / Old Calico of Blue — Carroll Loveday[w/m] *(Brewster)*; Oh Papa, Oh Daddy — Arthur Robsham[w/m] *(Brewster)*. COVER: Allie Bagley and two girls.

1076 Huckleberry Finn (closed before Broadway, 1950). Stars unknown.

Apple Jack / The Catfish Song / Come In, Mornin' / River Chanty / This Time Next Year — Maxwell Anderson[w] & Kurt Weill[m] *(Chappell)*. An unfinished musical being written by Weill at the time of his death. COVER: river and trees.

1077 Hulbert Follies (British, 1941). Jack Hulbert, Cicely Courtneidge.

My Romance [B] — Lorenz Hart[w] & Richard Rodgers[m] *(Chappell)*. A revue that toured England but never opened in London. COVER: Hulbert and Courtneidge.

1078 Hummin' Sam (Broadway, 1933). Gertrude Baby Cox, Madeline Belt.

I'll Be True But Blue / Jubilee / Pinchin' Myself — Alexander Hill[w/m] *(Harms)*. A black musical about horse racing; the musical lasted for only one performance. COVER: titles and designs.

1079 The Humming Bird (Broadway, 1920). Maude Fulton, Walter Wills.

Humming Bird — waltz — Frank Egan[w] & H. Knight Clark[m] *(Marks)*; Toinette — Maude Fulton[w/m] *(Marks)*. A comedy drama about an Apache dancer and her partner. COVER: Maude Fulton.

1080 Humpty Dumpty (*see also* Take a Chance) (Broadway, 1932). Ethel Merman, Eddie Foy, Jr.

Humpty Dumpty / I'm Way Ahead of the Game / Night / Turn Out the Light / You're an Old Smoothie — B.G. DeSylva[w/m] & Richard Whiting[w/m] & Herb N. Brown[w/m] *(Harms)*. *Humpty Dumpty* was a disaster on the road. It closed, was revised and reopened as *Take a Chance*. Jack Haley replaced Eddie Foy Jr. and the deleted songs were replaced by Vincent Youmans songs. COVER: Humpty Dumpty and animals.

1081 I, Anastasia (*see also* Anya) (closed before Broadway, 1981). Judy Kaye, Len Cariou.

Drawn to You [VS] / Here Tonight, Tomorrow Where [VS] / Homeward [VS] / If This Is Goodbye [VS] / Little Hands [VS] / My Kind of Love [VS] / Snowflakes and Sweethearts [VS] / That Song [VS] / Think Upon Something Beautiful [VS] / Two Waltzes [VS] — Robert Wright[w/m] & George Forrest[w/m] & S. Rachmaninoff[w/m] *(Frank)*. The musical *Anya* was a quick failure in 1965. It was revised and presented as *I, Anastasia* or *The Anastasia Game* in 1989 in Lowell, Massachusetts, where it failed again. COVER: Russian coat of arms.

1082 I and Albert (British, 1972). Polly James, Sven-Bertil Taube.

I and Albert [B] / Just You and Me [B] / This Gentle Land [B] / Victoria [B] — Lee Adams[w] & Charles Strouse[m] *(Morris)*; Victoria and Albert Waltz [B] — Charles Strouse[m] *(Morris)*. A musical by two Americans about the British Royal Family. It lasted almost four months. COVER: children's blocks with British scenes.

1083 I Can Get It for You Wholesale (Broadway, 1962). Elliott Gould, Barbra Streisand.

A Gift Today / Have I Told You Lately? / I Can Get It for You Wholesale — complete vocal score / Miss Marmelstein / Momma, Momma! / On My Way to Love / The Sound of Money / Too Soon / What's in It for Me? / Who Knows? — Harold Rome[w/m] *(Chappell)*. A musical about the garment district in New York; it ran for nine months. It had a serviceable score and book, but more importantly marked the great debut of Streisand. COVER: boy, girl, and boxes.

1084 I Do! I Do! (Broadway, 1966). Mary Martin, Robert Preston.

The Honeymoon Is Over / I Do, I Do / I Do! I Do! — complete vocal score / I Love My Wife [VS] / Love Isn't Everything / My Cup Runneth Over / Roll Up the Ribbons [VS] / Someone Needs Me [VS] / This House [VS] / Thousands of Flowers / Together Forever / What Is a Woman? / Where Are the Snows [VS] — Tom Jones[w] & Harvey Schmidt[m] *(Chappell)*. An intimate musical based on *The Fourposter* with pleasant songs and the charming Mary Martin and Robert Preston who kept it running for almost a year and a half. COVER 1: sketch of couple at home in arm chairs — cream color. COVER 2: sketch of heart — bright red.

1085 I Don't Care (closed before Broadway, 1923). Moher and Eldridge.

Crying for You / Linger Awhile — Ned Miller[w/m] & Chester Cohn[w/m] *(Feist)*. COVER: Moher and Eldridge.

1086 I Had a Ball (Broadway, 1964). Buddy Hackett, Richard Kiley.

Addie's at It Again / Affluent Society [VS] / Almost / Can It Be Possible [VS] / Coney Island, U.S.A. [VS] / Doctor Freud [VS] / Ev'rything I Want / Faith / The Fickle Finger of Fate / I Had a Ball / Neighborhood Song [VS] / The Other Half of Me / Think Beautiful [VS] / You Deserve Me [VS] — Jack Lawrence[w/m] & Stan Freeman[w/m]

(Morris). A musical with a carnival atmosphere that was lots of fun. It had some nice songs and excellent voices. Buddy Hackett's ad-libbing kept it going for almost six months. COVER: ferris wheel, roller coaster, and dancing girls.

1087 I Love a Lassie (closed before Broadway, 1919). Stars unknown.

Billy / Down Lover's Lane / Hop Scotch / I'm Going to Be a Vampire / Manana / Sweetheart of Mine / Tiddia Dum — Clifton Crawford[w/m] *(Harms)*. COVER: Scotch bagpipes.

1088 I Love My Wife (Broadway, 1977). Lenny Baker, Joanna Gleason.

By Threes [VS] / Ev'rybody Today Is Turning On [VS] / Hey There, Good Times / I Love My Wife / Love Revolution / Lovers on Christmas Eve [VS] / Married Couple Seeks Married Couple [VS] / Monica [VS] / A Mover's Life [VS] / Scream [VS] / Sexually Free [VS] / Someone Wonderful I Missed / We're Still Friends [VS] — Michael Stewart[w] & Cy Coleman[m] *(Notable)*. A very good musical about wife-swapping; the musical ran for two years. COVER: a heart and two couples.

1089 I Loved You Wednesday (Broadway, 1932). Humphrey Bogart, Jane Seymour.

I Loved You Wednesday — Abner Silver[w/m] & Walter Kent[w/m] & Milton Drake[w/m] *(Marks)*. A love story with one song. COVER: sketch of man and woman.

1090 I Married an Angel (Broadway, 1938). Vera Zorina, Vivienne Segal.

At the Roxy Music Hall [VS] / Did You Ever Get Stung? / How to Win Friends / I Married an Angel / I'll Tell the Man in the Street / Spring Is Here / Twinkle in Your Eye — Lorenz Hart[w] & Richard Rodgers[m] *(Robbins)*. A fantasy in which a man marries an angel. This production had a beautiful Rodgers and Hart score and a run of nine months. COVER: man and woman with cupid.

1091 I Must Love Someone (Broadway, 1939). Nancy Carroll, Scott Colton.

I Must Love Someone — Mack David[w] & Jerry Livingston[m] *(Famous)*. A melodrama with one song. COVER: Nancy Carroll.

1092 I Remember Mama (Broadway, 1979). Liv Ullmann, George Hearn.

Ev'ry Day Comes Something Beautiful / I Remember Mama [RC] / It Is Not the End of the World / A Little Bit More [RC] / Time / You Could Not Please Me More — Martin Charnin[w] & Richard Rodgers[m] *(M. C. A.)*. A poor musical with many problems including Rodgers' being ill, Ullmann's inability to sing, Cohen's fighting with everyone, and replacement of a lyricist. The score and book were terrible and the show folded after three months. COVER: Liv Ullmann and daughter.

1093 I Told You So *(see also* **Piggy**) (Broadway, 1927). Sam Bernard, Brooke Johns.

I'll Love You Just the Same — Lew Brown[w/m] & Cliff Friend[w/m] *(Remick)*. A rich-poor-boy-girl affair with nothing to recommend it; a failure. In its try-out, it was called *I Told You So* and *That's My Baby* but opened on Broadway as *Piggy*. COVER: flowers and designs.

1094 I Want You (Off Broadway, 1961). Al Mancini, Joshua Shelley.

Ain't It Funny / I Want You / Loyal American / A Perfect Man / Remarkable / The Street — Joe Crayhon[w/m] & Stefan Kanfer[w/m] & Jess Korman[w/m] *(Morris)*. A patriotic musical that folded after three performances. COVER: Uncle Sam and flag.

1095 I Would If I Could (Jewish, 1933). Sholom Secunda.

Bei Mir Bistu Shein — J. Jacobs[w] & Sholom Secunda[m] *(Trio)*. COVER: S. Secunda.

1096 Ice Capades of 1941 (Ice Show, 1941). Belita, Vera Hruba.

Blue September / I Hear America Singing — Mitchell Parish[w] & Peter DeRose[m] *(Robbins)*; Somewhere /

Yippi-i-ay! — John Latouche[w] & Peter DeRose[m] *(Robbins)*; The Yankee Doodle Polka — John Latouche[w] & Vernon Duke[m] *(Robbins)*. COVER: Vera Hruba, Belita, Lois Dworshak, and girls.

1097 Ice Capades of 1942 (Ice Show, 1942). Vera Hruba, Belita.

Forever and Ever — Jule Styne[w/m] & Sol Meyer[w/m] & George Brown[w/m] *(Mills)*. COVER: Belita.

1098 Ice Capades of 1943 (Ice Show, 1942). Vera Hruba.

The Guy with the Polka-Dot Tie — Sol Meyer[w] & Jule Styne[m] *(Mills)*; Love's Magic — Dorothy Mason[w] & Jacques Offenbach[m] *(Mills)*. COVER: ice skaters.

1099 Ice Capades of 1950 (Ice Show, 1950). Donna Atwood, Bobby Specht.

I Fell in Love with a Dream — Johnny Lange[w/m] & Eliot Daniel[w/m] *(Ice Capades)*; Toyshop Jamboree — Johnny Lange[w/m] & Eliot Daniel[w/m] *(Disney)*. COVER: Atwood and Specht.

1100 Ice Capades of 1954 (Ice Show, 1954). Donna Atwood, Bobby Specht.

Jingle Polka — Dixie Lou Thompson[w/m] & John Rarig[w/m] *(Sam Fox)*. COVER: ice skaters doing the polka.

1101 Ice Capades of 1957 (Ice Show, 1957). Bobby Specht, Rosemary Henderson.

I'm a Happy Guy / Old Man Winter / Ven Papa Vould Cut a Figure Eight / When You Are Seventeen / With All My Heart — Marilyn Bergman[w/m] & Alan Bergman[w/m] & Lew Spence[w/m] *(Chappell)*. COVER: a girl on ice skates.

1102 Ice Follies of 1939 (Ice Show, 1939). Bess Ehrhardt, Roy Shipstads.

Loveland in the Wintertime — Cliff Friend[w/m] & Dave Franklin[w/m] *(B V and C)*. COVER: Ehrhardt, Shipstads.

1103 Ice Follies of 1942 (Ice Show, 1942). Bess Ehrhardt, Roy Shipstads.

By Young Again / The Devil in My Angel's Eyes / My Heart Flies Blind / Romancing with My Lady Fair / We Will Always Be in Love — Bobby Worth[w/m] & Stanley Cowan[w/m] *(Melody Lane)* COVER: Bess Ehrhardt, Roy Shipstads.

1104 Ice Follies of 1949 (Ice Show, 1949). Frick and Frack.

Chickady Chay / I'm Gonna Find a Gal in Californy / The Lollypop Polka / Smooth Sailin' / Song Bird Singin' in a Bamboo Tree / The Swing Waltz / With a Rose in Your Hair — Larey Morey[w/m] *(Morey-Pearce)*. COVER: Bess Ehrhardt, Roy Shipstad.

1105 Ice Travaganza (Ice Show, 1964). Dick Button.

Everyone Knows / We Haven't Begun to Live — John Morris[w/m] & Gerald Freedman[w/m] *(Chappell)*. COVER: two ice skaters.

1106 Icetime (Ice Show, 1946). Freddie Trenkler, Joan Hyldoft.

Dream Waltz / I Do — Do You? — Jimmy Littlefield[w] & Johnny Fortis[m] *(Dorsey Bros.)*; Mary / Old King Cole / When the Minstrels Come to Town / Wonderful You — Jimmy Littlefield[w/m] *(Dorsey Bros.)*. COVER: a couple iceskating.

1107 I'd Rather Be Right (Broadway, 1937). George M. Cohan, Joy Hodges.

Ev'rybody Loves You [VS] / Have You Met Miss Jones? / I'd Rather Be Right (#1) / I'd Rather Be Right (#2) / Sweet Sixty-five / Take and Take and Take — Lorenz Hart[w] & Richard Rodgers[m] *(Chappell)*. A political satire that didn't quite make it. The author, the star, and the songwriters all hated each other. It did contain three good songs and ran nine months. COVER: a politician and the Washington Monument.

1108 Ideas Have Legs (*see also* **The Good Road**) (Regional, 1947). Stars unknown.

Change for Every Joe — Eleanor Purdy[w/m] *(Moral Rearmament)*; Come Along / Ideas Have Legs / The Spirit of the West — Cecil Broadhurst[w/m] *(Moral Rearmament)*; Families Can Be Fun / The Good Road — Alan Thornhill[w] & Paul Misraki[m] *(Moral Rearmament)*; Heartpower — Dorothy Saul[w] & Katharine Miller[m] & Marie Sanger[m] *(Moral Rearmament)*; Sorry Is a Magic

Little Word / Struggle Alley – Cecil Broadhurst[w] & Richard Hadden[m] *(Moral Rearmament)*; The Third Way – A. Garrett[w] & Katharine Miller[m] *(Moral Rearmament)*; Whatcha Gonna Do, Mister? – Cecil Broadhurst[w] & Svenerik Back[m] *(Moral Rearmament)*; The Whole World Is My Neighbor – Jessie Allen[w/m] & Marie Sanger[w/m] *(Moral Rearmament)*. A political revue which was also called *The Good Road*. COVER: sketch of families and friends.

1109 If Five Years Pass (Off Broadway, 1962). Richard Buck, Anne Francine.

If Five Years Pass / I'm Not Yours – Bix Reichner[w] & George Fischoff[m] *(Elliot)*. A Frederico Garcia Lorca drama with songs that failed. COVER: black and white.

1110 If the Shoe Fits (Broadway, 1946). Joe Besser, Florence Desmond.

But I Took Another Look / I Wish / I'm Not Myself To-night / In the Morning / My Business Man / This Is the End of the Story – June Carroll[w] & David Raksin[m] *(Chappell)*. The Cinderella story with great sets, but it failed after two weeks. COVER: Cinderella and Prince Charming.

1111 If Winter Comes (Broadway, 1922). Cyril Maude, Mabel Terry-Lewis.

If Winter Comes – Reginald Arkell[w] & H.M. Tennent[m] *(Chappell)*. An old melodrama with one song. COVER: Cyril Maude.

1112 If You Please (closed before Broadway, 1950). Frank Fay, Maurice Kelly.

Don't Look Now / Kiss Hello and Not Goodbye / Ta-Hy-Ta-Ho-Tahiti / What's a Girl to Do? / Wrapped in Arms – Frank Fay[w/m] *(Mills)*. A poor revue headed for Broadway but lasting only five days in San Francisco. COVER: dancing girls.

1113 I'll Say She Does (closed before Broadway, 1920). Roland Young, Juliette Day.

Settling Down / A Sunny May After noon / While the City Sleeps / You're All That I Need – B.G. DeSylva[w/m] *(Harms)*. COVER: flowers and designs.

1114 I'll Say She Is (Broadway, 1924). The Marx Brothers.

I'm Saving You for a Rainy Day / Only You! / The Thrill of Love / When Shadows Fall / Wonderful One – Will Johnstone[w] & Tom Johnstone[m] *(Harms)*; Tessie! Stop Teasin' Me – Brooke Johns[w/m] & Ray Perkins[w/m] *(Curtis)*. This was the four Marx Brothers' introduction to Broadway. The show had a weak plot but crazy antics and ran for nine months. COVER: a lady and her mirror.

1115 The Illustrators' Show (Broadway, 1936). Helen Lynd, Earl Oxford.

Bang – The Bell Rang! – Frank Loesser[w] & Irving Actman[m] *(Chappell)*; I've Walked in Moonlight – Milton Pascal[w] & Edgar Fairchild[m] *(Chappell)*; A Waltz Was Born in Vienna – Earle Crooker[w] & Frederick Loewe[m] *(Chappell)*. A revue by the Society of Illustrators created for art rather than theatre. It was a one week failure. COVER: artist and palette.

1116 Illya Darling (Broadway, 1967). Melina Mercouri, Orson Bean.

After Love / Illya Darling / Illya Darling – selections / Love, Love, Love / Ya Chara Bye-bye-bye-bye – Joe Darion[w] & Manos Hadjidakis[m] *(United Artists)*. A poor stage version of the movie *Never on Sunday* which ran nine months due to Mercouri. COVER: Melina Mercouri.

1117 I'm Getting My Act Together and Taking It on the Road (Off Broadway, 1978). Gretchen Cryer, Nancy Ford.

Dear Tom [VS] / Feel the Love [VS] / Happy Birthday [VS] / In a Simple Way I Love You [VS] / Lonely Lady [VS] / Miss America [VS] / Natural High [VS] / Old Friend [VS] / Put in a Package and Sold [VS] / Smile [VS] / Strong Woman Number [VS] – Gretchen Cryer[w] & Nancy Ford[m] *(Fiddleback)*. A musical about women's lib that became a surprise hit and ran for three years. COVER: Gretchen Cryer.

1118 I'm in Love (Jewish, 1946). Lilly Lilliana, Leon Liebgold.

Ich Vil Es Her n Nochamol — Jacob Jacobs[w] & I. Lillian[w] & Abraham Ellstein[m] *(Metro)*. COVER: Lilliana and Liebgold.

1119 I'm So Happy (Regional, 1918). Fred Bowers.

I Cannot Forget Your Eyes / I'm So Happy / Sunshine — Arthur Lamb[w] & Fred Bowers[m] *(Berlin)*. COVER: Fred Bowers and girls.

1120 I'm Solomon (Broadway, 1968). Dick Shawn, Karen Morrow.

In Love with a Fool / Something in His Eyes — Anne Croswell[w] & Ernest Gold[m] *(Morris)*. This musical opened in Baltimore as *In Someone Else's Sandals* and then became *I'm Solomon*. Except for the scenery, it was bad and lasted only seven performances in New York. COVER: the king and his sandals.

1121 In Bamville (*see also* **Chocolate Dandies**) (Broadway, 1924). Josephine Baker, Elisabeth Welch.

Dixie Moon / Jassamine / Jassamine Lane / Manda / Slave of Love / There's a Million Little Cupids in the Sky / There's No Place as Grand as Bandana Land / Thinking of Me — Noble Sissle[w/m] & Eubie Blake[w/m] *(Harms)*. A black musical about horse racing which ran for only three months. It toured as *In Bamville* but opened in New York as *The Chocolate Dandies*. COVER: colored circles and designs.

1122 In Dutch (closed before Broadway, 1924). Edward Gallagher, Al Shean.

Dipping in the Moonlight / Do You Love as I Love? — Irving Caesar[w] & Joseph Meyer[m] *(Harms)*; Twilight Serenade — Irving Caesar[w] & William Daly[m] & Joseph Meyer[m] *(Harms)*. COVER: lettering and designs.

1123 In Gay Company (Off Broadway, 1974). Rick Gardner, Gordon Ramsey.

The Days of the Dancing [VS] / Firemen's Song [VS] / Handsome Stranger [VS] / If He'd Only Be Gentle [VS] / I'm in Love with a Boy Who's Gay [VS] / Lament [VS] / True Confession [VS] / You Really Ought to Get Married [VS] — Fred Silver[w/m] *(Genesis 3)*. A gay musical revue that ran for seven months. COVER: four guys and a girl.

1124 In Heidelberg (*see also* **The Student Prince**) (Broadway, 1924). Roberta Beatty, Howard Marsh.

Deep in My Heart, Dear / Golden Days / Just We Two / May I Come to See You Dear To-night / Serenade — Dorothy Donnelly[w] & Sigmund Romberg[m] *(Harms)*. This sentimental operetta with a great score was one of the biggest hits of the musical theatre. It was called *In Heidelberg* during tryout but opened as *The Student Prince*. COVER: flowers and designs.

1125 In Love with Love (Broadway, 1923). Lynn Fontanne, Henry Hull.

In Love with Love — Dailey Paskman[w] & Rudolf Friml[m] *(Berlin)*. A drama and love story with a song by Friml. COVER: cats on a fence.

1126 In Person (*see also* **The Act**) (Broadway, 1977). Liza Minnelli, Barry Nelson.

Arthur [RC] / Bobo's [RC] / It's the Strangest Thing [RC] / Love Songs [CUT] [RC] / My Own Space [RC] / Only Game in Town [CUT] [RC] / Shine It On [RC] — Fred Ebb[w] & John Kander[m] *(Chappell)*. A musical about a fading actress. It kept going for six months thanks to Liza Minnelli. The try-out title was *In Person* but it opened as *The Act*. COVER: none.

1127 In the Moonlight (*see also* **Dew Drop Inn**) (Broadway, 1923). James Barton, Lee Kelso.

Goodbye — Cyrus Wood[w] & Alfred Goodman[m] *(Harms)*. A poor show that toured as *In the Moonlight* and opened as *Dew Drop Inn*. It lasted one month. COVER: titles and designs.

1128 In Trousers (Off Broadway, 1981). Catherine Cox, Tony Cummings.

I'm Breaking Down [VS] — William Finn[w/m] *(Warner Bros.)*. One of three plays in the *Falsetto* series. The only one that was unsuccessful with a run of two weeks. COVER: cast of show.

1129 Inner City (Broadway, 1971). Delores Hall, Linda Hopkins.

Deep in the Night [PC] / Riddle Song [PC] / Shadow of the Sun [PC] / Who Killed Nobody [PC] — Eve Merriam[w] & Helen Miller[m] *(Sunbeam)*. A poor musical of life in the big city with a run of three months. COVER: none.

1130 Innocent Eyes (Broadway, 1924). Mistinguett, Frances Williams.

Africa — Henry Creamer[w/m] & James Hanley[w/m] *(Shapiro, Bernstein)*; Croony Spoony Tune / Garden of Love / I'm Fed Up / On Broadway / On the Q.T. / Organdy Days — Tot Seymour[w] & Jean Schwartz[m] *(Harms)*; Hard Hearted Hannah — Jack Yellen[w/m] & Bob Bigelow[w/m] & Charles Bates[w/m] *(A Y and B)*; Hula Lou — Jack Yellen[w] & Milton Charles[m] & Wayne King[m] *(A Y and B)*; I'm for You — Tot Seymour[w] & G. Pearly[m] & F. Pearly[m] *(Harms)*; Innocent Eyes — McElbert Moore[w] & Jean Schwartz[m] & Fred Coots[m] *(Harms)*; La Java — Tot Seymour[w] & Maurice Yvain[m] *(Harms)*. A revue built around the French star Mistinguett. It bombed and she went back to Paris. COVER: Mistinguett, Frances Williams.

1131 Inside U.S.A. (Broadway, 1948). Jack Haley, Beatrice Lillie.

Blue Grass / First Prize at the Fair / Haunted Heart / Inside U.S.A. [PC] / My Gal Is Mine Once More / Rhode Island Is Famous for You — Howard Dietz[w] & Arthur Schwartz[m] *(Chappell)*. A revue about life in the U.S. with a pleasant score and the comedy of Lillie and Haley. It ran for one year. COVER: Beatrice Lillie, Jack Haley, and a map of the USA.

1132 International Beauty Tour (Regional, 1935). Nancy Corrigan, Mildred Melrose.

Beauty Parade — Andrew Donnelly[w/m] *(Marks)*. COVER: Nancy Corrigan and beautiful girls.

1133 International Revue (Nightclub, 1933). Paul Whiteman.

Any Way the Wind Blows / Broadway Lady / Crazy Walk / Paradise Waltz — Bud Green[w] & Sam Stept[m] *(Mills)*. COVER: Paul Whiteman.

1134 Into the Woods (Broadway, 1987). Bernadette Peters, Joanna Gleason.

Agony [VS] / Any Moment [VS] / Children Will Listen / Into the Woods [VS] / Into the Woods — complete score / It Takes Two [VS] / No More [VS] / No One Is Alone / Stay with Me — Stephen Sondheim[w/m] *(Warner Bros.)*. A fairy tale musical with some interesting songs and an uneven book, but it ran two years. COVER: people entering the woods.

1135 Ireland a Nation (Irish, 1920). Emmett Moore.

Irish Liberty — Charles Lawlor[w/m] & Alice Lawlor[w/m] *(Ireland)*. COVER: Charles Lawlor and Emmett Moore.

1136 Irene (Broadway, 1919). Edith Day, J.P. Bowden.

Alice Blue Gown / Castle of Dreams / Hobbies / Irene / Irene — complete vocal score / The Last Part of Ev'ry Party / The "Paul Jones" / Skyrocket / Talk of the Town / To Be Worthy / We're Getting Away with It — Joseph McCarthy[w] & Harry Tierney[m] *(Feist)*; Irene Valse [B] — Harry Tierney[m] *(Feist)*. A Cinderella story with a good book and some wonderful songs; it ran for a year and a half. COVER: There are two sets of covers. One cover shows Edith Day and the other set is letters.

1137 Irene (Broadway, 1973). Debbie Reynolds, Patsy Kelly.

Alice Blue Gown / The Family Tree / Irene / The Last Part of Every Party [VS] — Joseph McCarthy[w] & Harry Tierney[m] *(Feist)*; The Great Lover Tango [VS] — Charles Gaynor[w] & Otis Clements[m] *(Big Three)*; I Can Dream, Can't I? [B] [VS] — Irving Kahal[w] & Sammy Fain[m] *(EMI)*; If Only He Knew [B] [VS] — Norman Newell[w] & Michael Reed[m] *(E M I)*; I'm Always Chasing Rainbows — Joseph McCarthy[w] & Harry Carroll[m] *(Robbins)*; An Irish Girl — Charles Gaynor[w] & Otis Clements[m] *(Feist)*; Mother, Angel, Darling [VS] — Charles Gaynor[w/m] *(Big*

Three); Riviera Rage — Wally Harper[m] *(Notable)*; They Go Wild, Simply Wild, Over Me — Joseph McCarthy[w] & Fred Fisher[m] *(Feist)*; What Do You Want to Make Those Eyes at Me For? — Joseph McCarthy[w/m] & Howard Johnson[w/m] & Jimmy Monaco[w/m] *(Feist)*; The World Must Be Bigger Than an Avenue [VS] — Jack Lloyd[w] & Wally Harper[m] *(Big Three)*; You Made Me Love You — Joseph McCarthy[w] & James Monaco[m] *(Broadway)*. A revival of the 1919 hit that was entertaining without any charm. With an almost new score and a new book, it ran for two years. This was longer than the original. COVER: Debbie Reynolds.

1138 Irish Eyes (Irish, 1921). Walter Scanlon.

An Irish Song Will Live / Judy / My Galway Rose — George Kershaw[w] & Walter Scanlan[m] *(Berlin)*; Kathleen — Harry B. Smith[w] & Ted Snyder[m] *(Berlin)*. Another touring show that never reached Broadway. COVER: Walter Scanlan.

1139 Irma La Douce (Broadway, 1960). Stuart Damon, Elizabeth Seal.

Bravo [B] / Christmas Child / Dis-Donc, Dis-Donc / From a Prison Cell / Irma La Douce / Our Language of Love / She's Got the Lot / There Is Only One Paris for That — Julian More[w] & David Heneker[w] & Monty Norman[w] & Marguerite Monnot[m] *(Trafalgar)*; Bridge of Caulaincourt — piano selections — Marguerite Monnot[m] *(Trafalgar)*. A musical about a streetwalker; imported from France and England. It was fast moving with pleasant tunes and ran for well over a year. COVER: Irma La Douce.

1140 It Happens on Ice (Ice Show, 1940). Skippy Baxter, Betty Atkinson.

Between You and Me and the Lamp Post / What's on the Penny — Al Stillman[w] & Fred Ahlert[m] *(Robbins)*; Don't Blow That Horn, Gabriel — Al Stillman[w/m] & Will Hudson[w/m] & Vernon Duke[w/m] *(Robbins)*; Long Ago — Al Stillman[w] & Vernon Duke[m] *(Robbins)*; The Moon Fell in the River —

Mitchell Parish[w] & Peter DeRose[m] *(Robbins)*. COVER: three ice skaters.

1141 It Happens on Ice (Ice Show, 1941). Betty Atkinson, Skippy Baxter.

The Waltz of Memory — John Burger[w/m] *(Famous)*. COVER: a group of couples ice skating.

1142 It Pays to Sin (Broadway, 1933). Jane Starr, Leon Waycoff.

This Night Is Ours — Joe McCarthy[w/m] & Nell Finn[w/m] & Everett Wright[w/m] & Irving Bibo[w/m] *(Bibo-Lang)*. A comedy love story with one song. COVER: Jane Starr.

1143 It's a Bird ... It's a Plane ... It's Superman (Broadway, 1966).

Doing Good [VS] / I'm Not Finished Yet [VS] / It's Super Nice [VS] / It's Superman / Ooh, Do You Love Me [VS] / Pow! Bam! Zonk! [VS] / Revenge [VS] / So Long, Big Guy [VS] / The Strongest Man in the World [VS] / Superman Theme / We Don't Matter At All [VS] / We Need Him [VS] / What I've Always Wanted [VS] / Woman for the Man Who Has Everything [VS] / You've Got Possibilities / You've Got What I Need, Baby [VS] — Lee Adams[w] & Charles Strouse[m] *(Morris)*; Superman Love Theme / Superman March — Charles Strouse[m] *(Morris)*. A comic strip character in a musical that failed. It had a so-so book and ordinary songs. COVER: Superman over city.

1144 It's a Small World (World's Fair, 1963). Stars unknown.

It's a Small World — Richard Sherman[w/m] & Robert Sherman[w/m] *(Wonderland)*. A song presented at the Disney exhibit at the New York World's Fair. COVER: children and designs.

1145 It's Up to You! (closed before Broadway, 1919). Stars unknown.

I'd Rather Be a Friend of Yours / Jack in the Box / When I First Kissed You / Won't You Let Me Creep into Your Heart — A.G. Delamater[w] & William Peters[m] *(Harms)*. COVER: bubbles and designs.

1146 It's Up to You (*see also* **High**

and Dry) (Broadway, 1921). Charles King, Betty Pierce.

Bee Deedle Dee Dum Dey / Burglar Song / Those Oriental Blues / We Hate to Go—Harry Clarke^w & John McManus^m *(Witmark)*; The Boy Who Bangs a Drum / I'll Always Believe in You / I'll Tell the World / I'm Alright When I Dance Alone—E.A. Paulton^w & John McManus^m *(Witmark)*; Doveland—Francis DeWitt^w & Werner Janssen^m *(Witmark)*; Everytime I See You Dear / Firefly / I Never Thought of Dark / I Want a Home / I Wish You Would Leave Me Alone / Someone Console Me—E.A. Paulton^w & Manuel Klein^m *(Witmark)*; Havana—John McManus^{w/m} *(Witmark)*; In Our Little Castle in Air—Harry Clarke^w & John McManus^w & John McManus^m *(Witmark)*; Love Me / Man Is as Old as He Feels—Ray Perkins^{w/m} *(Witmark)*. A rags-to-riches failure. This show toured as *High and Dry* and opened as *It's Up to You.* COVER: a pretty girl.

1147 Jack and Jill (Broadway, 1923). Clifton Webb, Ann Pennington.

Concentrate / Voodo Man / Wallflower—Otto Harbach^w & Alfred Newman^m *(Remick)*; Dancing in the Dark—Oliver Deering^w & Muriel Pollock^m *(Remick)*; Hoping / It's the Nicest Sort of Feeling—Irving Caesar^w & William Daly^m *(Remick)*; I Love—Thou Lovest—Augustus Barratt^{w/m} & John Murray Anderson^{w/m} *(Remick)*; I Want a Pretty Girl—Otto Harbach^w & William Daly^m *(Remick)*; My Cherokee Rose / No Other Eyes—John Murray Anderson^{w/m} & Augustus Barratt^{w/m} *(Remick)*. A musical about love and telling the truth; it lasted for only ten weeks. COVER: a girl and a boy.

1148 Jack and Jill (British, 1934). Arthur Riscoe, Betty Ann Davies.

I'm on a See-Saw—Desmond Carter^w & Vivian Ellis^m *(Chappell)*. A hit musical that had a song published in the U.S. COVER: a couple on a see-saw.

1149 Jack of Hearts (Irish, 1923). Fiske O'Hara.

Beguilin' Smilin' Eyes / The Jaunting Car / Pretty Molly Malone—Florence Fink^w & George Gartlan^m *(H H and E)*. A touring show that never made it to Broadway. COVER: Fiske O'Hara.

1150 Jackpot (Broadway, 1944). Nanette Fabray, Betty Garrett.

I've Got a One Track Mind / Sugarfoot / There Are Yanks / What Happened?—Howard Dietz^w & Vernon Duke^m *(Harms)*. A poor musical with a wartime theme; the musical lasted for two months. COVER: three girls and three soldiers.

1151 Jacques Brel Is Alive and Well and Living in Paris (Off Broadway, 1968). Elly Stone, Mort Shuman.

Amsterdam [VS] / If We Only Have Love / Timid Frieda [VS]—Mort Shuman^{w/m} & Eric Blau^{w/m} & Jacques Brel^{w/m} *(Big Three)*; Days of the Waltz—Will Holt^{w/m} & Jacques Brel^{w/m} *(Leeds)*; The Desperate Ones [VS] / I Loved [VS] / Jackie [VS] / Old Folks [VS] / Sons Of [VS]—Eric Blau^{w/m} & Mort Shuman^{w/m} & Gerard Jouannest^{w/m} *(Big Three)*; Fanette—Eric Blau^{w/m} & Mort Shuman^{w/m} & Jacques Brel^{w/m} *(Hill and Range)*; Jacques Brel Is Alive—complete vocal score—Mort Shuman^{w/m} & Eric Blau^{w/m} & Jacques Brel^{w/m} & Gerard Jouannest^{w/m} *(Big Three)*; Marathon—Eric Blau^{w/m} & Jacques Brel^{w/m} *(Marks)*. A cabaret revue that ran for four years featuring the songs of Jacques Brel. COVER: Jacques Brel.

1152 Jamaica (Broadway, 1957). Lena Horne, Ricardo Montalban.

Ain't It de Truth / Coconut Sweet / Hooray for de Yankee Dollar [PC] / I Don't Think I'll End It All Today / Incompatibility / Leave de Atom Alone [PC] / Little Biscuit / Napoleon / Pity de Sunset [PC] / Pretty to Walk With / Push de Button / Savanna / Take It Slow, Joe / What Good Does It Do?—E.Y. Harburg^w & Harold Arlen^m *(Morris)*. Life and love on a tropical island were the basis of this musical which was not too good but ran for a year and a half because of the attraction of Lena Horne. COVER: cartoon characters and houses.

1153 Jay Flippens Frolics (closed before Broadway, 1928). Jay Flippen.

You're Just a Little Bit of Everything I Love — Jay C. Flippen$^{w/m}$ & Mack Gordon$^{w/m}$ & George Wiest$^{w/m}$ *(Mills)*. COVER: Jay Flippen.

1154 Jazz King (*see also* **Melody Man**) (Broadway, 1924). Eva Puck, Sammy White.

I'd Like to Poison Ivy / Moonlight Mama — Herbert Richard, Lorenz *(Marks)*. A comedy with songs that failed that was also called *The Melody Man*. The composers disguised their names for this one. COVER: a mad violinist and Puck and White.

1155 The Jazz Singer (Broadway, 1925). George Jessel, Sam Jaffe.

Home Pals — Joe Young^w & Sam Lewis^w & M.K. Jerome^m *(Remick)*. A drama, with songs, about a rabbi's son. COVER: George Jessel.

1156 J.B. (Broadway, 1959). Raymond Massey, Christopher Plummer.

J.B. Themes — David Amram^m *(Empress)*. A classical drama and winner of the Pulitzer Prize. COVER: shining light over trees.

1157 Jeeves (British, 1975). David Hemmings, Michael Aldridge.

Half a Moment — Alan Ayckbourn^w & Andrew Lloyd Webber^m *(Jeeves Music)*. Probably the only failure of Webber's, this was a musical version of the famous warehouse character Jeeves. The show lasted five weeks. COVER: yellow with black letters.

1158 Jekyll & Hyde (closed before Broadway, 1990). Chuck Wagner, Linda Eder.

Hospital Board [VS] / It's Over Now [VS] / Letting Go [VS] / Love Has Come of Age [VS] / A New Life [VS] / No One Knows Who I Am [VS] / No One Must Ever Know [VS] / Once Upon a Dream-Boy [VS] / Once Upon a Dream-Girl [VS] / Possessed [VS] / Retribution [VS] / Seduction [VS] / Someone Like You / This Is the Moment / Till You Came Into My Life [VS] / Transformation

[VS] / We Still Have Time [VS] — Leslie Bricusse^w & Frank Wildhorn^m *(Cherry Lane)*. An interesting musical with some good songs performed by the Alley Theatre in Texas. At this writing, a Broadway production is scheduled to open in December 1995. COVER: Jekyll, Hyde, and girl.

1159 Jennie (Boston) (Broadway, 1963). Mary Martin, Dennis O'Keefe.

Before I Kiss the World Goodbye / High Is Better Than Low / I Still Look at You That Way / On the Other Hand / Waitin' for the Evening Train / Where You Are — Howard Dietz$^{w/m}$ & Arthur Schwartz$^{w/m}$ *(Harms)*. A musical loosely based on Laurette Taylor's life. Backstage, there were constant fights involving the star, the songwriters, the producer, and the director. Since Mary Martin was married to the producer, she won. In addition, Dennis O'Keefe could not sing and had other problems so he was let go during the Boston try-out. COVER: Mary Martin in various outfits plus the name of Dennis O'Keefe as co-star.

1160 Jennie (New York) (Broadway, 1963). Mary Martin, George Wallace.

Before I Kiss the World Goodbye / Born Again / High Is Better Than Low / I Believe in Takin' a Chance / I Still Look at You That Way / Waitin' for the Evening Train / When You're Far Away from New York Town / Where You Are — Howard Dietz$^{w/m}$ & Arthur Schwartz$^{w/m}$ *(Harms)*. After numerous revisions and the replacement of the co-star, this musical opened in New York as a total disaster. It lasted ten weeks. Incidentally, Mary Martin turned down *Funny Girl* and *Hello Dolly* for this show. COVER: Mary Martin in various outfits, plus the name of George Wallace as co-star.

1161 Jerome Robbins Broadway (Broadway, 1989). Terrence Mann, Faith Prince.

America [VS] / Cool [VS] / Somewhere [VS] — Stephen Sondheim^w & Leonard Bernstein^m *(B.M.G.)*; Comedy

Tonight [VS] — Stephen Sondheim^{w/m} (B.M.G.); I Still Get Jealous [VS] / On a Sunday by the Sea [VS] — Sammy Cahn^w & Jule Styne^m (B.M.G.); I'm Flying [VS] — Carolyn Leigh^w & Mark Charlap^m (B.M.G.); Mr. Monotony — Irving Berlin^{w/m} (Berlin); New York, New York [VS] / Some Other Time [VS] / Ya Got Me [VS] — Betty Comden^w & Adolph Green^w & Leonard Bernstein^m (B.M.G.); Sunrise, Sunset [VS] / Tradition [VS] — Sheldon Harnick^w & Jerry Bock^m (B.M.G.); You Gotta Have a Gimmick [VS] — Stephen Sondheim^w & Jule Styne^m (B.M.G.). A wonderful dancing show with the best of Jerome Robbins' choreography. COVER: cast of the show and Broadway marquees.

1162 Jerry for Short (Broadway, 1929). Fiske O'Hara, Patricia Quinn.

Jerry for Short — Fiske O'Hara^{w/m} (Feist). A comedy about a newly rich couple in society. COVER: O'Hara and Quinn.

1163 Jerry's Girls (Broadway, 1986). Dorothy Loudon, Chita Rivera, Leslie Uggams.

Bosom Buddies [VS] / Chin Up, Ladies! [VS] / Dickie [VS] / Hello Dolly! [VS] / I Wanna Make the World Laugh [VS] / I Won't Send Roses [VS] / If He Walked Into My Life Today [VS] / I'll Be Here Tomorrow [VS] / It Only Takes a Moment [VS] / Jerry's Girls [VS] / Just Go to the Movies [VS] / Kiss Her Now [VS] / Look What Happened to Mabel [VS] / Mame [VS] / Man in the Moon [VS] / Milk and Honey [VS] / Movies Were Movies [VS] / Nelson [VS] / Open a New Window [VS] / Put On Your Sunday Clothes [VS] / Shalom [VS] / So Long, Dearie [VS] / Tap Your Troubles Away [VS] / Time Heals Everything [VS] / Two-a-Day [VS] / Voices [VS] / We Need a Little Christmas [VS] / Wherever He Ain't [VS] — Jerry Herman^{w/m} (Leonard). A rather over-long rehash of Herman songs performed by three professionals. COVER: four chorus girls.

1164 The Jest (Broadway, 1919). John Barrymore, Lionel Barrymore.

Madrigal of May — song and waltzes — Maurice Nitke^{w/m} (Stern). An Italian melodrama produced for the Barrymores. COVER: John Barrymore.

1165 Jesus Christ Superstar (Broadway, 1971). Yvonne Elliman, Ben Vereen.

Everything's Alright / Heaven on Their Minds / Hosanna / I Don't Know How to Love Him / I Only Want to Say (Gethsemane) / King Herod's Song / The Last Supper / Pilate's Dream / Superstar — Tim Rice^w & Andrew Lloyd Webber^m (Leeds). A rock opera with a biblical theme and a hit for two years. COVER: two angels.

1166 Jig Saw (British, 1920). Dolly Sisters.

Limehouse Nights — piano selections / Poppyland — piano selections / Swanee — piano selections — George Gershwin^m (Chappell); Poppyland — John Mears^w & B.G. DeSylva^w & George Gershwin^m (Chappell). A revue using some Gershwin songs. COVER: the Dolly Sisters.

1167 Jim Jam Jems (Broadway, 1920). Joe E. Brown, Frank Fay.

Ev'rybody But Me — Joe Goodwin^w & James Hanley^m (Shapiro, Bernstein); From Your Heart to Mine / I've Always Been Fond of Babies / Jim Jam Jems / The Magic Kiss / Raggedy Ann / Sweet Little Stranger / When the Right Little Girl Comes Along — Harry Cort^w & George Stoddard^w & James Hanley^m (Shapiro, Bernstein); I Used to Love You — Lew Brown^w & Albert Von Tilzer^m (Broadway). A reporter and society girl was the basis of this musical which lasted a few months and then toured as *Hello Lester!* COVER: girl in water with ship sailing away.

1168 Jimmie (Broadway, 1920). Frances White, Harry Delf.

Baby Dreams / Cute Little Two by Four / Jimmie / Ming Poo / Rickety Crickety / That's as Far as I Can Go — Otto Harbach^w & Oscar Hammerstein^w & Herbert Stothart^m (Harms). A musical about an inheritance that had some pleasant songs but lasted only two months. COVER: Frances White.

1169 Jimmy (Broadway, 1969). Anita Gillette, Julie Wilson.

I Only Wanna Laugh [VS] / Jimmy [VS] / What's Out There for Me? [VS] — Bill Jacob[w/m] & Patti Jacob[w/m] *(T R O)*. The life of Jimmy Walker and a ten week failure. COVER: Frank Gorshin as Jimmy.

1170 Jo (Off Broadway, 1964). Susan Browning, Joy Hodges.

Afraid to Fall in Love / Friendly Polka / I Like — William Dyer[w/m] & Don Parks[w/m] *(Sunbeam)*. *Little Women* set to music and a failure of ten weeks. COVER: a mirror with ribbons.

1171 Joan of Arkansaw (see also Always You) (Broadway, 1920). Helen Ford, Walter Scanlon.

Always You / Don't You Remember? / Drifting / I Never Miss / I'll Say So / Misterioso / Pousse Cafe / Same Old Places / Some Big Something / A String of Girls / Wonderful War — Oscar Hammerstein[w] & Herbert Stothart[m] *(Remick)*. The first show with book and lyrics by Oscar Hammerstein. It ran for only eight weeks. This show toured as *Joan of Arkansaw* and opened on Broadway as *Always You*. COVER: trees, sky, and designs.

1172 Joe Howard Revue (Regional, 1920). Joe Howard.

When It's Honeysuckle Time Way Down in Georgia — Arthur Freed[w] & Joe Howard[m] & Oliver Wallace[m] *(Musicland)*; You Are a Wonderful Girl — Arthur Freed[w] & Joe Howard[m] & Jack King[m] *(Musicland)*. A revue that toured the country but never reached Broadway. COVER: Joe Howard.

1173 John Henry (Broadway, 1940). Paul Robeson, Ruby Elzy.

Careless Love / Got a Head Like a Rock / I've Trompled All Over / Sundown in My Soul — Roark Bradford[w] & Jacques Wolfe[m] *(Chappell)*. A drama with music about a black man and his tragic life. It was too sad and closed in one week. COVER: silhouette of man with bale of cotton.

1174 John Murray Anderson's Almanac (Broadway, 1953). Hermione Gingold, Billy DeWolfe.

Acorn in the Meadow / Fini / You're Such a Part of Me — Richard Adler[w/m] & Jerry Ross[w/m] *(Frank)*; Anema E. Core — Mann Curtis[w] & Harry Akst[w] & Salve Desposito[m] *(Leeds)*; Earth and the Sky — John Rox[w/m] *(Frank)*; Hold 'em Joe — Harry Thomas[w/m] *(Folkways)*; If Every Month Were June — John Murray Anderson[w] & Henry Sullivan[m] *(Robbins)*; Mark Twain — Harry Belafonte[w/m] *(Folkways)*; My Love Is a Wanderer [VS] — Bart Howard[w/m] *(Hampshire)*; Tin Pan Alley — Joseph McCarthy[w] & Cy Coleman[m] *(Robbins)*. A very entertaining revue with pleasant songs and the great comedy of Gingold and DeWolfe. It was the debut of Adler and Ross and also featured Harry Belafonte. It had a run of six months. COVER: curtain and masks; girl with balloons; Harry Belafonte.

1175 Johnny Johnson (Broadway, 1936). Lee Cobb, Luther Adler.

Johnny Johnson — complete vocal score — Edward Heyman[w] & Paul Green[w] & Kurt Weill[m] *(Chappell)*; Listen to My Heart [VS] / Mon Ami, My Friend / Oh, Heart of Love / Oh the Rio Grande — Paul Green[w] & Kurt Weill[m] *(Chappell)*; To Love You and to Lose You — Edward Heyman[w] & Kurt Weill[m] *(Chappell)*. An anti-war musical with some good Kurt Weill music but which ran only two months. COVER: a soldier, a bird and the Statue of Liberty.

1176 Jollies of 1922 (Black, 1922). Stars unknown.

Give Me Your Love All the Time / Jungoland / Longing / Oo-La-La — Haven Gillespie[w] & Joe Bren[m] *(Browne)*; Kiddo — Joe Bren[w/m] *(Browne)*. A revue from Chicago. COVER: two black dancers.

1177 Jollyanna (see also Flahooley) (Regional, 1952). Mitzi Gaynor, Bobby Clark.

How Lucky Can You Get? — E.Y.

Harburg^w & Sammy Fain^m *(Chappell)*. A revised edition of the Broadway failure, *Flahooley* having a limited run by the Los Angeles Light Opera Co. Cover: a genie and his toys.

1178 Jonica (Broadway, 1930). Nell Roy, Bert Matthews.

Garden of Beautiful Girls / Here in My Heart / If You Were the Apple / One Step Nearer the Moon / Specially Made for You / Tie Your Cares to a Melody — Billy Moll^w & Joseph Meyer^m *(Shapiro, Bernstein)*; I Want Someone / Tonight or Never — William Friedlander^w/m *(Shapiro, Bernstein)*. A musical about a wedding with romance between the guests. It lasted five weeks. Cover: an artist painting a girl's face.

1179 Joseph and the Amazing Technicolor Dreamcoat (Broadway, 1981). Bill Hutton, Laurie Beecham.

Any Dream Will Do [vs] / Benjamin Calypso / Close Ev'ry Door to Me [vs] / A Coat of Many Colors [vs] / Hang On Now, Joseph [vs] / Jacob and Sons [vs] / Joseph and the Amazing Technicolor Dreamcoat — complete vocal score / Joseph's Dreams [vs] / One More Angel in Heaven [vs] / Pharaoh's Number Two [vs] / Poor, Poor Joseph [vs] / Seven Years [vs] / Song of the King [vs] — Tim Rice^w & Andrew Lloyd Webber^m *(Belwin-Mills)*. The first musical by Rice and Webber; a biblical setting. It ran for two years and has been revived many times. Cover: Joseph and his coat.

1180 Jotham Valley (Broadway, 1951). Leland Holland, Marion Clayton.

The Answer Man / Change in a Home on the Range / I'm the Luckiest Girl Alive / Look to the Mountains! / Nothing's Ever Quite Like This — Cecil Broadhurst^w & Frances Hadden^m *(Moral Rearmament)*; Jingle to My Spurs / The Omelet Song / Somewhere in the Heart of a Man / When I Grow Up / When I Point My Finger at My Neighbor — Cecil Broadhurst^w/m *(Moral Rearmament)*; Twicklehampton School for Girls — Cecil Broadhurst^w &

Alan Thornhill^w & Frances Hadden^m *(Moral Rearmament)*; Wonder Why — Cecil Broadhurst^w & Francis Hadden^m & George Fraser^m *(Moral Rearmament)*. A propaganda musical for Moral Rearmament that lasted three weeks. Cover: scenes of families and friends.

1181 Joy (Off Broadway, 1970). Oscar Brown, Jean Pace.

Afro Blue — Oscar Brown^w/m & Mongo Santamaria^w/m *(Marks)*; Brown Baby / Flowing to the Sea / Funky World / Time / Wimmen's Ways / Under the Sun [vs] — Oscar Brown^w/m *(Marks)*; Funny Feelin' / Much as I Love You / A New Generation / What Is a Friend? — Oscar Brown^w & Luiz Henrique^m *(Marks)*; If I Only Had — Oscar Brown^w & Charles Aznavour^m *(Marks)*; Mother Africa's Day — Oscar Brown^w & Sivuca^m *(Marks)*; Nothing But a Fool — Oscar Brown^w/m & L. Reis^w/m & A. Barbosa^w/m *(Marks)*; Sky and Sea [vs] — J. Alf^w/m *(Marks)*. An Oscar Brown concert that ran for six months. Cover: designs and letters.

1182 A Joyful Noise (Broadway, 1966). John Raitt, Susan Watson.

Ballad Maker [vs] / Barefoot Gal [vs] / Fool's Gold [vs] / I Say Yes [vs] / I'm Ready [vs] / A Joyful Noise [vs] / Longtime Traveling [vs] / Lord, You Sure Know How to Make a New Day [vs] / Love Was [vs] / Until Today [vs] / We Won't Forget to Write [vs] / Whither Thou Goest [vs] — Oscar Brand^w/m & Paul Nassau^w/m *(T R O)*. A musical about a folk singer. It lasted for 12 performances. Cover: a man and his guitar.

1183 Jubilee (Broadway, 1935). Mary Boland, Melville Cooper.

Begin the Beguine / Just One of Those Things / The Kling-Kling Bird (on the Top of the Divi-Divi Tree) / Me and Marie / A Picture of Me Without You / When Love Comes Your Way / Why Shouldn't I — Cole Porter^w/m *(Harms)*. A royal family in disguise go on the town. This show was a critical success with some gems by Cole Porter; however, the public stayed away. Mary Boland returned to Hollywood and the show folded after five months. *Begin the Beguine* was not liked and did not become a hit for several years. COVER: a crown.

1184 Judy (Broadway, 1927). Queenie Smith, Charles Purcell.

Judy, Who D'ya Love? / Poor Cinderella / Pretty Little Stranger / Start Stompin' / Wear Your Sunday Smile — Leo Robin[w] & Charles Rosoff[m] *(Harms)*. A good girl living with a bunch of bachelors made up this musical which lasted three months. COVER: designs and lettering.

1185 Judy Drops In (Broadway, 1921). Marian Mears.

Caring for No One But You — John H. Mears[w] & Earnest Golden[m] *(Feist)*. A comedy with one song. COVER: Marian Mears.

1186 Judy Forgot (closed before Broadway, 1920). Harriet Cruise.

Why Little Boy Blue Was Blue — Frederick Day[w/m] & Avery Hopwood[w/m] & Silvio Hein[w/m] *(Harms)*. COVER: Harriet Cruise.

1187 Julie (closed before Broadway, 1934). Paula Laurence, Lenore Ulric.

The Love in My Life / The Tea Leaves Say Goodbye — Jules Loman[w] & Allan Roberts[w] & Hugo Rubens[m] *(Harms)*. COVER: flowers and designs.

1188 Julius Caesar (Broadway, 1937). Orson Welles, Joseph Cotten.

Orpheus — Lucius' Song — William Shakespeare[w] & Marc Blitzstein[m] *(Schirmer)*. An Orson Welles Mercury Theatre production. COVER: lettering and designs.

1189 Jumbo (Broadway, 1935). Jimmy Durante, Gloria Grafton.

The Circus on Parade / Diavolo / Little Girl Blue / The Most Beautiful Girl in the World / My Romance / Over and Over Again — Lorenz Hart[w] & Richard Rodgers[m] *(Harms)*. A Billy Rose spectacle about a circus in the Hippodrome; the spectacle lasted six months but did not make any money. It

did, however, produce three great Rodgers and Hart songs. COVER: a circus scene.

1190 Jump for Joy (closed before Broadway, 1941). Herb Jeffries, Dorothy Dandridge.

Bli-Blip — Duke Ellington[w] & Sid Kuller[w] & Duke Ellington[m] *(Robbins)*; The Brown-Skin Gal in the Calico Gown / Chocolate Shake / I Got It Bad — Paul Webster[w] & Duke Ellington[m] *(Robbins)*; If Life Were All Peaches and Cream / The Tune of the Hickory Stick / Two Left Feet — Paul Webster[w] & Hal Borne[m] *(Robbins)*; Jump for Joy — Paul Webster[w] & Sid Kuller[w] & Duke Ellington[m] *(Robbins)*; Nothin' — Ray Golden[w] & Sid Kuller[w] & Hal Borne[m] *(Robbins)*. A black musical that toured and produced one terrific hit song. COVER: a dancer jumping for joy.

1191 Jumpers (Broadway, 1974). Brian Bedford, Remak Ramsay.

Beyond My Reach — Mort Goode[w] & Claus Ogerman[m] *(Glamorous Music)*. A British comedy which failed. COVER: naked girl with fish bowl.

1192 June Days (Broadway, 1925). Jay Flippen, Elizabeth Hines.

All I Want Is Love — James Kendis[w] & Hal Dyson[m] *(Harms)*; If You Knew Susie — B.G. DeSylva[w/m] *(Shapiro, Bernstein)*; June Days — Clifford Grey[w] & Cyrus Wood[w] & Stephen Jones[m] *(Harms)*; Remembering You / Why Is Love? — Clifford Grey[w] & Fred Coots[m] *(Harms)*. A musical set in a girl's school and a failure of ten weeks. COVER: roses.

1193 June Love (Broadway, 1920). Elsa Adler, Johnny Dooley.

Dear Love, My Love / Don't Keep Calling Me Dearie / The Flapper and the Vamp / June Love / Somebody Like You — Brian Hooker[w] & Rudolf Friml[m] *(Harms)*. A dreary musical about a widow looking for a husband. It lasted six weeks. COVER: flowers and designs.

1194 June Moon (Broadway, 1929). Lee Patrick, Philip Loeb.

June Moon / Montana Moon — Ring Lardner[w/m] & George Kaufman[w/m] *(Harms)*. A comedy with several songs. COVER: two deer and a moon.

1195 Jungle Drums at the Plantation Club (Nightclub, 1929). Stars unknown.

Jungle Drums / Up-Town Low-Down / You Do — Frank Bannister[w/m] *(Marks)*. COVER: two black couples.

1196 Juno (Broadway, 1959). Shirley Booth, Melvyn Douglas.

I Wish It So / The Liffey Waltz / My True Heart / One Kind Word / Poor Thing [PC] — Marc Blitzstein[w/m] *(Chappell)*. A very interesting musical about the Irish Revolution. With a good score by Blitzstein, but a poor book and miscasting of the stars, it lasted two weeks. COVER: Shirley Booth and Melvyn Douglas.

1197 Just a Minute (Broadway, 1919). Johnny Hines, Wellington Cross.

Because You're Different / I'm Going to Be Lonesome / Just Imagine / Little by Little / Melody / Some Other Girl — Harry Cort[w] & George Stoddard[w] & Harold Orlob[m] *(Shapiro, Bernstein)*; When You Dance with a Certain Girl — Harry Cort[w] & George Stoddard[w] & Harold Orlob[m] *(Schirmer)*. Keeping secret a million dollar inheritance was the subject of this one month failure. COVER: man followed by a group of girls.

1198 Just a Minute (Broadway, 1928). Helen Patterson, Morton Havel.

Anything Your Heart Desires / The Break-Me-Down / Heigh-Ho-Cheerio / I've Got a Cookie Jar But No Cookies / Pretty Petite and Sweet / We'll Just Be Two Commuters / You'll Kill 'Em — Walter O'Keefe[w] & Harry Archer[m] *(D B and H)*. One big vaudeville act that failed after ten weeks. COVER: girl sitting by giant clock with girls' faces.

1199 Just Because (Broadway, 1922). Queenie Smith, Charles Trowbridge.

Day Dream Bay / I'll Name My Dolly for You / Just Because! / Love — Just Simply Love / Oh, Those Jazzing Toes — Helen Woodruff[w] & Madelyn Sheppard[m] *(Harms)*. An "orphan story" that ran for five weeks. COVER: flowers and designs.

1200 Just Fancy (Broadway, 1927). Raymond Hitchcock, Eric Blore.

Coo-Coo / Dressed Up for Your Sunday Beau / Humpty-Dumpty / Shake, Brother! / Two Loving Arms / You Came Along — Leo Robin[w] & Philip Charig[m] & Joseph Meyer[m] *(Harms)*. An imaginary romance between a working girl and a prince. It ran ten weeks. COVER: flowers and designs.

1201 Just Married (Broadway, 1921). Vivian Martin, Lynne Overman.

Just Married — Adelaide Mathews[w] & Don Kendall[m] *(Feist)*. A comedy about a shipboard romance. COVER: Martin and Overman.

1202 Just My Luck (Jewish, 1947). Menasha Skulnik.

Shtarker Fun Liebe — Lillian Jacobs[w] & Abraham Ellstein[m] *(Metro)*. COVER: Abraham Ellstein and two stars.

1203 Katcha-Koo (closed before Broadway, 1921). Stars unknown.

I Never Knew What Love Could Do / I Was Always Rushing All the Girls I Knew — Maurice Baker[w/m] *(Baker)*. COVER: dancer in oriental outfit.

1204 Kathleen (closed before Broadway, 1921). Stars unknown.

Arabella / Don't Forget / Kathleen / Love Light — Luther Yantis[w] & Clayton Hotchkiss[m] *(Rogers)*. COVER: girl in checkered hat.

1205 Katja, the Dancer (Broadway, 1926). Lillian Davis, Allan Pryor.

Back to My Heart [B] — Percy Greenbank[w] & Vernon Duke[m] *(Chappell)*; If You Cared / Leander / Those Eyes So Tender / When Love's in the Air — Harry Graham[w] & Jean Gilbert[m] *(Harms)*; Just for Tonight — Clifford Grey[w] & Ralph Benatzki[m] & Maurie Rubens[m] *(Harms)*; Try a Little Kiss [B] — Percy Greenbank[w] & Arthur Wimperis[w] & Vernon Duke[m] *(Chappell)*. An

Austrian operetta by way of London. It had a four month run. COVER: lettering and designs.

1206 The Katzenjammer Kids (Regional, 1920). Stars unknown.

I Like Sadie, I Like Sam [VS] — Grace Hayward^{w/m} *(Gatts)*; San Francisco Cal [VS] / Song of the Katzenjammer Kids [VS] / Ten Little Sailors [VS] — Dave Wolf ^w & Don Bester^m *(Gatts)*. A touring musical that never went to Broadway. COVER: the Katzenjammer Kids.

1207 Kean (Broadway, 1961). Alfred Drake, Lee Venora.

Chime In / Elena / The Fog and the Grog / Inevitable / Sweet Danger / To Look Upon My Love / Willow, Willow, Willow — Robert Wright^{w/m} & George Forrest^{w/m} *(Empress)*. The life of a famous actor. It had a dreary book and score and lasted for only three months. COVER: an actor on stage.

1208 Keep It Clean (Broadway, 1929). Will Morrissey, Midge Miller.

All I Need Is Someone Like You — Charles Tobias^w & Harry Archer^m *(Shapiro, Bernstein)*; Broadway Mammy — Jimmy Duffy^{w/m} & Clarence Gaskill^{w/m} *(Shapiro, Bernstein)*; Doin' the Hot-Cha-Cha — Lester Lee^{w/m} *(Shapiro, Bernstein)*; Just a Little Blue for You — James Hanley^{w/m} *(Shapiro, Bernstein)*; Let Me Hold You in My Arms — Clarence Gaskill^{w/m} *(Shapiro, Bernstein)*; What Do You See in Me — Jack Murray^{w/m} & Lester Lee^{w/m} *(Shapiro, Bernstein)*. A very poor revue that lasted two weeks. COVER: a row of beautiful homes.

1209 Keep It in the Family (Broadway, 1967). Maureen O'Sullivan, Patrick Magee.

Keep It in the Family — Dorothy Fields^w & Cy Coleman^m *(Notable)*. A British comedy that lasted one week. COVER: sketch of girl with finger on lips.

1210 Keep Kool (Broadway, 1924). Hazel Dawn, Charles King.

By the Shalimar / Calicoquette / Dandelion Time / Dawn Will Come / Gypsy Anna / How You Gonna Keep Kool / Painted Rose — Paul Smith^w & Jack Frost^m *(Remick)*; Out Where the Pavement Ends — Jack Frost^{w/m} *(Remick)*. An ordinary revue with dull songs and skits that managed to run for five months. COVER: snow and frost.

1211 Keep Moving (Broadway, 1934). Tom Howard, Billy Taylor.

Hot-cha Chiquita / Now Is the Time / Wake Up, Sleepy Moon — Jack Scholl^w & Max Rich^m *(Harms)*. A two week run for another poor revue. COVER: a sketch of dancers.

1212 Keep Off the Grass (Broadway, 1940). Ray Bolger, Jimmy Durante.

Clear Out of This World / Crazy as a Loon / A Latin Tune, a Manhattan Moon, and You — Al Dubin^w & Jimmy McHugh^m *(Crawford)*; On the Old Park Bench / Two in a Taxi — Howard Dietz^w & Jimmy McHugh^m *(Crawford)*. A revue that had many show doctors along the way but still ended up a failure after five weeks. COVER: sketch of a scene in Central Park with various people.

1213 Keep Shufflin' (Broadway, 1928). Josephine Hall, Flournoy Miller.

Charlie, My Back Door Man — Con Conrad^w & Henry Creamer^w & Clarence Todd^m *(Harms)*; Give Me the Sunshine / Sippi — Con Conrad^w & Henry Creamer^w & Jimmy Johnson^m *(Harms)*; Got Myself Another Jockey Now / How Jazz Was Born / Willow Tree — Andy Razaf^w & Thomas Waller^m *(Harms)*; Pining — Henry Creamer^{w/m} & Clarence Todd^{w/m} *(Harms)*; 'Twas a Kiss in the Moonlight — Con Conrad^w & Henry Creamer^w & Stephen Jones^m *(Harms)*. A black musical with great dancing and only a fair book. It ran for three months. COVER: a row of men and ladies' legs and feet.

1214 Keith's Vaudeville (Regional, 1920). Aileen Stanley.

Jazz Vampire — Arthur Swanstrom^w & Carey Morgan^m *(Stern)*. COVER: Aileen Stanley.

1215 Kelly (Broadway, 1964). Don Francks, Eileen Rodgers.

Ballad to a Brute / Everyone Here Loves Kelly / Home Again / I'll Never Go There Anymore / It Kinda Makes Yuh Wonder — Eddie Lawrence[w] & Moose Charlap[m] *(Chappell)*. One of the biggest disasters in Broadway history. A huge flop of one night. COVER: man falling from bridge.

1216 The Kick Off (closed before Broadway, 1925). Stars unknown.

Canvasman's College Song [VS] / Congo College Song [VS] / Cornwall Days [VS] / Cornwall Forever [VS] / Goodnight Team [VS] / The Kick Off [VS] / My Alma Mammy [VS] / Song for the Bold and the Blues [VS] — Frank Craven[w/m] & Grantland Rice[w/m] & Silvio Hein[w/m] *(Feist)*. A college musical. COVER: a football player kicking.

1217 Kicks and Co. (closed before Broadway, 1961). Burgess Meredith, Al Freeman.

Ernest's Theme — Oscar Brown[m] *(Marks)*; Hazel's Hips / Love Is Like a Newborn Child / Mister Kicks / Opportunity, Please Knock / Virtue Is Its Own Reward / While I Am Still Young / Worldful of Grey — Oscar Brown[w/m] *(Marks)*. A musical about sex and racial problems; it lasted four days in its try-out in Chicago. COVER: Burgess Meredith.

1218 Kid Boots (Broadway, 1923). Eddie Cantor, Mary Eaton.

Alabamy Bound — Bud DeSylva[w/m] & Bud Green[w/m] & Ray Henderson[w/m] *(Shapiro, Bernstein)*; Along the Old Lake Trail / The Cake Eater's Ball / The Fountain of Youth / In the Swim at Miami / Keep Your Eye on the Ball / Let's Do and Say We Didn't / A Play-Fair Man! / Polly Put the Kettle On / The Same Old Way / The Social Observer / Someone Loves You After All / We've Got to Have More / When the Cocoanuts Call / When Your Heart's in the Game / Why Don't You Say So? — Joseph McCarthy[w] & Harry Tierney[m] *(Feist)*; The Dumber They Come the Better I Like 'Em — Harry DeCosta[w/m] & Eddie Cantor[w/m] & Fred Ahlert[w/m] *(Berlin)*; Farmer Took Another Load Away — Edgar Leslie[w/m] & Charles O'Flynn[w/m] & Larry Vincent[w/m] *(C and L)*; Goin' Home Blues — Willie Raskin[w] & George Olsen[m] & Ed Kilfeather[m] *(Robbins-Engel)*; Hot Ziggity — Eddie Cantor[w/m] & Jerry Benson[w/m] *(Breau, Tobias)*; Hottest Man in Town — Owen Murphy[w/m] & Jay Gorney[w/m] *(Robbins-Engel)*; If You Do-What You Do — Roy Turk[w/m] & Lou Handman[w/m] & Eddie Cantor[w/m] *(Berlin)*; If You Knew Susie — B.G. DeSylva[w/m] *(Shapiro, Bernstein)*; I'm Goin' South — Abner Silver[w/m] & Harry Woods[w/m] *(Witmark)*; It's Just That Feeling for Home — Sam Lewis[w/m] & Joe Young[w/m] & Fred Ahlert[w/m] *(W B and S)*; The King Isn't King Anymore — Edgar Leslie[w] & James Monaco[m] *(C and L)*; Mah-Jong — Billy Rose[w/m] & Con Conrad[w/m] *(Witmark)*; Mee Too — Harry Woods[w/m] & Charles Tobias[w/m] & Al Sherman[w/m] *(Shapiro, Bernstein)*; Morning — Roy Turk[w/m] & Abner Silver[w/m] *(Berlin)*; Oh! How I Love My Darling! — Edgar Leslie[w] & Harry Woods[m] *(C and L)*; Rock-a-bye Baby Days — Harold Christy[w] & Abner Silver[m] & Saul Bernie[m] *(Feist)*; Rosie — Lew Brown[w/m] & Eddie Cantor[w/m] & Henry Santly[w/m] *(Shapiro, Bernstein)*; A Sunkist Cottage in California — George Olsen[w/m] & Louis Hirsch[w/m] & Ed Kilfeather[w/m] *(Robbins-Engel)*. Eddie Cantor was a golf caddie and bootlegger in a book show which was more like a revue. With songs changing nightly, this mediocre show kept running for more than a year. COVER: Eddie Cantor, Mary Eaton and golfer.

1219 Kiddie Karnival (Regional, 1928). Madeline Lawson.

China / Come Down to the Seashore with Me / Does Anybody Want a Little Kewpie? / Let's Make Ev'ry Day a May Day / Mister Sandman / When Pat Rooney Dances a Waltz / When the Sun Smiles on Erin — Jack Darrell[w/m]

& Sam Cantor^w/m & Sam Lewis^w/m & Lew Hays^w/m *(Darrell)*. Cover: kids in various poses.

1220 Kiddie Karnival (Regional, 1934). Norma Wayne.

Ach Du Lieber Darling / The Babies on Parade / Fickle Heart / Gun Moll Gerty / Kiddie Days — Jack Darrell^w/m & Sam Cantor^w/m & Sam Lewis^w/m & Lew Hays^w/m *(Darrell)*; I Know — Jack Darrell^w & Lew Hayes^m *(Darrell)*; Mother's Dancing Doll — Jack Darrell^w & Marie Schroeder^m *(Darrell)*. Cover: kids in various poses.

1221 Kiki (Broadway, 1921). Lenore Ulric, Sam Hardy.

Kiki — Schuyler Greene^w & Zoel Parenteau^m *(Harms)*. A hit comedy with one song. Cover: Lenore Ulric.

1222 Kill That Story (Broadway, 1934). Gloria Grafton, James Bell.

Two Cigarettes in the Dark — Paul F. Webster^w & Lew Pollack^m *(D B and H)*. A comedy with a moderate run. Cover: Gloria Grafton.

1223 The King and I (Broadway, 1951). Yul Brynner, Gertrude Lawrence.

Getting to Know You / Hello, Young Lovers / I Have Dreamed / I Whistle a Happy Tune / The King and I — complete vocal score / My Lord and Master / Shall We Dance? / Something Wonderful / We Kiss in a Shadow — Oscar Hammerstein^w & Richard Rodgers^m *(Williamson)*; March of the Siamese Children — Richard Rodgers^m *(Williamson)*. One of the great musicals, running three years, with many revivals. The stars were perfectly cast and the score was beautiful. Cover: Siamese artifacts and statement "Gertrude Lawrence in *The King and I.*"

1224 The King and I (Broadway, 1977). Yul Brynner, Constance Towers.

The King and I — nine songs (1977) — Oscar Hammerstein^w & Richard Rodgers^m *(Williamson)*. A beautiful revival of this hit show. Cover: red designs and statement "Yul Brynner in *The King and I.*" Cover: red designs with Yul Brynner's name in large letters as star billing.

1225 King of Song (Jewish, 1934). Herman Yablokoff.

Give Me Back My Heart — Herman Yablokoff^w/m *(Kammen)*. A musical from the Second Avenue theatre. Cover: Herman Yablokoff.

1226 King of the Whole Damn World! (Off Broadway, 1962). Alan Howard, Tom Pedi.

Who's Perfect — Robert Larimer^w/m *(Saunders)*. A musical about the "village" that lasted one month. Cover: black and white with titles only.

1227 A Kingdom for a Cow (British, 1935). Webster Booth, Vivienne Chatterton.

As Long as I Love / Two Hearts — Desmond Carter^w & Kurt Weill^m *(Chappell)*; A Kingdom for a Cow — piano selections — Kurt Weill^m *(Chappell)*. During a brief period of residence in England, Weill wrote this musical which failed. Cover: a silly knight riding a cow.

1228 Kismet (*see also* **Timbuktu!**) (Broadway, 1953). Alfred Drake, Doretta Morrow.

And This Is My Beloved / Baubles, Bangles and Beads / He's in Love / Kismet — complete score / Night of My Nights / Sands of Time / Stranger in Paradise — Robert Wright^w/m & George Forrest^w/m & A. Borodin^w/m *(Frank)*. A lavish spectacle with lovely melodies and good singers. It ran for eighteen months. Cover: oriental designs.

1229 The Kiss Burglar (Broadway, 1919). Marie Carroll, Louise Mink.

Because You Do Not Know / The Girl I Can't Forget / I Want to Learn to Dance / The Little Black Sheep / The Mantelpiece Tragedy / On the Shimmering Glimmering Nile / One Day / The Rose / Since I Met Wonderful You / Solitaire Lane — Glen MacDonough^w & Raymond Hubbell^m *(Harms)*. A musical about a grand duchess and a kiss. It ran three months. Cover: a couple embracing.

1230 Kiss Me (closed before Broadway, 1919). Stars unknown.

Kiss Me – William Friedlander[w/m] *(Remick).* COVER: titles and designs.

1231 Kiss Me (Broadway, 1927). Fred Santley, Joseph Macaulay.

I Have Something Nice for You / Kiss Me / Pools of Love / Rose of Iran – Derick Wulff[w] & Winthrop Cortelyou[m] *(Harms).* A musical set in a harem with a run of four weeks. COVER: flowers and designs.

1232 Kiss Me Again (closed before Broadway, 1919). Fred Bowers.

If I Ever Get You – Arthur Lamb[w] & Fred Bowers[m] *(Bowers);* Kiss Me Again / Someone / Who's Going to Love All – William Tracey[w] & Fred Bowers[m] *(Bowers);* Ragtime Wedding Blues – Victor Scott[w/m] *(Bowers).* COVER: Fred Bowers.

1233 Kiss Me, Kate (Broadway, 1948). Alfred Drake, Patricia Morison.

Always True to You in My Fashion / Another Op'nin', Another Show / Bianca / Brush Up Your Shakespeare / From This Moment On / I Am Ashamed That Women Are So Simple / I Hate Men / I Sing of Love / I'm Afraid Sweetheart, I Love You [VS] [CUT] / I've Come to Wive It Wealthily in Padua / Kiss Me, Kate – complete score / So in Love / Tom, Dick or Harry / Too Darn Hot / We Open in Venice / We Shall Never Be Younger [PC] [CUT] / Were Thine That Special Face / Where Is the Life That Late I Led? / Why Can't You Behave? / Wunderbar – Cole Porter[w/m] *(Harms).* Cole Porter's best score in one of the best shows on Broadway. A beautiful production with a good book, talented singers, perfect staging and direction. It ran two and one half years. *From This Moment On* was published and dropped from *Out of This World.* It was used and published in the movie *Kiss Me, Kate.* It was then re-published with the original stage cover of *Kiss Me, Kate.* COVER: red, white and blue stars and shapes.

1234 Kiss of the Spider Woman (Broadway, 1993). Chita Rivera, Brent Carver.

Anything for Him / The Day After That / Dear One / Dressing Them Up / I Do Miracles / The Kiss of the Spider Woman / The Morphine Tango / Only in the Movies / Over the Wall-2 / She's a Woman / Where You Are – Fred Ebb[w] & John Kander[m] *(Fiddleback).* A strange and beautiful musical about a jailed homosexual and his fantasies. A failure in its early try-out, it was revised, presented in Toronto and London and went on to be a smash hit in New York. It was especially helped by a sensational performance by Chita Rivera. COVER: Chita Rivera.

1235 Kissing Time (British, 1919). George Grossmith, Phyllis Dare.

I Was So Young [B] – Irving Caesar[w] & Al Bryan[w] & George Gershwin[m] *(Chappell).* A version of *The Girl Behind the Gun* with a Gershwin song added. It had a run of one year. COVER: Grossmith and Dare.

1236 Kissing Time (Broadway, 1920). Paul Frawley, Edith Taliaferro.

As Long as the World Goes Round / Beware / Bill and Coo / Kikeri-Kee / Kissimee / Love's Telephone / Mini-Bells Are Ringing – George Hobart[w] & Ivan Caryll[m] *(Chappell);* Come Back to Me – Clifford Grey[w] & Ivan Caryll[m] *(Chappell);* It's the Nicest Sort of Feeling – Irving Caesar[w] & William Daly[m] *(Harms);* Kissing Time – Irving Caesar[w] & Ivan Caryll[m] *(Chappell).* An old fashioned musical about a pretend marriage. It lasted nine weeks. COVER: flowers and ferns.

1237 Kittiwake Island (Off Broadway, 1960). Kathleen Murray, Lainie Kazan.

I'd Gladly Walk to Alaska [VS] / If Love's Like a Lark [VS] / When a Robin Leaves Chicago [VS] – Arnold Sundgaard[w] & Alec Wilder[m] *(Hampshire).* A musical about life on a small island. It lasted one week. COVER: Alec Wilder.

1238 Kitty's Kisses (Broadway, 1926). Dorothy Dilley, John Boles.

I'm in Love – Gus Kahn[w] & Otto Harbach[w] & Con Conrad[m] *(Harms);*

Kitty's Kisses / Thinking of You — Gus Kahn[w] & Con Conrad[m] *(Harms)*; Step on the Blues — Otto Harbach[w] & Con Conrad[m] & Will Donaldson[m] *(Harms)*. A musical love story dealing with a lost handbag. Its best feature was the spectacular dancing which kept the show running for almost six months. COVER: a pair of lips and lettering.

1239 Klick-Klick (closed before Broadway, 1921). Joseph Santley, Ivy Sawyer.

You and Me and You — Kenneth Webb[w] & Roy Webb[m] *(Witmark)*. COVER: Santley and Sawyer sitting on the moon.

1240 Knickerbocker Holiday (Broadway, 1938). Walter Huston, Ray Middleton.

Ballad of the Robbers [VS] / Dirge for a Soldier [VS] / How Can You Tell an American? [VS] / It Never Was Anywhere You / It Never Was You / Knickerbocker Holiday — complete vocal score / May and January [VS] / One Indispensable Man [VS] / Our Ancient Liberties [VS] / The Scars [VS] / September Song / There's Nowhere to Go But Up / To War [VS] / Washington Irving's Song [VS] / We Are Cut in Twain [VS] / Will You Remember Me? / Young People Think About Love [VS] — Maxwell Anderson[w] & Kurt Weill[m] *(Crawford)*. This musical had only a moderate run but a lovely Kurt Weill score including *September Song*. COVER: top hat, cane, gloves, and lettering.

1241 Kosher Kitty Kelly (Broadway, 1925). Fred Santley, Helen Shipman.

Dancing Toes / Kosher Kitty Kelly / Never to Leave You Again / When We Can Be in Love — Leon De Costa[w/m] *(Harms)*. A not-so-great attempt to recreate *Abie's Irish Rose;* however, it ran five months. COVER: lettering and designs.

1242 The Kosher Widow (Jewish, 1959). Molly Picon, Irving Jacobson.

All I Want Baby Is You / Am Yisroel Chai! / The Hutska / No Greater Love — Sheldon Secunda[w] & Sholom Secunda[m] *(Mills)*. COVER: a lady with parasol.

1243 Kwamina (Broadway, 1961). Sally Ann Howes, Terry Carter.

Another Time, Another Place / I'm Seeing Rainbows / Nothing More to Look Forward To / Ordinary People / Something Bit / What Happened to Me Tonight? [PC] / What's Wrong with Me? — Richard Adler[w/m] *(Chappell)*. An interesting failure about an interracial love affair in Africa. This was Adler's first solo show. COVER: African dancer with mask.

1244 The Lace Petticoat (Broadway, 1927). Dick Powell, Vivian Hart.

The Engagement / Playthings of Love — Howard Johnston[w] & Emil Gerstenberger[m] *(Harms)*; The Girl That I Adore / Little Lace Petticoat — Carle Carlton[w] & Emil Gerstenberger[m] *(Harms)*. A New Orleans musical that lasted two weeks. COVER: girl in beautiful gown.

1245 Ladies First (Broadway, 1918). Nora Bayes, William Kent.

All My Life — Nora Bayes[w/m] & Harry Akst[w/m] & Irving Fisher[w/m] *(Harms)*; Happy Days / Home Life / I'm Always Happy with a Crowd of Girls / Just What a Girl Can Do / Kaiser Bill / My Comparative Love / War Garden — Harry B. Smith[w] & Baldwin Sloane[m] *(Harms)*; I'll Tell the World — Al Weeks[w] & Nora Bayes[m] & Seymour Simons[m] *(Remick)*; Just Like a Gipsy / Tell Me — Nora Bayes[w/m] & Seymour Simons[w/m] *(Remick)*; Just the Two of Us — Seymour Simons[w/m] *(Berlin)*; M-A-Y-B-E — Edgar Leslie[w/m] & Harry Ruby[w/m] *(Berlin)*; Me and You — Nora Bayes[w] & Irving Fisher[m] & Harry Akst[m] *(Harms)*; Prohibition Blues — Ring Lardner[w] & Nora Bayes[m] *(Remick)*; The Real American Folk Song (plain) — Ira Gershwin[w] & George Gershwin[m] *(Chappell)*; Some Wonderful Sort of Someone — Schuyler Greene[w] & George Gershwin[m] *(Harms)*; Ten Little Bottles — Ballard MacDonald[w] & James Monaco[m] *(Shapiro, Bernstein)*; When I Build a

Home / Without You — Nora Bayes[w] & Irving Fisher[m] *(Harms)*. A musical about women's suffrage and a moderate hit for four months with two early Gershwin songs. COVER: Nora Bayes.

1246 The Lady (Broadway, 1923). Mary Nash, Marcel Marelli.

Give Her a Violet — Martin Brown[w/m] *(Harms)*. A melodrama with one song. COVER: Mary Nash.

1247 Lady, Be Good! (Broadway, 1924). Fred and Adele Astaire.

Fascinating Rhythm / The Half of It, Dearie, Blues / Hang On to Me / Little Jazz Bird / The Man I Love / Oh, Lady Be Good! / So Am I — Ira Gershwin[w] & George Gershwin[m] *(Harms)*; I'd Rather Charleston [B] — Desmond Carter[w] & George Gershwin[m] *(Harms)*; It's All the Same to Me — Chick Endor[w/m] *(Berlin)*; Something About Love [B] — Lou Paley[w] & George Gershwin[m] *(Harms)*; Swiss Miss [B] — George Gershwin[m] *(Harms)*; Who Takes Care of the Caretaker's Daughter — Chick Endor[w/m] *(Shapiro, Bernstein)*. This show was Broadway at its best with a jazzy score, art deco sets, and the Astaires. It ran for nine months and produced several Gershwin standards. COVER: butterflies and circles.

1248 Lady Billy (Broadway, 1920). Mitzi, Boyd Marshall.

Come to Arcady with Me / Good-Bye / Just Plant a Kiss / The Legend / Love Comes Like a Butterfly / The Matchless English Language / The Tune They Play / A Vision — Zeld Sears[w] & Harold Levey[m] *(Harms)*; The Hand That Spanks the Baby — piano selections — Harold Levey[m] *(Harms)*. This musical involved a lady posing as the gardener's son. It had a pleasant book but dreary music. Mitzi kept it running for six months. COVER: Mitzi.

1249 Lady Butterfly (Broadway, 1923). Florenz Ames, Allen Kearns.

Kiss Time / Lady Butterfly / My Cottage in Sunshine Lane / Sway with Me / Waltz Time / Wonderful You — Clifford Grey[w] & Werner Janssen[m] *(Harms)*. A terrible plot about luggage mix-ups. Despite a poor score, a lot of good dance numbers kept it going for four months. COVER: lettering and designs.

1250 The Lady Comes Across (Broadway, 1942). Joe E. Lewis, Ronald Graham.

I'd Like to Talk About the Weather [PC] / Lady [PC] / Summer Is A-Comin' In [PC] / This Is Where I Came In [PC] / You Took Me by Surprise [PC] — John Latouche[w] & Vernon Duke[m] *(Miller)*. A spy story that lasted three performances on Broadway after a million problems on the road. COVER: none.

1251 Lady Do (Broadway, 1927). Karyl Norman, Nancy Welford.

Blah! But Not Too Blue / Buddy Rose [ABQ] / Dreamy Montmartre / In the Long Run [ABQ] / Lady Do / Little Miss Small Town [ABQ] / Live Today — Love Today [ABQ] / My Castle in Sorrento [ABQ] / O Sola Mi — Whose Soul Are You? [ABQ] / On Double Fifth Avenue / Paris Taught Me Zis [ABQ] / You Can't Eye a Shy Baby [ABQ] — Sam Lewis[w] & Joe Young[w] & Abel Baer[m] *(Feist)*. A poor show with female impersonator Karyl Norman. It ran seven weeks. COVER: a girl's face.

1252 Lady Fair (*see also* The Desert Song) (Broadway, 1926). Robert Halliday, Vivienne Segal.

Dreaming in Paradise / "It" / Let's Have a Love Affair / Love's Dear Yearning / One Alone #1 / One Alone #2 / The Riff Song / Romance — Otto Harbach[w] & Oscar Hammerstein[w] & Sigmund Romberg[m] *(Harms)*. A smash hit in the old operetta style with good Romberg music. It was based on the French-Arab troubles in North Africa. It tried out as *Lady Fair,* but opened as *The Desert Song.* COVER: an Arab and a girl on the desert.

1253 Lady Fingers (Broadway, 1929). Louise Brown, John Price.

Ga-Ga / Let Me Weep on Your Shoulder / Open Book / Raise the Dust / Slow Down / Something to Live For / Turn to Me / You're Perfect —

Edward Eliscu[w] & Joseph Meyer[m] *(Harms)*; I Love You More Than Yesterday / Sing — Lorenz Hart[w] & Richard Rodgers[m] *(Harms)*. A musical involving a bank robbery. With two Rodgers and Hart songs, it had a run of four months. COVER: lady fingers with jewels.

1254 Lady in Ermine (Broadway, 1922). Wilda Bennett, Walter Woolf.

Dear Old Land of Mine / I'll Follow You to Zanzibar / The Lady in Ermine — Cyrus Wood[w] & Alfred Goodman[m] *(Harms)*; Marianna — Harry Graham[w] & Jean Gilbert[m] *(Harms)*; My Silhouette — Harry Graham[w] & Cyrus Wood[w] & Jean Gilbert[m] & Alfred Goodman[m] *(Harms)*; When Hearts Are Young — Cyrus Wood[w] & Sigmund Romberg[m] & Alfred Goodman[m] *(Harms)*. A moderate hit of seven months about romance between a colonel and a lady. COVER: an ermine curtain.

1255 The Lady in Red (Broadway, 1919). Neil Moore, Ann Herndon.

China Dragon Blues / Play Me That Tune — Irving Caesar[w] & Will Donaldson[m] *(Harms)*; I Want Somebody — Anne Caldwell[w] & Richard Winterberg[m] *(Harms)*; Some Wonderful Sort of Someone — Schuyler Greene[w] & George Gershwin[m] *(Harms)*; Something About Love — Lou Paley[w] & George Gershwin[m] *(Harms)*; Where's the Girl for Me — Harry B. Smith[w] & Jerome Kern[m] *(Harms)*. This musical about an artist and his dream girl lasted six weeks. COVER: candles and red letters.

1256 Lady in the Dark (Broadway, 1941). Gertrude Lawrence, Danny Kaye.

Girl of the Moment / Jenny / Lady in the Dark — complete vocal score / My Ship / One Life to Live / Princess of Pure Delight / Tchaikovsky / This Is New — Ira Gershwin[w] & Kurt Weill[m] *(Chappell)*. Another hit musical that had everything including wonderful music, sets, and stars. It ran over a year. COVER: Gertrude Lawrence.

1257 Lady Kitty, Inc. (closed before Broadway, 1920). Kitty Gordon, Donald MacDonald.

Anywhere Is Home Sweet Home with You / Moonbeams / Once in a Lifetime / One Little Girl / Say It Once Again / To Live to Love One Girl / You Can Dance Your Way into My Heart — Irving Caesar[w] & Melville Alexander[w] & Paul Lannin[m] *(Harms)*; I Always Give the Wrong Impression — Irving Caesar[w] & Paul Lannin[m] *(Harms)*; Perfume of Paradise — Irving Caesar[w] & Alfred Solman[m] *(Harms)*. Kitty Gordon was advertised as *The International Beauty*. The play folded in Baltimore. COVER: Kitty Gordon.

1258 Lady Luck (British, 1927). Laddie Cliff, Leslie Henson.

If I Were You [B] / Sing [B] — Lorenz Hart[w] & Richard Rodgers[m] *(Chappell)*. A musical play with Laddie Cliff that ran for nine months in London. COVER: letters and designs.

1259 Lady Mary (British, 1928). George Grossmith, Helen Gilliland.

If You're a Friend of Mine [B] — Harry Graham[w] & Jerome Kern[m] *(Chappell)*. A musical play in London that ran for six months. COVER: black and white cover.

1260 Lady of the Lamp (Broadway, 1920). George Gaul, Brandon Hurst.

All the World Is My Dreaming Place — Earl Carroll[w/m] *(Shapiro, Bernstein)*. An Earl Carroll production with a moderate run. COVER: a beautiful lady by a lamp.

1261 Lady Precious Stream (Broadway, 1936). Helen Chandler, Bramwell Fletcher.

Lady Precious Stream — Milton Pascal[w] & Edgar Fairchild[m] *(Marks)*. A moderate hit about a Chinese daughter avoiding an arranged marriage. COVER: sketch of Chinese Lady.

1262 Lady Purple (closed before Broadway, 1920). Stars unknown.

Celebrate with Me / Girl of My Dreams / The Kind of a Girl / Queen of the Vamp / Violets So Blue / Wine from Women and Song / Wonderful

Boy — George Deisroth[w] & Milton Leichtman[m] *(Hummer)*. COVER: lady in purple and two gentlemen.

1263 A Lady Says Yes (Broadway, 1945). Carole Landis, Arthur Maxwell.

I Wonder Why You Wander / Take My Heart with You / Without a Caress / You're More Than a Name and Address — Stanley Adams[w] & Fred Spielman[m] & Arthur Gershwin[m] *(Grand)*. A dream fantasy that lasted 11 weeks. COVER: a beautiful lady on steps.

1264 Laffing Room Only (Broadway, 1944). Olsen and Johnson.

Feudin' and Fightin' — plain cover / Gotta Get Joy [ABQ] — Al Dubin[w] & Burton Lane[w] & Burton Lane[m] *(Chappell)*; Got That Good-Time Feeling / Mother Mississippi [ABQ] / Stop That Dancing / Sunny California / You Excite Me [ABQ] — Burton Lane[w/m] *(Chappell)*. Al Dubin started to write these songs and became ill. They were finished by Burton Lane. This revue had a moderate run but the public was tired of the same Olsen-Johnson comedy. COVER: Olsen and Johnson.

1265 La-La-Lucille! (Broadway, 1919). Janet Velie, John Hazzard.

The Best of Everything / From Now On / The Love of a Wife / Nobody But You / Somehow It Seldom Comes True / Tee-Oodle-Um-Bum-Bo — B.G. DeSylva[w] & Arthur Jackson[w] & George Gershwin[m] *(Harms)*; There's More to the Kiss Than the Sound — plain cover — Irving Caesar[w] & George Gershwin[m] *(Harms)*. This was Gershwin's first complete Broadway score. It was not exceptional. This show with a thin plot ran for 13 weeks. COVER: curtains and lamps.

1266 The Land of Make Believe (Regional, 1922). Elinore Harris.

Jackie Coogan — The Kid — William Dailey[w] & B. Bentley[m] *(Harmony)*. A show in San Francisco billed as a spectacular production. COVER: Elinore Harris.

1267 Land of Romance (Irish, 1922). Fiske O'Hara.

A Broth of a Boy — Florence Fink[w] & George Gartlan[m] *(H H and E)*; The Land o' Romance — Rachel Michel[w] & George Gartlan[m] *(H H and E)*. COVER: Fiske O'Hara.

1268 Land of Romance (*see also* **Castles in the Air**) (Broadway, 1926). Vivienne Segal, Harold Murray.

First Kiss of Love / Girls and the Gimmies / I Would Like to Fondle You / Land of Romance / Lantern of Love / Other Fellow's Girl / True Love and a Ring / When Romance Is Gone / When the Only One Meets the Only One — Raymond Peck[w] & Percy Wenrich[m] *(Feist)*. A royal romance with a run of five months. It toured as *Land of Romance* and opened on Broadway as *Castles in the Air*. COVER: a troubadour serenading a lady in the window.

1269 The Lark (Broadway, 1955). Julie Harris, Boris Karloff.

Soldier's Song / Spring Song / The Lark — French and Latin Choruses — Leonard Bernstein[w/m] *(Schirmer)*. A French play about Joan of Arc which ran for seven months. Background music by Bernstein. COVER: a sword.

1270 Lassie (Broadway, 1920). Dorothy Dickson, Carl Hyson.

Bonnie Sweet Kitty / Boo-Hoo / Croodlin' Doo / Dilly-Dally-O / Echo / Fairy Whispers / Lassie / Lovely Corals / The Piper of Dundee / The Tea Cup and the Spoon — Catherine Cushing[w] & Hugo Felix[m] *(Harms)*. An orphan's story with the beautiful voice of Dorothy Dickson and some good dancing. It lasted four months. COVER: a girl in Scottish plaids.

1271 The Last Savage (Opera, 1964). Nicolai Gedda, Teresa Stratas.

How Can My Lips Deny It? — Gian Carlo Menotti[w/m] *(Colombo)*. A Menotti opera that lasted for only a few performances at the Met. COVER: red and black letters.

1272 The Last Sweet Days of Isaac (Off Broadway, 1970). Austin Pendleton, Fredricka Weber.

Herein Lie the Seeds of Revolution /

I Can't Live in Solitary / I Want to Walk to San Francisco / My Most Important Moments Go By / A Transparent Crystal Moment / Yes, I Know That I'm Alive—Gretchen Cryer[w] & Nancy Ford[m] *(Hill and Range)*. This "rock musical" was a super hit Off Broadway and ran for over a year. COVER: a sketch of man and woman with radio and trumpet.

1273 Last Waltz (Broadway, 1921). James Barton, Eleanor Painter.

A Baby in Love—Harold Atteridge[w] & Alfred Goodman[m] & Ralph Benatzky[m] *(Tama)*; The Charming Ladies—Harold Atteridge[w] & Alfred Goodman[m] *(Tama)*; The Gallant Cavalier / Hail Sparkling Wine / The Last Waltz—Edward Dunn[w] & Oscar Straus[m] *(Tama)*; The Last Waltz—fox trot / The Last Waltz—waltzes—Oscar Straus[m] *(Toma)*; Live for Today—Harold Atteridge[w] & Alfred Goodman[m] & A. Weran[m] *(Tama)*; Mama, Mama / The Mirror Song / Now Fades My Golden Love Dream / O-La-La / Roses Out of Reach / Two Little Dimples / When Spring Buds Are Breaking—Edward Dunn[w] & Oscar Straus[m] *(Tama)*; The Next Dance with You—Harold Atteridge[w] & Alfred Goodman[m] & L. Friedman[m] *(Tama)*; The Whip Hand—Harold Atteridge[w] & Rudolf Nelson[m] *(Tama)*. An old fashioned operetta with Straus waltzes that had a moderate run of five months. COVER: lady in gown with mask.

1274 Late Nite Comic (Broadway, 1987). Robert LuPone, Teresa Tracy.

Clara's Dancing School [VS] / Gabrielle [VS] / It Had to Happen Sometime [VS] / Late Nite Comic [VS] / Relax with Me Baby [VS] / When I Am Movin' [VS]—Brian Gari[w/m] *(Warner Bros.)*. A failed musical about a comedian. COVER: a night comic.

1275 Latin Quarter (Nightclub, 1946). Stars unknown.

Latin Quarter Souvenir Songs—24 standards—Various Composers *(Robbins)*. COVER: male and female Apache dancers.

1276 Latin Quarter (Nightclub, 1956). Stars unknown.

I Lost My Cherie in Paree [VS] / Plastered in Paris—Sammy Gallop[w] & Al Goodhart[m] *(Waner Music)*; Jamaica Way [VS] / The Parisian Doodle-a-do [VS] / Parisian Honeymoon [VS] / When You Whisper Cherie [VS]—Lou Walters[w/m] & Art Waner[w/m] *(Waner Music)*. COVER: beautiful show girl.

1277 Laugh and Be Happy (Jewish, 1950). Leo Fuchs, Lilly Lilliana.

Ein Mol in Lebn / Just My Luck / Lach un Sai Freilach—Jacob Jacobs[w] & I. Lillian[w] & Sholom Secunda[m] *(Metro)*. COVER: Leo Fuchs, Edmund Zayenda, Lily Lilliana.

1278 The Laugh Parade (Broadway, 1931). Ed Wynn, Lawrence Gray.

Gotta Go to Town / I Wish I Could Laugh at Love / Love Me Forever / The More You Hurt Me / Ooh That Kiss / The Torch Song / You're My Everything—Mort Dixon[w] & Joe Young[w] & Harry Warren[m] *(Harms)*. An Ed Wynn carnival with a good score by Harry Warren and a run of seven months. COVER: six toy soldiers.

1279 Leader of the Pack (Broadway, 1985). Ellie Greenwich, Patrick Cassidy.

Leader of the Pack—George Morton[w/m] & Jeff Barry[w/m] & Ellie Greenwich[w/m] *(Warner Bros.)*. A disaster made up of pop songs of the early '60s written by Barry and Greenwich. COVER: a motorcycle.

1280 Leaning on Letty (closed before Broadway, 1936). Charlotte Greenwood.

Moon Melody—serenade—Martin Broones[w/m] *(Schirmer)*. One of a series of *Letty* comedies done by Greenwood. This one toured everywhere but New York. COVER: Charlotte Greenwood.

1281 Leave It to Jane (Off Broadway, 1959). George Segal, Kathleen Murray.

Cleopatterer [VS] / The Crickets Are Calling [VS] / I'm Going to Find a Girl [VS] / Leave It to Jane [VS] / Poor Prune [VS] / The Siren's Song [VS] / The Sun Shines Brighter [VS] / Wait

Till Tomorrow [VS] — P.G. Wodehouse[w] & Jerome Kern[m] *(Harms)*. A campy revival of the 1917 show which ran for years. COVER: "Jane."

1282 Leave It to Me (*see also* **Sweetheart Time**) (Broadway, 1925). Mary Milburn, Eddie Buzzell.

How Different Things Would Be / Little Song in My Heart / Marian / Tahiti Sweetie — Ballard MacDonald[w] & Walter Donaldson[m] *(Harms)*. This musical started out as *Leave It to Me*. It was revised and opened on Broadway as *Sweetheart Time*. The revisions didn't help and this rags-to-riches musical folded. COVER: flowers and lettering.

1283 Leave It to Me (Broadway, 1938). William Gaxton, Mary Martin.

Far Away / From Now On / Get Out of Town / I Want to Go Home / Information, Please [VS] / Most Gentlemen Don't Like Love / My Heart Belongs to Daddy / Taking the Steps to Russia / To-morrow / Vite, Vite, Vite [VS] — Cole Porter[w/m] *(Chappell)*. A musical dealing with Russia and world peace. It was blessed with some good Porter songs, the comedy of Victor Moore plus Sophie Tucker and Mary Martin. COVER: William Gaxton, Victor Moore.

1284 The Left-Over (*see also* **Lollipop**) (Broadway, 1924). Ada May, Harry Puck.

Deep in My Heart / Going Rowing / Honey Bun / It Must Be Love — Zelda Sears[w] & Vincent Youmans[m] *(Harms)*. This show tried out as *The Left-Over* but opened as *Lollipop*. A poor book with a Cinderella theme and some promising Youmans tunes. It ran for five months. COVER: Ada May.

1285 Lend an Ear (Broadway, 1948). Carol Channing, Gene Nelson.

After Hours [BW] / Doin' the Old Yahoo Step [BW] / Friday Dancing Class [BW] / Give Your Heart a Chance to Sing / I'm Not in Love [BW] / I'm on the Lookout / Molly O'Reilly / Neurotic You and Psychopathic Me / Romantic'lly Inclined [BW] / Three Little Queens of the Silver Screen [BW] /

When Someone You Love Loves You / Who Hit Me? — Charles Gaynor[w/m] *(Southern)*. A clever revue which included a mini-musical. The talented cast was headed by Carol Channing and Gene Nelson and ran for well over a year. COVER: theatre balconies with silhouettes of people.

1286 Let 'em Eat Cake (Broadway, 1933). William Gaxton, Victor Moore.

Blue, Blue, Blue / Let 'em Eat Cake / Mine / On and On and On / Till Then [CUT] / Union Square — plain cover — Ira Gershwin[w] & George Gershwin[m] *(Harms)*. A sequel to *Of Thee I Sing* which became a quick failure even though it had a good score by Gershwin. COVER: shirt, collar, neck tie.

1287 Let 'er Go Letty (closed before Broadway, 1921). Charlotte Greenwood, Stuart Wilson.

Bermuda [ABQ] / Lend Us a Daddy [ABQ] / My Little Sea Shell [ABQ] / We Gotta Find a New Kentucky Home / What a Position for Me [ABQ] / A Wonderful Time Was Had by All [ABQ] — Ballard MacDonald[w] & James Hanley[m] *(Shapiro, Bernstein)*. One of the many "Letty" shows done by Greenwood. This edition never reached Broadway. COVER: Charlotte Greenwood.

1288 Let Freedom Sing (Broadway, 1942). Mitzi Green, Betty Garrett.

The House I Live In — plain — Lewis Allan[w] & Earl Robinson[m] *(Chappell)*. A poor revue by some untalented young people; it lasted only one week. COVER: black and white.

1289 Let It Ride! (Broadway, 1961). George Gobel, Sam Levene.

Ev'rything Beautiful / Hey Jimmy Joe John Jim Jack / His Own Little Island / Just an Honest Mistake / Let It Ride / Love, Let Me Know — Jay Livingston[w/m] & Ray Evans[w/m] *(Schirmer)*. A dull musical with an ordinary score that lasted two months. COVER: three people on a horse.

1290 Let Me Hear the Melody (closed before Broadway, 1951). Melvyn Douglas, Anthony Quinn.

Hi-Ho — Ira Gershwin[w] & George Gershwin[m] *(Gershwin)*. A musical which folded in Philadelphia. It used some unknown Gershwin music. It resulted in the first publication of this song, cut from *Shall We Dance*. COVER: sketch of George and Ira.

1291 Let's Face It (Broadway, 1941). Danny Kaye, Eve Arden.

Ace in the Hole / Ev'rything I Love / Farming / I Hate You Darling / Jerry, My Soldier Boy / Let's Not Talk About Love / A Little Rumba Numba / Revenge [PC] [CUT] / Rub Your Lamp / You Irritate Me So — Cole Porter[w/m] *(Chappell)*. A war-time musical about soldiers and their wives with a pleasant Porter score and the clowning of Danny Kaye which gave it a run of a year and a half. COVER: soldier and girls in jeep.

1292 Let's Go (Regional, 1919). Fanchon and Marco.

Debutante's Engagement Book / La Paloma Girl / Mack Sennett Girls / When the Jazz Band Plays "Let's Go" — Fanchon and Marco[w/m] *(D and W)*. A San Francisco revue. COVER: Fanchon and Marco.

1293 Let's Go (Regional, 1942). Stars unknown.

Eyes of the U.S.A. — May Mc-Kague[w/m] *(Edwards)*. A Hollywood revue. COVER: chorus girls.

1294 Let's Keep It That Way (Nightclub, 1955). Stars unknown.

It's Love, It's Romance — Sammy Ostrow[w] & Gordon Vanderburg[m] *(Souvenir)*. COVER: Vick Masters.

1295 Letty Pepper (Broadway, 1922). Charlotte Greenwood, Ray Raymond.

Bluebird Blues / Coo-ee-doo / Every Little Miss / Greenbaum / I Love to Dance / Lanky Letty Pepper / Lavender and Lace / Ray of Sunshine / Sittin' Pretty / What Could Be Sweeter? — Leo Wood[w] & Irving Bibo[w] & Werner Janssen[m] *(Feist)*; You Teach Me — Ballard MacDonald[w] & James Hanley[m] *(Shapiro, Bernstein)*. A poor musical with Greenwood as Letty. It

lasted four weeks. COVER: Charlotte Greenwood.

1296 Lew Leslie's International Revue (Broadway, 1930). Gertrude Lawrence, Harry Richman.

Cinderella Brown / Exactly Like You / I'm Feelin' Blue / International Rhythm / I've Got a Bug in My Head / Keys to Your Heart / On the Sunny Side of the Street — Dorothy Fields[w] & Jimmy McHugh[m] *(Shapiro, Bernstein)*; There's Danger in Your Eyes, Cherie! — Harry Richman[w/m] & Jack Meskill[w/m] & Pete Wendling[w/m] *(Berlin)*. A very talented cast with no material except a couple of good songs. It had a short run of three months. COVER: sketch of two dancers.

1297 The Liar (Broadway, 1950). Melville Cooper, Paula Lawrence.

Lack-a-Day / Out of Sight, Out of Mind / What's in a Name? — Edward Eager[w] & John Mundy[m] *(Chappell)*. A musical set in 16th century Italy. It lasted one week. COVER: sketch of man and two women.

1298 Lido Lady (British, 1926). Cicely Courtneidge, Jack Hulbert.

Atlantic Blues [B] / Here in My Arms [B] / I Want a Man [B] / Lido Lady [B] / Morning Is Midnight [B] / A Tiny Flat Near Soho Square [B] / Try Again Tomorrow [B] / What's the Use? [B] / You're on the Lido Now [B] — Lorenz Hart[w] & Richard Rodgers[m] *(Chappell)*; My Heart Is Sheba Bound — piano selections [B] / I Must Be Going [B] — Richard Rodgers[m] *(Chappell)*. A hit for Rodgers and Hart that ran for a year and a half. COVER: lettering and designs.

1299 The Life and Adventures of Nicholas Nickleby (Broadway, 1982). Roger Rees, Emily Richard.

The Life and Adventures of Nicholas Nickleby — eight songs [VS] [B] — Stephen Oliver[w/m] *(Novello)*. Incidental music for the eight hour British drama. It had a limited run. COVER: Nicholas Nickleby.

1300 Life and Times of Dorian Gray (Off Broadway, 1939). Jeron Criswell.

I Was Just Around the Corner / Victorian Waltz — Arthur Jones[w/m] & Louise Howard[w/m] *(H and C)*. COVER: scenes from the play.

1301 Life Begins at 8:40 (Broadway, 1934). Ray Bolger, Bert Lahr.

At Exactly 8:40 (Life Begins) / I Couldn't Hold My Man (I Look Bad in a Uniform) / Spring Fever — Ira Gershwin[w] & E.Y. Harburg[w] & Harold Arlen[m] *(USO);* Fun to Be Fooled / Let's Take a Walk Around the Block / Shooein' the Mare / What Can You Say in a Love Song? / You're a Builder Upper — Ira Gershwin[w] & E.Y. Harburg[w] & Harold Arlen[m] *(Harms)*. A revue that lasted for six months with some very good Arlen songs. COVER: sketch of a lady smoking.

1302 Life Is Like That (Broadway, 1930). Doris Covert, Edward Pawley.

Lavender and Old Lace — Clifford Lang[w/m] & Jack Hyman[w/m] *(Harms)*; Weary Soul — Helen Kaminsky[w] & Hazel Chisholm[m] *(Harms)*. A melodrama about a jealous wife. It lasted one month. COVER: Doris Covert.

1303 Life of the Party (closed before Broadway, 1942). Margaret Dumont, Charles Ruggles.

One Robin Doesn't Make a Spring / Somehow — Earle Crooker[w] & Frederick Loewe[m] *(Chappell)*. A comedy with music that folded in Detroit. The first union of Lerner's book and Loewe's music. COVER: dancing boy and girl in cowboy outfits.

1304 Li'l Abner (Broadway, 1956). Edith Adams, Peter Palmer.

If I Had My Druthers / It's a Nuisance Having You Around / Jubilation T. Cornpone / Li'l Abner — complete vocal score / Love in a Home / Namely You / Otherwise [VS] / Unnecessary Town — Johnny Mercer[w] & Gene DePaul[m] *(Commander)*. The Dogpatch musical hit that had a fine score, great dancing, a fine sense of humor and a run of almost two years. COVER: all the Dogpatch characters.

1305 Liliom (Broadway, 1921). Joseph Schildkraut, Eva La Gallienne.

The Thieves Song — Benjamin Glazer[w] & Deems Taylor[m] *(Tama)*. A big dramatic hit of the '20s which later became *Carousel*. COVER: Joseph Schildkraut and another man.

1306 Lily Dale (*see also* Chickens *and* Glory) (Broadway, 1921). Helen Groody, Jack Clifford.

Friendly Eyes / The Kindly Little Things We Do [ABQ] / Let's Show You to the Girls [ABQ] / The Little White House with the Green Blinds / Mother's Wedding Dress / The Nine O'Clock Bell / Post Office, Parlor Games [ABQ] / Saw Mill River Road [ABQ] / The Tenor Married the Soprano [ABQ] / Three Little Peas in a Pod [ABQ] / Underneath the Lantern Glow / We've Got to Build [ABQ] — Joseph McCarthy[w] & Harry Tierney[m] *(Feist)*. A rags-to-riches failure, this show toured as *Chickens* and *Lily Dale* but opened as *Glory*. COVER: beautiful girls with chickens and a white house.

1307 Linger Longer Letty (Broadway, 1919). Charlotte Greenwood, Olin Howard.

Climbing the Ladder of Love / Did You, My Boy? / It's Just the Movement / Let's Pretend / Mechanical Doll / Strawberry Glide — Bernard Grossman[w] & Alfred Goodman[m] *(Feist)*; Linger Longer Letty — Oliver Morosco[w] & Alfred Goodman[m] *(Feist)*; Oh, By Jingo — Lew Brown[w] & Albert Von Tilzer[m] *(Feist)*; Slow Town Is Jazz Town Now / Ten to One You Fall — Bernard Grossman[w] & George Yoerger[w] & Alfred Goodman[m] *(Feist)*; Twentieth Century Lullaby — Bernard Grossman[w] & George Yoerger[w] & W. Frisch[m] & Alfred Goodman[m] *(Feist)*. Another "Letty" show that failed. COVER: flowers and designs.

1308 Listen Dearie (closed before Broadway, 1926). Fred Hildebrand, Ann Milburn.

Moonlight on the Ganges — Chester Wallace[w] & Sherman Myers[m] *(Harms)*; Tit for Tat / Why Should We Be Wasting Time? — Charles Gilpin[w/m] *(Harms)*. COVER: roses on a vine.

1309 Listen Lester (Broadway, 1918). Clifton Webb, Ada Mae Weeks.

I Was a Very Good Baby / I Wonder If It's You / I'd Love To / Listen Lester — complete vocal score / Oh! You Sweet Stuff / Show a Little Something New / Waiting / When the Shadows Fall / Who Was the Last Girl? — Harry Cort[w] & George Stoddard[w] & Harold Orlob[m] *(Shapiro, Bernstein)*; Ev'ry Little Village Has a Broadway — A. Santly[w/m] & B. Bratton[w/m] & C. Downs[w/m] *(Shapiro, Bernstein)*. A hit of nine months involving lost love letters. It had ordinary music but great dancing. COVER 1: girl on telephone. COVER 2: orange and grey designs. COVER 3: six girls dancing around a boy.

1310 Listen to Me (closed before Broadway, 1921). Virginia O'Brien, Charles Gates.

The Devilish Blues / Doctor Cupid / Letters / Listen to Me / Oh! You Kewpie Kandy Doll / Our Bungalow in Winter Time / Where's the Girl for Me — Charles George[w/m] *(Witmark)*. COVER: boy and girl on telephones.

1311 The Little Blue Devil (Broadway, 1919). Bernard Granville, Lillian Lorraine.

All the Comforts of Home / I'm So Sympathetic / The Little Blue Devil / My Might Have Been / Peter Pan / Red Riding Hood / A Stroller in Dreamland — Harold Atteridge[w] & Harry Carroll[m] *(Berlin)*; Out of a Clear Sky — Sam Lewis[w] & Joe Young[w] & Jan Rubini[m] & Sal Santaella[m] *(Berlin)*. A flop. With two Ziegfeld stars, the show involved a fraudulent scheme to get ahead. COVER: a dancing girl.

1312 The Little Clown (Jewish, 1920). Molly Picon, Herman Sheratsky.

Die Bist Mein Glick — Molly Picon[w] & Joseph Rumshinsky[m] *(Trio)*. COVER: Picon and Rumshinsky.

1313 Little Devil (Jewish, 1928). Molly Picon, Herman Sheratsky.

The Little Devil — three selections — Molly Picon[w] & I. Lilian[w] & J. Rumshinsky[m] *(Trio)*. COVER: Molly Picon

and balloons.

1314 The Little Dog Laughed (British, 1939). Flanagan and Allen.

F.D.R. Jones — Harold Rome[w/m] *(Chappell)*; The Girl Who Loves a Soldier / Run, Rabbit, Run! / Noel Gay[w/m] & Ralph Butler[w/m] *(Mills)*. A hit revue which used a Rome song and also had two songs published in the U.S. COVER: sketch of park scene; Flanagan and Allen.

1315 The Little Dog Laughed (closed before Broadway, 1940). Mili Monti, Joseph Vitale.

Easy Does It / I Have a Song / I Want Romance / Of the People Stomp / You're Your Highness to Me — Harold Rome[w/m] *(Chappell)*. A way-out fantasy with a terrible book produced to showcase *Mili Monti*. It folded fast! COVER: Milli Monti and dog.

1316 Little Jesse James (Broadway, 1923). Miriam Hopkins, Allen Kearns.

The Blue Bird / Come On, Let's Step, Step Around / From Broadway to Main Street [ABQ] / I Love You / I'm Me and You're You [ABQ] / Knocking Book Worms [ABQ] / Little Jack Horner [ABQ] / Little Jesse James / My Home Town in Kansas / Quiet Afternoon [ABQ] / Such Is Life / Suppose I Had Never Met You / Talk It Over [ABQ] — Harlan Thompson[w] & Harry Archer[m] *(Feist)*. This show had practically nothing — a modest set, mediocre score, and a poor romantic plot — but for some reason it ran for almost a year. COVER: cowgirl with cowboys and Indians.

1317 The Little Kangaroo (closed before Broadway, 1922). Marjorie Gateson, Allen Kearns.

Come Down Miss Price Love / Everything Is Coming Rosie's Way [ABQ] / I Want to Live [ABQ] / Kangaroo Ragout [ABQ] / Kissland / Lady Butterfly / Song to Order / When You're Away from Me [ABQ] / Your Heart Is Palpitating [ABQ] — James Powers[w] & Werner Janssen[m] *(Feist)*. COVER: a kangaroo and dancing people.

1318 Little Mary Sunshine (Off Broadway, 1959). Eileen Brennan, John McMartin.

Do You Ever Dream of Vienna? / Little Mary Sunshine / Little Mary Sunshine — complete vocal score / Look for a Sky of Blue / Mata Hari [VS] / Once in a Blue Moon / Such a Merry Party — Rick Besoyan$^{w/m}$ *(Valando)*. A take-off on the old operettas with a talented cast and a good score. It ran for three years. COVER: a smiling face.

1319 Little Me (Broadway, 1962). Sid Caesar, Virginia Martin.

Deep Down Inside / Dimples / Here's to Us / Le Grand Boom Boom / I've Got Your Number / Little Me / On the Other Side of the Tracks / Poor Little Hollywood Star / Real Live Girl / To Be a Performer — Carolyn Leigh^w & Cy Coleman^m *(Morris)*. A moderate hit with some good songs by Coleman and the clowning of Sid Caesar. COVER: One set of covers shows five hands with cocktail glasses and the other set shows Sid Caesar wearing six different hats.

1320 Little Me (Broadway, 1982). James Coco, Jessica James.

Don't Ask a Lady / I Wanna Be Yours — Carolyn Leigh^w & Cy Coleman^m *(Notable)*. A revised edition of the 1962 musical that folded quickly. It added two new Coleman songs. COVER: a girl surrounded by suitors.

1321 Little Miracle Town (World's Fair, 1939). Stars unknown.

Parade of the Wooden Soldiers — Victor Oliver^w & Leon Jessel^m *(Marks)*. A midget show that was presented at the World's Fair in 1939. COVER: a sketch of midgets in various outfits in the palm of a man's hand.

1322 Little Miss Bluebeard (Broadway, 1923). Irene Bordoni, Eric Blore.

The Gondola and the Girl — Percy Graham Paul^w & Ray Goetz^w & Paul Rubens^m *(Chappell)*; I Won't Say I Will — B.G. DeSylva^w & Arthur Francis (IG)^w & George Gershwin^m *(Harms)*; So This Is Love — Ray Goetz$^{w/m}$ *(Harms)*; Who'll Buy My Violets? — Ray Goetz^w & Jose Padilla^m *(Harms)*. A comedy with music that had a moderate run due to Irene Bordoni. COVER: Irene Bordoni (two covers with photo and two covers with sketch).

1323 Little Miss Charity (Broadway, 1920). Marjorie Gateson, Frank Moulan.

Angel Town / Crinoline Girl / Dance Me Around / Eyes of Youth / I Think So Too / Little Miss Charity / Step Inside / That Certain Something / When Love Comes to Your Heart / A Woman's Touch — Edward Clark^w & S. Henry^m & M. Savin^m *(Stern)*. A woman trying to give away her fortune was the basis of this story. It was poor all around and folded quickly. COVER: six girls in different costumes.

1324 Little Miss Raffles (*see also* The Hotel Mouse) (Broadway, 1922). Vivienne Segal, Lawrence Grossmith.

I'll Dream of You — Clifford Grey^w & Armand Vecsey^m *(Chappell)*; Little Mother / Manana / Romance — Clifford Grey^w & Ivan Caryll^m & Armand Vecsey^m *(Chappell)*; Santiago — Clifford Grey^w & Ivan Caryll^m *(Chappell)*. This musical, about a robbery, was called *Little Miss Raffles* on try-out and *Hotel Mouse* on Broadway. When it opened on Broadway the leading stars were changed. It was a quick failure. COVER: designs and lettering.

1325 Little Miss Vamp (Regional, 1921). Winnie Lightner, Newton Alexander.

It's a Wonderful World After All — Newton Alexander$^{w/m}$ *(Rossiter)*. A Chicago musical that never reached New York. COVER: Winnie Lightner and Newton Alexander.

1326 Little Nellie Kelly (Broadway, 1922). Charles King, Elizabeth Hines.

All in the Wearing / All My Boys / Dancing My Worries Away / The Great New York Police / The Hinkey Dee / The Name of Kelly / Nellie Kelly, I Adore You / Pretty Girls / Till My Luck Comes Rolling Along / Voice in

My Heart / When I Hear the Mocking Bird / You Remind Me of My Mother — George M. Cohan^{w/m} *(Witmark)*. A story of an Irish girl finding true love. This moderate hit ran for six months. COVER: one girl and a lot of gentlemen plus George M.

1327 A Little Night Music (Broadway, 1973). Len Cariou, Glynis Johns.

A Little Night Music — Stephen Sondheim^m *(Revelation)*; Bang! [VS] / Every Day a Little Death [VS] / The Glamorous Life [VS] / Liaisons [VS] / A Little Night Music — complete vocal score / The Miller's Son / Remember? / Send In the Clowns / Silly People [VS] / Two Fairy Tales [VS] / You Must Meet My Wife — Stephen Sondheim^{w/m} *(Revelation)*. The music and lyrics were exceptional, the cast was superb and it ran one and a half years. COVER: a tree and the moon.

1328 Little Old New York (Broadway, 1920). Genevieve Tobin, Donald Meek.

Do You Hear Me Calling? — Rida Johnson Young^w & William Schroeder^m *(Harms)*. A melodrama with one song. COVER: Genevieve Tobin.

1329 A Little Racketeer (Broadway, 1932). Queenie Smith, John Garrick.

Here's to Night / Inside Looking Out / Whiling My Time Away — Edward Eliscu^w & Henry Sullivan^m *(Harms)*; I'll Ballyhoo You / Starry Sky — Edward Eliscu^w & Dmitri Tiomkin^m *(Miller)*. A musical with a silly plot and a lot of problems. It lasted six weeks. COVER: Queenie Smith.

1330 The Little Rascals (closed before Broadway, 1987). Ronn Carroll, Betsy Joslyn.

Not Much of a Dog [VS] — Joe Raposo^{w/m} *(Jonico)*. A new musical that tried out at Goodspeed in Connecticut but never made it to Broadway. COVER: Joe Raposo.

1331 Little Shop of Horrors (Off Broadway, 1982). Ellen Greene, Lee Wilkof.

Dentist! [VS] / Don't Feed the Plants [VS] / Git It! [VS] / Grow for Me [VS] / Little Shop of Horrors [VS] / The Meek Shall Inherit [VS] / Skid Row (Downtown) [VS] / Somewhere That's Green [VS] / Suddenly Seymour [VS] / Ya Never Know [VS] — Howard Ashman^w & Alan Menken^m *(Warner Bros.)*. A hilarious musical about a man-eating plant; the musical lasted for years Off Broadway. COVER: huge plant holding girl.

1332 Little Show (Broadway, 1929). Clifton Webb, Fred Allen.

Can't We Be Friends? — Paul James^w & Kay Swift^m *(Harms)*; Caught in the Rain — Howard Dietz^w & Henry Sullivan^m *(Harms)*; Get Up on a New Routine — piano selections / The Theme Song — piano selections — Arthur Schwartz^m *(Harms)*; I Guess I'll Have to Change My Plan / I've Made a Habit of You — Howard Dietz^w & Arthur Schwartz^m *(Harms)*; A Little Hut in Hoboken — Herman Hupfeld^{w/m} *(Harms)*; Moanin' Low — Howard Dietz^w & Ralph Rainger^m *(Harms)*; Or What Have You? — Grace Henry^w & Morris Hamilton^m *(Harms)*. A smash revue that gave the world several standard songs, Dietz and Schwartz, and Webb and Allen. COVER: an elegant couple watching a stage performance.

1333 Little Simplicity (Broadway, 1918). Walter Catlett, Marjorie Gateson.

Boomerang / Follow the Boys / I Cannot Leave You / Military Fox Trot — Rida Johnson Young^w & Augustus Barratt^m *(Shapiro, Bernstein)*; It's Worthwhile Waiting for Someone — Joseph McCarthy^w & Harry Tierney^m *(M and F)*; My Caravan / When the Whistle Blows — Augustus Barratt^{w/m} *(Shapiro, Bernstein)*. A minor musical about an Algerian flower girl loving an American; the musical ran three months. COVER: a pretty girl with flowers.

1334 Little Tommy Tucker (British, 1930). Melville Cooper, Jane Welch.

I Have No Words — Desmond

Carter[w] & Arthur Schwartz[m] *(Chappell)*; Out of the Blue — Desmond Carter[w] & Arthur Schwartz[m] & Vivian Ellis[m] *(Chappell)*. This show lasted only two months but the song *I Have No Words* later became *Something to Remember You By* with Carter's lyrics replaced by Howard Dietz lyrics. COVER: lettering and designs.

1335 The Little Whopper (Broadway, 1919). Sydney Grant, Vivienne Segal.

Bye-Bye, My Little Wifie / If You Go, I'll Die! / I'm Lonely / It's Great to Be Married / I've Got to Leave You / Oh! What a Little Whopper / 'Round the Corner / Sweet Dreams / Twinkle, Little Star! / We'll Build a Cute Little Nest / You'll Dream and I'll Dream — Otto Harbach[w] & Bide Dudley[w] & Rudolf Friml[m] *(Schirmer)*; I Have a Date [B] / Let It Be Soon [B] — Otto Harbach[w] & Bide Dudley[w] & Rudolf Friml[m] *(Feldman)*; I Shall Be Calling to You [B] — Clifford Grey[w] & Willy Redstone[m] *(Feldman)*. Elopement problems were the basis of this moderate hit with pleasant Friml songs. It ran six months. COVER: One set of covers is a baby on the telephone and the other is a man and woman whispering.

1336 The Littlest Revue (Off Broadway, 1956). Tammy Grimes, Joel Grey.

Born Too Late / Good Little Girls / Madly in Love / You're Far from Wonderful — Ogden Nash[w] & Vernon Duke[m] *(Saunders)*; Game of Dance — Sol Berkowitz[m] *(Saunders)*; The Shape of Things — Sheldon Harnick[w/m] *(Saunders)*; Summer Is A-Comin' In — John Latouche[w] & Vernon Duke[m] *(Saunders)*. A small revue with some good people and good songs but which lasted only four weeks. COVER: a group of people in a pyramid on stage.

1337 Livin' the Life (Off Broadway, 1957). Alice Ghostley, James Mitchell.

Late Love / Livin' the Life / Someone — Bruce Geller[w] & Jack Urbont[m] *(Schirmer)*. Based on Mark Twain stories, this musical lasted three weeks.

COVER: riverboat and couple dancing.

1338 Liza (Broadway, 1922). Irvin C. Miller, Will Cook.

I've Got Those Runnin' Wild Blues / Liza / Love Me / Planning — Maceo Pinkard[w/m] *(Harms)*; Lovin' Sam — Jack Yellen[w] & Milton Ager[m] *(A Y and B)*; My Old Man — Nat Vincent[w] & Maceo Pinkard[m] *(Harms)*. A black musical that became a moderate hit due more for its dancing than its music. COVER: titles and designs.

1339 Liza (Broadway, 1974). Liza Minnelli.

Best of Friends / Liza with a "Z" / On Stage / Ring Them Bells — Fred Ebb[w] & John Kander[m] *(Hanson)*. An evening with Liza at the Winter Garden with a limited run engagement. COVER: Liza Minnelli.

1340 Lizzie Borden (Opera, 1967). Stars unknown.

Abbie's Bird Song / Lizzie Borden — complete vocal score — Kenward Elmslie[w] & Jack Beeson[m] *(Boosey, Hawkes)*; Margret's Garden Aria — Jack Beeson[w/m] *(Boosey, Hawkes)*. A limited run of an opera commissioned by the New York City Opera. COVER: letters and designs.

1341 Load of Coal at Connie's Inn (Nightclub, 1929). Jean Starr, Maude Russell.

Honeysuckle Rose / My Fate Is in Your Hands [PC] / Zonky — Andy Razaf[w] & Thomas Waller[m] *(Santly Bros.-Joy)*. COVER: black girl dancing; girl with flowers in a garden.

1342 Lock Up Your Daughters (closed before Broadway, 1960). Nancy Dussault, George Irving.

If I'd Known You / I'll Be There / Is This the Happy Ending? / Lock Up Your Daughters / Lovely Lover / When Does the Ravishing Begin? — Laurie Johnson[w] & Lionel Bart[m] *(Sam Fox)*. An imported British musical that didn't make it in the U.S. and folded in Boston. COVER: Nancy Dussault, Frederick Jaeger.

1343 The Logic of Larry (Irish, 1919). Barry McCormack.

Dear Mother of Mine—Arthur Grant^{w/m} *(Grant)*. COVER: Barry McCormack.

1344 Lola (closed before Broadway, 1922). Helen Shipman.

At the End of the Road / Lola Waltz—Close in Your Arms / My Little Sea Shell Told Me So—Ballard MacDonald^w & James Hanley^m *(Shapiro, Bernstein)*; Close Your Eyes—Francis DeWitt^w & Werner Janssen^m *(Witmark)*. COVER: Helen Shipman.

1345 Lola in Love (closed before Broadway, 1922). Carl Dietz, Florence Earle.

Give Me One Day / I Mean No-One-Else-But-You / If Wives Were Put on Sale / A Perfect Model for Your Arms—Irving Caesar^w & Hugo Hirsch^m *(Harms)*. COVER: a Spanish senorita sitting on garden wall.

1346 Lolita, My Love (closed before Broadway, 1971). Dorothy Loudon, John Neville.

Going, Going, Gone [PC] / How Far Is It to the Next Town? [PC] / In the Broken Promise Land of Fifteen / Lolita / Tell Me, Tell Me [PC]—Alan Jay Lerner^w & John Barry^m *(Morris)*. This musical, based on the famous novel, opened and closed in Philadelphia. It was quickly revised and opened again in Boston where it folded for good. COVER: lettering and designs.

1347 Lollipop *(see also* **The Left-Over**) (Broadway, 1923). Ada May, Harry Puck.

Deep in My Heart / Going Rowing / Honey-Bun / It Must Be Love / Take a Little One Step / Tie a String Around Your Finger—Zelda Sears^w & Vincent Youmans^m *(Harms)*; Havana—M. Schonberger^w & Abe Lyman^w & John Schonberger^m *(Jack Mills)*. The pre–Broadway title was *The Left-Over*. This show had a poor book with a Cinderella theme and promising Youman songs. It ran five months. COVER: Ada May.

1348 London Calling (British, 1922). Gertrude Lawrence, Noel Coward.

Carrie [B] / Other Girls [B] / Parisian Pierrot [B] / Prenez Gard Lisette [B] / Russian Blues [B] / Tamarisk Town [B] / What Love Means to Girls Like Me [B] / When My Ship Comes Home [B]—Noel Coward^{w/m} *(Keith Prowse)*; Sentiment [B]—Noel Coward^{w/m} & Philip Braham^{w/m} *(Keith Prowse)*; You Were Meant for Me [B]—Eubie Blake^{w/m} & Noble Sissle^{w/m} *(Keith Prowse)*. A revue that ran nine months and became *Charlot's Revue* in New York. COVER: Gertrude Lawrence, Noel Coward, Maisie Gay.

1349 Lonely Hearts (Broadway, 1933). Stars unknown.

Tell Me That You Love Me—Al Silverman^w & C.A. Bixio^m *(Harms)*. A limited run production by Leonidoff. COVER: Radio City Music Hall and the orchestra.

1350 A Lonely Romeo (Broadway, 1919). Lew Fields, Eleanor Henry.

Any Old Place with You—Lorenz Hart^w & Richard Rodgers^m *(Remick)*; Candy Jag / Don't Do Anything Till You Hear from Me / I Want a Lonely Romeo / Influenza Blues / Sweets to the Sweet / Underneath a Big Umbrella—Robert Smith^w & Malvin Franklin^m *(Remick)*; I Guess I'm More Like Mother Than Like Father—Raymond Egan^w & Richard Whiting^m *(Remick)*; Jolly Me / One I Love, Two I Love / Save a Little Daylight for Me / Wait for Me / You Never Can Tell—Robert Smith^w & Robert H. Bowers^m *(Remick)*; A Lonely Romeo—complete score—Hart^{w/m} & Rodgers^{w/m} & Smith^{w/m} & Franklin^{w/m} & Egan^{w/m} & Whiting^{w/m} & Bowers^{w/m} & Spencer^{w/m} *(Remick)*; Will o' Wisp—Robert Smith^w & Malvin Franklin^m & Otis Spencer^m *(Remick)*; Will o' Wisp Fox Trot—Malvin Franklin^m & Otis Spencer^m *(Remick)*. Includes the first Broadway song of Rodgers and Hart; an ordinary musical that ran for only ten weeks. COVER: a gentleman with a group of ladies.

1351 Long Live America! (Jewish, 1939). Miriam Kressyn.

Di in Di Zin in Di Shtern — Jacob Jacobs[w] & Alexander Olshanetsky[m] *(Trio)*. COVER: Itzek Feld, an American flag and eagle.

1352 Look Ma, I'm Dancin'! (Broadway, 1948). Nancy Walker, Harold Lang.

If You'll Be Mine / I'm Not So Bright / I'm Tired of Texas / The Little Boy Blues / Shauny O'Shay / Tiny Room / The Way It Might Have Been — Hugh Martin[w/m] *(Chappell)*. A wonderful dancing show plus Nancy Walker and some pleasant songs. It ran six months. COVER: ballet dancers.

1353 Look to the Lilies (Broadway, 1970). Shirley Booth, Al Freeman.

Follow the Lamb! [VS] / I, Yes Me! That's Who [VS] / I'd Sure Like to Give It a Shot [VS] / Look to the Lilies [VS] / One Little Brick at a Time [VS] / Some Kind of Man [VS] / There Comes a Time [VS] — Sammy Cahn[w] & Jule Styne[m] *(Chappell)*. A poor musical with a bad score and two miscast actors. It lasted three weeks. COVER: a nun with a man ringing a church bell.

1354 Look to the Rainbow (British, 1985). Jack Gilford, Michael Cantwell.

Time, You Old Gypsy Man — E.Y. Harburg[w] & Philip Springer[m] *(Warner Bros.)*. COVER: a sketch of Harburg.

1355 Look Who's Here (Broadway, 1920). Cecil Lean, Cleo Mayfield.

Bell Hop Blues / I Cannot Understand / I Wonder What She's Thinking of Now / If I Had Only Met You / I'll Make Bubbles / Love / Love Had Come to Stay / My Heart's a Roomy Hotel / Since My Wife Got Fat / Tia-Da-Tia-Da-Dee — Edward Paulton[w] & Silvio Hein[m] *(Harms)*. A musical about marital problems. It lasted ten weeks. COVER: Cecil Lean, Cleo Mayfield.

1356 Look Who's Here (closed before Broadway, 1932). Bert Walton.

Counting the Stars / I Guess I Love You / Ladies Who Dance Like This / A Penthouse for a Song — Arthur Swanstrom[w/m] *(Southern)*. A revue produced by RKO studios to introduce

a flock of new faces. COVER: a dancer.

1357 Lorelei (Broadway, 1974). Carol Channing, Dody Goodman.

Bye Bye Baby [VS] / Diamonds Are a Girl's Best Friend [VS] / Homesick Blues [VS] / I Love What I'm Doing [VS] / It's Delightful Down in Chile [VS] / A Little Girl from Little Rock [VS] / Mamie Is Mimi [VS] — Leo Robin[w] & Jule Styne[m] *(C.M.P.)*; I Won't Let You Get Away / Lorelei / Men! — Betty Comden[w] & Adolph Green[w] & Jule Styne[m] *(Stratford)*. A rehash of *Blondes* with some new songs. It was a so-so show that Channing kept running for nine months. COVER: Carol Channing.

1358 Lost in the Stars (Broadway, 1949). Todd Duncan, Inez Matthews.

Big Mole / A Bird of Passage — choral edition / A Little Gray House / Lost in the Stars / Lost in the Stars — complete score / Stay Well / Thousands of Miles / Trouble Man — Maxwell Anderson[w] & Kurt Weill[m] *(Chappell)*. Kurt Weill's last musical. It had a good score but a poor book and a nine month run. COVER: native huts and titles.

1359 Louie the 14th (Broadway, 1925). Leon Errol, Ethel Shutta.

The Crossword Puzzle / Don't Let Anybody Vamp Your Man / Homeland / Little Peach / Pep / Sweetheart of Mine / True Hearts — Arthur Wimperis[w] & Sigmund Romberg[m] *(Harms)*; Edelweiss — Clifford Grey[w] & Sigmund Romberg[m] *(Harms)*; Give a Little, Get a Little Kiss / My First Love Letter — Irving Caesar[w] & Sigmund Romberg[m] *(Harms)*. A lavish Ziegfeld production with Errol's adventures at a dinner party. It had ordinary Romberg songs but lasted nine months because of the comedy and settings. COVER: cartoon of Leon Errol and girls.

1360 Louisiana Lady (Broadway, 1947). George Baxter, Edith Fellows.

The Cuckoo-Cheena / The Night Was All to Blame / That's Why I Want to Go Home / When You Are Close to

Me — Monte Carlo^w & Alma Sanders^m *(Chappell)*. A musical set in New Orleans in a bordello; an awful book and score. It had a run of four performances. COVER: a lady on a balcony.

1361 Louisiana Purchase (Broadway, 1940). Victor Moore, Vera Zorina.

Dance with Me / Fools Fall in Love / I'd Love to Be Shot from a Cannon with You [PC] / It'll Come to You / It's a Lovely Day Tomorrow / Latins Know How / The Lord Done Fixed Up My Soul / Opening Chorus [VS] — Louisiana Purchase / Opening Letter [VS] — Louisiana Purchase / Outside of That I Love You / Sex Marches On [VS] / What Chance Have I with Love / Wild About You / You Can't Brush Me Off / You're Lonely and I'm Lonely — Irving Berlin^{w/m} *(Berlin)*. A very entertaining musical dealing with politics in Louisiana. A good score by Berlin, a good book, and some talented actors. It ran for a year. COVER: William Gaxton, Vera Zorina, Victor Moore, Irene Bordoni.

1362 Love and Kisses (*see also* The Gingham Girl) (Broadway, 1922). Helen Ford, Eddie Buzzell.

Business Is Bad / Forty Second Street Strut / Just as Long as You Have Me / Tell Her While the Waltz Is Playing / The Twinkle in Your Eye — Neville Fleeson^w & Albert Von Tilzer^m *(Harms)*. This musical ran nine months in New York. A charming story about two small-towners in the big city. It toured as *Love and Kisses* but opened on Broadway as *The Gingham Girl.* COVER: a vase filled with flowers.

1363 Love and Let Love (Broadway, 1951). Ginger Rogers, Tom Helmore.

Just One Kiss — Ned Washington^w & Victor Young^m *(Young)*. A short-lived comedy with Ginger Rogers. COVER: Ginger Rogers.

1364 Love Bet (Irish, 1924). Frederick Bowers.

When the Stars Are Shining — Walter Decker^w & Fred Bowers^m *(Marks)*. COVER: Frederick Bowers.

1365 Love Birds (Broadway, 1921). Pat Rooney, Marion Brent.

Can Mary Do Without Me / Fat, Fat, Fatima / I Love to Go Swimmin' with Wimmen / In Bokara, Miss O'Hara / Is It Hard to Guess / A Little Dream That Lost Its Way / Trousseau Incomplete / Two Little Love Birds / When the Cat's Away — Ballard MacDonald^w & Sigmund Romberg^m *(Witmark)*; Molly O'Malley and Me — Pat Rooney^{w/m} & J. Kendis^{w/m} & A. Brockman^{w/m} *(Witmark)*. A romantic story with poor music by Romberg. It ran three months. COVER: tree branches and birds.

1366 Love Call (closed before Broadway, 1926). Grace La Rue.

Himmelbett / Love's Call — waltz song / My Little Nest of Heavenly Blue / You Ask Me What Is Love — Sigmund Spaeth^w & Franz Lehar^m *(Marks)*. COVER: a dancing lady.

1367 Love Call (closed before Broadway, 1925). Stars unknown.

Dipping in the Moonlight — Irving Caesar^w & Joseph Meyer^m *(Harms)*; Show Me How to Make Love — Irving Caesar^w & Harry Rosenthal^m *(Harms)*; We Two — Irving Caesar^w & Franz Lehar^m *(Harms)*. COVER: designs and lettering.

1368 The Love Call (*see also* Bonita *and* My Golden West) (Broadway, 1927). Berna Dean, John Barker.

Eyes That Love / Good Pals / I Live, I Die for You / The Rangers Song / 'Tis Love! — Harry B. Smith^w & Sigmund Romberg^m *(Harms)*. A poor musical about rangers and Indians. It toured as *Bonita* and *My Golden West* before opening on Broadway as *The Love Call.* It had a short run. COVER: cowgirl riding a horse.

1369 The Love Doctor (*see also* The Carefree Heart) (British, 1957). Ian Carmichael, Joan Heal.

The Carefree Heart / I Would Love You Still / Promised / Rich Man, Poor Man / Who Is? You Are! / Would I Were — Robert Wright^{w/m} & George

Forrest[w/m] *(Frank)*. An attempt to revive a musical that closed before Broadway. The name was changed to *Love Doctor* but it still folded after two weeks. COVER: sketch of man and other people.

1370 Love Dreams (Broadway, 1921). Vera Michelena, Tom Powers.

Any Time Is Love Time / Drinking Song / Entre Nous / Here, There and Everywhere / I'm Looking for a Lonesome Girl / Knights of the Table / Love Dreams / My Dream of Love Is You / Pity Me / Reputation / Toddle Top Whirl / Two Is Company / Where Smoke Rings Go — Oliver Morosco[w] & Werner Janssen[m] *(Feist)*. A soap-opera-type operetta that had nothing. It lasted five weeks. COVER: troubadour serenading beside a castle.

1371 Love for Sale (closed before Broadway, 1919). Kitty Gordon.

Ask Me Why / The Dimple on My Knee [ABQ] / Girls I Have Loved [ABQ] / Give Me a Thrill [ABQ] / The Greatest Lover / I'll Break Into Your Heart [ABQ] / My Shantung Flower [ABQ] / Oh, Kitty [ABQ] / Rainbow of Love [ABQ] / Spanish Jazz / Wall Street Blues [ABQ] — Tom Johnstone[w/m] & Harry Auracher[w/m] *(Stern)*. COVER: Kitty Gordon.

1372 Love from Judy (British, 1952). Jeannie Carson, Adelaide Hall.

Daddy Long Legs [B] / Go and Get Your Old Banjo [B] / Love from Judy [B] / Love from Judy — complete vocal score [B] / My True Love [B] — Hugh Martin[w] & Jack Gray[w] & Hugh Martin[m] *(Chappell)*; I Ain't Going to Marry — piano selections [B] / Here We Are — piano selections [B] — Hugh Martin[m] *(Chappell)*. A musical about an orphan. A big London hit running for 18 months. COVER: sketch of man and dancers.

1373 Love in 32 Bars (Off Broadway, 1941). Stars unknown.

Sometime [PC] — Perry Lafferty[w/m] *(BMI)*. This is listed as a "Columbia Workshop Production." COVER: none.

1374 Love-Knots (closed before Broadway, 1922). Stars unknown.

Love-Knots / Moonlight in Springtime / One Little Smile — Alonzo Price[w] & Antonio Bafunno[m] *(Harms)*. COVER: flowers and designs.

1375 Love Laughs (Broadway, 1919). Jessie Glendinning, Janet Velie.

Love Laughs — Leon De Costa[w/m] *(Remick)*. A comedy with one song; the production lasted two weeks. COVER: Jessie Glendinning.

1376 The Love Letter (Broadway, 1921). Fred and Adele Astaire.

Canzonetta / Dreaming / First Love / The Girl at Home / I'll Return for You / I'll Say I Love You / My Heart Beats for You / The Only Girl / Scandal Town / Upside-Down / We Were in Love — William Le Baron[w] & Victor Jacobi[m] *(Harms)*. In this musical, a girl dreams of lovers and love letters. This was a poor musical with a run of four weeks. When this show folded, Victor Jacobi died of heart break at the age of 37. COVER: letters and designs.

1377 Love Letters (closed before Broadway, 1920). Elizabeth Brice.

Somebody Like You — Howard Rogers[w] & Nat Shilkret[m] *(Remick)*. COVER: Elizabeth Brice.

1378 Love Life (Broadway, 1948). Nanette Fabray, Ray Middleton.

Economics / Green-up Time / Here I'll Stay / I Remember It Well [RC] / Is It Him or Is It Me / Love Song / Mr. Right / My Kind of Night [RC] / Susan's Dream / This Is the Life / Women's Club Blues [RC] — Alan Jay Lerner[w] & Kurt Weill[m] *(Chappell)*. A musical fantasy of a marriage covering several decades in American history. A lovely score and two talented leads kept it going for eight months. COVER: jugglers, acrobats, singers, and other characters.

1379 Love Match (closed before Broadway, 1968). Patricia Routledge, Michael Allinson.

I Hear Bells [PC] / I Think I May Want to Remember Today [VS] / The Little Part of Me That's Mine [PC] / Next Time [VS] / Today Is the First

Day [VS] / Woman Looking for Love [PC] — Richard Maltby, Jr.[w] & David Shire[m] *(Chappell)*. A Broadway bound musical that folded in Los Angeles. Patricia Routledge portrayed Queen Victoria in this dull over-long book with some pleasant songs by Maltby and Shire which were used later in their two revues. COVER: none.

1380 The Love Song (Broadway, 1925). Allan Pryor, Evelyn Herbert.

Fair Land of Dreaming / Love Song — Remember Me / Love Song — You Will Forget / Love Will Find You Someday / You Will Forget — Harry B. Smith[w] & Edward Kunneke[m] *(Harms)*; He Writes a Song / It Is Love / Only a Dream — Harry B. Smith[w] & Jacques Offenbach[m] *(Harms)*; Yes or No — Harry B. Smith[w] & Jacques Offenbach[m] & Edward Kunneke[m] *(Harms)*. An imported operetta with a short run. COVER: flowers and designs.

1381 The Love Thief (Jewish, 1931). Molly Picon, Leon Gold.

In Meine Augen Bisti Shein — Molly Picon[w] & N. Stuchkoff[w] & Joseph Rumshinsky[m] *(CNF)*. COVER: Picon and Gold.

1382 Lovely Ladies, Kind Gentlemen (Broadway, 1970). Kenneth Nelson, Ron Husmann.

Call Me Back [VS] / Find Your Own Cricket [VS] / Lovely Ladies, Kind Gentlemen [VS] / One More for the Last One [VS] / One Side of World [VS] / Simple Words [VS] / This Time [VS] / With a Snap of My Finger [VS] / You've Broken a Fine Woman's Heart [VS] — Stan Freeman[w/m] & Frank Underwood[w/m] *(T R O)*. The Teahouse of the August Moon set to music with a poor show. It lasted two weeks. COVER: a geisha girl.

1383 Lovely Lady *(see also* **Ain't Love Grand)** (Broadway, 1927). Edna Leedom, Donald Brian.

At the Barbecue — Harry Steinberg[w] & Eddie Ward[w] & Dave Stamper[m] & Harold Levey[m] *(Shapiro, Bernstein)*; Breakfast in Bed / Just Say the Word / Lost Step / Lovely Lady / Make

Believe You're Happy — Cyrus Wood[w] & Dave Stamper[m] & Harold Levey[m] *(Shapiro, Bernstein)*; One Step to Heaven — Raymond Klages[w] & Jesse Greer[m] *(Robbins)*. An ordinary show with a short run. It toured as *Ain't Love Grand,* but opened as *Lovely Lady.* COVER: Edna Leedom. Some covers show Mitzi as the star of this show.

1384 Love's Old Sweet Song (Broadway, 1940). Walter Huston, Jessie Royce Landis.

Of All the Things I Love / The Years — William Saroyan[w] & Paul Bowles[m] *(Chappell)*. A Saroyan comedy that lasted for only a month. COVER: letters and designs.

1385 Lovesong (Off Broadway, 1976). Jess Richards, Melanie Chartoff.

April Child [VS] — Kenneth Pressman[w] & Michael Valenti[m] *(Belwin Mills)*; A Birthday [VS] — Christina Rossetti[w] & Michael Valenti[m] *(Belwin Mills)*; Echo [VS] — Henry Comor[w] & Michael Valenti[m] *(Belwin Mills)*; An Epitaph [VS] — Richard Crashaw[w] & Michael Valenti[m] *(Belwin Mills)*; I Remember [VS] — Thomas Hood[w] & Michael Valenti[m] *(Belwin Mills)*; If Ever Two Were One [VS] — Anne Bradstreet[w] & Michael Valenti[m] *(Belwin Mills)*; Jenny Kiss'd Me [VS] — Leigh Hunt[w] & Michael Valenti[m] *(Belwin Mills)*; A Rondelay [VS] — Peter Motteaux[w] & Michael Valenti[m] *(Belwin Mills)*; So We'll Go No More A-Roving [VS] — George Gordon[w] & Michael Valenti[m] *(Belwin Mills)*; Song [VS] — Thomas Lodge[w] & Michael Valenti[m] *(Belwin Mills)*; Sophia [VS] — Edwin Dulchin[w] & Michael Valenti[m] *(Belwin Mills)*; What Is a Woman Like? [VS] — Henry Comor[w] & Michael Valenti[m] *(Belwin Mills)*; What Is Love? [VS] — Walter Raleigh[w] & Michael Valenti[m] *(Belwin Mills)*. A revue based on love themes. It lasted three weeks. COVER: birds and designs.

1386 Luana (Broadway, 1930). Lillian Bond, Doris Carson.

Aloha / In Your Cradle of Love /

Luana / My Bird of Paradise / My Hills of Rome / Son of the Sun / A World of Melody — J. Keirn Brennan^w & Rudolf Friml^m *(Schirmer)*. A musical about a South Sea island princess that lasted two weeks. COVER: One set of covers shows lettering only and the other set shows a South Sea island scene.

1387 Luckee Girl (Broadway, 1928). Irene Dunne, Irving Fisher.

Come On and Make Whoopee — Mann Holiner^w & Werner Janssen^m *(Harms)*; A Flat in Montmartre — Maurice Yvain^{w/m} & Lew Pollack^{w/m} *(Harms)*; Friends and Lovers / I Love You So / I'll Take You to the Country / In Our Little Studio / Magic Melody — Max Lief^w & Nathaniel Lief^w & Maurice Yvain^m *(Harms)*. An imported French musical about a girl in love. It was a flop of ten weeks. COVER: designs and letters.

1388 Lucky (Broadway, 1927). Mary Eaton, Paul Whiteman.

Cingalese Girls / Dancing the Devil Away / The Same Old Moon — Otto Harbach^{w/m} & Bert Kalmar^{w/m} & Harry Ruby^{w/m} *(Harms)*; That Little Something / When the Bo-Tree Blossoms Again — Bert Kalmar^w & Harry Ruby^w & Jerome Kern^m *(Harms)*; Ballet — piano selections / Cingalese Village — piano selections — Jerome Kern^m *(Harms)*. A musical about a pearl diver that lasted for two months. COVER: Whiteman, Santley, Sawyer, Eaton, Catlett, Gallagher, and Keeler.

1389 A Lucky Break *(see also* **Broke!)** (Broadway, 1925). George Mac-Farlane, Lucille Sears.

Rainbow / When the Hurdy-Gurdy Plays / With You Beside Me — Zelda Sears^w & Harold Levey^m *(Harms)*. A poor-man-makes-good musical that flopped. The try-out title was *Broke* but it went to Broadway as *A Lucky Break*. COVER: George MacFarlane.

1390 Lucky Days (Jewish, 1943). Menasha Skulnik, Lilly Lilliana.

Ich Veis Nit Vi Me Tit Es — Isidore Lillian^w & Sholom Secunda^m *(Metro)*. COVER: S. Secunda, M. Skulnik.

1391 Lulu *(see also* **The Girl in the Private Room)** (closed before Broadway, 1920). Queenie Smith.

All's Fair in Love and War / And Then Came a Carriage / Dancing the Razza-ma-tazz / Different Days / Filled with Flowers / Goodbye, Take Care / I Love My Art / Look for the Rainbow / My Old New Jersey Home / Silver Wedding Day / Some Things Cannot Be Explained / A Table for Two — Edward Clark^w & Gitz Rice^m *(Shapiro, Bernstein)*; You're Just as Beautiful at Sixty — Howard Rogers^w & Leo Edwards^m *(Shapiro, Bernstein)*. This musical toured as *Lulu* and *The Girl in the Private Room*. COVER: a girl and her suitors.

1392 Lulu Belle (Broadway, 1926). Lenore Ulric, Henry Hull.

Lulu Belle — Leo Robin^w & Richard Myers^m *(Harms)*. A drama about a loose woman; some music. COVER: Lenore Ulric.

1393 Lunchtime Follies (War, 1942). Milton Berle, Shirley Booth.

The Ballad of Sloppy Joe / Dear Joe / The Lady's on the Job / The Men Behind the Man Behind the Gun [PC] / On That Production Line / On Time / That's My Pop / Victory Symphony, Eight to the Bar — Harold Rome^{w/m} *(Leeds)*; Buddy on the Nightshift [VS] — Oscar Hammerstein^w & Kurt Weill^m *(Coda)*; Schickelgruber [VS] — Howard Dietz^w & Kurt Weill^m *(Coda)*; The Song of the Free [PC] — Archibald MacLeish^w & Kurt Weill^m *(Chappell)*; A Quiet Girl — Marc Blitzstein^{w/m} *(Chappell)*. A series of lunchtime entertainments for production workers for morale. COVER: entertainers with crowds.

1394 Lute Song (Broadway, 1946). Mary Martin, Yul Brynner.

Bitter Harvest / The Lute Song / Mountain High — Valley Low / See the Monkey / Vision Song / Where You Are / Willow Tree — Bernard Hanighen^w & Raymond Scott^m *(Capitol)*.

An exotic musical about a Chinese couple; it lasted for only two months. COVER: Mary Martin.

1395 Luv (Broadway, 1964). Eli Wallach, Anne Jackson.

LUV — Will Holt[w] & Irving Joseph[m] *(Frank)*. A hit comedy by Murray Schisgal. COVER: sketch of couple with a third man.

1396 The Lyric Revue (British, 1951). Graham Payn, Dora Bryan.

Don't Make Fun of the Fair [VS] — Noel Coward[w/m] *(Chappell)*. A hit revue in London with one Noel Coward song. COVER: Noel Coward.

1397 Lysistrata (Broadway, 1972). Melina Mercouri, Evelyn Russell.

Spirit of Love [PC] / A Woman's Hands [PC] — Michael Cacoyannis[w] & Peter Link[m] *(Gravel)*. A musical based on the classic drama. The musical lasted one week. COVER: none.

1398 Mack and Mabel (Broadway, 1974). Bernadette Peters, Robert Preston.

Big Time [VS] / Hundreds of Girls / I Promise You a Happy Ending / I Wanna Make the World Laugh [VS] / I Won't Send Roses / Look What Happened to Mabel [VS] / Movies Were Movies [VS] / Tap Your Troubles Away / Today I'm Gonna Think About Me [CUT] — plain cover / When Mabel Comes in the Room / Wherever He Ain't — Jerry Herman[w/m] *(Morris)*. A musical about silent films. The musical folded after two months. It had a lot of faults but it still had a good score and was interesting. COVER: sketch of camera and silent movie characters.

1399 Macushla (Irish, 1920). John Hamilton, Chauncey Olcott.

The Girl I'll Call My Sweetheart Must Look Like You — Chauncey Olcott[w/m] & Dan Sullivan[w/m] *(Witmark)*; I Never Met Before a Girl Like You — George Graff[w] & Chauncey Olcott[m] & Cass Freeborn[m] *(Witmark)*; I'll Miss You Old Ireland / Macushla Asthore / She's Irish / That's How the Shannon Flows / Who Knows / Word from an Irishman's Tongue — J. Keirn

Brennan[w] & Ernest Ball[m] *(Witmark)*; Ireland You're the Motherland — Thomas Meehan[w] & Arthur Grant[m] *(Witmark)*; My Land — Bartley Costello[w] & Chauncey Olcott[m] & Ernest Ball[m] *(Witmark)*; 'Tis an Irish Girl I Love and She's Just Like You — J. Keirn Brennan[w] & Alfred Dubin[w] & Ernest Ball[m] *(Witmark)*. A production billed as a play with music. COVER: Chauncey Olcott.

1400 The Mad Show (Off Broadway, 1966). Linda Lavin, Paul Sand.

The Boy From... [VS] — Stephen Sondheim[w] & Mary Rodgers[m] *(Burthern)*; Eccch! [PC] / The Gift of Maggie / Misery Is / The Real Thing [PC] / Snappy Answers [PC] / Who Dunit? [PC] / World, World Mad [PC] — Marshall Barer[w] & Mary Rodgers[m] *(Burthern)*; Hate Song [PC] / You Never Can Tell [PC] — Steven Vinaver[w] & Mary Rodgers[m] *(Burthern)*; Well, It Ain't [PC] — Larry Siegel[w] & Mary Rodgers[m] *(Burthern)*. A clever revue that ran for over two years. COVER: none.

1401 Madame Aphrodite (Off Broadway, 1961). Nancy Andrews, Jack Drummond.

Beautiful / The Girls Who Sit and Wait / Only, Only Love / Take a Good Look Around — Jerry Herman[w/m] *(Morris)*. A musical about a rooming house; the musical lasted one week. COVER: a hand with many rings putting drops in a cook pot.

1402 Madame Pagliacci (Jewish, 1938). Jennie Goldstein, Max Rosen.

Oi, Hob Ich a Meidele — David Myerowitz[w] & Sam Medoff[m] *(Metro)*. COVER: Jennie Goldstein.

1403 Madame Pompadour (Broadway, 1922). Wilda Bennett, Frederick Lewis.

I'll Be Your Soldier / Oh Joseph / One Two / Magic Moments / Serenade Madame Pompadour — Clare Kummer[w] & Leo Fall[m] *(Harms)*. An old fashioned operetta that folded after ten weeks. COVER: Madame Pompadour.

1404 The Madcap (*see also* **Green**

Fruit) (Broadway, 1927). Mitzi, Arthur Treacher.

Honey, Be My Honey Bee / Something to Tell / Stop, Go! — Clifford Grey[w] & Fred Coots[m] & Maurie Rubens[m] *(Harms)*; Odle-De-O — CliffordGrey[w] & Maurie Rubens[m] *(Harms)*. A French farce which flopped after three months. It was called *Green Fruit* in try-out and opened as *The Madcap*. COVER: columns and designs.

1405 The Madwoman of Central Park West (Off Broadway, 1979). Phyllis Newman.

My New Friends [VS] — Leonard Bernstein[w/m] *(Boosey, Hawkes)*. A one woman show that ran for ten weeks. COVER: none.

1406 Magdalena (Broadway, 1948). John Raitt, Irra Petina.

Bon Soir, Paris / The Emerald Song / Food for Thought / Magdalena / My Bus and I / The Singing Tree — Robert Wright[w] & George Forrest[w] & Heitor Villa-Lobos[m] *(Robbins)*. A lavish musical with a South American background and Villa-Lobos music. It flopped after 11 weeks. It was probably a little classy for most theatre goers. COVER: Irra Petina, John Raitt, Dorothy Sarnoff, Hugo Haas, and sketches.

1407 Maggie (Broadway, 1953). Keith Andes, Betty Paul.

Charm / My Mind's on You / What Every Woman Knows / You Become Me — William Roy[w/m] *(Chappell)*. A five performance flop based on the famous play *What Every Woman Knows*. COVER: girl with puppets.

1408 Maggie Flynn (Broadway, 1968). Shirley Jones, Jack Cassidy.

The Game of War [VS] / How About a Ball [VS] / I Won't Let It Happen [VS] / Learn How to Laugh [VS] / Look Around Your Little World / Maggie Flynn / Mr. Clown / Nice Cold Mornin' [VS] / Pitter Patter / The Thank You Song / What Does He Think? / Why Can't I Walk Away? — Hugo Peretti[w/m] & Luigi Creatore[w/m] & George D. Weiss[w/m] *(Valando)*. A musical set in

the Civil War period that survived only ten weeks. COVER: sketch of Jones, Cassidy, and other characters.

1409 The Magic Melody (Broadway, 1919). Charles Purcell, May Marbe.

Dear Heart of Mine / Down by the Nile / Dream Girl Give Back My Dream to Me / Gianina / Lips! Lips! Lips! / Little Church Around the Corner / Love Makes the World Go Round / Melodie of Dance / Night of Love / Once Upon a Time / Two's Company, Three's a Crowd / We Take It, Just Take It from You / When You're in Right / You Know and I Know — Frederic Kummer[w] & Sigmund Romberg[m] *(Witmark)*; Magic Melody Waltz — Sigmund Romberg[m] *(Witmark)*. A musical about a composer and his family; a poor Romberg score. It was a failure of four months. COVER: boy playing a lyre and girl in heart.

1410 The Magic Ring (*see also* Minnie and Me) (Broadway, 1923). Mitzi, Sydney Greenstreet.

Broken Hearts / Deep in Someone's Heart / Famous Falls / The Hand Organ / Homesick / A Love Song / Malaiya / When I Walk with Minnie — Zelda Sears[w] & Harold Levey[m] *(Harms)*. A poor rags-to-riches musical with an oriental setting that ran for three months. It was called *Minnie and Me* while trying out but opened as *The Magic Ring*. COVER: Mitzi. If you look carefully, some of the covers state "Dances by Julian Alfred" and some covers say "Dances by Dave Bennett."

1411 The Magic Show (Broadway, 1974). Doug Henning, Anita Morris.

Before Your Very Eyes [VS] / Charmin's Lament [VS] / Lion Tamer — plain cover / Solid Silver Platform Shoes [VS] / Style [VS] / Sweet, Sweet, Sweet [VS] / Two's Company [VS] / Up to His Old Tricks [VS] / West End Avenue [VS] — Stephen Schwartz[w/m] *(Belwin Mills)*. A glorified magic show that ran for over four years. COVER: Doug Hemming and magic acts.

1412 The Magnolia Lady (Broadway, 1924). Ruth Chatterton, Ralph Forbes.

The French Lesson / Moon Man / My Heart's in the Sunny South / The Old Red Gate / Tiger Lily Lou — Anne Caldwell[w] & Harold Levey[m] *(Harms)*. A dreary musical about a rich Southern family going poor. It lasted six weeks. COVER: Ruth Chatterton.

1413 Maid of the Mountains (Broadway, 1918). Sidonie Espero, William Danforth.

A Bachelor Gay / Dirty Work / Dividing the Spoils — Clifford Harris[w] & Harold Fraser-Simson[m] *(Feist)*; Farewell / Friendship and Love / Good People Gather 'Round / Husbands and Wives / I Understand / Live for Today / Love Will Find a Way / My Life Is Love / New Moon / Over There / Paradise for Two — Harry Graham[w] & Harold Fraser-Simson[m] *(Feist)*; Waiting for You — Marcus Connelly[w] & Gitz Rice[m] *(Feist)*; When You're in Love — Clifford Harris[w] & A. Valentine[w] & James Tate[m] *(Feist)*. This musical ran for four years in London and lasted four weeks on Broadway. COVER: a young girl carrying flowers.

1414 Maid to Love (*see also* The Right Girl) (Broadway, 1921). Charles Purcell, Helen Montrose.

Aladdin / Call of Love / Cocktail / Girls All Around Me / Look for the Girl / Look into My Eyes / Love's Little Journey / Love's Romantic Sea / Oriental Serenade / Rocking Chair Fleet / There's an Old Flame Burning / We Were Made to Love / When Everything Is Harmony — Raymond Peck[w] & Percy Wenrich[m] *(Feist)*. A rich-to-poor-to-rich musical that lasted only three months. This show toured as *Maid to Love* but opened as *The Right Girl* on Broadway. COVER: flowers and designs.

1415 Maid to Measure (British, 1948). Jessie Matthews, Tommy Fields.

Time May Change — Leigh Stafford[w] & Hugh Wade[m] *(Shapiro, Bernstein)*. A song published in the U.S. from a hit London revue starring Jessie Matthews. COVER: Jessie Matthews and Tommy Fields.

1416 The Maiden Voyage (*see also* Honeymoon Cruise) (closed before Broadway, 1925). Stars unknown.

A Honeymoon Cruise / Hot Patootie Land [ABQ] / I Am Angling for You [ABQ] / I Want You / Just One More Waltz with You [ABQ] / Oui! Oui! [ABQ] / Pango Moon / Persian Skies [ABQ] / Pompadour [ABQ] / Rain! Rain! Rain! / The Whole World's Doing It Now [ABQ] — Arthur Swanstrom[w] & Carey Morgan[m] *(Feist)*. This show toured as *The Maiden Voyage* and as *Honeymoon Cruise*. COVER: a group of people boarding a yacht.

1417 Make a Wish (Broadway, 1951). Nanette Fabray, Helen Gallagher.

Over and Over / Paris, France / Suits Me Fine / That Face [ABQ] / What I Was Warned About / When Does This Feeling Go Away? — Hugh Martin[w/m] *(Morris)*. This musical, about an orphan in Paris, was very charming with talented people and pleasant songs but it lasted only three months. COVER: girl staring at a French scene. This score was published with two sets of covers. One set is black, blue and white and the other is just blue and white.

1418 Make It Snappy (Broadway, 1922). Eddie Cantor, Georgie Hale.

Bashful Baby — A. Sizemore[w/m] & B. Shrigley[w/m] *(Remick)*; Blossom Time / Bouquet of Girls / Desert Rose / Doing the Eddie Cantor / I'm Wild About Wild Men / Jazza Painted Jazza-Ma-Renos / Lovable Eyes / My Fragonard Girl / My Vision in Vermillion — Harold Atteridge[w] & Jean Schwartz[m] *(Remick)*; Don't — Joe Goodwin[w] & Murray Roth[w] & James Hanley[m] *(Shapiro, Bernstein)*; Fly Home to Your Nest — Louis Breau[w/m] *(Belwin)*; Gay Butterfly on the Wheel / Hooch Rhythm — Alfred Bryan[w] & Jean Schwartz[m] *(Remick)*; How Ya Gonna ----- Your Mind on Dancing — Lew

Brown[w] & James Hanley[m] *(Shapiro, Bernstein)*; I Love Her—She Loves Me—Irving Caesar[w] & Eddie Cantor[w] & Irving Caesar[m] *(Harms)*; I'm Hungry for Beautiful Girls—Billy Rose[w] & Wilbur Held[w] & Fred Fisher[m] *(Fred Fisher)*; Keep It Under Your Hat—Eddie Cantor[w/m] & Charles Tobias[w/m] & Louis Breau[w/m] *(Bee-Tee)*; Little Rover—Gus Kahn[w] & Walter Donaldson[m] *(Shapiro, Bernstein)*; Lovin' Sam—Jack Yellen[w] & Milton Ager[m] *(A Y and B)*; My Yiddisha Mammy—Alex Gerber[w/m] & Jean Schwartz[w/m] & Eddie Cantor[w/m] *(Witmark)*; Seven or Eleven / Where the Bamboo Babies Grow—Lew Brown[w] & Walter Donaldson[m] *(Shapiro, Bernstein)*; The Sheik of Araby—Harry B. Smith[w] & Francis Wheeler[w] & Ted Snyder[m] *(Berlin)*; Snuggle Pups Cantor—Eddie Cantor[w/m] *(Cantor)*; Sophie—Abner Silver[w/m] *(Witmark)*; To-Morrow—Roy Turk[w/m] & J. Russel Robinson[w/m] *(Berlin)*; Waikiki—Bert Kalmar[w/m] & Harry Ruby[w/m] *(Berlin)*; When You're Married—Fred Fisher[w/m] & Eddie Cantor[w/m] *(Fred Fisher)*. A Winter Garden revue that featured Cantor and some vaudeville acts. It lasted only three months. COVER: Eddie Cantor, Lillian FitzGerald.

1419 Make Mine Manhattan (Broadway, 1948). David Burns, Sid Caesar.

Gentleman Friend / I Don't Know Her Name / I Fell in Love with You / My Brudder and Me / Phil the Fiddler / Saturday Night in Central Park—Arnold Horwitt[w] & Richard Lewine[m] *(Harms)*. A hit revue with good sketches and pleasant songs. It ran for over a year. COVER: sketches of people in New York.

1420 Making Mary (closed before Broadway, 1931). Stars unknown.

You Know How to Say Lovely Things—Harold Orlob[w/m] & Grace Johnson[w/m] & Harold Lewis[w/m] *(Shapiro, Bernstein)*. COVER: face of a girl.

1421 Mamba's Daughters (Broadway, 1939). Ethel Waters, Canada Lee.

Lonesome Walls—DuBose Heyward[w] & Jerome Kern[m] *(Chappell)*. A heavy drama with Ethel Waters and this one Kern song. It ran for five months. COVER: lettering and designs.

1422 Mame (Broadway, 1966). Angela Lansbury, Beatrice Arthur.

Bosom Buddies [VS] / Gooch's Song [VS] / If He Walked into My Life / It's Today [VS] / Mame / Mame—complete vocal score / The Man in the Moon [VS] / My Best Girl / Open a New Window / St. Bridget [VS] / That's How Young I Feel [VS] / We Need a Little Christmas—Jerry Herman[w/m] *(Morris)*. A smash hit musical based on *Auntie Mame*. It had a wonderful score and a talented cast and ran over three years. Like Dolly, everyone wanted to play Mame and it was done at various times by Ginger Rogers, Ann Sothern, Susan Hayward and many others. COVER: "Mame."

1423 Mamie Smith and Her Gang (Black, 1927). Mamie Smith.

I Ain't Gonna Shake It No More—Bama Bound[w/m] *(Marks)*; Lenox Avenue Blues / Mama's Got What Papa Wants—Mamie Smith[w/m] & Lew Porter[w/m] *(Marks)*; There'll Be No Freebies—Quinton Redd[w/m] *(Marks)*. COVER: Mamie Smith.

1424 The Man from Wicklow (Irish, 1927). Fiske O'Hara.

I Love and Adore But Thee—George Gatlan[w/m] *(Feist)*; My Old Irish Mother and Ireland / The Princess of My Heart / What Shall I Say—Fiske O'Hara[w] & Bartley Costello[w] & Cass Freeborn[m] *(Feist)*. COVER: Fiske O'Hara.

1425 Man in the Moon (Broadway, 1963). Bil Baird Puppets.

Worlds Apart—Sheldon Harnick[w] & Jerry Bock[m] *(Valando)*. A puppet show with music presented for a limited run. COVER: a boy and girl puppet.

1426 Man of LaMancha (Broadway, 1965). Richard Kiley, Joan Diener.

Aldonza / The Barber's Song [RC] / The Dubbing [VS] / Dulcinea / Golden

Helmet [RC] / I Really Like Him / I'm Only Thinking of Him [RC] / The Impossible Dream / It's All the Same [RC] / Knight of the Woeful Countenance / Little Bird, Little Bird / A Little Gossip / Man of LaMancha / Man of LaMancha — complete score / Mask of Evil [RC] / The Psalm [RC] / To Each His Dulcinea / What Do You Want of Me? [RC] — Joe Darion[w] & Mitch Leigh[m] *(Sam Fox)*. The legend of Don Quixote set to music and a hit for six years. It had an adventurous story and talented actors plus a hit song, *The Impossible Dream*. COVER: sketch of a knight and a girl.

1427 The Man of Tomorrow (Jewish, 1941). Leon Gold.

Der Mensh Fun Morgn — Chaim Tauber[w] & Sholom Secunda[m] *(Metro)*. COVER: Sholom Secunda, Leon Gold, Samuel Goldenburg.

1428 The Man Who Came to Dinner (Broadway, 1939). Monty Woolley, Edith Atwater.

The Man Who Came to Dinner — promotion song — Barnett Hart[w/m] *(Berlin)*; What Am I to Do? — published in play script only — Cole Porter[w/m] *(Chappell)*. A smash comedy that ran for two years with a good story and Monty Woolley. This incidental song was thrown in to support a "Noel Coward" type character. COVER: Monty Woolley.

1429 Man with a Load of Mischief (Off Broadway, 1966). Reid Shelton, Virginia Vestoff.

Any Other Way / Come to the Masquerade / Hulla-Baloo-Balay / Little Rag Doll / Make Way for My Lady / Man with a Load of Mischief / Once You've Had a Little Taste / A Wonder — John Clifton[w] & Ben Tarver[w] & John Clifton[m] *(Scope)*. A period piece with a run of six months. COVER: a medieval man and woman.

1430 Mandragola (closed before Broadway, 1925). Stars unknown.

Only Love Is the Life / A Woman Knows All — Alfred Kreymborg[w] & Ignatz Waghalter[m] *(Harms)*. COVER: lettering and designs.

1431 Manhattan Mary (Broadway, 1927). Ed Wynn, George White.

Broadway / The Five-Step / I'd Like You to Love Me / It Won't Be Long Now / Just a Cozy Hide-Away / Just a Memory / Manhattan Mary / My Bluebird's Home Again / Nothing But Love — B.G. DeSylva[w] & Lew Brown[w] & Ray Henderson[m] *(Harms)*. A musical which was really a revue. Ed Wynn kept this show running for eight months. COVER: a skyscraper.

1432 Manhattan Music Hall (Lew Brown) (Nightclub, 1934). Carolyn Marsh.

You Get a Lot of Help — Lew Brown[w] & Harry Akst[m] *(Witmark)*. COVER: Carolyn Marsh.

1433 Manhattan Music Hall (Jack Pomeroy) (Nightclub, 1934). Kathleen Karr.

Dancing My Dinner Down / Plodding Along / Spring Is Blue / Zazu, Zazu, Zee — Abe Tuvin[w] & Donald Heywood[m] *(Marks)*. COVER: Kathleen Karr and chorus girls.

1434 The Manhatters (Broadway, 1927). Ben Bernie, Aida Ward.

Close Your Eyes / Down on the Delta / Nigger Heaven Blues — George Oppenheimer[w] & Alfred Nathan[m] *(D B and H)*; Under the Moon — Ev-Lyn[w/m] & Francis Wheeler[w/m] & Ted Snyder[w/m] *(Berlin)*. A poor revue transferred from the Village. It lasted eight weeks. COVER: titles and designs.

1435 March of the Falsettos (Off Broadway, 1981). Stephen Bogardus, Michael Rupert.

Father to Son [VS] / Four Jews in a Room Bitching [VS] / Games I Play [VS] / I Never Wanted to Love You [VS] / Making a Home [VS] / March of the Falsettos [VS] / A Marriage Proposal [VS] / Marvin at the Psychiatrist [RC] / My Father's a Homo [RC] — William Finn[w/m] *(Warner Bros.)*. The first of three one-act plays by William Finn about a gay relationship. It was highly acclaimed and was later redone as one part of the hit musical *Falsettos*. COVER: a scene from the play.

1436 Marching By (Broadway, 1932). Guy Robertson, Desiree Taylor.

I Love You, My Darling — George Hirst[w] & Edward Eliscu[w] & Jean Gilbert[m] *(Harms)*; I've Gotta Keep My Eye on You — Mack Gordon[w] & Harry Revel[m] *(Harms)*; Marching By — Harry Clarke[w] & Gus Edwards[m] *(Harms)*. A German operetta re-vamped by Harry B. Smith. This was his last Broadway show and it ran for a week and a half. COVER: a dancing girl.

1437 Marching with Johnny (closed before Broadway, 1943). Beatrice Kay, David Brooks.

Let's End the Beguine [PC] — Henry Meyers[w] & Edward Eliscu[w] & Jay Gorney[m] *(Mills)*. This touring musical emphasized labor's contribution to the war. It folded in Philadelphia. Most of the material for this show came from two previous failures, *The New Meet the People* and *They Can't Get You Down*. COVER: none.

1438 Marcus Show of 1920 (Nightclub, 1920). Charles Abbate.

Smile with Me — Charles Abbate[w/m] *(Marcus)*. COVER: Charles Abbate and chorus girls.

1439 Marcus Show of 1921 (closed before Broadway, 1921). Stars unknown.

Bohemia / California / I've Got a New One / Love Me If You Dare / Too Late — Little Girl — Too Late / You're Like a Rose — Jack Lait[w] & Charlie Abot[m] *(Remick)*. COVER: a girl with flowers.

1440 Mardi Gras (Regional, 1965). Stars unknown.

Come Along Down / I'd Know That Smile / The Kind of a Girl for Me / The Mardi Gras Waltz / Mumbo Jumbo / Someone I Could Love / When I Take My Lady — Carmen Lombardo[w/m] & John J. Loeb[w/m] *(Lombardo)*. An original musical produced for a summer run at Jones Beach in N.Y. COVER: a sketch of carnival characters.

1441 Margery Daw (*see also* Mar-

jorie) (Broadway, 1924). Skeets Gallagher, Ethel Shutta.

Happy Ending / What Do You Say — Clifford Grey[w] & Herbert Stothart[m] *(Harms)*; Hollywood / Margery / Monastery — Clifford Grey[w] & Stephen Jones[m] *(Harms)*. A musical about producing a play. The try-out title was *Margery Daw* but it opened on Broadway as *Marjorie* and lasted four months. COVER: designs and lettering.

1442 Maria Golovin (Broadway, 1958). Patricia Neway, Ruth Kobart.

Maria Golovin — complete vocal score — Gian Carlo Menotti[w/m] *(Belwin-Mills)*. A husband and wife war tragedy that lasted five performances on Broadway. COVER: a scene from the musical.

1443 Marie Galante (French, 1934). Florelle, Inkijinoff.

Les Filles de Bordeaux [F] / Le Grand Lustucru [F] / J'Attends un Navire [F] / Le Roi d'Aquitaine [F] / Le Train du Ciel [F] — Jacques Deval[w] & Kurt Weill[m] *(Heugel)*; Marche de l'Armee Panemeenne [F] / Scene au Dancing [F] — Kurt Weill[m] *(Heugel)*. An unsuccessful musical written in Paris by Weill after fleeing from Berlin. COVER: a lady holding a mask with an ocean liner sailing away.

1444 Marinka (Broadway, 1945). Joan Roberts, Harry Stockwell.

Cab Song / One Last Love Song / One Touch of Vienna / Sigh by Night / Treat a Woman Like a Drum / Turn On the Charm — George Marion[w] & Emmerich Kalman[m] *(Remick)*. An old fashioned operetta with a moderate run. COVER: couple dancing before a castle.

1445 Marjolaine (1446) (Broadway, 1922). Peggy Wood, Irving Beebe.

Cuddle Up Together / Don't / Here Away / Marjolaine / O Love of Mine! / River of Dreams / The Syringa Tree / Wonderland — Brian Hooker[w] & Hugo Felix[m] *(Harms)*; I Want You — Anne Caldwell[w] & Hugo Felix[m] *(Harms)*; Nesting Place — John H. Mears[w/m] & Earnest Golden[w/m]

(Harms). A musical about a parent's and children's romances with nothing to recommend it except Peggy Wood. It ran four months. COVER: two sets of covers. One set had straight orange and grey lines and one had flowers.

1446 Marjorie (*see also* **Margery Daw**) (Broadway, 1924). Skeets Gallagher, Ethel Shutta.

Forty Second Street Moon / My Twilight Rose — Clifford Grey[w] & Sigmund Romberg[m] *(Harms)*; Happy Ending / What Do You Say — Clifford Grey[w] & Herbert Stothart[m] *(Harms)*; Hollywood / Margery / Monastery — Clifford Grey[w] & Stephen Jones[m] *(Harms)*; Shuffle Your Troubles Away — Henry Creamer[w] & James Hanley[m] *(Harms)*; Yesterday — Clifford Grey[w] & Herbert Stothart[m] & P.H. Culkin[m] *(Harms)*. A musical about producing a play. It lasted four months. The try-out title was *Margery Daw* but it opened on Broadway as *Marjorie*. COVER: lettering and designs.

1447 Married Alive (*see also* **Darling of the Day**) (Broadway, 1968). Vincent Price, Patricia Routledge.

It's Enough to Make a Lady Fall in Love [PC] / I've Got a Rainbow Working for Me [PC] / Let's See What Happens [PC] / Not on Your Nellie [PC] / Under the Sunset Tree [PC] — E.Y. Harburg[w] & Jule Styne[m] *(Chappell)*. A short run musical with a pleasant score by Harburg and Styne plus the talented Patricia Routledge. It had a poor book and a dull performance from Vincent Price. The try-out title was *Married Alive* but it opened on Broadway as *Darling of the Day*. COVER: none.

1448 Marry Me a Little (Off Broadway, 1981). Suzanne Henry, Craig Lucas.

So Many People [VS] / What More Do I Need [VS] — Stephen Sondheim[w/m] *(Valando)*. A revue based on Sondheim songs with a New York theme. It lasted three months. The balance of the songs used are listed with their respective shows. COVER: Sondheim.

1449 La Martinique Revue (Nightclub, 1944). Rose Marie.

Ma-Ma-Marie — Sunny Skylar[w] & Irving Fields[m] *(Marks)*. COVER: Rose Marie.

1450 Mary (Broadway, 1920). Jack McGowan, Janet Velie.

Anything You Want to Do, Dear / Deeper / The Love Nest / Mary / That Farm Out in Kansas / Tom-Tom-Toddle / Waiting / We'll Have a Wonderful Party — Otto Harbach[w] & Louis Hirsch[m] *(Victoria)*. A rags-to-riches love story with a great score and dancing. It lasted six months and had many road companies touring the U.S. It produced several hit songs such as *The Love Nest*. COVER: flowers and designs.

1451 Mary Jane McKane (Broadway, 1923). Mary Hay, Hal Skelly.

Come On and Pet Me / Flannel Petticoat Girl / My Boy and I / Toodle-Oo — Oscar Hammerstein[w] & William Duncan[w] & Vincent Youmans[m] *(Harms)*; Stick to Your Knitting / Thistle Down — Oscar Hammerstein[w] & William Duncan[w] & Herbert Stothart[m] *(Harms)*. A poor secretary story with some good Youmans songs. It ran five months. COVER: flowers and designs.

1452 Mask and Wig (Red Rhumba) (College, 1936). University of Pennsylvania Students.

Havana / You Can't Judge a Book by Its Cover — Moe Jaffe[w] & Clay Boland[m] *(Berlin)*; Just Because I Looked at You — Clay Boland[w/m] & Tommy Smith[w/m] *(Berlin)*; Too Good to Be True — Clay Boland[w/m] *(Berlin)*; When You Love — Moe Jaffe[w] & Harry Barris[w] & Clay Boland[m] *(Berlin)*. COVER: lettering and designs.

1453 Mask and Wig (This Mad Whirl) (College, 1936). University of Pennsylvania Students.

An Apple a Day / Foolish Fascination / Let's Take a Trip to Jamaica / Something Has Happened to Me / This Mad Whirl / Whirligig / You're My Best Bet — Moe Jaffe[w] & Clay Boland[m] *(Words and Music)*. COVER: faces and masks.

1454 Mask and Wig (Fifty Fifty) (College, 1937). University of Pennsylvania Students.

Gypsy in My Soul / I Live the Life I Love / It's Corny But It's Fun / Open Your Heart — Moe Jaffe[w] & Clay Boland[m] *(Words and Music)*. COVER: faces and masks.

1455 Mask and Wig (All Around the Town) (College, 1938). University of Pennsylvania Students.

There's No Place Like Your Arms / When I Go A-Dreamin' / Ya Got Me — Bickley Reichner[w] & Clay Boland[m] *(Lincoln)*. COVER: man's and woman's face.

1456 Mask and Wig (Great Guns) (College, 1939). University of Pennsylvania Students.

I've Got My Eye on You / When I Climb Down from My Saddle — Bickley Reichner[w] & Clay Boland[m] *(Lincoln)*; Stop! It's Wonderful — Bickley Reichner[w/m] & Clay Boland[w/m] *(Lincoln)*. COVER: two masks.

1457 Mask and Wig (High as a Kite) (College, 1940). University of Pennsylvania Students.

High as a Kite / I'll Sing Your Praises / My Gal / Not So Long Ago — Bickley Reichner[w] & Clay Boland[m] *(Marks)*. COVER: Franklin with a key and a kite.

1458 Mask and Wig (Out of This World) (College, 1941). University of Pennsylvania Students.

Fifty Million Sweethearts Can't Be Wrong / Stars Over the Schoolhouse / That Solid Old Man — Bickley Reichner[w] & Clay Boland[m] *(Melrose)*. COVER: outer space and the earth with musical notes.

1459 Mask and Wig (Paoli Local) (College, 1942). University of Pennsylvania Students.

Sighted Dame — Loved Same — Eddie DeLange[w/m] & Clay Boland[w/m] & Moe Jaffe[w/m] & Bickley Reichner[w/m] *(Mills)*. COVER: naked dancing girl.

1460 Mask and Wig (Red Points and Blue) (College, 1944). University of Pennsylvania Students.

As You Were / Big Three Polka / How Do You Like Your Romance? / Talkin' to Your Picture / You Give Ice Away — Moe Jaffe[w] & Bickley Reichner[w] & Clay Boland[m] *(Mills)*. COVER: smiling face with cap and gown.

1461 Mask and Wig (Hep to the Beat) (College, 1945). University of Pennsylvania Students.

How to Play Boogie Woogie — Clay Boland[w/m] *(Mills)*. COVER: girl at piano.

1462 Mask and Wig (John Paul Jones) (College, 1946). University of Pennsylvania Students.

Don't Say We're Through / It's Spring / Jam That Licorice Stick / Reasonable Facsimile / Sentiment and Stuff — Moe Jaffe[w] & Darrell Smith[w] & Clay Boland[m] *(Words and Music)*; Gypsy in My Soul — Moe Jaffe[w] & Clay Boland[w] & Clay Boland[m] *(Words and Music)*. COVER: a bust of John Paul Jones.

1463 Mask and Wig (Chris Crosses) (College, 1946). University of Pennsylvania Students.

Christmas Eve — Dale Wood[w] & Clarence Kelley[w] & Clay Boland[m] *(Words and Music)*; Holiday — Fred Waring[w] & Moe Jaffe[w] & Clay Boland[m] *(Words and Music)*; I Live the Life I Love — Clay Boland[w/m] *(Words and Music)*; I'll Take You All Over the World — Clay Boland[w/m] *(Boland)*; Interlude — Moe Jaffe[w] & Nick Wells[w] & Clay Boland[m] *(General)*; It's the Same the Whole World Over — Moe Jaffe[w/m] & Clay Boland[w/m] & Dwight Latham[w/m] *(General)*; She Told Him Emphatic'lly "No" — Saxie Dowell[w/m] & Bickley Reichner[w/m] & Clay Boland[w/m] *(Boland)*. COVER: a map of the world, three ships, and Columbus.

1464 Mask and Wig (Juleo and Romiet) (College, 1947). University of Pennsylvania Students.

Happy Go Lucky — Moe Jaffe[w] & Clay Boland[m] *(Words and Music)*; If Love Can Happen — Dale Wood[w] & Michael Grace[w] & Clay Boland[m] & Eddie DeLange[m] *(Cecille)*. COVER: musical notes and scales.

1465 Mask and Wig (Adamant Eve) (College, 1949). University of Pennsylvania Students.

Got You Right Where I Want You / Your Life Is My Life — Bickley Reichner^w & Clay Boland^m *(Elliot)*; I Didn't Know It Was That Good / Kissing Me — Moe Jaffe^w & Clay Boland^m *(General)*; Love Is — Clay Boland^{w/m} *(Simon);* Watch That First Step — Moe Jaffe^{w/m} & Clay Boland^{w/m} *(General).*COVER: boy, girl, apple, snake.

1466 Mass (Broadway, 1971). Alan Titus, David Cryer.

Almighty Father / Gloria Tibi / Mass — complete vocal score / Sanctus / A Simple Song / The Word of the Lord — Stephen Schwartz^w & Leonard Bernstein^w & Leonard Bernstein^m *(Boosey, Hawkes).* A spectacular musical work written for the opening of the Washington Kennedy Center. It also played for one week in Philadelphia and three weeks at the Metropolitan Opera House in N.Y. COVER: letters with a steeple and cross.

1467 Mata Hari (*see also* Ballad for a Firing Squad) (closed before Broadway, 1967). Marisa Mell, Pernell Roberts.

Maman / There Is No You [PC] — Martin Charnin^w & Edward Thomas^m *(Morris).* One of the biggest disasters in theatre history. Miscast stars and a poor score closed this musical in Washington after two weeks. It was revised and opened Off Broadway as *Ballad for a Firing Squad* but failed again. COVER: wounded soldiers.

1468 The Matinee Girl (Broadway, 1926). James Hamilton, Jack Squire.

Like-a-Me, Like-a-You / Only One — McElbert Moore^w & Frank Grey^m & McElbert Moore^m *(Harms).* A girl-chases-boy musical that lasted for three weeks. COVER: an audience staring at a stage.

1469 May Wine (Broadway, 1935). Leo Carroll, Walter Slezak.

Dance, My Darlings / I Built a Dream One Day / Just Once Around

the Clock / Somebody Ought to Be Told / Something New Is in My Heart — Oscar Hammerstein^w & Sigmund Romberg^m *(Chappell).* A 19th century plot musical with a pleasant Romberg score. It ran six months. COVER: girls with flowers.

1470 Maybe I'm Doing It Wrong (Off Broadway, 1982). Deborah Rush, Mark Linn-Baker.

Short People — Randy Newman^{w/m} *(Warner Bros.).* A short-lived revue using Randy Newman songs. COVER: Randy Newman.

1471 Mayfair and Montmartre (British, 1922). Alice Delysia, Evelyn Laye.

The Bandit Band [B] / The Blue Boy Blues [B] / Cocktail Time [B] / Olga (Come Back to the Volga) [B] / The Sponge [B] — Cole Porter^{w/m} *(Chappell)*; Do It Again (Please Do It Again) [B] — B.G. DeSylva^w & George Gershwin^m *(Chappell)*; Drifting Along with the Tide [B] / My Lady [B] / South Sea Isles [B] — Arthur Jackson^w & George Gershwin^m *(Chappell)*; Peaches [B] — P.G. Wodehouse^w & Jerome Kern^m *(Chappell).* A Cochran revue in London with songs by famous American composers. COVER: flowers and lettering.

1472 Mayflowers (Broadway, 1925). Joseph Santley, Ivy Sawyer.

Mayflowers — Clifford Grey^w & Frank Tours^m *(Harms)*; Put Your Troubles in a Candy Box — Clifford Grey^w & Fred Coots^m *(Harms)*; The Road of Dreams — Donovan Parsons^w & Clifford Grey^w & Pat Thayer^m *(Harms)*; Seven Days / Take a Little Stroll with Me — Clifford Grey^w & Edward Kunecke^m *(Harms).* A musical about a girl's romantic dreams; the work lasted ten weeks. COVER: silhouette of girl with flowers.

1473 Mayor (Broadway, 1985). Lenny Wolfe, Ilene Kristen.

Ballad [VS] / Good Times / Hootspa [VS] / How'm I Doin' [VS] / I Want to Be the Mayor [VS] / I'll Never Leave You / The Last "I Love New York"

Song [VS] / March of the Yuppies [VS] / Mayor / My City / What You See Is What You Get [VS] / You Can Be a New Yorker, Too [VS] / You're Not the Mayor [VS] — Charles Strouse^{w/m} *(Columbia)*. A small musical about the mayor of New York; it ran for eight months. COVER: a sketch of the mayor.

1474 Maytime in Erin (Irish, 1922). Walter Scanlon.

The Dawning of Love / My Lady Fair / Some Day — Walter Scanlan^{w/m} *(Berlin)*; I Was a Pilgrim in Loveland / Meself / Mother's Paisley Shawl / A Puff o' Me Pipe and a Song — George Kershaw^w & Walter Scanlan^m *(Berlin)*. COVER: Walter Scanlan.

1475 Me and Juliet (Boston) (Broadway, 1953). Isabel Bigley, Bill Hayes.

I'm Your Girl / Keep It Gay / Marriage Type Love / No Other Love / A Very Special Day — Oscar Hammerstein^w & Richard Rodgers^m *(Williamson)*. COVER: a yellow and purple cover with sketch of backstage people.

1476 Me and Juliet (New York) (Broadway, 1953). Isabel Bigley, Bill Hayes.

Big Black Giant / I'm Your Girl / It Feels Good / It's Me / Keep It Gay / Marriage Type Love / Me and Juliet — complete vocal score / No Other Love / That's the Way It Happens / A Very Special Day / We Deserve Each Other — Oscar Hammerstein^w & Richard Rodgers^m *(Williamson)*. A backstage musical with a poor book and an ordinary score; it somehow managed to survive for almost a year. COVER: a red, white, and purple cover with a sketch of backstage people.

1477 Me and My Girl (British, 1937). Lupino Lane, George Graves.

Me and My Girl / Lambeth Walk — Douglas Furber^w & Noel Gay^m *(Mills)*. Two songs published in the U.S. from the smash hit musical of London. COVER: Lupino Lane.

1478 Me and My Girl (Broadway, 1986). Robert Lindsay, Maryann Plunkett.

Hold My Hand [VS] — Harry Graham^w & Maurice Elwin^m & Noel Gay^m *(Leonard)*; Lambeth Walk [VS] / Me and My Girl [VS] — Douglas Furber^w & Noel Gay^m *(Leonard)*; Leaning on a Lamp-Post [VS] / Love Makes the World Go Round [VS] / Once You Lose Your Heart [VS] — Noel Gay^{w/m} *(Leonard)*; The Sun Has Got His Hat On [VS] / Take It on the Chin [VS] — Ralph Butler^{w/m} & Noel Gay^{w/m} *(Leonard)*; Thinking of No One But Me [VS] / You Would If You Could [VS] — Douglas Furber^{w/m} & Noel Gay^{w/m} *(Leonard)*. A hit revival of the old British musical. It was a lavish production featuring Robert Lindsay. COVER: man in royal outfit and lamp post.

1479 Me for You (*see also* Heads Up) (Broadway, 1929). Ray Bolger, Victor Moore.

I Can Do Wonders with You / Me for You! / My Man Is on the Make / Ship Without a Sail / Sky City — Lorenz Hart^w & Richard Rodgers^m *(Harms)*. A slight musical about rum. The show had several good Rodgers songs and ran four months. Its try-out title was *Me for You* but it opened on Broadway as *Heads Up*. COVER: flowers and designs.

1480 The Me Nobody Knows (Broadway, 1970). Carl Thomas, Hattie Winston.

Black [VS] / Dream Babies [VS] / How I Feel / If I Had a Million / Let Me Come In / Light Sings / Sounds / This World / The Tree [VS] / War Babies [PC] — Will Holt^w & Gary W. Friedman^m *(Valando)*. A revue about the thoughts of children set to music. It lasted a year and a half. COVER: designs and letters.

1481 Mecca (Broadway, 1920). Gladys Hanson, John Nicholson.

The Chinaman's Song / A Fool There Was / Hast Thou Been to Mecca? / In the Dance / Love in My Breast / My King of Love / When Love Knocked Upon the Door — Oscar Asche^w & Percy Fletcher^m *(Harms)*. An Arabian Nights spectacle that ran for four months. COVER: a group of men riding camels.

1482 The Medium (Broadway, 1947). Marie Powers, Claramae Turner.

The Black Swan / The Medium — complete vocal score — Gian-Carlo Menotti[w/m] *(Schirmer)*. A double bill of two short operas, *The Telephone* and *The Medium*. They ran for six months. COVER: a half naked child clinging to a curtain.

1483 Medium Rare (Regional, 1960). Bob Dishy, Jean Arnold.

The Tempo of the Times — Carolyn Leigh[w] & Cy Coleman[m] *(Morris)*. A hit revue in Chicago that ran for three years but never went to N.Y. It had music by Bock and Harnick; Strouse and Adams; and Leigh and Coleman. COVER: the devil and three dancers.

1484 Meet Me in St. Louis (Regional, 1960). Stars unknown.

Almost / The Boy Next Door / Diamonds in the Starlight / Have Yourself a Merry Little Christmas / How Do I Look? / If I Had an Igloo / A Raving Beauty / Skip to My Lou / The Trolley Song / What's-His-Name / You Are for Loving — Hugh Martin[w/m] & Ralph Blane[w/m] *(Feist)*; Meet Me in St. Louis, Louis — Andrew Sterling[w] & Kerry Mills[m] *(Feist)*. A stage version of the popular movie for the Municipal Opera in St. Louis on a limited run. COVER: exposition buildings and fireworks.

1485 Meet Me in St. Louis (Broadway, 1989). George Hearn, Betty Garrett.

The Boy Next Door / The Trolley Song — Hugh Martin[w/m] & Ralph Blane[w/m] *(Belwin)*; Meet Me in St. Louis, Louis — Andrew Sterling[w] & Kerry Mills[m] *(Belwin)*. A revised version of the 1960 St. Louis production. COVER: boy and girl with little girl in pigtails.

1486 Meet Miss Jones (Black, 1947). Stars unknown.

Don't Lose Your Head / I've Got to Be Lovely to Harry / You're My Rose — Flournoy E. Miller[w] & James Johnson[m] *(Mills)*. COVER: tropical dancer and palm tree.

1487 Meet My Sister (Broadway, 1930). Bettina Hall, George Grossmith.

Always in My Heart / The Devil May Care / She Is My Ideal — Ralph Benatzky[w/m] *(Harms)*. A German musical about divorce. It ran four months. COVER: a string of hearts and green leaves.

1488 Meet the People (Broadway, 1940). Nanette Fabray, Peggy Ryan.

The Bill of Rights / In-Chi-Chi-Castenango / Let's Steal a Tune / Meet the People / The Stars Remain / Voulez-Vous, Mrs. Yifnif? / We Have Sandwiches — Henry Myers[w] & Jay Gorney[m] *(Mills)*; Elmer's Wedding Day — Sid Kuller[w/m] & Ray Golden[w/m] *(Mills)*; A Fellow and a Girl / It's the Same Old Dream — Edward Eliscu[w] & Jay Gorney[m] *(Mills)*; No Lookin' Back / Union Label — Henry Myers[w] & Edward Eliscu[w] & Jay Gorney[m] *(Mills)*. A fast moving topical revue that lasted for five months on Broadway after a cross country tour. COVER: silhouettes of a row of people.

1489 Meet the People (Nightclub, 1955). Mickey Calin, Janet Gaylord.

You, and Your Broken Heart! — Henry Myers[w] & Edward Eliscu[w] & Jay Gorney[m] *(Mills)*. A small edition of the 1940 revue in the Cafe Theatre of Hotel Paramount. COVER: skyscrapers.

1490 Melody (Broadway, 1933). Gypsy Rose Lee, Everett Marshall.

Give Me a Roll on a Drum / I'd Write a Song / In My Garden / Melody / Melody — complete vocal score / Never Had an Education / Pompadour / Tonight May Never Come Again / You Are the Song — Irving Caesar[w] & Sigmund Romberg[m] *(Harms)*. Another dull love story in the operetta style from Romberg. It lasted ten weeks. It was the last show for the great set designer Urban and the last show at the Casino Theatre. COVER: letters and designs.

1491 Melody Man (*see also* **Jazz King**) (Broadway, 1924). Eva Puck, Sammy White.

I'd Like to Poison Ivy / Moonlight Mama — Herbert$^{w/m}$ & Richard$^{w/m}$ & Lorenz$^{w/m}$ *(Marks)*. A comedy that flopped. The composers disguised their names. It was called *Jazz King* out of town. COVER: a mad violinist with Puck and White.

1492 The Melting of Molly (Broadway, 1918). Charles Purcell, Gladys Walton.

Dancing School [ABQ] / Darling / Dear Old Gown / Floating Down a Moonlight Stream / I Want My Husband [ABQ] / Jazz, How I Love to Hear It [ABQ] / Lodger [ABQ] / Oh! Doctor, Doctor / Wedding by Proxy [ABQ] / You Remember Me / You Win [ABQ] — Cyrus Wood^w & Sigmund Romberg^m *(Shapiro, Bernstein)*; Jazz All Your Troubles Away — Augustus Barratt^w & Sigmund Romberg^m *(Shapiro, Bernstein)*. A silly plot about obesity and marriage and nothing else. It lasted ten weeks. COVER: beautiful girl on a garden wall.

1493 Memphis Bound! (Broadway, 1945). Bill Robinson, Avon Long.

Growin' Pains / The Nightingale, the Moon and I / Old Love — Don Walker$^{w/m}$ & Clay Warnick$^{w/m}$ *(Crawford)*. A takeoff on Gilbert and Sullivan in the South with a run of one month. COVER: a Mississippi river boat.

1494 Mercenary Mary (Broadway, 1925). Allen Kearns, Madeleine Fairbanks.

Beautiful Baby / Charleston Mad / Come On Along / Everything Is Going to Be All Right / Get Your Woman / Honey I'm in Love with You / I've Got to Be a Chaste Woman / Just You and I and the Baby / Mercenary Mary / Over a Garden Wall / That's When a Feller Needs a Friend / They Still Look Good to Me / Tomorrow / Waiting — William Friedlander$^{w/m}$ & Con Conrad$^{w/m}$ *(Feist)*. A silly plot about an inheritance. This show lasted four months.

It moved to London where it turned out to be a long running smash hit. COVER: a girl in furs with car and chauffeur.

1495 Mercenary Mary (British, 1925). Sonnie Hale and "June."

Dipping in the Moonlight [B] — Irving Caesar^w & Joseph Meyer^m *(Chappell)*; A Girl in Your Arms [B] — Irving Caesar^w & Jay Gorney^m *(Chappell)*; I Am Thinking of You [B] — Irving Caesar^w & Louis Hirsch^m *(Chappell)*; I'm a Little Bit Fonder of You [B] — Irving Caesar$^{w/m}$ *(Chappell)*; Tie a String Around Your Finger [B] — Zelda Sears^w & Vincent Youmans^m *(Chappell)*. This musical — with minor revisions — was a huge success in London with two British touring companies. COVER: letters and designs.

1496 The Merchant of Venice (Regional, 1921). Robert Mantell, Andrew Byrne.

Jessica Speak — Andrew Byrne$^{w/m}$ *(Byrne Music)*. A touring company of the Shakespeare classic. COVER: Robert Mantell.

1497 The Merchant of Venice (Regional, 1956). Stars unknown.

In Belmont Is a Lady — Leslie Bridgewater^m *(Robbins)*. A song from a touring production of the classic. COVER: a piano.

1498 Merlin (Broadway, 1983). Doug Henning, Chita Rivera.

Beyond My Wildest Dreams [VS] / He Who Knows the Way [VS] / I Can Make It Happen [VS] / It's About Magic [VS] / Put a Little Magic in Your Life [VS] / Satan Rules [VS] / Something More [VS] / We Haven't Fought a Battle in Years [VS] — Don Black^w & Elmer Bernstein^m *(Leonard)*. A poor magic show that posed as a musical. It had nothing going for it but it did run six months. COVER: Doug Hemming, Chita Rivera, and magic acts.

1499 Merrily We Roll Along (Broadway, 1934). Herbert Steiner, Jessie Royce Landis.

Life Begins with Love — Charles

Tobias[w] & Joseph Cooper[m] *(Witmark)*. A hit comedy by Kaufman and Hart. COVER: a couple arm in arm.

1500 Merrily We Roll Along (Broadway, 1981). Jim Walton, Lonny Price.

Good Thing Going / The Hills of Tomorrow [VS] / Honey [VS] / Like It Was [VS] / Merrily We Roll Along [VS] / Merrily We Roll Along – complete vocal score / Not a Day Goes By / Old Friends [VS] / Our Time [VS] – Stephen Sondheim[w/m] *(Revelation)*. This musical was based on the hit Kaufman-Hart comedy of 1934. The book and direction were lacking but the score was fine. COVER: three people on roof top with large neon sign. The first issues of the two single songs list Ron Field as choreographer and the second edition lists Larry Fuller.

1501 Merry Go Round (Broadway, 1927). Marie Cahill, Frances Gershwin.

Hogan's Alley – Morrie Ryskind[w] & Howard Dietz[w] & Jay Gorney[m] *(Feist)*; I've Got a Yes Girl / New York Town / Sentimental Silly / Something Tells Me / Tampa / What D'ye Say? – Morrie Ryskind[w] & Howard Dietz[w] & Henry Souvaine[m] & Jay Gorney[m] *(Feist)*. A four month run of a small revue with some talented young people. COVER: sketch of dancers.

1502 Merry-Go-Round (Nightclub, 1951). Bert Wheeler, Lou Holtz.

Look Younger, Live Longer / Three Little Wolves from Hollywood / To Be or Not to Be in Love – Sam Coslow[w/m] *(Mills)*. COVER: chorus girls.

1503 The Merry Malones (Broadway, 1927). Polly Walker, Alan Edwards.

Blue Skies, Gray Skies / Charming / The Easter Sunday Parade / A Feeling in Your Heart / God Is Good to the Irish / Like the Wandering Minstrel / Molly Malone / Our Own Way of Going Along / Roses Understand / Tee Teedle Tum Di Dum / To Heaven on the Bronx Express / The Yankee Father in the Yankee Home – George M. Cohan[w/m] *(Witmark)*. A poor girl–rich boy romance with a pleasant Cohan

score. It ran six months. COVER: George M. Cohan, a boy and a girl.

1504 Merry Mary Brown (closed before Broadway, 1919). Charles Judels, Vera Michelena.

Chinaland / Everybody Falls for Mary Brown / In the Eyes of the World / My Lady Fair / When It's Onion Time in Spain / When the Clocking on the Stocking Looks at You – Bernard Grossman[w] & Alfred Goodman[m] *(Harms)*. COVER: flower baskets and designs.

1505 Merry, Merry (Broadway, 1925). William Frawley, Marie Saxon.

Every Little Note / I Was Blue / It Must Be Love / Little Girl / My Own / Oh, Wasn't It Lovely [ABQ] / Poor Pierrot [ABQ] / Spanish Mick [ABQ] / Step, Step Sisters [VS] / Ten Step [ABQ] / We Were a Vow [VS] / What a Life / You're the One [ABQ] – Harlan Thompson[w] & Harry Archer[m] *(Feist)*. A pleasant backstage musical that ran for five months. COVER: a row of dancing chorus girls.

1506 The Merry Widow (Broadway, 1943). Jan Kiepura, Marta Eggerth.

I Love You So / Vilia – Adrian Ross[w] & Franz Lehar[m] *(Chappell)*; Kuiawiak – Jan Kiepura[w] & Henri Wienlawski[m] *(Chappell)*. A successful and lavish revival of the old operetta. This new production ran for nine months. COVER: Kiepura and Eggerth.

1507 The Merry Widow (Broadway, 1964). Patrice Munsel, Bob Wright.

Vilia – Forman Brown[w] & Franz Lehar[m] *(Morris)*. A limited four week run at Lincoln Center of this operetta which originated at the Civic Opera in L.A. COVER: a beautiful chandelier.

1508 Merry Wives of Gothan (*see also* **Fanshastics**) (Broadway, 1924). Grace George, Laura Hope Crews.

Heart o' Mine – Laurence Eyre[w] & Victor Herbert[m] *(Harms)*. A comedy about two Irish orphans with a song by Victor Herbert. This song was also published as being from the play *Fanshastics*. COVER: plain black and white cover.

1509 The Merry World (Broadway, 1926). Alexander Gray, Salt and Pepper.

Deauville / Don't Fall in Love with Me / Sort o' Lonesome — Herman Hupfeld^{w/m} *(Harms)*; Golden Gates of Happiness / Sunday / Why Should We Be Wasting Time? — Clifford Grey^w & Fred Coots^m *(Harms)*; I Fell Head Over Heels in Love — Donovan Parsons^w & Pat Thayer^m *(Feist)*; My Cutey's Due at Two-to-Two To-day — Leo Robin^w & Albert Von Tilzer^m *(B B and L)*; Wall Flower — Billy Frisch^{w/m} & Roy Bergere^{w/m} & Jack Pepper^{w/m} *(Marks)*; Whispering Trees — Herbert Reynolds^w & Fred Coots^m *(Harms)*; White Rose, Red Rose — R. Moreiti^{w/m} *(Harms)*. This revue was imported from London and was panned severely. After ten weeks, it closed and toured for a short time as *Passions of 1924* and then *The Passing Show of 1924.* COVER: flowers and designs.

1510 Messin' Around (Broadway, 1929). Cora LaRedd, Bamboo Mc-Carver.

Get Away from That Window / Harlem Town / I Don't Love Nobody But You / I Need You / Messin' Around / Put Your Mind Right on It / Roust-About / Shout On! / Skiddle-De Skow / Sorry That I Strayed Away from You / Your Love I Crave — Perry Bradford^w & Jimmy Johnson^m *(Witmark)*. A poor black revue with some good dancing. The show lasted four weeks. COVER: flowers and designs.

1511 Michael Todd's Mexican Hayride (Broadway, 1944). June Havoc, Bobby Clark.

Abracadabra / Carlotta / Count Your Blessings / Girls / The Good-Will Movement / I Love You / It Must Be Fun to Be You / It's Just Yours [VS] [CUT] / Sing to Me, Guitar / There Must Be Someone for Me — Cole Porter^{w/m} *(Chappell)*. Bobby Clark was a crook in Mexico in this hit musical. With a lavish production, Bobby Clark, and a hit song, *I Love You,* this musical ran well over a year. COVER: a lady bullfighter.

1512 Michael Todd's Peep Show (Broadway, 1950). Lina Romay, Clifford Guest.

Blue Night / Love at Sundown — Chakraband^w & N. Tongyai^w & H.M. Bhumibol^m *(Shapiro, Bernstein)*; Desire — Walter Mourant^w & Raymond Scott^m *(Gateway)*; Francie / Stay with the Happy People — Bob Hilliard^w & Jule Styne^m *(Morris)*; Gimme the Shimmy! — Harold Rome^{w/m} *(Chappell)*; Pocketful of Dreams — Harold Rome^{w/m} *(Chappell)*; Violins from Nowhere — Herb Magidson^w & Sammy Fain^m *(B V and C)*; You've Never Been Loved — Sam Stept^{w/m} & Dan Shapiro^{w/m} *(B V and C)*. A glorified burlesque show that ran for nine months. COVER: chorus girls, Margaret Whiting, Ray Anthony, Lilly Christine, oriental dancer.

1513 Michael Todd's Theatre Cafe (Nightclub, 1940). Stars unknown.

I Hear America Singing — Mitchell Parish^w & Peter DeRose^m *(Robbins)*; Not a Star in Sight — Ray Noble^{w/m} *(Robbins)*. A lavish revue in the Theatre Cafe in Chicago that was incidentally billed as the world's largest nightclub. COVER: three chorus girls.

1514 The Midnight Rounders (Broadway, 1921). Eddie Cantor, Harold Murray.

Angels / Rebecca — Bert Kalmar^{w/m} & Harry Ruby^{w/m} *(Berlin)*; Anna in Indiana — Billy Gorman^{w/m} & Eddie Gorman^{w/m} & Harry Rose^{w/m} *(Broadway)*; Baby — Charles Tobias^w & William Polla^m *(Church)*; Georgia Rose — Alex Sullivan^w & Jimmy Flynn^w & Harry Rosenthal^m *(Feist)*; Grieving for You — Joe Gibson^{w/m} & Joe Ribaud^{w/m} & Joe Gold^{w/m} *(Feist)*; I Never Knew I Could Love Anybody — Paul Whiteman^{w/m} & Tom Pitts^{w/m} & Ray Egan^{w/m} & Roy Marsh^{w/m} *(Feist)*; I Want My Mammy — George Wehner^w & Louis Breau^m *(Shapiro, Bernstein)*; If You Knew — Eddie Cantor^{w/m} & Harry Tobias^{w/m} & James Blyler^{w/m} *(Berlin)*; Ireland — Eddie Cantor^{w/m} & W.C. Polla^{w/m} & Charles

Tobias^{w/m} (Church); Ladies Man—Dapper Dan—Lew Brown^w & Albert Von Tilzer^m (Broadway); Lena from Palesteena—Lew Brown^w & Albert Von Tilzer^m (Shapiro, Bernstein); Ma!—Sidney Clare^w & Con Conrad^m (Fisher); Mama! Mama! Pap's Got a Lot of Lovin' / Wana—Cliff Friend^{w/m} (Fisher); My Sunny Tennessee—Bert Kalmar^{w/m} & Harry Ruby^{w/m} & Herman Ruby^{w/m} (Berlin); Nobody's Baby—Benny Davis^{w/m} & Lester Santly^{w/m} & Milton Ager^{w/m} (Feist); Now I Lay Me Down to Sleep—Sidney Mitchell^w & George Meyer^m (Remick); Oh Dear—Cliff Friend^{w/m} & Jimmy Blyler^{w/m} (Fisher); O-H-I-O / That Doesn't Mean a Thing—Jack Yellen^w & Abe Olman^m (Forster); Scandinavia—Ray Perkins^{w/m} (Stark, Cowan); Vision Girl—Noble Sissle^{w/m} & Eubie Blake^{w/m} (Feist); Wana—Cliff Friend^{w/m} (Jack Mills); What-cha-gonna Do When There Ain't No Jazz?—Edgar Leslie^{w/m} & Pete Wendling^{w/m} (Stark, Cowan); Who Cares?—Jack Yellen^w & Milton Ager^m (A Y and B); Why Do I Care for You—Jack Yellen^w & Albert Hay Malotte^m (A Y and B); Wimmin—Fred Fisher^{w/m} (Fisher). A typical Eddie Cantor revue that ran only six weeks. COVER: Eddie Cantor, Jane Green, Jim Blyler.

1515 A Midsummer Night's Dream (Regional, 1958). June Havoc, Barbara Barrie.

Court Song [VS] / Anonymous^w & Marc Blitzstein^m (Schirmer); Lullaby [VS]—William Shakespeare^w & Marc Blitzstein^m (Schirmer); Sweet Is the Rose [VS]—Amoretti^w & Marc Blitzstein^m (Schirmer). Songs written for a summer production at the Shakespeare Theatre in Stratford, Conn. COVER: lettering.

1516 Milk and Honey (Broadway, 1961). Molly Picon, Robert Weede.

As Simple as That / Chin Up, Ladies! / I Will Follow You / Independence Day Hora / Let's Not Waste a Moment / Milk and Honey / Milk and Honey—complete vocal score / Shalom / That Was Yesterday / There's No Reason in the World—Jerry Herman^{w/m} (Morris). A musical set in Israel with pleasant Herman tunes and the performance of Molly Picon. It ran for almost one and one half years. COVER: musical note and designs.

1517 Million Dollar Doll in Paris (closed before Broadway, 1920). Harold Orr.

Girlie in a Kimono / Girls, Girls, Girls / The Girls I Used to Fancy / Let Me Stick Along with You / Three Little Words—Louis Weslyn^{w/m} (Stern). This musical was produced by Harvey Orr for the incomparable comedian Harold Orr. COVER: Harold Orr and a sketch of a girl in short dress.

1518 Minnie and Me (see also The Magic Ring) (Broadway, 1923). Mitzi, Sydney Greenstreet.

Broken Hearts / Hand Organ / Homesick / A Love Song / When I Walk with Minnie—Zelda Sears^w & Harold Levey^m (Harms). A rags-to-riches musical that ran three months. It was called Minnie and Me on try-out and The Magic Ring on Broadway. COVER: Mitzi.

1519 Minnie's Boys (Broadway, 1970). Shelley Winters, Lewis J. Stadlen.

Be Happy / Empty / He Gives Me Love / Mama, a Rainbow / Minnie's Boys Theme—Ninety Third Street / Rich Is / Where Was I When They Passed Out Luck? / You Don't Have to Do It for Me [VS] / You Remind Me of You—Hal Hackady^w & Larry Grossman^m (Valando). A poor imitation of the Marx Brothers with a bad score and a terrible book; it lasted ten weeks. COVER: a sketch of the five Marx Brothers.

1520 Mis' Nelly of N'Orleans (Broadway, 1919). Mrs. Fiske, Frederic Burt.

N'Orleans Waltz—Bernard Glasser^m (Witmark). A drama with the famous actress. COVER: Minnie Madern Fiske.

1521 Les Miserables (Broadway, 1987). Judy Kuhn, Colin Wilkinson.

At the End of the Day [VS] / Bring Him Home [VS] / Castle on a Cloud [VS] / Do You Hear the People Sing? [VS] / Drink with Me to Days Gone By [VS] / Empty Chairs at Empty Tables [VS] / A Heart Full of Love [VS] / In My Life [VS] / Little Fall of Rain [VS] / Little People / Master of the House [VS] / Stars [VS] / Who Am I [VS] — Alain Boublil[W] & Herb Kretzmer[W] & Claude-Michel Schonberg[m] *(Leonard)*; I Dreamed a Dream / Love Montage [B] / On My Own [B] — Alain Boublil[W] & Herb Kretzmer[W] & Claude-Michel Schonberg[m] *(MacIntosh)*. A musical based on the famous French novel that is part opera and part spectacle. A huge hit in many capitals of the world. COVER: little girl with sad face.

1522 Miss Calico (*see also* Africana) (Broadway, 1927). Ethel Waters.

I'm Coming Virginia — Will Marion Cook[W] & Donald Heywood[m] *(Robbins- Engel)*. A small black revue that was expanded and taken to Broadway as *Africana*. COVER: a girl returning to her southern mansion.

1523 Miss Emily Adam (Off Broadway, 1960). Cherry Davis, Robert Fitch.

Dear Old Friend / Love Is / Your Valentine — James Lipton[W] & Sol Berkowitz[m] *(Chappell)*. A small musical that lasted for two weeks. COVER: black lettering.

1524 Miss Happiness (*see also* Cynthia) (closed before Broadway, 1926). William Gaxton, Peggy Hope.

I Want to Be a Liberty Belle / Let's Make Believe / Open Your Arms / That's Happiness — George Stoddard[W] & Jay Gorney[m] *(Shapiro, Bernstein)*. A musical that toured as *Miss Happiness* and *Cynthia*. COVER: girl in evening gown on couch.

1525 Miss Liberty (Broadway, 1949). Eddie Albert, Allyn McClerie.

Business for a Good Girl Is Bad [PC] [CUT] / Extra! Extra! / Falling Out of Love Can Be Fun / Give Me Your Tired, Your Poor / Homework / The Hon'rable Profession of the Fourth Estate / I'd Like My Picture Took / Just One Way to Say I Love You / Let's Take an Old-Fashioned Walk / Little Fish in a Big Pond / Me an' My Bundle / Miss Liberty / Mr. Monotony / The Most Expensive Statue in the World / Mrs. Monotony [PC] / Only for Americans / Paris Wakes Up and Smiles / The Policeman's Ball / What Do I Have to Do to Get My Picture in the Paper / You Can Have Him — Irving Berlin[w/m] *(Berlin)*. A musical about the Statue of Liberty with a poor book and a passable Berlin score. It ran for nine months though. COVER: sketch of a winking girl and other characters.

1526 Miss Millions (Broadway, 1919). Vinton Freedley, Valli Valli.

Don't Say Goodbye / Dreams / The Farmer's Daughter / I Know That I'm in Love / If You Just Wait a Little While / Mary — R.H. Burnside[W] & Raymond Hubbell[m] *(Harms)*. A rags-to-riches musical that lasted for only six weeks. COVER: flowers and designs.

1527 Miss Saigon (Broadway, 1991). Jonathan Pryce, Lea Salonga.

The American Dream [VS] / Bui-doi [VS] / The Heat Is On in Saigon [VS] / I Still Believe [VS] / I'd Give My Life for You [VS] / If You Want to Die in Bed [VS] / The Last Night of the World [VS] / The Movie in My Mind [VS] / Now That I've Seen Her [VS] / Sun and Moon [VS] / Why God Why? — Richard Maltby, Jr.[W] & Alain Boublil[W] & Claude-Michel-Schonberg[m] *(Leonard)*. A modern version of *Madama Butterfly* which had a spectacular staging but nothing else and was a big hit. COVER: the moon, a face, a sword, and symbols.

1528 Mr. President (Broadway, 1962). Robert Ryan, Nanette Fabray.

Don't Be Afraid of Romance / Empty Pockets Filled with Love / The First Lady / Glad to Be Home / I'm Gonna Get Him / In Our Hide-Away / Is He the Only Man in the World / It Gets Lonely in the White House / I've Got to Be Around / Laugh It Up / Let's Go Back to the Waltz / Meat and Potatoes

/ Once Every Four Years / Opening of Mr. President [PC] / Pigtails and Freckles / Poor Joe / The Secret Service / Song for Belly Dancer / They Love Me / This Is a Great Country / Washington Twist — Irving Berlin[w/m] *(Berlin)*. A White House musical with a poor Irving Berlin score but a great performance by Nanette Fabray. It had a huge advance sale which kept it going for eight months. COVER: red, white, and blue stars.

1529 Mr. Strauss Goes to Boston (Broadway, 1945). George Rigaud, Virginia MacWatters.

Going Back Home / I Never Know When to Stop / Into the Night / Mr. Strauss Goes to Boston / What's a Girl Supposed to Do / Who Knows — Robert Sour[w] & Robert Stolz[m] *(BMI)*. An operetta about Mr. Strauss' visit to Boston where he stayed only 12 performances. COVER: violinist on stage before an audience.

1530 Mr. Whittington (British, 1934). Jack Buchanan, Elsie Randolph.

Like Monday Follows Sunday [B] — Clifford Grey[w] & Rex Newman[w] & Douglas Furber[w] & John Green[m] *(Chappell)*; Oceans of Time [B] — Clifford Grey[w] & Greatrex Newman[w] & Douglas Furber[w] & John Green[m] *(Chappell)*; The Sun Is Around the Corner [B] / Weep No More, My Baby [B] / What a Pleasant Surprise [B] / Who Do You Think You Are? [B] / Whoops for Derby Day [B] — Edward Heyman[w] & John Green[m] *(Chappell)*. A musical about a playboy who is ruined and then regains his fortune to marry the girl he loves. It was a smash hit in London and ran for over a year with some good songs by John Green. COVER: Jack Buchanan.

1531 Mr. Wonderful (Broadway, 1956). Sammy Davis, Olga James.

Ethel, Baby / Jacques d'Iraque / Mr. Wonderful / Too Close for Comfort / There [VS] / Without You I'm Nothing — Jerry Bock[w/m] & Larry Holofcener[w/m] & George Weiss[w/m] *(Laurel)*. A musical about a nightclub enter-

tainer which was pretty bad except for Sammy Davis and two hit songs which kept it running for one year. COVER: silhouette of Sammy Davis.

1532 Mistress of the Inn (closed before Broadway, 1957). Stars unknown.

Here and Now / In Love with a Lovely Life / The Monkey in My Mind / My Masculine Man / Never Let Your Dander Down / Restless Rover / Simpatico / Tan-tivy — Don Walker[w] & Ira Wallach[w] & Don Walker[m] *(Donald)*. COVER: silhouette of lady's head.

1533 Models of 1925 (closed before Broadway, 1925). Myra Brown, Johnny Getz.

In Orange Time — George Stoddard[w] & Charles Maynard[m] *(Wintz)*. COVER: Brown and Getz.

1534 Molly (Broadway, 1973). Kaye Ballard, Swen Swenson.

Go in the Best of Health / High Class Ladies and Elegant Gentlemen [ABQ] / I Want to Share It with You [ABQ] / I Was There [ABQ] / If Everyone Got What They Wanted [ABQ] / In Your Eyes [ABQ] / I've Got a Molly / A Piece of the Rainbow [ABQ] / There's Gold on the Trees [ABQ] — Leonard Adelson[w] & Jerry Livingston[m] *(Sam Fox)*. A musical based on the old radio series *The Goldbergs*. It was pretty bad and closed in eight weeks. COVER: Kaye Ballard in window.

1535 Molly Darling (Broadway, 1922). Jack Donahue, Mary Millburn.

Dear Little Gad-a-Bout / Mellow Moon / Melody Dreams / Someone / Syncopate — Phil Cook[w] & Tom Johnstone[m] *(Harms)*; When All Your Castles Come Tumbling Down — Arthur Francis (IG)[w] & Milton Schwarzwald[m] *(Harms)*; You Know What to Do — Phil Cook[w] & Milton Schwarzwald[m] & Tom Johnstone[m] *(Harms)*. A musical set in a radio station. It was very interesting but ran only three months. COVER: a well dressed girl in a plush garden.

1536 Molly Darling (Regional, 1962). Stars unknown.

The Heart That Broke Was Mine — Fran Landesman[w/m] & Tommy Wolf[w/m] *(Wolf-Mills)*. A limited run musical for the Municipal Opera in St. Louis about the city of St. Louis. COVER: plain red letters.

1537 Molly Dear (Irish, 1918). Andrew Mack.

America Made a Man / Good-bye, So Long, My Little Sweetheart / It's a Long, Long Way to My Home Town / It's You, Only You, That I Love — Andrew Mack[w/m] *(Feist)*. COVER: Andrew Mack.

1538 Money (Nightclub, 1963). George Coe, David Rounds.

How Can I Tell? / Who Wants to Work? — David Axelrod[w] & Tom Whedon[w] & Sam Pottle[m] *(Morris)*. A cabaret revue at the Upstairs at the Downstairs. COVER: dollar signs.

1539 Monkey Business (Regional, 1926). Olsen and Johnson.

Bohemia / Dream House / My Sweet Egyptian Rose [ABQ] / Pretty Girls Are Like Jewels [ABQ] / Tell Me Gypsy Maid [ABQ] / When Me and Mr. Kitty Step Out [ABQ] / Where the Daffodils Grow — Earle Foxe[w] & Lynn Cowan[m] *(Sherman Clay)*. A West Coast revue. COVER: a bunch of monkeys.

1540 Monkey Shines of 1921 (closed before Broadway, 1921). Stars unknown.

Sleeping Beauty — Clinton Faudre[w] & Kenneth Burton[m] *(H and D)*. COVER: a monkey with top hat.

1541 Monsieur Beaucaire (Broadway, 1919). Marion Green, John Clarke.

English Maids / Gold and Blue and White / Honour and Love / Honours of War [VS] / I Do Not Know [VS] / Lightly, Lightly [VS] / Monsieur Beaucaire — complete vocal score / Philomel / Red Rose / Say No More [VS] / That's a Woman's Way / Under the Moon / We Are Not Speaking [VS] / What Are Names [VS] / When I Was King of the Bath [VS] — Adrian Ross[w] & Andre Messager[m] *(Feist)*. An imported European hit musical set in the court of French royalty. The costumes, setting and drama kept this old fashioned operetta running for five months. COVER: an elegant gentleman kissing a lady's hand.

1542 Monte Cristo, Jr. (Broadway, 1919). Charles Purcell, Chic Sale.

Are You Stepping Out Tonight / Come Back to Me / Flutter On by My Broadway Butterfly / Girl in Every Port / Hoop-Ti-Do / Jazzamarimba Dance / Military Wedding Glide / Monte Cristo / My Lady's Dress / Sentimental Nights / Sugar Baby / Sweetheart Special / There's a World of Beauty in You / They're All My Type — Harold Atteridge[w] & Sigmund Romberg[m] & Jean Schwartz[m] *(Remick)*; I Always Think I'm Up in Heaven — Sam Lewis[w] & Joe Young[w] & Maurice Abrahams[m] *(Berlin)*; Sahara — Alfred Bryan[w] & Jean Schwartz[m] *(Remick)*; Who Played Poker with Pocahontas? — Sam Lewis[w] & Joe Young[w] & Fred Ahlert[m] *(Berlin)*. A vaudeville type musical spectacle about a man dreaming he is Monte Cristo. It was showy enough to run for 30 weeks. COVER: girl in brief outfit with sword and pirate's hat.

1543 Monte Proser's C'est la Vie (Nightclub, 1955). Stars unknown.

The Moon Must Have Followed Me Home — Bob Hilliard[w] & Milton DeLugg[m] *(Morris)*. COVER: singer Tim Kirby.

1544 A Month of Sundays (closed before Broadway, 1951). Nancy Walker, Richard Kiley.

Looking for a Bluebird / Semi-Tropical Island / So Right / You Have to Have Love — B.G. Shevelove[w] & Albert Selden[m] *(Spitzer)*. This Broadway bound musical folded in Philadelphia. It was a musical about an excursion boat and its passengers with a terrible book and score. COVER: sketch of a ship, the moon, and various characters.

1545 Moon Over Mulberry Street (Broadway, 1935). Betty Kashman, Cornel Wilde.

Moon Over Mulberry Street—Raymond Egan[w] & Harry Tierney[m] *(Marks)*. A comedy about a poor Italian family on Mulberry Street. COVER: Betty Kashman.

1546 Moonlight (Broadway, 1924). Julia Sanderson, Frank Crumit.

Aren't We All [ABQ] / The Daffy-Dill / Don't Put Me Out of Your Heart [ABQ] / Fair Weather Friends [ABQ] / Forever / Hoi Polloi / Honeymoon Blues / I Love Them All [ABQ] / In a Bungalow / Moonlight—complete vocal score / On Such a Night / One Note [ABQ] / Say It Again / Tell Me Am I Shooting at the Moon / Turn On the Popular Moon / When I'm Gliding [ABQ]—William Friedlander[w] & Con Conrad[m] *(Marks)*; Hold Me / How Do I Know? / I Can't Live Without Love / Old Man in the Moon—William Friedlander[w/m] *(Marks)*. A small intimate musical about a "love bet" with a pleasant score and book. It ran five months. COVER: a house, a garden, and the moon.

1547 Moonlight and Honeysuckle (Broadway, 1919). Ruth Chatterton, Sydney Booth.

Abandonado—waltz—Guillermo Posadas[m] *(Sherman Clay)*. A silly comedy about a woman testing the true love of her three suitors. COVER: Ruth Chatterton.

1548 Moonshine (Nightclub, 1920). The Versatile Sextette.

Oh! What a Tune—Nat Vincent[w] & Irving Aaronson[m] & Al Lentz[m] *(Witmark)*. COVER: the Versatile Sextette.

1549 More Cheers (closed before Broadway, 1935). Stars unknown.

Moon Over Napoli [PC]—Irving Berlin[w/m] *(Berlin)*. A sequel to *As Thousands Cheer* that was announced but never produced. COVER: none.

1550 Morris Gest Midnight Whirl (Broadway, 1919). Dorothy Dickson, Bernard Granville.

Care-Free Cairo Town—John Wolcott[w/m] *(Harms)*; Limehouse Nights / Poppyland—John H. Mears[w] & Buddy DeSylva[w] & George Gersh-win[m] *(Harms)*; Peggy—Harry Williams[w] & Neil Moret[m] *(Feist)*; Your Baby for All the Time—John Wolcott[w/m] *(Remick)*. A limited run of a revue on the roof of the Century Theatre. COVER: Dorothy Dickson; dancing chorus girl.

1551 The Most Happy Fella (Broadway, 1956). Robert Weede, Jo Sullivan.

Big D / Don't Cry / I Like Ev'rybody / Joey, Joey, Joey / The Most Happy Fella / The Most Happy Fella—complete vocal score / My Heart Is So Full of You / Somebody, Somewhere / Standing on the Corner / Warm All Over—Frank Loesser[w/m] *(Frank)*. A musical version of the hit drama *They Knew What They Wanted* that turned into a smash hit. A sentimental love story, sweeping melodies, and excellent voices kept this show running for 19 months. COVER: The music was published with two covers. One set was red and green with a sketch of a smiling Tony and the other was yellow and blue with a vague sketch of Tony.

1552 A Most Immoral Lady (Broadway, 1928). Alice Brady, Austin Fairman.

The Endless Kiss—Hugo Felix[w/m] *(Berlin)*. A comedy about blackmail that had a moderate run. COVER: Alice Brady.

1553 A Mother's Kisses (closed before Broadway, 1968). Beatrice Arthur, Bill Callaway.

There Goes My Life [PC]—Richard Adler[w/m] *(T R O)*. A musical about a Jewish mother and her son. It folded in Baltimore after three weeks on the road. COVER: none.

1554 The Mountain Man (Broadway, 1921). Sidney Blackmer, Chester Morris.

Through All the World—Claire Kummer[w/m] *(Wagner)*. A poor mountaineer becomes a millionaire in this drama. COVER: Sidney Blackmer.

1555 Mrs. Patterson (Broadway, 1954). Eartha Kitt, Avon Long.

Be Good, Be Good, Be Good / If I Was a Boy / Mrs. Patterson / My Daddy Is a Dandy / Tea in Chicago—James

Shelton^{w/m} *(Garland)*; I Wish I Was a Bumble Bee — Charles Sebree^w & Greer Johnson^w & James Shelton^m *(Garland)*. A play with music about a day-dreaming black girl. It got poor reviews and lasted three months. COVER: Eartha Kitt.

1556 Much Ado About Love (*see also* **The Firebrand of Florence)** (Broadway, 1945). Melville Cooper, Lotte Lenya.

Life, Love and Laughter / A Rhyme for Angela / Sing Me Not a Ballad / You're Far Too Near Me — Ira Gershwin^w & Kurt Weill^m *(Chappell)*. An Italian conspiracy with a rich Kurt Weill score plus Gershwin lyrics but it failed. It was called *Much Ado About Love* in try-out but opened as *The Firebrand of Florence*. COVER: lettering and designs.

1557 Mulligan's Follies (Nightclub, 1922). Charles DeHaven, Fred Nice.

Beautiful Fish of the Sea / Climbing the Stairway of Love / Somewhere There Is a Rainbow — James S. Royce^{w/m} *(Witmark)*. COVER: two boys and two girls dressed as clowns.

1558 Murder at the Vanities (Broadway, 1933). Woods Miller, Beryl Wallace.

Dust in Your Eyes — Irving Newman^{w/m} & Lionel Newman^{w/m} *(Harms)*; Love and Kisses — Phil Baker^{w/m} & Sid Silvers^{w/m} *(Berlin)*; Me for You Forever — Edward Heyman^w & Richard Myers^m *(Harms)*; Savage Serenade — Herman Hupfeld^{w/m} *(Harms)*; Sweet Madness — Ned Washington^w & Victor Young^m *(Harms)*; Weep No More My Baby — Edward Heyman^w & John Green^m *(Harms)*; You Love Me — Herman Hupfeld^{w/m} *(Harms)*. A murder backstage at the *Vanities* which Carroll used as an excuse for another edition of his *Vanities*. It did well enough to last six months at his rival's theatre, Ziegfeld's New Amsterdam. COVER: silhouette of naked dancing girl.

1559 Murray Anderson's Almanac (Broadway, 1929). Jimmo Savo, Trixie Friganza.

Educate Your Feet / Nightingale Song / Tinkle! Tinkle! / Wait for the Happy Ending — Jack Yellen^w & Milton Ager^m *(A Y and B)*; I Can't Remember the Words — Jack Yellen^w & Milton Ager^m & Henry Lodge^m *(A Y and B)*; I May Be Wrong — Harry Ruskin^w & Henry Sullivan^m *(A Y and B)*; Same Old Moon — Clifford Orr^w & John Murray Anderson^w & Henry Sullivan^m *(A Y and B)*. A poor revue that lasted eight weeks and yielded one hit song, *I May Be Wrong*. COVER: dancing girls.

1560 Music Box Idea (Hollywood) (Nightclub, 1929). Fanchon and Marco.

That Music Box Tune — Virginia Spencer^{w/m} *(Campbell)*. COVER: Wanda Allen.

1561 Music Box Revue (#1) (Broadway, 1921). Irving Berlin, Ivy Sawyer.

At the Court Around the Corner / Behind the Fan / Everybody Step / In a Cozy Kitchenette Apartment / I'm a Dumbbell (not published) / Legend of the Pearls / My Little Book of Poetry / Say It with Music / Schoolhouse Blues / Tell Me with a Melody [B] / They Call It Dancing — Irving Berlin^{w/m} *(Berlin)*. A hit revue that opened the Music Box Theatre. It ran for one year with good songs and production numbers. COVER: girl dancing on music box.

1562 Music Box Revue (#2) (Broadway, 1922). William Gaxton, Charlotte Greenwood.

Bring on the Pepper / Crinoline Days / Dancing Honeymoon / Diamond Horseshoe / I'm Looking for a Daddy Long Legs / Lady of the Evening / The Little Red Lacquer Cage / Mont Martre / Pack Up Your Sins and Go to the Devil / Porcelain Maid / Take a Little Wife / Three Cheers for the Red, White, and Blue (not published) / Will She Come from the East? — Irving Berlin^{w/m} *(Berlin)*. Another hit revue with excellent comedy, songs, and lavish production numbers that ran nine months. COVER: a music box and dancing girls.

1563 Music Box Revue (#3) (Broadway, 1923). Grace Moore, Bob Benchley.

Chick! Chick! — composer unknown *(Berlin)*; Climbing Up the Scale / Learn to Do the Strut / Little Butterfly / Maid of Mesh / One Girl / An Orange Grove in California / Tell Me with a Bedtime Story / The Waltz of Long Ago / What'll I Do — Irving Berlin[w/m] *(Berlin)*. The score and comedy for the third revue were not as good as the first two and the run was several months shorter. COVER: dancer and music box.

1564 Music Box Revue (#4) (Broadway, 1924). Fanny Brice, Bobby Clark.

Alice in Wonderland / All Alone / The Call of the South / Don't Send Me Back to Petrograd / Don't Wait Too Long / The Happy New Year Blues [PC] / I Want to Be a Ballet Dancer (not published) / In the Shade of a Sheltering Tree / Listening / Rockabye Baby / Tell Her in the Springtime / Tokio Blues / Unlucky in Love / Where Is My Little Old New York / Who — Irving Berlin[w/m] *(Berlin)*; The Black Bottom Blues — George Wintz[w] & Baldy Wetzel[m] *(Wintz)*; Polly of Hollywood — B.G. DeSylva[w/m] & James Hanley[w/m] *(Shapiro, Bernstein)*. With shorter runs every year, Berlin ended this series of revues with the fourth edition. It had great talent, but lesser material, and ran only six months. COVER: music box and dancing girl.

1565 Music Hath Charms (*see also* **Annina**) (Broadway, 1934). Constance Carpenter, Truman Gaige.

Cavaliers / Love / Maria / My Heart Is Yours / My Palace of Dreams / Romance / Sweet Fool — Rowland Leigh[w] & John Shubert[w] & Rudolf Friml[m] *(Schirmer)*. Written for Maria Jeritza and Allan Jones, it was called *Annina* in its try-out tour. They were replaced by Natalie Hall and Robert Halliday and the title was changed to *Music Hath Charms*. It was still a big flop! COVER: man serenading a lady on terrace.

1566 Music in May (Broadway, 1929). Greek Evans, Gertrude Lang.

Every Month Is May / Unto My Heart — J. Keirn Brennan[w] & Emil Berte[m] *(Harms)*; Glory of Spring / High, High, High! / I Found a Friend / Lips That Laugh at Love / No Other Love / There's Love in the Heart I Hold — J. Keirn Brennan[w] & Maury Rubens[m] *(I.C.L.A.)*; I'd Like to Love Them All — J. Keirn Brennan[w] & Maury Rubens[m] & Phil Svigals[m] *(I.C.L.A.)*; I'm in Love — J. Keirn Brennan[w] & Emil Berte[m] & Maury Rubens[m] *(Harms)*. An imported operetta with a Cinderella type theme which ran ten weeks. COVER: One cover is a girl with flowers and the other is a girl with swan.

1567 Music in My Heart (*see also* **Song Without Words**) (Broadway, 1947). Charles Freerick, Vivienne Segal.

The Balalaika Serenade / Flower Song — waltz / Love Is a Game for Soldiers / Love Song / Once Upon a Time / Song of the Troika / Stolen Kisses / While There's a Song to Sing — Forman Brown[w] & P. Tchaikovsky[m] *(Robbins)*. An operetta using the music of Tchaikovsky and running three months in N.Y. It played in L.A. as *Song Without Words*. COVER: a man playing a piano.

1568 Music in the Air (Broadway, 1932). Walter Slezak, Natalie Hall.

And Love Was Born / I Am So Eager / I'm Alone / In Egern on the Tegern See / I've Told Ev'ry Little Star / Music in the Air — complete vocal score / One More Dance / The Song Is You / There's a Hill Beyond a Hill / We Belong Together / When the Spring Is in the Air — Oscar Hammerstein[w] & Jerome Kern[m] *(Harms)*. One of Jerome Kern's most beautiful scores for this operetta style musical which ran for almost a year. COVER: flowers and designs.

1569 Music in the Air (Broadway, 1951). Jack Pickens, Charles Winninger.

All the Things You Are / I've Told

Ev'ry Little Star / The Song Is You / There's a Hill Beyond a Hill / When Spring Is in the Air — Oscar Hammerstein[w] & Jerome Kern[m] *(Harms)*. A lavish revival of this great musical that lasted only seven weeks. Included in this show was the song *All the Things You Are* from the failed musical *Very Warm for May*. COVER: a brown and grey cover with flowers and designs.

1570 Music Is (Broadway, 1976). Christopher Hewett, David Holliday.

Should I Speak of Loving You [PC] — Will Holt[w] & Richard Adler[m] *(Music of the Times)*. A terrible musical version of Shakespeare's *Twelfth Night* that lasted eight performances. COVER: none.

1571 Music Man (Broadway, 1957). Barbara Cook, Robert Preston.

Gary, Indiana [VS] / Goodnight, My Someone / It's You / Lida Rose / Marian the Librarian [RC] / My White Knight [VS] / The Music Man — complete vocal score / Seventy-Six Trombones / Till There Was You / The Wells Fargo Wagon [VS] / Ya Got Trouble — Meredith Willson[w/m] *(Frank)*. A musical dealing with a con-man in a small town was the basis of this show which ran for over three years. A charming period piece with good songs and talented singers. COVER: man with trumpet holding girl.

1572 Musicland (closed before Broadway, 1919). Stars unknown.

Cutest Little Daddy / Thanks — Herbert Stanwood[w] & Anatol Friedland[m] *(Stern)*. COVER: singers and chorus girls on stage.

1573 My Album of Memories (Regional, 1928). Roger Reichert, Marie Voldo.

Does Anybody Want a Little Kewpie? — Jack Darrell[w/m] *(Darrell)*; Don't Cha? — Etta Becker[w] & Edna Martin[m] *(Darrell)*; Runaway Boy — Johnny Lombardi[w/m] *(Darrell)*. A juvenile talent show. COVER: Reichert and Voldo.

1574 My Boy Friend (closed before Broadway, 1924). Stars unknown.

All Alone in a Crowd / Dancing on a Dime / Evelyn — Harold Christy[w] & Jack Lait[w] & Con Conrad[m] *(Harms)*. COVER: lettering and designs.

1575 My China Doll (closed before Broadway, 1923). Barbara Brunell.

Jazzmania / The Land of Dreams / My China Doll / Tale the Blue Bells Told / The Wedding of My China Doll and Me — Charles George[w/m] *(Forster)*. COVER: girl in fur coat with parrot.

1576 My Darlin' Aida (Broadway, 1952). Dorothy Sarnoff, William Olvis.

King Cotton / Me and Lee / My Darlin' Aida / Why Ain't We Free? — Charles Friedman[w] & Giuseppe Verdi[m] *(Chappell)*. A ponderous adaptation of the opera, this version lasted only 11 weeks. COVER: a southern mansion.

1577 My Dear Public (Broadway, 1943). David Burns, Nanette Fabray.

Feet on the Sidewalk — Sammy Lerner[w/m] & Gerald Marks[w/m] *(Chappell)*; Now That I'm Free — Irving Caesar[w/m] & Sammy Lerner[w/m] & Irma Hollander[w/m] *(Chappell)*; Rain on the Sea / This Is Our Private Love Song — Irving Caesar[w/m] & Sammy Lerner[w/m] & Gerald Marks[w/m] *(Chappell)*; There Ain't No Color Line Around the Rainbow — Irving Caesar[w/m] *(Chappell)*. This show folded in Philadelphia on its try-out in 1942. It was revised, recast and opened on Broadway for a run of five weeks. Critics complained of the poor material. COVER: designs and lettering.

1578 My Fair Lady (*see also* **Tell Me More**) (Broadway, 1925). Alexander Gray, Lou Holtz.

Baby / Kickin' the Clouds Away / My Fair Lady / Tell Me More! / Three Times a Day / Why Do I Love You — B.G. DeSylva[w] & Ira Gershwin[w] & George Gershwin[m] *(Harms)*. A boy-chases-girl musical with very good dancing but no hit Gershwin tunes. It had a run of three months. The try-out title was *My Fair Lady*, but it opened on Broadway as *Tell Me More*. COVER: flowers, hat boxes, designs.

1579 My Fair Lady (Broadway, 1956). Julie Andrews, Rex Harrison.

Come to the Ball [CUT] [RC] / Get Me to the Church on Time / I Could Have Danced All Night / I've Grown Accustomed to Her Face / Just You Wait / My Fair Lady — complete vocal score / On the Street Where You Live / Rain in Spain (lyrics) / Show Me / Why Can't the English / With a Little Bit of Luck / Without You / Wouldn't It Be Loverly — Alan Jay Lerner[w] & Frederick Loewe[m] *(Chappell)*; Rain in Spain (solo) — Frederick Loewe[m] *(Chappell)*. A blockbuster hit that ran for over six years with many revivals. This show had everything including wonderful music, talented actors, good book, beautiful sets and costumes and great direction. COVER: Shaw with Rex Harrison and Julie Andrews as puppets.

1580 My Fair Lady (Broadway, 1976). Ian Richardson, Christine Andreas.

Get Me to the Church on Time / My Fair Lady [VS] (seven songs) — Alan Jay Lerner[w] & Frederick Loewe[m] *(Chappell)*. A 20th anniversary production with a new cast and a run of one year. COVER: a slight variation on original cover with Shaw and puppets Harrison and Andrews.

1581 My Favorite Year (Broadway, 1992). Lainie Kazan, Tim Curry.

Funny [VS] / If the World Were Like the Movies [VS] / Larger Than Life [VS] / Manhattan (The Night Is Young) [VS] / My Favorite Year [VS] / Professional Show Bizness Comedy [VS] / Rookie in the Ring [VS] / Shut Up and Dance [VS] / Twenty Million People [VS] / Welcome to Brooklyn [VS] — Lynn Ahrens[w] & Stephen Flaherty[m] *(Warner Bros.)*. A limited run production by Lincoln Center based on the movie. The book, songs, and people were rather dull and the show did not go on to Broadway as hoped. COVER: young man, camera, skyscrapers.

1582 My Girl (Broadway, 1924). Jane Taylor, Russell Mack.

Before the Dawn / Desert Isle / Fellow Like Me / It Never Will Get You a Thing / A Little Place of Your Own / Lovesick / Rainbow of Jazz / A Solo on the Drum / There Was a Time / They Say / You and I / You Women — Harlan Thompson[w] & Harry Archer[m] *(Feist)*. Breaking into society was the theme of this ordinary musical that ran six months. COVER: a girl in furs.

1583 My Golden Girl (Broadway, 1920). Edna May Oliver, Ned Sparks.

Darby and Joan / I Want You / I'd Like a Honeymoon with You / If We Had Met Before / In Venice / Little Nest for Two / My Golden Girl / Name the Day / Oh, Day in June / Ragtime Terpsichore / Shooting Star / Song Without Many Words — Fred Kummer[w] & Victor Herbert[m] *(Harms)*. A divorce story with a second rate Victor Herbert score that lasted for three months. COVER: lettering and designs.

1584 My Golden Girl (*see also* **My Princess**) (Broadway, 1927). Hope Hampton, Donald Meek.

Follow the Sun to the South / Girls, Good-bye! / My Mimosa / Prince Charming — Dorothy Donnelly[w] & Sigmund Romberg[m] *(Harms)*. A musical about an heiress and society with bland Romberg songs and a run of 20 performances. It was called *My Golden Girl* on its try-out tour and opened as *My Princess*. COVER: Hope Hampton.

1585 My Golden West (*see also* **Bonita** *and* **The Love Call**) (Broadway, 1927). Berna Dean, John Barker.

Eyes That Love / Good Pals / I Live, I Die for You / Rangers Song / 'Tis Love — Harry B. Smith[w] & Sigmund Romberg[m] *(Harms)*. This show toured as *My Golden West* and *Bonita* and opened on Broadway as *Love Call*. A poor short-lived musical about rangers and Indians. COVER: a cowgirl on a horse.

1586 My Havana Girl (closed before Broadway, 1921). Stars unknown.

Baby Days / Girl o' Mine / I Want My Wedding Played in Ragtime / I'll Miss You / I've Had a Lot of Girlies / Money — William Mayhew[w] & George

Kennedy[m] *(Hodges Music)*; My Havana Girl — Billy Arnold[w] & Albert Mitchell[m] *(Hodges Music)*. Cover: girl watching a horse race.

1587 My L.A. (Regional, 1951). Stars unknown.

Heaven Help Us / On the Seventh Day He Rested / Our Little Gray Home in the Red / Something for the Books / That's My L.A. / Twist My Arm — Paul F. Webster[w] & Sammy Fain[m] *(Chappell)*; A Thousand Burning Bridges — Bob Hilliard[w] & Sammy Fain[m] *(Chappell)*. A limited run revue in L.A. that never made it to N.Y. Cover: a cartoon sketch of places and things in L.A.

1588 My Lady Friends (Broadway, 1919). Jack Norworth, Clifton Crawford.

I Want to Spread a Little Sunshine — Clifton Crawford[w/m] *(Harms)*. A comedy about a Bible printer, his fortune, and his girl friends. Cover: Jack Norworth.

1589 My Lucky Day (Jewish, 1952). Edmund Zayenda, Selma Kaye.

My Lucky Day — Jacob Jacobs[w] & Joseph Rumshinsky[m] *(Metro)*. A musical from the Second Avenue Theatre. Cover: Edmund Zayenda, Selma Kaye.

1590 My Magnolia (Broadway, 1926). Eddie Hunter, Paul Bass.

Baby Mine [ABQ] / Baby Wants [ABQ] / Gallopin' Dominoes [ABQ] / Gee Chee — Charleston [ABQ] / Laugh Your Blues Away [ABQ] / Magnolia / Parade of the Christmas Dinner [ABQ] / Shake Your Duster [ABQ] / Sundown Serenade [ABQ] / Sweet Popopper [ABQ] — Alex Rogers[w] & C. Luckeyth Roberts[m] *(R and R)*. An all-black revue notable only for its dancing. It lasted for four performances. Cover: girl's face in the middle of a flower.

1591 My Maryland (Broadway, 1927). Evelyn Herbert, Nathaniel Wagner.

The Boys in Gray / Mother / Silver Moon / Won't You Marry Me? / Your Land and My Land — Dorothy Don-nelly[w] & Sigmund Romberg[m] *(Harms)*. *My Maryland* had a successful try-out run in Philadelphia of 40 weeks before N.Y. This Civil War musical with a rousing story and songs was a hit in N.Y. with a run for 40 weeks. Cover: an old mansion and flowers.

1592 My One and Only (Broadway, 1983). Tommy Tune, Twiggy.

Blah-Blah-Blah [VS] / Funny Face [VS] / He Loves and She Loves [VS] / High Hat [VS] / How Long Has This Been Going On? [VS] / I Can't Be Bothered Now [VS] / In the Swim [VS] / My One and Only [VS] / Nice Work If You Can Get It [VS] / 'S Wonderful [VS] / Soon [VS] / Strike Up the Band [VS] — Ira Gershwin[w] & George Gershwin[m] *(Warner Bros.)*; Boy Wanted [VS] — Arthur Francis (IG)[w] & George Gershwin[m] *(Warner Bros.)*; Kickin' the Clouds Away [VS] — B.G. DeSylva[w] & Ira Gershwin[w] & George Gershwin[m] *(Warner Bros.)*; My One and Only — Ira Gershwin[w] & George Gershwin[m] *(New World)*. A revised version of *Funny Face* with songs from other Gershwin productions. It was a smash hit with smart sets and dazzling choreography. Cover: Tommy Tune and Twiggy.

1593 My Princess (*see also* **My Golden Girl**) (Broadway, 1927). Hope Hampton, Donald Meek.

Follow the Sun / Girls, Goodbye / I Wonder Why / My Mimosa / Prince Charming — Dorothy Donnelly[w] & Sigmund Romberg[m] *(Harms)*. A society and heiress musical with ordinary Romberg songs with a run of only two weeks. Cover: Hope Hampton.

1594 My Romance (closed before Broadway, 1948). Anne Jeffreys, Charles Fredericks.

Magic Moment — Rowland Leigh[w] & Denes Agay[m] *(Century)*; No One's Heart — Rowland Leigh[w] & Fred Jay[w] & Irving Reid[w] & Denes Agay[m] *(Century)*; You're Near and Yet So Far — Rowland Leigh[w] & Philip Redowski[m] *(Century)*. A fantasy about old romances. It was pretty bad and folded after several months on the road. It was revised and opened on Broadway several months later under the same title. COVER: Anne Jeffreys and Charles Fredericks.

1595 My Romance (Broadway, 1948). Anne Jeffreys, Lawrence Brooks.

Bella Donna / Desire / From Now Onward / If Only / In Love with Romance — Rowland Leigh^w & Sigmund Romberg^m *(Harms)*. A revised edition of a show that had folded on the road. The new score by Romberg was the last in his lifetime. The show was still poor and lasted three months. COVER: flowers and designs.

1596 Mystery Moon (Broadway, 1930). Arthur Campbell, Pauline Dee.

It's All OK / Mystery Moon / One Night in the Rain — Monte Carlo$^{w/m}$ & Alma Sanders$^{w/m}$ *(Harms)*. A musical about a road company with problems. It lasted for one performance. COVER: the moon and a naked girl.

1597 The Mystery of Edwin Drood (Broadway, 1985). Betty Buckley, Cleo Laine.

Both Sides of the Coin [VS] / Don't Quit While You're Ahead [VS] / The Garden Path to Hell [VS] / A Man Could Be Quite Mad [VS] / Moonfall [VS] / Never the Luck [VS] / Off to the Races [VS] / Perfect Strangers [VS] / There You Are [VS] / Two Kinsmen [VS] / The Writing on the Wall [VS] — Rupert Holmes$^{w/m}$ *(Warner Bros.)*. A mystery musical that was a hit with a fun book, a great performance by George Rose, and a pleasant score. It had a run of one year. COVER: a lady dressed as a man with cigar.

1598 Nancy (closed before Broadway, 1926). Nancy Welford.

And the Moonlight's Calling You / Just a Bunch of Wild Flowers / Loving You / Nancy / Rum-Dum-Dum-Dum — William Clifford^w & Jean Schwartz^m *(Harms)*. COVER: sketch of girl with book and boy with roses plus Nancy Welford.

1599 National Lampoon's Lemmings (Off Broadway, 1973). John Belushi, Chevy Chase.

National Lampoon Lemmings — vocal selections (30 songs) — various composers *(Cherry Lane)*. This revue of sketches and songs ran for almost a year at the Village Gate. The *Vocal Selection Book* includes songs used in this show, the radio program, and on record albums. COVER: a sketch of a group of weird people.

1600 Natja (Broadway, 1925). Alexander Clark, Madeline Collins.

Beside the Star of Glory / Eyes That Haunt Me / For Queen and for Country / Home and Glory / I Hear Love Call Me / In My Homeland / A Lady Who Lives for Love / The Magic of Moonlight and Love / Shall I Tell Him / There Is a Garden in Loveland / Ups and Downs — Harry B. Smith^w & Karl Hajos^m & P. Tchaikovsky^m *(Feist)*. A musical with a Russian background that lasted four weeks. COVER: girl in peasant costume.

1601 Naughty Cinderella (Broadway, 1925). Irene Bordoni, Nat Pendleton.

Do I Love You? — E. Ray Goetz^w & H. Christine^m & E. Ray Goetz^m *(Harms)*; I Love the Moon — Paul Rubens$^{w/m}$ & E. Ray Goetz$^{w/m}$ *(Harms)*; Mia Luna — E. Ray Goetz$^{w/m}$ *(Harms)*; That Means Nothing to Me — A.L. Keith$^{w/m}$ & Lee Sterling$^{w/m}$ *(Harms)*. A romantic drama with Bordoni and several songs. COVER: One set of covers with only the face of Bordoni and another with Bordoni with a parasol.

1602 The Naughty Diana (*see also* **Diana Comes to Town**) (closed before Broadway, 1923). Stars unknown.

Dreams / Goodnight, the Sun Is Shining / I've Found Love at Last / My Heart Is Paging Yours — Cyrus Wood^w & Will Ortmann^m *(Harms)*; I Have a Rendezvous — Cyrus Wood^w & Willy Engel-Berger^m *(Harms)*. This show toured as *Naughty Diana* and *Diana Comes to Town*. COVER: lettering and designs.

1603 Naughty Mamzelle (Nightclub, 1924). Tom Martelle.

Naughty Mamzelle – Tom Martelle[w/m] *(Century)*. A female impersonator show. COVER: Tom Martelle.

1604 Naughty-Naught '00 (Broadway, 1937). Alexander Clark, Barbara Hunter.

Love Makes the World Go Round / Zim-Zam-Zee – Ted Fetter[w] & Richard Lewine[m] *(Chappell)*. A recreation of the gay '90s era. A melodrama with music that lasted almost six months. COVER: a couple in a gay '90s outfit.

1605 Naughty Naughty (Broadway, 1946). John Cromwell, Teddy Hart.

When We're in Love – Ted Fetter[w] & Richard Lewine[m] *(Chappell)*. A failed attempt to revive the 1937 hit. It ran two weeks. COVER: sketch of lady in gay '90s outfit.

1606 Naughty Riquette (*see also* **Riquette**) (Broadway, 1926). Mitzi, Alexander Gray.

Brother of Mine / In Armenia / Make Believe You're Mine / Plant Some Roses – Harry B. Smith[w] & Oscar Strauss[m] *(Harms)*; I May – Harry B. Smith[w] & Maurie Rubens[m] & Kendall Burgess[m] *(Harms)*; Someone – Harry B. Smith[w] & Alfred Goodman[m] & Maurie Rubens[m] *(Harms)*. A telephone operator is the subject of this musical which ran 11 weeks. It was originally called *Riquette* but opened as *Naughty Riquette*. COVER: girl at switchboard.

1607 Ned Wayburn's Gambols (Broadway, 1927). Libby Holman, Lew Hearn.

Church Around the Corner / Crescent Moon / Little Dream That's Coming True / Palm Beach Walk / Savannah Stomp / Ship of Love – Morrie Ryskind[w] & Walter Samuels[m] *(Harms)*; The Sun Will Shine – Morrie Ryskind[w] & Arthur Schwartz[m] *(Harms)*; What Is the Good? – Clifford Grey[w] & Lew Kessler[m] *(Harms)*. A minor revue with outstanding dancing that lasted for three weeks. COVER: lettering and designs.

1608 Nellie Bly (Broadway, 1946). William Gaxton, Victor Moore.

Aladdin's Daughter [PC] / All Around the World [PC] / Fogarty and Mandolin Girls [PC] / Fogarty and Nellie Bly Parade [PC] / Fogarty the Great [PC] / Harmony [PC] / How About a Date? [PC] / I Did It for the Missus [PC] / Just My Luck [PC] / May the Best Man Win [PC] / Nellie Bly [PC] / No News Today [PC] / Sky High [PC] / Start Dancin' [PC] / That's Class [PC] / There's Nothing Like Travel [PC] / You May Not Love Me [PC] / You Never Saw That Before [PC] – Johnny Burke[w] & James Van Heusen[m] *(B and V H)*. Nellie Bly's trip around the world lasted only two weeks on Broadway. COVER: none.

1609 The Nervous Set (Broadway, 1959). Larry Hagman, Richard Hayes.

The Ballad of the Sad Young Men / How Do You Like Your Love? [PC] / I've Got a Lot to Learn About Life / Spring Can Really Hang You Up the Most [BW] / Travel the Road of Love – Fran Landesman[w] & Tommy Wolf[m] *(Empress)*. A pleasant little musical with one good song, *Ballad of the Sad Young Men*. It lasted only three weeks. COVER: sketch of a nervous character.

1610 Never Too Late (Broadway, 1962). Paul Ford, Maureen O'Sullivan.

Never Too Late – Sheldon Harnick[w] & Jerry Bock[m] *(Valando)*. A smash hit comedy directed by George Abbott that ran for two and one half years. COVER: an alarm clock.

1611 The New Dictator (*see also* **The Girl from Home**) (Broadway, 1920). Frank Craven, Marion Sunshine.

I Miss a Place Called Home / It's a Wonderful Spot / I've Got a Great Idea / Just Say Goodbye / Manana / Money / Nine Little Missionaries / Ocean Blues / Sometime / Wireless Heart / You're the Nicest Girl I Ever Met – Frank Craven[w] & Silvio Hein[m] *(Harms)*. A South American revolution set to music and a quick failure. The try-out title was *The New Dictator* but it opened on Broadway as *The Girl from Home*. COVER: lettering and designs.

1612 New Faces (British, 1940). Judy Campbell.

A Nightingale Sang in Berkeley Square — Eric Maschwitz[w] & Manning Sherwin[m] *(Shapiro, Bernstein)*. A hit revue in London supplied this hit song which became a standard in the U.S. COVER: Judy Campbell.

1613 New Faces of 1934 (Broadway, 1934). Imogene Coca, Henry Fonda.

'Cause You Won't Play House — E.Y. Harburg[w] & Morgan Lewis[m] *(Harms)*; Lamplight — James Shelton[w/m] *(Harms)*; Music in My Heart — June Sillman[w] & Warburton Guilbert[m] *(Harms)*; You're My Relaxation — Robert Sour[w] & Charles Schwab[m] *(Harms)*. A clever revue with talented young people and a run of 20 weeks. COVER: cartoon sketch of man and woman.

1614 New Faces of 1936 (Broadway, 1936). Ralph Blane, Imogene Coca.

It Must Be Religion — Forman Brown[w/m] *(Chappell)*; It's High Time I Got the Low-Down on You — Edward Heyman[w] & Joseph Meyer[m] *(Chappell)*; Love Is a Dancer — Jean Sothern[w] & Muriel Pollock[m] *(Chappell)*; My Last Affair — Haven Johnson[w/m] *(Chappell)*; My Love Is Young / You Better Go Now — Bickley Reichner[w] & Robert Graham[m] *(Chappell)*; Tonight's the Night — June Sillman[w] & Alex Fogarty[m] *(Chappell)*; Your Face Is So Familiar — Edwin Gilbert[w] & Alex Fogarty[m] *(Chappell)*. Another edition which was average but lasted almost six months on Broadway. COVER: a tree with blossoms and a new face in each blossom.

1615 New Faces of 1943 (Broadway, 1942). John Lund, Alice Pearce.

Animals Are Nice — J.B. Rosenberg[w] & Lee Wainer[m] *(Marks)*; Hey, Gal! / New Shoes — June Carroll[w] & Will Irwin[m] *(Marks)*; I Loved You Well! (Well! Well!) / Love, Are You Raising Your Head Again? — June Carroll[w] & Lee Wainer[m] *(Marks)*; Yes, Sir, I've Made a Date! — Jack Rosenberg[w] & Lee Wainer[m] *(Marks)*. An ordinary edition which ran only three months. COVER: photographs of the new faces.

1616 New Faces of 1952 (Broadway, 1952). Alice Ghostley, Eartha Kitt.

Boston Beguine — Sheldon Harnick[w/m] *(Santly Bros.-Joy)*; Guess Who I Saw Today — Murray Grand[w/m] & Elisse Boyd[w/m] *(Santly Bros.-Joy)*; He Takes Me Off His Income Tax / Love Is a Simple Thing / Monotonous / Penny Candy — June Carroll[w] & Arthur Seigel[m] *(Santly Bros.-Joy)*; I'm in Love with Miss Logan — Ronny Graham[w/m] *(Santly Bros.-Joy)*; Lizzie Borden — Michael Brown[w/m] *(Santly Bros.-Joy)*. The best edition of this series with some good songs and wonderful talent and a run of one year. COVER: a sketch of new faces. Some of the covers state sketches staged by John Beal and some state staged by Roger Price.

1617 New Faces of 1956 (Broadway, 1956). Jane Connell, Tiger Haynes.

April in Fairbanks — Murray Grand[w/m] *(Hill and Range)*; The Boy Most Likely to Succeed / Don't Wait / Tell Her / The White Witch — June Carroll[w] & Arthur Seigel[m] *(Hill and Range)*; Girls 'n' Girls 'n' Girls — Irvin Graham[w/m] *(Hill and Range)*; The Greatest Invention — Sid Silvers[w/m] & Matt Dubey[w/m] & Harold Karr[w/m] *(Hill and Range)*; Hurry — Murray Grand[w] & Elisse Boyd[w] & Murray Grand[m] *(Hill and Range)*; Love at an Auction [PC] / Rouge [PC] — Murray Grand[w/m] *(Morris)*; Perfect Night / Scratch My Back — Marshall Barer[w] & Dean Fuller[m] *(Hill and Range)*; Too Many Questions — Paul Nassau[w/m] *(Hill and Range)*. An edition with poor songs but some great performers. It ran six months. COVER: caricature of a face.

1618 New Faces of 1962 (Broadway, 1962). Marian Mercer, Travis Hudson.

Depends On How You Look at Things / I Want You to Be the First One to Know / Love Is Good for You / The Other One — June Carroll[w] & Arthur Seigel[m] *(Consolidated)*; Over the River and into the Woods — Jack Holmes[w/m] *(Consolidated)*. A very poor edition of this series that lasted for three weeks. COVER: a caricature of a face.

1619 New Faces of 1968 (Broadway, 1968). Madeline Kahn, Robert Klein.

The Girl in the Mirror / A New Waltz — Fran Minkoff[w] & Fred Hellerman[m] *(Warner Bros.)*; Hungry — Murray Grand[w/m] *(Warner Bros.)*; Philosophy — Hal Hackady[w] & Carl Friberg[m] *(Warner Bros.)*; Where Is Me? — June Carroll[w] & Arthur Seigel[m] *(Warner Bros.)*; Where's the Waltz? — Paul Nassau[w] & Alonzo Levister[m] *(Warner Bros.)*. The final edition in this series was very poor and lasted only six weeks. COVER: a caricature of a face.

1620 A New Girl (*see also* **She's a Good Fellow**) (Broadway, 1919). Joseph Santley, Ivy Sawyer.

The Bull Frog Patrol / The First Rose of Summer / Ginger Town / Happy Wedding Day / Home Sweet Home / Jubilo / Letter Song / Oh, You Beautiful Person / Semiramis [ABQ] / Some Party / Teacher, Teacher / Wine Woman and Song [ABQ] — Anne Caldwell[w] & Jerome Kern[m] *(Harms)*. This show, dealing with impersonations, had a moderate run and a pleasant score by Kern. The try-out title was *A New Girl*. COVER: lettering and designs.

1621 New Girl in Town (Broadway, 1957). Gwen Verdon, Thelma Ritter.

At the Check Apron Ball / Did You Close Your Eyes? / Flings / Here We Are Again / If That Was Love / It's Good to Be Alive / Look at 'Er / New Girl in Town — theme / Sunshine Girl / You're My Friend, Ain'tcha? — Bob Merrill[w/m] *(Chappell)*. A musical version of *Anna Christie* that turned out to be a hit due to Gwen Verdon's dancing and Thelma Ritter's comedy plus a pleasant score by Bob Merrill. It ran over a year. COVER: girl with suitcase sitting at a bar.

1622 The New Meet the People (Broadway, 1941). Stars unknown.

Crispus Attucks — Robert Meltzer[w] & Edward Eliscu[w] & Phil Moore[m] *(Mills)*; Damn the Torpedos — Henry Myers[w] & Edward Eliscu[w] & Jay Gorney[m] *(Robbins)*; The Four Freedoms / He Was All Right Here / It's No Fun Eating Alone / Juarez and Lincoln / Let's Go Out and Ring Doorbells / Love in a Changing World / Mama, It's Saturday Night / You're Good for My Morale — Henry Myers[w] & Edward Eliscu[w] & Jay Gorney[m] *(Mills)*; Little Miss Jesse James — Jack Brooks[w] & Norman Berens[m] *(Mills)*; Meet the People — Henry Myers[w] & Jay Gorney[m] *(Mills)*. A new edition of the topical revue which was a minor hit. COVER: sketches of people's faces.

1623 The New Meet the People of 1944 (closed before Broadway, 1944). Stars unknown.

Four Rivers — Henry Myers[w] & Edward Eliscu[w] & Jay Gorney[m] *(Mills)*; Damn the Torpedos — Henry Myers[w] & Edward Eliscu[w] & Jay Gorney[m] *(Robbins)*. A new revised edition of this revue that got nowhere. COVER: an inkwell, books, and Eddie Cantor.

1624 The New Moon (Broadway, 1928). Evelyn Herbert, Robert Halliday.

The Girl on the Prow / I'm Just a Sentimental Fool / Liar / Lover, Come Back to Me / Marianne / 'Neath a New Moon / New Moon — complete vocal score / One Kiss / One Kiss Is Waiting for One Man / Softly, as in a Morning Sunrise / Stout Hearted Men / Try Her Out at Dances / Wanting You / When I Close My Eyes! — Oscar Hammerstein[w] & Sigmund Romberg[m] *(Harms)*; Funny Little Sailor Man — piano selections / Love Is Quite a Simple Thing — piano selections — Sigmund Romberg[m] *(Harms)*. A smash hit operetta with glorious voices and songs with a run of well over a year. COVER: a pirate girl, a pirate, and a ship.

1625 The New Plantation (Nightclub, 1925). Stars unknown.

Dinah / Hot-Foot'n — Sam Lewis[w] & Joe Young[w] & Harry Akst[m] *(Waterson)*.

A revue at the Plantation Club, 49th and Broadway. It introduced the hit *Dinah*. COVER: dancing girls and a parrot.

1626 New York Exchange (Broadway, 1926). Sydney Shields, Donn Cook.

Wonderful, Wonderful You — Irving Bibo[w] & Jack LeSoir[m] & Ray Doll[m] *(B B and L)*. A melodrama with one song. COVER: a potted tree.

1627 The New Yorkers (Broadway, 1927). Jean Sothern, Tamara Draisin.

Floating Thru the Air / Romany [ABQ] — Henry Myers[w] & Arthur Schwartz[m] *(Marks)*; Nothing Left But Dreams [ABQ] / A Side Street Off Broadway / You're My "So and So" [ABQ] — Henry Myers[w] & Edgar Fairchild *(Marks)*; Slow River / Welcome Home, Your Hubby [ABQ] — Henry Myers[w] & Charles Schwab[m] *(Marks)*. A poor revue that lasted for six weeks. COVER: Jean Sothern.

1628 The New Yorkers (Broadway, 1930). Hope Williams, Ann Pennington.

The Great Indoors / I Happen to Like New York / I'm Getting Myself Ready for You / Just One of Those Things / Let's Fly Away / Love for Sale / Take Me Back to Manhattan / Where Have You Been? — Cole Porter[w/m] *(Harms)*. A tale of bootlegging and other New York characters with a witty Cole Porter score and some great people. It was a hit but closed early due to the big bank failure. COVER: a group of sophisticated New Yorkers.

1629 Nice Goin' (closed before Broadway, 1939). Mary Martin, Bert Wheeler.

Blow Me Down / I Shoulda Stood in Bed / I've Gone Off the Deep End / That Sarong Number / The Wind at My Window — Leo Robin[w] & Ralph Rainger[m] *(Crawford)*. After singing *Daddy*, Mary Martin was rushed into stardom as the lead of this show and proved totally inadequate in a leading role. The show was poor and folded in Boston. COVER: Mary Martin and

sketch of sailor and girl.

1630 Nice Goings On (British, 1933). Leslie Henson, Zelma O'Neal.

I Know the Kind of Girl [B] — Douglas Furber[w] & Arthur Schwartz[m] *(Chappell)*; Sweet One [B] / Twixt the Devil and the Deep Blue Sea [B] / What a Young Girl Ought to Know [B] / Whatever You Do [B] / With You Here and Me Here [B] — Frank Eyton[w] & Arthur Schwartz[m] *(Chappell)*; You're an Old Smoothie [B] — B.G. DeSylva[w/m] & Richard Whiting[w/m] & Herb Brown Nacio[w/m] *(Chappell)*. A hit comedy for Henson as a poor clerk trying to get ahead on the job. It ran six months. COVER: Leslie Henson.

1631 Nice to See You (Nightclub, 1953). George White.

Nice to See You — Jack Yellen[w] & Irving Caesar[w] & Belle Fenstock[m] *(Caesar)*; Rain in My Heart — Jack Yellen[w] & Irving Caesar[w] & Lou Cobey[m] *(Caesar)*; This Time — Irving Caesar[w] & Sydney Green[m] *(Caesar)*; When I Come Home — Irving Caesar[w] & Joe Meyer[m] *(Caesar)*. A revue presented by George White at the Versailles, N.Y. COVER: George White.

1632 Nick & Nora (Broadway, 1991). Barry Bostwick, Joanna Gleason.

As Long as You're Happy [VS] / Boom Chicka Boom [VS] / Class [VS] / Everybody Wants to Do a Musical [VS] / Is There Anything Better Than Dancing? [VS] / Look Who's Alone Now [VS] / Married Life [VS] / May the Best Man Win [VS] / Men [VS] / Swell [VS] — Richard Maltby, Jr.[w] & Charles Strouse[m] *(Belwin)*. A disastrous musical version of *The Thin Man*. After many previews, it was a quick failure. COVER: plain cover with title only.

1633 Nic-Nax of 1926 (Broadway, 1926). Gitz Rice, Ralph Riggs.

Do the Doodledoo / Everything Is High Yellow Now / Mary McNally / Oh! Daddy / Sesquicentennial / Syncopassion / When the Sun Kissed the Rose Goodbye — Gitz Rice[w/m] *(Wit-*

mark); For a Girl Like You – Joe Goodwin[w] & Gitz Rice[m] *(Witmark)*; I Have Forgotten You Almost – Anna Fitziu[w] & Gitz Rice[m] *(Witmark)*; Without the One You Love – Gitz Rice[w] & Werner Janssen[m] *(Witmark)*. An amateur-type revue that lasted 13 performances. COVER: three girls, pen and pencil, and inkwell.

1634 Nifties (1923) (Broadway, 1923). Helen Broderick, Frank Crumit.

Are You Here, Maggie Mooney, Are You Here? – Gus Van[w/m] & Joe Schenck[w/m] & C.W. Murphy[w/m] & Worton David[w/m] *(Harms)*; At Half Past Seven – B.G. DeSylva[w] & George Gershwin[m] *(Harms)*; Calico Days / The Old Gray Owl – Ray Perkins[w/m] *(Witmark)*; Fabric of Dreams – B.G. DeSylva[w] & Arthur Francis (IG)[w] & Raymond Hubbell[m] *(Harms)*; If You Will Marry Us – Bert Kalmar[w/m] & Harry Ruby[w/m] *(Berlin)*; Little Brown Road – Frank Crumit[w/m] *(Harms)*; Nashville Nightingale – Irving Caesar[w] & George Gershwin[m] *(Harms)*; An Old Time Tune / Sweet Alice / Where Are the Old Pals of Yesterday? – Gus Van[w/m] & Joe Schenck[w/m] *(Harms)*; That Bran' New Gal o' Mine – Gus Van[w/m] & Joe Schenck[w/m] & Benny Davis[w/m] & Harry Akst[w/m] *(Witmark)*. A talented cast in a so-so revue that lasted six weeks. COVER: Sam Bernard, William Collier.

1635 A Night at the Copa (Nightclub, 1946). Stars unknown.

For Those in Love – Benny Davis[w/m] & Ted Murray[w/m] *(Robbins)*. COVER: palm trees and drums.

1636 Night Boat (Broadway, 1920). Louise Groody, Hal Skelly.

Bob White / Chick! Chick! Chick! / Don't You Want to Take Me? / A Heart for Sale / I Love the Lassies / I'd Like a Lighthouse / Left All Alone Again Blues / The Lorelei / Rip Van Winkle and His Little Men / Whose Baby Are You – Anne Caldwell[w] & Jerome Kern[m] *(Harms)*; Good-Night Boat – Anne Caldwell[w] & Frank Craven[w] & Jerome Kern[m] *(Harms)*;

My Spanish Rose – Anne Caldwell[w] & Jose Padilla[m] *(Harms)*; Some Fine Day – piano selection – Jerome Kern[m] *(Harms)*. A musical, dealing with a river boat, that had a funny book and good Kern tunes. It ran for nine months. COVER: plain black and white covers.

1637 Night Cruise of 1934 (Nightclub, 1934). Stars unknown.

Faces / You're Grand / You're Something to Write Home About – Allen Boretz[w] & Walter Samuels[m] *(Harms)*. A revue on board a floating nightclub. COVER: a ship with sails.

1638 A Night in California (Jewish, 1927). A. Lebedeff, Bella Mysell.

A Yidish Meidel Darf a Yidishen Boy – J. Jacobs[w] & A. Olshanetsky[m] *(Metro)*. COVER: Lebedeff and Mysell.

1639 A Night in Paris (Broadway, 1926). Ray Bolger, Eleanor Painter.

Fascinating Lady / Louisiana / When – McElbert Moore[w] & J. Fred Coots[m] & Maurie Rubens[m] *(Harms)*; Looking at the World – Tommie Malie[w/m] & Jimmy Steiger[w/m] *(Weil)*; The Newport Glide – Clifford Grey[w] & J. Fred Coots[m] & Maurie Rubens[m] *(Harms)*; What a Life – George Little[w/m] & Joe Goodwin[w/m] & Larry Shay[w/m] *(Broadway)*; Why Should We Be Wasting Time? – Ed Conrad[w] & McElbert Moore[w] & J. Fred Coots[m] & Maurie Rubens[m] & Alfred Goodman[m] *(Harms)*. An ordinary revue with pleasant songs, dances, and young talent that ran for nine months. COVER: the Eiffel Tower.

1640 A Night in Spain (Broadway, 1927). Phil Baker, Sid Silvers.

De-Dum-Dum / Room for Two / Simple Spanish Maid – Alfred Bryan[w] & Jean Schwartz[m] *(Harms)*; Did You Mean It? – Phil Baker[w/m] & Sid Silvers[w/m] & Abe Lyman[w/m] *(Shapiro, Bernstein)*; Love and Kisses – Phil Baker[w/m] & Sid Silvers[w/m] *(Berlin)*; Nothin' – Roy Turk[w/m] & Lou Handman[w/m] *(Shapiro, Bernstein)*; Rainy Day – Phil Baker[w/m] & Sid Silvers[w/m] *(Remick)*; Under the Clover Moon –

Ted Healy$^{w/m}$ *(Berlin)*. A revue with a Spanish flavor and some good comedians that ran for six months. COVER: Ted Healy; letters and designs; Phil Baker and Sid Silvers; Marion Harris.

1641 A Night in Venice (Broadway, 1929). Ted Healy, Anne Seymour.

I'm for You / Sliding Down a Silver Cloud — J. Keirn Brennan^w & Lee David^m *(Harms)*; Loose Ankles — Moe Jaffe^w & Clay Boland^m & Maurie Rubens^m *(Harms)*; One Night of Love — J. Keirn Brennan^w & Maury Rubens^m *(Harms)*. A revue of ordinary vaudeville that ran for 20 weeks. COVER: a gondolier serenading a lady on balcony.

1642 A Night Off (closed before Broadway, 1919). Stars unknown.

I Like You / If One Finds a Girl Who's Fainted / I'm a Watchin', I'm a Waitin' — Melville Raymond^w & Hugo Frey^m *(Harms)*. COVER: letters and designs.

1643 A Night Out (British, 1920). Stanley Holloway, Leslie Henson.

It's a Sad Day at This Hotel [VS] / Look Around [VS] / Our Hotel [VS] / Why Didn't We Meet Before [VS] — Clifford Grey^w & Cole Porter^m *(Chappell)*. A hit comedy in London, running for nine months, with four Cole Porter songs. COVER: three dancers in costumes with balloons.

1644 A Night Out (closed before Broadway, 1925). Zelda Edwards, Robert Greig.

I Want a Yes Man — Clifford Grey^w & Irving Caesar^w & Ira Gershwin^w & Vincent Youmans^m *(Harms)*; Kissing / Like a Bird on the Wing / Sometimes I'm Happy — Clifford Grey^w & Irving Caesar^w & Vincent Youmans^m *(Harms)*. A musical based on the 1920 British comedy hit. It folded in Philadelphia after two weeks. COVER: a man and woman in dress clothes on the town.

1645 The Nightingale (Broadway, 1926). Stanley Lupino, Eleanor Painter.

Breakfast in Bed / Enough Is Enough / May Moon / Two Little Ships / When I Meet You — P.G. Wodehouse^w & Armand Vecsey^m *(Harms)*; Josephine / Once in September — Clifford Grey^w & Armand Vecsey^m *(Harms)*. A musical about a sad love affair with little substance. It lasted only 12 weeks. COVER: girl in hoop skirt with flowers.

1646 Nightingale (Off Broadway, 1982). Stars unknown.

Nightingale — complete vocal score — Charles Strouse$^{w/m}$ *(Schirmer)*. A children's opera based on Andersen's fairy tale. A limited run by the Children's Theatre. COVER: red title only.

1647 Nikki (Broadway, 1931). Frank Chapman, Adele Dixon.

Now I Know / On Account of "I Love You" / Taking Off — James Dyrenforth^w & Philip Charig^m *(Harms)*. A poor musical about exaviators; it lasted four weeks. COVER: a speeding airplane.

1648 Nina Rosa (Broadway, 1930). Guy Robertson, Jack Sheehan.

Adored One / I'm a Daughter of Peru / Nina Rosa / Payador / Serenade of Love / There Can Only Be Only One for Me / Your Rose / Your Smiles, Your Tears — Irving Caesar^w & Sigmund Romberg^m *(Harms)*; Gaucho March — piano selections — Sigmund Romberg^m *(Harms)*; My First Love, My Last Love — Irving Caesar^w & Otto Harbach^w & Sigmund Romberg^m *(Harms)*; Nina Rosa — complete vocal score — Irving Caesar$^{w/m}$ & Otto Harbach$^{w/m}$ & Sigmund Romberg$^{w/m}$ *(Harms)*. An American in Peru falls in love with a native girl. It was a pleasant musical that ran four months. COVER: a senorita with shawl.

1649 Nine (Broadway, 1982). Karen Akers, Taina Elg.

Amor [VS] / Be Italian [VS] / Be on Your Own / Bells of Saint Sebastian [VS] / Call from the Vatican [VS] / Folies Bergeres [VS] / Getting Tall [VS] / Guido's Song [VS] / I Can't Make This Movie [VS] / My Husband Makes Movies [VS] / Nine [VS] / Only with You / Simple / Unusual Way / Waltz from Nine [VS] — Maury Yeston^(w/m) *(Belwin Mills)*. A musical about an Italian movie director which had a so-so score but a great set and fabulous direction by Tommy Tune. It kept running for almost two years. COVER: Raul Julia and a large nine.

1650 Nine-Fifteen Revue (Broadway, 1930). Ruth Etting, Paul Kelly.

Bring Him Back Here [ABQ] — composers unknown *(Harms)*; Get Happy — Ted Koehler^w & Harold Arlen^(w/m) *(Remick)*; Knockin' on Wood / One Way Street — Edward Eliscu^w & Richard Myers^m *(Harms)*; A Purty Little Thing — Will Johnstone^w & Philip Broughton^m *(J and B)*; Up Among the Chimney Pots — Paul James^w & Kay Swift^m *(Harms)*; Winter and Spring — Edward Eliscu^w & Rudolf Friml^m *(Harms)*; You Wanted Me, I Wanted You — Harold Arlen^(w/m) & Ted Koehler^(w/m) *(Remick)*. A musical revue written and performed by some of the best talent in show business; it ran one week. COVER: a girl's face and a list of 34 contributors to sketches and songs.

1651 No Foolin' (aka **Ziegfeld American Revue, Ziegfeld Follies of 1926, Ziegfeld Palm Beach Girl,** and **Ziegfeld Palm Beach Nights**) (Broadway, 1926). Charles King, James Barton.

Every Little Thing You Do / Honey, Be Mine — Gene Buck^w & James Hanley^m *(Harms)*; Florida, the Moon and You — Gene Buck^w & Rudolf Friml^m *(Harms)*; No Foolin' — Gene Buck^(w/m) & James Hanley^(w/m) *(Harms)*; Wasn't It Nice? — Irving Caesar^w & Rudolf Friml^m *(Harms)*. This poor Ziegfeld revue lasted for three months on Broadway. It went through many changes on its try-out tour. Ziegfeld was in a legal battle with the title *Ziegfeld Follies* and could not use that title. He opened a new theatre in Florida and called this show *Palm Beach Nights* and *Palm Beach Girl*. In the next city, it was *American Revue,* followed by *No Foolin'* due to the hit song in it. Ziegfeld regained the words

Ziegfeld Follies and the post–Broadway tour gave it the title of *Ziegfeld Follies of 1926.* COVER: palm tree, beach house, and the ocean.

1652 No for an Answer (Broadway, 1941). Martin Wolfson, Carol Channing.

The Purest Kind of Guy / Sing Out! — Marc Blitzstein^(w/m) *(People's Songs Magazine)*. A radical musical dealing with a hotel workers strike. With no backing, it had three staged readings. COVER: none.

1653 No, No, Nanette (Broadway, 1925). Louise Groody, Charles Winninger.

The Boy Next Door — Schuyler Greene^w & Otto Harbach^w & Vincent Youmans^m *(Harms)*; I Don't Want a Girlie — B.G. DeSylva^w & Vincent Youmans^m *(Harms)*; I Want to Be Happy / Tea for Two / Too Many Rings Around Rosie / "Where Has My Hubby Gone?" Blues / You Can Dance with Any Girl at All — Irving Caesar^w & Vincent Youmans^m *(Harms)*; I've Confessed to the Breeze / No, No, Nanette! / Santa Claus — Otto Harbach^w & Vincent Youmans^m *(Harms)*; No, No Nanette — complete vocal score — Schuyler Greene^w & Otto Harbach^w & Irving Caesar^w & Vincent Youmans^m *(Harms)*. A smash hit portraying the flapper era. It had a good book, a talented cast, and a score that included *Tea for Two* and *I Want to Be Happy.* It ran for only nine months on Broadway but it had touring companies all over the country. COVER: letters and designs.

1654 No, No, Nanette (Broadway, 1971). Ruby Keeler, Jack Gilford.

The Call of the Sea [VS] / I Want to Be Happy / Tea for Two / Too Many Rings Around Rosie / You Can Dance with Any Girl at All / "Where Has My Hubby Gone?" Blues — Irving Caesar^w & Vincent Youmans^m *(Warner Bros.)*; I've Confessed to the Breeze [VS] / No, No, Nanette [VS] / Peach on the Beach [VS] / Telephone Girlie [VS] / Waiting for You [VS] — Otto Harbach^w & Vincent Youmans[m] *(Warner Bros.)*; Take a Little One-Step — Zelda Sears[w] & Vincent Youmans[m] *(Warner Bros.)*. A smash hit revival of the 1925 musical. It was given a lavish production with a very talented cast and ran for over two years with many road companies following. COVER: girls with flowers, champagne, bubbles.

1655 No Other Girl (*see also* **The Belle of Quakertown** *and* **The Town Clown**) (Broadway, 1923). Eddie Buzzell, Helen Ford.

Doing the Town / Honduras / In the Corner of My Mind / No Other Girl / You Flew Away from the Nest — Bert Kalmar[w/m] & Harry Ruby[w/m] *(Berlin)*. A short lived musical about a highway. This show toured as the *Belle of Quakertown* and *The Town Clown* but opened on Broadway as *No Other Girl*. COVER: a Quaker girl.

1656 No Strings (Broadway, 1962). Richad Kiley, Diahann Carroll.

Be My Host / Eager Beaver / La-La-La / Loads of Love / Look No Further / Love Makes the World Go / "Maine" / The Man Who Has Everything / No Strings / No Strings — complete vocal score / Nobody Told Me / The Sweetest Sounds / You Don't Tell Me — Richard Rodgers[w/m] *(Williamson)*. A musical about an interracial love affair in Paris with a wonderful score by Rodgers and a lovely performance by Diahann Carroll. It ran for almost two years. COVER: the Eiffel Tower and two people.

1657 No Time for Sergeants (Broadway, 1955). Andy Griffith, Don Knotts.

There's No Time for Sergeants — Marcille McRae[w/m] & Cecil Rutherford[w/m] *(Chappell)*. A long running comedy hit with one song. COVER: soldier and civilian hanging on to one parachute.

1658 Nobody's Girl (*see also* **Holka-Polka** *and* **Spring in Autumn**) (Broadway, 1925). Orville Harrold, Patti Harrold.

Holka-Polka / Home of My Heart / In a Little While / Spring in Autumn / When Love Is Near — Gus Kahn[w] & Ray Egan[w] & William Ortmann[m] *(Harms)*. This quick flop toured the country as *Nobody's Girl* and *Spring in Autumn* before reaching Broadway as *Holka Polka*. COVER: Ilse Marvenga.

1659 Nobody's Perfect (*see also* **Sugar**) (Broadway, 1972). Robert Morse, Cyril Ritchard.

Doing It for Sugar [RC] / The People in My Life [RC] — Bob Merrill[w] & Jule Styne[m] *(Chappell)*. This musical version of *Some Like It Hot* had great comedy from Morse and Ritchard plus some nice period songs by Jule Styne. It ran 15 months and was called *Nobody's Perfect* in the early stages, but opened as *Sugar*. COVER: none.

1660 Not Tonight, Josephine (closed before Broadway, 1920). Ben Linn, Mlle. Florie.

It Can't Keep on Raining Forever / I've a Parasol for You Dear / Love Dreams / Not Tonight, Josephine — Ed Hutchinson[w] & Seymour Furth[m] *(Joe Morris)*. COVER: Ben Linn, Mlle. Florie.

1661 Nothing But Love (Broadway, 1919). Donald Meek, Marion Sunshine.

Ask the Stars / I'll Remember You / Moonbeam / Take Me Home / When I Walk Out with You / Wonderful Man — Frank Stammers[w] & Harold Orlob[m] *(Harms)*. A musical about a dual personality; the musical lasted four weeks. COVER: letters and designs.

1662 Nowhere to Go But Up (Broadway, 1962). Dorothy Loudon, Tom Bosley.

Baby, Baby / A Couple of Clowns / Here I Am [PC] / Nowhere to Go But Up / Out of Sight, Out of Mind / When a Fella Needs a Friend — James Lipton[w] & Sol Berkowitz[m] *(Chappell)*. A musical about prohibition that lasted one week. COVER: two men hanging on to an angel.

1663 Nunsense (Off Broadway, 1986). Christine Anderson, Marilyn Farina.

Growing Up Catholic [VS] / I Could've Gone to Nashville [VS] / I Just

Want to Be a Star [VS] / Lilacs Bring Back Memories [VS] / Nunsense Is Habit-Forming [VS] / Turn Up the Spotlight [VS] / We've Got to Clean Out The Freezer [VS] — Dan Groggin^{w/m} *(Warner Bros.)*. A comedy hit about five nuns. COVER: sketch of five nuns.

1664 Nuts and Bolts (Army, 1943). Army Camp Show.

Take a Walk / This Is America — Heinz Freiberg^{w/m} *(Miller)*. A musical revue for factory workers during World War II. COVER: the American eagle and flags.

1665 Nymph Errant (British, 1933). Gertrude Lawrence, David Burns.

Back to Nature with You — piano selections [B] / Castle — piano selections [B] / The Cocotte — piano selections [B] / Georgia Sand — piano selections [B] / Neauville-Sur-Mer — piano selections [B] — Cole Porter^m *(Chappell)*; Experiment [B] / How Could We Be Wrong? [B] / It's Bad for Me [B] / Nymph Errant [B] / The Physician [B] / Solomon [B] / When Love Comes Your Way [B] / You're Too Far Away [VS] — Cole Porter^{w/m} *(Chappell)*. A sort of shocking musical about a nymphomaniac with a run of 20 weeks in London. The only production in the U.S. was a four week run at the Equity Theatre in N.Y. in 1982. COVER: a map of the world.

1666 O Mistress Mine (British, 1936). Yvonne Printemps, Pierre Fresnay.

Goodbye, Little Dream, Goodbye [B] — Cole Porter^{w/m} *(Chappell)*. A British play that included one current Cole Porter song. COVER: Yvonne Printemps.

1667 The O'Brien Girl (Broadway, 1921). Ada Mae Weeks, Truman Stanley.

The Conversation Step / I Wonder How I Ever Passed You By / I'm All Excited / Indian Prance / The Last Dance / Learn to Smile / My Little Canoe / That O'Brien Girl / There Can't Be Any Harm in Saying Just

Goodbye — Otto Harbach^w & Louis Hirsch^m *(Victoria)*. A rags-to-riches story in an ordinary musical that ran 20 weeks. COVER: flowers and designs.

1668 Oddities of 1920 (Nightclub, 1923). Peggy Ross.

Dreamy Melody — Ted Koehler^{w/m} & Frank Magine^{w/m} & C. Naset^{w/m} *(Remick)*. COVER: Peggy Ross.

1669 Of Thee I Sing (Broadway, 1931). William Gaxton, Victor Moore.

Because, Because / The Illegitimate Daughter / Love Is Sweeping the Country / Of Thee I Sing / Of Thee I Sing — complete vocal score / The Senator from Minnesota [VS] / Who Cares? / Wintergreen for President [VS] — Ira Gershwin^w & George Gershwin^m *(Harms)*. One of the great American musicals with a brilliant book and score; the musical ran over one year. COVER: a couple on the steps of the Capitol.

1670 Of Thee I Sing (Broadway, 1952). Jack Carson, Betty Oakes.

Because, Because / Love Is Sweeping the Country / Mine / Of Thee I Sing / Who Cares? / Wintergreen for President — Ira Gershwin^w & George Gershwin^m *(New World)*. A revival of the hit musical that folded after nine weeks. COVER: sketch of two men with political signs.

1671 Of "V" We Sing (Broadway, 1942). Betty Garrett, Phil Leeds.

Don't Sing Solo — Roslyn Harvey^w & George Kleinsinger^m *(Marks)*; We Have a Date — Roslyn Harvey^w & Lou Cooper^m *(Marks)*. A revue with young people that poked fun at American life. It lasted ten weeks. COVER: girl in red, white, and blue holding a poster.

1672 Off to Buffalo (Broadway, 1939). Joe Cook, Hume Cronyn.

Ain't That Something Now / Sorry Dear — Dave Oppenheim^{w/m} & Milton Berle^{w/m} & Henry Tobias^{w/m} *(Mills)*. A comedy with songs that lasted one week. COVER: Joe Cook.

1673 The O'Flynn (Broadway, 1934). George Houston, Lucy Monroe.

Child of Erin / A Lovely Lady / The

Man I Love Is Here — Russell Janney[w] & Franklin Hauser[m] *(Mills)*; Jamie — Brian Hooker[w] & Russell Janney[w] & Franklin Hauser[m] *(Mills)*; So You Will Walk with Me / Song of My Heart — Brian Hooker[w] & Franklin Hauser[m] *(Mills)*. A terrible imitation of *Vagabond King* that lasted one week. COVER: George Houston.

1674 Oh, Baby (Regional, 1920). Charles Abbate.

Bachelor Days / Dixie I Love You / Salvation Army Girl / Smile with Me — Charles Abbate[w/m] *(Marcus)*. COVER: Charles Abbate and chorus girls.

1675 Oh, Brother! (Broadway, 1981). Larry Marshall, Judy Kaye.

I to the World / A Loud and Funny Song / Oh, Brother! / What Do I Tell People This Time? — Donald Driver[w] & Michael Valenti[m] *(Mac)*. Shakespeare's *Comedy of Errors* in a Persian setting. It was a poor musical that lasted less than two weeks. COVER: a camel with sunglasses and turban.

1676 Oh, Calcutta! (Broadway, 1969). Bill Macy, Margo Sappington.

Ballerina [VS] / Dick and Jane [VS] / Freeze Music [VS] / Green Pants [VS] / Jack and Jill [VS] — Robert Dennis[w/m] *(United Artists)*; Clarence and Mildred [VS] / Oh, Calcutta! (with lyrics) [VS] — Stanley Walden[w/m] *(United Artists)*; Exchanges of Information [VS] / I Don't Have a Song to Sing [VS] / I Want It [VS] / Sincere Replies [VS] — Peter Schickele[w/m] *(United Artists)*; I Like the Look [VS] — Robert Dennis[w/m] & Peter Schickele[w/m] *(United Artists)*; I'm an Actor [VS] — Stanley Walden[w/m] & Peter Schickele[w/m] & Robert Dennis[w/m] *(United Artists)*; Much Too Soon [VS] — Robert Dennis[w/m] & Jacques Levy[w/m] & Peter Schickele[w/m] & Stanley Walden[w/m] *(United Artists)*; Oh, Calcutta! (instrumental) [VS] — Stanley Walden[m] *(United Artists)*. A musical, with complete nudity, that ran for several years. COVER: black and white cover with titles only.

1677 Oh Captain! (Broadway,

1958). Tony Randall, Susan Johnson.

All the Time / It's Never Quite the Same / Life Does a Man a Favor / The Morning Music of Montmartre / Surprise / We're Not Children / You Don't Know Him / You're So Right for Me — Jay Livingston[w/m] & Ray Evans[w/m] *(Chappell)*. A musical version of the hit British movie that didn't make it. It lasted five months! COVER: sketch of a girl cooking, wearing only a small apron.

1678 Oh Coward! (Off Broadway, 1972). Roderick Cook, Jamie Ross.

Chase Me, Charlie [VS] / Dance, Little Lady [VS] / Don't Put Your Daughter on the Stage, Mrs. Worthington [VS] / Has Anybody Seen Our Ship? [VS] / Here and Now / I Went to a Marvelous Party [VS] / If Love Were All [VS] / I'll Follow My Secret Heart [VS] / I'll See You Again [VS] / Let's Say Goodbye [VS] / London Is a Little Bit of All Right [VS] / London Pride [VS] / Mad About the Boy [VS] / Mad Dogs and Englishmen [VS] / Matelot [VS] / Men About Town [VS] / Nina [VS] / The Party's Over Now [VS] / Play, Orchestra, Play [VS] / A Room with a View [VS] / Sail Away [VS] / Someday I'll Find You [VS] / Something Very Strange [VS] / The Stately Homes of England [VS] / This Is a Changing World [VS] / Three White Feathers [VS] / We Must All Be Very Kind to Auntie Jessie [VS] / We Were Dancing [VS] / Why Do the Wrong People Travel? [VS] / World Weary [VS] / You Were There [VS] / Zigeuner [VS] — Noel Coward[w/m] *(Chappell)*. A successful revue using the music of Noel Coward. COVER: Noel Coward.

1679 Oh, Earnest! (Broadway, 1927). Marjorie Gateson, Vivian Marlowe.

Give Me Some One / He Knows Where the Rose Is in Bloom / Let's Pretend — Francis DeWitt[w] & Robert Hood Bowers[m] *(Harms)*. A musical version of an Oscar Wilde classic that lasted seven weeks. COVER: a vase filled with flowers.

1680 Oh Johnny! (closed before Broadway, 1928). Stars unknown.

The Longest Way 'Round Is the Sweetest Way Home—J. Keirn Brennan[w] & James Royce[m] *(Feist)*. There were 13 other songs listed on the cover but probably not published. COVER: letters and designs.

1681 Oh Joy! (Black, 1922). Whitney and Tutt.

Bamboo Isle [ABQ] / Down at the Jamboree [ABQ] / Intoxicating Jazz [ABQ] / Ja Da Blues [ABQ] / Sally Sue / Smile on Sue / Struttin' Along—James Vaughan[w/m] & J. Edgar Dowell[w/m] & Eddie Kamnetz[w/m] *(Kay-Stern)*; My Dawg—Bert Murphy[w/m] *(Kay-Stern)*; That Da-Da Strain—Mamie Medina[w] & J. Edgar Dowell[m] *(Williams)*; When You're Crazy Over Daddy—J. Edgar Dowell[w/m] & Eddie Kamnetz[w/m] *(Kay-Stern)*. COVER: letters and designs.

1682 Oh, Kay! (Broadway, 1926). Gertrude Lawrence, Victor Moore.

Bride and Groom [VS] / Dear Little Girl [VS] / Don't Ask [VS] / The Woman's Touch [VS]—Ira Gershwin[w] & George Gershwin[m] *(Warner Bros.)*; Clap Yo' Hands / Do-Do-Do / Fidgety Feet / Maybe / Show Me the Town / Someone to Watch Over Me—Ira Gershwin[w] & George Gershwin[m] *(Harms)*; Finale of Act 1 (piano selections)—George Gershwin[m] *(Harms)*; Heaven on Earth / Oh, Kay!—Ira Gershwin[w] & Howard Dietz[w] & George Gershwin[m] *(Harms)*. A prohibition musical loaded with great Gershwin tunes and Gertrude Lawrence. It lasted eight months. COVER: flowers and designs.

1683 Oh, Kay! (Broadway, 1990). Angela Teek, Brian Mitchell.

Ask Me Again—Ira Gershwin[w] & George Gershwin[m] *(Warner Bros.)*. David Merrick revived this hit with a black cast. It turned out to be a big disaster; however, this unknown Gershwin song was added to the score, and then published for the first time. COVER: plain cover with Warner logo.

1684 Oh Mama (Broadway, 1925). Alice Brady, John Cromwell.

Just a Kiss—Cyrus Wood[w] & Arthur Johnston[m] *(Berlin)*; Oh Mama!—Herman Ruby[w] & Arthur Johnston[m] *(Berlin)*. A comedy with several songs. COVER: Alice Brady.

1685 Oh, Mamma! (Broadway, 1919). Frank Fay, Julia Kellety.

I Never Knew How Much I Loved You—Frank Fay[w] & Dave Dreyer[m] *(Von Tilzer)*; Ooh! La, La—I'm Having a Wonderful Time—Bud Green[w] & Ed Nelson[m] *(Stasny)*. A play with several songs. COVER: Frank Fay and Julia Kellety.

1686 Oh, My Dear! (*see also* **Ask Dad**) (Broadway, 1918). Ivy Sawyer, Joseph Santley.

Boat Song / Childhood Days / City of Dreams / Come Where Nature Calls / I Shall Be All Right Now / I Wonder Whether / I'd Ask No More / If They Ever Parted You from Me / It Sort of Makes a Fellow Stop and Think / The Land Where Journeys End / You Never Know—P.G. Wodehouse[w] & Louis Hirsch[m] *(Harms)*; Go Little Boat—P.G. Wodehouse[w] & Jerome Kern[m] *(Harms)*; I Love a Musical Comedy Show / Now and Then But Not All the Time / Sas'prilla, Women and Song—Alfred Bryan[w] & Jean Schwartz[m] *(Remick)*. The last of the Princess Theatre shows, since without Kern, they ended. This show with poor music lasted six months. It was called *Ask Dad* on its try-out tour but opened as *Oh, My Dear!* COVER: flowers and letters.

1687 Oh, Oh, Cindy! (Regional, 1920). Stars unknown.

Da De Dum Dee Means Dance to Me / Love Is Like a Game of Cards / You've Been the Light of My Life—Maurice Baker[w/m] *(Rogers)*. COVER: boy and girl dressed as clowns.

1688 Oh! Oh! Nurse (Broadway, 1925). James Doyle, Gertrude Vanderbilt.

Is It Any Wonder? / My Lady Love—Goodnight / Way Out in Rainbow Land—Monte Carlo[w] & Alma Sanders[m] *(Shapiro, Bernstein)*. A musical set in a hospital and regarded by the critics as terrible. It lasted four weeks. COVER: lady in nurse's uniform.

1689 Oh, Please! (Broadway, 1926). Beatrice Lillie, Charles Purcell.

I Know That You Know / I'm Waiting for a Wonderful Girl / Like He Loves Me / Nicodemus — Anne Caldwell^w & Vincent Youmans^m *(Harms)*. A musical about a jealous wife with Beatrice Lillie miscast in a straight role. It had one hit song but lasted only ten weeks. COVER: a water fountain and a tree.

1690 Oh Say Can You Sing (Off Broadway, 1937). Stars unknown.

Night After Night — Sid Kuller^w & Ray Golden^w & Phil Charig^m *(Chappell)*. A musical presented by the Federal Theatre WPA. COVER: sketch of girl sitting on musical note; red, white, and blue stars.

1691 Oh, Teacher! (Broadway, 1928). Paige Sisters.

Playmates — James Dietrich^{w/m} & Larry Spier^{w/m} & Sam Coslow^{w/m} *(Spier and Coslow)*. A small revue presented by Paramount-Publix in between showings of their new movie features.

1692 Oh! U Baby! (Off Broadway, 1921). Tommy Levene.

Oh — U — Baby — Tommy Levene^w & P. Brady^m *(Levene)*. A female impersonator show. COVER: Tommy Levene as a chorus girl.

1693 Oh, Uncle (see also Oh, What a Girl) (Broadway, 1919). Frank Fay, Sam Ash.

Baby — Gus Kahn^w & Egbert Van Alstyne^m *(Remick)*; Breeze Through the Trees / Dainty Little Girl Like You / Nice Sweet Kiss / One Little Girl I Know — Edgar Smith^w & Charles Jules^m & Jacques Presburg^m *(Schirmer)*; Gimme This — Gimme This — Gimme That — Wolfe Gilbert^{w/m} & Nat Vincent^{w/m} *(Gilbert-Friedland)*; I Never Knew That I Loved You — Frank Fay^w & Dave Dreyer^m *(Von Tilzer)*; Prince Charming — Edward Clark^w & Charles Jules^m & Jacques Presburg^m

(Schirmer). A musical about a nephew and uncle chasing the same girl. It lasted for eight weeks. It was called *Oh, Uncle* in try-out but opened on Broadway as *Oh, What a Girl.* COVER: a man and woman in elegant clothes.

1694 Oh, What a Girl (see also Oh, Uncle) (Broadway, 1919). Frank Fay, Sam Ash.

Baby — Gus Kahn^w & Egbert Van Alstyne^m *(Remick)*; The Breeze Through the Trees / Dainty Little Girl Like You / Nice, Sweet Kiss / Oh, What a Girl! — Edgar Smith^w & Charles Jules^m & Jacques Presburg^m *(Schirmer)*; Gimme This — Gimme This — Gimme That — Wolfe Gilbert^{w/m} & Alex Sullivan^{w/m} & Nat Vincent^{w/m} *(G and F)*; I'm Way Ahead of the Times — Murray Kissen^w & Joe Burns^w & Jack Glogau^m *(M and F)*; Prince Charming — Edward Clark^w & Charles Jules^m & Jacques Presburg^m *(Schirmer)*; You'd Be Surprised — Irving Berlin^{w/m} *(Berlin)*. A musical about a nephew and uncle chasing the same girl; it lasted eight weeks. It was called *Oh, Uncle* in try-out but opened on Broadway as *Oh, What a Girl.* COVER: a man and woman in elegant clothes.

1695 Oh, What a Lovely War (Broadway, 1964). Victor Spinetti, Reid Shelton.

Old Soldiers Never Die [PC] / When This Lousy War Is Over [PC] — Charles Chilton^{w/m} *(T R O)*. A British import of an anti-war musical. This poor musical ran only three months. COVER: none.

1696 The Oil Islands (German, 1929). Stars unknown.

Song of the Brown Islands [VS] — Lion Feuchtwanger^w & Kurt Weill^m *(T R O)*. A German play with one song by Kurt Weill. It was first published in 1958 in *Weill Song Album* (HH). COVER: Kurt Weill.

1697 O-Kay for Sound (British, 1936). Stars unknown.

There's a New World — Jimmy Kennedy^{w/m} & Michael Carr^{w/m} *(Mills)*. A song published in the U.S. from a hit revue. COVER: clouds.

1698 Okay U.S.A. (Army, 1944). Stars unknown.

I Was Down Texas Way [VS] / My Chicago [VS] / The Tall Pines [VS] / Tonight in San Francisco [VS] / A Trip Round the U.S.A. [VS] / You're OK, U.S.A.! [VS] — Frank Loesser[w/m] *(Army Script)*; When He Comes Home — Frank Loesser[w/m] *(Words and Music)*. A soldier show from the Special Services Division for production in military establishments. COVER: the Statue of Liberty and a big red, white, and blue star.

1699 Oklahoma! (*see also* **Away We Go**) (Broadway, 1943). Alfred Drake.

I Can't Say No / Many a New Day / Oh, What a Beautiful Mornin' / Oklahoma / Oklahoma — complete vocal score / Out of My Dreams / People Will Say We're in Love / The Surrey with the Fringe on Top / When I Go Out Walking with My Baby [VS] [CUT] — Oscar Hammerstein[w] & Richard Rodgers[m] *(Williamson)*. A musical set in Kansas that was a smash hit and ran for five and one half years on Broadway. It had talented young people, an Agnes DeMille ballet, and many Rodgers and Hammerstein hit songs. This show opened in New Haven as *Away We Go* but changed its title in Boston. COVER: houses, trees, and fields.

1700 Oklahoma (Broadway, 1979). Laurence Guittard, Christine Andreas.

All er Nothin' / The Farmer and the Cowman / I Can't Say No / Kansas City / Many a New Day / Oh, What a Beautiful Mornin' / Oklahoma! / Out of My Dreams / People Will Say We're in Love / Pore Jud / Surrey with the Fringe on Top — Oscar Hammerstein[w] & Richard Rodgers[m] *(Williamson)*. An excellent revival that lasted for nine months. COVER: beautiful colored cover of boy and girl dancing.

1701 Ol' Man Satan (Broadway, 1932). Walter Richardson, Lawrence Chenault.

Home Beyond the River — Donald Heywood[w/m] *(Schirmer)*. A religious drama with a black cast that lasted three weeks. COVER: Walter Richardson, river and trees.

1702 Old Bill, M.P. (Broadway, 1926). Charles Coburn, Charles Jordan.

Vi-o-lets — A. Bairnsfather[w/m] & Abel Baer[w/m] *(Berlin)*. A continuation of the character from *The Better Ole.* It lasted only three weeks. COVER: sketch of Charles Coburn.

1703 The Old Maid and the Thief (Opera, 1939). Robert Weede, Dorothy Sarnoff.

Old Maid and the Thief / Steal Me, Sweet Thief — complete vocal score — Gian Carlo Menotti[w/m] *(Belwin Mills)*. The New York City Opera Company performed this show. COVER: plain cover with titles only.

1704 Oliver! (Broadway, 1963). Georgia Brown, Clive Revill.

As Long as He Needs Me / Consider Yourself / Food Glorious Food [VS] / I'd Do Anything / It's a Fine Life / Oom-Pah-Pah / Where Is Love? / Who Will Buy? — Lionel Bart[w/m] *(Hollis);* Oliver — complete vocal score — Lionel Bart[w/m] *(Lakeview)*. A very entertaining musical with a good score, great sets, Georgia Brown, and a run of two years. COVER: a sad boy's face.

1705 Olympic Games of Barcelona (Concert, 1992). Jose Carreras, Sarah Brightman.

Amigos Para Siempre — Don Black[w] & Andrew L. Webber[m] *(Really Useful)*. A special song written for Olympic opening. COVER: Carreras and Brightman.

1706 Olympus on My Mind (Broadway, 1986). Lewis J. Stadlen, Tom Wopat.

Heaven on Earth / Something of Yourself — Barry Harman[w] & Grant Sturiale[m] *(Chappell)*. A musical set in old Greece that became a moderate hit. COVER: sketch of girl in brief outfit with jewels and furs.

1707 On a Clear Day You Can See Forever (Broadway, 1965). John Cullum, Barbara Harris.

Come Back to Me / Hurry! It's Lovely Up Here! / Melinda / On a Clear Day You Can See Forever / On a Clear Day You Can See Forever — complete vocal score / On the S.S. Bernard Cohn / She Wasn't You / Wait Till We're Sixty-Five / What Did I Have That I Don't Have / When I'm Being Born Again — Alan Jay Lerner[w] & Burton Lane[m] *(Chappell)*. A musical dealing with extrasensory perception that had a wonderful performance by Barbara Harris and a lovely score by Lerner and Lane. It ran for nine months. Cover: window frame with flower pot.

1708 On the Town (Broadway, 1944). Nancy Walker, Betty Comden.

Carried Away (long version) [VS] / I Can Cook Too (long version) [VS] / I Feel Like I'm Not Out of Bed Yet (long version) [VS] / Lonely Town (long version) [VS] / Lucky to Be Me (long version) [VS] / New York, New York (long version) [VS] / Some Other Time (long version) [VS] / Ya Got Me (long version) [VS] — Betty Comden[w] & Adolph Green[w] & Leonard Bernstein[m] *(Warner Bros.)*; I Can Cook Too / Lonely Town / Lucky to Be Me / New York, New York / Some Other Time / Ya Got Me — Betty Comden[w] & Adolph Green[w] & Leonard Bernstein[m] *(Witmark)*. A musical that developed from a ballet about three sailors on the loose in New York. This hit had wonderful dialogue and songs plus some great comedy and dancing. It ran over a year. Cover: three sailors.

1709 On the Town (Broadway, 1971). Bernadette Peters, Phyllis Newman.

Lonely Town / New York, New York / On the Town — vocal selections of six songs (1971) / Some Other Time — Betty Comden[w] & Adolf Green[w] & Leonard Bernstein[m] *(Warner Bros.)*. A lavish revival of the hit musical that had no oomph. It closed after nine weeks. Cover: three sailors and the skyscrapers of New York.

1710 On the Twentieth Century (Broadway, 1978). Madeline Kahn, John Cullum.

Five Zeros [VS] / I Rise Again [VS] / I've Got It All [VS] / The Legacy [VS] / Life Is Like a Train [VS] / Mine [VS] / Never [VS] / On the Twentieth Century / Our Private World / Repent [VS] / She's a Nut [VS] / Sign, Lilly Sign [VS] / Together [VS] / Veronique [VS] — Betty Comden[w] & Adolph Green[w] & Cy Coleman[m] *(Notable)*. This musical is a battle of the sexes on a cross-country train trip. It was a lavish art-deco production and the audience applauded the scenery more than the play. This was an old-fashioned type operetta that lasted for a year. Cover: a well-dressed couple boarding a train.

1711 On with the Dance (British, 1925). Alice Delysia, Nigel Bruce.

Cosmopolitan Lady [B] / First Love [B] / I'm So in Love [B] / Ladybird [B] / Poor Little Rich Girl [B] — Noel Coward[w/m] *(A H and C)*. A Charles Cochran revue that became a London hit and ran for over six months. Cover: Alice Delysia.

1712 On with the Show (Broadway, 1954). Irra Pettina, Robert Wright.

Remember the Night / Set Me Free / Somehow I've Always Known / What's My Fatal Charm? — Elizabeth Miele[w] & Frederico Valerio[m] *(Chappell)*. This musical's try-out title was *On with the Show*. At the last minute, before opening on Broadway, the title was changed to *Hit the Trail*. It was so bad it closed after four performances and no music was issued with the Broadway title of *Hit the Trail*. Cover: stagecoach arriving in Western town.

1713 On Your Toes (Broadway, 1936). Ray Bolger, Monty Woolley.

Glad to Be Unhappy / The Heart Is Quicker Than the Eye / It's Got to Be Love / On Your Toes / On Your Toes — complete vocal score / Quiet Night / There's a Small Hotel / Too Good for the Average Man — Lorenz Hart[w] & Richard Rodgers[m] *(Chappell)*; Slaughter on Tenth Avenue (ballet cover) — Richard Rodgers[m] *(Chappell)*. A hit musical with some of Rodgers and Hart's best songs and two wonderful Balanchine ballets. Cover: a ballerina.

1714 On Your Toes (Broadway, 1954). Vera Zorina, Bobby Van.

Glad to Be Unhappy / The Heart Is Quicker Than the Eye / It's Got to Be Love / On Your Toes / Quiet Night / There's a Small Hotel / Too Good for the Average Man—Lorenz Hart[w] & Richard Rodgers[m] *(Chappell).* A lavish revival of this hit that seemed dated. It had two wonderful dancing stars and Elaine Stritch but it ran for only eight weeks. Cover: a boy and a girl ballet dancer.

1715 On Your Toes (Broadway, 1983). Lara Teeter, Natalia Makarova.

On Your Toes—vocal selections of eight songs (1983)—Lorenz Hart[w] & Richard Rodgers[m] *(Chappell).* Another lavish revival of this musical, which although dated, had some excellent dancers who could not act. Even so, it ran for 15 months. Cover: Lara Teeter, Natalia Makarova.

1716 Once on This Island (Broadway, 1991). La Chanze, Sheila Gibbs.

Forever Yours [VS] / The Human Heart [VS] / Mama Will Provide [VS] / Rain [VS] / Some Girls [VS] / Ti Moune [VS] / Waiting for Life [VS] / We Dance [VS]—Lynn Ahrens[w] & Stephen Flaherty[m] *(Warner Bros.).* A musical with a Caribbean setting, a pleasant score and some good dancing. It was a moderate hit. Cover: vivid sketch of tropical dancers.

1717 Once Upon a Mattress (Broadway, 1959). Carol Burnett, Joe Bova.

Happily Ever After [VS] / In a Little While / Normandy / Sensitivity [VS] / Shy / Very Soft Shoes [VS] / Yesterday I Loved You—Marshall Barer[w] & Mary Rodgers[m] *(Chappell).* An Off Broadway hit due to the comedy of Carol Burnett. It moved to Broadway and ran for a year. Cover: sketch of lady on a pile of mattresses.

1718 Once Upon a Time (closed before Broadway, 1933). Stars unknown.

Once Upon a Time [PC]—Cole Porter[w/m] *(Chappell).* This song was from an unproduced Cole Porter musical. Cover: none.

1719 Ondine (Broadway, 1954). Audrey Hepburn, Mel Ferrer.

Ondine—Robert Mellin[w] & Ulpio Minucci[m] *(Mellin).* A romantic drama and a hit for Hepburn and Ferrer. Cover: strange sketches of girls, castles, horses, flowers.

1720 One Damn Thing After Another (British, 1927). Jessie Matthews, Sonnie Hale.

Danse Grotesque a la Negre—piano selections [B] / Idles of the King [B] / Make Hey! Make Hey! [B] / Minuet [B] / One Damn Thing After Another [B] / Sandwich Girls [B] / Shuffle [B]—Richard Rodgers[m] *(Chappell);* I Need Some Cooling Off [B] / My Heart Stood Still [B] / My Lucky Star [B]—Lorenz Hart[w] & Richard Rodgers[m] *(Chappell).* A hit revue in London. Cover: letters and designs.

1721 One Dark Night (Nightclub, 1940). Stars unknown.

Alone Again / Sharpest Man in Town—Johnny Lange[w/m] & Lew Porter[w/m] *(Mills).* Cover: musical notes and letters.

1722 One for the Money (Broadway, 1939). Alfred Drake, Gene Kelly.

I Only Know / Once Upon a Time / Teeter Totter Tessie—Nancy Hamilton[w] & Morgan Lewis[m] *(Chappell).* A minor revue with some great young talent that ran three months. Cover: letters and designs.

1723 "110 in the Shade" (Broadway, 1963). Inga Swenson, Robert Horton.

Everything Beautiful Happens at Night / Gonna Be Another Hot Day [VS] / Is It Really Me? / Little Red Hat [VS] / Love, Don't Turn Away / A Man and a Woman / 110 in the Shade [B] / 110 in the Shade—complete vocal score / Pretty 18 [PC] [CUT] / Raunchy [VS] / Simple Little Things / Too Many People Alone—Tom Jones[w] & Harvey Schmidt[m] *(Chappell).* A charming musical based on the *Rainmaker.* It had a lovely score and some talented actors but ran for only nine months due to a surplus of bigger hits on Broadway. COVER: girl leaning on post under a hot sun.

1724 One in a Million (Jewish, 1920). Molly Picon, Moses Feder.

Prost in Pushit — Molly Picon[w] & Abe Ellstein[m] *(Trio)*. COVER: Molly Picon.

1725 One Kiss (Broadway, 1923). Louise Groody, Oscar Shaw.

Just a Little Love / One Kiss / There Are Some Things You Never Forget / Up There / When We Are Married / Your Lips — Clare Kummer[w] & Maurice Yvain[m] *(Harms)*. A musical about young love. The musical, imported from France, lasted 12 weeks. COVER: One cover is yellow and grey with designs and the other is pink and blue with designs.

1726 One Mo' Time (Off Broadway, 1979). Vernel Bagneris, Topsy Chapman.

After You've Gone [VS] — Henry Creamer[w/m] & Turner Layton[w/m] *(Mayfair)*; Hindustan — Oliver Wallace[w/m] & Harold Weeks[w/m] *(Hansen)*; One Mo' Time [VS] — Vernel Bagneris[w/m] *(Hansen)*. A musical called a "1920s black vaudeville show." It was a moderate hit. COVER: Sylvia Williams.

1727 One Night Stand (closed before Broadway, 1980). Jack Weston, Charles Kimbrough.

Long Way from Home [PC] / There Was a Time [PC] — Herb Gardner[w] & Jule Styne[m] *(Chappell)*. COVER: none.

1728 One of the Canebiere (closed before Broadway, 1935). Stars unknown.

After That I Don't Remember — Mitchell Parish[w] & Vincent Scotto[m] *(Mills)*. COVER: titles and designs.

1729 One of Those Girls (closed before Broadway, 1922). DeLyle Alda.

Buy a Paper / Y-O-U — Arthur Swanstrom[w] & Carey Morgan[m] *(Berlin)*. COVER: DeLyle Alda.

1730 One Shining Moment (closed before Broadway, 1983). Kevin Anderson.

Imitate the Sun [VS] — Leslie Bricusse[w/m] & Allan Jay Friedman[w/m] *(Stage and Screen)*. A musical about John F. Kennedy that folded in Chicago. COVER: Leslie Bricusse.

1731 One Sunny Day (*see also* **Sunny Days**) (Broadway, 1928). Jeanette MacDonald, Lynne Overman.

Hang Your Hat on the Moon / One Sunny Day / Really and Truly — Clifford Grey[w] & William Duncan[w] & Jean Schwartz[m] *(Harms)*. A musical about a French man and his mistress that closed in three months. It was called *One Sunny Day* in try-out but opened as *Sunny Days*. COVER: a hat box and flowers.

1732 One Touch of Venus (Broadway, 1943). John Boles, Mary Martin.

Foolish Heart / Speak Low / That's Him / The Trouble with Women / Westwind — Ogden Nash[w] & Kurt Weill[m] *(Chappell)*; How Much I Love You [VS] / I'm a Stranger Here Myself [VS] / One Touch of Venus [VS] / Very, Very, Very [VS] / Way Out West in Jersey [VS] / Wooden Wedding [VS] — Ogden Nash[w] & Kurt Weill[m] *(T R O)*. Venus comes to life in this hit musical. It had witty dialogue and beautiful songs plus Mary Martin in a beautiful Mainbocher gown. It ran for one and one half years. COVER: the head of a marble statue.

1733 Open Your Eyes (British, 1930). Marie Burke, Ella Logan.

Happily Ever After [B] / Jack and Jill [B] / Open Your Eyes [B] / Such a Funny Feeling [B] / Too, Too Divine [B] / You'd Do for Me — I'd Do for You [B] — Collie Knox[w] & Vernon Duke[m] *(A H and C)*. This musical played two weeks in Glasgow in 1929 and was closed by Equity for non-payment of actors' salaries. It reopened with a new cast in 1930 and after a brief tour, opened in London where it lasted three weeks. COVER: pretty girl with red hat and closed eyes.

1734 Operette (British, 1938). Hugh French, Peggy Wood.

Countess Mitzi [B] / Dearest Love [B]

/ Gypsy Melody [B] / Operette [B] / Operette – complete vocal score [B] / Stately Homes of England [B] / Where Are the Songs We Sing [B] – Noel Coward[w/m] *(Chappell)*. A musical about performing a musical that was over-written and under-composed. It got very poor reviews and lasted only four months. COVER: a well dressed couple dancing.

1735 The Optimists (Broadway, 1928). Luella Gear, Melville Gideon.

Amapu – Edward Knoblock[w] & Melville Gideon[m] *(Feist)*; Little Lacquer Lady – Clifford Seyler[w] & Melville Gideon[m] *(Feist)*; Practically True to You / Spare a Little Love – Clifford Grey[w] & Melville Gideon[m] *(Feist)*. An American version of the British hit *Co-optimists* that lasted three weeks. COVER: designs and letters.

1736 Orange Blossoms (Broadway, 1922). Edith Day, Hal Skelly.

A Dream of Orange Blossoms / In Hennequeville / A Kiss in the Dark / Legend of the Glowworm / The Lonely Nest / Orange Blossoms – complete vocal score / Then Comes the Dawning / This Time It's Love / Way Out West in Jersey – B.G. DeSylva[w] & Victor Herbert[m] *(Harms)*. A short-lived musical about an inheritance. A poor Victor Herbert score. COVER: dancing girl and castle.

1737 Orchids Preferred (Broadway, 1937). Eddie Foy, Jr., Benay Venuta.

Boy, Girl, Moon / The Dying Swan [ABQ] / Echoes of Love [ABQ] / A Girl for the Man-About-Town [ABQ] / I'm Leaving the Bad Girls for Good / A Million Dollars / Selling a Song [ABQ] / Three Little Pigs [ABQ] / What Are You Going to Do About Love? – Fred Herendeen[w] & Dave Stamper[w] *(Marks)*. A musical about bar girls and true love that lasted for one week. COVER: a pretty girl and a pink orchid.

1738 Originalities (Irish, 1922). James Kilpatrick.

Little Home for Two – B.C. Hilliam[w/m] *(Witmark)*. COVER: Kilpatrick and Hilliam.

1739 Oui Madame (*see also* **Some Colonel**) (closed before Broadway, 1920). Dorothy Maynard, Georgia O'Ramey.

Every Hour Away from You Is Sixty Minutes Lost / He Wanted to Go and He Went / If I Saw Much of You / Over the Garden Wall / Play Me Something I Can Dance To / When You Know Me Better / Where Were You / The Wooing of the Violin – Robert Smith[w] & Victor Herbert[m] *(Harms)*. This musical opened in March 1920 and played Philadelphia and Boston as *Oui Madame*. It opened in Stamford, Connecticut, in October as *Some Colonel* where shortly thereafter, it folded. COVER: dancers, circles, and flowers.

1740 Our Nell (*see also* **Hayseed**) (Broadway, 1922). Mr. and Mrs. James Barry.

By and By / Walking Home with Angeline – Brian Hooker[w] & George Gershwin[m] *(Harms)*; Innocent Ingenue Baby – Brian Hooker[w] & William Daly[m] & George Gershwin[m] *(Harms)*; Old New England Home – Brian Hooker[w] & William Daly[m] *(Harms)*. A terrible musical of five weeks that toured as *Hayseed* and opened as *Our Nell*. COVER: letters and designs.

1741 Out of the Bottle (British, 1932). Arthur Riscoe, Frances Day.

Everything But You [B] / Put That Down in Writing [B] / We've Got the Moon and Sixpence [B] / When Things Go Wrong [B] – Clifford Grey[w] & Oscar Levant[m] *(Chappell)*. A fantasy about a genie in a bottle with spectacular scenic effects but nothing else. It had a run of three months. COVER: letters and designs.

1742 Out of This World (Broadway, 1950). Charlotte Greenwood, David Burns.

Cherry Pies Ought to Be You / Climb Up the Mountain / From This Moment On / Hark to the Song of the Night / I Am Loved / No Lover / Nobody's Chasing Me / Oh, It Must Be Fun [VS] [CUT] / Use Your Imagination

/ What Do You Think About Men? [PC] / Where, Oh Where / You Don't Remind Me — Cole Porter^{w/m} *(Chappell)*. A Cole Porter flop that ran for only 20 weeks. This was a lavish production with some good and clever Porter songs but a terrible book and some uneven singing voices. COVER: a face of stars and a big eye.

1743 Out There (Broadway, 1918). Laurette Taylor, George Arliss.

I Want to Go Home — Gitz Rice^{w/m} *(Feist)*. A limited run play — with outstanding actors — produced to raise money for the Red Cross. COVER: Laurette Taylor.

1744 The Outrageous Mrs. Palmer (Broadway, 1920). Ray Hackett, Mary Young.

Boy of My Dreams — A. McDermott^{w/m} & A. Comstock^{w/m} *(Harms)*. A comedy-drama with one song. COVER: Mary Young.

1745 Over Here! (Broadway, 1974). Maxene Andrews, Patty Andrews.

The Big Beat [VS] / Buy a Victory Bond [VS] / Charlie's Place [VS] / Don't Shoot the Hooey to Me, Louie! [VS] / Dream Drummin' [VS] / The Good-Time Girl [VS] / The Grass Grows Green [VS] / Hey, Yvette! [VS] / My Dream for Tomorrow [VS] / No Goodbyes / Over Here! [VS] / Since You're Not Around [VS] / Soft Music [VS] / Wait for Me, Marlena [VS] / Wartime Wedding [VS] / We Got It [VS] / Where Did the Good Times Go? — Richard Sherman^{w/m} & Robert Sherman^{w/m} *(New York Times)*. A musical about wartime entertainers that recaptured some of the spirit of the '40s. It had a lavish setting, good dancing but a poor score and ran for one year. COVER: a patriotic cover with dancers and musicians.

1746 The Overseas Revue (aka **Toot Sweet**) (Broadway, 1919). Elizabeth Brice, Will Morrissey.

America's Answer / Blighty Bound / Charge of the Song Brigade / Elephant Skid / Eyes of the Army / Give Him Back His Job / Just 'Round the Corner / Keep Your Eye on Little Mary Brown / Madelon / Rose of Verdun / Salvation Sal / Toot Suite — Raymond Egan^w & Richard Whiting^m *(Remick)*. The first complete Broadway score of Richard Whiting's. The songs were war oriented and only passable. This show toured as *The Overseas Revue* and opened on Broadway as *Toot Sweet*. It ran only five weeks. COVER: dancing girl in brief costume.

1747 The Overtons (Broadway, 1945). June Knight, Arlene Francis.

Two Hearts in Danger — Archie Gottler^w & Jerome Gottler^m *(Shapiro, Bernstein)*. A comedy with one song and a run of six months. COVER: June Knight.

1748 Pacific 1860 (British, 1946). Mary Martin, Graham Payn.

Bright Was the Day [B] / His Excellency Regrets [B] / I Saw No Shadow [B] / One, Two, Three [B] / Pacific 1860 — complete vocal score [B] / This Is a Changing World [B] / Uncle Harry [B] — Noel Coward^{w/m} *(Chappell)*. A South Pacific romance that was given a beautiful production and included some of the best and worst of Noel Coward songs. It ran for three months. COVER: sketch of a lady and map of an island.

1749 Pacific Overtures (Broadway, 1976). Yuki Shimoda, Mako.

Pacific Overtures — complete vocal score / Pretty Lady [VS] — Stephen Sondheim^{w/m} *(Revelation)*. The early invasion of Japan by Americans was the subject of this musical which was an artistic success but a financial failure. It ran for six months. COVER: red, white, and blue flag and Japanese actor.

1750 Padlocks of 1927 (Broadway, 1927). Jay Flippen, Texas Guinan.

Brass Button Blues / Here I Am / Hot Heels / It's Tough to Be a Hostess / Let's Make Whoopee / Stupid Melody — Billy Rose^w & Ballard MacDonald^w & Lee David^m *(Shapiro, Bernstein)*; I Haven't Got You / Say It with a Red, Red Rose — Billy Rose^w &

Jesse Greer[m] *(Robbins)*; If I Had a Lover — Billy Rose[w] & Ballard MacDonald[w] & Henry Tobias[m] *(Shapiro, Bernstein)*; The Tap Tap / Tell Her in the Summertime / Texas and Barnum and Cohan / Tom Tom Days — Billy Rose[w] & Ballard MacDonald[w] & Jesse Greer[m] *(Shapiro, Bernstein)*. A revue which poked fun at the Wales Padlock Act. It was kept running for three months by the antics of Texas Guinan. COVER: Texas Guinan and padlock on door.

1751 Padlocks of 1929 (Broadway, 1929). Harry Shannon and His Orchestra.

For You, Baby / Wake Up Your Feet / When I Dream — Mack Gordon[w/m] & George Wiest[w/m] *(Shapiro, Bernstein)*. A follow-up to the 1927 revue that folded quickly. COVER: dancing chorus girls.

1752 Page Miss Glory (Broadway, 1934). Dorothy Hall, James Stewart.

Dawn — Paul F. Webster[w] & Lew Pollack[m] *(Crawford)*. A short lived comedy about a beauty contest. COVER: Dorothy Hall.

1753 Page Miss Venus (closed before Broadway, 1921). Stars unknown.

Any Time [ABQ] / Fireside Dreams / Lost Paradise [ABQ] / Love Makes the World Go Round [ABQ] / Page Miss Venus [ABQ] Polka Dot [ABQ] / Tell Us the Story of Love / Won't You Be My Little Kewpie [ABQ] — Leon De Costa[w/m] *(Marks)*. COVER: girl in evening gown with beautiful peacock.

1754 Page Mr. Cupid (closed before Broadway, 1920). Stars unknown.

I Can't Do This and I Can't Do That / A Little Wigwam for Two / Love Is an Old-Fashioned Feeling / My Little Dancing Heart / Page Mister Cupid / There Is Life in the Old Boy Yet / Why Didn't I Meet You Long Ago — Blanche Merrill[w] & Jean Schwartz[m] *(Remick)*. COVER: a girl, a page, and a cupid.

1755 Paging Danger (Broadway, 1931). Dolores DeMonde, Eric Dressler.

Paging Danger — Claire Carvalho[w] & Mort Barrett[m] *(Miller)*. A quick flop

involving Russian royalty as servants. COVER: designs and letters.

1756 Paint Your Wagon (New York) (Broadway, 1951). James Barton, Olga San Juan.

Another Autumn / Carino Mio / I Still See Elisa / I Talk to the Trees / I'm on My Way / Paint Your Wagon — complete vocal score / They Call the Wind Maria / Wand'rin' Star — Alan Jay Lerner[w] & Frederick Loewe[m] *(Chappell)*. A Gold Rush musical with some good songs but a dull book. It ran for nine months. COVER: the second edition of this show lists seven songs and the three star names.

1757 Paint Your Wagon (Philadelphia) (Broadway, 1951). James Barton, Olga San Juan.

Carino Mio / I Still See Elisa / I Talk to the Trees / Sh! / They Call the Wind Maria — Alan Jay Lerner[w] & Frederick Loewe[m] *(Chappell)*. COVER: the first edition cover of this show lists five songs but does not list the stars.

1758 Pair o' Fools (closed before Broadway, 1926). Max Dill, S. William Kolb.

Come to Me Tonight / Dreamland Faces / First Time You Kissed Me / Let's Sow a Wild Oat / No One Else / Tell Me Little Star / When You Smile — Byron Gay[w/m] *(Sherman Clay)*; Hello, Hello, Sandy / Honky Tonky Toddle / In a Taxi Cab / Isn't It Strange / Keepin' Out of Trouble / Tell Me That You Love Me — Arthur Freed[w/m] *(Sherman Clay)*. This musical opened in San Francisco with two big comedians and then played Chicago where it folded. COVER: stars and designs with Freed's music in gold cover and Gay's music in orange cover.

1759 The Pajama Game (Broadway, 1954). John Raitt, Janis Paige.

Hernando's Hideaway / Hey There / I'm Not at All in Love / A New Town Is a Blue Town [PC] / The Pajama Game — complete vocal score / Small Talk / Steam Heat / There Once Was a Man — Richard Adler[w/m] & Jerry Ross[w/m] *(Frank)*. This musical covered life and love in a pajama factory. It had wonderful choreography and a bunch of hit songs and ran for two and one half years. COVER: girl in extra large pajamas.

1760 The Pajama Game (Broadway, 1973). Hal Linden, Barbara McNair.

Hernando's Hideaway / Once-a-Year Day (polka) / Pajama Game — selections (1973) seven songs — Richard Adler[w/m] & Jerry Ross[w/m] *(Frank)*. A poor revival of this hit musical that lasted for only two months. COVER: boy, girl, and pajamas.

1761 The Pajama Lady (closed before Broadway, 1930). Lester Allen, John Barker.

Down Through the Ages / One, Two, Three / Three Guesses — John Mercer[w] & Phil Charig[m] & Richard Myers[m] *(Harms)*; Let's Suppose — Robert Smith[w] & Phil Charig[m] & Richard Myers[m] *(Harms)*. COVER: girl in evening gown on deck of ship.

1762 Pal Joey (Broadway, 1940). Gene Kelly, Vivienne Segal.

Bewitched / Den of Iniquity [VS] / Do It the Hard Way / I Could Write a Book / Pal Joey — complete vocal score / Plant You Now, Dig You Later / You Mustn't Kick It Around — Lorenz Hart[w] & Richard Rodgers[m] *(Chappell)*. A musical about a gigolo that was considered "a foul well" in 1940. It had two great leading actors and a bunch of hit songs. This production ran for one year. COVER: a sidewalk canopy of a New York apartment building.

1763 Pal Joey (Broadway, 1950). Harold Lang, Vivienne Segal.

Bewitched / Do It the Hard Way / Happy Hunting Horn / I Could Write a Book / Plant You Now, Dig You Later / Take Him / You Mustn't Kick It Around / What Is a Man? — Lorenz Hart[w] & Richard Rodgers[m] *(Chappell)*. A successful revival that now got good reviews. The original star returned with a new Joey. The show ran for 18 months which was longer than the original. COVER: lady with orchids and gigolo with dollars.

1764 The Palais Revue of 1920 (Nightclub, 1920). Stars unknown.

Lady Fortune / Thousand and One Nights — Andre Sherri[w] & A. Baldwin Sloane[m] *(Witmark)*. COVER: a girl with a wild head-dress plus two lamps.

1765 Palladium Frolics (Nightclub, 1936). Stars unknown.

The Beat of Feet in the Street / Put Down an Empty Glass / The Wotcha-Ma-Callit — Mitchell Parish[w] & Lou Leaman[m] *(Mills)*; Love Is a Ripple on the Water — Mitchell Parish[w] & Harry Carroll[m] *(Mills)*. COVER: silhouette of band leader and musicians.

1766 Panama Hattie (Broadway, 1940). Ethel Merman, James Dunn.

All I've Got to Get Now Is My Man / Fresh as a Daisy / I'm Throwing a Ball Tonight [VS] / I've Still Got My Health / Let's Be Buddies / Make It Another Old-fashioned, Please / My Mother Would Love You / Visit Panama / Who Would Have Dreamed? — Cole Porter[w/m] *(Chappell)*. A bar girl trying to make society was the subject of this Cole Porter hit. It contained one hit song and ran for a year only because of the great Merman. COVER: palm trees and water.

1767 Pan-American Casino Revue (Nightcub, 1937). Stars unknown.

Bluebonnet / Don't You Know or Don't You Care — Irving Kahal[w] & Sammy Fain[m] *(Feist)*. COVER: girl with sombrero.

1768 Papierene Kinder (Jewish, 1936). Chaim Tauber.

Mein Shteitale Moliff — Chaim Tauber[w] & Manny Fleischman[m] *(Kammen)*; Papierene Kinder — Morris Rund[w] & David Meyerowitz[m] *(Kammen)*. A musical from the Bronx. COVER: Chaim Tauber.

1769 Parade (Broadway, 1935). Jimmy Savo, Eve Arden.

Life Could Be So Beautiful / You Ain't So Hot — Paul Peters[w] & George Sklar[w] & Jerome Moross[m] *(Harms)*. A very leftist political musical that lasted only five weeks. COVER: a parade of dolls.

1770 Parade (Off Broadway, 1960). Dody Goodman, Charles Nelson Reilly.

Next Time I Love / Show Tune in 2/4 / There's No Tune Like a Show Tune / Wonderful World of the Two-a-Day / Your Good Morning / Your Hand in Mine — Jerry Herman^{w/m} *(Morris)*. A revue that ran for three months. COVER: balloons.

1771 Paradise Alley (closed before Broadway, 1922). Stars unknown.

Always Look for a Rainbow — Howard Johnson^w & Carle Carlton^m *(Feist)*; Any Old Alley Is Paradise Alley / Bonnie [ABQ] / Come Down to Argentine [ABQ] / Happiness [ABQ] / If We Could Live on Promises [ABQ] / I'm Only Human, That's All [ABQ] / In This Automatical World [ABQ] / What You Could Be If You Had Me [ABQ] / When I Made the Grade with O'Grady [ABQ] / Your Way or My Way [ABQ] — Howard Johnson^w & Harry Archer^m & Carle Carlton^m *(Feist)*. This musical folded on the road in 1922. It was revised and opened on Broadway in 1924. COVER: a wonderful cartoon of a couple dancing on sidewalk with trash cans, etc.

1772 Paradise Alley (Broadway, 1924). Helen Shipman, Charles Derickson.

As Long as They Keep On Makin' 'Em [ABQ] / The Bobbed Hair Bandit [ABQ] / The First Nighters [ABQ] / Friendship / Happiness [ABQ] / Musical Comedy Show [ABQ] / Paradise Alley / Promises [ABQ] / Success [ABQ] / Rolland from Holland [ABQ] / What the Future Holds for Me [ABQ] / When I Made the Grade [ABQ] — Howard Johnson^w & Harry Archer^m & Carle Carlton^m *(Feist)*; Chimes — Howard Johnson^w & Harry Archer^m *(Feist)*; Put On the Ritz — Howard Johnson^w & Irving Bibo^m *(Feist)*; Tell Me Truly — Howard Johnson^w & Carle Carlton^m *(Feist)*. A revised edition of the 1922 failure, a rags-to-riches story that lasted eight weeks. COVER: a girl in a dancing pose.

1773 Paradise Island (Regional, 1961). William Gaxton, Arthur Treacher.

Beyond the Clouds / The Coconut Wireless / It's a Great Day for Hawaii / Never Any Time to Play / Paradise Island — Carmen Lombardo^{w/m} & John Jacob Loeb^{w/m} *(Keys-Hansen)*. A summer musical produced by Guy Lombardo at the Jones Beach theatre. COVER: tropical hut, girls and drums.

1774 Paradise Parade (5th edition) (Nightclub, 1935). Stars unknown.

Hand in Hand in Heaven / Tambourine Jamboree / We're Off to a Wonderful Start — Milton Drake^w & Ben Oakland^m *(Harms)*. COVER: silhouettes of dancers.

1775 Paradise Parade of 1935 (Nightclub, 1935). Stars unknown.

Bells of Monterey / Prayin' in Rhythm / Wearing My Heart on My Sleeve — Ned Washington^w & Sam Stept^m *(Mills)*. COVER: a naked dancer.

1776 Paradise Parade of 1936 (Nightclub, 1936). Stars unknown.

Avenue of Trees / From the Circle to the Square — Milton Drake^w & Ben Oakland^m *(Harms)*. COVER: two girls in evening gowns dancing.

1777 Paradise Revue (Nightclub, 1933). Stars unknown.

I've Got to Pass Your House to Get to My House — Lew Brown^{w/m} *(D B and H)*. COVER: a row of dancing girls.

1778 Paradise Revue (Prevue also called **Venus in Paradise**) (Nightclub, 1939). Richard Himber and orchestra.

Bimini Bounce / It's Getting Fair and Warmer / Love's the Thing That Makes the World Go Round / Manhattan Merry Go Round / Tails, Top-Hat, and You — Charles Barnes^w & Marjery Fielding^m *(Mills)*. COVER: Richard Himber.

1779 Paradise Revue of 1938 (Nightclub, 1938). Stars unknown.

Swingin' with the Wind / Things They Do in Hollywood — Dave Oppenheim^{w/m} & Henry Tobias^{w/m} *(Exclusive)*; You Walked Out of the Picture — Little Jack Little^{w/m} & Dave

Oppenheim[w/m] & Henry Tobias[w/m] *(Exclusive)*. COVER: a girl's leg with high heel.

1780 Paradise Revue of 1939 (Nightclub, 1939). Russ Morgan and orchestra.

Angelita / Blue Night / I Can't Say It Too Many Times / The Jitteroo — Teddy Powell[w/m] & Leonard Whitcup[w/m] *(Exclusive)*. COVER: Russ Morgan.

1781 Pardon Me (closed before Broadway, 1927). Stars unknown.

Catch a Hunk o' Rhythm / Dreaming My Life Away / Giving the Devil His Due — Morrie Ryskind[w] & Charles Rosoff[m] *(Harms)*; Pardon Me — Ralph Murphy[w] & Harold Lewis[m] *(Harms)*; Sophisticated Baby / What About You and Me — Morrie Ryskind[w] & Harold Lewis[m] *(Harms)*. COVER: a couple in elegant clothes, a big car, and a chauffeur.

1782 Pardon My English (Broadway, 1933). Jack Pearl, Lyda Roberti.

Isn't It a Pity? / I've Got to Be There / The Lorelei / The Luckiest Man in the World / My Cousin in Milwaukee / So What? / Where You Go, I Go — Ira Gershwin[w] & George Gershwin[m] *(New World)*; Two Waltzes in C (Tonight) [VS] — George Gershwin[m] *(New World)*. A musical set in Germany that was troubled from the beginning. It was a disaster except for some great Gershwin songs and it lasted only five weeks. COVER: cartoon of man and woman.

1783 Pardon Our French (Broadway, 1950). Olsen and Johnson.

A Face in the Crowd / I Oughta Know More About You / I'm Gonna Make a Fool Out of April / There's No Man Like a Snowman — Edward Heyman[w] & Victor Young[m] *(Morris)*. This musical started out as a small revue in California titled *A La Carte*. It took over the songs and actors and added Olsen and Johnson, whose day was past. It ran three months. COVER: Olsen and Johnson, Eiffel Tower, and girl in a brief costume.

1784 Paris (Broadway, 1928). Irene Bordoni, Louise Hale.

An' Furthermore / Wob-a-Ly Walk — Bud Green[w] & Harry Warren[m] *(Shapiro, Bernstein)*; Don't Look at Me That Way / The Heaven Hop / The Land of Going to Be / Let's Do It / Let's Misbehave / Quelque-Chose / Two Little Babes in the Wood / Vivienne / Which? — Cole Porter[w/m] *(Harms)*. An intimate musical with Bordoni chasing her man. It had witty songs and a run of six months. COVER: Irene Bordoni.

1785 Paris in Spring (closed before Broadway, 1930). Stars unknown.

Don't Ask Too Much of Love / The Moon Shines Down / Until We Kiss — John Mercer[w] & Emmerich Kalman[m] *(Harms)*; What Have I Done? — Fritz Rotter[w] & Desmond Carter[w] & Walter Jurman[m] *(Harms)*. COVER: a tree branch and blossoms.

1786 Paris '90 (Broadway, 1952). Cornelia Otis Skinner.

Calliope / The Waltz I Heard in a Dream — Kay Swift[w/m] *(Chappell)*. A one woman show with Skinner playing many different characters. It ran three months. COVER: Cornelia Otis Skinner.

1787 Paris Toujours (Moulin Rouge) (Nightclub, 1956). Stars unknown.

Awaken, My Lonely One / The Day the Blues Began — Pony Sherrell[w/m] & Phil Moody[w/m] *(American Academy)*. COVER: the Eiffel Tower and can-can dancers.

1788 Park Avenue (Broadway, 1946). Leonora Corbett, Arthur Margretson.

Don't Be a Woman If You Can [VS] / For the Life of Me / Goodbye to All That / Land of Opportunities [PC] / There's No Holding Me — Ira Gershwin[w] & Arthur Schwartz[m] *(Harms.)* A musical about a socialite and her affairs. It had a poor book, poor music and lasted only nine weeks. It was Ira Gershwin's last Broadway show! COVER: lady walking a dog on Park Avenue.

1789 A Party with Comden and Green (Broadway, 1977). Betty Comden, Adolf Green.

Catch Our Act at the Met [VS] / Dance Only with Me [VS] / If You Hadn't But You Did [VS] / Just in Time [VS] / The Party's Over [VS] — Betty Comden^w & Adolph Green^w & Jule Styne^m *(Stratford)*; French Lesson [VS] — Betty Comden^w/m & Adolph Green^w/m & Roger Edens^w/m *(Stratford)*; I Said Good Morning [VS] — Betty Comden^w & Adolph Green^w & Andre Previn^m *(Stratford)*. A revue of Comden and Green songs by the authors. It was previously done on Broadway in 1958. COVER: Comden and Green.

1790 Passing Parade of 1922 (Nightclub, 1922). Stars unknown.

Mystic Night / Pretty Butterfly / Those Cadets on Parade / Vanity / Where the Sweet Tulips Grow — Ted Koehler^w/m & Frank Magine^w/m *(Marigold)*. COVER: two beautiful peacocks.

1791 The Passing Show of 1918 (Broadway, 1918). Fred and Adele Astaire.

Baby — Gus Kahn^w & Egbert Van Alstyne^m *(Remick)*; Dreaming of a Sweet Tomorrow — Eugene Howard^w & Willie Howard^w & Frank Magine^m & Phil Goldberg^m *(Feist)*; Dress Dress Dress / The Duchess of Devonshire / The Galli-Curci Rag / My Baby-Talk Lady / Squab Farm — Harold Atteridge^w & Sigmund Romberg^m *(Remick)*; Go West Young Girl — Harold Atteridge^w & Russell Tarbox^m *(Remick)*; I Really Can't Make My Feet Behave / Oh You Vampire Girls — Harold Atteridge^w & Jean Schwartz^m & Sigmund Romberg^m *(Remick)*; I'm Forever Blowing Bubbles — Jean Kenbrovin^w & John Kellette^m *(Remick)*; I'm Over Here and You're Over There / Salome / Trombone Jazz — Harold Atteridge^w & Jean Schwartz^m *(Remick)*; Meet Me in Bubble Land — Casper Nathan^w & Joe Manne^w & Isham Jones^m *(Berlin)*; My Holiday Girls — Harold Atteridge^w & Augustus Barratt^m *(Remick)*; On the Level You're a Little Devil — Joe Young^w & Jean Schwartz^m *(Berlin)*; Peachie — Jack Yellen^w & Albert Gumble^m *(Remick)*; Smiles — Will Callahan^w & Lee Roberts^m *(Remick)*; Tell Me — Will Callahan^w & Max Kortlander^m *(Remick)*; That Soothing Serenade — Harry DeCosta^w/m *(Witmark)*; Venetian Moon — Gus Kahn^w & Phil Goldberg^m & Frank Magine^m *(Remick)*; Won't You Buy a War Stamp — Harold Atteridge^w & Ray Perkins^m *(Remick)*. A better than average revue with some jazzy numbers and the Astaires but a run of only four months. COVER: Howard Brothers, Emily Miles; sketch of girl dancing on the moon.

1792 The Passing Show of 1919 (Broadway, 1919). James Barton, Charles Winninger.

Allah, You Know Me, Al — Edgar Leslie^w & Pete Wendling^m & Fred Ahlert^m *(Berlin)*; America's Popular Song / Dreamy Florence / In a Love Boat with You / Kiss Burglar — Harold Atteridge^w & Jean Schwartz^m & Sigmund Romberg^m *(Remick)*; Come On to That Creole Dance — Eugene West^w & Joe Gold^m *(Harris)*; Honolulu Eyes — Howard Johnson^w & Violinsky^m *(Feist)*; It's Always Summertime in the Winter Garden / Orient / Solomon — Alfred Bryan^w & Jean Schwartz^m *(Remick)*; Lovable Moon / Roads of Destiny / Tumble In — Harold Atteridge^w & Jean Schwartz^m *(Remick)*; Molly Malone — Hale Byers^w & Chris Schonberg^m *(Remick)*; My Isle of Golden Dreams — Gus Kahn^w & Walter Blaufuss^m *(Remick)*; So Long, Sing Song — Harold Atteridge^w & Sigmund Romberg^m *(Remick)*; You've Got Mischief in Your Eyes — Benjamin Burt^w/m *(Remick)*. A revue with a lot of girls but nothing else as the Shuberts were very cheap. The music was poor but the chorus girls kept this show running for nine months. COVER: chorus girl sitting on post.

1793 The Passing Show of 1921 (Broadway, 1921). Marie Dressler, Howard Brothers.

Becky from Babylon—Alex Gerber^w & Abner Silver^m *(Witmark)*; Carolina Rolling Stone—Mitchell Parish^w & Eleanor Young^m & Harry Squires^m *(Morris)*; Charm School—Alfred Bryan^w & Jean Schwartz^m *(Remick)*; Dance of the Blues / I'm Oriental / My Lady of the Lamp / Where Is the Beautiful Face—Harold Atteridge^w & Lew Pollack^m *(Remick)*; Dream of My Last Waltz with You—Gus Kahn^w & Charles Drury^m & George Rath^m *(Remick)*; How Is It by You?—Ray Perkins^{w/m} & John Bratton^{w/m} *(Witmark)*; I Was a Soldier—Johnny Burke^{w/m} *(Remick)*; In Little Old New York / Ta-Hoo / When There's No One to Love—Harold Atteridge^w & Jean Schwartz^m *(Remick)*; June Moon—Joe Lyons^w & Frank Magine^m & Charley Straight^m *(Broadway)*; Kentucky Blues—Clarence Gaskill^{w/m} *(Witmark)*; Let's Have a Rattling Good Time—Alfred Bryan^w & Jean Schwartz^m *(Remick)*; Michigan—Alex Gerber^w & Malvin Franklin^m *(Witmark)*; My Sunny Tennessee—Bert Kalmar^{w/m} & Harry Ruby^{w/m} & Herman Ruby^{w/m} *(Mills)*; Nightingale—Harold Atteridge^w & Alfred Bryan^w & Jean Schwartz^m & Lew Pollack^m *(Remick)*; She's the Mother of Broadway Rose—Max Freedman^w & Nelson Ingham^w & Willie Howard^m & George McConnell^m *(Fisher)*; Spanish Love—Willie Howard^{w/m} & Gene Howard^{w/m} & Alex Gerber^{w/m} & Abner Silver^{w/m} *(Witmark)*; The Sweetest Melody—Abner Silver^{w/m} *(Witmark)*; Underneath Hawaiian Skies—Fred Rose^w & Ernie Erdman^m *(Feist)*; Weep No More / When Caruso Comes to Town—Sidney Mitchell^w & Sidney Clare^w & Lew Pollack^m *(Broadway)*; When I Hear Them Play a Dixie Melody—Frank Shubert^{w/m} & Sam Howard^{w/m} *(Empire City)*; Wonderful Kid—Willie Howard^w & Sidney Clare^w & Lew Pollack^m *(Berlin)*. The Shuberts

skipped a passing show in 1920. This edition was just passable but ran six months. COVER: chorus girl on post; Howard Brothers; the Rath Brothers.

1794 The Passing Show of 1922 (Broadway, 1922). Howard Brothers, Fred Allen.

American Jazz / I Came—I Saw—I Fell / Orphans of the Storm / Underneath a Pretty Hat—Harold Atteridge^w & Alfred Goodman^m *(Remick)*; Carolina in the Morning—Gus Kahn^w & Walter Donaldson^m *(Remick)*; Diamond Girl / Radiance—Jack Stanley^w & Alfred Goodman^m *(Remick)*; Do You, Don't You, Will You, Won't You—George Little^{w/m} & Larry Schaetzlein^{w/m} & Willie Howard^{w/m} & Gene Howard^{w/m} *(Remick)*; Georgia Cabin Door—Mitchell Parish^w & Eleanor Young^m & Harry Squires^m *(Morris)*; Got to Cool My Doggies Now—Bob Schafer^{w/m} & Babe Thompson^{w/m} & Spencer Williams^{w/m} *(Williams)*; I Love Me—Jack Hoins^w & Will Mahoney^w & Edwin Weber^m *(Broadway)*; Mississippi Moon—M. Gunsky^w & Nat Goldstein^m *(Goldstein)*; Silver Swanee—Eddie Cantor^w & Jean Schwartz^m *(Remick)*; Sonja—A. Beda^w & Eugene Partos^m *(Marks)*; Ten-Ten-Tennessee—Joe Young^w & Sam Lewis^w & George Meyer^m *(Berlin)*; Wanita—Sam Coslow^{w/m} & Al Sherman^{w/m} *(Stark, Cowan)*. Another ordinary edition, running three months, that was sparked by Fred Allen and *Carolina in the Morning.* COVER: Howard Brothers; sketch of masks and designs.

1795 The Passing Show of 1923 (Broadway, 1923). George Jessel, Phil Baker.

The Ball Begins / Love Lit Eyes—Harold Atteridge^w & Sigmund Romberg^m *(Harms)*; Gaby Doll / Girl at the Rainbow's End—Harold Atteridge^w & Jean Schwartz^m & Sigmund Romberg^m *(Harms)*; Golfing Blues / Jackie Coogan / Kissable Lips / My Dutch Lady—Harold Atteridge^w & Jean Schwartz^m *(Harms)*; Lotus Flower /

Rose of the Morning—Cyrus Wood[w] & Sigmund Romberg[m] *(Harms)*; Nearer and Dearer—Haven Gillespie[w] & Egbert Van Alstyne[m] *(Remick)*. A weak edition with terrible songs and weak comedy that ran three months. COVER: colored blocks and designs.

1796 The Passing Show of 1924 (Broadway, 1924). James Barton, Olga Cook.

A Beaded Bag / Mooching Along—Alex Gerber[w] & Sigmund Romberg[m] & Jean Schwartz[m] *(Harms)*; The Day Will Come—Ted Lewis[w/m] & Ed East[w/m] *(A Y and B)*; Dublinola / When Knighthood Was in Flower—Harold Atteridge[w] & Jean Schwartz[m] & Sigmund Romberg[m] *(Harms)*; Hoo's Little Who Is Oo—Alex Gerber[w] & Jean Schwartz[m] *(Harms)*; If You Knew Susie—B.G. DeSylva[w/m] *(Shapiro, Bernstein)*. A very poor and very cheap edition produced by the Shuberts. It ran three months and was the last production in this series by the Shuberts. COVER: Ted Lewis; colored blocks and designs.

1797 The Passion Flower (Broadway, 1920). Nance O'Neil, Edna Walton.

The Passion Flower—Irving Berlin[w/m] *(Berlin)*. A melodrama of love and murder that ran for five months. COVER: Nance O'Neil.

1798 Patsy (closed before Broadway, 1926). Stars unknown.

The Bally Baloo / If I Were King / Peculiar Tune / Strolling the Avenue / What Can a Poor Girl Do?—Clifford Grey[w] & Magnus Ingleton[w] & I.B. Kornblum[m] *(Harms)*. COVER: flowers and designs.

1799 Paulette (British, 1931). Mireille Perrey, Paul England.

Don't Tell a Soul—Harry Pepper[w/m] *(Mills)*. This musical was a bomb in London lasting two weeks. COVER: blue designs and letters.

1800 Peace (Off Broadway, 1969). Essie Borden, Julie Kurnitz.

America the Beautiful [VS]—Kathleen Lee Bates[w] & Al Carmines[m] *(Chappell)*; Just Sit Around [VS] / Peace Anthem [VS] / Summer's Nice [VS] / Things Starting to Grow Again [VS] / Up in Heaven [VS]—Tim Reynolds[w] & Al Carmines[m] *(Chappell)*. A minstrel musical taking place on Earth and in Heaven. It ran six months. COVER: a big "Peace" sign leading to the clouds.

1801 Peaches (closed before Broadway, 1923). Stars unknown.

Ev'ry Heart Has a Dream / I Wish I Could Believe You / Insignificant Me / Listen Mister Verdi / Passers By / Ring for Rosy / Wake Me Up with a Kiss—Robert Smith[w] & Max Steiner[m] *(Harms)*. COVER: a peach, branch, and leaves.

1802 Peek-a-Boo (of 1921) (closed before Broadway, 1921). Bobby Clark, Paul McCullough.

Cuddle [ABQ] / Cuttin' Up Critter [ABQ] / Every Trouble Is Like a Bubble [ABQ] / Hitch Your Wagon to a Star / I Want a Syncopated Wedding [ABQ] / In the Days of Peek-a-Boo [ABQ] / The Life of the Party [ABQ] / My Melody Dream Girl / Ornamental Oriental Land [ABQ] / Try a Manicure [ABQ]—P.D. Cook[w] & Harry Archer[m] *(Feist)*. COVER: girl in clown outfit with a cupid.

1803 Peek-a-Boo (of 1924) (Nightclub, 1924). Billy Carola.

Sweet California—Jack Lauria[w] & Vic Lauria[m] *(Marks)*. COVER: Billy Carola.

1804 Peg (Broadway, 1983). Peggy Lee.

One Beating a Day—Peggy Lee[w/m] *(Notable)*. A very dull one woman show of the life and music of Peggy Lee. It lasted five performances. COVER: Peggy Lee.

1805 Peg (Peg o' My Heart) (closed before Broadway, 1984). Ann Morrison, George Ede.

Manhattan Hometown [VS] [B] / When a Woman Has to Choose [VS] [B]—David Heneker[w/m] *(Chappell)*; Peg o' My Heart [VS] [B]—Alfred Bryan[w] & Fred Fisher[m] *(Chappell)*. This musical was panned in London in 1984 where it ran four months. This revised version played a limited engagement in New Hampshire with the hope of going to Broadway. COVER: a girl on a swing.

1806 Peg o' My Dreams (Broadway, 1924). Chester Hale, Suzanne Keener.

Love's Young Dream / Peg o' My Dreams / A Rainbow Waiting for You — Anne Caldwell[w] & Hugo Felix[m] *(Harms)*. A poor musical version of *Peg o' My Heart* that lasted for one month. COVER: a dog with a big bow, a suitcase, and an umbrella.

1807 Peggy (closed before Broadway, 1921). Skeets Gallagher, Russell Mack.

The Dream Boat / The Kiss Trot / Peggy o' Mine / Wonderful Hindoo — Fred Caryll[w] & Lou Dymond[m] *(Shapiro, Bernstein)*. COVER: a lady with a rose sitting in a large hat box.

1808 Peggy-Ann (Broadway, 1926). Helen Ford, Edith Meiser.

A Little Birdie Told Me So / Maybe It's Me / A Tree in the Park / Where's That Rainbow — Lorenz Hart[w] & Richard Rodgers[m] *(Harms)*; Chuck It! — piano selections / Havana — piano selections — Richard Rodgers[m] *(Harms)*. A musical involving dream psychology with a pleasant score and a run of nine months on Broadway. COVER: letters and designs.

1809 Peggy-Ann (British, 1927). Dorothy Dickson.

The Country Mouse [B] — Desmond Carter[w] & Richard Rodgers[m] *(Harms)*; Give That Little Girl a Hand [B] [PC] / Hello! [B] / Howdy to Broadway [B] [PC] — Lorenz Hart[w] & Richard Rodgers[m] *(Harms)*. A very poor version in London of the American hit that lasted only three months. COVER: letters and designs.

1810 Penny Plain (British, 1951). Laurier Lister.

Janette [RC] — Hugh Martin[w/m] *(Chappell)*. A hit revue with contributions by many composers. It ran for over a year. COVER: none.

1811 Perfect Fishel (Jewish, 1936). Menashe Skulnik.

Dos Zelbe Fun Dir Tzu Hern — Isidor Lillien[w] & Joseph Rumshinsky[m] *(Metro)*. COVER: Skulnik and Rumshinsky.

1812 The Perfect Fool (Broadway, 1921). Ed Wynn, Janet Velie.

Daisy / Girls, Pretty Girls / Old Home Week in Maine / She Loves Me, She Loves Me Not / Typewriter Song / Visions That Pass in the Night — Ed Wynn[w/m] *(Harms)*; A Doll House — Ed Wynn[w/m] & Harry Richman[w/m] & Lou Davis[w/m] *(Harms)*; My Log-Cabin Home — Irving Caesar[w] & B.G. DeSylva[w] & George Gershwin[m] *(Harms)*; No One Else But That Girl of Mine — Irving Caesar[w] & George Gershwin[m] *(Harms)*; Stealing — Ed Wynn[w/m] *(Feist)*; Sweetheart, Will You Answer Yes? — Al Wilson[w/m] & James Brennan[w/m] & Rolf Piquet[w/m] *(Marks)*. A revue with the crazy Ed Wynn that ran for almost nine months. COVER: flowers and designs.

1813 A Perfect Lady (*see also* **Sweet Little Devil**) (Broadway, 1924). Constance Binney, Marjorie Gateson.

Hey! Hey! Let 'er Go! / The Jijibo / Mah-Jongg / Pepita / Someone Believes in You / Under a One-Man Top / Virginia, Don't Go Too Far! — B.G. DeSylva[w] & George Gershwin[m] *(Harms)*. The story of a gold-digger and a good girl with some interesting Gershwin songs that have been forgotten. It had a run of 15 weeks and the try-out title was *A Perfect Lady*. COVER: flowers and designs.

1814 The Perfect Marriage (Broadway, 1932). George Gaul, Edith Barrett.

There's Always Tomorrow — Arthur Goodrich[w/m] *(Harms)*. A drama about a golden wedding and memories of married life. It was a flop of one week. COVER: sketch of a man's and woman's face.

1815 Perfect '36 (Nightclub, 1936). Stars unknown.

Are You Thrilling / Beating the Goombay / Boy Meets Girl / Give Me a Martial Air / I'm Clay in Your Hands / The Wiggly-Woggly-Walk / With a Dollar in Your Pocket / You're a

Standout — Allan Roberts[w] & Jules Loman[w] & Francis Shuman[m] *(Mills)*. COVER: a naked dancer.

1816 La Perichole (Broadway, 1956). Stars unknown.

The Letter Song / A Spaniard Knows — Maurice Valency[w] & Jacques Offenbach[m] *(Boosey, Hawkes)*. A new up-dated version of the Offenbach operetta performed at the Metropolitan Opera. COVER: a lady in peasant outfit.

1817 Personal Appearance (Broadway, 1934). Gladys George, Phil Sheridan.

April Woman — Laurence Harris[w/m] *(Harms)*. A comedy about a famous movie star on a personal appearance tour. It ran nine months. COVER: sketch of red-headed woman with flowers.

1818 Peter Pan (Broadway, 1924). Marilyn Miller, Leslie Banks.

Peter Pan, I Love You — Robert King[w/m] & Ray Henderson[w/m] *(Shapiro, Bernstein)*; The Sweetest Thing in Life — B.G. DeSylva[w] & Jerome Kern[m] *(Harms)*. This version of *Peter Pan* ran for three months. COVER: Marilyn Miller as Peter Pan.

1819 Peter Pan (Broadway, 1950). Jean Arthur, Boris Karloff.

My House / Never-Land / Peter, Peter / Pirate Song — choral arrangement / Plank Round — choral arrangement / Who Am I? — Leonard Bernstein[w/m] *(Schirmer)*. Jean Arthur was Peter Pan in this play with music. It ran nine months. COVER: sketches of all the characters in *Peter Pan*.

1820 Peter Pan (Broadway, 1954). Mary Martin, Cyril Ritchard.

Captain Hook's Waltz / Distant Melody / Never Never Land / Wendy — Betty Comden[w] & Adolph Green[w] & Jule Styne[m] *(Morris)*; I Won't Grow Up / I'm Flying / I've Gotta Crow / Tender Shepherd — Carolyn Leigh[w] & Mark Charlap[m] *(Morris)*. This version had a run of four months and a showing on TV. COVER: Mary Martin.

1821 Peter Pan (British, 1960). Jacqueline DeBief.

Never Never Land [B] — Betty Comden, Adolf Green[w] & Jule Styne[m] *(Morris)*. This production was performed on ice in England. COVER: a sketch of Peter Pan and Wendy.

1822 Peter Pan (Regional, 1974). Stars unknown.

Hook's Hook / Peter Pan — selections (1974) — vocal selections of ten songs / Youth, Joy and Freedom — Tom Adair[w/m] & Jule Styne[w/m] *(Morris)*. A touring production by NBC using the 1954 version with some new songs. COVER: a sketch of Peter Pan and Tinker Bell.

1823 Peter Pan (Broadway, 1979). Sandy Duncan, George Rose.

I Won't Grow Up — Carolyn Leigh[w] & Mark Charlap[m] *(Morris)*; Never Never Land — Betty Comden[w] & Adolf Green[w] & Jule Styne[m] *(Morris)*; Peter Pan — vocal selections of eight songs (1979) — Carolyn Leigh[w] & Betty Comden[w] & Adolf Green[w] & Mark Charlap[m] & Jule Styne[m] *(Morris)*. This production with Sandy Duncan ran for 18 months. COVER: Sandy Duncan.

1824 Peter Pan (British, 1982). Stars unknown.

Peter's First Tune [B] [VS] / Peter's Second Tune [B] [VS] / Mrs. Darling's Lullaby [B] [VS] — Stephen Oliver[w/m] *(Novello)*. A production of the Royal Shakespeare Company in London in 1982 with a limited run. COVER: sketch of Peter Pan.

1825 Petticoat Fever (Broadway, 1935). Dennis King, Oscar Shaw.

Love Tiptoed Through My Heart — Irene Alexander[w] & Frederick Loewe[m] *(Harms)*; Something to Remember — Billy Hill[w] & Karl Vacek[m] *(Shapiro, Bernstein)*. *A farce set in Labrador starring Dennis King who was replaced by Oscar Shaw. It had a run of four months.* COVER 1: a heart and designs. COVER 2: Oscar Shaw and Eskimos.

1826 PFC Mary Brown (Army Show, 1944). Soldiers.

First Class Private Mary Brown /

The WAC Hymn—Frank Loesser[w/m] *(Famous)*; PFC Mary Brown—vocal selections—Frank Loesser[w/m] *(Army Script)*. A WAC show that toured camps during the war. COVER: titles only.

1827 Phantom of the Opera (Broadway, 1925). Stars unknown.

If You Would Believe in Me—George Bennett[w] & Jack Glogau[m] *(Moss)*. This is listed as a production at B.S. Moss Colony Theatre in New York. COVER: theatre marquee surrounded by the audience waiting to enter.

1828 Phantom of the Opera (Broadway, 1988). Sarah Brightman, Michael Crawford.

All I Ask of You / The Music of the Night [B]—Charles Hart[w] & Richard Stilgoe[w] & Andrew L. Webber[m] *(Really Useful)*; Angel of Music [VS] / Masquerade [VS] / The Point of No Return [VS] / Prima Donna [VS] / Think of Me [VS] / Wishing You Were Somehow Here Again [VS]—Charles Hart[w] & Richard Stilgoe[w] & Andrew L. Webber[m] *(Leonard)*; The Phantom of the Opera [B]—Mike Batt[w] & Richard Stilgoe[w] & Andrew L. Webber[m] *(Really Useful)*. This super-hit with a lavish setting and dramatic songs has been running in major cities for more than five years and shows no signs of stopping. COVER: Michael Crawford, Sarah Brightman, and a mask and rose.

1829 Phantom of the Opera (closed before Broadway, 1992). Stars unknown.

Home [VS] / Melodie de Paris [VS] / My True Love [VS] / This Place Is Mine [VS] / You Are Music [VS] / You Are My Own [VS]—Maury Yeston[w/m] *(Cherry Lane)*. A new version of the *Phantom* that has had several regional try-outs. COVER: the Phantom as the base of a candlestick holder, with a girl in the flame.

1830 Phi Phi (British, 1922). Clifton Webb, Evelyn Laye.

The Ragtime Pipes of Pan [B]—Cole Porter[w/m] *(Chappell)*. A poor revue that ran for four months in London. COVER: a Greek warrior and his lady.

1831 Philemon (Off Broadway, 1975). Dick Latessa, Leila Martin.

The Greatest of These [VS] / I Love His Face [VS]—Tom Jones[w] & Harvey Schmidt[m] *(Leonard)*. A musical set in ancient Rome with Christians and Romans fighting. It was a heavy musical that has had numerous regional and little theatre productions but never on Broadway. COVER: Jones and Schmidt.

1832 Phinney's Rainbow (College, 1948). Students.

How Do I Know? / Phinney's Rainbow / Still Got My Heart—Stephen Sondheim[w/m] *(BMI)*. The first published music of Sondheim's for his college show. COVER: a rainbow line and letters.

1833 Phoebe of Quality Street (Broadway, 1921). Shaun Glenville, Dorothy Ward.

The Autumn Sun / Dawn Grows to Morning / Dream of Joy / Oh, Let Us Be Merry / Paddy Dear, Oh Stop Your Teasin' / Promise of the Rainbow / Waltzing Is Spreading from Land to Land—Edward Dunn[w] & Walter Kollo[m] *(Tama)*. A terrible version of the Barrie classic that lasted two weeks. COVER: flowers and designs.

1834 Phoenix '55 (Off Broadway, 1955). Nancy Walker, Joshua Shelley.

All Around the World / A Funny Heart / Never Wait for Love—David Craig[w] & David Baker[m] *(Chappell)*. A small revue which ran for three months due to Nancy Walker. COVER: the Phoenix symbol.

1835 Pickings (Harry Carroll) (Regional, 1925). Stars unknown.

Chop Sticks / In Our Orange Grove / Locker of Davey Jones / Mission Bells / Oriental Pearl / Pretty Pickings / Rosie Posie's—Ballard MacDonald[w] & Harry Carroll[m] & Arthur Freed[m] *(Sherman Clay)*; Hay Foot Straw Foot / Hot Steps / I'm a Pickford That Nobody Picked—Ballard MacDonald[w] & Harry Carroll[m] *(Sherman Clay)*. A musical presented at Arthur Freed's Orange Grove Theatre for a limited run. COVER: a dancing girl on stage.

1836 Pickwick (Broadway, 1965). Harry Secombe, Charlotte Rae.

If I Ruled the World / There's Something About You — Leslie Bricusse[w] & Cyril Ornadel[m] *(Chappell)*; I'll Never Be Lonely Again — Leslie Bricusse[w/m] *(Chappell)*. This musical based on a Dickens story was a modest London hit. It had one hit song but only lasted seven weeks on Broadway. COVER: a horse and carriage loaded with people.

1837 Pieces of Eight (Nightclub, 1960). Stars unknown.

Clandestine / Orientale — Martin Charnin[w] & Robert Kessler[m] *(Marks)*. COVER: the entrance to Downstairs at the Upstairs.

1838 Pierrot Players (closed before Broadway, 1920). Stars unknown.

Balm / A Modest Little Thing / Swish / The World Is Waiting for the Sunrise — Eugene Lockhart[w/m] *(Chappell)*; In Your Wedding Gown — Ray Roberts[w/m] & Eugene Lockhart[w/m] *(Chappell)*. COVER: a man dressed as Pierrot.

1839 Piggy (*see also* **I Told You So**) (Broadway, 1927). Sam Bernard, Brooke Johns.

Didn't It? / Ding Dong Dell / I Need a Little Bit, You Need a Little Bit / I Wanna Go Voom Voom / It Just Had to Happen / It's Easy to Say Hello / Let's Stroll Along and Sing a Song of Love / A Little Change of Atmosphere / The Music of a Little Rippling Stream / Oh Baby / When — Lew Brown[w] & Cliff Friend[m] *(Remick)*. A failure about a rich and poor boy and girl. In try-out it was called *I Told You So* and *That's My Baby*. COVER: hearts and flowers.

1840 Pin Wheel Revue (Broadway, 1922). Frank Fay, Raymond Hitchcock.

Oh Say — Oh Sue! — Irving Caesar[w] & Joseph Meyer[m] *(Harms)*; Silver Stars — Percy Wenrich[w/m] *(Feist)*. A minor revue with some good dancing but a short life. COVER: stars, pin wheels, and designs.

1841 Pins and Needles (Broadway, 1922). Edith Gould, Harry Pilcer.

Ah! Ah! Ah! / Jungle Bungalow / Melancholies / My Lady's Vanity Bag / Souvenirs / Sunny Sunbeams / Syncopated Minuet — Ballard MacDonald[w] & James Hanley[m] *(Shapiro, Bernstein)*; The Little Tin Soldier — Darl MacBoyle[w] & James Hanley[m] *(Shapiro, Bernstein)*; South Sea Sweetheart — Irving Caesar[w] & Maurice Yvaine[m] *(Harms)*. A revue that was imported from London and lasted five weeks. COVER: Edith Gould and Harry Pilcer.

1842 Pins and Needles (Broadway, 1937). Union workers Hy Goldstein, Ruth Rubinstein.

Back to Work / Chain Store Daisy / Cream of Mush Song [PC] / Doing the Reactionary / Four Little Angels of Peace / General Unveiled / It's Better with a Union Man / I've Got the Nerve to Be in Love / Mene, Mene, Tekel [BW] / Nobody Makes a Pass at Me / Not Cricket to Picket / One Big Union for Two / Papa Don't Love Mama Any More / Pins and Needles — complete vocal score / Sing Me a Song with Social Significance / Stay Out, Sammy! / Sunday in the Park / We Sing America [BW] / What Good Is Love / When I Grow Up [BW] — Harold Rome[w/m] *(Mills)*. A hit musical revue by the Ladies Garment Workers Union with interesting songs by Harold Rome and a run of three years. COVER: union worker sewing boss's pants.

1843 Pipe Dream (Broadway, 1955). Helen Traubel, Bill Johnson.

All at Once You Love Her / Everybody's Got a Home / The Man I Used to Be / The Next Time It Happens / Pipe Dream — complete vocal score / Suzy Is a Good Thing / Sweet Thursday — Oscar Hammerstein[w] & Richard Rodgers[m] *(Williamson)*. A musical version of Steinbeck's "Sweet Thursday" with some pleasant Rodgers songs but an uneven book and a miscast leading lady. It ran for only 30 weeks and lost money. COVER: sketch of various characters from the show.

1844 Pippin (Broadway, 1972). John Rubinstein, Ben Vereen.

Corner of the Sky / Extraordinary [VS] / The Goodtime Ladies Rag / I Guess I'll Miss the Man / Just Between the Two of Us / Kind of Woman [VS] / Love Song [VS] / Magic to Do [VS] / Morning Glow / No Time At All [VS] / Pippin [VS] / Pippin — complete vocal score / Simple Joys [VS] / Spread a Little Sunshine [VS] / With You [VS] — Stephen Schwartz^w/m *(Belwin Mills)*. This musical involved a boy searching for himself in the time of Charlemagne. It could have been an ordinary show except for the wonderful staging of Bob Fosse and the performance of Ben Vereen which kept it going for almost five years. COVER: clowns in poses of the title.

1845 The Pirates of Penzance (Broadway, 1981). Linda Ronstadt, Rex Smith.

Pirates of Penzance — complete vocal score — William S. Gilbert^w & Arthur Sullivan^m *(Goldfeder)*; Poor Wandering One — William S. Gilbert^w & Arthur Sullivan^m *(Goldfeder)*. A Joseph Papp production of this old operetta that became a smash hit because of the staging and the actors. It ran for two years. COVER: sketch of a pirate.

1846 Pitter Patter (Broadway, 1920). James Cagney, Helen Bolton.

Bagdad on the Subway / Jazzing It Up in Havana / Meet Your True Love Half Way / Since You Came Into My Life / The Wedding Blues / You Can Never Tell — William Friedlander^w/m *(Harms)*; I Saved a Waltz for You / Pitter Patter — Will Hough^w & William Friedlander^m *(Harms)*; Send for Me — Will Hough^w/m & William Friedlander^w/m *(Harms)*. A poor musical with a riches-to-rags-to-riches story that lasted three months. COVER: a rainbow and clouds.

1847 Plain and Fancy (Broadway, 1954). Barbara Cook, Shirl Conway.

City Mouse, Country Mouse / Follow Your Heart / It Wonders Me / Plain We Live / Plenty of Pennsylvania / This Is All Very New to Me / Young and Foolish — Arnold Horwitt^w & Albert Hague^m *(Chappell)*. A hit musical about Amish farmers in Lancaster. It had an interesting book and a pleasant score with one hit song, *Young and Foolish*. It ran for over a year. COVER: hex signs and birds.

1848 Plain Jane (Broadway, 1924). Lorraine Manville, Charles McNaughton.

Don't Take Your Troubles to Bed / If Flowers Could Speak — Phil Cook^w/m & Tom Johnstone^w/m *(Harms)*; Plain Jane / Road to Love — Phil Cook^w & Tom Johnstone^m *(Harms)*. True love and a rag doll were the themes of this poor musical that lasted two weeks. COVER: sketch of Plain Jane.

1849 Plantation Follies (*see also* Dixie to Broadway) (Broadway, 1924). Florence Mills, Shelton Brooks.

Dixie Dreams / I'm a Little Blackbird Looking for a Bluebird / Jazz Time Came from the South / Mandy Make Up Your Mind — Grant Clarke^w & Roy Turk^w & George Meyer^m & Arthur Johnston^m *(Berlin)*. A black revue with great dancing and Florence Mills. The try-out title was *Plantation Follies*. COVER: black men singing and dancing along the river.

1850 Plantation Revue (Broadway, 1922). Florence Mills, Ulysses Thompson.

Gee! But I Hate to Go Home Alone — Joe Goodwin^w & James Hanley^m *(Shapiro, Bernstein)*; Hawaiian Night in Dixieland — Roy Turk^w/m & J. Russel Robinson^w/m *(Berlin)*; He Used to Be Your Man — Robert Kelly^w/m *(Blues Music)*. A poor black revue that lasted four weeks at the 48th Street Theatre. COVER: Chappelle and Stinette; Negroes picking cotton; sketch of nightclub scene.

1851 Play It Again, Sam (Broadway, 1969). Woody Allen, Anthony Roberts.

Play It Again, Sam — Hal Hackady[w] & Larry Grossman[m] *(Valando)*. A hit comedy by and with Woody Allen. COVER: sketch of Woody Allen and girls.

1852 Playgirls (Nightclub, 1970). Julie Wilson, Marilyn Maxwell.

Playgirls / Us — Jackie Barnett[w/m] *(Robbins)*. COVER: Julie Wilson, Dagmar, Marilyn Maxwell, Patrice Wymore, and chorus girls.

1853 Pleasure Bound (*see also* Well Well Well) (Broadway, 1929). Phil Baker, Aileen Stanley.

Just Suppose — Sid Silvers[w] & Moe Joffee[w] & Phil Baker[m] & Maury Rubens[m] *(Shubert)*; My Melody Man — Charles Tobias[w] & Sidney Clare[w] & Peter DeRose[m] *(Berlin)*; Park Avenue Strut / Sweet Little Mannikin Doll — Moe Joffee[w] & Harold Atteridge[w] & Phil Baker[m] & Maury Rubens[m] *(Shubert)*; The Things That Were Made for Love — Charles Tobias[w] & Irving Kahal[w] & Peter DeRose[m] *(Berlin)*; We'll Get Along / Why Do You Tease Me? — Max Lief[w] & Nathaniel Lief[w] & Muriel Pollock[m] *(Shubert)*. A revue with nothing to recommend it. It ran four months. The try-out title was *Well Well Well*. COVER: Aileen Stanley; Phil Baker; sketch of couple dressed in elegant clothes.

1854 Pleasures and Palaces (closed before Broadway, 1965). John McMartin, Phyllis Newman.

Ah, to Be Home Again [PC] / Barabanchik [PC] / Far, Far, Far Away [PC] / In Your Eyes [PC] / Pleasures and Palaces [PC] / Thunder and Lightning [PC] / Truly Loved [PC] — Frank Loesser[w/m] *(Frank)*. A musical about Catherine the Great. It was given a lavish production but had a terrible book. This show folded in Detroit and was Frank Loesser's last musical. COVER: none.

1855 Policy Kings (Black, 1939). Stars unknown.

Deed I Do Blues [ABQ] / Dewey Blues [ABQ] / Gonna Hit the Numbers Today [ABQ] / Harlem Woogie / Havin' a Ball [ABQ] / Walkin' My Baby Back Home [ABQ] / You, You, You! — Louis Douglass[w] & James Johnson[m] *(Joe Davis)*. COVER: silhouette of speaker and audience.

1856 Polly (closed before Broadway, 1924). Stars unknown.

All the World Is Loving / Beware the 'Gator [ABQ] / How Happy They'll Be [ABQ] / Is It the Wind? / Rumble On / Something / Shooting Stars [ABQ] / Try a Little Step [ABQ] / You Have Taught Me How to Smile [ABQ] — Margaret Mayo[w] & Audrey Kennedy[w] & Hugo Felix[m] *(Feist)*. COVER: an empty stage and curtains.

1857 Polly (Broadway, 1928). Fred Allen, Lucy Monroe.

Comme Ci, Comme Ca / Heel and Toe / On with the Dance / Polly / What Can Be Sweeter? — Irving Caesar[w] & Philip Charig[m] *(Harms)*; Sing a Song in the Rain — Douglas Furber[w] & Irving Caesar[w] & Harry Rosenthal[m] *(Harms)*; Sweet Liar — Irving Caesar[w] & Herbert Stothart[m] *(Harms)*; When a Fellow Meets a Flapper on Broadway — Irving Caesar[w] & Philip Charig[m] *(Harms)*. A musical — involving a silly love triangle — that lasted two weeks. COVER: girl watching a polo player on horseback.

1858 Polly and Her Pals (closed before Broadway, 1920). Stars unknown.

Different Eyes / In My Land / An Old Fashioned Bride / Polar Bear Shiver / Underneath a Southern Moon / What a Wonderful Girl You Are — Harry Hume[w] & Hampton Durand[m] *(Harms)*. This show was advertised as a "musical comedy adapted from Cliff Sterrett's cartoon." COVER: cartoon characters, flowers and designs.

1859 Polly of Hollywood (Broadway, 1927). John Agee, Hugh Herbert.

Company Manners / Kisses That You Gave to Me / New Kind of Rhythm / Texas Stomp / Wanting You — Will Morrissey[w/m] & Edmund Joseph[w/m] *(Shapiro, Bernstein)*. This musical about a small town girl in Hollywood lasted three weeks. COVER: Polly and camera man.

1860 Polly Preferred (Broadway, 1923). David Burns, Genevieve Tobin.

Red Moon — Lew Brown[w] & John Traver[w] & Henri DeMartini[m] & Max Kortlander[m] *(Shapiro, Bernstein)*. A comedy about a chorus girl trying to make good. It was a moderate hit of six months. COVER: Genevieve Tobin.

1861 Polonaise (Broadway, 1945). Marta Eggerth, Jan Kiepura.

Just for Tonight / Wait for Tomorrow — John Latouche[w] & Frederic Chopin[m] & Bronislaw Kaper[m] *(Chappell)*; The Next Time I Care / Stranger — John Latouche[w] & Bronislaw Kaper[m] *(Chappell)*. A Polish uprising set to Chopin's music with a moderate run of three months. COVER: sketch of castle.

1862 Poor Little Ritz Girl (Broadway, 1920). Charles Purcell, Eleanor Griffith.

The Bombay Bombashay — Alex Gerber[w] & Sigmund Romberg[m] & Ray Perkins[m] *(Witmark)*; Boomerang (not published) / Lady Raffles Behave / Let Me Drink in Your Eyes (not published) / Love Will Call / Love's Intense in Tents / Will You Forgive Me (not published) / You Can't Fool Your Dreams — Lorenz Hart[w] & Richard Rodgers[m] *(Remick)*; Dear Heart — Bide Dudley[w] & Ted Barron[m] *(Harms)*; I Love to Say Hello to the Girls / In the Land of Yesterday / Pretty Ming Toy / When I Found You — Alex Gerber[w] & Sigmund Romberg[m] *(Witmark)*; Mary, Queen of Scots — Herbert Fields[w] & Richard Whiting[m] *(Remick)*. A musical about a girl and a boy renting the same apartment. It was supposed to be a full Rodgers-Hart score but at the last minute it was changed to half Rodgers and half Romberg. It ran only 12 weeks. COVER: Remick has girl driving car and Witmark has girl with chauffeur driven car.

1863 Poppy (Broadway, 1923).

Madge Kennedy, W.C. Fields.

Alibi Baby — Howard Dietz[?] & Dorothy Donnelly[w] & Arthur Samuels[m] *(Harms)*; Hang Your Sorrows in the Sun / Picnic Party with You — Dorothy Donnelly[w] & John Egan[m] *(Harms)*; Mary / What Do You Do Sunday, Mary? — Irving Caesar[w] & Stephen Jones[m] *(Harms)*; Someone Will Make You Smile — Irving Caesar[w] & Rudolf Sieczynski[m] *(Harms)*; Steppin' Around — piano selections — Monte Carlo[m] & Alma Saunders[m] *(Harms)*; Two Make a Home — Dorothy Donnelly[w] & Stephen Jones[m] & Arthur Samuels[m] *(Harms)*; When You Are in My Arms — Dorothy Donnelly[w] & Niclas Kempner[m] *(Harms)*. A rags-to-riches musical with the only redeeming feature being W.C. Fields, who caused it to run almost a year. *Alibi Baby* is credited to Donnelly but is supposed to be by Howard Dietz. COVER: One set of covers is pink with Madge Kennedy and the other set is yellow with a full view of W.C. Fields and a musical instrument.

1864 Porgy (Broadway, 1927). Frank Wilson, Evelyn Ellis.

Porgy — eleven spirituals — Traditional *(B B and L)*. The original production of the play that later became a classic musical. It ran six months. COVER: a row of houses with people in windows.

1865 Porgy and Bess (Broadway, 1935). Todd Duncan, Anne Brown.

Bess, You Is My Woman / I Got Plenty o' Nuttin' / Porgy and Bess — complete vocal score — DuBose Heyward[w] & Ira Gershwin[w] & George Gershwin[m] *(Gershwin)*; It Ain't Necessarily So / Oh Bess, Oh Where's My Bess / There's a Boat Dats Leavin' Soon for New York — Ira Gershwin[w] & George Gershwin[m] *(Gershwin)*; My Man's Gone Now / Summertime / A Woman Is a Sometime Thing — DuBose Heyward[w] & George Gershwin[m] *(Gershwin)*. Life on Catfish Row was the basis for this black musical. It had a tragic story and a wonderful Gershwin score; however, the first production lasted only three months. Over the years, with many important revivals, it has become a classic. COVER: man, woman, houses and skyscrapers in black and white.

1866 Porgy and Bess (Broadway, 1976). Abraham Lind-Oquenda, Clamma Dale.

It Ain't Necessarily So — Ira Gershwin[w] & George Gershwin[m] *(Leonard)*; Porgy and Bess — vocal selections of seven songs (1976) — Ira Gershwin[w] & DuBose Heyward[w] & George Gershwin[m] *(Chappell)*. A successful tour by the Houston Grand Opera Company. It ran in New York for three months. COVER: Porgy and Bess and scenes from the musical.

1867 Portofino (Broadway, 1958). Helen Gallagher, Georges Guetary.

Isn't It Wonderful [PC] / Portofino [PC] — Richard Ney[w] & Louis Bellson[m] *(Sunbeam)*. American tourists in Italy were the basis of this disaster which lasted three performances. COVER: none.

1868 Pot of Gold (College, 1912). Cole Porter and students.

Longing for Dear Old Broadway [VS] — Cole Porter[w/m] *(Chappell)*. A show at Yale. COVER: Cole Porter.

1869 Pousse Cafe (Broadway, 1966). Theodore Bikel, Travis Hudson.

C'est Comme Ca / Let's / Thank You Ma'am — Marshall Barer[w] & Duke Ellington[m] *(Tempo)*. A terrible musical based on *The Blue Angel* with a run of three performances. COVER: red and white designs.

1870 Present Arms (Broadway, 1928). Charles King, Joyce Barbour.

Blue Ocean Blues / Crazy Elbows / Do I Hear You Saying / Down by the Sea / I'm a Fool, Little One / A Kiss for Cinderella / You Took Advantage of Me — Lorenz Hart[w] & Richard Rodgers[m] *(Harms)*; Tell It to the Marines — piano selections — Richard Rodgers[m] *(Harms)*. A musical about a marine with some good songs but a run of only 20 weeks. COVER: a row of hands and rifles.

1871 Prettybelle (closed before Broadway, 1971). Angela Lansbury, Jon Cypher.

How Could I Know? [PC] / I Met a Man [VS] / I'm in a Tree [VS] / Individual Thing [VS] / Prettybelle [VS] / To a Small Degree [PC] / When I'm Drunk I'm Beautiful [VS] — Bob Merrill[w] & Jule Styne[m] *(Valando)*. Angela Lansbury as an alcoholic and mental patient in a strange musical that folded in Boston. COVER: "Prettybelle."

1872 Primrose (British, 1924). Heather Thatcher, Leslie Henson.

Boy Wanted [B] / Isn't It Wonderful [B] / Naughty Baby [B] / Primrose — complete vocal score [B] / Wait a Bit, Susie [B] — Desmond Carter[w] & Ira Gershwin[w] & George Gershwin[m] *(Chappell)*; The Country Side [B] / That New-Fangled Mother of Mine [B] — Desmond Carter[w] & George Gershwin[m] *(Chappell)*; Some Far-Away Someone [B] — Ira Gershwin[w] & B.G. DeSylva[w] & George Gershwin[m] *(Chappell)*. A hit musical in London that ran seven months. It had some good Gershwin songs and involved an author, his heroine, and complications. COVER: flowers, ribbons, designs.

1873 The Prince and the Pauper (Off Broadway, 1963). John Davidson, Carol Blodget.

Coronation Song / Do This, Do That / Ev'rybody Needs Somebody to Love / Finale of Prince and the Pauper / Garbage Court Round / In a Storybook / I've Been A-Begging / King Foo-Foo the First / Oh, Pity the Man / The Prince Is Mad / The Tree and the Sun / Why Don't We Switch? / With a Sword in My Buckle — Verna Tomasson[w] & George Fischoff[m] *(Felsted)*. A children's musical of the classic story that ran for 20 weeks. COVER: a sketch of the prince and the pauper.

1874 Princess April (Broadway, 1924). Tessa Kosta, Nathaniel Wagner.

Dreamy Eyes / In Rainbow Land / Love Clock / Love of Mine / One Piece Blues / Princess April / Tantalizing April — Monte Carlo[w/m] & Alma Saunders^w/m *(Marks)*. A "poor Irish girl" musical that lasted three weeks. COVER: Tessa Kosta.

1875 Princess Charming (Broadway, 1930). George Grossmith, Portia Grafton.

I Love Love — Walter O'Keefe^w & Robert Dolan^m *(Harms)*; I Must Be One of Those Roses / I'll Be There / I'll Never Leave You / Just a Friend of Mine / Never Mind How / Trailing a Shooting Star / You — Arthur Swanstrom^w & Albert Sirmay^m & Arthur Schwartz^m *(Harms)*; I'm Designed for Love — Arthur Swanstrom^w & Albert Sirmay^m *(Harms)*. An imported British operetta about a princess and a commoner that lasted seven weeks. COVER: flowers and silhouette of girl in hoop skirt.

1876 Princess Flavia (*see also* **A Royal Pretender**) (Broadway, 1925). Evelyn Herbert, Douglass Dumbrille.

Convent Bells Are Ringing / I Dare Not Love You / Marionettes / Only One / Twilight Voices / What Do I Care? / Yes or No — Harry B. Smith^w & Sigmund Romberg^m *(Harms)*. A poor imitation of *The Student Prince*; it ran 19 weeks and toured. The try-out title was *A Royal Pretender*. COVER: a crown and sceptre.

1877 Princess Ting-ah-Ling (closed before Broadway, 1930). Stars unknown.

My Dream Prince — Charles Roos^w & Francesco DeLeone^m *(Sam Fox)*. COVER: sketch of Chinese girl and lanterns.

1878 Princess Virtue (Broadway, 1921). Tessa Kosta, Frank Moulan.

Dear Sweet Eyes / I'd Like to Be a Wave / Life Is All Sunshine / Little Red Riding Hood / Princess Virtue / Smoke Rings / When I Meet Love — B.C. Hilliam^w/m & Gitz Rice^w/m *(Witmark)*. A romance in Paris that lasted for two weeks. COVER: flowers and designs.

1879 A Private Affair (Broadway, 1936). Oscar Shaw, Florence Britton.

The Scene Changes — Billy Hill^w/m *(Shapiro, Bernstein)*. A comedy that failed after three weeks. COVER: Oscar Shaw.

1880 Private Lives (Broadway, 1931). Gertrude Lawrence, Noel Coward.

Someday I'll Find You — Noel Coward^w/m *(Harms)*. A Noel Coward comedy that ran for 20 weeks. COVER: Gertrude Lawrence, Noel Coward.

1881 Promenade (Off Broadway, 1969). Alice Playten, Madeline Kahn.

Capricious and Fickle [VS] / Cigarette Song [VS] / A Flower [VS] / I Saw a Man [VS] / The Moment Has Passed [VS] / Unrequited Love [VS] — Maria I. Fornes^w & Al Carmines^m *(Chappell)*; Promenade Theme — Al Carmines^m *(Chappell)*. A hit musical pitting good against evil in a "Candide-like" story. It had great sets, talented singers, a good plot-line and a run of eight months. COVER: naked girl jumping out of large box surrounded by other characters.

1882 Promises, Promises (Broadway, 1968). Jerry Orbach, Jill O'Hara.

Christmas Day / A Fact Can Be a Beautiful Thing [VS] / Half as Big as Life [VS] / I'll Never Fall in Love Again / It's Our Little Secret [VS] / Knowing When to Leave / Let's Pretend We're Grownup [RC] [CUT] / Promises, Promises / Promises, Promises — complete vocal score / She Likes Basketball [VS] / Tick Tock Goes the Clock [RC] [CUT] / Turkey Lurkey Time [VS] / Upstairs [VS] / Wanting Things / What Am I Doing Here [RC] [CUT] / Where Can You Take a Girl? [VS] / Whoever You Are, I Love You / You'll Think of Someone [VS] / A Young Pretty Girl Like You [VS] — Hal David^m & Burt Bacharach^m *(Morris)*. This was a hit musical based on the movie *The Apartment*. It had an excellent score and cast and ran three years. COVER: five girls and a large key.

1883 The Provincetown Follies (Broadway, 1935). Beatrice Kay, Marie Alverez.

Rain Over Manhattan — Arthur

Jones$^{w/m}$ *(Shapiro, Bernstein)*; Red Sails in the Sunset — Jimmy Kennedy^w & Hugh Williams^m & Will Grosz^m *(Shapiro, Bernstein)*; Restless River — Mary Schaeffer$^{w/m}$ *(Shapiro, Bernstein)*. A poor revue that lasted two months. COVER: Connie Boswell; designs and lettering.

1884 The Punch Bowl (British, 1924). Hermione Baddeley, Sonnie Hale.

All Alone [B] / What'll I Do [B] — Irving Berlin$^{w/m}$ *(F D and H)*; Chili Bom Bom [B] — Cliff Friend^w & Walter Donaldson^m *(F D and H)*. A hit revue in London that ran for almost 18 months. COVER: Sonnie Hale, Norah Blaney.

1885 Puppets (Broadway, 1925). Miriam Hopkins, Henry Gordon.

Love May Find Me Today — Clifford Grey^w & Isidore Luckstone^m *(Harms)*. A melodrama of a war romance that had a brief run. COVER: Miriam Hopkins.

1886 The Pure in Heart (Broadway, 1934). Dorothy Hall, James Bell.

Can't Find My Way — Edward Heyman^w & Richard Myers^m *(Harms)*. A drama about a small town girl trying to make it on Broadway. It ran one week. COVER: designs and letters.

1887 Purlie (Broadway, 1969). Linda Hopkins, Cleavon Little.

Big Fish, Little Fish [VS] / Down Home [VS] / First Thing Monday Mornin' [VS] / He Can Do It / I Got Love / New Fangled Preacher Man [VS] / Purlie / Walk Him Up the Stairs / The World Is Comin' to a Start [VS] — Peter Udell^w & Gary Geld^m *(Mourbar)*. A musical about a young black preacher trying to help his fellow men. With a rousing score and book it had a run of almost two years. COVER: sketch of Purlie and a girl.

1888 The Purple Cow (closed before Broadway, 1924). Stars unknown.

Any Man Is Easy / Magical Isle / Only One / What You Don't Know, Won't Hurt You — Gelett Burgess^w & Edwin Helms^m *(Harms)*. COVER: flowers and designs.

1889 Put and Take (*see also* **Chocolate Brown**) (closed before Broadway, 1921). Andrew Tribble, Mildred Smallwood.

Beedle Em Boo / I Can't Forget the Dear Old Folks at Home / Land of Creole Girls / The Meanest Man in the World / My June Love / Put and Take / Separation Blues / Snag 'em Blues — Spencer Williams$^{w/m}$ *(Bradford)*; Chocolate Brown — Spencer Williams$^{w/m}$ *(Irvin Miller)*; Georgia Rose — Alex Sullivan^w & Jimmy Flynn^w & Harry Rosenthal^m *(Feist)*; Nervous Blues / Old Time Blues — Perry Bradford$^{w/m}$ *(Bradford)*; Stop! Rest a While — L. Wolfe Gilbert$^{w/m}$ & Tim Brymn$^{w/m}$ *(Gilbert)*. A black revue that started out as *Chocolate Brown* and later became *Put and Take*. COVER: boy and girl spinning a top.

1890 Put It in Writing (Off Broadway, 1963). Jane Connell, Bill Hinnant.

Walking Down the Road — Alan Kohan$^{w/m}$ & William Angelos$^{w/m}$ *(Morris)*. A small revue that lasted for three weeks. COVER: a Hirschfeld sketch of girl with champagne glass.

1891 Puzzles of 1925 (Broadway, 1925). Elsie Janis, Helen Broderick.

The Do I or Don't I Blues / You've Got to Dance — Elsie Janis$^{w/m}$ *(Berlin)*; The Doo-Dab — Bert Kalmar$^{w/m}$ & Harry Ruby$^{w/m}$ *(Berlin)*; Je Vous Aime — Arthur Beiner$^{w/m}$ *(Harms)*; Look Who's Here — Ray Klages^w & Ken Whitmer^m *(Robbins-Engel)*; Titina — Bertal Maubon^w & E. Ronn^w & Leo Daniderff^m *(Harms)*; You're Just a Flower from an Old Bouquet — Gwynne Denni^w & Lucien Denni^m *(Jenkins)*. A revue of vaudeville acts dominated by Elsie Janis who kept it running for three months. COVER: Elsie Janis; lettering and designs.

1892 Queen High (Broadway, 1926). Charles Ruggles, Luella Gear.

Beautiful Baby / Don't Forget — B.G. DeSylva^w & James Hanley^m *(Harms)*; Cross Your Heart / Everything Will Happen for the Best / Gentlemen Prefer Blondes / You'll

Never Know — B.G. DeSylva^w & Lewis Gensler^m *(Harms)*; My Lady — Frank Crummit$^{w/m}$ & Ben Jerome$^{w/m}$ *(Harms)*. A musical dealing with business partners. With a funny story and good songs, it ran for a year. COVER: a big red heart.

1893 Queen o' Hearts (Broadway, 1922). Nora Bayes, Harry Richman.

Dear Little Girlie — Nora Bayes^w & Dudley Wilkinson^m *(Harms)*; Ding, Dong, Ding! / Tom-Tom / You Need Someone, Someone Needs You — Oscar Hammerstein^w & Lewis Gensler^m *(Harms)*; Dreaming Alone — Oscar Hammerstein^w & Dudley Wilkinson^m *(Harms)*; Mammy's Carbon Copy — Harry Richman$^{w/m}$ & Bill Dugan$^{w/m}$ & Lou Davis$^{w/m}$ *(Harms)*; That's That! — Nora Bayes$^{w/m}$ & Harry Richman$^{w/m}$ & Dudley Wilkinson$^{w/m}$ *(Harms)*. A musical, dealing with a matrimonial agency, that lasted for only five weeks. COVER: Nora Bayes.

1894 The Queen's Taste (*see also* **Angela**) (Broadway, 1928). Jeanette MacDonald, Florenz Ames.

I Can't Believe It's True / Love Is Like That / Regal Romp — Mann Holiner^w & Alberta Nichols^m *(I.C.L.A)*. A musical about a royal marriage; the musical lasted five weeks. The try-out title was *The Queen's Taste*. COVER: girl with crown receiving jewels from pages.

1895 A Quiet Place (Opera, 1984). Robert Galbraith, Beverly Morgan.

A Quiet Place — complete score — Leonard Bernstein$^{w/m}$ & Stephen Wadsworth$^{w/m}$ *(B and B)*. A full three act opera which incorporates the short opera *Trouble in Tahiti*. COVER: titles and designs.

1896 The Rabbi's Sweetheart (Jewish, 1937). Michal Michalesko, Lucy Levin.

Shir Hashirm — Chaim Tauber^w & Manny Fleischman^m *(Trio)*. COVER: Michalesko and Levin.

1897 Radio City Music Hall (Broadway, 1934). Jan Peerce.

Blue Bird of Happiness — Edward Heyman^w & Sandor Harmati^m *(Harms)*. COVER: Jan Peerce.

1898 Radio City Music Hall (Broadway, 1935). Stars unknown.

Let's Rub Noses — Al Silverman^w & Joseph Meyer^m *(Harms)*. COVER: Two penguins and ice.

1899 Radio City Music Hall Christmas Spectacular (Broadway, 1987). Rockettes.

It's Christmas in New York — Billy Butt$^{w/m}$ *(Shattinger)*. COVER: Christmas trees.

1900 The Radio Girl (Jewish, 1929). Molly Picon.

Es Ziht Es Briht — I. Lillian^w & J.M. Rumshinsky^m *(Trio)*. COVER: Molly Picon.

1901 The Ragged Edge (closed before Broadway, 1927). Stars unknown.

Kid Baby — Warburton Guilbert$^{w/m}$ *(Harms)*. A melodrama that folded in Chicago. COVER: girl on knees begging a man.

1902 Ragged Robin (Irish, 1921). Chauncey Olcott.

Click of Her Little Brogans — J. Keirn Brennan^w & Ernest Ball^m *(Witmark)*; The Eyes That Come from Ireland — Richard LeGallienne^w & Chauncey Olcott^m *(Witmark)*; I Used to Believe in Fairies — George Spink$^{w/m}$ *(Witmark)*; If You'll Remember Me — George Graff^w & Ernest Ball^m *(Witmark)*; The Laugh with a Tear in It — Manuel Klein^w & Chauncey Olcott^m *(Witmark)*; Michael McGinnity — Chauncey Olcott$^{w/m}$ & Manuel Klein$^{w/m}$ *(Witmark)*; Sweet Girl of My Dreams — Chauncey Olcott$^{w/m}$ & Dan Sullivan$^{w/m}$ *(Witmark)*; When — Chauncey Olcott$^{w/m}$ *(Ricordi)*. COVER: Chauncey Olcott.

1903 Raggedy Ann (Broadway, 1986). Ivy Austin, Elizabeth Austin.

Blue [VS] / Rag Dolly [VS] — Joe Raposo$^{w/m}$ *(Jonico)*. This musical toured Russia and then opened on Broadway. It was pretty bad and lasted for five performances. COVER: Joe Raposo.

1904 Rags (Broadway, 1986). Larry Kert, Judy Kuhn.

Blame It on the Summer Night [VS] / Brand New World [VS] / Children of the Wind (show) [VS] / Children of the Wind (standard) [VS] / Dancing with the Fools [VS] / For My Mary [VS] / Penny a Tune [VS] / Rags [VS] / Three Sunny Rooms [VS] / Wanting [VS] / Yankee Boy [VS] — Stephen Schwartz[w] & Charles Strouse[m] *(Belwin)*. This musical about Jewish immigrants had a poor book, a fair score, and Teresa Stratas. It ran for four performances. COVER: the Statue of Liberty and immigrants.

1905 Rah-Rah-Daze (Regional, 1930). Fred Waring and Orchestra.

I'm in the Mood / So Beats My Heart for You / What's the Use of Lovin' — Bat Ballard[w/m] & Charles Henderson[w/m] & Tom Waring[w/m] *(D B and H)*. A touring concert starring Fred Waring and his Pennsylvanians. COVER: a college boy and girl.

1906 Rah! Rah! Rah! (Broadway, 1929). Stars unknown.

More Than Anybody — Del Porter[w/m] *(Famous)*. A short musical program performed in large cities in between showings of new Paramount movies. COVER: silhouette of couple on balcony.

1907 Railroads on Parade (New York World's Fair, 1939). Stars unknown.

Mile After Mile — Charles Alan[w] & Buddy Bernier[w] & Kurt Weill[m] *(Crawford)*. Music for a railroad show. COVER: a speeding train.

1908 Rain or Shine (Broadway, 1928). Joe Cook, Nancy Welford.

Add a Little Wiggle / Breakfast with You / Forever and Ever / Rain or Shine / Who's Going to Get You — Jack Yellen[w] & Milton Ager[m] *(A Y and B)*; All I Need Is You! — Richard Lynch[w/m] *(Hollis)*; Feelin' Good — Jack Yellen[w] & Owen Murphy[m] *(A Y and B)*; Oh Baby — Owen Murphy[w/m] *(A Y and B)*; Roustabout Song — Jack Yellen[w] & Owen Murphy[m] & Milton Ager[m] *(A Y and B)*. A hit musical with a circus background and ordinary music. The star Joe Cook kept it going for almost a year using his vaudeville clowning. COVER: girl with umbrella outside circus tent.

1909 Rainbo Charms (Nightclub, 1933). Stars unknown.

Tripping Along — Jerry Sullivan[m] & Harry Hosford[m] *(Jack Mills)*. COVER: a picture of the cast in costume.

1910 Rainbow (British, 1923). Grace Hayes.

All Over Town [B] — Lou Paley[w] & Clifford Grey[w] & George Gershwin[m] *(Harms)*; Beneath the Eastern Moon [B] / Good-night My Dear [B] / In the Rain [B] / Moonlight in Versailles [B] / Oh! Nina [B] / Strut Lady with Me [B] / Sunday in London Town [B] / Sweetheart [B] — Clifford Grey[w] & George Gershwin[m] *(Harms)*; Innocent Ingenue Baby [B] — Brian Hooker[w] & Clifford Grey[w] & William Daly[m] & George Gershwin[m] *(Harms)*. A poor revue with bland Gershwin tunes. It lasted only three months. COVER: a colored rainbow and clouds.

1911 Rainbow (Broadway, 1928). Libby Holman, Brian Donlevy.

Hay, Straw / I Like You as You Are / I Want a Man / The One Girl — Oscar Hammerstein[w] & Vincent Youmans[m] *(Youmans)*; Who Am I — Gus Kahn[w] & Vincent Youmans[m] *(Youmans)*. A musical set in gold rush days that was a complete disaster and lasted three weeks. COVER: pioneer and covered wagon.

1912 Rainbow Jones (Broadway, 1974). Ruby Persson, Gil Robbins.

Free and Easy / We All Need Love / Who Needs the Love of a Woman — Jill Williams[w/m] *(Morris)*. A girl and her fantasies that lasted for one performance. COVER: black and white cover with title only.

1913 Rainbow Rose (Broadway, 1926). Jack Squire, Jack Whiting.

All the Time / First Last and Only / If You Were Someone Else / Something Seems to Tell Me / When the

Hurdy Gurdy Plays — Owen Murphy[w/m] *(Harms)*; Let's Run Away and Get Married — Harold Levey[w/m] & Owen Murphy[w/m] *(Harms)*; Rainbow — Zelda Sears[w] & Harold Levey[m] *(Harms)*. A musical about a wealthy man separating out his true friends; it ran seven weeks. COVER: roses, broken down fence, old house.

1914 Raisin (*see also* **Didn't You Hear That Thunder?**) (Broadway, 1973). Virginia Capers, Deborah Allen.

Alaiyo [VS] / He Come Down This Morning [VS] / It's a Deal [VS] / Man Say [VS] / Measure the Valleys [VS] / Not Anymore [VS] / Runnin' to Meet the Man [VS] / Sidewalk Tree [VS] / Sweet Time [VS] / A Whole Lotta Sunlight [VS] / Whose Little Angry Man [VS] / Yes Sir, No Sir! [VS] / You Done Right [VS] — Robert Brittain[w] & Judd Woldin[m] *(Blackwood)*. A hit musical about a black family trying to get ahead. A competent score and good acting kept it going for two years. It was called *Didn't You Hear the Thunder* in try-out. COVER: a rainbow with a man upside down at the end.

1915 Raisin' Cain (Black, 1923). Buck and Bubbles.

Raisin' Cain — Joseph Trent[w] & Donald Heywood[m] *(Jack Mills)*. A musical that toured the black circuit. The story took place partly in Africa and partly in N.Y. COVER: Buck and Bubbles and a black dancing girl.

1916 The Ramblers (Broadway, 1973). Clark and McCullough.

All Alone Monday / California Skies / Like You Do / We Won't Charleston / Whistle — Bert Kalmar[w] & Harry Ruby[m] *(Harms)*; Oh! How We Love Our Alma Mater / You Smiled at Me — Bert Kalmar[w/m] & Harry Ruby[w/m] *(Harms)*. A hit musical with the two great comedians loose on a movie set. It had good songs and ran for nine months. COVER: Clark and McCullough.

1917 Rang Tang (Broadway, 1927). Aubrey Lyles, Flournoy Miller.

Brown / Harlem / Jungle Rose / Monkey Land / Rang Tang / Sambo's Banjo / Sammy and Topsy / Summer Nights / Zulu Fifth Avenue — Jo Trent[w] & Ford Dabney[m] *(Feist)*. A black musical with a fair score and excellent dancing. It lasted three months. COVER: black man beating a drum with three dancers.

1918 The Real Ambassadors (Regional, 1962). Louis Armstrong, Carmen McRae.

The Real Ambassadors — vocal selections of 15 songs — Iola Brubeck[w] & Dave Brubeck[w] & Dave Brubeck[m] *(Hansen)*. A musical play involving a jazz group and singers first presented at the Monterey Jazz Festival. COVER: Louis Armstrong.

1919 Really Rosie (Off Broadway, 1980). Tisha Campbell, Bibi Humes.

Alligators All Around [VS] / Avenue P [VS] / The Awful Truth [VS] / The Ballad of Chicken Soup [VS] / Chicken Soup with Rice [VS] / My Simple Humble Neighborhood [VS] / One Was Johnny [VS] / Pierre [VS] / Really Rosie #1 [VS] / Really Rosie #2 [VS] / Screaming and Yelling [VS] / Such Sufferin' [VS] — Maurice Sendak[w] & Carole King[m] *(Columbia)*. A children's musical based on the cartoon character. It ran almost nine months. COVER: cartoon of Rosie and friends.

1920 The Red Cat (Broadway, 1934). Francis Lister, Ruth Weston.

He's the Man I Adore / You Have to Live a Little — Dana Suesse[w/m] *(Harms)*. A nightclub performer impersonates a baron in this drama that lasted two weeks. COVER: a red cat with a fan.

1921 The Red Devil Battery Sign (closed before Broadway, 1975). Claire Bloom, Anthony Quinn.

Hombre — Sidney Lippman[m] *(Croma Music)*. A Tennessee Williams drama that lasted for two weeks in Boston. COVER: black and white with title only.

1922 Red, Hot and Blue! (Broadway, 1936). Ethel Merman, Bob Hope.

Down in the Depths / Goodbye, Little Dream, Goodbye / It's Delovely / A

Little Skipper from Heaven Above / Ours / The Ozarks Are Callin' Me Home / Perennial Debutante [VS] / Red, Hot and Blue / Ridin' High / What a Great Pair We'll Be [VS] / When Your Troubles Have Started [VS] [CUT] / You're a Bad Influence on Me / You've Got Something — Cole Porter^{w/m} *(Chappell)*. This musical, about a lottery, had some Cole Porter hits, the comedy of Hope and Durante, plus Ethel Merman; however, it ran for only five months. COVERS: a red, white, and blue cover with Capitol building in background. The other cover is red, white, and blue without the Capitol in the background.

1923 The Red Mill (Broadway, 1945). Eddie Foy, Jr., Dorothy Stone.

Badinage — Victor Herbert^m *(Schuberth)*; Because You're You / Every Day Is Ladies Day with Me / The Isle of Our Dreams / Moonbeams / The Red Mill — complete vocal score / Streets of New York — Henry Blossom^w & Victor Herbert^m *(Witmark)*. A hit revival of the old Herbert operetta that ran 18 months and toured. COVER: a windmill and the cast of the show.

1924 Red Pepper (Broadway, 1922). Thomas Heath, James McIntyre.

Dreamy Hollow — Owen Murphy^{w/m} *(Remick)*; It Must Be You — Howard Rogers^w & Albert Gumble^m & Herman Paley^m *(Remick)*; Levee Land / Senora / Strut Your Stuff — Howard Rogers^w & Albert Gumble^m *(Remick)*; Oh Sing-a-loo — Lew Brown^w & Sidney Mitchell^w & Lew Pollack^m *(Broadway)*. A poor musical about horseracing that lasted three weeks. COVER: a horse and a horse race.

1925 The Red Robe (Broadway, 1928). Violet Carson, Walter Woolf.

Believe in Me — Harry B. Smith^w & Arthur Schwartz^m *(Harms)*; Home of Mine / If I Could Forget / Oh, How the Girls Adore Me / A Soldier of Fortune / What Have You Got to Say? / Where the Banners Lead / You and I Are Passers By — Harry B. Smith^w & Jean Gilbert^m *(Harms)*; I've Got It — Mann Holiner^w & Alberta Nichols^m *(Harms)*; King of the Sword — J. Keirn Brennan^w & Robert Stolz^m & Maurie Rubens^m *(Harms)*; Laugh at Life — J. Delany Dunn^w & Maurie Rubens^m *(Harms)*; Wings of Romance — Cyrus Wood^w & Jean Gilbert^m *(Harms)*. An old fashioned operetta set in France with cardinals and counts. It had an ordinary book and score, a great performance by Walter Woolf, but a run of only 20 weeks. COVER: a nobleman with large hat and sword.

1926 The Red Robin (closed before Broadway, 1933). Stars unknown.

Yodel-o-de-ay — Jack Scholl^w & Max Rich^m & Jean Schwartz^m *(Bibo-Lang)*. COVER: man and woman, a Swiss chalet, and the Alps.

1927 Red, White and Blue (closed before Broadway, 1950). Larry Storch, Bob Carroll.

All American Rainbow — Bob Hilliard^w & Victor Young^m *(Alamo)*; Away from Home — Jack Elliott^w & David Rose^m *(Alamo)*; The Mask Waltz — Leo Robin^w & David Rose^m *(Alamo)*; These Foolish Monkeys — Jack Scholl^w & M.K. Jerome^m *(Alamo)*. A patriotic revue presented by the American Legion. After two months it folded in Chicago. COVER: cartoon sketches of various American-type characters.

1928 Red, White and Maddox (Broadway, 1969). Jay Garner, Georgia Allen.

Jubilee Joe — Don Tucker^{w/m} *(Valando)*; Red, White and Maddox — Don Tucker^m *(Valando)*. A musical based on an imaginary character like Lester Maddox of Atlanta and what would have happened if he had become President. It lasted five weeks. COVER: red, white, and blue letters.

1929 Redemption (Broadway, 1921). John Barrymore.

No More at Evening (Redemption Gypsy Song) — Maurice Nitke^{w/m} & Alex Ivanoff^{w/m} *(Marks)*; Redemption Waltzes — Maurice Nitke^m *(Marks)*. A production of the Tolstoy classic with John Barrymore produced on a limited run. COVER: a scene from the play.

1930 Redemption (Broadway, 1928). Charlotte Schultz, Alexander Moissi.

Redemption (fox-trot ballad) / Redemption (waltz ballad) — Mitchell Parish[w] & Sam Perry[m] *(Lewis Music)*. A revival of the Tolstoy classic for a limited run. COVER: a lady playing the piano.

1931 Redhead (Broadway, 1959). Gwen Verdon, Richard Kiley.

I Feel Merely Marvelous / I'm Back in Circulation / It Doesn't Take a Minute / Just for Once / Look Who's in Love / My Girl Is Just Enough Woman for Me / Redhead — complete vocal score / The Right Finger of My Left Hand / Two Faces in the Dark — Dorothy Fields[w] & Albert Hague[m] *(Chappell)*. A musical with a "Jack the Ripper" theme and a pleasant score. It ran for over a year because of the direction of Bob Fosse and the dancing of Gwen Verdon. COVER: a sketch of Gwen Verdon as the Redhead.

1932 Regina (Broadway, 1949). Priscilla Gillette, Brenda Lewis.

The Best Thing of All / Blues / Chinkypin / Greedy Girl / The Rain (choral arrangement) / Regina — complete vocal score / Summer Day / What Will It Be? — Marc Blitzstein[w/m] *(Chappell)*. An opera based on *The Little Foxes* that had a superb cast and a beautiful score. It lasted only seven weeks. COVER: designs and letters.

1933 The Rejuvenation of Aunt Mary (closed before Broadway, 1923). May Robson.

Everytime / Please Come Marry Me — Frank W. Beaston[w/m] *(Witmark)*; Southern Lullaby — Ray Mack[w] & Frank W. Beaston[m] *(Witmark)*. COVER: May Robson.

1934 Remote Control (Broadway, 1929). Frank Beaston, Louise Barrett.

Tune In on My Heart — Buddy Valentine[w/m] & Gene Johnston[w/m] *(Feist)*. A melodrama about a radio an-

nouncer that lasted for ten weeks. COVER: face of a beautiful girl and a remote control thermostat.

1935 Requiem (Broadway, 1985). Sarah Brightman, Placido Domingo.

Pie Jesu — Andrew Lloyd Webber[w/m] *(Really Useful)*. A concert version of this religious musical at the Episcopal Church in Manhattan. COVER: letters and designs.

1936 Return to the Forbidden Planet (Off Broadway, 1991). Gabriel Barre, Allison Briner.

Return to the Forbidden Planet — vocal selections of 20 songs — various composers *(Leonard)*. A musical from London about life on a space ship. It did not have any original music but used rock type songs from the '60s. It lasted six months. COVER: a space ship, a space man, and girl.

1937 Reuben, Reuben (closed before Broadway, 1955). Eddie Albert, Kaye Ballard.

Be with Me / The Hills of Amalfi / Miracle Song / Monday Morning Blues / Never Get Lost — Marc Blitzstein[w/m] *(Chappell)*. A strange musical which dealt with suicide and circus acts. It had some talented performers and a few interesting songs. The public could not understand it, so it folded in Boston. COVER: lettering and designs.

1938 Reunion in Vienna (Broadway, 1931). Lynn Fontanne, Alfred Lunt.

I'll Make You Love Me — Erno Beda[w] & Eisemann Mihaly[m] *(Marks)*; Reunion in Vienna — Roy Turk[w] & Vee Lawnhurst[m] *(Berlin)*. A hit comedy produced by the Theatre Guild; it ran for seven months. COVER: Lunt and Fontanne being serenaded by musicians.

1939 Re-United (Nightclub, 1922). Weber and Fields.

Chloe Cling to Me — Lorenz Hart[w] & Herbert Fields[w] & Joe Trounstine[m] *(Berlin)*; The Pelican — Lorenz Hart[w] & Herbert Fields[w] & A. Clapson[m] *(Marks)*. Music from a vaudeville act that reunited Weber and Fields. COVER: a boy and girl in an embrace; a pelican.

1940 Revenge with Music (Broadway, 1934). Charles Winninger, Libby Holman.

If There Is Someone Lovelier Than You / Maria / That Fellow Manuelo / Wand'ring Heart / When You Love Only One / You and the Night and the Music — Howard Dietz[w] & Arthur Schwartz[m] *(Harms)*. A musical with a Spanish setting. The book and settings were meant for an operetta and the songs did not fit in. The show produced two hit songs but ran only 20 weeks. COVER: sketch of a face, a house, and some people.

1941 La Revue des Ambassadeurs (Nightclub, 1928). Morton Downey, Fred Waring.

Almiro / Alpine Rose [VS] / Baby, Let's Dance [VS] / Blue Hours [VS] / Fish [VS] / Fountain of Youth [VS] / Hans / In a Moorish Garden [VS] / The Lost Liberty Blues [VS] / Military Maids / Old Fashioned Girl / Pilot Me [VS] / You and Me — Cole Porter[w/m] *(Harms)*. A nightclub revue with a limited run at the Ambassadeurs in Paris. COVER: lettering and designs.

1942 Revue Please! (British, 1933). Beatrice Lillie, Lupino Lane.

Hoops / Louisiana Hayride — Howard Dietz[w] & Arthur Schwartz[m] *(Chappell)*. This was a revue starring Bea Lillie with a short run. It utilized two hit Dietz-Schwartz songs. COVER: letters and designs.

1943 Revuette of 1930 (Nightclub, 1930). George Arthur.

Why Leave Me — George Arthur[w/m] *(Harms)*. COVER: George Arthur.

1944 Rex (Broadway, 1976). Nicol Williamson, Tom Aldredge.

As Once I Loved You / Away from You / Dear Jane [CUT] [RC] / Elizabeth (lullaby) [RC] / Eternal Stars [CUT] [RC] / I'll Miss You [CUT] [RC] / No Song More Pleasing [RC] / Te Deum [PC] / Tell Me [CUT] [RC] — Sheldon Harnick[w] & Richard Rodgers[m] *(Williamson)*. A musical dealing with Henry VIII with a dreary book and an ordinary score. It had a run of five weeks. COVER: titles and designs.

1945 Rhapsody in Black (Broadway, 1931). Ethel Waters, Al Moore.

I'm Feelin' Blue — Dorothy Fields[w] & Jimmy McHugh *(Shapiro, Bernstein)*; Till the Real Thing Comes Along — Mann Holiner[w/m] & L. Freeman[w/m] & Saul Chaplin[w/m] & Sammy Cahn[w/m] *(Shapiro, Bernstein)*; What's Keeping My Prince Charming? / You Can't Stop Me from Lovin' You — Mann Holiner[w] & Alberta Nichols[m] *(Shapiro, Bernstein)*. A singing vaudeville show with Waters and the Cecil Mack Choir. It lasted ten weeks. COVER: silver and black letters and designs.

1946 Rhyth-Mania (at the Cotton Club) (Nightclub, 1931). Aida Ward, Cab Calloway.

Between the Devil and the Deep Blue Sea / Breakfast Dance / Get Up, Get Out, Get Under the Sun / I Love a Parade [BW] / Kickin' the Gong Around / 'Neath the Pale Cuban Moon / Without Rhythm — Ted Koehler[w] & Harold Arlen[m] *(Mills)*. A Cotton Club revue with a limited run. It produced one hit song. COVER: four black dancers.

1947 Ride the Winds (Off Broadway, 1974). Chip Zien, Irving Lee.

Every Days / Loving You / That Touch / You're Loving Me — John Driver[w/m] *(Dramatis)*. A musical set in old Japan that lasted three performances. COVER: a Japanese warrior with a kite.

1948 The Right Girl (see also Maid to Love) (Broadway, 1921). Charles Purcell, Helen Montrose.

Aladdin / The Call of Love / The Cocktail Hour / Girls All Around Me / Look for the Girl / Look into Your Eyes / Love's Little Journey / Love's Romantic Sea / Lovingly Yours / Oriental Serenade / The Right Girl / The Rocking Chair Fleet / Thre's an Old Flame Burning / We Were Made to Love / You Can Trust Me / You'll Get Nothing from Me — Raymond Peck[w] & Percy Wenrich[m] *(Feist)*. A rich-to-poor-to-rich musical lasting three months. The try-out title was *Maid to Love*. COVER: flowers, branches, and designs.

1949 Right This Way (Broadway, 1937). Guy Robertson, Joe E. Lewis.

Don't Listen to Your Heart / Love Design — Marianne Waters$^{w/m}$ & Brad Greene$^{w/m}$ *(Marlo)*; Doughnuts and Coffee / I Can Dream, Can't I? / I Love the Way We Fell in Love / I'll Be Seeing You — Irving Kahal^w & Sammy Fain^m *(Marlo)*. A show dealing with romance in Paris that had two hit songs but lasted only two weeks. COVER: girl in evening gown with her arm — right this way.

1950 Ring 'Round the Moon (Broadway, 1950). Neva Patterson, Denholm Elliott.

Invitation Waltz — Richard Addinsell^m *(Chappell)*. A hit French comedy that lasted only eight weeks in the U.S. COVER: plain cover with titles only.

1951 The Rink (Broadway, 1984). Liza Minnelli, Chita Rivera.

All the Children in a Row [VS] / Blue Crystal [VS] / Chief Cook and Bottle Washer [VS] / Colored Lights [VS] / Marry Me [VS] / The Rink [VS] / Under the Roller-Coaster [VS] / Wallflowers [VS] / We Can Make It [VS] — Fred Ebb^w & John Kander^m *(Fiddleback)*. A musical set in an abandoned roller rink. It was boring and had a terrible score but lasted six months due to the attraction of Minnelli. COVER: Rivera and Minnelli in profile.

1952 Rio Rita (Broadway, 1927). Walter Catlett, Ada May.

Are You There? / Following the Sun Around / If You're in Love You'll Waltz / I'm Out on the Loose Tonight / The Kinkajou / The Rangers Song / Rio Rita / Rio Rita — complete vocal score / Sweetheart — Joseph McCarthy^w & Harry Tierney^m *(Feist)*. The opening attraction at the Ziegfeld Theatre was an old fashioned operetta. Ziegfeld's extra lavish production far outshone the serviceable score and the book about the Texas Rangers. It was

a hit and ran for 15 months. COVER: The original cover is a pale orange, shows a senorita, and lists six songs. The second cover is bright blue, shows four people, and lists eight songs.

1953 Rip Van Winkle (closed before Broadway, 1953). Stars unknown.

Now He's Gone / Stolen Moments — Morton DaCosta^w & Edwin McArthur^m *(Chappell)*. COVER: a sketch of Rip Van Winkle.

1954 Ripples (Broadway, 1926). Fred Stone, Dorothy Stone.

Anything May Happen Any Day — Graham John^w & Jerome Kern^m *(Harms)*; Babykins / There's Nothing Wrong in a Kiss — Irving Caesar^w & Graham John^w & Oscar Levant^m *(Harms)*; I'm a Little Bit Fonder of You / Ripples — Irving Caesar$^{w/m}$ *(Harms)*; I'm Afraid — Irving Caesar^w & Graham John^w & Albert Sirmay^m *(Harms)*; Is It Love / Talk with Your Heel and Toe — Irving Caesar^w & Oscar Levant^m *(Harms)*; You Never Can Tell About Love — Benny Davis^w & Fred Coots^m *(D C and E)*. A poor musical built around the Stone family dealing with bootleggers and such. It ran seven weeks. COVER: the Four Stones.

1955 Riquette *(see also* **Naughty Riquette)** (Broadway, 1926). Mitzi, Alexander Gray.

Brother of Mine / In Armenia / Make Believe You're Mine / Plant Some Roses — Harry B. Smith^w & Oscar Strauss^m *(Harms)*; I May — Harry B. Smith^w & Maurie Rubens^m & Kendall Burgess^m *(Harms)*; Some One — Harry B. Smith^w & Alfred Goodman^m & Maurie Rubens^m *(Harms)*. A musical about a telephone operator that ran 11 weeks. The try-out title was *Riquette*. COVER: girl at switchboard.

1956 The Rise and Fall of the City of Mahagonny (Off Broadway, 1970). Barbara Harris, Estelle Parsons.

Mahagonny — melody — Kurt Weill$^{w/m}$ & Bert Brecht$^{w/m}$ *(Harms)*; The Rise ·d Fall of the City of Mahagonny —

complete score—Kurt Weill[w/m] & Bert Brecht[w/m] *(Universal).* An updated revival of this Weill work that lasted one week. COVER: green cover with piano.

1957 Rise and Shine (British, 1935). Binnie Hale, Jack Whiting.

Rise 'n' Shine [B]—B.G. DeSylva[w] & Vincent Youmans[m] *(Chappell).* A big Drury Lane production that lasted five weeks. COVER: an air view of London including the Thames, bridges, and other items.

1958 The Rise of Rosie O'Reilly (Broadway, 1923). Jack McGowan, Virginia O'Brien.

Born and Bred in Brooklyn / A Darned Good Cry / I Never Met a Girl Like You / In the Slums / Keep-a-Countin' Eight / Let's You and I Just Say Goodbye / Love Dreams / The Marathon Step / Poor Old World / A Ring to the Name of Rosie / When June Comes Along with a Song—George M. Cohan[w/m] *(Witmark).* A cheap imitation of *Little Nellie Kelly* that ran for 12 weeks. COVER: George M. Cohan, Rosie, and the Brooklyn Bridge.

1959 Ritzie (*see also* **White Lights #1** *and* **White Lights #2)** (Broadway, 1927). Rosalie Claire, Sam Ash.

Don't Throw Me Down / Eyeful of You / Sitting in the Sun / Skiddle-De-Doo / Show Girl—Al Dubin[w] & Fred Coots[m] *(Marks);* I'll Keep on Dreaming of You—Fred Coots[w/m] & Al Dubin[w/m] & Walter Rode[w/m] *(Marks).* A poor backstage musical that lasted for a month. It toured as *White Lights,* then *Ritzie,* but opened in New York as *White Lights.* COVER: playgirl with a cigarette holder on playboy's shoulder.

1960 The River (Off Broadway, 1977). Stars unknown.

It's Never That Easy [VS] / Song of Me [VS] / Travel [VS]—Richard Maltby, Jr.[w] & David Shire[m] *(Fiddleback).* This was a musical that was planned for Off Broadway but never made it. COVER: titles only.

1961 Riverwind (Off Broadway, 1962). Helon Blount, Lawrence Brooks.

Riverwind / Sew the Buttons On—John Jennings[w/m] *(Saunders).* A small musical about a tourist home on the banks of the Wabash. With a very pleasant score and show, it ran for over a year. COVER: water, grass, and trees.

1962 Roads of Destiny (Broadway, 1919). Florence Reed.

Roads of Destiny Waltz—Paul Eisler[m] *(Harms).* A melodrama that had a short run on Broadway. COVER: Florence Reed.

1963 The Roar of the Greasepaint—The Smell of the Crowd (Broadway, 1965). Anthony Newley, Cyril Ritchard.

The Beautiful Land [VS] / Feeling Good / It Isn't Enough [VS] / The Joker / Look at That Face / My First Love Song [VS] / My Way [VS] / Nothing Can Stop Me Now / Put It in the Book [VS] / Sweet Beginning [VS] / That's What It Is to Be Young [VS] / Things to Remember [VS] / This Dream / What a Man! [VS] / Where Would You Be Without Me? [VS] / Who Can I Turn To / With All Due Respect [VS] / A Wonderful Day Like Today—Leslie Bricusse[w/m] & Anthony Newley[w/m] *(T R O).* A sort of sequel to *Stop the World* but not as good. An allegory of "haves" and "have nots," it produced several hit songs but ran only six months. COVER: a sketch of Newley and Ritchard.

1964 The Robber Bridegroom (Off Broadway, 1974). Raul Julia, Rhonda Coullet.

Deeper in the Woods / Nothin' Up / Sleepy Man—Alfred Uhry[w] & Robert Waldman[m] *(Macmillan).* This was a small production of this musical before it was enlarged for Broadway. It had a limited run of one week. COVER: sketch of the robber bridegroom and other characters.

1965 Robber Bridegroom (Broadway, 1976). Barry Bostwick, Rhonda Coullet.

Deeper in the Woods [VS] / Goodbye Salome [VS] / Love Stolen [VS] / Next to Lovin' [VS] / Nothin' Up [VS] / The Only Home I Know [VS] / Over the Hill [VS] / Papa's Gonna Make It Alright [VS] / The Pickers Are Comin' [VS] / Raise the Flag [VS] / Sleepy Man [VS] / Violets and Silverbells [VS] / Why Am I Me? [VS] — Alfred Uhry[w] & Robert Waldman[m] *(Macmillan)*. This folk musical about a bridegroom searching for his bride lasted only four months. COVER: a sketch of the robber bridegroom.

1966 Robert and Elizabeth (closed before Broadway, 1982). Leigh Berry, Mark Jacoby.

The Girls That Boys Dream About [B] / I Know Now [B] / I Said Love [B] / The World Outside [B] / You Only to Love Me [B] — Ronald Millar[w] & Ron Grainer[m] *(Erle Music)*. This musical version of the *Barretts of Wimpole Street* was a big London hit of almost 1,000 performances. This lavish production at the Paper Mill Playhouse was well received but got no offers for Broadway. COVER: street lamps, designs, and lettering.

1967 Roberta *(see also* **Gowns by Roberta***)* (Broadway, 1933). Bob Hope, Lyda Roberti.

I'll Be Hard to Handle — Bernard Dougall[w] & Jerome Kern[m] *(Harms)*; Let's Begin / Smoke Gets in Your Eyes / Something Had to Happen / The Touch of Your Hand / Yesterdays — Otto Harbach[w] & Jerome Kern[m] *(Harms)*; Roberta — complete vocal score — Otto Harbach[w] & Bernard Dougall[w] & Jerome Kern[m] *(Harms)*. This was Kern's last big Broadway show; it dealt with the fashion world in Paris. It ran for nine months with a wonderful score and many hit songs. The try-out title was *Gowns by Roberta*. COVER: a model beside a curtain.

1968 Robinson Crusoe (closed before Broadway, 1933). Stars unknown.

I Will Always Love You / Over a Southern Sea — Louis Weslyn[w] & Hal Dyson[m] *(Marks)*; Sunshine Follows the Rain — Hal Dyson[w/m] *(Marks)*. COVER: five girls in beach attire and a parrot.

1969 Rock-a-Bye Baby (Broadway, 1918). Louise Dresser, Frank Morgan.

The Big Spring Drive / I Believed All They Said / I Never Thought / The Kettle Song / Little Tune, Go Away / Lullaby / My Boy / Not You / Nursery Fanfare / One, Two, Three / There's No Better Use for Time Than Kissing — Herbert Reynolds[w] & Jerome Kern[m] *(Harms)*. This was a musical about a woman stranded at a "Baby Inn." A pleasant Jerome Kern score and fairly good reviews could not keep it going more than 11 weeks. COVER 1 is pale blue, black, and white with flowers and lists nine songs. COVER 2 is bright blue with a couple in hammock and lists 11 songs.

1970 The Rocky Horror Show (Broadway, 1975). Tim Curry, Kim Milford. Vocal Selections:

Charles Atlas Song / Charles Atlas Song — reprise / Damn It Janet / Don't Dream It / Eddie's Teddy / Hot Patootie — Bless My Soul / I Can Make You a Man / I Can Make You a Man Reprise / I'm Going Home / Once in a While / Over at the Frankenstein Place / Planet Shmamet Janet / Science Fiction/Double Feature / Science Fiction Reprise / Super Heroes / Sweet Transvestite / Sword of Damocles / Time Warp / Time Warp Reprise / Toucha, Toucha, Toucha, Touch Me / Whatever Happened to Saturday Night / Wild and Untamed Things — Richard O'Brien[w/m] *(Druidcrest Music)*. This was a London hit, making fun of old horror movies, that lasted four weeks in N.Y. COVER: Frank N. Furter, a transvestite.

1971 Roly Boly Eyes (Broadway, 1919). Eddie Leonard, Queenie Smith.

A Bungalow for Two / Dippy Doodlums / Just a Girl, Just a Boy / Old Fashioned Flower / Your Voice I

Hear — Edgar Woolf[w] & Eddy Brown[m] & Louis Gruenberg[m] *(Shapiro, Bernstein)*; Ida, Sweet as Apple Cider — Eddie Leonard[w/m] *(Marks)*. A musical about a man falsely accused of a crime. It ran three months and introduced "Ida." COVER: a smiling girl with pretty eyes.

1972 Romance Isle (Broadway, 1929). Stars unknown.

If I Had My Way — Ruben Cowan[w/m] *(Famous)*. A small musical performed in between showings in Paramount theatres in large cities. COVER: silhouette of a girl and a flower.

1973 Romance! Romance! (Broadway, 1988). Scott Bakula, Alison Fraser.

Goodbye, Emil [VS] / How Did I End Up Here? [VS] / I'll Always Remember the Song [VS] / It's Not Too Late / The Little Comedy [VS] / The Night It Had to End / Romance! Romance! / Romantic Notions / Words He Doesn't Say — Barry Harman[w] & Keith Herrmann[m] *(Warner Bros.)*. Two one act musicals that were very charming. The subject was romance and it lasted nine months. COVER: the title in a big heart.

1974 Romany Love (closed before Broadway, 1925). Geraldine Farrar.

We Two — William Carey Duncan[w] & Irving Caesar[w] & Franz Lehar[m] *(Harms)*. COVER: Geraldine Farrar.

1975 Rosalie (Broadway, 1928). Marilyn Miller, Jack Donahue.

Beautiful Gypsy / Ev'rybody Knows I Love Somebody / How Long Has This Been Going On? / Rosalie / Show Me the Town / Yankee Doodle Rhythm — Ira Gershwin[w] & George Gershwin[m] *(Harms)*; Follow the Drums — piano selections — George Gershwin[m] *(Harms)*; Hussars March / West Point Song / Why Must We Always Be Dreaming — P.G. Wodehouse[w] & Sigmund Romberg[m] *(Harms)*; Oh Gee, Oh Joy! / Say So! — P.G. Wodehouse[w] & Ira Gershwin[w] & George Gershwin[m] *(Harms)*.

This was a lavish Ziegfeld production for Marilyn Miller as a princess in love with a commoner. It ran ten months. COVER: Marilyn Miller.

1976 Rosalinda (Broadway, 1942). Dorothy Sarnoff, Gene Barry.

Ballet-Wine, Woman, and Song; [VS] / Waltz Selection [VS] — Johann Strauss[m] *(Boosey Hawkes)*; Brother Mine [VS] / Drinking Song [VS] / Entr'acte [VS] / Laughing Song / Oh Jiminy [VS] / Orlofsky's Song — Paul Kerby[w] & Johann Strauss[m] *(Boosey, Hawkes)*. An excellent revival of the old classic *Fledermaus*; the revival 15 months. COVER: lady with mask and fan.

1977 Rose Briar (Broadway, 1922). Billie Burke.

Give Me the Moon — Booth Tarkington[w] & Donald McGibeny[m] *(Harms)*; Love and the Moon — Booth Tarkington[w] & Jerome Kern[m] *(Harms)*. A Ziegfeld production for Billie Burke as a singer involved in a divorce case. It ran three months. COVER: Billie Burke.

1978 The Rose Girl (Broadway, 1920). Charles Purcell, Mabel Withee.

Beauty's Candy Shop / Come On Girls, Let's Go / Dear Little Rose Girl / Down Where the Mortgages Grow / The Girl You Never Have Kissed / I Love the Love That's New / If You Have Proteges / If You Keep Them Wondering / I'm a One Girl Boy / Magnetism / May and September / A Nice Little Girl on the Side / Something New / That One Sweet Hour / That's New / There Comes a Some Day / When Our Sundays Are Blue / When That Somebody Comes — William Duncan[w] & Anselm Goetzl[m] *(Witmark)*; In the Heart of a Crimson Rose — William Duncan[w] & Shep Camp[m] *(Witmark)*; Ma! — Sidney Clare[w] & Con Conrad[m] *(Fisher)*; My Old New Jersey Home — Ballard MacDonald[w] & Nat Vincent[m] *(Shapiro, Bernstein)*; Wondrous Midnight Eyes — Kay Reese[w] & Anselm Goetzl[m] *(H and D)*. A musical about a girl who flees to Paris to avoid a marriage. It was a very dull musical that lasted three months. COVER: a girl surrounded by roses.

1979 Rose Marie (Broadway, 1924). Mary Ellis.

The Call / Door of My Dreams / Indian Love Call / Lak Jeem / Rose Marie / Totem Tom-Tom — Otto Harbach[w] & Oscar Hammerstein[w] & Rudolf Friml[m] *(Harms)*; Hard Boiled Herman / Why Shouldn't We — Otto Harbach[w] & Oscar Hammerstein[w] & Herbert Stothart[m] *(Harms)*; Indian Cabin and Empire Scene — piano selections — Herbert Stothart[m] & Rudolf Friml[m] *(Harms)*; The Mounties / Rose Marie — complete vocal score — Otto Harbach[w] & Oscar Hammerstein[w] & Rudolf Friml[m] & Herbert Stothart[m] *(Harms)*. A love story set in the Canadian Rockies became one of the biggest hit musicals in the century. With Friml's best score and some big production numbers, this show ran for a year and a half. It toured and toured and played for years in all the capitals of the world. COVER: flowers and designs.

1980 Rose Marie (Regional, 1950). Patrice Munsel, Wally Cassel.

Indian Love Call / Rose Marie / Totem Tom-Tom — Otto Harbach[w] & Oscar Hammerstein[w] & Rudolf Friml[m] *(Harms)*; Mam'selle / Waltz Song — Forman Brown[w] & Rudolf Friml[m] *(Harms)*; The Mounties — Otto Harbach[w] & Oscar Hammerstein[w] & Herbert Stothart[m] & Rudolf Friml[m] *(Harms)*; Whenever Night Falls — Otto Harbach[w] & Rudolf Friml[m] *(Harms)*; Why Shouldn't We — Otto Harbach[w] & Oscar Hammerstein[w] & Herbert Stothart[m] *(Harms)*. This revival had a limited run by the Los Angeles Civic Opera with some new Friml songs. COVER: roses and designs.

1981 Rose of China (Broadway, 1919). Oscar Shaw, June Richardson.

Bunny Dear / College Spirit / Down on the Banks of the Subway / Tao Loved His Li / Yale / Yesterday — P.G. Wodehouse[w] & Armand Vecsey[m] *(Harms)*; In Our Bungalow — Oscar Shaw[w] & P.G. Wodehouse[w] & Armand Vecsey[m] *(Harms)*. This was a musical about an American boy and Chinese girl. It was a big hit in its pre-Broadway tour, a failure of six weeks on Broadway, and a smash hit in Chicago after Broadway. COVER: designs and lettering.

1982 Rose of Killarney (Irish, 1924). Gerald Griffin.

Ireland Is Heaven to Me — Gerald Griffin[w/m] & Charles Harrison[w/m] & Fred Rose[w/m] *(Browne)*; Just Day Dreams — Gerald Griffin[w] & Gerald Sullivan[m] *(Browne)*; My Sweet Killarney Rose — Gerald Griffin[w/m] & Bartley Costello[w/m] & Roy Barton[w/m] *(Browne)*. COVER: Gerald Griffin.

1983 The Rose of Stamboul (Broadway, 1922). James Barton, Tessa Kosta.

Girls from the Cultured West / Little Blue Book / No More Girls / Rose Feast / The Rose of Stamboul / When We Are Honeymooning — Harold Atteridge[w] & Leo Fall[m] *(Tama)*; Lovey Dove / Mazuma / My Heart Is Calling / Time, Only Time, Dear — Harold Atteridge[w] & Sigmund Romberg[m] *(Tama)*; Ting-a-Ling / A Waltz It Should Be — Harold Atteridge[w] & Leo Fall[m] & Sigmund Romberg[m] *(Tama)*; Why Do They Die — William Jerome[w] & Alex Gerber[w] & Jean Schwartz[m] *(Witmark)*. A dull musical about a pasha's daughter. It ran three months.

1984 Rosso's Song Review of 1927 (Nightclub, 1927). Stars unknown.

Bring Back the World — A. Collins[w/m] *(McClure)*; Forever — Billy Hill[w/m] *(McClure)*; I'll Make You Smile / I'm Just a 'Wearying for You / Poor Little Butterfly / There's a Little Lovin' — Harley Rosso[w] & Billy Kelly[m] *(McClure)*. COVER: a beautiful butterfly.

1985 The Rothschilds (Broadway, 1970). Hal Linden, Leila Martin.

Everything [VS] / I'm in Love, I'm in Love! / In My Own Lifetime / One Room / Rothschild and Sons [VS] /

Sons [VS] / Valse de Rothschild — Sheldon Harnick[w] & Jerry Bock[m] *(Valando)*. A musical about the Rothschild family that was quite ordinary but ran for over a year. COVER: the Rothschild coat of arms.

1986 Round the Town (Broadway, 1924). Harry Fox.

Liza Jane / Poor Little Wallflow'r — Ned Wever[w] & Alfred Nathan[m] *(Harms)*. A musical revue on the Century roof. COVER: letters and designs.

1987 Roundabout (British, 1949). Bobby Howes, Pat Kirkwood.

Roundabout — Ken Attiwill[w] & Edward Horan[m] *(Shapiro, Bernstein)*. A musical that lasted three weeks in London with a song published in the United States. COVER: circus tents and musical notes.

1988 Roxy's Premiere Radio City (Broadway, 1932). Ray Bolger, Lew Fields.

Happy Times / Hey! Young Fella / Journey's End / With a Feather in Your Cap — Dorothy Fields[w] & Jimmy McHugh[m] *(Robbins)*. COVER: a picture of Roxy and a sketch of Radio City in New York.

1989 Royal Palm Revue (Nightclub, 1940). Tony Martin, Rudy Vallee.

I'll Be Seeing You — Irving Kahal[w] & Sammy Fain[m] *(Marlo)*; Love Song of Renaldo — Irving Kahal[w] & Sammy Fain[m] *(Shapiro, Bernstein)*. COVER: Harry Richman, Tony Martin, Rudy Vallee, Abe Lyman, and others.

1990 A Royal Pretender (*see also* **Princess Flavia**) (Broadway, 1925). Evelyn Herbert, Douglass Dumbrille.

I Dare Not Love You / Marionettes / Only One / What Do I Care? — Harry B. Smith[w] & Sigmund Romberg[m] *(Harms)*. A poor imitation of *Student Prince* with a run of 19 weeks and tour. The try-out title was *A Royal Pretender*. COVER: a crown and sceptre.

1991 The Royal Vagabond (Broadway, 1919). Tessa Kosta, Dorothy Dickson.

Charming — Joseph McCarthy[w] & Harry Tierney[m] *(M and F)*; Democ-racy / I Want Someone to Love Me / Just for You and You Alone / Love Is Love / Love of Mine / Nice Little Girl on the Side / Talk / Thistledown Girl / What You Don't Know Won't Hurt You / When the Cherry Blossoms Fall / When the World Is Upside Down — William Duncan[w] & Anselm Goetzl[m] *(Witmark)*; Goodbye, Bargravia / Here Come the Soldiers / In a Kingdom of Our Own — George M. Cohan[w/m] *(Witmark)*; Milady's Perfume — Joseph McCarthy[w] & John Mears[w] & Harry Tierney[m] *(M and F)*; Revolutionary Rag — Irving Berlin[w/m] *(Harms)*; Royal Vagabong — complete vocal score — Joseph McCarthy[w/m] & Harry Tierney[w/m] & William Duncan[w/m] & Anselm Goetzl[w/m] & George M. Cohan[w/m] & John Mears[w/m] & Irving Berlin[w/m] *(Witmark)*; A Wee Bit of Lace — George M. Cohan[w] & Harry Tierney[m] *(M and F)*. A revolution in Bargravia was the subject of this musical. It was very ordinary but it lasted six months. COVER 1 is blue and gold with a crown. COVER 2 is red and blue with a vagabond's face. COVER 3 is red and blue with a man in wig and lace with a cane.

1992 The Rubicon (Broadway, 1922). Dorothy Tierney, Kenneth Hill.

Whistle a Tune — Neville Fleeson[w] & Albert Von Tilzer[m] *(Von Tilzer)*. A comedy about a love triangle that had a short life. COVER: a well dressed lady in a field of flowers.

1993 Rudy Vallee's Punch Bowl Revue (Nightclub, 1936). Rudy Vallee.

Hold Me Close — Jimmie Lee[w] & Karl C. Lillie[m] *(Southern)*. COVER: Rudy Vallee and punch bowl.

1994 Rufus LeMaire's Affairs (1st edition and on tour) (Broadway, 1927). Ted Lewis, Sophie Tucker.

Boulevard Strut / Bring Back Those Minstrel Days / Down Where the Morning Glories Twine / The Golden Girl / Jingly Tune / Love May Not Hide / Remember Cameo / Scandalizing Fashion / Wandering in Dreamland / When I Think About Girls I Fell For /

You'll Learn How, Bye and Bye — Ballard MacDonald[w] & Martin Broones[m] *(Shapiro, Bernstein)*; I Can't Get Over a Girl Like You — Harry Ruskin[w] & Martin Broones[m] *(Shapiro, Bernstein)*; I'll Take the Key and Lock Him Up — Bob Schafer[w] & Jack Hauser[w] & Artie Dunn[m] *(Broadway Music)*. This show was a failure on Broadway but had a successful post-Broadway tour with Sophie Tucker. COVER: flowers and designs with the names of Sophie Tucker and Ted Lewis.

1995 Rufus LeMaire's Affairs (1st edition) (Broadway, 1927). Charlotte Greenwood, Ted Lewis. Second cast.

Boulevard Strut / The Golden Girl / Jingly Tune / Love May Not Hide / Minstrel Days / Remember Cameo / Scandalizing Fashion / Wandering in Dreamland / When I Think About the Girls I Fell For / Where the Morning Glories Twine — Ballard MacDonald[w] & Martin Broones[m] *(Shapiro, Bernstein)*; I Can't Get Over a Girl Like You — Harry Ruskin[w] & Martin Broones[m] *(Shapiro, Bernstein)*. This revue was a failure on Broadway with Greenwood and Lewis but a big hit on tour with Sophie Tucker and Ted Lewis. COVER: flowers and designs with the names of Charlotte Greenwood and Ted Lewis.

1996 Rufus LeMaire's Affairs (2nd edition) (Broadway, 1927). Ted Lewis, Bobbe Arnst.

Hosanna / Love Baby / Nagasacki Butterfly / Rose of the Studio / When the Eenie-Meenies Do the Minie Mo — Billy Rose[w] & Jesse Greer[m] *(Shapiro, Bernstein)*; Lily — Ballard MacDonald[w/m] & Harry Warren[w/m] & Martin Broones[w/m] *(Shapiro, Bernstein)*; Since Henry Ford Apologized to Me — Billy Rose[w] & Ballard MacDonald[w] & Dave Stamper[m] *(Shapiro, Bernstein)*; Underneath the Wabash Moon — Billy Rose[w] & Dave Stamper[m] *(Shapiro, Bernstein)*; Wah-Wah! — Ballard MacDonald[w] & Martin Broones[m] *(Shapiro, Bernstein)*; You'll Find a Beautiful Face / You'll Find the End of the Rainbow — Billy Rose[w] & Ballard MacDonald[w] & Jesse Greer[m] *(Shapiro, Bernstein)*. COVER: designs and lettering.

1997 Rugantino (Broadway, 1964). Nino Manfredi, Ornella Vanoni.

Ciumachella / The Lights of Roma — Carl Sigman[w] & Armando Trovajoli[m] *(Harms)*. A hit Italian musical about early Rome adapted by Alfred Drake. It ran three weeks. COVER: the cast of the show.

1998 Rumple (Broadway, 1957). Eddie Foy, Gretchen Wyler.

Coax Me / The First Time I Spoke of You / How Do You Say Goodbye? / In Times Like These / Wish — Frank Reardon[w] & Ernest Schweikert[m] *(Chappell)*. A musical about a fading cartoonist that lasted five weeks. COVER: Eddie Foy with umbrella.

1999 Runnin' Wild (Broadway, 1923). Adelaide Hall, Cecil Mack.

Charleston / Ginger Brown / Love Bug / Old Fashioned Love / Open Your Heart / Snow Time — Cecil Mack[w/m] & Jimmy Johnson[w/m] *(Harms)*; Easy Goin' Man — Darl MacBoyle[w/m] & Turner Layton[w/m] *(Remick)*; Heart Breakin' Jo — Porter Grainger[w/m] & Jo Trent[w/m] *(Harms)*; I Don't Know Nobody — Jo Trent[w/m] & Will Donaldson[w/m] *(Fred Fisher)*. A black musical that got good reviews and ran for 20 weeks. COVER: red and black designs; Miller and Lyles.

2000 Sadie Thompson (Broadway, 1944). June Havoc, Ralph Dumke.

If You Can't Get the Love You Want / Life's a Funny Present from Someone / The Love I Long For / Poor as a Churchmouse / Sailing at Midnight / When You Live on an Island — Howard Dietz[w] & Vernon Duke[m] *(Paramount)*. A musical version of the classic *Rain* written for Ethel Merman but played by June Havoc. It had some lovely Duke songs, but a dreary book, and lasted for two months. COVER: a beautiful colored sketch of Sadie Thompson.

2001 Sail Away (Broadway, 1961). Elaine Stritch, Alice Pearce.

Don't Turn Away from Love / Go Slow, Johnny / Later Than Spring / Sail Away / Something Very Strange / This Is a Changing World / When You Want Me / Where Shall I Find Him / Why Do the Wrong People Travel? — Noel Coward[w/m] *(Chappell)*. Elaine Stritch was a cruise hostess in this musical that lasted only five months. COVER: sketch of people on deck of ship.

2002 St. Louis Woman (Broadway, 1946). Pearl Bailey, Ruby Hill.

Any Place I Hang My Hat Is Home / I Had Myself a True Love / I Wonder What Became of Me [BW] / Legalize My Name / Ridin' on the Moon — Johnny Mercer[w] & Harold Arlen[m] *(D B and H)*; Cakewalk Your Lady / A Woman's Prerogative [VS] — Johnny Mercer[w] & Harold Arlen[m] *(Crawford)*; Come Rain or Come Shine / Li'l Augie Is a Natural Man [RC] / Lullaby [VS] — Johnny Mercer[w] & Harold Arlen[m] *(Chappell)*. This musical, involving a jockey and a beauty, had a lovely Arlen score and some great dancing but the poor book held it back and it lasted only three months. COVER: a black couple doing the cakewalk.

2003 The Saint of Bleecker Street (Broadway, 1954). Virginia Copeland, Gabrielle Ruggiero.

The Saint of Bleecker Street — complete vocal score — Gian-Carlo Menotti[w/m] *(Schirmer)*. An opera about murder and incest; the opera lasted only 11 weeks. COVER: a saint.

2004 Salad Days (Off Broadway, 1958). Barbara Franklin, Richard Easton.

I Sit in the Sun [B] / It's Easy to Sing [B] / Oh! Look at Me [B] / The Time of My Life [B] [VS] / We Said We Wouldn't Look Back [B] — Dorothy Reynolds[w/m] & Julian Slade[w/m] *(Robbins)*; Salad Days — complete vocal score [B] — Dorothy Reynolds[w/m] & Julian Slade[w/m] *(F D and H)*. A long running hit in London, this musical fantasy lasted only ten weeks in the

U.S. COVER: a piano on wheels, chairs, and an empty park.

2005 Sally (Broadway, 1920). Leon Errol, Marilyn Miller.

The Church 'Round the Corner / You Can't Keep a Good Girl Down — P.G. Wodehouse[w] & Clifford Grey[w] & Jerome Kern[m] *(Harms)*; Look for the Silver Lining / Whip-Poor-Will — B.G. DeSylva[w] & Jerome Kern[m] *(Harms)*; The Lorelei — Anne Caldwell[w] & Jerome Kern[m] *(Harms)*; On with the Dance / Sally / The Schnitza Komisski / Wild Rose — Clifford Grey[w] & Jerome Kern[m] *(Harms)*; Sally — complete vocal score — P.G. Wodehouse[w] & B.G. DeSylva[w] & Clifford Grey[w] & Anne Caldwell[w] & Jerome Kern[m] *(Harms)*. Marilyn Miller was a dishwasher to a Broadway star in this musical. It had just about everything including a lavish production, wonderful songs, a good book, great comedy, and a star. It ran 18 months. COVER: Marilyn Miller, Leon Errol.

2006 Sally (British, 1921). Dorothy Dickson, Leslie Henson.

Sally — Valse [B] — Jerome Kern[m] *(Chappell)*; Whose Baby Are You? [B] — Anne Caldwell[w] & Jerome Kern[m] *(Chappell)*. This American hit was also a hit in London and ran for over a year. COVER: a girl dancing on the clouds.

2007 Sally (Broadway, 1948). Bambi Linn, Willie Howard.

Church 'Round the Corner — P.G. Wodehouse[w] & Clifford Grey[w] & Jerome Kern[m] *(Harms)*; Look for the Silver Lining — B.G. DeSylva[w] & Jerome Kern[m] *(Harms)*; The Siren's Song — P.G. Wodehouse[w] & Jerome Kern[m] *(Harms)*; Wild Rose — Clifford Grey[w] & Jerome Kern[m] *(Harms)*. A revival of the hit musical that lacked everything and lasted for only a month. COVER: a flower and designs.

2008 Sally, Irene and Mary (Broadway, 1922). Jean Brown, Eddie Dowling.

After the Clouds Roll By / Dance of the Radium / How I've Missed You Mary / I Wonder Why / Jimmie / Old Fashioned Gown / Our Home Sweet

Home / Time Will Tell / When a Regular Boy Loves a Regular Girl—Raymond Klages[w] & Fred Coots[m] *(Remick)*. This musical was a take-off on the three hit musicals of the year. It was the story of three girls and their beaux with an ordinary score but good comedy that ran nine months. COVER: flowers, ribbons, and designs.

2009 Saluta (Broadway, 1934). Milton Berle, Ann Barrie.

Chill in the Air—Will Morrissey[w] & Frank D'Armond[m] *(Shapiro, Bernstein)*; Just Say the Word—Milton Berle[w] & Frank D'Armond[m] *(Shapiro, Bernstein)*; We, Incorporated—Milton Berle[w] & Maurice Sigler[w] & Frank D'Armond[m] *(Shapiro, Bernstein)*. Milton Berle produced this opera in Italy in competition with *Il Duce*. It was a poor musical that lasted five weeks. COVER: stripes and designs.

2010 Salute to Spring (closed before Broadway, 1936). Guy Robertson, Bernice Claire.

April Day / One Robin / Salute to Spring / Somehow / A Waltz Was Born in Vienna—Earle Crooker[w] & Frederick Loewe[m] *(Chappell)*. A musical about an artist's colony that had a summer try-out. COVER: a robin, flowers, and buildings.

2011 Salvation (Off Broadway, 1969). C.C. Courtney, Joe Morton.

Daedalus [VS] / Gina [VS] / Let the Moment [VS] / Let's Get Lost in Now [VS] / Tomorrow Is the First Day of the Rest of My Life—C.C. Courtney[m] & Peter Link[m] *(Chappell)*; Forever / If You Let Me Make Love to You / In Between—C.C. Courtney[w/m] & Peter Link[w/m] *(Chappell)*. A rock musical that was a moderate hit and ran for six months. COVER: a cross with light bulbs.

2012 Sancho Panza (Broadway, 1923). Otis Skinner, Robert Robson.

When Her Lips Surrender—Hugo Felix[w/m] *(Berlin)*. A comedy with a Don Quixote theme that lasted only five weeks. COVER: Otis Skinner.

2013 Sandhog (Off Broadway, 1954). Jack Cassidy, Alice Ghostley.

Johnny-O / Katie O'Sullivan / Sandhog—complete score / Twins—Waldo Salt[w] & Earl Robinson[m] *(Chappell)*. An interesting musical about building tunnels that ran only six weeks. COVER: boy and girl in tunnel.

2014 Sap of Life (Off Broadway, 1961). Kenneth Nelson, Jerry Dodge.

She Loves Me Not [VS] / Watching the Big Parade Go By [VS]—Richard Maltby, Jr.[w] & David Shire[m] *(Fiddleback)*. A musical about young love; the musical lasted six weeks. COVER: Maltby and Shire.

2015 Saratoga (Broadway, 1959). Howard Keel, Carol Lawrence.

Dog Eat Dog [VS] / A Game of Poker / Goose Never Be a Peacock / Love Held Lightly / The Man in My Life / The Parks of Paris [VS] / Petticoat High [VS] / Saratoga / You for Me [VS]—Johnny Mercer[w] & Harold Arlen[m] *(Morris)*. A musical version of the famous novel with lavish sets but nothing else. It lasted ten weeks and was Arlen's last score. COVER: men and women in a New Orleans courtyard.

2016 Sarava (Broadway, 1979). P.J. Benjamin, Tovah Feldshuh.

Sarava—N. Richard Nash[w] & Mitch Leigh[m] *(Cherry Lane)*. A musical version of a hit movie that dragged on for four months. COVER: black and white cover with titles and designs.

2017 Sari (Broadway, 1930). Mitzi, Boyd Marshall.

Ha-Za-Za / Love Has Wings / Love's Own Sweet Song / My Faithful Stradivari / Softly Thro' the Summer Night—C. Cushing[w] & E. Heath[w] & Emmerich Kalman[m] *(Marks)*. An attempt to revive an old hit musical with the original star. It lasted two weeks. COVER: Mitzi.

2018 Satellite (Broadway, 1935). Noel Francis, Barbara Weeks.

The Girl Was Beautiful / Satellite—Manny Kurtz[w] & Samuel Pokrass[m] *(Mills)*; Honestly—Mitchell Parish[w] & Samuel Pokrass[m] *(Mills)*. A comedy with three sisters as chorus girls. It lasted one performance. COVER: Noel Francis, Barbara Weeks, Joyce White.

2019 Satires of 1920 (*see also* **Alley Up!** *and* **Sunkist**) (Broadway, 1920). Fanchon and Marco.

Ain't We Got Fun — Gus Kahn[w] & Raymond Egan[w] & Richard Whiting[m] *(Remick)*; Grieving for You — Joe Gibson[w/m] & Joe Ribaud[w/m] & Joe Gold[w/m] *(Feist)*; The I Dun-No-Wat / I Want to Meet You Some Day in California / The Love a Gipsy Knows / My Sweetie's Smile / Pollyanna / A Pretty Dance Is Like a Violin — Fanchon and Marco[w/m] *(Remick)*. A revue poking fun at the movies. It toured as *Alley Up!* and *Satires of 1920* and opened as *Sunkist*, but it failed. COVER: Arthur West and Miss Fanchon.

2020 Saturday Night (closed before Broadway, 1954). Jack Cassidy.

Class [PC] / So Many People [VS] — Stephen Sondheim[w/m] *(Chappell)*. This was Sondheim's first full score written for Broadway. It was put aside for work on *West Side Story* and *Gypsy*. After *Gypsy* opened, Jule Styne was to produce it for a December 1959 opening at the 46th Street Theatre with Bob Fosse as director. During the early auditions, Sondheim withdrew the musical saying he would rather go forward than backward. COVER: Stephen Sondheim.

2021 Save Me the Waltz (Broadway, 1938). John Emery, Jane Wyatt.

Save Me the Waltz — Buddy Bernier[w] & Hans Barth[m] *(Crawford)*. A comedy that lasted one week about a royal marriage. COVER: a couple waltzing.

2022 Say, Darling (Broadway, 1958). David Wayne, Vivian Blaine.

Dance Only with Me / It's the Second Time You Meet That Matters / Let the Lower Light Be Burning / My Little Yellow Dress / Say, Darling / Something's Always Happening on the River / Try to Love Me as I Am — Betty Comden[w] & Adolph Green[w] & Jule Styne[m] *(Stratford)*. A musical about creating a musical. It was passable but nothing more and lasted nine months. COVER: sketch of a stage show in rehearsal.

2023 Say Hello to Harvey (closed before Broadway, 1981). Donald O'Connor, Patricia Routledge.

Bring It to the Bar [VS] / Do It in Style [VS] / I Recommend Pleasant [VS] / I'd Rather Look at You [VS] / Perfect Person [VS] / Say Hello to Harvey [VS] / We Like the Same Things [VS] — Leslie Bricusse[w/m] *(Stage and Screen)*. A musical based on the hit comedy *Harvey* that folded on the road. COVER: Leslie Bricusse.

2024 Say Mama (Regional, 1921). Stars unknown.

Jack and Jill [PC] — Lorenz Hart[w] & Richard Rodgers[m] *(Feist)*. A musical written for and performed at two Akron Club benefits. COVER: none.

2025 Say When (Broadway, 1928). Dorothy Fitzgibbon, Alison Skipworth.

Cheerio — James Walker[w] & Jesse Greer[m] *(Robbins)*; Give Me a Night / My One Girl — W. Franke Harling[w/m] *(Harms)*; How About It? / One Step to Heaven / Say When — Raymond Klages[w] & Jesse Greer[m] *(Robbins)*; In My Love Boat — Max Lief[w] & Nathaniel Lief[w] & Comtesse de Segonzac[m] *(Robbins)*; No Room for Anybody in My Heart for You / Who's the Boy — Max Lief[w] & Nathaniel Lief[w] & Ray Perkins[m] *(Harms)*. A "love triangle" musical that lasted for two weeks. COVER: Harms' cover has a man and woman sitting on a divan and Robbins' cover has four men and a woman in evening clothes.

2026 Say When (Broadway, 1934). Bob Hope, Harry Richman.

Don't Tell Me It's Bad / Isn't It June / It Must Have Been the Night / Let's Take Advantage of Now / Put Your Heart in a Song / Say When / So Long for Ever So Long / Torch Parade / When Love Comes Swingin' Along — Ted Koehler[w] & Ray Henderson[m] *(Harms)*. This shipboard romance received good reviews but lasted only nine weeks. COVER: a girl with a glass of champagne.

2027 Scandal (Broadway, 1919). Charles Cherry, Francine Larrimore.

A Kiss to Remember Me By — Cosmo Hamilton[w/m] & Ed Breier[w/m] & Edward Weinstein[w/m] *(Stern)*. A comedy about a lie and a marriage that had a short run. COVER: Cherry and Larrimore.

2028 The Scarlet Pimpernel (closed before Broadway, 1992). Linda Eder.

Home Again [VS] / I'll Forget You [VS] / Marguerite [VS] / Now When the Rain Falls [VS] / Our Separate Ways [VS] / The Scarlet Pimpernel [VS] / Storybook [VS] / There Never Was a Time [VS] / They Seek Him Here [VS] / When I Look at You [VS] / You Are My Home — Nan Knighton[w] & Frank Wildhorn[m] *(Warner Bros.)*; Pimpernel Fanfare [VS] — Frank Wildhorn[m] *(Warner)*. A musical written for Broadway and recorded by Angel records. COVER: Linda Eder.

2029 School Belles (closed before Broadway, 1924). Stars unknown.

His Photograph / Write Me a Letter — Dorothy Donnelly[w] & Nat Ayer[m] *(Harms)*. COVER: three girls in front of a blackboard.

2030 School for Husbands (Broadway, 1933). Osgood Perkins, Stuart Casey.

Kiss and Never Tell / Yes — Ma Ma! — Edward Rickett[w/m] *(Witmark)*. A limited run revival of the Molière classic. COVER: letters and designs.

2031 The School for Scandal (Broadway, 1931). Ethel Barrymore, Arthur Treacher.

Lady Teazle Minuet — Maurice Nitke[m] *(Empire City)*. A three week revival of the Sheridan comedy. COVER: Ethel Barrymore.

2032 Sea Legs (Broadway, 1937). Charles King, Dorothy Stone.

Catalina / Dark Stranger / Infatuation / Opposite Sex / Ten O'Clock Town / Touched in the Head / Wake Me Up a Star — Arthur Swanstrom[w] & Michael Cleary[m] *(Marks)*. A stowaway, a romance, and a cat make up this silly musical that lasted two weeks. COVER: five chorus girls kicking on the deck of a ship.

2033 The Second Little Show (Broadway, 1930). J.C. Flippen, Gloria Grafton.

Foolish Face / I Like Your Face / Lucky Seven / What a Case I've Got on You! / You're the Sunrise — Howard Dietz[w] & Arthur Schwartz[m] *(Harms)*; Practising Up on You — Phil Charig[w/m] *(Harms)*; Sing Something Simple — Herman Hupfeld[w/m] *(Harms)*; Tired of Love — Ted Fetter[w] & Del Cleveland[m] *(Harms)*. An inferior revue that lasted for only eight weeks. COVER: a boy and girl dancing in the spotlight.

2034 Second Marriage (Jewish, 1953). Edmund Zayenda, Miriam Kressyn.

S'vet Zein Git — Jacob Jacobs[w] & Manny Fleischman[m] *(Metro)*. COVER: Zayenda and Kressyn.

2035 Second Nine O'Clock Revue (closed before Broadway, 1933). Stars unknown.

Pale Moonlight — Bud Cooper[w] & Ed Lambert[w] & Jean Talbot[m] *(Harms)*; Sing a Little Jingle — Bud Cooper[w] & Jean Talbot[m] *(Harms)*. COVER: a dancing girl and a large clock at nine o'clock.

2036 The Secret Garden (Broadway, 1991). Daisy Eagan, Mandy Patinkin.

A Bit of Earth [VS] / Clusters of Crocus [VS] / Come to My Garden / The Girl I Mean to Be [VS] / Hold On / How Could I Ever Know? / If I Had a Fine White House [VS] / Lily's Eyes [VS] / Race You to the Top of the Morning [VS] / Round-Shouldered Man [VS] / Where in the World [VS] / Wick [VS] / Winter's on the Wing [VS] — Marsha Norman[w] & Lucy Simon[m] *(Warner Bros.)*. A musical based on the classic novel. It was beautifully produced but long winded and draggy. COVER: faces, flowers, and a snake.

2037 The Secret Life of Walter Mitty (Off Broadway, 1964). Marc London, Cathryn Damon.

Confidence / Fan the Flame / Hello, I Love You, Goodbye / Marriage Is for Old Folks / The Secret Life / Walking with Peninnah — Earl Shuman[w] & Leon Carr[m] *(April)*. A musical about the dreams of Walter Mitty that ran for three months. COVER: Walter Mitty with dreams in his head.

2038 See-Saw (Broadway, 1919). Guy Robertson, Elizabeth Hines.

Good Bye! Hello! / The Happiest Moment I've Ever Known / I Just Want Jazz / Peep-Peep / See-Saw / When Two Hearts Discover / When You Dance / Won't You Come and Join the Navy? / A World Full of Girls / You'll Have to Find Out — Earl Derr Biggers[w] & Louis Hirsch[m] *(Victoria)*. A poor musical about a love triangle that lasted 11 weeks. COVER: a well dressed couple on a see-saw.

2039 See-Saw (Broadway, 1973). Michelle Lee, Ken Howard.

He's Good for Me [VS] / I'm Way Ahead [VS] / In Tune [VS] / It's Not Where You Start / My City [VS] / Nobody Does It Like Me / Poor Everybody Else [VS] / Ride Out the Storm / Seesaw / Spanglish [VS] / Welcome to Holiday Inn [VS] / We've Got It [VS] / You're a Lovable Lunatic [VS] — Dorothy Fields[w] & Cy Coleman[m] *(Notable)*. A musical based on the hit drama. It had a wonderful cast, great songs, super dancing, and a run of nine months. COVER: a bunch of people on one see-saw.

2040 The Selling of the President (Broadway, 1972). Pat Hingle, Karen Morrow.

Stars of Glory / Take My Hand / We're Gonna Live It Together — Jack O'Brien[w/m] & Bob James[w/m] *(Morris)*. A dreadful musical about elections. It lasted five performances. COVER: the Presidential seal.

2041 Selwyn's Snapshots of 1921 (Broadway, 1921). Lew Fields, Nora Bayes.

Deburau / Every Girlie Wants to Be a Sally / Happyland / In Indiana / Irene Rosenstein — Alex Gerber[w] & Malvin Franklin[m] *(Witmark)*; Remember the Rose — Sidney Mitchell[w] & Seymour Simons[m] *(Remick)*; Satur-day — Sidney Mitchell[w] & Harry Brooks[m] *(Remick)*; Yokohama Lullaby — Grant Clarke[w] & James Monaco[m] *(Shapiro, Bernstein)*. An evening of vaudeville that lasted six weeks. COVER: Lew Fields, Nora Bayes, DeWolf Hopper.

2042 Send Me No Flowers (Broadway, 1960). David Wayne, Nancy Olson.

Send Me No Flowers — George Weiss[w/m] & Will Lorin[w/m] *(Aries Music)*. A comedy about a man who thinks he is going to die. It lasted five weeks. COVER: a man saying "don't."

2043 Sensations (Off Broadway, 1970). John Savage, Judy Gibson.

I Cannot Wait / Lonely Children / Lying Here / The Morning Sun / Sensations / Sounds — Paul Zakrzewski[w] & Wally Harper[m] *(Notable)*. An updated Romeo and Juliet with drugs and violence. It lasted two weeks. COVER: designs and lettering.

2044 Set to Music (Broadway, 1939). Beatrice Lillie, Richard Haydn.

I Went to a Marvelous Party / I'm So Weary of It All / Mad About the Boy / Never Again / The Stately Homes of England / Three White Feathers — Noel Coward[w/m] *(Chappell)*. An American version of Noel Coward's London hit *Words and Music*. It was very British and lasted four months only because of Bea Lillie. COVER: Beatrice Lillie.

2045 Seven Lively Arts (Broadway, 1944). Beatrice Lillie, Bert Lahr.

The Band Started Swinging a Song / Ev'ry Time We Say Goodbye / Frahngee-Pahnee / Hence It Don't Make Sense / Is It the Girl? / Only Another Boy and Girl / When I Was a Little Cuckoo / Wow-Ooh-Wolf — Cole Porter[w/m] *(Chappell)*. Billy Rose purchased the Ziegfeld Theatre and celebrated with this poor revue. It had two good Cole Porter songs but poor comedy skits and cheap sets. It lasted almost six months. COVER: theatre masks and designs.

2046 Seven o' Hearts (closed before Broadway, 1922). Will Kraemer.

Tain't Nobody's Biz-ness If I Do — Porter Grainger[w/m] & Everett Robbins[w/m] *(Williams)*. COVER: Kraemer and six chorus girls.

2047 The Seven Year Itch (Broadway, 1952). Vanessa Brown, Tom Ewell.

The Girl Without a Name — Scott Olsen[w/m] & Dana Suesse[w/m] *(Marks)*; That Girl — Eddie Bracken[w] & Dana Suesse[m] *(Marks)*. A romantic comedy set in New York City that lasted almost three years. COVER: Eddie Bracken, Tom Ewell and Vanessa Brown.

2048 Seventeen (Broadway, 1951). Kenneth Nelson, Dick Kallman.

After All It's Spring / Headaches and Heartaches / I Could Get Married Today / Nobody Ever Felt Like This Before / Ooh, Ooh, Ooh, What You Do to Me! / Reciprocity / Summertime Is Summertime / Things Are Gonna Hum This Summer — Kim Gannon[w] & Walter Kent[m] *(Leeds)*. A charming little musical about puppy love with pleasant tunes and people. It lasted five months. COVER: a boy flirting with a girl.

2049 "1776" (Broadway, 1969). Ken Howard, William Daniels.

But, Mr. Adams [VS] / Cool, Cool Considerate Men [VS] / The Egg [VS] / He Plays the Violin / Is Anybody There? / The Lees of Old Virginia [VS] / Molasses to Rum [VS] / Momma, Look Sharp / Piddle, Twiddle, and Resolve [VS] / Sit Down, John [VS] / Till Then [VS] / Yours, Yours, Yours! — Sherman Edwards[w/m] *(Schirmer)*. A musical about the signing of the Declaration of Independence that was quite theatrical and entertaining. It lasted three years. COVER: an American eagle with flag emerging from a British egg.

2050 Seventh Heaven (Broadway, 1955). Gloria De Haven, Ricardo Montalban.

Blessings / C'est la Vie / If It's a Dream / Love Sneaks Up on You / A Man with a Dream / A "Miss You" Kiss / Remarkable Fellow / Where Is That Someone for Me — Stella Unger[w] & Victor Young[m] *(Chappell)*. A musical version of the movie classic that was rather ordinary and lasted only one month. COVER: sketch of embracing couple and clouds.

2051 "70, Girls, 70" (Broadway, 1971). Mildred Natwick, Lillian Roth.

Believe [VS] / Boom Ditty Boom [VS] / Broadway, My Street [VS] / Coffee (in a cardboard cup) [VS] / Do We? [VS] / The Elephant Song / Go Visit Your Grandmother [VS] / Home [VS] / Old Folks [VS] / 70, Girls 70 [VS] / Yes — Fred Ebb[w] & John Kander[m] *(Valando)*. A charming musical that lasted less than a month. It had some great older actors and a pleasant score and story but never caught on! COVER: an old lady with a fur, and a cat with a firecracker.

2052 Shady Lady (Broadway, 1933). Helen Kane, Jack Donahue.

Anyway the Wind Blows / Get Hot Foot / Swingy Little Thingy — Bud Green[w/m] & Sam Stept[w/m] *(Mills)*; Everything But My Man — Charles Kenny[w] & Serge Walter[m] *(Mills)*; Farewell, Time to Go / Time to Go / Where Oh Where Can I Find Love? — Stanley Adams[w] & Jesse Greer[m] *(Mills)*; Isn't It Swell to Dream — Bud Green[w] & Stanley Adams[w] & Sam Stept[m] & Jesse Greer[m] *(Mills)*. A musical about a painter and a model that lasted almost a month. COVER: a dancing girl.

2053 Shake Your Feet (British, 1927). Stars unknown.

All I Want to Do [B] — Joe Burke[w/m] & Walter Donaldson[w/m] *(F D and H)*. A British revue with one Donaldson song. It lasted only a short time in London. COVER: sketch of girl with large bow.

2054 Shamrock (Irish, 1923). Pat Rooney, Marion Bent.

Anastasia Reilly — William Halligan[w/m] *(Remick)*; I Want a Girl Like Mother Was / Irish Moon / Shamrock / The Two Best Girls I Love — Cliff Hess[w/m] & Joseph Santley[w/m] *(Remick)*. COVER: Pat Rooney, Marion Bent.

2055 Shangri-La (Broadway, 1956). Jack Cassidy, Alice Ghostley.

Lost Horizon / Second Time in Love / Shangri-la — Jerome Lawrence[w] & Robert Lee[w] & Harry Warren[m] *(Morris)*. A musical version of *Lost Horizon*. It had talented people but nothing else and lasted two weeks. COVER: red and white squares.

2056 Sharlee (Broadway, 1923). Juliette Day, Sydney Grant.

Heart Beats / Honeymoon Row / Little Drops of Water / Love To-day / Princess Nicotine / Sharlee — Alex Rogers[w] & C. Luckeyth Roberts[m] *(Shapiro, Bernstein)*. This musical had a nightclub singer searching for romance. The search ended in three weeks. COVER: a pretty girl in a flowing gown.

2057 She Loves Me (Broadway, 1963). Barbara Cook, Daniel Massey.

Days Gone By / Dear Friend / Grand Knowing You / Ilona [VS] / She Loves Me / Tonight at Eight / Will He Like Me? — Sheldon Harnick[w] & Jerry Bock[m] *(Valando)*; Vanilla Ice Cream [BW] — Sheldon Harnick[w] & Jerry Bock[m] *(Warner Bros.)*. This story, which had been done many times on the stage and in the movies, was turned into a charming musical. It had everything including a talented cast, a lovely score, and a good book yet it ran for only nine months and suffered a loss. It has been revived many times. COVER: a cupid with a smile on his face.

2058 She Loves Me Not (Broadway, 1933). Dwight Wiman, Tom Weatherly.

After All, You're All I'm After / She Loves Me Not — Edward Heyman[w] & Arthur Schwartz[m] *(Harms)*. Dealing with a girl escaping the mob, this comedy ran for seven months. COVER: silhouette of lady with a large daisy.

2059 She Shall Have Music (Off Broadway, 1955). Sherry Davis, Betty Oakes.

Who Are You? — Dede Meyer[w/m] *(Chappell)*. A musical version of the play *The Country Wife* that lasted six weeks. COVER: a lady in evening gown holding a mask.

2060 She Took a Chance (closed before Broadway, 1918). Ray Raymond, Eddie Dowling.

Always Wear a Smile / Any Time New York Goes Dry / Everytime I Look at You / Happiness / Just to Make the World a Little Brighter / Love Has Come to Me / No One Would Steal You from Me / One Hundred Years from Now / Susie from Sioux City / There's No Time Like Now / There's Something About You / When You Love and Your Lover Is Away — Henry Blossom[w] & Uda Waldrop[m] *(Witmark)*. This musical played Boston and Washington and then folded. COVER: flowers and designs.

2061 She Walked Home (closed before Broadway, 1929). Stars unknown.

I Do / I Got a Lucky Break / Rosette / You're My Temptation — Don Hunt[w/m] *(Harms)*. COVER: a girl in a fur coat walking down the road.

2062 Shelter (Broadway, 1973). Marcia Rodd, Susan Browning.

Changing [PC] — Gretchen Cryer[w] & Nancy Ford[m] *(Multimood)*. A charming little musical about a writer of TV commercials. With mostly excellent reviews it still ran only four weeks. COVER: none.

2063 Shenandoah (Broadway, 1975). John Cullum, Donna Theodore.

Freedom / It's a Boy [VS] / I've Heard It All Before [VS] / Meditation [VS] / Next to Lovin' [VS] / The Only Home I Know [VS] / Over the Hills [VS] / Papa's Gonna Make It Alright [VS] / Pass the Cross to Me / The Pickers a Are Comin' [VS] / Raise the Flag [VS] / Violets and Silverbells [VS] / We Make a Beautiful Pair / Why Am I Me? [VS] — Peter Udell[w] & Gary Geld[m] *(Morris)*. A musical set in the Civil War period and how it affected innocent farmers. With some rousing singing and dancing and a sympathetic story, it ran for two and one half years. COVER:

a quilt showing a peaceful farm and fields.

2064 Sherlock Holmes (British, 1989). Stars unknown.

Anything You Want to Know [B] [VS] / The Best of You, Best of Me [B] [VS] / Down the Apples 'n' Pears [B] [VS] / Her Face [B] [VS] / London Is London [B] [VS] / Million Years Ago, or Was It Yesterday? [B] [VS] / No Reason [B] [VS] / Sherlock Holmes [B] [VS] / Without Him, There Can Be No Me [B] [VS] — Leslie Bricusse[w/m] *(E M I)*. A musical mystery that ran three months in London and is scheduled to tour on Broadway in early 1996. COVER: Sherlock Holmes.

2065 Sherry (Broadway, 1967). Dolores Gray, Clive Revill.

Au Revoir / How Can You Kiss Those Good Times Goodbye? / Imagine That [VS] / Maybe It's Time for Me / Putty in Your Hands [VS] / Sherry! — James Lipton[w] & Laurence Rosenthal[m] *(Chappell)*. This musical, based on *The Man Who Came to Dinner,* suffered through many problems including the death of George Sanders, a weak score and a poor book. It lasted two months. COVER: Sheridan Whiteside cracking the whip over everyone. The single sheets feature George Sanders in *Sherry* and were issued out of town. Sanders was replaced by Clive Revill and the vocal selections book plus the title song shows Clive Revill in *Sherry.*

2066 She's a Good Fellow (*see also* **A New Girl**) (Broadway, 1919). Joseph Santley, Ivy Sawyer.

The Bull Frog Patrol / First Rose of Summer / A Happy Wedding Day / Home Sweet Home / I Want My Little Gob / I've Been Waiting for You All the Time / Jubilo / Just a Little Line / Oh! You Beautiful Person / Some Party / Teacher, Teacher — Anne Caldwell[w] & Jerome Kern[m] *(Harms)*. A show dealing with love and impersonations. It had a pleasant score and a run of four months. The try-out title was *A New Girl.* COVER: black and white with titles only.

2067 She's My Baby (Broadway, 1927). Beatrice Lillie, Clifton Webb.

A Baby's Best Friend / How Was I to Know? / If I Were You / A Little House in Soho / Morning Is Midnight / When I Go on the Stage / Whoopsie / You're What I Need — Lorenz Hart[w] & Richard Rodgers[m] *(Harms)*. A musical with Webb and Lillie posing as husband and wife to get money. With a poor book and score, Bea Lillie kept it going for two months. COVER: flowers and designs.

2068 Shim Sham Revue (Nightclub, 1934). Stars unknown.

I Do, I Do, I Do / Keep Moving / Sweetness of It All / Without That Man — J.C. Lewis[w] & Charlie Kisco[m] *(Robbins)*. COVER: Times Square and three dancing girls.

2069 Shinbone Alley (*see also* **Archy and Mehitabel**) (Broadway, 1957). Eartha Kitt, Eddie Bracken.

Cheerio My Deario / Flotsam and Jetsam / The Stranger / Way Down Blues / A Woman Wouldn't Be a Woman — Joe Darion[w] & George Kleinsinger[m] *(Chappell)*. A musical based on *Archy and Mehitabel*, a cockroach and a cat. *Shinbone Alley* failed after six weeks. COVER: Eartha Kitt and Eddie Bracken.

2070 Ship Shapes (closed before Broadway, 1930). Stars unknown.

A Ship Passing By / A Someone Like You — Stewart Baird[w] & Peggy Ellis[m] & Lew Kessler[m] *(Harms)*. COVER: a ship in full sail.

2071 Shmendrik (Jewish, 1925). Molly Picon, Jacob Kalich.

Shmendrik — Molly Picon[w] & Joseph Rumshinsky[m] *(Kammen)*. COVER: Molly Picon.

2072 Shoestring '57 (Nightclub, 1957). Dody Goodman, George Marcy.

Love Is a Feeling — Norman Gimbel[w] & Moose Charlap[m] *(Morris)*; There's Always One Day More — Carolyn Leigh[w] & Philip Springer[m] *(Morris)*. COVER: a sketch of some cartoon-like characters.

2073 Shoestring Revue (Nightclub, 1929). Stars unknown.

Hoboken Seidel / I'm Not Me, I'm You / Racket / Want to Go Places / Where Are You / Words and Music — Stanley Adams[w] & William Irwin[m] *(Mills)*; I Know It Won't Work Out — Sterling Holloway[w] & William Irwin[m] *(Mills)*. COVER: dancers, ribbons, and designs.

2074 Shoestring Revue (Nightclub, 1955). Dody Goodman, Beatrice Arthur.

Someone's Been Sending Me Flowers — Sheldon Harnick[w] & David Baker[m] *(Leeds)*. COVER: black and white with title only.

2075 Shoot the Works (Broadway, 1931). George Murphy, Imogene Coca.

Begging for Love [BW] — Irving Berlin[w/m] *(Berlin)*; Do What You Like — Leo Robin[w/m] & Phil Charig[w/m] *(Harms)*; Don't Ask Me Why — Joe Young[w] & Robert Stolz[m] *(Harms)*; Hot Moonlight — E.Y. Harburg[w] & Jay Gorney[m] *(Harms)*; How's Your Uncle? — Dorothy Fields[w] & Jimmy McHugh[m] *(Robbins)*; It's in the Stars / Poor Little Doorstep Baby — Max Lief[w] & Nathaniel Lief[w] & Michael Cleary[m] *(Harms)*; Muchacha — E.Y. Harburg[w] & Jay Gorney[m] & Vernon Duke[m] *(Harms)*. A poor revue produced on a shoestring budget. The revue lasted 11 weeks. COVER: stars and designs; chorus girls and Broadway.

2076 Shootin' Star (closed before Broadway, 1946). David Brooks, Doretta Morrow.

Footloose / Friendly Country / Sometime Tomorrow — Sol Kaplan[w] & Bob Russell[m] *(Famous)*. A musical about Billy the Kid that folded in Boston. COVER: cowboy and dance hall girls.

2077 The Shop Girl (British, 1920). Thorpe Bates.

Louisiana Lou — Leslie Stuart[w/m] *(Harms)*. A hit revival in London of an 1894 musical. This song was published in the U.S. COVER: titles and designs.

2078 Shotgun Weddin' (closed before Broadway, 1950). Christie Nicholas.

Houseboat on the Mississippi / In Love at Last / There's a Ring Around the Moon — Glenn Hughes[w/m] & Nicholas Russo[w/m] *(Peer)*. COVER: Christie Nicholas.

2079 Show Boat (Broadway, 1927). Norma Terris, Helen Morgan.

After the Ball — Charles Harris[w/m] *(Harris)*; Bill — P.G. Wodehouse[w] & Oscar Hammerstein[w] & Jerome Kern[m] *(Harms)*; Can't Help Lovin' Dat Man / Make Believe / Ol' Man River / Why Do I Love You — Oscar Hammerstein[w] & Jerome Kern[m] *(Harms)*; Show Boat — complete score — P.G. Wodehouse[w] & Oscar Hammerstein[w] & Jerome Kern[m] *(Harms)*. The best musical of the century with a wonderful story, a great score, and a lavish production. COVER: blue and orange flowers and lyre. The first sheet music for *Show Boat* was issued on November 30, 1927 in Cleveland with the blue and orange lyre cover. After an engagement in Philadelphia, it opened in N.Y. on December 27, 1927. Early in 1928, the sheet music was reissued with the "gang-plank" cover.

2080 Show Boat (British, 1928). Edith Day, Paul Robeson.

Captain Andy [B] / Cotton Blossom [B] (piano selections) / Hey, Fellah [B] / Julie's Lament [B] / Misery [B] / Valon's Theme [B] — Jerome Kern[m] *(Chappell)*. *Show Boat* was a hit in London and ran for one year. All the usual songs were issued plus a piano selection of some rare songs. COVER: the gangplank cover.

2081 Show Boat (Broadway, 1932). Helen Morgan, Norma Terris.

Bill — P.G. Wodehouse[w] & Oscar Hammerstein[w] & Jerome Kern[m] *(Harms)*; Can't Help Lovin' Dat Man / Make Believe / Ol' Man River / Why Do I Love You? / You Are Love — Oscar Hammerstein[w] & Jerome Kern[m] *(Harms)*; Goodbye My Lady Love — Joseph Howard[w/m] *(Mills)*. A Ziegfeld revival with the original cast. It opened May 19, 1932, just before Ziegfeld died on July 22, 1932. COVER: the gangplank cover.

2082 Show Boat (Broadway, 1946). Jan Clayton, Carol Bruce.

After the Ball — Charles Harris[w/m] *(Harris)*; Bill — P.G. Wodehouse[w] & Oscar Hammerstein[w] & Jerome Kern[m] *(Harms)*; Can't Help Lovin' Dat Man / Make Believe / Nobody Else But Me / Ol' Man River / Why Do I Love You / You Are Love — Oscar Hammerstein[w] & Jerome Kern[m] *(Harms)*. A hit revival that opened January 5, 1946, and ran for a year plus a long tour. Jerome Kern died November 11, 1945, after writing his last song for this show, *Nobody Else But Me.* COVER: blue cover with man, woman, show boat and flowers.

2083 Show Boat (British, 1971). Cleo Laine, Jan Waters.

Bill — P.G. Wodehouse[w] & Oscar Hammerstein[w] & Jerome Kern[m] *(Chappell)*; Can't Help Lovin' Dat Man / I Still Suits Me / Make Believe / Ol' Man River / Why Do I Love You? / You Are Love — Oscar Hammerstein[w] & Jerome Kern[m] *(Chappell)*. A lavish revival in London that ran two years. It was noteworthy, because it included all the minor songs. COVER: titles and designs.

2084 Show Girl (Broadway, 1929). Jimmy Durante, Ruby Keeler.

Do What You Do / Feeling Sentimental / Harlem Serenade / I Must Be Home by Twelve O'Clock / Liza / So Are You — Ira Gershwin[w] & Gus Kahn[w] & George Gershwin[m] *(New World)*; Mississippi Dry — J. Russel Robinson[w] & Vincent Youmans[m] *(Youmans)*. A lavish production with good Gershwin songs but a run of only three months. Ziegfeld had used all the big stars of the period except Jolson, who was well paid by the Shuberts. He finally got him — in a way. Jolson ran down the aisle every night singing *Liza* to calm Ruby Keeler who was descending a high staircase but afraid of height. COVER: titles and designs.

2085 Show Girl (Broadway, 1961). Carol Channing, Jules Munshin.

The Girl in the Show / My Kind of Love — Charles Gaynor[w/m] *(Frank)*. An almost one woman show with Carol Channing over-doing her Lorelei mannerisms. It had a run of three months. COVER: Carol Channing.

2086 The Show Is On (Broadway, 1936). Beatrice Lillie, Bert Lahr.

At Ease You Rookies (Parade Night) [VS] — Norman Zeno[w] & Will Irwin[m] *(USO)*; Buy Yourself a Balloon — Herman Hupfeld[w/m] *(Chappell)*; By Strauss — Ira Gershwin[w] & George Gershwin[m] *(Chappell)*; Casanova — song and ballet [PC] / Now — Ted Fetter[w] & Vernon Duke[m] *(Chappell)*; Finale Marches On [VS] — E.Y. Harburg[w] & Ted Fetter[w] & Vernon Duke[m] *(USO)*; It's So Easy to Lose — Ted Fetter[w] & Hoagy Carmichael[m] *(Chappell)*; Little Old Lady — Stanley Adams[w/m] & Hoagy Carmichael[w/m] *(Chappell)*; Long as You Got Your Health — E.Y. Harburg[w] & Norman Zeno[w] & Will Irwin[m] *(Chappell)*; Shakespearean Opening [VS] — Howard Dietz[w] & Arthur Schwartz[m] *(USO)*; Show Is Through (The Show Is On) [VS] — Ted Fetter[w] & Hoagy Carmichael[m] *(USO)*; What a Dummy Love Has Made of Me — Norman Zeno[w] & Will Irwin[m] *(Chappell)*. A moderate hit revue with some great talent and songs from many composers. It was beautifully staged by Vincente Minnelli and ran for seven months. COVER: Beatrice Lillie and Bert Lahr.

2087 Show Me Where the Good Times Are (Broadway, 1970). Cathryn Damon, Christopher Hewett.

Show Me Where the Good Times Are — Kenneth Jacobson[w] & Rhoda Roberts[m] *(Valando)*. A musical set in New York in 1913 that lasted three weeks. COVER: a man and woman dancing.

2088 Showboat Revue (Nightclub, 1933). Bobby Sanford.

Rhythm on the River — Billy Tracy[w] & Jack Palmer[m] *(Mills)*; Rock-a-Bye River / You Excite Me! — Mitchell

Parish[w] & Frank Perkins[m] *(Mills)*. COVER: a girl in costume and dancers.

2089 Shuffle Along (Broadway, 1921). Eubie Blake, Noble Sissle.

Ain't It a Shame — W.A. Hann[w/m] & Joseph Simms[w/m] & Al Brown[w/m] *(Witmark)*; Ain't-cha Coming Back, Mary Ann, to Maryland / I'm Just Simply Full of Jazz / Oriental Blues / Pickaninny Shoes / Serenade Blues — Noble Sissle[w] & Eubie Blake[m] *(Witmark)*; Baltimore Buzz / Bandanna Days / Daddy Won't You Please Come Home / Dear Li'l Pal / Don't Love Me Blues / Everything Reminds Me of You / Good Night, Angeline / Gypsy Blues / If You've Never Been Vamped by a Brown Skin / I'm Craving for That Kind of Love / I'm Just Wild About Harry / In Honeysuckle Time / Kentucky Sue / Liza Quit Vamping Me (not published) / Love Will Find a Way / Low Down Blues / Old Black Joe and Uncle Tom / Shuffle Along / Sing Me to Sleep, Dear Mammy / Vision Girl — Noble Sissle[w/m] & Eubie Blake[w/m] *(Witmark)*; Long Gone — Chris Smith[w] & W.C. Handy[m] *(Handy)*. A black musical put together on a shoestring. The plot was simple but the music and dancing kept this show going for 15 months. COVER: a row of dancing feet. The first set of covers states "Nikko Producing Co. Offers 'Shuffle Along.'" The second set says "Shuffle Along Co. Presents 'Shuffle Along.'"

2090 Side by Side by Sondheim (Broadway, 1977). Millicent Martin, Julie McKenzie.

I Never Do Anything Twice [BW] — Stephen Sondheim *(Leeds)*. A hit British revue of Sondheim songs imported to the U.S. with the British cast. It ran one year. COVER: titles only.

2091 Sidewalks of New York (Broadway, 1927). Eddie Dowling, Ray Dooley.

Goldfish Glide / Headin' for Harlem / Just a Little Smile from You / Play-Ground in the Sky / When You Were Sweet Sixteen / Wherever You Are — Eddie Dowling[w/m] & James Hanley[w/m]

(Shapiro, Bernstein). A pleasant musical about a design contest and young love. It ran three months. COVER: a row of skyscrapers.

2092 Sigh No More (British, 1945). Joyce Grenfell, Cyril Ritchard.

I Wondered What Happened to Him [B] / Matelot [B] / Music Hath Charms [B] / Never Again [B] / Nina [B] / Parting of the Ways [B] / Sigh No More [B] / That Is the End of the News [B] / Wait a Bit, Joe [B] — Noel Coward[w/m] *(Chappell)*; Oh, Mr. DuMaurier [B] — Joyce Grenfell[w] & Richard Addinsell[m] *(Keith Prowse)*. A Noel Coward revue that ran for only six months but contained some good Coward songs. COVER: Joyce Grenfell; musical instruments.

2093 The Sign of the Rose (Broadway, 1933). Stars unknown.

The Sign of the Rose — Lew Brown[w] & Leo Edwards[m] *(Shapiro, Bernstein)*. A melodrama with a short run. COVER: George Beban.

2094 Silk Stockings (Broadway, 1955). Don Ameche, Hildegarde Neff.

All of You / As On Through the Seasons We Sail / Give Me the Land [VS] [CUT] / It's a Chemical Reaction That's All / Josephine / Paris Loves Lovers / Satin and Silk / Siberia / Silk Stockings / Stereophonic Sound / Without Love — Cole Porter[w/m] *(Chappell)*. Cole Porter's last musical with many hit songs, a great cast and a run of over one year. COVER: gift boxes with ribbons.

2095 Silks and Satins (Broadway, 1920). William Demarest, Aileen Stanley.

Around the Town / I've Shaken Everything I've Got / Like Honey / Midsummer Maiden / Step Along with Me / Sunday's Child — Louis Weslyn[w] & Leon Rosebrook[m] *(Remick)*; Chili Bean — Lew Brown[w] & Albert Von Tilzer[m] *(Broadway)*; I Want to Be Somebody's Baby — Jesse Greer[w/m] & Ed Smalle[w/m] *(Von Tilzer)*; I'm Just a Sentry / That Colored Jazzoray — Arthur Freed[w/m] & Oliver Wallace[w/m]

(Remick); My Little Bimbo – Grant Clarke^w & Walter Donaldson^m *(Berlin)*; My Rose of Memory – Lloyd Garrett^w & Leon Rosebrook^m *(Remick)*; Nanking Blues – Louis Weslyn^w & William Rock^w & Leon Rosebrook^m *(Remick)*; This Is the End of Me Now – Raymond Egan^w & Henry Marshall^m *(Remick)*; Was Mrs. Macbeth Really Sleeping? – Louis Weslyn^w & Ethel Rosemon^w & Leon Rosebrook^m *(Remick)*. A poor revue that lasted seven weeks. COVER: Aileen Stanley; a pretty girl in silks and satins.

2096 The Silver Fox (Broadway, 1921). Vivienne Osborne, Lawrence Grossmith.

Frankie – Jack Snyder$^{w/m}$ *(Jack Snyder Music)*. A melodrama that had a short run. COVER: Vivienne Osborne.

2097 The Silver Screen (Nightclub, 1942). Joe E. Howard, Charles King.

Keep 'em Smiling – Fred Rose$^{w/m}$ & Milton Ager$^{w/m}$ *(A Y and B)*. COVER: titles only.

2098 Silver Slipper (Nightclub, 1924). Van and Schenck.

Whose Izzy Is He – Lew Brown$^{w/m}$ & Bud Green$^{w/m}$ & Murray Sturm *(Shapiro, Bernstein)*. COVER: Van and Schenck.

2099 The Silver Swan (Broadway, 1929). Edward Nell, Vivian Hart.

Cigarette / I Love You, Adore You / The Lonely Road / Love Letters – William Brady^w & H. Maurice Jacquet^m *(Feist)*; Till I Met You – William Brady^w & Alonzo Price^w & H. Maurice Jacquet^m *(Feist)*. An old fashioned operetta involving soldiers and opera singers. It lasted two weeks. COVER: a beautiful inn with a balcony and a courtyard.

2100 Simple Simon (Broadway, 1930). Ed Wynn, Ruth Etting.

Cottage in the Country – Walter Donaldson$^{w/m}$ *(Donaldson)*; Don't Tell Your Folks / He Dances on My Ceiling / He Was Too Good to Me / I Can Do Wonders with You / I Still Believe in You / Send for Me / Sweetenheart / Ten Cents a Dance – Lorenz Hart^w &

Richard Rodgers^m *(Harms)*; Cottage in the Country – Walter Donaldson$^{w/m}$ *(Donaldson)*. A lavish Ziegfeld production with Ed Wynn and his fairy tale dreams. In addition to the great comedy, it had Ruth Etting and *Ten Cents a Dance*. It ran only four months. COVER: Ed Wynn and Ruth Etting.

2101 Simply Heavenly (Broadway, 1957). Claudia McNeil, John Bowie.

Did You Ever Hear the Blues? / Gatekeeper of My Castle / Good Old Girl / Let's Ball Awhile / Look for the Morning Star / Simply Heavenly / When I'm in a Quiet Mood – Langston Hughes^w & David Martin^m *(Bourne)*. A good play with a weak score about a poor black man torn between two loves and his dreams. It was a success Off Broadway but ran less than two months on Broadway. COVER: girl winking at a boy.

2102 The Sin of Pat Muldoon (Broadway, 1957). James Barton, Elaine Stritch.

The Sin of Pat Muldoon – Richard Adler$^{w/m}$ *(Andrew)*. A comedy that lasted five performances. COVER: Pat Muldoon in bed.

2103 Sinbad (Broadway, 1918). Al Jolson, Kitty Doner.

Alexander's Band Is Back in Dixieland / Darktown Dancin' School – Jack Yellen^w & Albert Gumble^m *(Remick)*; Bagdad / Bedalumbo – Harold Atteridge^w & Al Jolson^m *(Schirmer)*; Beauty and the Beast / I Hail from Cairo / It's Wonderful / Our Ancestors / The Rag Lad of Bagdad / Raz-Ma-Taz / A Thousand and One Arabian Nights – Harold Atteridge^w & Sigmund Romberg^m *(Schirmer)*; By the Honeysuckle Vine / Chloe / I Gave Her That – B.G. DeSylva$^{w/m}$ & Al Jolson$^{w/m}$ *(Harms)*; Cleopatra – Alfred Bryan^w & Harry Tierney^m *(Remick)*; Dixie Rose / Swanee Rose – Irving Caesar^w & B.G. DeSylva^w & George Gershwin^m *(Harms)*; Down Yonder – L. Wolfe Gilbert$^{w/m}$ *(Gilbert Music)*; Hello Central! Give Me No

Man's Land—Sam Lewis[w] & Joe Young[w] & Jean Schwartz[m] *(Berlin)*; How'd You Like to Be My Daddy?—Joe Young[w] & Sam Lewis[w] & Ted Snyder[m] *(Berlin)*; I'll Say She Does—B.G. DeSylva[w/m] & Gus Kahn[w/m] & Al Jolson[w/m] *(Remick)*; I'll Sing You a Song—Henry Creamer[w/m] & Turner Layton[w/m] *(Witmark)*; I'll Tell the World—B.G. DeSylva[w/m] & Harold Atteridge[w/m] *(Schirmer)*; I'm Not Jealous—Harry Pease[w] & Ed Nelson[m] & Fred Mayo[m] *(Stasny)*; I've Got the Blue Ridge Blues—Charles Mason[w] & Charles Cooke[m] & Richard Whiting[m] *(Remick)*; Let the Little Joy Bell Ring—Cliff Friend[w/m] *(Berlin)*; My Mammy—Joe Young[w] & Sam Lewis[w] & Walter Donaldson[m] *(Berlin)*; "N" Everything—B.G. DeSylva[m] & Gus Kahn[m] & Al Jolson[m] *(Remick)*; O-H-I-O—Jack Yellen[w] & Abe Olman[m] *(Forster)*; Swanee—Irving Caesar[w] & George Gershwin[m] *(Harms)*; Sweetie Mine—Sidney Mitchell[w] & Cliff Hess[w] & Al Jolson[m] *(Feist)*; Tell That to the Marines—Harold Atteridge[w] & Jean Schwartz[m] & Al Jolson[m] *(Berlin)*; War Babies—Ballard MacDonald[w] & Ed Madden[w] & James Hanley[m] *(Shapiro, Bernstein)*; Why Do They All Take the Night Boat to Albany—Joe Young[w] & Sam Lewis[w] & Jean Schwartz[m] *(Berlin)*. A typical Al Jolson musical with a slight book about travels to exotic places. It ran 20 weeks and toured all over. It is remembered only for *Swanee* and *My Mammy*. COVER: Al Jolson.

2104 Sing for Your Supper (Broadway, 1939). Paula Laurence, Sonny Tufts.

Ballad for Americans [BW]—John Latouche[w] & Earl Robinson[m] *(Robbins)*; Imagine My Finding You Here—Robert Sour[w] & Ned Lehac[m] *(Marks)*; Papa's Got a Job—Robert Sour[w] & Hector Troy[w] & Harold Rome[w] & Ned Lehac[m] *(Marks)*; The Story of a Horn—Robert Sour[w] & Lee Wainer[m] *(Marks)*. A topical revue produced by the WPA Federal Theatre

that ran seven weeks. COVER: Uncle Sam with a dancer and a cook.

2105 Sing Muse! (Off Broadway, 1961). Karen Morrow, Brandon Maggart.

In Our Little Salon for Two / The Wrath of Achilles / Your Name May Be Paris—Erich Segal[w] & Joe Raposo[m] *(Morris)*. A musical centered around Greek mythology characters. It lasted five weeks. COVER: a boy and girl in Greek costumes with lyre.

2106 Sing Out, Sweet Land (Broadway, 1944). Alfred Drake, Bibi Osterwald.

Sing Out, Sweet Land—15 Folk Songs—Traditional *(Northern Music)*. A review of American life over the centuries with a run of three months. COVER: various American people in different poses and costumes.

2107 Sing Out the News (Broadway, 1938). Hiram Sherman, Will Geer.

F.D.R. Jones / How Long Can Love Keep Laughing / My Heart Is Unemployed / One of These Fine Days / Ordinary Guy / Plaza 6-9423 [PC] / Yip-Ahoy [PC]—Harold Rome[w/m] *(Chappell)*. An entertaining topical revue that lasted three months and produced the hit song *F.D.R. Jones*. COVER: newspapers and girl singing.

2108 Singin' in the Rain (British, 1983). Tommy Steele, Roy Castle.

Be a Clown [B] [VS]—Cole Porter[w/m] *(I.M.P.)*; Fascinating Rhythm [B] [VS]—Ira Gershwin[w] & George Gershwin[m] *(I.M.P.)*; Fit as a Fiddle [B] [VS]—Arthur Freed[w] & Al Hoffman[m] & Al Goodhart[m] *(I.M.P.)*; Good Morning [B] [VS] / Singin' in the Rain [B] [VS] / Temptation [B] [VS] / Would You [B] [VS] / You Are My Lucky Star [B] [VS]—Arthur Freed[w] & Nacio Herb Brown[m] *(I.M.P.)*; I Can't Give You Anything But Love [B] [VS]—Dorothy Fields[w] & Jimmy McHugh[m] *(I.M.P.)*; Moses [B] [VS]—Betty Comden[w] & Adolph Green[w] & Roger Edens[m] *(I.M.P.)*; Too Marvellous for Words [B] [VS]—Johnny Mercer[w] & Richard Whiting[m] *(I.M.P.)*. A hit musical based on the great movie with a very talented cast and the most lavish production ever seen on the British stage. COVER: Tommy Steele, Roy Castle, and two girls.

2109 Singin' the Blues (Broadway, 1931). Mantan Moreland, Ashley Cooper.

It's the Darndest Thing / Singin' the Blues — Dorothy Fields[w] & Jimmy McHugh[m] *(Robbins)*. A Negro drama with some songs with a run of six weeks on Broadway. COVER: musical notes.

2110 Singing Out Loud (and other productions) (Carnegie Hall Tribute, 1993). Liza Minnelli, Dorothy Loudon.

Water Under the Bridge — Stephen Sondheim[w/m] *(Warner Bros.)*. A song first performed at Carnegie Hall as a tribute to Sondheim. COVER: black and blue with title only.

2111 The Singing Rabbi (Broadway, 1931). Florenz Ames, Boris Thomashefsky.

Answer with a Kiss [ABQ] / Cry of Israel [ABQ] / Honor Thy Father and Mother [ABQ] / I'm Wide Awake When I Dream / Only Your Heart Can Tell / Playing on the Harpsichord [ABQ] / Yonkele and Rifkele [ABQ] — L. Wolfe Gilbert[w] & Harry Lubin[m] *(Marks)*. The story of a Jewish family emigrating to New York. It was a big hit downtown, but uptown only four performances. COVER: a Jewish candlestick.

2112 Siomka's Wedding (Jewish, 1930). Paul Burstein, Lillian Lux.

Mit Dir Alein — Louis Markowitz[w/m] & Maurice Rauch[w/m] *(Trio)*. A musical at the Hopkinson Theatre in Brooklyn. COVER: Paul Burstein, Lillian Lux.

2113 Sitting Pretty (Broadway, 1924). Queenie Smith, Frank McIntyre.

All You Need Is a Girl / Bongo on the Congo / Enchanted Train / Mr. and Mrs. Rorer / On a Desert Island with You / Shadow of the Moon / Shufflin' Sam / Tulip Time in Sing Sing / Worries / A Year from Today — P.G. Wodehouse[w] & Jerome Kern[m] *(Harms)*; Sitting Pretty — Jerome Kern[w] & P.G. Wodehouse[w] & Jerome

Kern[m] *(Harms)*. A musical about a crook going straight for love. It had a good score but a run of only three months. COVER: a couple sitting on a wall surrounded by flowers.

2114 1600 Pennsylvania Avenue (Broadway, 1976). Ken Howard, Patricia Routledge.

Bright and Black [BW] / I Love My Wife [RC] / Nation That Wasn't There [RC] / Pity the Poor [VS] / President Jefferson March [BW] / The Red, White and Blues [VS] / Seena [VS] / Take Care of This House [BW] / We Must Have a Ball [VS] — Alan Jay Lerner[w] & Leonard Bernstein[m] *(Music of the Times)*. A story of life in the White House and a dreadful musical that lasted one week. COVER: the White House.

2115 Skating Vanities (closed before Broadway, 1942). Ben Klassen, Bobby May.

You're Invited to Attend a Dream — Vic Mizzy[w/m] & Irving Taylor[w/m] *(Santly Bros.–Joy)*. This was a roller-skating show. COVER: a row of chorus girls.

2116 Skirts (British, 1944). Air Force Men.

Jumping to the Juke Box [B] / The Little Brown Suit My Uncle Bought Me [B] / My Pin-Up Girl [B] — Harold Rome[w/m] *(Peter Maurice)*; Skirts [B] — Frank Loesser[w/m] *(Peter Maurice)*. A special Air Force revue produced at the Cambridge Theatre in London. COVER: a dancing girl with British and American flags and two tired looking GIs.

2117 Sky High (Broadway, 1925). Joyce Barbour, Willie Howard.

The Barber of Seville — Clifford Grey[w] & Maurie Rubens[m] & Carlton Kelsey[m] *(Harms)*; Give Your Heart in June Time — Clifford Grey[w] & Harold Atteridge[w] & Victor Herbert[m] *(Harms)*; If You Knew Susie — B.G. DeSylva[w/m] *(Shapiro, Bernstein)*; Keep On Croonin' a Tune — Sammy Fain[w/m] & Irving Weill[w/m] & Jimmy McHugh[w/m] *(Jack Mills)*; Let It Rain — James Kendis[w/m] & Hal yson^w/m *(Harms)*; Trim Them All—Clifford Grey^w & Carlton Kelsey^m & Maurie Rubens^m *(Harms)*. The clowning of Willie Howard as a valet kept this poor show going for six months. COVER: flowers and designs.

2118 The Sky's the Limit (Broadway, 1934). Joe Smith, Charles Dale.

Love in My Life—Jules Loman^w & Allan Roberts^w & Walter Kent^m *(Harms)*. A comedy that lasted only three weeks. COVER: bird on skyscraper surrounded by clouds.

2119 Skyscraper (Broadway, 1965). Julie Harris, Peter Marshall.

Ev'rybody Has the Right to Be Wrong! / The Gaiety [VS] / I'll Only Miss Her When I Think of Her / Local 403 [VS] / More Than One Way / An Occasional Flight of Fancy / Opposites / Run for Your Life!—Sammy Cahn^w & James Van Heusen^m *(Harms)*. Julie Harris was in this poor musical version of *Dream Girl* that ran seven months. COVER: Julie Harris on a metal beam beside an unfinished skyscraper.

2120 Sleepy Hollow (Broadway, 1948). Gil Lamb, Mary McCarty.

The Gray Goose / Here and Now / Things That Lovers Say—Miriam Battista^w & Russell Maloney^w & George Lessner^m *(Chappell)*; I'm Lost—Ruth Aarons^w & George Lessner^m *(Chappell)*. A dreadful musical based on the Rip Van Winkle legend. It lasted 12 performances. COVER: a boy and three girls dancing.

2121 Small Wonder (Broadway, 1948). Jack Cassidy, Joan Diener.

I Like a Man Around the House / Nobody Told Me—Phyllis McGinley^w & Baldwin Bergersen^m *(Chappell)*; Show Off / When I Fall in Love—Albert Selden^w/m *(Chappell)*. A poor revue that lasted for four months. COVER: a small man looking at a map of the world.

2122 Smarty (aka **Funny Face**) (Broadway, 1927). Fred and Adele Astaire.

Dance Alone with You / How Long Has This Been Going On? / Let's Kiss and Make Up / 'S Wonderful / What Am I Gonna Do? / The World Is Mine—Ira Gershwin^w & George Gershwin^m *(New World)*. A hit musical with the best of Gershwin and the Astaires and a minor plot that didn't matter. It was called *Smarty* on the road but opened in N.Y. as *Funny Face*. COVER: red and black letters and designs.

2123 Smile (Broadway, 1986). Marsha Waterbury, Jeff McCarthy.

Disneyland [VS] / In Our Hands [VS] / Smile [VS]—Howard Ashman^w & Marvin Hamlisch^m *(Chappell)*. A musical about beauty pageants that was pretty bad and lasted only six weeks. COVER: Marvin Hamlisch.

2124 Smile at Me (Broadway, 1935). Jack Osterman, Dorothy Morrison.

Caribbean [ABQ] / Fiesta in Madrid [ABQ] / Goona Goona [ABQ] / I'm Dreaming While We're Dancing / Is This the End [ABQ] / Tired of the South [ABQ]—Gerald Dolin^w/m & Edward Lambert^w/m *(Sherman Clay)*; Smile at Me—Edward Lambert^w/m *(Sherman Clay)*; You're a Magician—Edward Lambert^w & Gerald Dolin^m *(Sherman Clay)*. A poor revue that lasted three weeks. COVER: lettering and designs.

2125 Smile, Smile, Smile (*see also* **Comedy**) (Off Broadway, 1973). Rudy Toronto, Chip Zien.

Open Your Heart / Smile, Smile, Smile—Hugo Peretti^w/m & Luigi Creatore^w/m & George D. Weiss^w/m *(Colgems)*. A revised version of a musical called *Comedy* that folded in Boston in 1972. It was a fantasy musical that lasted only one week the second time around. COVER: a cartoon of a smiling face.

2126 Smiles (Broadway, 1930). Fred and Adele Astaire.

Be Good to Me / If I Were You, Love—Ring Lardner^w & Vincent Youmans^m *(Youmans)*; Carry On, Keep Smiling / He Came Along [BW] [CUT] / More Than Ever (not published)—Harold Adamson^w & Vincent Youmans^m *(Youmans)*; I'm Glad I Waited—

Harold Adamson^w & Clifford Grey^w & Vincent Youmans^m *(Youmans)*; Time on My Hands – Harold Adamson^w & Mack Gordon^w & Vincent Youmans^m *(Youmans)*. This was the story of an orphan adopted by three soldiers. Ziegfeld was fighting with the author and replaced him which resulted in a poor book. In spite of lavish urban sets, great talents, and some good songs, the show ran for only two months. COVER: lettering and designs. One cover is blue and silver and the other is orange and black.

2127 Smiles of 1921 (closed before Broadway, 1921). Stars unknown.

All the World Rolls Around / Land of Romance – Lucille Palmer^w/m & Emile DeRecat^w/m *(Harms)*; Mary Jane – Emile DeRecat^w/m *(Harms)*; My Beautiful Garden of Dreams / My Poppy Maid – Lucille Palmer^w/m *(Harms)*. COVER: baskets of flowers and ribbons.

2128 Smilin' Through (Broadway, 1919). Jane Cowl, Henry Stephenson.

Smilin' Through – Arthur Penn^w/m *(Witmark)*. An old fashioned love story that was a big hit and had many revivals. COVER: Jane Cowl.

2129 Smiling Faces (Broadway, 1932). Fred Stone, Dorothy Stone.

Do Say You Do – Mack Gordon^w & Harold Adamson^w & Harry Revel^m *(Miller)*; I Stumbled Over You and Fell in Love / In a Little Stucco in the Sticks / Quick Henry, the Flit! / Sweet Little Stranger / There Will Be a Girl – Mack Gordon^w & Harry Revel^m *(Miller)*. This is a story of a movie star and her loves while filming a movie. It was dreadful and lasted one month. COVER: Fred Stone and Paula Stone. The cover shows Paula but she was replaced by Dorothy Stone.

2130 Smiling the Boy Fell Dead (Off Broadway, 1961). Danny Meehan, Warren Wade.

If I Felt Any Younger / More Than Ever Now / Two by Two / A World to Win – Sheldon Harnick^w & David Baker^m *(Valando)*. This musical about

America as the land of opportunity and opportunists had a good book, pleasant songs, and great stars but ran only three weeks. COVER: a boy dancing with a smile.

2131 Smiling Through (*see also* **Through the Years**) (Broadway, 1931). Michael Bartlett, Reginald Owen.

Drums in My Heart / It's Every Girl's Ambition / Kathleen Mine / Kinda Like You / Through the Years / You're Everywhere – Edward Heyman^w & Vincent Youmans^m *(Miller)*. A musical version of the old classic with some good songs but a run of only two weeks. The try-out title was *Smiling Through*, but it opened as *Through the Years*. COVER: titles and designs.

2132 Snap Into It (Broadway, 1929). Stars unknown.

Lonesome Little Doll – Rubey Cowan^w & Phil Boutelje^m *(Shapiro, Bernstein)*. A short musical presented by Paramount-Publix in between showings of their movies at larger theatres. COVER: four girls dressed as clowns.

2133 Snoopy! (Off Broadway, 1982). Terry Kirwin, David Garrison.

Clouds / Daisy Hill / Don't Be Anything Less / Friend / I Know Now / Just One Person / Poor Sweet Baby / Where Did That Little Dog Go? / The World According to Snoopy – Hal Hackady^w & Larry Grossman^m *(Chappell)*; Woodstock's Theme – Larry Grossman^m *(Chappell)*. A musical version of the cartoon character. This version toured the country for six months in 1976 and closed. It reopened Off Broadway in 1982 and lasted 20 weeks. COVER: Snoopy!

2134 Snow White and the Seven Dwarfs (Broadway, 1979). Mary Jo Salerno, Richard Bowne.

Bluddle-Uddle-Um-Dum [VS] / The Dwarf's Yodel Song [VS] / Heigh-Ho [VS] / I'm Wishing [VS] / One Song [VS] / Some Day My Prince Will Come [VS] / Whistle While You Work [VS] / With a Smile and a Song [VS] – Larry Morey^w & Frank Churchill^m *(Bourne)*;

Welcome to the Kingdom [VS] / Will I Ever See Her Again [VS] — Joe Cook[w] & Jay Blackton[m] *(Bourne)*. A stage version of the movie with a run of one month, a tour, and a second run of two months. COVER: Snow White, Seven Dwarfs, Prince Charming, and the Queen.

2135 So Proudly We Hail! (College, 1938). Alan Jay Lerner, Vinton Freedley, Jr.

Came the Dawn / Rainbow in the Sky — David Lannon[w] & Benjamin Welles[m] *(Chappell)*; Chance to Dream — Alan Jay Lerner[w/m] *(Chappell)*. A show at Harvard with probably the first song published by Lerner. COVER: a mask and ivy with red and black designs.

2136 So This Is Paris (*see also* **Hello Paris**) (Broadway, 1930). Polly Walker, Chic Sale.

Deep Paradise / Nobody Else / Prairie Blues / Wind Me Around Your Finger — Charles Locke[w] & Russell Tarbox[m] *(Harms)*. A newly rich oil man goes to Paris in this poor musical that lasted four weeks. The try-out title was *So This Is Paris!* COVER: a man with a suitcase and sketches of Paris life.

2137 The Social Register (Broadway, 1937). Lenore Ulric, Sidney Blackmer.

The Key to My Heart — Ira Gershwin[w] & Louis Alter[m] *(Harms)*. A comedy about a show girl and her loves that ran three months. COVER: Lenore Ulric.

2138 Softly (closed before Broadway, 1965). Stars unknown.

That's a Fine Kind o' Freedom — Martin Charnin[w] & Harold Arlen[m] *(Morris)*. A musical with complete score by Arlen and Charnin, and with book by Hugh Wheeler. Never produced. COVER: white cover with red titles and two flying birds.

2139 Some Colonel (*see also* **Oui Madame**) (closed before Broadway, 1920). Dorothy Maynard, Georgia O'Ramey.

Every Hour Away from You / He Wanted to Go and He Went / If I Saw Much of You / Over the Garden Wall / Play Me Something I Can Dance To / When You Know Me Better / Where Were You / The Wooing of the Violin — Robert Smith[w] & Victor Herbert[m] *(Harms)*. This musical played Philadelphia and Boston as *Oui Madame*. After several months of touring, it became *Some Colonel*. It ran for eight months on the road and folded. COVER: dancers, circles, and flowers.

2140 Some Day (closed before Broadway, 1925). Charles King, Inez Courtney.

I Looked at You / If You Like Me / Some Day / Virginia Town — Neville Fleeson[w] & Albert Von Tilzer[m] *(Harms)*. COVER: man, woman and children and cottage in the country.

2141 Some Girl (closed before Broadway, 1925). Tommy Martelle.

Cross-word Puzzle of Love / Listen to the Pipes of Pan / Melody of Love / Merely Mary Ann / Oh, What a Girl! / Over the Garden Wall — George Kershaw[w] & Ed Smalle[m] *(Marks)*. A female impersonator musical. COVER: Tommy Martelle as a boy and as a girl.

2142 Some Girl (Jewish, 1930). Molly Picon, Boris Rosenthal.

Jenke! / Oi Is Dus a Meidel — Molly Picon[w] & Murray Rumshisky[m] *(Trio)*. COVER: Molly Picon.

2143 Some Night (Broadway, 1918). Charles Fulton, Charles Hall.

Alone in a Great Big World / By My Window I'll Be Waiting / Send Me a Real Girl / Something That Money Can't Buy / With the Boy I Love — Harry Delf[w/m] *(Witmark)*. A war musical that lasted three weeks. COVER: soldier dreaming of his girl.

2144 Somebody's Sweetheart (Broadway, 1918). William Kent, Walter Scanlon.

American Beauty Rose / Dearie, I Love You / Follow Me / Girl of My Heart / On Wings of Doubt / Somebody's Sweetheart / Song of the Fiddle / Sultana / Then I'll Marry You /

Twinkle — Alonzo Price[w] & Antonio Bafunno[m] *(Harms)*; In the Old Fashioned Way / It Gets Them All / Spain — Arthur Hammerstein[w/m] & Herbert Stothart[w/m] *(Shapiro, Bernstein)*. A musical about a jealous gypsy in Spain that lasted for six months. COVER: One cover has a girl with a violin and the other has a branch of roses and birds.

2145 Something for the Boys (Broadway, 1943). Ethel Merman, Betty Garrett.

By the Mississinewah / Could It Be You? / He's a Right Guy / Hey, Good Lookin' / I'm in Love with a Soldier Boy / The Leader of a Big-Time Band / See That You're Born in Texas / Something for the Boys / When My Baby Goes to Town — Cole Porter[w/m] *(Chappell)*. A bright, bubbly musical with Ethel Merman next door to an Army camp in Texas. It had some pleasant Cole Porter songs and a lavish production by Mike Todd. It ran over a year. COVER: red, white and blue stars and designs.

2146 Something Gay (Broadway, 1935). Walter Pidgeon, Tallulah Bankhead.

You Are So Lovely and I'm So Lonely — Lorenz Hart[w] & Richard Rodgers[m] *(Rodart)*. A comedy dealing with jealousy that ran for two months. COVER: Tallulah Bankhead.

2147 Something More! (Broadway, 1964). Barbara Cook, Ronny Graham.

Come Sta? / One Long Last Look / Something More! / That Faraway Look / You Gotta Taste All the Fruit — Marilyn Bergman[w] & Alan Bergman[w] & Sammy Fain[m] *(Chappell-Styne)*. A family moves from Mineola to Italy to enjoy life. The show lasted only two weeks. COVER: cartoon sketches of all kinds of people in various forms of enjoyment.

2148 Something's Afoot (Broadway, 1976). Tessie O'Shea, Neva Small.

Carry On [VS] / I Don't Know Why I Trust You [VS] / The Legal Heir [VS] / The Man with the Ginger Mustache [VS] / A Marvelous Weekend [VS] /

Something's Afoot [VS] / You Fell Out of the Sky — James McDonald[w/m] & David Vos[w/m] & Bob Gerlach[w/m] & Ed Linderman[w/m] *(Times Music)*. A musical murder mystery that lasted almost two months. COVER: a sketch of the ten characters in the musical.

2149 Sometime (Broadway, 1918). Mae West, Ed Wynn.

Any Kind of Man / Baby Doll / Beautiful Night / Dearie / Keep On Smiling / No One But You / Oh Argentine / Picking Peaches / Sometime / Sometime — complete vocal score / Spanish Maid / Tune You Can't Forget — Rida J. Young[w] & Rudolf Friml[m] *(Schirmer)*; Smiles (piano selections) — Rudolf Friml[m] *(Schirmer)*. A story of love and jealousy with serviceable music by Friml. The clowning of Mae West and Ed Wynn kept it going for nine months. COVER: dull green cover with titles only.

2150 The Son-Daughter (Broadway, 1919). Lenore Ulric, Thomas Findlay.

In the Bamboo Tree — David Belasco[w] & Anselm Goetzl[m] *(Witmark)*; Son-Daughter Intermezzo — Anselm Goetzl[m] *(Witmark)*; Who Comes in My Garden — George Scarborough[w] & David Belasco[w] & Anselm Goetzl[m] *(Witmark)*. A drama of Chinese people living in New York with ties in old China. It ran for six months. COVER: Lenore Ulric.

2151 Song and Dance (Broadway, 1985). Bernadette Peters, Christopher D'Amboise.

Capped Teeth and Caesar Salad [VS] / Come Back with the Same Look [VS] / It's Not the End of the World [PC] / Take That Look Off Your Face (#2) [VS] / Tell Me on a Sunday [VS] / Unexpected Song / You Made Me Think You Were in Love [VS] — Don Black[w] & Andrew Lloyd Webber[m] *(Leonard)*; English Girls / Finale — What Have I Done? [VS] / First Letter Home [VS] / I Love New York [VS] / Let Me Finish [VS] / Nothing Like You've Ever Known [VS] / Second Letter Home [VS] / So Much to Do in New York (#1) [VS]

/ So Much to Do in New York (#2) [VS] / So Much to Do in New York (#3) [VS] / Take That Look Off Your Face (#1) [VS] / Third Letter Home [VS] — Richard Maltby^w & Don Black^w & Andrew L. Webber^m *(Leonard)*. A lonely British girl in New York and a ballet made up this unusual musical. With a great solo performance by Peters and some good Webber songs, it ran for over a year. COVER: Bernadette Peters.

2152 Song of Love (closed before Broadway, 1941). James Melton.

You Haunt My Heart — Richard Brooks^w & Erich W. Korngold^m & Johann Strauss^m *(A.M.P.)*. COVER: James Melton.

2153 Song of Norway (Regional, 1944). Irra Patina, Lawrence Brooks.

At Christmastime / Freddy and His Fiddle / I Love You / Midsummer's Eve / Now / Strange Music / Three Loves — Robert Wright$^{w/m}$ & George Forrest$^{w/m}$ & Edvard Grieg$^{w/m}$ *(Chappell)*. This was an operetta based on Grieg's music, produced for a limited run in California. COVER: a green cover with a Norwegian scene.

2154 Song of Norway (Broadway, 1944). Irra Patina, Lawrence Brooks.

Song of Norway — Broadway (seven separate songs) (1944) — Robert Wright$^{w/m}$ & George Forrest$^{w/m}$ & Edvard Grieg$^{w/m}$ *(Chappell)*. A hit musical from California based on Grieg's music. It ran for over two years. COVER: a blue cover with dancing scene from the musical.

2155 Song of Norway (Broadway, 1960). Stars unknown.

Song of Norway — Jones Beach (seven separate songs) (1960) — Robert Wright$^{w/m}$ & George Forrest$^{w/m}$ & Edvard Grieg$^{w/m}$ *(Chappell)*. A production of the hit operetta by Guy Lombardo at Jones Beach, N.Y., for a summer run. COVER: a Viking ship.

2156 Song of the Flame (Broadway, 1925). Tessa Kosta, Guy Robertson.

Cossack Love Song / Song of the Flame / Vodka / You Are You — Otto Harbach^w & Oscar Hammerstein^w & Herbert Stothart^m & George Gershwin^m *(Harms)*; The Field (Russian folk songs) / I Was There (Russian folk songs) / In the Village (Russian folk songs) / The Pines of the Village (Russian folk songs) — Traditional *(Harms)*; Great Big Bear / Wander Away — Otto Harbach^w & Oscar Hammerstein^w & Herbert Stothart^m *(Harms)*; Midnight Bells / The Signal — Otto Harbach^w & Oscar Hammerstein^w & George Gershwin^m *(Harms)*; Tartar (piano selections) — George Gershwin^m *(Harms)*. A musical dealing with the Russian revolution. It was staged as a spectacle and ran for six months. COVER: Russian peasants listening to a revolutionary.

2157 Song of the Free (Concert, 1942). Stars unknown.

Song of the Free — Archibald MacLeish^w & Kurt Weill^m *(Chappell)*. A concert piece written by Weill. COVER: black and white with title only.

2158 Song Without Words (see also Music in My Heart) (Regional, 1945). Charles Frederick, Vivienne Segal.

Balalaika Serenade / Kiss Me Tonight / Night Wind / Song of the Troika — Forman Brown^w & Franz Steininger^m & P. Tchaikovsky^m *(Robbins)*. This was an attempt to produce another *Song of Norway* — this time with Tchaikovsky. This musical played L.A. as *Song Without Words* and opened in N.Y. as *Music in My Heart* for a short run. COVER: a lady in formal dress with umbrella.

2159 The Song Writer (Broadway, 1928). Georgie Price, Mayo Methot.

Sing Me a Song of the South — Georgie Price$^{w/m}$ & Abner Silver$^{w/m}$ *(Shapiro, Bernstein)*; You Are My Heaven — Herb Magidson$^{w/m}$ & Georgie Price$^{w/m}$ *(Shapiro, Bernstein)*; You're Gone — Phil Baker$^{w/m}$ & Georgie Price$^{w/m}$ & Sid Silvers$^{w/m}$ *(Shapiro, Bernstein)*. A play with music about a song writer that lasted less than two months. COVER: Georgie Price.

2160 Sonny (Broadway, 1921). Carl Randall, Emma Dunn.

Dream / Hometown Blues / I Wonder / I'm in Love Dear / My Dear Old Chum / Peaches / Sonny — George Hobart[w] & Raymond Hubbell[m] *(Harms)*. A musical with a war story theme. It was dreadful and lasted almost a month. COVER: designs and lettering.

2161 Sons o' Fun (Broadway, 1941). Olsen and Johnson.

Happy in Love / Let's Say Goodnight with a Dance / Oh, Auntie! — Jack Yellen[w] & Sammy Fain[m] *(Feist)*. A revue with the old material of Olsen and Johnson. Carmen Miranda and Ella Logan kept the show going for six months. COVER: Olsen and Johnson with Carmen Miranda and Ella Logan.

2162 Sons o' Guns (*see also* **Carry On**) (Broadway, 1929). Lily Damita, Jack Donahue.

Cross Your Fingers / I'm That Way Over You / It's You I Love / Let's Merge / May I Say I Love You / Over Here / Red Hot and Blue Rhythm / Sentimental Melody / There's a Rainbow on the Way / Why? — Arthur Swanstrom[w/m] & Benny Davis[w/m] & Fred Coots[w/m] *(D C and E)*. A war musical set in France with urban sets, pleasant tunes, and lots of chorus girls. It ran for nine months. The try-out title was *Carry On!* COVER #1: red and blue with Donahue, Damita, and chorus girls. COVER #2: blue and orange with Jack Donahue, Gina Malo, and scene from play. COVER #3: blue and orange with Harry Richman, Gina Malo, and scene from play.

2163 Sons o' Guns (British, 1930). Bobby Howes.

Yours Sincerely — Lorenz Hart[w] & Richard Rodgers[m] *(Chappell)*. This American musical was a hit in London, wherein this Rodgers tune was added. It ran for six months. COVER: red and blue cover with row of chorus girls.

2164 Soon (Broadway, 1971). Barry Bostwick, Nell Carter.

One More Time [PC] / Soon [PC] — Scott Fagan[w/m] & Joe Kookoolis[w/m] *(Colgems)*. A rock musical about a group of struggling musicians. It lasted three performances. COVER: none.

2165 Sophie (Broadway, 1963). Libi Staiger, Art Lund.

Don't Look Back / Fight for the Man [CUT] [RC] / I Love You Today / I Want the Kind of a Fella [RC] / I'll Show Them All / I'm a Red Hot Mama / One Little Thing [CUT] [RC] / Patsy [RC] / Queen of the Burlesque Wheel [RC] / Sunshine Face [RC] / They've Got a Lot to Learn / When I'm in Love / When You Carry Your Own Suitcase / Who Are We Kidding [RC] / You'd Know It [CUT] [RC] / You've Got to Be a Lady — Steve Allen[w/m] *(Rosemeadow)*. A musical with a poor score and a lackluster recreation of Sophie Tucker. It had a run of one week. COVER: a sketch of Sophie with a suitcase at the stage door.

2166 Sophisticated Ladies (Broadway, 1981). Gregory Hines, Judith Jamison.

Bli-Blip [VS] — Duke Ellington[w/m] & Sid Kuller[w/m] *(Belwin Mills)*; Caravan [VS] — Duke Ellington[w/m] & Irving Mills[w/m] & Juan Tizol[w/m] *(Belwin Mills)*; Do Nothin' Till You Hear from Me / Don't Get Around Much Anymore [VS] — Duke Ellington[w/m] & Bob Russell[w/m] *(Belwin Mills)*; Drop Me Off in Harlem [VS] — Nick Kenny[w] & Duke Ellington[m] *(Belwin Mills)*; Hit Me with a Hot Note [VS] — Don George[w] & Duke Ellington[m] *(Belwin Mills)*; I Got It Bad [VS] — Duke Ellington[w/m] & Paul F. Webster[w/m] *(Belwin Mills)*; I Let a Song Go Out of My Heart — Duke Ellington[w/m] & Irving Mills[w/m] & Henry Nemo[w/m] & John Redmond[w/m] *(Belwin Mills)*; I'm Beginning to See the Light [VS] — Don George[w/m] & Duke Ellington[w/m] & Harry James[w/m] & John Hodges[w/m] *(Belwin Mills)*; I'm Just a Lucky So and So [VS] — Duke Ellington[w/m] & Mack David[w/m] *(Belwin Mills)*; Imagine My Frustration [VS] — Bill Strayhorn[w] & Gerald Wilson[w] & Duke Ellington[m] *(Belwin Mills)*; In a Sentimental Mood — Duke Ellington[w/m] & Irving

Mills^{w/m} & Manny Kurtz^{w/m} *(Belwin Mills)*; It Don't Mean a Thing — Duke Ellington^{w/m} & Irving Mills^{w/m} *(Belwin Mills)*; Just Squeeze Me [VS] — Lee Gaines^{w} & Duke Ellington^{m} *(Belwin Mills)*; Love You Madly [VS] — Duke Ellington^{w/m} & Luther Henderson^{w/m} *(Belwin Mills)*; Mood Indigo — Duke Ellington^{w/m} & Irving Mills^{w/m} & Albany Bigard^{w/m} *(Belwin Mills)*; Satin Doll [VS] — DukeEllington^{w/m} & Johnny Mercer^{w/m} & Billy Strayhorn^{w/m} *(Belwin Mills)*; Solitude — Duke Ellington^{w/m} & Eddie DeLange^{w/m} & Irving Mills^{w/m} *(Belwin Mills)*; Something to Live For — Duke Ellington^{w/m} & Billy Strayhorn^{w/m} *(Belwin Mills)*; Sophisticated Lady — Duke Ellington^{w/m} & Irving Mills^{w/m} & Mitchell Parish^{w/m} *(Belwin Mills)*; Take the "A" Train [VS] — Billy Strayhorn^{w/m} & Delta Rhythm^{w/m} *(Belwin Mills)*. A revue using the music of Duke Ellington and terrific choreography. It ran for two years. COVER: Duke Ellington and a group of ladies.

2167 The Sound of Music (Broadway, 1959). Mary Martin, Theodore Bikel.

Climb Ev'ry Mountain / Do-Re-Mi / Edelweiss / The Lonely Goatherd / Maria / My Favorite Things / An Ordinary Couple / Sixteen Going on Seventeen / The Sound of Music / The Sound of Music — complete vocal score — Oscar Hammerstein^{w} & Richard Rodgers^{m} *(Williamson)*. A musical about the Trapp family of Austria with a solid book, talented stars and some wonderful songs that became standards. It was the last Broadway show of Oscar Hammerstein's and ran for three and one half years before becoming a successful movie. COVER #1: red and gold with banjo and flute stating "Mary Martin in *Sound of Music.*" COVER #2: red and gold with banjo and flute stating "Florence Henderson in *Sound of Music.*" COVER #3: red and gold with banjo and flute stating "Martha Wright in *Sound of Music.*"

2168 South Pacific (Broadway, 1949). Mary Martin, Ezio Pinza.

Bali Ha'I / A Cock-Eyed Optimist / Dites-Moi / Happy Talk / Honeybun / I'm Gonna Wash That Man Right Outa My Hair / Now Is the Time [VS] [CUT] / Some Enchanted Evening / South Pacific — complete vocal score / There Is Nothin' Like a Dame / This Nearly Was Mine / A Wonderful Guy / Younger Than Springtime / You've Got to Be Carefully Taught — Oscar Hammerstein^{w} & Richard Rodgers^{m} *(Williamson)*. A super-hit musical that ran almost five years. It had a glorious romantic story and two great stars. It produced more than half a dozen hit songs. COVER #1: island with palm trees and ocean, stating "Mary Martin and Ezio Pinza in *South Pacific.*" COVER #2: island with palm trees and ocean, stating "Mary Martin and Ray Middleton in *South Pacific.*" COVER #3: island with palm trees and ocean with no stars listed.

2169 Spades Are Trump (Nightclub, 1930). Stars unknown.

Rollin' Down the River — Stanley Adams^{w} & Thomas Waller^{m} *(Santly Bros.-Joy)*. COVER: man in small boat on the river.

2170 Speakeasy (Broadway, 1927). Dorothy Hall, Leo G. Carroll.

Forever and a Day — Irving Bibo^{w} & John Philip Sousa^{m} *(B B and L)*. A short lived melodrama about an innocent girl lost in N.Y. COVER: pink and white designs with title only.

2171 Spice of Life (closed before Broadway, 1920). Stars unknown.

Cuddle and Kiss — Bert Kalmar^{w} & Harry Ruby^{w} & M.K. Jerome^{m} *(Berlin)*. COVER: beautiful chorus girl and clown.

2172 Spice of 1922 (Broadway, 1922). Georgie Price, Sam Hearn.

Angel Child — George Price^{w/m} & Abner Silvar^{w/m} & Benny Davis^{w/m} *(Witmark)*; Dreams for Sale — Herbert Reynolds^{w/m} & James Hanley^{w/m} *(Shapiro, Bernstein)*; I'll Stand Beneath Your Window Tonight — Jerry

Benson$^{w/m}$ & Jimmy McHugh$^{w/m}$ & George Price$^{w/m}$ *(Jack Mills)*; I'm in Love with You—Kenneth Keith^w & Arman Kaliz^m *(Shapiro, Bernstein)*; In My Little Red Book—McElbert Moore^w & Fred Coots^m *(Harms)*; A Little Side Street in Paree / Old-Fashioned Cakewalk—Jack Stanley^w & James Hanley^m *(Shapiro, Bernstein)*; Love Tunes—George Price$^{w/m}$ & Sam Hearn$^{w/m}$ *(A Y and B)*; My Dixie—Sidney Mitchell^w & Maceo Pinkard^m *(Broadway)*; Swanee Sway / Two Little Wooden Shoes—James Hanley$^{w/m}$ & Jack Stanley$^{w/m}$ *(Shapiro, Bernstein)*; 'Way Down Yonder in New Orleans—Henry Creamer$^{w/m}$ & Turner Layton$^{w/m}$ *(Shapiro, Bernstein)*; The Yankee Doodle Blues—Irving Caesar^w & B.G. DeSylva^w & George Gershwin^m *(Harms)*. A revue with some good dancing. It ran only ten weeks but produced one hit song, *New Orleans.* COVER: Georgie Price; Adele Rowland; sketch of pretty girl riding a rocket.

2173 The Spider (Broadway, 1928). John Halliday, Paul Harvey.

A Kiss Before the Dawn—Ray Perkins$^{w/m}$ *(Marks)*. A mystery melodrama that lasted two weeks. COVER: a silhouette of a man about to kiss a woman.

2174 Spoon River Anthology (Broadway, 1963). Betty Garrett, Robert Elston.

Spoon River Anthology—17 folk songs—Traditional *(Warner Bros.)*. A musical about a small town. It utilized traditional folk songs and lasted three months. COVER: a sketch of various characters in a small town.

2175 Spread It Around (British, 1936). Dorothy Dickson, Hermione Gingold.

These Foolish Things—Holt Marvell^w & Jack Strachey^m & Harry Link^m *(Berlin)*. A hit revue that ran for over six months and produced this standard. COVER: a singing group.

2176 Spring in Autumn (*see also* **Holka-Polka** *and* **Nobody's Girl**)

(Broadway, 1925). Orville Harrold, Patti Harrold.

Good Fellow Days / Holka-Polka / Home of My Heart / In a Little While / Spring in Autumn / This Is My Dance / When Love Is Near—Gus Kahn^w & Raymond Egan^w & Will Ortmann^m *(Harms)*. This two week flop toured the country as *Nobody's Girl* and *Spring in Autumn,* but opened as *Holka Polka.* COVER: flowers and vines.

2177 Spring Is Here (Broadway, 1929). Charles Ruggles, Lillian Taiz.

Baby's Awake Now / Rich Man, Poor Man / Why Can't I? / With a Song in My Heart / You Never Say Yes / Yours Sincerely—Lorenz Hart^w & Richard Rodgers^m *(Harms)*. A musical about two girls and their romances with some beautiful Rodgers songs and a run of three months. COVER: titles and designs.

2178 Springtime in Mayo (Irish, 1920). Fiske O'Hara.

A Bit o' the Brogue / The Top of the Morning—Anna Nichols^w & George Gartlan^m *(Feist)*; Don't You Love to Dream of Dear Old Ireland—Leo Wood^w & George Gartlan^m *(Feist)*; Springtime in Mayo—Anna Nichols^w & Fiske O'Hara^w & George Gartlan^m *(Feist)*. A touring "Melody-Drama" that never reached N.Y. COVER: Fiske O'Hara.

2179 Springtime of Youth (Broadway, 1922). Grace Hamilton, Harold Murray.

In Brazil / Just Like a Doll / Pretty Polly / Starlight of Hope / Youth and Spring—Cyrus Wood^w & Sigmund Romberg^m *(Harms)*; There May Bloom a Rose for Me—Harry B. Smith^w & Sigmund Romberg^m *(Harms)*. A love story set in New England in 1812 that lasted two months. COVER: designs and lettering.

2180 The Squealer (Broadway, 1928). Zelda Santley, Robert Bentley.

My Jimmy—Robert Sterlin$^{w/m}$ *(Shapiro, Bernstein)*. A melodrama about a dope peddler and cabaret singer. It lasted two months. COVER: Zelda Santley.

2181 S.S. Bear Mountain (Nightclub, 1938). Kay Parsons.

Beware Love's in the Air / The Hornpipe Hop / I Can't Keep You Out of My Dreams / In a Houseboat on the Hudson / There's So Much You Can Say with a Lovely Bouquet — Dave Oppenheim[w/m] & Jacques Krakeur[w/m] *(Mills)*. COVER: Kay Parsons.

2182 Stags at Bay (College, 1935). Students.

East of the Sun / Love and a Dime — Brooks Bowman[w/m] *(Santly Bros.-Joy)*; Will Love Find a Way — Brooks Bowman[w] & K.B. Alexander[m] *(Santly Bros.-Joy)*. COVER: boy, girl and eclipse.

2183 Stairway Idea (Nightclub, 1928). Fanchon and Marco.

Stairway of Dreams — Gene Stone[w] & Adrian Mack[m] *(Johnston)*. COVER: a chorus girl.

2184 Star and Garter (Broadway, 1942). Bobby Clark, Gypsy Rose Lee.

Brazilian Nuts — Al Stillman[w] & Dorival Caymmi[m] *(Robbins)*; Bunny, Bunny, Bunny — Harold Rome[w/m] *(Robbins)*; I Don't Get It — Sis Willner[w] & Doris Tauber[m] *(Robbins)*. A burlesque show kept going for 18 months by the antics of Bobby Clark and the presence of Gypsy Rose Lee. COVER: Bobby Clark, Gypsy Rose Lee, and chorus girls.

2185 Star Dust (closed before Broadway, 1931). Stars unknown.

Pick Me Up and Lay Me Down [VS] — Cole Porter[w/m] *(Chappell)*. Cole Porter finished the complete score for this musical that was never produced. The balance of the unused score went into future musicals including *I Get a Kick Out of You* (*Anything Goes*) and part of the score for *Gay Divorce*. COVER: Cole Porter.

2186 Stardust (closed before Broadway, 1990). Betty Buckley, Karen Ziemba.

Belle of the Ball [VS] / Forgotten Dreams [VS] / Sleigh Ride [VS] / The Syncopated Clock [VS] — Mitchell Parish[w] & Leroy Anderson[m] *(Belwin)*; Carolina Rolling Stone — Mitchell Parish[w] & Eleanor Young[m] & Harry Squires[m] *(Belwin)*; Ciao, Ciao, Bambina [VS] — Mitchell Parish[w] & Domenico Modugno[m] *(Belwin)*; Deep Purple [VS] — Mitchell Parish[w] & Peter DeRose[m] *(Belwin)*; Dixie After Dark [VS] / Sidewalks of Cuba [VS] — Mitchell Parish[w] & Ben Oakland[m] & Irving Mills[m] *(Belwin)*; Don't Be That Way [VS] — Mitchell Parish[w] & Benny Goodman[m] & Edgar Sampson[m] *(Belwin)*; Evenin' [VS] — Mitchell Parish[w] & Harry White[m] *(Belwin)*; Hands Across the Table [VS] — Mitchell Parish[w] & Jean Delettre[m] *(Belwin)*; I Would If I Could But I Can't [VS] — Mitchell Parish[w] & Bing Crosby[m] & Alan Grey[m] *(Belwin)*; It Happens to the Best of Friends — Mitchell Parish[w] & Rube Bloom[m] *(Belwin)*; A Little Bit Older [VS] — Mitchell Parish[w] & Joe Harnell[m] *(Belwin)*; Midnight at the Onyx [VS] / Sophisticated Swing [VS] — Mitchell Parish[w] & Will Hudson[m] *(Belwin)*; Moonlight Serenade [VS] — Mitchell Parish[w] & Glenn Miller[m] *(Belwin)*; One Morning in May [VS] / Star Dust [VS] — Mitchell Parish[w] & Hoagy Carmichael[m] *(Belwin)*; Organ Grinder's Swing [VS] — Mitchell Parish[w] & Irving Mills[m] & Will Hudson[m] *(Belwin)*; Riverboat Shuffle — Mitchell Parish[w] & Hoagy Carmichael[m] & Dick Voynow[m] & Irving Mills[m] *(Belwin)*; Ruby [VS] — Mitchell Parish[w] & Heinz Roemheld[m] *(Belwin)*; The Scat Song [VS] [SCAT] — Mitchell Parish[w] & Frank Perkins[m] & Cab Calloway[m] *(Belwin)*; Sentimental Gentleman from Georgia [VS] / Stars Fell on Alabama [VS] — Mitchell Parish[w] & Frank Perkins[m] *(Belwin)*; Sophisticated Lady [VS] — Mitchell Parish[w] & Duke Ellington[m] & Irving Mills[m] *(Belwin)*; Stairway to the Stars — Mitchell Parish[w] & Matt Malneck[m] & Frank Signorelli[m] *(Belwin)*; Sweet Lorraine [VS] — Mitchell Parish[w] & Cliff Burwell[m] *(Belwin)*; Take Me in Your Arms [VS] — Mitchell Parish[w] & Fred

Markush^m *(Belwin)*; Tell Me Why [VS] — Mitchell Parish^w & Michael Edwards^m & Sigmund Spaeth^m *(Belwin)*; Wealthy, Shmelthy, as Long as You're Healthy [VS] / You're So Indiff'rent [VS] — Mitchell Parish^w & Sammy Fain^m *(Belwin)*. This revue of Parish songs opened on Broadway in 1987. It was a rather small scale production and ran three months before folding, due to financial problems. It was restaged and given a lavish production at the Opera House in Washington. COVER: a beautiful sketch by Erte of a girl in a flowing gown.

2187 Starlight Express (British, 1984). Ray Shell, Jeff Shankley.

A.C./D.C. [B] [VS] / He Whistled at Me [B] [VS] / Light at the End of the Tunnel [B] / Only He / Rolling Stock [B] [VS] / Starlight Express [B] [VS] / Uncoupled [B] [VS] — Richard Stilgoe^w & Andrew Lloyd Webber^m *(Really Useful)*. A musical on roller skates with actors portraying various trains. It was a huge spectacle with only serviceable music and yet has been running for ten years in London. COVER: a vague sketch of a speeding train with headlight.

2188 Starlight Express (Broadway, 1987). Andrea McArdle, Robert Torti.

Engine of Love [VS] / I Am the Starlight [VS] / Make Up My Heart [VS] / Next Time You Fall in Love [BW] / One Rock and Roll Too Many [VS] / Only You [VS] / Pumping Iron [VS] / Starlight Express / There's Me [VS] — Richard Stilgoe^w & Andrew Lloyd Webber^m *(Leonard)*; The Race Is On [VS] — Andrew Lloyd Webber^m *(Leonard)*. This roller-skating spectacle, which has been running in London for years, ran for less than two years on Broadway, followed by a national tour. COVER: a vague sketch of a speeding train with spotlight.

2189 Starlight Roof (British, 1947). Barbara Perry.

South America, Take It Away! [B] — Harold Rome^{w/m} *(Feldman)*. A Hippodrome revue that ran for 18 months. COVER: a boy pulling at a curtain.

2190 Stars and Gripes (Army, 1943). Soldier show.

The Army Service Forces / Hup! Tup! Thrup! Four! / Jumping to the Jukebox / Little Brown Suit My Uncle Bought Me / Love Sometimes Has to Wait / My Pin-Up Girl — Harold Rome^{w/m} *(Leeds)*; Mail Call — Thom Conroy^w & Tony Sacco^m *(Mills)*; My Man with a European Tan — A. DeLorenzo^w & Tony Sacco^m *(Mills)*. A musical revue that toured the Army camps. COVER: red, white and blue patriotic cover.

2191 Stars in Your Eyes (Broadway, 1939). Ethel Merman, Jimmy Durante.

All the Time / I'll Pay the Check / It's All Yours / Just a Little Bit More / A Lady Needs a Change / Terribly Attractive / This Is It — Dorothy Fields^w & Arthur Schwartz^m *(Chappell)*. A musical about a movie star and her love affairs. It had an ordinary score and book and ran three months. COVER: sketch of a movie star surrounded by crew.

2192 Stars of Tomorrow (Regional, 1935). Marilyn Weinrauch, Ann Pardes.

Does Anybody Want a Little Kewpie? / When Pat Rooney Steps — Jack Darrell^{w/m} *(Darrell)*; Gun Moll Gerty — Jack Darrell^{w/m} & Marie Kister^{w/m} *(Darrell)*; Skipping Rope — Jack Darrell^{w/m} & Marie Schroeder^{w/m} *(Darrell)*. COVER: various child stars in talent contest.

2193 Stars of Tomorrow (Regional, 1936). Baby Mae, Norma Wayne.

Ach Du Lieber Darling — Jack Darrell^{w/m} & Marie Kister^{w/m} *(Darrell)*; I'm a Little Boolie Bear — Jack Darrell^{w/m} & Marie Schroeder^{w/m} & Art Darvo^{w/m} *(Darrell)*. COVER: child stars in talent contest.

2194 Stars of Tomorrow (Regional, 1939). Freddie Krimm.

Here I Am, Uncle Sam — Jack Darrell^{w/m} *(Darrell)*. COVER: child stars in talent contest.

2195 Stars on Ice (Ice Show, 1941). Stars unknown.

I Never Saw It to Fail / The World Waltzes — Irvin Graham[w/m] *(BMI)*. COVER: a sketch of a row of ice skaters.

2196 Stars on Ice (Ice Show, 1942). Vivienne Allen, Skippy Baxter.

Big Broad Smile / Gin Rummy / Juke Box Saturday Night / Little Jack Frost — Al Stillman[w] & Paul McGrane[m] *(Mutual)*; Like a Leaf Falling in the Breeze — Al Stillman[w] & James Littlefield[m] *(Mutual)*. COVER: Ice skater and stars.

2197 Starting Here, Starting Now (Off Broadway, 1977). Loni Ackerman, George Lee Andrews. Vocal Selections:

Autumn / Barbara / Crossword Puzzle / Flair / I Don't Remember Christmas / I Hear Bells / I Think I May Want to Remember Today / A Little Bit Off / One Step / Song of Me / Starting Here, Starting Now / Today Is the First Day — / Travel / Watching the Big Parade Go By — Richard Maltby, Jr.[w] & David Shire[m] *(Fiddleback)*; What About Today? — David Shire[w/m] *(Fiddleback)*. A revue featuring some good songs by Maltby and Shire. It ran three months. COVER: letters and designs.

2198 Steppin' High (Black, 1924). Hazel Myers, Dike Thomas.

The Charleston Crave [ABQ] / Drifting Back Home [ABQ] / Love, Love, Why Do You Seem So Hard to Hold / My Mammy's Blues / Sunshine Mae [ABQ] / What'll You Do [ABQ] / The Whole World Seems Wrong / You're Not the Only One That's Lonesome [ABQ] — John Spikes[w/m] & Benjamin Spikes[w/m] *(Sherman Clay)*. COVER: a black girl steppin' high.

2199 Stepping Sisters (Broadway, 1930). Helen Raymond, Grace Huff.

Shadows Were Falling / Your Loving Arms — Hector Carlton[w] & Iver Peterson[m] *(Harms)*. A comedy with songs; it lasted two months. COVER: two girls all dressed up and dancing.

2200 The Stepping Stones (Broadway, 1923). Fred Stone, Dorothy Stone.

Brittany Scene (piano selections) / Everybody Calls Me Little Red Riding Hood / In Love with Love / Little Angel Cake (piano selections) / Once in a Blue Moon / Our Lovely Rose / Pie / Raggedy Ann / Stepping Stones / The Stepping Stones — complete vocal score / Wonderful Dad — Anne Caldwell[w] & Jerome Kern[m] *(Harms)*; I Saw the Roses and Remembered You — Herbert Reynolds[w] & Jerome Kern[m] *(Harms)*. A musical on the Little Red Riding Hood theme. It had a beautiful Jerome Kern score and ran seven months. COVER: Raggedy Ann and Andy.

2201 Sterling Silver (Off Broadway, 1979). Lee Roy Reams, Karen Jablons.

The Age of Elegance [VS] / Closing Time [VS] / The Days of the Dancing [VS] / I Do Like London [VS] / A Simple Song [VS] / Someone in My Life [VS] — Fred Silver[w/m] *(Genesis 3)*. A revue of humorous songs that lasted for four shows. COVER: Fred Silver.

2202 Steve (closed before Broadway, 1923). Eugene O'Brien.

Lovetime in Eden — Rida J. Young[w] & William Schroeder[m] *(Harms)*; Steve — George Kershaw[w] & Ted Snyder[m] *(Berlin)*. A drama written for the movie star. It was headed for Broadway but folded in Chicago. COVER: Eugene O'Brien.

2203 Still Dancing (British, 1925). Stars unknown.

Lady of the Moon [B] — Noble Sissle[w/m] & Eubie Blake[w/m] *(Chappell)*. COVER: lettering and designs.

2204 Stop Flirting (aka **For Goodness Sake**) (British, 1923). Fred and Adele Astaire.

All by Myself [B] (piano selections) / Opening Chorus of Act One [B] (piano selections) — George Gershwin[m] *(Harms)*; The Best of Everything [B] — B.G. DeSylva[w] & Arthur Jackson[w] & George Gershwin[m] *(Warner Bros.)*; Every Day [B] / Oh Gee! Oh Gosh! [B] — Arthur Jackson[w] & William Daly[m] *(Harms)*; I'll Build a Stairway to Paradise [B] — B.G. DeSylva[w] & Arthur

Francis (IG)^w & George Gershwin^m *(Harms)*; The Oom-Pah Trot [B] — William Daly^m & Paul Lannin^m *(Harms)*; Someone [B] — Arthur Francis (IG)^w & George Gershwin^m *(Harms)*; The Whichness of the Whatness [B] — Arthur Jackson^w & William Daly^m & Paul Lannin^m *(Harms)*. This show was a revised edition of the American musical *For Goodness Sake*. It was a hit for six months. COVER: flowers and designs.

2205 Stop the Press (British, 1935). Dorothy Dickson.

Easter Parade [B] / How's Chances? [B] / Lonely Heart [B] — Irving Berlin$^{w/m}$ *(Chappell)*; How Can I Hold You Close Enough? [B] — E.Y. Harburg^w & Edward Heyman^w & John Green^m *(Chappell)*; Revolt in Cuba [B] — piano selections — Irving Berlin^m *(Chappell)*; You and the Night and the Music [B] — Howard Dietz^w & Arthur Schwartz^m *(Chappell)*. A London version of *As Thousands Cheer* with music by various composers. It had a moderate run. COVER: a newspaper with a big splash of ink.

2206 Stop the World — I Want to Get Off (Broadway, 1962). Anthony Newley, Anna Quayle.

Gonna Build a Mountain / Lumbered [VS] / Meilinki Meilchik [VS] / Once in a Lifetime / Someone Nice Like You / Typically English [VS] / What Kind of Fool Am I? — Leslie Bricusse$^{w/m}$ & Anthony Newley$^{w/m}$ *(Ludlow)*. An allegorical musical with Newley as Mr. Littlechap. It produced several hit songs and ran for 18 months. COVER: a dopey looking man balanced on a round globe.

2207 Stop the World — I Want to Get Off (Broadway, 1978). Sammy Davis, Jr., Wendy Edmead.

All American [VS] / Glorious Russian [VS] / Gonna Build a Mountain / I Wanna Be Rich [VS] / Life Is a Woman / Lumbered [VS] / Meilinki Meilchik [VS] / Once in a Lifetime / Someone Nice Like You [VS] / Typically English [VS] / What Kind of Fool Am I? —

Leslie Bricusse$^{w/m}$ & Anthony Newley$^{w/m}$ *(TRO)*. A revival of the hit musical that toured the U.S. for a year but played only three weeks on Broadway. COVER: Sammy Davis, Jr., and a bunch of girls.

2208 Stovepipe Hat (closed before Broadway, 1944). Bob Kennedy, Ann Warren.

The Great Man Says / Lady Lovely / Softly My Heart Is Singing — Edward Heyman^w & Harold Spina^m *(Chappell)*. A musical about Lincoln that folded after ten days in New Haven and Boston. COVER: a large stovepipe hat.

2209 La Strada (Broadway, 1969). Larry Kert, Bernadette Peters.

Everything Needs Something [PC] / Sooner or Later [PC] / Starfish [PC] — Martin Charnin^w & Elliot Lawrence^m *(Morris)*. A musical version of the Fellini film that lasted one performance. The playbill states that the music and lyrics were by Lionel Bart; however, most of the music was written by Lawrence and Charnin. COVER: none.

2210 The Straw Hat Revue (Broadway, 1939). Imogene Coca, Danny Kaye.

Four Young People / Our Town — James Shelton$^{w/m}$ *(Chappell)*; Give Me Some Men [VS] / Here He Comes Now — finale [VS] / It Really Doesn't Matter [VS] / It's Lonely on the Lone Prairie [VS] / L'Amour Toujours [VS] / Love Will Find a Way [VS] / Mario and Mary Sue Ann's Entrance [VS] / Oh, Mary Sue Ann [VS] / One Moment Alone [VS] / So This Is Venice [VS] — Sylvia Fine$^{w/m}$ *(USO)*. A small revue that played summer theatres with the talents of Alfred Drake, Imogene Coca, Danny Kaye, and Jerome Robbins; however, it lasted only two months on Broadway. COVER: a large straw hat with four girls.

2211 Street Scene (Broadway, 1947). Polyna Stoska, Anne Jeffreys.

A Boy Like You / Lonely House / Moon-Faced, Starry-Eyed / We'll Go Away Together / What Good Would the Moon Be? — Langston Hughes[w] & Kurt Weill[m] *(Chappell)*; Street Scene — complete vocal score — Langston Hughes[w] & Elmer Rice[w] & Kurt Weill[m] *(Chappell)*. An operatic musical based on the Rice play. It was very long and melodramatic but it had a beautiful score by Weill. It lasted five months then entered the operatic repertory. COVER: the entrance to an apartment building with people on doorsteps and in windows.

2212 The Street Singer (Broadway, 1929). Guy Robertson, Queenie Smith.

From Now On — Edward Eliscu[w] & Richard Myers[m] *(Harms)*; Go One Better — Graham John[w] & Sam Timberg[m] *(Harms)*; Jumping Jimminy / Playboy of Dreams / You Might Have Known I Loved You / You've Made Me Happy Today — Graham John[w] & Niclas Kempner[m] *(Harms)*. A flower girl becomes a Follies girl in Paris in this show. It had a poor score but great dancing and a run of six months. COVER: a small house, a street lamp, and a bridge.

2213 The Streets of New York (Broadway, 1931). Dorothy Gish, Rommey Brent.

Whoa, Emma! — John Reid[w/m] *(Marks)*. A limited run revival of the old classic. It ran for 11 weeks. COVER: man with mustache singing.

2214 The Streets of New York (Off Broadway, 1963). David Cryer, Gail Johnston.

Arms for the Love of Me / If I May / Love Wins Again — Barry Alan Grael[w] & Richard Chodosh[m] *(Chappell)*. A musical version of the old classic play. It was a lovely production that ran nine months. COVER: a lady putting down a man offering her money.

2215 The Streets of Paris (Broadway, 1939). Bobby Clark and Abbott and Costello.

Danger in the Dark / Doin' the Chamberlain / In My Memoirs / Is It Possible? / Reading, Writing, and Rhythm / Rendezvous Time in Paree / Robert the Roue from Reading, PA [ABQ] / South American Way / We Can Live on Love — Al Dubin[w] & Jimmy McHugh[m] *(Harms)*; History Is Made at Night — Harold Rome[w/m] *(Chappell)*. A smash hit revue loaded with talent including Bobby Clark, Carmen Miranda, Jean Sablon, and Abbott and Costello. It was a great comedy with good songs and ran for nine months. COVER: streets with lamp posts.

2216 Strider (Broadway, 1979). Gerald Hiken, Roger DeKoven.

Darling's Romance [VS] / Live Long Enough [VS] / Oh, Mortal [VS] / Serpuhovsky's Romance [VS] / Serpuhovsky's Song [VS] / Song of the Herd [VS] / Troika [VS] / Warm and Tender [VS] — Steve Brown[w] & M. Rozovsky[m] & S. Vetkin[m] *(Macmillan)*. A Russian musical play about the life of a horse. The play lasted six months. COVER: three dancers.

2217 Strike a New Note (British, 1943). Yvette, Sid Field.

I'm Gonna Get Lit Up — Hubert Gregg[w/m] & John Klenner[w/m] *(Shapiro, Bernstein)*. An American publication of a song from a hit London revue that ran over 18 months. COVER: the singer Yvette.

2218 Strike Me Pink (*see also* **Forward March**) (Broadway, 1932). Lupe Velez, Jimmy Durante.

Home to Harlem / I Hate to Think That You'll Grow Old, Baby / It's Great to Be Alive / Let's Call It a Day / Ooh, I'm Thinking / Strike Me Pink — Lew Brown[w/m] & Ray Henderson[w/m] *(Harms)*. The first version of this revue was called *Forward March* and folded. It was rewritten and opened as *Strike Me Pink* and became a moderate hit of four months. COVER: a sketch of a bunch of chorus girls.

2219 Strike Up the Band (closed before Broadway, 1927). Jimmy Savo, Morton Donney.

The Man I Love / Meadow Serenade [PC] / Military Dancing Drill / Seventeen and Twenty-One / Strike Up the

Band / Yankee Doodle Rhythm—Ira Gershwin[w] & George Gershwin[m] *(Harms)*. This version of *Strike Up the Band* had a bitter anti-war book and closed after a few weeks' try-out. COVER: girl beating a drum. Cover states that Edgar Selwyn presents the Gershwin-Kaufman musical with book by George S. Kaufman.

2220 Strike Up the Band (Broadway, 1930). Bobby Clark, Paul McCullough.

Hangin' Around with You / I Mean to Say / I Want to Be a War Bride / I've Got a Crush on You / Mademoiselle in New Rochelle / Soon / Strike Up the Band / Strike Up the Band—complete vocal score—Ira Gershwin[w] & George Gershwin[m] *(Harms)*. A satire on big business policies with the great comedy team and wonderful Gershwin songs. COVER: girl beating drum. The cover states that Edgar Selwyn presents Clark and McCullough in *Strike Up the Band* with book by Morrie Ryskind.

2221 Strip for Action (closed before Broadway, 1956). Yvonne Adair, Jerome Courtland.

Dame Crazy / The Good Old Days of Burlesque [ABQ] / I Just Found Out About Love / Kicking Up a Storm [ABQ] / Love Me as Though There Were No Tomorrow / My Papa from Panama [ABQ] / Song and Dance Man [ABQ] / Strip for Action / Too Young to Go Steady—Harold Adamson[w] & Jimmy McHugh[m] *(Robbins)*. A musical about a burlesque show entertaining at the Brooklyn Navy Yard. The book was terrible but it did have some good songs. After a month on the road, it folded in Pittsburgh. COVER: two strippers.

2222 Strut Miss Lizzie (Broadway, 1922). Henry Creamer, Turner Layton.

Argentina / Beware of the Chickens / Buzz Mirandy / I'm Nobody's Gal / In Yama / Way Down Yonder in New Orleans—Henry Creamer[w/m] & Turner Layton[w/m] *(Shapiro, Bernstein)*; Breakin' the Leg / Dear Old Southland / I Love Sweet Angeline / Mandy /

Strut Miss Lizzie—Henry Creamer[w/m] & Turner Layton[w/m] *(Jack Mills)*. A poor black revue that lasted two months. COVER: Mills shows chubby black girl; Shapiro Bernstein shows elegant blonde lady with suitors.

2223 The Student Gypsy (Broadway, 1963). Dom DeLuise, Eileen Brennan.

My Love Is Yours / Romance / Seventh Heaven Waltz / Somewhere / Ting-a-Ling Dearie / Very Much in Love—Rick Besoyan[w/m] *(Valando)*. A take-off on operetta a la *Little Mary Sunshine*. It didn't work and was canceled after two weeks. COVER: a gypsy with a rose in his mouth.

2224 The Student Prince (*see also* **In Heidelberg**) (Broadway, 1924). Howard Marsh, Ilsa Marvenga.

Arrival of the Prince (piano selections)—Sigmund Romberg[m] *(Harms)*; Deep in My Heart, Dear / Drinking Song / Golden Days / Just We Two / Serenade / The Student Prince—complete vocal score / Students March Song—Dorothy Donnelly[w] & Sigmund Romberg[m] *(Harms)*. This sentimental musical with a wonderful score by Romberg is one of the classics of the musical theatre with many revivals. The try-out title was *In Heidelberg*. COVER: flowers and designs.

2225 The Studio Girl (closed before Broadway, 1927). Stars unknown.

Because I Love You / Moonlight and Love and All / There's No One as Sweet as Trilby / Way Down in Barbizon—J. Keirn Brennan[w] & William Ortmann[m] *(Harms)*. COVER: flowers and designs.

2226 Subways Are for Sleeping (Broadway, 1961). Carol Lawrence, Sydney Chaplin.

Be a Santa / Comes Once in a Lifetime / How Can You Describe a Face? / I Just Can't Wait [PC] / I'm Just Taking My Time / Ride Through the Night / Who Knows What Might Have Been—Betty Comden[w] & Adolph Green[w] & Jule Styne[m] *(Strat-*

ford). A musical about two love affairs in New York. Other than a couple of pleasant Styne songs, it had nothing else. It ran for six months due to David Merrick's outlandish ads. COVER: a girl hanging on a subway strap, napping with alarm clock in hand.

2227 Sue Dear (Broadway, 1922). Bradford Kirkbride, Olga Steck.

By Radiophone [ABQ] / Da-Da-Daddy Dear / Dance Me Darling, Dance Me [ABQ] / Foolishment [ABQ] / Hiram Skinner's Comb [ABQ] / Key to My Heart [ABQ] / Lady Lingerie / Lady of Dreams [ABQ] / Lorayne [ABQ] / The Love Ship / Lover's Lane with You / Love's Corporation / My Little Full Blown Rose / Pidgie Widgie / Smile and Forget / That Samson and Delilah Melody / Up on Riverside [ABQ] – Bide Dudley[w] & Frank Grey[m] *(Feist)*. A musical with a Cinderella plot and nothing else. It lasted three months. COVER: sketch of a pretty young girl.

2228 Sugar (*see also* **Nobody's Perfect**) (Broadway, 1972). Robert Morse, Cyril Ritchard.

All You Gotta Do Is Tell Me [RC] [CUT] / It's Always Love [RC] / The Kind of Beauty That Drives Men Mad [RC] / Nice Ways [RC] [CUT] / The People in My Life [CUT] [RC] / Sugar / We Could Be Close [RC] – Bob Merrill[w] & Jule Styne[m] *(Chappell)*. An underrated version of the hit movie *Some Like It Hot*. It had great comedy with Morse and Ritchard plus some nice period songs by Styne. It ran 15 months. COVER: sketch of girls with musical instruments.

2229 Sugar Babies (Broadway, 1979). Ann Miller, Mickey Rooney.

Cuban Love Song [VS] – Herbert Stothart[w/m] & Dorothy Fields[w/m] & Jimmy McHugh[w/m] *(McHugh)*; Don't Blame Me [VS] / I Can't Give You Anything But Love [VS] – Dorothy Fields[w] & Jimmy McHugh[m] *(McHugh)*; Down at the Gaiety Burlesque [VS] / Let Me Be Your Sugar Baby [VS] / Mister Banjo Man [VS] – Arthur Malvin[w/m] *(McHugh)*; Exactly

Like You / On the Sunny Side of the Street – Dorothy Fields[w] & Jimmy McHugh[m] *(Shapiro, Bernstein)*; A Good Old Burlesque Show [VS] – Arthur Malvin[w/m] & Jimmy McHugh[w/m] *(McHugh)*; I Feel a Song Comin' On [VS] – Jimmy McHugh[w/m] & Dorothy Fields[w/m] & George Oppenheimer[w/m] *(McHugh)*; I Just Want to Be a Song and Dance Man [VS] – Harold Adamson[w] & Jimmy McHugh[m] *(McHugh)*; I'm Keepin' Myself Available for You [VS] / In Lou'siana [VS] / Sally [VS] – Arthur Malvin[w] & Jimmy McHugh[m] *(McHugh)*; I'm Shooting High [VS] – Ted Koehler[w] & Jimmy McHugh[m] *(McHugh)*; Sugar Baby Bounce – Jay Livingston[w/m] & Ray Evans[w/m] *(Hansen)*; Warm and Willing [VS] – Jimmy McHugh[w/m] & Jay Livingston[w/m] & Ray Evans[w/m] *(McHugh)*; When You and I Were Young Maggie Blues [VS] – Jack Frost[w/m] & Jimmy McHugh[w/m] *(McHugh)*; You Can't Blame Your Uncle Sammy [VS] – Al Dubin[w/m] & Jimmy McHugh[w/m] & Irwin Dash[w/m] *(McHugh)*. A musical revue about burlesque utilizing the songs of Jimmy McHugh. It was very fast moving and funny. Ann Miller and Mickey Rooney kept it going for three years. COVER: a beautiful colored cartoon sketch of burlesque queens and comic.

2230 Sugar Hill (Broadway, 1931). Flournoy Miller, Aubrey Lyles.

Chivaree / Far-Away Love / I Don't Want Any Labor in My Job / Keep 'em Guessing / My Sweet Hunk o' Trash / Peace, Sister, Peace / Stay Out of the Kitchen / That Was Then / You Can't Lose a Broken Heart – Flournoy Miller[w] & James Johnson[m] *(Mills)*; Somethin's Gonna Happen to Me and You / Yes, I Love You Honey – Jo Trent[w] & Jimmy Johnson[m] *(Harms)*. A black musical about bootlegging and crime that lasted for 11 performances. COVER: sketch of a boy and girl dancing.

2231 Suite Sixteen (closed before Broadway, 1919). Stars unknown.

Beauty Dance / The First Step /

Fond of Girlies / Good Bye / I Dare You / I Want Some Loe / I'd Like to Plant a Smile / If I Were You / Joy Out of Life / Quaker Song / The Reason Why / Suspicion / Teach Me / Wiggle Waggle — Edward Paulton^w & Silvio Hein^m *(Church)*. COVER: letters and designs.

2232 Summer Wives (Broadway, 1936). Smith and Dale.

The Chatterbox / Mickey / My Love Carries On / Play Me an Old Time Two-Step — Dolph Singer^w & Sam Morrison^m *(Famous)*; I Wrote a Song for You — Dolph Singer^w & William Dunham^w & Sam Morrison^m *(Famous)*; Us on a Bus — Tot Seymour^w & Vee Lawnhurst^m *(Famous)*. A comedy about a country club and its entertainers. It lasted one week. COVER: Smith and Dale with Helen Charleston.

2233 The Sun Never Sets (British, 1938). Todd Duncan, Adelaide Hall.

My Love Is Like the River — Desmond Carter^w & Kenneth Leslie-Smith^m *(Chappell)*; River God — Cole Porter^w/m *(Chappell)*. A melodrama with music about the racial problem in Africa. It lasted one month. COVER: a tropical river scene.

2234 Sun Showers (Broadway, 1923). Harry Delf, Tom Dingle.

Each Little Jack Is Some Girl's Little John [ABQ] / Everything Is Beautiful in Someone's Eyes / Get Him on a Moonlight Night [ABQ] / A Greenwich Village Chambermaid [ABQ] / He Loves Me [ABQ] / How Do You Doodle? [ABQ] / If Old Folks Could Only See Us Now [ABQ] / It Always Happens for the Best [ABQ] / My Little Jail-Bird / Sunshowers / Worth While Waiting For / You Beside Me [ABQ] / You Can Speak Without Compunction [ABQ] / Yours Truly — Harry Delf^w/m *(Feist)*. A band of school teachers trying to get a raise was the subject of this poor musical. It lasted six weeks. COVER: a church, a little village, clouds, and a rainbow.

2235 Sunbonnet Sue (closed before Broadway, 1923). Olga Cook, Chester Fredericks.

Little Boy Blue Jeans / Love Is a Garden of Roses / 'Member When? / She's the Same Old Sunbonnet Sue — Robert Smith^w & Gus Edwards^m *(Harms)*. COVER: Olga Cook.

2236 Sunday in the Park with George (Broadway, 1984). Bernadette Peters, Mandy Patinkin.

Beautiful [VS] / Children and Art [VS] / Finishing the Hat [VS] / Move On [VS] / Putting It Together [BW] / Sunday [VS] / Sunday in the Park with George — complete vocal score — Stephen Sondheim^w/m *(Revelation)*. A musical based on a painting that was much too arty for the general public. It won many awards, and curiosity probably kept it going for 18 months. COVER: man and woman walking in park — part painting and part real.

2237 Sunkist *(see also* **Alley Up!** *and* **Satires of 1920)** (Broadway, 1920). Fanchon and Marco.

Ain't We Got Fun — Gus Kahn^w & Raymond Egan^w & Richard Whiting^m *(Remick)*; The I-Dun-No-Wat / I Want to Meet You Some Day in California / The Love a Gipsy Knows / My Sweetie's Smile / Pollyanna / Pretty Dance Is Like a Violin — Fanchon and Marco^w/m *(Remick)*. A Hollywood revue poking fun at the movies. It toured as *Satires of 1920* and *Alley-Up* and opened as *Sunkist* for a very brief run. COVER: girl in evening gown holding a ball.

2238 Sunny (Broadway, 1925). Marilyn Miller, Cliff Edwards.

Dream a Dream / D'Ye Love Me? / Sunny / Sunshine / Two Little Lovebirds / Who? — Otto Harbach^w & Oscar Hammerstein^w & Jerome Kern^m *(Harms)*; I'll Say to You and You Say to Me / Just a Little Thing Called Rhythm — Chick Endor^w & Eddie Ward^m *(Harms)*; I'm Moving Away — Irving Caesar^w/m & Cliff Edwards^w/m *(Harms)*; Paddlin' Madelin' Home — Harry Woods^w/m *(Shapiro, Bernstein)*. A lovely musical with little plot about a circus girl. The dancing of Marilyn Miller and the beautiful songs of

Jerome Kern, however, gave it a run of 15 months. COVER: girl with flowers surrounded by trees.

2239 Sunny (British, 1926). Binnie Hale, Jack Buchanan.

At the Hunt Ball [B] (piano selections) — Jerome Kern^m *(Chappell)*; I Might Grow Fond of You [B] / I've Looked for Trouble [B] / Let's Say Goodnight [B] / When We Get Our Divorce [B] — Desmond Carter^w & Jerome Kern^m *(Chappell)*; Sunny — complete vocal score [B] — Desmond Carter^{w/m} & Otto Harbach^{w/m} & Oscar Hammerstein^{w/m} & Jerome Kern^{w/m} *(Chappell)*. This American musical, with some changes and new songs, had a ten month run at the Hippodrome. COVER: girl with flowers and designs.

2240 Sunny Days (*see also* **One Sunny Day**) (Broadway, 1928). Jeanette MacDonald, Lynne Overman.

Hang Your Hat on the Moon / One Sunny Day / Really and Truly / 'Sno Use Talking / So Do I — Clifford Grey^w & William Duncan^w & Jean Schwartz^m *(Harms)*. A musical dealing with a French man and his mistress. It lasted three months. The try-out title was *One Sunny Day* but it opened on Broadway as *Sunny Days*. COVER: a hat box and flowers.

2241 Sunny River (Broadway, 1941). Vicki Charles, Tom Ewell.

Along a Winding Road / Call It a Dream / Eleven Levee Street / Lordy / Sunny River — Oscar Hammerstein^w & Sigmund Romberg^m *(Chappell)*. A sad love story set to music. It was a poor musical that lasted almost a month. COVER: a tropical style house with palm tree, river, and boats.

2242 Sunset Boulevard (British, 1993). Patti LuPone, Kevin Anderson.

As If We Never Said Goodbye / The Perfect Year / Too Much in Love to Care / With One Look — Don Black^w & Christopher Hampton^w & Andrew Lloyd Webber^m *(Really Useful)*. The famous Gloria Swanson movie set to music with good and bad reviews. COVER: the Sunset Boulevard street sign.

2243 Sun-Up (Broadway, 1923). Lucille LaVerne.

It's Sun-Up Now — Eugene Lockhart^{w/m} *(Lockhart)*. A comedy drama that turned out to be a big hit. COVER: Lucille LaVerne.

2244 Susannah (Opera, 1957). Beverly Sills.

Ain't It a Pretty Night / The Trees on the Mountains — Carlisle Floyd^{w/m} *(Boosey, Hawkes)*. This production was commissioned by the New York City Opera Company. COVER: black and white titles only.

2245 Suzanne (closed before Broadway, 1925). Stars unknown.

All the Time Is Loving Time / Any Loon Can Write a Tune / I Heard the Blue-Bird / Little One / Maybe I Will / Oh! Henry! / The Only Boy / Suzanne / What Do You Do When I'm Gone / When a Rolls Rolls into a One Horse Town — William Duncan^{w/m} & Harold Orlob^{w/m} *(Feist)*. COVER: sketch of a girl in a big wide skirt and a startled look.

2246 Suzette (Broadway, 1921). Marie Astroba, John Cherry.

Bagdad / Dreams of Tomorrow / Gypsy Rose / Honey Love Moon / Suzette / Sweetheart Mine — Roy Dixon^w & Arthur Gutman^m *(Feist)*. A silly musical that lasted for four performances. COVER: girl in turban with large feathers. Six other songs are listed but probably not published.

2247 Swanee Music Revue (Nightclub, 1933). Kate Smith.

You're Gonna Lose Your Gal — Joe Young^w & James Monaco^m *(A Y and B)*. COVER: Kate Smith.

2248 Sweeney Todd (Broadway, 1979). Angela Lansbury, Len Cariou.

Ballad of Sweeney Todd [VS] / By the Sea [VS] / Green Finch and Linnet Bird [VS] / Johanna / Not While I'm Around / Pretty Women / Sweeney Todd — complete vocal score / Wait [VS] — Stephen Sondheim^{w/m} *(Revelation)*. An operatic version of the mad barber and baker that is Sondheim's greatest achievement. It was a fascinating story with two of the most talented people on Broadway. It ran for over a year, toured, and has had many revivals. COVER: a cartoon of woman with rolling pin and man with razor.

2249 Sweet Adeline (Broadway, 1929). Helen Morgan, Charles Butterworth.

Don't Ever Leave Me / Here Am I / Out of the Blue / The Sun About to Rise / 'Twas Not So Long Ago / Why Was I Born? — Oscar Hammerstein[w] & Jerome Kern[m] *(Harms)*; A Girl Is on Your Mind (piano selections) — Jerome Kern[m] *(Harms)*; Indestructible Kate / She Is Doing It All for Baby — Irene Franklin[w] & Jerry Jarnigan[m] *(Harms)*. A musical about a singer's rise to stardom with some lovely Jerome Kern songs. With good reviews, it was in for a long run and then C-R-A-S-H! COVER: a girl dancing on stage watched by a gentleman with champagne.

2250 Sweet and Low (*see also* **Corned Beef and Roses**) (Broadway, 1931). James Barton, Fannie Brice.

Cheerful Little Earful — Ira Gershwin[w] & Billy Rose[w] & Harry Warren[m] *(Remick)*; He's Not Worth Your Tears / Would You Like to Take a Walk — Mort Dixon[w] & Billy Rose[w] & Harry Warren[m] *(Remick)*; I'd Rather Have You — Abner Silver[w/m] & Alan Walker[w/m] *(Silver)*; The King's Horses — Noel Gay[w/m] & Harry Graham[w/m] *(Feist)*; Overnight — Billy Rose[w] & Charlotte Kent[w] & Louis Alter[m] *(Robbins)*; Sweet So and So — Ira Gershwin[w] & Joseph Meyer[m] & Philip Charig[m] *(Harms)*. This revue was called *Corned Beef and Roses,* then *Sweet and Low.* Later, some of it was absorbed into *Billy Rose's Crazy Quilt.* It had a few good songs and ran for six months. COVER: three cartoon characters.

2251 Sweet Bye and Bye (closed before Broadway, 1946). Dolores Gray, Walter O'Keefe.

Just Like a Man / Low and Lazy / An Old Fashioned Tune / Round About / Sweet Bye and Bye — Ogden Nash[w] & Vernon Duke[m] *(Harms)*. A futuristic type musical that didn't work and folded in Philadelphia. COVER: sketch of a flying rocket ship.

2252 Sweet Charity (Broadway, 1966). Gwen Verdon, John McMartin.

Baby Dream Your Dream / Big Spender / Gimme a Rain Check / Give Me a Rain Check / I Love to Cry at Weddings / If My Friends Could See Me Now! / I'm a Brass Band / I'm the Bravest Individual / Poor, Everybody Else / So What Now? [PC] [CUT] / Sweet Charity / Sweet Charity — complete vocal score / Sweet Charity Theme / There's Gotta Be Something Better Than This / Too Many Tomorrows / Where Am I Going? / You Should See Yourself / You Wanna Bet — Dorothy Fields[w] & Cy Coleman[m] *(Notable)*. A hit musical about a dance hostess that had hit songs by Cy Coleman, a touching book by Neil Simon, and super choreography by Bob Fosse. It ran 18 months. COVER: Gwen Verdon. The first set of covers show a small figure of Verdon with a pink background and state "Book by Bert Lewis." The second set of covers show a larger picture of Verdon with white background and state "Book by Neil Simon."

2253 Sweet Charity (Broadway, 1986). Michael Rupert, Debbie Allen.

Big Spender / If My Friends Could See Me Now / Rhythm of Life [VS] — Sweet Charity — vocal selections of 13 songs (1986) — Dorothy Fields[w] & Cy Coleman[m] *(Notable)*. A revival of the hit musical with a new dancing star. This production ran for almost a year. COVER: Debbie Allen.

2254 Sweet Lady (closed before Broadway, 1926). Inez Courtney, Harry Puck.

Be Naughty [ABQ] / Hot Water [ABQ] / Just Want You [ABQ] / The Mauve Decade [ABQ] / On a Side Street / To Make You Love Me [ABQ] / Yoo Hoo, Sweet Lady — Bud Green[w] & Delos Owen[m] & Thomas Ball[m] *(Shapiro,*

Bernstein); Hot Rhythm — Bud Green[w] & Delos Owen[m] *(Shapiro, Bernstein)*; I Adore You — Ballard MacDonald[w] & Sam Coslow[w] & Rene Mercier[m] *(Shapiro, Bernstein)*. COVER: an elegant lady, with fan, being kissed on the hand by a gentleman.

2255 Sweet Little Devil (*see also* A Perfect Lady) (Broadway, 1924). Constance Binney, Marjorie Gateson.

Hey! Hey! Let 'er Go! / The Jijibo / Mah-Jongg / Pepita / Someone Believes in You / Under a One-Man Top / Virginia, Don't Go Too Far! — B.G. DeSylva[w] & George Gershwin[m] *(Harms)*. A musical about a good and a bad girl with some interesting Gershwin songs that have been forgotten. It ran for 15 weeks. The try-out title was *A Perfect Lady*. COVER: Constance Binney in large reed chair.

2256 Sweet Moments (Jewish, 1930). William Siegel, Louis Freiman.

Sweet Moments — Isidor Lillian[w] & Sholom Secunda[m] *(Trio)*. COVER: Sholom Secunda.

2257 The Sweetheart Shop (Broadway, 1920). Helen Ford, Dan Healy.

Didn't You? / I Want to Be a Bride / I'd Like to Teach You the ABC's / Is There Any Little Thing I Can Do? / The Long Road of Love / My Caravan / The Sweetheart Shop / The Syringa Tree — Anne Caldwell[w] & Hugo Felix[m] *(Harms)*; Life Is a Whirling Carousel (piano selections) / Mr. Postman (piano selections) — Hugo Felix[m] *(Harms)*; Waiting for the Sun to Come Out — Arthur Francis (IG)[w] & George Gershwin[m] *(Harms)*. A romantic musical that was a long running hit in Chicago but lasted only seven weeks on Broadway. COVER 1: blue and gray with trees, flowers, and birds. COVER 2: red and gray with sculptured designs. Incidentally, *Waiting for the Sun to Come Out* was Arthur Francis' (Ira Gershwin's) first published song.

2258 Sweetheart Time (*see also* Leave It to Me) (Broadway, 1926). Eddie Buzzell, Mary Milburn.

A Girl in Your Arms — Irving Caesar[w] & Jay Gorney[m] *(Harms)*; Marian / One Way Street — Ballard MacDonald[w] & Walter Donaldson[m] *(Harms)*; Sweetheart Time / Time for Love / Two by Four / Who Loves You as I Do? — Irving Caesar[w] & Joseph Meyer[m] *(Harms)*; There's Something in Sympathy — Henry Myers[w] & Fred Coots[m] *(Harms)*. This rags-to-riches musical started out as *Leave It to Me*, opened on Broadway as *Sweetheart Time,* and folded after four months. COVER: flowers and designs.

2259 Sweethearts (Broadway, 1947). Bobby Clark, Marjorie Gateson.

Every Lover Must Meet His Fate / I Might Be Your Once in a While / Jeanette and Her Little Wooden Shoes / Pretty as a Picture / Sweethearts — Robert Smith[w] & Victor Herbert[m] *(Schirmer)*. A revival of the old classic that survived for nine months because of Bobby Clark's comedy. COVER: Bobby Clark and a scene from the musical.

2260 Swing It! (Broadway, 1937). George Booker, James Boxwill.

Ain't We Got Love / By the Sweat of Your Brow / Green and Blue / Huggin' and Muggin' — Cecil Mack[w/m] & Milton Reddie[w/m] & Eubie Blake[w/m] *(Mills)*. A musical from the Federal Theatre Project about two entertainers trying to make it in Harlem. It was a rather ordinary show and lasted only two months. COVER: dancers, musicians, buildings, piano keyboard.

2261 The Swing Mikado (Broadway, 1939). Edward Fraction, Gladys Boucree.

The Flowers That Bloom in the Spring / My Object All Sublime (the Mikado's Song) / Three Little Maids from School / Tit Willow / A Wandering Minstrel I — W.S. Gilbert[w] & Arthur Sullivan[m] *(Marks)*. This version of the Mikado was a five month hit in Chicago. It ran ten weeks in New York. COVER: the Mikado swinging.

2262 Swingin' the Dream (Broadway, 1939). Benny Goodman, Louis Armstrong.

Darn That Dream / Moonland / Peace, Brother! / Swingin' a Dream / There's Gotta Be a Weddin' — Eddie DeLange[w] & Jimmy Van Heusen[m] *(B V and C)*; Love's a Riddle — Eddie DeLange[w] & Jimmy Van Heusen[w] & Alec Wilder[m] *(B V and C)*; Spring Song — Eddie DeLange[w] & Jimmy Van Heusen[m] & Benny Goodman[m] *(B V and C)*. A musical version of *Midsummer Night's Dream*. It was a lavish production with great jazz stars but a run of only 13 performances. COVER: a cartoon sketch of Goodman, Armstrong, and Shakespeare.

2263 Swissing the Swiss (Nightclub, 1927). Stanley Chapman.

There's Everything Nice About You — Alfred Bryan[w] & Arthur Terker[w] & Peter Wendling[m] *(Waterson)*. COVER: Stanley Chapman.

2264 Symphony in Brown (Nightclub, 1942). Stars unknown.

Life Could Be a Cakewalk with You — Ted Koehler[w] & Harold Arlen[m] *(Chappell)*. COVER: letters and titles only.

2265 Tails Up! (British, 1918). J. Campbell, Phyllis Titmuss.

The Story of Peter Pan [B] — NoelCoward[w/m] & Doris Joel[w/m] *(Darewski)*. A hit revue that ran for over one year and produced Coward's first theatre song. COVER: black and white titles.

2266 Take a Chance (*see also* **Ginger**) (Broadway, 1923). Letta Corder, Walter Douglas.

Don't Forget / Oh Doctor Koo-ay / Teach Me How — H. Phillips[w] & Harold Orlob[m] *(Harms)*. A musical about parachutes; the musical lasted one month. The try-out title was *Take a Chance*. COVER: flowers.

2267 Take a Chance (*see also* **Humpty Dumpty**) (Broadway, 1932). Ethel Merman, Jack Haley.

Eddie Was a Lady / Turn Out the Light / You're an Old Smoothie — B.G. DeSylva[w] & Richard Whiting[m] & Herb Brown Nacio[m] *(Harms)*; I Want to Be with You / My Lover / Oh How I Long to Belong to You / Rise 'n' Shine /

Should I Be Sweet? / So Do I — B.G. DeSylva[w] & Vincent Youmans[m] *(Harms)*. This show started out as *Humpty Dumpty* and folded on the road. It was revised and opened as *Take a Chance*. This story of producing a revue ran for over six months. COVER: Ethel Merman, Jack Haley, Jack Whiting.

2268 Take Five (Nightclub, 1957). Ronny Graham, Ellen Hanley.

Perfect Stranger [VS] — Bart Howard[w/m] *(T R O)*. COVER: Bart Howard.

2269 Take It from Me (Broadway, 1919). Vera Michelena, Jack McGowan.

The Call of the Cozy Little Home / Camouflage / Explanations / Good, Bad, Beautiful Broadway / I Like to Linger in the Lingerie / The Kiss / A Penny for Your Thoughts / Take It from Me / Take It from Me — complete vocal score / The Tanglefoot / To Have and to Hold / Tomorrow / What Makes the Tired Business Man So Tired — Will Johnstone[w] & Will Anderson[m] *(Witmark)*. A musical about a man who inherits a department store; the show lasted three months. COVER: a pretty girl's face.

2270 Take Me Along (Philadelphia) (Broadway, 1959). Jackie Gleason, Walter Pidgeon.

Little Green Snake / Nine O'Clock / Promise Me a Rose / Staying Young / Take Me Along — Bob Merrill[w/m] *(Hansen)*. COVER: red, white, blue with sketches of characters stating "*Take Me Along*" with "Jackie Gleason, Walter Pidgeon, Eileen Herlie" in small letters.

2271 Take Me Along (New York) (Broadway, 1959). Jackie Gleason, Walter Pidgeon.

But Yours / I Get Embarrassed / I Would Die / Little Green Snake / Nine O'Clock / Promise Me a Rose / Sid, Old Kid / Staying Young / Take Me Along — Bob Merrill[w/m] *(Hansen)*. A musical version of O'Neill's *Ah, Wilderness*. It was a hit and ran for over one year; however, there was nothing memorable about it. COVER:

red, white, blue with sketches of characters stating in large letters "Jackie Gleason, Walter Pidgeon, Eileen Herlie in *Take Me Along.*"

2272 Take the Air (Broadway, 1927). Will Mahoney, Greek Evans.

Ham and Eggs in the Morning — Al Dubin[w] & Con Conrad[m] & Abner Silver[m] *(Harms)*; Just Like a Wild, Wild Rose / Lullaby / Maybe I'll Baby You / Wings — Gene Buck[w] & Dave Stamper[m] *(Harms)*; On a Pony for Two — Gene Buck[w] & James Hanley[m] *(Harms)*; Someone, Someday, Somewhere — Clifford Grey[w] & Rudolph Friml[m] *(Harms)*; We'll Have a New Home in the Mornin' — Gene Buck[w/m] & J. Russel Robinson[w/m] & Willard Robison[w/m] *(Harms)*; You're the First Thing I Think of in the Morning — Billy Tracey[w] & Jack Stanley[m] *(Broadway)*. An aviation musical that ran for six months but was forgettable. COVER: girl standing on airplane wings.

2273 Taking My Turn (Off Broadway, 1983). Margaret Whiting, Tiger Haynes.

Fine for the Shape I'm In [VS] / Good Luck to You [VS] / I Am Not Old [VS] / It Still Isn't Over [VS] / Pick More Daisies [VS] / Taking My Turn [VS] / This Is My Song [VS] / Two of Me [VS] — Will Holt[w] & Gary Friedman[m] *(T R O)*. A musical about the older generation. It was a hit for almost a year. COVER: a large daisy.

2274 The Tales of Rigo (Broadway, 1927). Hyman Adler, Mira Nirska.

In Romany / Zita — Ben Schwartz[w/m] *(Harms)*. An operetta-musical about gypsies; it lasted one week. COVER: flowers and designs.

2275 Talk About Girls (Broadway, 1927). William Frawley, Jane Taylor.

All the Time Is Loving Time / Love Birds / A Lovely Girl / Maybe I Will — Irving Caesar[w] & Harold Orlob[m] *(Harms)*; Talk About Girls — Irving Caesar[w] & Stephen Jones[m] *(Harms)*. A musical about a small town boy making good. It lasted three per-

formances. COVER: four girls.

2276 Tambourines to Glory (Broadway, 1963). Louis Gossett, Hilda Simms.

Moon Outside My Window — Langston Hughes[m] & Jobe Huntley[m] *(Chappell)*. A play with music about a gospel church in Harlem. It lasted three weeks. COVER: a large tambourine.

2277 Tan Town Topics Revue (Nightclub, 1926). Stars unknown.

Charleston Bound / I've Found a New Baby / Senorita Mine — Spencer Williams[w] & Ed Rector[w] & Fats Waller[m] & Clarence Williams[m] *(Williams)*. COVER: gentleman with guitar serenading a lady on balcony.

2278 Tangerine (Broadway, 1921). Julia Sanderson, Joseph Cawthorn.

Civilization / Dance Tangerine / Hallucination of Love / Hawaiian Blues / In Our Mountain Bower / Isle of Tangerine / It's Your Carriage That Counts / Listen to Me / Love Is a Business / Multiplied by Eight / There Is a Sunbeam / Tropical Vamps / We Never Grow Old / You and I — Howard Johnson[w] & Monte Carlo[m] & Alma Saunders[m] *(Feist)*; Give Me Your Love — Monte Carlo[w/m] & Alma Saunders[w/m] & Carle Carlton[w/m] *(Feist)*; It's Great to Be Married / Man Is the Lord of It All / Ode to the Sun / A Point to Bear in Mind / The Spice of Love / Stolen Sweets / The Voice at the End of the Line — Howard Johnson[w] & Monte Carlo[m] & Alma Saunders[m] & Carle Carlton[m] *(Feist)*; Lords of Creation — Howard Johnson[w] & Jean Schwartz[m] *(Feist)*; She Was Very Dear to Me — Ben Burt[w/m] *(Feist)*; Sweet Lady — Howard Johnson[w] & Frank Crumit[m] & Dave Zoob[m] *(Feist)*. A hit musical about alimony and an imaginary world. It had a very good book but ordinary music and ran for more than nine months. COVER: One set of covers is the face of Julia Sanderson and a parrot and the other set is a sketch of a dancing girl.

2279 Tangletoes (Broadway, 1925). Mildred MacLeod, Walker Ellis.

Tangletoes—Gertrude Purcell^w & Vincent Rose^m *(Feist)*. A play about a chorus girl that lasted three weeks. COVER: sketch of girl in clown outfit.

2280 The Tap Dance Kid (Broadway, 1983). Hinton Battle, Hattie Winston. Vocal Selections:

Another Day / Class Act / Dance If It Makes You Happy / Dancing Is Everything / Dipsey's Comin' Over / Fabulous Feet / I Could Get Used to Him / I Remember How It Was / Man in the Moon / My Luck Is Changing / Someday [VS] / Tap Tap [VS]—Robert Lorick^w & Henry Krieger^m *(Leonard)*. A boy's dreams of being a tap dancer were the topic of this musical. It had a poor book but the dancing kept it on for 18 months. COVER: a group of dancers in a scene from the musical.

2281 Tars and Spars (Military, 1944). Victor Mature, Sid Caesar.

Apprentice Seaman [VS] / Arm in Arm / Civilian / Farewell for Awhile / Palm Beach [VS] / Silver Shield— Howard Dietz^w & Vernon Duke^m *(Fischer)*. This revue toured the country during the war to recruit people for the Coast Guard. COVER: silver and gray cover with Coast Guard insignia.

2282 Tattle Tales (closed before Broadway, 1920). Cliff Edwards, Jimmy Hussey.

I'm an Indian Assassin [ABQ] / Rose of the Rotisserie [ABQ] / Tip-Tip Tippy Canoe—Ballard MacDonald^w & James Hanley^m *(Shapiro, Bernstein)*; I'm Out on Strike for a Beautiful Girl [ABQ] / In Watermelon Time / Lead Me to Laughter [ABQ] / Life Without a Cigarette [ABQ] / Star Eyes / Taps [ABQ] / Tattle Tales [ABQ] / Those Mason-Dixon Blues / When the Statues Come to Life [ABQ] / You've Got to Keep on Moving [ABQ]— Howard Johnson^w & Archie Gottler^m *(Feist)*; Sadie Harrowtiz—Howard Johnson^w & Archie Gottler^m *(Fischer)*; You've Got to Give the Babies a Bottle—Howard Johnson^{w/m} & Milton Ager^{w/m} *(Feist)*. COVER: two pilgrims and a dog.

2283 Tattle Tales (closed before Broadway, 1930). Stars unknown.

Another Case of Blues—John Mercer^w & Richard Myers^m *(Harms)*; Counting the Sheep / Just a Sentimental Tune—Max Lief^w & Nathaniel Lief^w & Louis Alter^m *(Harms)*; My Impression of You—Herb Magidson^{w/m} & Ned Washington^{w/m} & Michael Cleary^{w/m} *(Harms)*. COVER: sketch of two couples with fingers to mouth—shhh!

2284 Tattle Tales (Broadway, 1933). Frank Fay, Guy Robertson.

The First Spring Day—Edward Eliscu^w & Howard Jackson^m *(Harms)*; I'll Take an Option on You—Leo Robin^w & Ralph Rainger^m *(Harms)*. A poor revue that started in Hollywood and came to Broadway for three weeks. Barbara Stanwyck was in the cast. COVER: Frank Fay, Guy Robertson, Janet Reade.

2285 The Teahouse of the August Moon (Broadway, 1953). David Wayne, John Forsythe.

Sakura / Teahouse of the August Moon—John Patrick^w & Dai Keong Lee^m *(Chappell)*. A smash hit comedy about the army occupation of Japan and the conflicts. COVER: a Japanese lady and a soldier having tea.

2286 Ted Lewis Frolic (closed before Broadway, 1923). Ted Lewis.

Back Home / Beautiful Girls / Beyond the Moonbeam Trail / Change Your Step / Non Stop Lovin' Man / Paisley Shawl / Struttin' School / Tick! Tock! / Twinkle, Twinkle Little Star—Jack Yellen^w & Milton Ager^m *(A Y and B)*. COVER: Ted Lewis.

2287 The Telephone (Broadway, 1947). Marilyn Cotlow, Frank Rogier.

The Telephone—complete vocal score—Gian-Carlo Menotti^{w/m} *(Schirmer)*. A one-act opera performed with *The Medium*. These two short operas ran for six months, appearing on the same program. COVER: cartoon of a woman waiting for the telephone to ring.

2288 Tell a Vision (closed before Broadway, 1931). Stars unknown.

Furnished Rooms / Gone Again /

Pal — Andrew White[w] & Lew Daly[m] *(Harms)*. This musical was billed as a Musical Radio Absurdity which meant it could have been a radio or stage musical. COVER: boy courting girl while the moon is winking.

2289 Tell Her the Truth (Broadway, 1932). John Sheehan, Andrew Tombes.

Happy the Day / Hooch! Caroline! / Sing, Brothers! — R.P. Weston[w] & Bert Lee[w] & Jack Waller[m] & Joseph Tunbridge[m] *(Chappell)*. A musical farce which was a success in England but a one week flop in New York. COVER: sketch of woman's face.

2290 Tell Me Again (closed before Broadway, 1928). Stars unknown.

Tell Me Again — Harry Clarke[w] & Percy Wenrich[m] *(Feist)*. COVER: a vague sketch of girl in a gown.

2291 Tell Me More (*see also* **My Fair Lady**) (Broadway, 1925). Alexander Gray, Lou Holtz.

Baby / Kickin' the Clouds Away / My Fair Lady / Tell Me More / Three Times a Day / Why Do I Love You — B.G. DeSylva[w] & Ira Gershwin[w] & George Gershwin[m] *(Harms)*; Love I Never Knew (piano selections) / Where the Delicatessen Flows (piano selections) — George Gershwin[m] *(Harms)*. A boy-chases-girl musical with good dancing but no hit songs. It had a run of six months. The try-out title was *My Fair Lady* but it opened on Broadway as *Tell Me More*. COVER: hat boxes and flowers.

2292 Tell Me More (British, 1925). Leslie Henson.

Murderous Monty [B] — Desmond Carter[w] & George Gershwin[m] *(Harms)*; Love I Never Knew (piano selections) [B] / Tell Me More — Opening Act One (piano selections) [B] / Where the Delicatessen Flows (piano selections) [B] — George Gershwin[m] *(Harms)*. The American musical presented in London with a few new songs added. It was a moderate hit. COVER: hat boxes and flowers (same as American cover).

2293 Tell Me on a Sunday (British, 1979). Marti Webb.

Capped Teeth and Caesar Salad [B] [VS] / Come Back with the Same Look in Your Eyes [B] / I'm Very You, You're Very Me [B] [VS] / It's Not the End of the World (#1) [B] [VS] / It's Not the End of the World (#2) [B] [VS] / Let Me Finish (#1) [B] [VS] / Let Me Finish (#2) [B] [VS] / Let's Talk About You [B] [VS] / Letter Home to England [B] [VS] / Nothing Like You've Ever Known [B] [VS] / Second Letter Home [B] [VS] / Sheldon Bloom [B] [VS] / Take That Look Off Your Face (#1) [B] [VS] / Take That Look Off Your Face (#2) [B] [VS] / Tell Me on a Sunday [B] / You Made Me Think You Were in Love [B] [VS] — Don Black[w] & Andrew Lloyd Webber[m] *(Really Useful)*. The first version of act one of *Song and Dance*. It was done as a concert piece before the stage version. COVER: Marti Webb.

2294 Telling the Tale (British, 1918). Marie Blanche, Nancy Gibbs.

Altogether Too Fond of You [BW] — Cole Porter[w/m] & James Heard[w/m] & Melville Gideon[w/m] *(Vogel)*. A musical based on an old French farce that ran three months in London. COVER: black and white with titles only.

2295 The Temporary Mrs. Smith (closed before Broadway, 1946). Luba Malina, Howard St. John.

Lovely Me — Jeff Bailey[w] & Arthur Seigel[m] *(Chappell)*. A fading Hollywood star with financial problems was the subject of this show. It folded in Wilmington. COVER: boy smiling at girl.

2296 Tenderloin (Broadway, 1960). Maurice Evans, Eileen Rodgers.

Artificial Flowers / Good Clean Fun / I Wonder What It's Like / Lovely Laurie / My Gentle Young Johnny / My Miss Mary / Tommy, Tommy — Sheldon Harnick[w] & Jerry Bock[m] *(Valando)*. A musical about the "Tenderloin" district of New York. It had nothing memorable but lasted six months. COVER: letters and designs.

2297 Texas, Li'l Darlin' (Broadway, 1949). Kenny Delmar, Mary Hatcher.

The Big Movie Show in the Sky / Hootin' Owl Trail / Horseshoes Are

Lucky / It's Great to Be Alive / A Month of Sundays / Politics [RC] / The Yodel Blues — Johnny Mercer[w] & Robert Emmett Dolan[m] *(Chappell)*. A musical dealing with Texas politics with an ordinary score and book. It had a run of nine months. COVER: a house on a hill with a big star.

2298 Thank You So Much (British, 1934). Stars unknown.

Dancing with My Shadow — Harry Woods[w/m] *(Joe Morris)*; I'm Lost for Words — Eddie DeLange[w/m] & Archie Fletcher[w/m] & Joe Burke[w/m] *(Joe Morris)*. These two songs were published in the U.S. and were used in a British revue. COVER: a dancing couple and a couple on a balcony.

2299 Thanks for Tomorrow (Nightclub, 1938). Stars unknown.

Funny Kind of Love / Silhouette — Beatrice Rodick[w/m] & Jewel Bennett[w/m] *(Mills)*. COVER: designs and lettering.

2300 That Casey Girl (closed before Broadway, 1923). Eddie Foy.

I Love Rosie Casey — William Jerome[w] & Jean Schwartz[m] *(Jack Mills)*. COVER: black and white cover with titles only.

2301 That's a Good Girl (British, 1928). Jack Buchanan, Elsie Randolph.

Chirp-Chirp! [B] — Ira Gershwin[w] & Joseph Meyer[m] & Philip Charig[m] *(Chappell)*; Let Yourself Go! [B] / The One I'm Looking For / Sweet So-and-So [B] — Douglas Furber[w] & Ira Gershwin[w] & Joseph Meyer[m] & Philip Charig[m] *(Chappell)*. A hit London musical that ran for nine months. It included music by Americans. COVER: red and black letters and designs.

2302 That's Gratitude (Broadway, 1930). Frank Craven, George Barbier.

Gratitude — Frank Craven[w] & Raymond Hubbell[m] *(Shapiro, Bernstein)*. A comedy about two friends; the show ran for six months. COVER: black and white cover with titles only.

2303 That's It (Nightclub, 1919). Fanchon and Marco.

Midnight Maid — Joe Meyer[w/m] & Ben Black[w/m] *(Sherman Clay)*. COVER: Fanchon and Marco dancing before a large clock.

2304 That's My Boy (closed before Broadway, 1924). Karyl Norman.

In a World of Our Own / Paris Rose / Play That Melody of Love / Wonderful Mother — Billy DuVal[w] & Robert Simonds[m] *(Remick)*; Me and the Boy Friend — Sidney Clare[w] & Jimmie Monaco[m] *(Remick)*; Somebody Like You — Cliff Friend[w] & Walter Donaldson[m] *(Remick)*. A musical starring the female impersonator. COVER: Karyl Norman.

2305 That's the Ticket (closed before Broadway, 1948). Loring Smith, Kaye Ballard.

I Shouldn't Love You / The Money Song / Take Off the Coat / You Never Know What Hit You (When It's Love) — Harold Rome[w/m] *(Crawford)*. A musical involving politics that lasted for one week in Philadelphia. COVER: a knight in armor on horseback with a girl.

2306 The Theme of Love (Broadway, 1929). Stars unknown.

The Dream of My Heart — Rubey Cowan[w] & Phil Bartholomae[w] & Phil Boutelje[m] *(Famous)*. This was a mini-stage show produced by Paramount-Publix in between showings of their latest films at large movie theatres. COVER: a stage, a screen, and curtains.

2307 There You Are (Broadway, 1932). Hyman Adler, Robert Capron.

Legend of the Mission Bells / Lovers' Holiday / Wings of the Morning — William Heagney[w/m] & Tom Connell[w/m] *(Chappell)*. A poor imitation of *Rio Rita* that lasted for one week. COVER: black and white cover with titles only.

2308 They Can't Get You Down (closed before Broadway, 1941). Gene Barry, Jan Clayton.

It's No Fun Eating Alone / Love in a Changing World / On the Banks of the Mildew River [ABQ] / That Mittel-Europa of Mine [ABQ] / They Can't Get You Down / Twenty-Five Bucks a Week / When a Bachelor Takes a Bride

[ABQ] — Henry Myers[w] & Edward Eliscu[w] & Jay Gorney[m] *(Mills)*. Some of the material in this Hollywood revue was also used in *Marching with Johnny* and *The New Meet the People 1941*. COVER: dancing girls and stars.

2309 They're Playing Our Song (Broadway, 1979). Robert Klein, Lucie Arnaz.

Fallin' [VS] / Fill In the Words [VS] / I Still Believe in Love [VS] / If You Really Knew Me [VS] / Just for Tonight [VS] / They're Playing Our Song / When You're in My Arms [VS] — Carole B. Sager[w] & Marvin Hamlisch[m] *(Chappell)*. A musical about songwriters that was entertaining and ran over two years. COVER: a boy and girl kissing beside a large musical note.

2310 The Third Little Show (Broadway, 1931). Beatrice Lillie, Ernest Truex.

Any Little Fish [B] [CUT] — Noel Coward[w/m] *(Chappell)*; Falling in Love — Earle Crooker[w] & Henry Sullivan[m] *(Robbins)*; I'll Putcha Pitcha in the Papers — Max Lief[w] & Nathaniel Lief[w] & Michael Cleary[m] *(Robbins)*; I've Lost My Heart — Grace Henry[w] & Morris Hamilton[m] *(Robbins)*; Mad Dogs and Englishmen — Noel Coward[w/m] *(Robbins)*; Say the Word — Harold Adamson[w] & Burton Lane[m] *(Robbins)*; When Yuba Plays the Rumba on the Tuba — Herman Hupfeld[w/m] *(Robbins)*; You Forgot Your Gloves — Edward Eliscu[w] & Ned Lehac[m] *(Robbins)*; You Might as Well Pretend — Edward Eliscu[w] & Ted Fetter[w] & William Lewis[m] *(Robbins)*. This was the third and last revue in this series. It kept going for four months by Bea Lillie. COVER: Beatrice Lillie, Ernest Truex.

2311 13 Daughters (Broadway, 1961). Don Ameche, Sylvia Syms.

Good-bye Is Hard to Say / A House on the Hill / Lei of Memories / Let-a-go Your Heart / Puka Puka Pants / Throw a Petal in the Stream / You Set My Heart to Music — Eaton Magoon[w/m] *(Ross Jungnickel)*. A musical about a Chinese family in Hawaii; the musical

lasted three weeks. COVER: sketch of a hula girl.

2312 13 Days to Broadway (closed before Broadway, 1983). Stars unknown.

You There in the Back Row [VS] — Barbara Fried[w] & Cy Coleman[m] *(Notable)*. A musical that was announced but never produced. COVER: Cy Coleman.

2313 This Is the Army (Broadway, 1942). Irving Berlin, Gary Merrill.

American Eagles / The Army's Made a Man Out of Me / Closing [VS] / The Fifth Army's Where My Heart Is [PC] / How About a Cheer for the Navy / I Get Along with the Aussies [PC] / I Left My Heart at the Stage Door Canteen / I'm Getting Tired So I Can Sleep / Jap-German Sextette [VS] / The Kick in the Pants [PC] / Ladies of the Chorus [VS] / My British Buddy (soldiers and flags cover) / My Sergeant and I Are Buddies / Opening — The Army and the Shuberts Depend on You [VS] / Opening of Act 2 — The Jane Cowl Number [VS] / Opening — Some Dough for the Army Relief [VS] / That Russian Winter / That's What the Well-Dressed Man in Harlem Will Wear / There Are No Wings on a Fox-Hole (guns on cover) / This Is the Army, Mister Jones / This Time (plain cover) / Ve Don't Like It [PC] / What Are We Gonna Do with All the Jeeps (plain) / With My Head in the Clouds / Yip Yip Yaphanker's Intro [VS] — Irving Berlin[w/m] *(This Is the Army Music Co.)*. This Army show played Broadway for three months and toured overseas and nationally. COVER: marching soldiers with flag.

2314 This Year of Grace (Broadway, 1928). Noel Coward, Beatrice Lillie.

Caballero / Dance Little Lady / Little Women [B] / Lorelei / Mary Make Believe / A Room with a View / Teach Me to Dance Like Grandma / Try to Learn to Love / World Weary — Noel Coward[w/m] *(Harms)*; Dream Is Over — A Dream of Youth [VS] / I'm Mad About You [B] / It Doesn't Matter

How Old You Are [VS] / This Year of Grace — complete vocal score — Noel Coward^{w/m} *(Chappell)*. This witty revue with Coward and Lillie ran for only 20 weeks in N.Y. but 40 weeks in London. COVER: colored letters and designs.

2315 This'll Make You Whistle (British, 1936). Jack Buchanan, Elsie Randolph.

Cocktail Time / Don't Count Your Chickens / I Don't Give a Continental / I Make a Motion / I'm Never Too Busy for You / Keep Your Eye in the Sky / There Isn't Any Limit to My Love / Without Rhythm / You've Got the Wrong Rhumba — Maurice Sigler^{w/m} & Al Goodhart^{w/m} & Al Hoffman^{w/m} *(Mills)*; Crazy with Love / I'm in a Dancing Mood / My Red Letter Day — Maurice Sigler^{w/m} & Al Goodhart^{w/m} & Al Hoffman^{w/m} *(Crawford)*; This'll Make You Whistle — Maurice Sigler^{w/m} & Al Goodhart^{w/m} & Al Hoffman^{w/m} *(Berlin)*. A hit musical whose whole score was published in the U.S. by three different publishers. COVER: Jack Buchanan.

2316 Three After Three (closed before Broadway, 1940). Simone Simon, Mitzi Green.

Break It Up, Cinderella (as Break It Now, Buck Private [VS]) / Wait Till You See Me in the Morning [VS] — Johnny Mercer^w & Hoagy Carmichael^m *(USO)*; Darn Clever, These Chinee (not published) / Everything Happens to Me (not published) / How Nice for Me [PC] / I Walk with Music / Ooh! What You Said / The Rumba Jumps / Way Back in 1939 A.D. / What'll They Think of Next — Johnny Mercer^w & Hoagy Carmichael^m *(Mercer and Morris)*; Give, Baby, Give — Gladys Shelley^w & Irving Gellers^m & Otis Spencer^m *(Mills)*. After four months on the road, this show folded in Detroit in early 1940. It was recast, revised, and opened several months later for a brief seven week run as *Walk with Music*. COVER: three girls

chasing three men.

2317 Three Cheers (Broadway, 1928). Patsy Kelly, Will Rogers.

Because You're Beautiful / Maybe This Is Love / Pompanola / Two Boys — B.G. DeSylva^{w/m} & Lew Brown^{w/m} & Ray Henderson^{w/m} *(D B and H)*; Let's All Sing the Lard Song — Anne Caldwell^w & Leslie Sarony^m *(Harms)*; My Silver Tree / Orange Blossom Home / Someone Else Is Blue — Anne Caldwell^w & Raymond Hubbell^m *(Harms)*. A musical involving filming a movie on an island. It was an ordinary show that ran six months. COVER: sketch of a large crowd cheering.

2318 Three Little Business Men (closed before Broadway, 1923). Stars unknown.

Oh! Say the Word — El Gee^w & Joseph Cherniavsky^m *(Marks)*. COVER: a chorus girl holding a man in the palm of her hand.

2319 Three Little Girls (Broadway, 1930). Harry Puck, Bettina Hall.

Love Comes Only Once in a Life Time — Stella Unger^w & Harold Stern^m & Harry Perella^m *(Harms)*; Love's Happy Dream / Prince Charming — Harry B. Smith^w & Walter Kollo^m *(Harms)*. An imported operetta with a Maytime theme. The operetta lasted three months. COVER: three girls in evening gowns descending staircase.

2320 The Three Musketeers (Broadway, 1928). Vivienne Segal, Dennis King.

Ev'ry Little While / Love Is the Sun / Ma Belle / My Sword and I / Queen of My Heart — Clifford Grey^w & Rudolf Friml^m *(Harms)*; March of the Musketeers — P.G. Wodehouse^w & Clifford Grey^w & Rudolf Friml^m *(Harms)*; Your Eyes — P.G. Wodehouse^w & Rudolf Friml^m *(Harms)*. A lavish Ziegfeld production of the Dumas classic. It was a hit and lasted nine months.

2321 Three of Us (Vaudeville, 1922). Sylvia Dakin.

In Old Loveland — Charles Harrison^{w/m} & Will Harrison^{w/m} *(Harrison and Dakin)*. A musical that toured the Keith Theatre vaudeville circuit. COVER: Sylvia Dakin.

2322 Three Showers (Broadway, 1920). Paul Frawley, Anna Wheaton.

B. Is the Note [ABQ] / Baby Lamb / Dancing Tumble-Tom / He Raised Everybody's Rent But Katie's / How Wonderful You Are / If and But / I'll Have My Way [ABQ] / It Must Be Love / It's Always the Fault of the Men [ABQ] / Love Me Sweetheart Mine / The Old Love Is the True Love / One of the Boys [ABQ] / Open Your Heart / Pussyfoot / There's a Way Out / Where Is the Love? [ABQ] / You May Be the World to Your Mother — Henry Creamer^{w/m} & Turner Layton^{w/m} *(Harris)*. An old fashioned musical about romance. It was very ordinary and lasted six weeks. COVER: three young ladies holding umbrellas in a pouring rainstorm.

2323 Three Sisters (British, 1934). Charlotte Greenwood, Stanley Holloway.

Circus Queen [B] / Here It Comes [B] / Now That I Have Springtime [B] / Somebody Wants to Go to Sleep [B] — (piano selections) Jerome Kern^m *(Harms)*; Funny Old House [B] / Hand in Hand [B] / I Won't Dance [B] / Keep Smiling [B] / Lonely Feet [B] / Roll On, Rolling Road [B] / What Good Are Words? [B] / You Are Doing Very Well [B] — Oscar Hammerstein^w & Jerome Kern^m *(Harms)*. A musical produced at the Drury Lane with some lovely Kern songs but a run of only two months. COVER: letters and designs.

2324 Three Star Gypsy (closed before Broadway, 1992). Stars unknown.

The Eleven O'Clock Song [VS] / A Love Letter to Broadway [VS] — Leslie Bricusse^{w/m} *(Stage and Screen)*. A musical announced for Broadway. COVER: Leslie Bricusse.

2325 Three to Make Music (Regional, 1958). Stars unknown.

It Takes Three to Make Music — Mary Rodgers^w & Linda Melnick^m *(Chappell)*. A children's musical commissioned by Thomas Scherman and the Little Orchestra. COVER: a lady conductor with small children.

2326 Three to Make Ready (Broadway, 1946). Arthur Godfrey, Ray Bolger.

Barnaby Beach / A Lovely Lazy Kind of Day / Oh, You're a Wonderful Person / The Old Soft Shoe / Tell Me the Story — Nancy Hamilton^w & Morgan Lewis^m *(Chappell)*. A revue with a lot of talented people but poor music. It ran nine months. COVER: letters and designs.

2327 Three Waltzes (Broadway, 1937). Kitty Carlisle, Michael Bartlett.

The Days of Old / I Sometimes Wonder / Our Last Valse — Clare Kummer^w & Oscar Straus^m *(Chappell)*; I Found My Love — Clare Kummer^w & Edwin Gilbert^w & Oscar Straus^m *(Chappell)*; Maytime in the Air / Springtime in the Air / To Love Is to Live — Clare Kummer^w & Johann Strauss Sr.^m *(Chappell)*. A dated operetta imported from Vienna. It was a cheap production by the Shuberts and lasted almost four months. COVER: three couples waltzing.

2328 Three Wishes for Jamie (Broadway, 1952). John Raitt, Anne Jeffreys.

April Face / Goin' on a Hayride / It Must Be Spring / It's a Wishing World / Love Has Nothing to Do with Looks / My Heart's Darlin' / Trottin' to the Fair — Ralph Blane^{w/m} *(Chappell)*. A pleasant little musical with an Irish theme that lasted almost three months. COVER: a boy and girl in love.

2329 The Threepenny Opera (aka **Die Dreigroschenoper** (Off Broadway, 1954). Lotte Lenya, Jo Sullivan.

Army Song [VS] / Ballad of Dependency [VS] / Ballad of the Easy Life [VS] / Barbara Song [VS] / Instead Of [VS] / Love Song [VS] / Mack the Knife / Pirate Jenny [VS] / Solomon Song [VS] / Tango Ballad [VS] / Useless Song [VS] — Marc Blitzstein^w & Bert Brecht^w & Kurt Weill^m *(Warner Bros.)*.

An English adaptation of the German musical that ran for over six years and produced the hit *Mack the Knife*. COVER: a sketch of some characters from the play.

2330 Three's a Crowd (Broadway, 1930). Clifton Webb, Fred Allen.

All the King's Horses — Alex Wilder^(w/m) & Edward Brandt^(w/m) & Howard Dietz^(w/m) *(Harms)*; Body and Soul — Edward Heyman^w & Robert Sour^w & Frank Eyton^w & John Green^m *(Harms)*; Forget All Your Books — Howard Dietz^w & Sam Lerner^w & Burton Lane^m *(Harms)*; Moment I Saw You — Howard Dietz^w & Arthur Schwartz^m *(Harms)*; Out in the Open Air — Howard Dietz^w & Ted Pola^w & Burton Lane^m *(Harms)*; Practising Up on You — Howard Dietz^w & Phil Charig^m *(Harms)*; Right at the Start of It / Something to Remember You By — Howard Dietz^w & Arthur Schwartz^m *(Harms)*; Yaller — Henry Myers^w & Charles Schwab^m *(Harms)*. A smash revue with hit songs and a talented cast that ran eight months. COVER: Clifton Webb, Fred Allen, Libby Holman.

2331 Through the Years (*see also* **Smiling Through**) (Broadway, 1931). Michael Bartlett, Reginald Owen.

Drums in My Heart / It's Every Girl's Ambition / Kathleen Mine / Kinda Like You / Through the Years / You're Everywhere — Edward Heyman^w & Vincent Youmans^m *(Miller)*. A musical version of the old classic with some good Youmans songs but a run of only two weeks. The try-out title was *Smiling Through* but it opened on Broadway as *Through the Years*. COVER: letters and designs.

2332 Thumbs Up! (Broadway, 1935). Bobby Clark, Paul McCullough.

Autumn in New York — Vernon Duke^(w/m) *(Harms)*; Continental Honeymoon — Ballard MacDonald^(w/m) & James Hanley^(w/m) *(Harms)*; Eileen Avourneen — John Murray Anderson^w & Henry Sullivan^m *(Harms)*; Flamenco / Lily Belle May June — Earle Crooker^w

& Henry Sullivan^m *(Harms)*; Gotta See a Man About His Daughter — Jean Herbert^(w/m) & Karl Stark^(w/m) & James Hanley^(w/m) *(Harms)*; Moody and Blue — Sammy Lerner^w & Gerald Marks^m *(Harms)*; Soldier of Love — Irving Caesar^(w/m) & Gerald Marks^(w/m) & Sammy Lerner^(w/m) *(Harms)*; Zing! Went the Strings of My Heart — James Hanley^(w/m) *(Harms)*. This was not a great revue but it produced two hit songs and lasted four months. COVER: a cartoon version of the Statue of Liberty on Roman columns.

2333 Tick-Tack-Toe (Broadway, 1920). Herman Timberg, Pearl Eaton.

The Dardanella Blues — Fred Fisher^w & Johnny Black^m *(Fisher)*; Hoppy Poppy Girl / I Want to Go Back to Philadelphia, Pa. / I'd Like to Know Why I Fell in Love with You / A Lesson in Love / Love Is a Game of Cards / My Manicure Maid — Herman Timberg^(w/m) *(M and F)*; Sweet Mamma — Fred Rose^(w/m) & George Little^(w/m) & Peter Frost^(w/m) *(Jack Mills)*. This revue of poor material lasted four weeks on Broadway. A tour was arranged for it with Sophie Tucker to recoup its losses, but this folded quickly, also. COVER: chorus girl in costume; Sophie Tucker and musicians.

2334 Tickets Please (Broadway, 1950). Grace and Paul Hartman.

Darn It Baby, That's Love / The Moment I Looked in Your Eyes / Restless / Television's Tough on Love / You Can't Take It with You — Joan Edwards^(w/m) & Lyn Duddy^(w/m) *(Chappell)*. A pleasant revue with nothing memorable and a run of six months. COVER: Grace and Paul Hartman.

2335 Tickle Me (Broadway, 1920). Frank Tinney, Allen Kearns.

Come Across / Famous You and Simple Me / If a Wish Could Make It So / India Rubber / Little Hindoo Man / Tickle Me / Until You Say Goodbye / We've Got Something — Otto Harbach^w & Oscar Hammerstein^w & Herbert Stothart^m *(Harms)*; A Perfect Lover (piano selections) / You're the

Type (piano selections) — Herbert Stothart[m] *(Harms)*. A musical about making a movie with the antics of Frank Tinney helping it to last six months. COVER: a large feather and designs.

2336 Tillie's Nightmare (closed before Broadway, 1919). Marie Dressler.

Bon Jour Marie / Here's the Latest Thing / How Could You Expect Me to Know? / I Like You, I Do / Old Gentleman Jazz / Sweethearts of Yesterday / There's Nothing Sweeter Than a Kiss from a Beautiful Girl — Alex Gerber[w] & A. Baldwin Sloane[m] *(Witmark)*. COVER: Marie Dressler.

2337 Timbuktu! (*see also* **Kismet**) (Broadway, 1978). Eartha Kitt, Melba Moore.

And This Is My Beloved / Baubles, Bangles and Beads / Bored / He's in Love / My Magic Lamp / Night of My Nights / Not Since Nineveh / Sands of Time / Stranger in Paradise — Robert Wright[w/m] & George Forrest[w/m] & A. Borodin[w/m] *(Frank)*; Golden Land, Golden Life / In the Beginning, Woman — Robert Wright[w/m] & George Forrest[w/m] *(Frank)*. A new version of *Kismet* with an all black cast and a lavish production. It lasted 30 weeks. COVER: a parade of people in white costumes and carrying umbrellas.

2338 Time (closed before Broadway, 1920). Dorothy Francis.

Sunset — Clare Kummer[w/m] *(Remick)*. COVER: Dorothy Francis.

2339 A Time for Singing (Broadway, 1966). George Hearn, Tessie O'Shea.

Far from Home / How Green Was My Valley / I Wonder If / I'd Be a Fine One to Marry [PC] [CUT] / I'm Always Wrong [PC] / I'm Not Afraid [PC] [CUT] / I've Nothing to Give You [PC] / Let Me Love You / Of the 53 Men [PC] [CUT] / There Is Beautiful You Are / A Time for Singing / When He Looks at Me / Why Would Anyone Want to Get Married? [PC] — Gerald Freeman[w] & John Morris[w] & John Morris[m] *(Chappell)*. A musical version of *How Green*

Was My Valley that lasted only five weeks. COVER: a small village in a green valley.

2340 Time, Place and Girl (Black, 1930). Stars unknown.

You Do — Joseph Bannister[w/m] & Joseph Howard[w/m] *(Marks)*. A black version of the 1906 hit. COVER: three black guys and one black girl.

2341 Time Remembered (Broadway, 1957). Richard Burton, Helen Hayes.

Ages Ago / Time Remembered — Vernon Duke[w/m] *(Chappell)*. A drama, translated from the French, that became a big hit partly due to its star power. COVER: Helen Hayes, Richard Burton, Susan Strasberg.

2342 The Time, the Place, and the Girl (Broadway, 1942). Joe Howard, Vicki Cummings.

Falling in Love / Have You Found Heaven / The Keeley Cure / Let Me Ride by Your Side in the Saddle / Love Is a Will o' the Wisp / Penny for Your Thoughts, Junior Miss / Put On Your Rubbers / They Can't Ration My Love / The Time, the Place and the Girl / Travelling Man — William Friedlander[w] & Joe Howard[m] *(Marks)*; There's Something in My Eye — Joe Howard[w/m] & Bob Randolph[w/m] & Lina Romay[w/m] & Bill Bird[w/m] *(Marks)*. A revival of the hit musical from 1906 that folded after one week. COVER 1: a park bench, a clock, and a girl, Irene Hilda. COVER 2: a red cover with a clock and the titles.

2343 Tip-Toes (Broadway, 1925). Queenie Smith, Allen Kearns.

Harlem River Chanty (choral arrangement) / It's a Great Little World / Looking for a Boy / Nice Baby / Nightie-Night / Sweet and Low-Down / That Certain Feeling / These Charming People / When Do We Dance? — Ira Gershwin[w] & George Gershwin[m] *(Harms)*; Tip-Toes, Opening of Act One (piano selections) — George Gershwin[m] *(Harms)*. A musical about a vaudeville group stranded in Florida. It was a big hit due to the cast and the great songs and ran for six months. COVER: flowers and designs.

2344 Tip Top (Broadway, 1920). Fred Stone, Duncan Sisters.

Baby Sister Blues — Henry Marshall[w/m] & Marion Sunshine[w/m] *(Remick)*; Don't Bring Me Posies — Billy McCabe[w] & Clarence Jennings[w] & Fred Rose[m] *(Berlin)*; Feather Your Nest — Kendis Brockman[w/m] & Howard Johnson[w/m] *(Feist)*; Finders Is Keepers — Tom Brown[w/m] & Jack Frost[w/m] *(Remick)*; The Girl I Never Met / The Girl Who Keeps Me Guessing / I Want a Lily / Lantern of Love / Sweet Dreams / Wonderful Girl, Wonderful Boy — Anne Caldwell[w] & Ivan Caryll[m] *(Chappell)*; Humming — Louis Breau[w/m] & Ray Henderson[w/m] *(Harms)*; I Don't Belong on a Farm — Arthur Swanstrom[w] & Dorothy Clark[m] *(Harms)*; I Want to Be Somebody's Baby — Jesse Greer[w/m] & Ed Smalle[w/m] *(Von Tilzer)*; I Want to See My Ida Hoe in Idaho — Alex Sullivan[w] & Bert Rule[m] *(Witmark)*; I'll Say I Love You — William LeBaron[w] & Victor Jacobi[m] *(Harms)*; Oh, Sing-a-loo — Lew Brown[w] & Sidney Mitchell[w] & Lew Pollack[m] *(Broadway)*; Russian Rag — George Cobb[m] *(Rossiter)*; Sweet Baby Mine — Tom Brown[w/m] & Jack Frost[w/m] *(Sam Fox)*; Wabash Blues — Dave Ringle[w] & Fred Meinken[m] *(Feist)* When Shall We Meet Again — Raymond Egan[w] & Richard Whiting[m] *(Remick)*; Wireless Heart — Anne Caldwell[w] & Silvio Hein[m] *(Chappell)*. A silly plot that was almost a revue but Fred Stone and the Duncan Sisters kept this show going for 30 weeks. COVER: Fred Stone and designs.

2345 To Live Another Summer (Broadway, 1971). Rivka Raz, Yona Atari.

Give Me a Star — Hayim Hefer[w] & David Krivochei[m] *(Cimino)*; To Live Another Summer — vocal selections of 17 songs — Hayim Hefer[w] & Dov Seltzer[m] *(Cimino)*. An Israeli revue that ran for five months. COVER: the cast of the musical on stage.

2346 Tobacco Road (Broadway, 1933). James Barton, Dean Jagger.

Along Tobacco Road — Tina Glenn[w] & Jesse Greer[m] *(Glenn Music)*. A drama about poor white trash in the South. It ran for eight years. COVER: James Barton.

2347 Tommy (Regional, 1973). Ted Neeley.

Pinball Wizard / See Me, Feel Me / Tommy, Can You Hear Me? — Peter Townsend[w/m] *(Warner Bros.)*; Tommy — complete vocal score — Peter Townsend[w/m] & John Entwistle[w/m] & Keith Moon[w/m] *(Fabulous)*. A national tour in concert form of this rock opera. COVER: birds, clouds, faces, lines.

2348 Tonight at 8:30 (Broadway, 1936). Gertrude Lawrence, Noel Coward.

Has Anybody Seen Our Ship? / Men About Town [BW] / Play, Orchestra, Play / We Were Dancing / You Were There — Noel Coward[w/m] *(Chappell)*. A series of short plays with music that were successful in N.Y. and London. COVER: Noel Coward and Gertrude Lawrence.

2349 Tonight at 8:30 (Broadway, 1948). Gertrude Lawrence, Graham Payn.

Play, Orchestra, Play / Then / We Were Dancing / You Were There — Noel Coward[w/m] *(Chappell)*. A limited run revival of the Noel Coward hit. COVER: Gertrude Lawrence, Graham Payn.

2350 Too Many Girls (Broadway, 1939). Desi Arnaz, Eddie Bracken.

All Dressed Up / 'Cause We Got Cake [VS] / Give It Back to the Indians / I Didn't Know What Time It Was / I Like to Recognize the Tune / Love Never Went to College / She Could Shake the Maracas / Too Many Girls [PC] — Lorenz Hart[w] & Richard Rodgers[m] *(Chappell)*. A college musical that became a hit for Rodgers and Hart and produced one standard song. It ran for 30 weeks. COVER: a football player and girls.

2351 Toot Toot (Broadway, 1918). Louise Groody, William Kent.

Every Girl in All America / Girlie / Honeymoon Land / I Will Knit a Suit o' Dreams / If (There's Anything You Want) / If You Only Care Enough / Let's Go / Tee-Pee / When You Wake Up Dancing — Berton Braley[w] & Jerome Kern[m] *(Harms)*; It's Greek to Me — piano selections / Yankee Doodle on the Line — piano selections — Jerome Kern[m] *(Harms)*; The Last Mile Home — Emil Breitenfeld[w/m] *(Harms)*; You're So Cute, Soldier Boy — Edgar A. Woolf[w] & Anatol Friedland[m] *(Gilbert-Friedland)*. A war romance with an ordinary score and a run of only five weeks. COVER: soldier and girl with baggageman and boxes.

2352 Top Banana (Broadway, 1951). Rose Marie, Phil Silvers.

Be My Guest / My Home Is in My Shoes / OK for TV / Only If You're in Love / Sans Souci / That's for Sure / Top Banana — Johnny Mercer[w/m] *(Chappell)*. A musical about a TV comedian. Phil Silvers kept it going for almost a year. COVER: comedian, dancing girls, and TV cameras.

2353 Top Hole (Broadway, 1924). Ernest Glendinning, Clare Stratton.

Everytime the Clock Ticks / Happy / Love Is a Sandman / Safe in Your Heart / Star Dust — Eugene Conrad[w] & Robert Braine[m] *(Berlin)*; Imagine Me Without My You — Ira Gershwin[w] & Lewis Gensler[m] *(Harms)*; In California / Is It Any Wonder? / There's Always Room for a Smile / You Must Come Over Eyes — Owen Murphy[w] & Jay Gorney[m] *(Harms)*; Then You Know That You're in Love — Owen Murphy[w/m] & Harry Richman[w/m] & Jay Gorney[w/m] *(Harms)*; There Is Music in an Irish Song — Owen Murphy[w/m] & Jay Gorney[w/m] *(Harms)*. A musical about golf that lasted for three months. COVER: Berlin's cover is a sketch of a goofy golfer with instruction book and Harms' cover is fancy designs and lettering.

2354 Top Speed (Broadway, 1929). Lester Allen, Ginger Rogers.

Goodness Gracious / Hot and Bothered / I'll Know and She'll Know / Keep Your Undershirt On / Reaching for the Moon / Sweeter Than You / What Would I Care? — Bert Kalmar[w/m] & Harry Ruby[w/m] *(Harms)*. Two poor clerks at a rich resort were the basis of this three month run musical. COVER: a group of people watching a speed boat race.

2355 Topics of 1923 (*see also* The Courtesan) (Broadway, 1923). Donald Brian, Nancy Carroll.

Garden of Evil / In the Cottage of My Heart / Just Like a Diamond / Love in a Haystack / On a Beautiful Evening / When You Love / Yankee Doodle Oo-La-La — Harold Atteridge[w] & Jean Schwartz[m] *(Harms)*. This show was written for Alice Delysia, a European singer. It was a total failure. It toured as *The Courtesan* and opened as *Topics of 1923*. COVER: lettering and designs.

2356 Toplitzky of Notre Dame (Broadway, 1946). Warde Donovan, Betty Jane Watson.

I Wanna Go to City College / Let Us Gather at the Goal Line / Love Is a Random Thing / Wolf Time / You Are My Downfall — George Marion[w] & Sammy Fain[m] *(Harms)*. Another college and football musical which was quite ordinary and lasted only two months. COVER: football player, goal posts, and large football.

2357 Topsy and Eva (Broadway, 1923). The Duncan Sisters.

Do Re Mi / High Brow Colored Lady / I Never Had a Mammy / Kiss Me / Land of Long Ago / Lickin's / Moon Am Shinin' / Rememb'ring / Sighing — Duncan Sisters[w/m] *(Berlin)*; Happy-Go-Lucky Days — Al Wilson[w/m] & James Brennan[w/m] *(Wilson)*; In Sweet Onion Time — Duncan Sisters[w/m] & Sam Coslow[w/m] *(Duncan)*; In the Autumn / Just in Love with Me / Um Um Da Da / Under a Lover's Moon / We'll Dance Through Life — Duncan Sisters[w/m] *(Wilkes)*; Stick in the Mud — Duncan Sisters[w/m] *(Duncan)*. A musical version of *Uncle Tom's*

Cabin that ran for 20 weeks. COVER: the Duncan Sisters. This production was also published with the White Sisters on the cover.

2358 Topsy and Eva (closed before Broadway, 1942). Duncan Sisters.

Jerk Mazurk / Land of the Free / Locked in the Cradle / Love Is a Merry Go Round — Duncan Sisters^{w/m} *(Edwards)*. A revival of the 1923 musical with the original cast. The revival closed in L.A. COVER: the Duncan sisters and sketches of black and white girl.

2359 Touch and Go (Broadway, 1949). Peggy Cass, Helen Gallagher.

Be a Mess! [VS] / Funny Old Little Old World / It Will Be All Right / This Had Better Be Love / Wish Me Luck — Jean Kerr^w & Walter Kerr^w & Jay Gorney^m *(Chappell)*. A clever revue that arrived when revues were on the way out. It lasted five months. COVER: a well dressed couple riding a merry-go-round.

2360 Tovarich (Broadway, 1963). Vivien Leigh, Jean Pierre Aumont.

All for You / I Go to Bed [ABQ] / I Know the Feeling / Lullaby for a Princess / Make a Friend / Nitchevo! [ABQ] / The Only One / Opportunity [ABQ] / Stuck with Each Other [ABQ] / Uh-Oh / Wilkes Barre, Pa. / You Love Me [ABQ] — Anne Croswell^w & Lee Pockriss^m *(Marks)*. Russian royalty serving as servants in Paris were the basis of this poor musical which ran for almost nine months due to the presence of Vivien Leigh. COVER: a crown, a sword, and a broom.

2361 The Town Clown (*see also* **The Belle of Quakertown** *and* **No Other Girl**) (Broadway, 1923). Eddie Buzzell, Helen Ford.

Doing the Town / Honduras / In the Corner of My Mind / It's the Dancer You Love / No Other Girl — Bert Kalmar^w & Harry Ruby^m *(Berlin)*. A short lived musical about building a highway. This show toured as *The Belle of Quakertown* and *The Town Clown* before opening as *No Other Girl*. COVER: a clown staring into a mirror.

2362 Town Gossip (closed before Broadway, 1921). Helen Broderick, Grace Moore.

Argentina / Golden Evenings of Autumn Time / I Have Something Nice / Just Like the Sunshine / Teaching the Baby to Walk — George Stoddard^w & Ned Wayburn^w & Harold Orlob^m *(Harms)*. COVER: fancy designs and lettering.

2363 The Toy Shop (closed before Broadway, 1924). Joseph Howard, Jannette Gilmore.

Driftwood — Gus Kahn^w & Lee Gold^m *(Berlin)*; I Can't Get the One I Want — Billy Rose^w & Herman Ruby^w & Lou Handman^m *(Berlin)*; Levee Lou — Charles Harris^w & Joseph Howard^m *(Harris)*. COVER: Joseph Howard, Jannette Gilmore.

2364 Transatlantic Rhythm (British, 1936). Stars unknown.

Breakfast in Harlem [B] / Spanish Jake [B] — Irving Caesar^{w/m} & Sammy Lerner ^{w/m} & Gerald Marks^{w/m} *(Chappell)*; Holiday Sweetheart / I Heard a Song in a Taxi — Irving Caesar^w & Desmond Carter^w & Ray Henderson ^m *(Chappell)*. A revue with music mostly by Americans and some of the songs published in the U.S. COVER: The American cover has a couple in a taxi and the British cover has titles and designs.

2365 Treasure Girl (Broadway, 1928). Gertrude Lawrence, Paul Frawley.

Feeling I'm Falling / Got a Rainbow / I Don't Think I'll Fall in Love Today / K-ra-zy for You / Oh, So Nice / What Are We Here For? / Where's the Boy? Here's the Girl — Ira Gershwin^w & George Gershwin^m *(Harms)*. This musical about an ambitious woman had a good score by the Gershwins but a terrible book. It lasted only two months. COVER: flowers, designs, and lettering.

2366 A Tree Grows in Brooklyn (Broadway, 1951). Shirley Booth, Johnny Johnston.

Growing Pains / If You Haven't Got a Sweetheart / I'll Buy You a Star / I'm Like a New Broom / Look Who's Dancing / Love Is the Reason / Make the Man Love Me—Dorothy Fields[w] & Arthur Schwartz[m] *(Harms)*. A wonderful musical based on the popular novel. It was given a lovely production, with a good score by Schwartz and the talents of Shirley Booth, but it ended in the red after playing almost nine months. COVER: a young smiling girl carrying flowers.

2367 Treemonisha (Broadway, 1975). Kathleen Battle, Kenneth Hicks.

Aunt Dinah Has Blowed de Horn / A Real Slow Drag / Treemonisha—vocal selections of 13 songs—Scott Joplin[w/m] *(Chappell)*. A reconstruction of a lost ragtime opera by the Houston Opera Company. It was a beautiful production brought in for a limited run of eight weeks. COVER: a group of people dancing.

2368 A Trial Honeymoon (closed before Broadway, 1924). Stars unknown.

Take Me to a Petting Party—Harold Orlob[w/m] *(Harms)*. COVER: flowers and designs.

2369 Tricks (Broadway, 1971). Rene Auberjonois, Walter Bobbie.

How Sweetly Simple / Life Can Be Funny / Love or Money / Man of Spirit / Tricks / Who Was I?—Lonnie Burstein[w] & Jerry Blatt[m] *(Unichappell)*. A musical version of Moliere's *De Scapin* that lasted one week on Broadway. COVER: people dressed as clowns.

2370 A Trip to Hitland (closed before Broadway, 1920). Stars unknown.

I'm Tellin' You / Underneath the Skies—Nat Vincent[w/m] & Billy Baskette[w/m] *(Rossiter)*; Laughing Vamp / We'll Still Be Together—Billy Frisch[w/m] & Bernie Grossman[w/m] *(Rossiter)*; Mammy's Apron Strings / Wow—Will Donaldson[w/m] & Sam Ehrlich[w/m] *(Rossiter)*; Scissors—Leon Flatow[w/m] & Bobby Jones[w/m] *(Rossiter)*; Think of Me / You're Just Around the Corner from Heaven—Al Siegel[w/m] & Jimmie Brown[w/m] *(Ros-*

siter). COVER: a girl in veils carrying flowers.

2371 Trouble in Tahiti (Broadway, 1955). Alice Ghostley, John Tyers.

Trouble in Tahiti—complete vocal score—Leonard Bernstein[w/m] *(Schirmer)*. A triple bill called *All in One* consisting of a one act opera, a one act drama by Tennessee Williams, and a concert by Paul Draper. It lasted six weeks. COVER: a man and woman with umbrellas walking away from each other.

2372 Troubles of 1920 (Nightclub, 1920). George Jessel.

I'm My Mamma's Baby Boy—George Jessel[w/m] & Roy Turk[w/m] & Louis Silvers[w/m] *(Berlin)*. COVER: George Jessel and sketch of mother and son.

2373 Troubles of 1922 (Nightclub, 1922). George Jessel, Courtney Sisters.

Baby Blue Eyes / Dear Old Southland / Deedle Deedle Dum—Walter Hirsch[w/m] & George Jessel[w/m] & Jesse Greer[w/m] *(Richmond-Robbins)*; I've Got the Lovesick Blues / Jig Walk / Snap to a Pretty Melody—Irving Mills[w/m] & Cliff Friend[w/m] *(Jack Mills)*; When You and I Were Young Maggie Blues—Jack Frost[w/m] & Jimmy McHugh[w/m] *(Jack Mills)*. COVER: George Jessel and the Courtney Sisters.

2374 Troubles of 1923 (Nightclub, 1923). George Jessel.

Little Rover—Gus Kahn[w] & Walter Donaldson[m] *(Shapiro, Bernstein)*. COVER: George Jessel and a sketch of mother.

2375 Tumble In (Broadway, 1919). Zelda Sears, Charles Ruggles.

Argentines, the Portuguese, and the Greeks—Arthur Swanstrom[w] & Carey Morgan[m] *(Stern)*; I've Told My Love / The Laugh / Limbo-Land / A Little Chicken Fit for Old Broadway / Snuggle and Dream / Thoughts That I Wrote on the Leaves of My Heart / The Trousseau Ball / The Wedding Blues / Won't You Help Me Out? / You'll Do It All Over Again—Otto Harbach[w] & Rudolph Friml[m] *(Schirmer)*. This musical involved a group of people quarantined in an apartment for a week. It had a weak score and book and lasted only three months. COVER: letters and designs. Some covers show a girl in a large jar; others show a group of five assorted people staring out window.

2376 Twinkle Toes (Nightclub, 1920). Stars unknown.

My Garden of Memory / Twinkle Toes / The World Is Mine — Z. Myers[w] & I. B. Kornblum[m] *(Stern)*. COVER: beautiful colored cover showing a dancing girl.

2377 Twinkle Twinkle (Broadway, 1926). Joe E. Brown, Ona Munson.

Find a Girl / Get a Load of This / Twinkle Twinkle / You Know I Know / You're the One — Harlan Thompson[w] & Harry Archer[m] *(Harms)*; Sweeter Than You — Bert Kalmar[w/m] & Harry Ruby[w/m] *(Harms)*; Whistle — Bert Kalmar[w] & Harry Ruby[m] *(Harms)*. A musical about a Hollywood star seeking peace and quiet. It had nothing going for it except Joe E. Brown whose clowning helped it last for 20 weeks. COVER: a skyline and twinkling stars.

2378 Two Bouquets (Broadway, 1938). Patricia Morison, Marcy Westcott.

The Bashful Lover — Eleanor Farjeon[w] & Herb Farjeon[w] & C. Moulton[m] *(Chappell)*; I Sent a Letter to My Love / Sweet Blossoms — Eleanor Farjeon[w] & Herb Farjeon[w] & M. Pinsuti[m] *(Chappell)*; Toddy's the Drink for Me — Eleanor Farjeon[w/m] & Herb Farjeon[w/m] *(Chappell)*. A London hit involving a mix-up between two couples. It was a failure of seven weeks. COVER: Patricia Morison, Marcy Westcott and flowers.

2379 Two by Two (Broadway, 1970). Danny Kaye, Madeline Kahn.

Everything That's Gonna Be, Has Been [PC] / Hey, Girlie [PC] / I Do Not Know a Day I Did Not Love You / An Old Man / Something Doesn't Happen / Something, Somewhere / Two by Two / Two by Two — complete vocal score / When It Dries [VS] / You [VS] / You Have Got to Have a Rudder on the Ark [VS] — Martin Charnin[w] & Richard Rodgers[m] *(Williamson)*. A musical about Noah and his ark. There wasn't much to it but Danny Kaye kept it going for almost a year. COVER: Danny Kaye, animals and the ark.

2380 Two for the Show (Broadway, 1940). Eve Arden, Alfred Drake.

At Last It's Love / A House with a Little Red Barn / How High the Moon — Nancy Hamilton[w] & Morgan Lewis[m] *(Chappell)*. An ordinary revue that produced one hit song and lasted four months. COVER: plain gray cover with letters and designs.

2381 Two Gentlemen of Verona (Broadway, 1971). Raul Julia, Clifton Davis.

Calla Lily Lady [VS] / Eglamour [VS] / Hot Lover [VS] / I Am Not Interested in Love [VS] / I Love My Father / Love Has Driven Me Sane [VS] / Love Me [VS] / Love's Revenge [VS] / Mansion [VS] / Night Letter [VS] / Summer, Summer / Symphony [VS] / What a Nice Idea [VS] / What Does a Lover Pack? [VS] — John Guare[w] & Galt MacDermott[m] *(Chappell)*; Who Is Sylvia? [VS] — William Shakespeare[w] & Galt MacDermott[m] *(Chappell)*. A musical based on a Shakespearean play. It was produced by Joseph Papp for Central Park's free concerts. It turned into a big hit and ran for 18 months. COVER: sketch of black and white girl.

2382 Two Little Girls in Blue (Broadway, 1921). Madeline Fairbanks, Oscar Shaw.

Dolly / Rice and Shoes — Arthur Francis (IG)[w] & Schuyler Greene[w] & Vincent Youmans[m] *(Harms)*; The Gypsy Trail — Irving Caesar[w] & Paul Lannin[m] *(Harms)*; Honeymoon / Just Like You — Arthur Francis (IG)[w] & Paul Lannin[m] *(Harms)*; Oh Me! Oh My! / Who's Who with You / You Started Something — Arthur Francis (IG)[w] & Vincent Youmans[m] *(Harms)*; Orienta — Irving Caesar[w] & Schuyler

Greene[w] & Vincent Youmans[m] *(Harms)*. A musical involving a mix-up with twins. It was Youmans' first Broadway score and turned into a moderate hit running almost five months. COVER: two girls on deck of ship.

2383 Two Little Girls in Blue (British, 1927). Barry Twins, Barrie Oliver.

Somebody's Sunday [B] — Vernon Duke[w/m] *(Chappell)*. This American musical with the Youmans score and one Duke song folded on its pre–London tour. COVER: the Barry Twins.

2384 Two on the Aisle (Broadway, 1951). Bert Lahr, Dolores Gray.

Catch Our Act at the Met [VS] / Everlasting / Give a Little — Get a Little / Hold Me — Hold Me — Hold Me / How Will He Know / If You Hadn't But You Did [VS] / So Far — So Good [PC] / There Never Was a Baby Like My Baby — Betty Comden[w] & Adolph Green[w] & Jule Styne[m] *(Morris)*. A very entertaining revue with some good songs and the talents of Lahr and Gray. It ran nine months. COVER: Bert Lahr and Dolores Gray.

2385 Two Weeks with Pay (closed before Broadway, 1957). Stars unknown.

Teatime on Fifth Avenue — Margaret Neas[m] *(Melody Lane)*. COVER: black and white cover with title only.

2386 Two's Company (Broadway, 1952). Bette Davis, David Burns.

Good Little Girls / It Just Occurred to Me — Sammy Cahn[w] & Vernon Duke[m] *(Remick)*; Just Like a Man / Out of a Clear Blue Sky / Roundabout — Ogden Nash[w] & Vernon Duke[m] *(Remick)*. An interesting revue with Bette Davis trying to sing and dance. There were a few good skits and some pleasant songs; however, it closed after 11 weeks due to Bette Davis' sudden illness. COVER: sketch of Bette Davis and designs.

2387 Typical Topical Tales (Nightclub, 1923). Lou Miller, Alice Bradford.

A Girl Like You — Lou Miller[w/m] *(Berlin and Horowitz)*. COVER: Alice Bradford.

2388 Under the Bamboo Tree (Broadway, 1922). Herbert Hoey.

While Miami Dreams — Raymond Egan[w] & Richard Whiting[m] *(Remick)*. A short lived comedy. COVER: Herbert Hoey.

2389 Underworld (closed before Broadway, 1962). Stars unknown.

Love Me [RC] — John Hollander[w] & Lester Judson[w] & Jerome Moross[m] *(Chappell)*. A musical that was never produced.

2390 The Unicorn (Broadway, 1957). N.Y. City Ballet.

The Unicorn — complete vocal score — Gian Carlo Menotti[w/m] *(Schirmer)*. A madrigal fable for chorus and dancers performed on a limited run. COVER: black and white cover with titles only.

2391 The Unsinkable Molly Brown (Broadway, 1960). Tammy Grimes, Harve Presnell.

Are You Sure? / Bea-u-ti-ful People of Denver / Belly Up to the Bar, Boys / Bon Jour / Chick-a-Pen / Dolce Far Niente / I Ain't Down Yet (march) / I Ain't Down Yet (vocal) / If I Knew / I'll Never Say No / I've A'ready Started In / Keep-a-Hoppin' / Leadville Johnny Brown [VS] / Unsinkable Molly Brown — complete vocal score — Meredith Willson[w/m] *(Frank)*. A rags-to-riches story set in the old West. It was very entertaining with a good score, lavish production and two talented leads. It ran for 18 months. COVER: Molly Brown in rowboat with paddle.

2392 Up and Doing (British, 1940). Leslie Henson, Binnie Hale.

Falling in Love with Love [B] / Sing for Your Supper [B] / This Can't Be Love [B] — Lorenz Hart[w] & Richard Rodgers[m] *(Victoria)*; London Pride [B] — Noel Coward[w/m] *(Chappell)*. A smash hit revue in London that ran for 15 months. It was interrupted by the blitz. COVER: Leslie Henson, Binnie Hale.

2393 Up and Down (Black, 1922). Salem Tutt Whitney, J. Homer Tutt.

That Da-Da Strain — Mamie Medina[w] & J. Edgar Dowell[m] *(Williams)*. COVER: Gertrude Saunders.

2394 Up in Central Park (*see also* **Central Park)** (Broadway, 1944). Wilbur Evans, Betty Bruce.

April Snow / The Big Back Yard / Carousel in the Park / Close as Pages in a Book / The Fireman's Bride / It Doesn't Cost You Anything to Dream / When You Walk in the Room — Dorothy Fields[w] & Sigmund Romberg[m] *(Williamson)*. An old fashioned operetta about New York and politicians that was a big hit. It was called *Central Park* in try-out but opened as *Up in Central Park*. COVER: horses and carriages in Central Park.

2395 Up in Mabel's Room (Broadway, 1919). Hazel Dawn, Enid Markey.

Up in Mabel's Room — Alex Gerber[w] & Abner Silver[m] *(Witmark)*. A comedy hit that ran for seven months. COVER: Hazel Dawn.

2396 Up in the Clouds (Broadway, 1921). Skeets Gallagher, Grace Moore.

Betsy Ross / Friends / Girl You Marry / Happiness / How Dry I Am / I See Your Face / Jean / Last Girl / Look-a-Look / Rum-Tum-Tiddle / Up in the Clouds / Wonderful Something — Will Johnstone[w] & Tom Johnstone[m] *(Up in the Clouds Music)*. A musical about a Hollywood star with a poor score and book. It lasted three months. COVER: girl in the clouds with an eagle flying.

2397 Up She Goes (Broadway, 1922). Donald Brian, Skeets Gallagher.

Bobbin' About / First Step You Take / Journey's End / Lady Luck / Let's Kiss / Nearing the Day / Settle Down and Travel / Takes a Heap of Love / Ty-Up — Joseph McCarthy[w] & Harry Tierney[m] *(Feist)*. The story of a young couple and their proposed bungalow. It had a very good book and pleasant score, and ran 30 weeks. COVER 1: a purple cover with circles. COVER 2: blue

and yellow; couple with flowers.

2398 Up Stage and Down (Broadway, 1919). Phillip Leavitt, Ralph Engelsman.

Asiatic Angles / Butterfly Love / Love Is Not in Vain / Twinkling Eyes — Richard Rodgers[w/m] *(Harms)*; Love Me by Parcel Post — Mortimer Rodgers[w] & Richard Rodgers[m] *(Harms)*. Performed one time as a benefit at the Waldorf Astoria. COVER: letters and designs.

2399 Up with the Lark (British, 1927). Anita Elison, Henry Wenman.

The Girl Is You and the Boy Is Me [B] / Tweet, Tweet [B] — B.G. DeSylva[w] & Lew Brown[w] & Ray Henderson[m] *(Harms)*; I'm in Love Again [B] — Cole Porter[w/m] *(Harms)*. A musical adapted from a French farce about young love. It toured for one month with a set score and group of actors. This score and the actors were thrown out before the London opening and a new cast plus some proven American hits were inserts. It ran three months. COVER: purple and green designs and lettering.

2400 Up with the People (Regional, 1965). Stars unknown.

Freedom Isn't Free / Gee I'm Looking Forward to the Future / Ride of Paul Revere / Up the Holler / Up with People / What Color Is God's Skin / Which Way America? — Paul Colwell[w/m] & Ralph Colwell[w/m] *(Up with the People Music)*. A touring musical to preach living together peacefully in America. COVER: a group of Americans from all walks of life.

2401 Ups-a-Daisy (Broadway, 1928). Luella Gear, Bob Hope.

Hot! / I Can't Believe It's True / Sweet One / Ups-a-Daisy / Will You Remember, Will You Forget — Robert Simon[w] & Lewis Gensler[m] *(Harms)*; Oh, How Happy We'll Be / Oh, How I Miss You Blues! — Robert Simon[w] & Clifford Grey[w] & Lewis Gensler[m] *(Harms)*. A musical dealing with mountain climbing. It was very ordinary but it ran nine months. COVER: a couple riding a seesaw.

2402 Urban Blight (Off Broadway, 1978). Faith Prince, Rex Robbins.

Life Story [VS] / Miss Byrd [VS] / One of the Good Guys [VS] / There's Nothing Like It [VS] / Three Friends [VS] / You Wanna Be My Friend [VS] — Richard Maltby, Jr.ʷ & David Shireᵐ *(Fiddleback)*; Three Friends Chaser [VS] — David Shireᵐ *(Fiddleback)*. This was a review of life in New York featuring songs that were used in *Closer Than Ever* and *Urban Blight*. Cover: titles only.

2403 USO Stage Door Canteen (Broadway, 1942). Stars unknown.

Buckle Down Buck Private — Ralph Blaneʷ/ᵐ & Hugh Martinʷ/ᵐ *(Crawford)*. The theme song of the Stage Door Canteen in New York during World War II. Cover: a soldier and a flag.

2404 A Vagabond Hero (closed before Broadway, 1939). Ruby Mercer, Hope Emerson.

Bonjour, Goodbye [PC] — Charles Lockeʷ & Vernon Dukeᵐ *(Robbins)*; I Cling to You [PC] / Shadow of Love [PC] — Charles Lockeʷ & Ted Fetterʷ & Vernon Dukeᵐ *(Robbins)*. A musical based on Cyrano de Bergerac that folded after two weeks. It was also called *The White Plume*. Cover: none.

2405 The Vagabond King (Broadway, 1926). Dennis King, Carolyn Thomson.

Huguette Waltz / Love for Sale / Love Me Tonight / Only a Rose / Someday / Song of the Vagabonds / The Vagabond King — complete vocal score / Vagabond King Waltz — Brian Hookerʷ & Rudolf Frimlᵐ *(Waterson)*. A romantic swashbuckling operetta with a grand production that lasted 15 months. Cover 1: shows Dennis King. Cover 2: shows Katherine DeVaucelles. Cover 3: is a red and purple cover with a sketch rather than a photo.

2406 Valmouth (Off Broadway, 1960). Anne Francine, Elly Stone.

I Loved a Man / Little Girl Baby / Magic Fingers / My Big Best Shoes / What Do I Want with Love? — Sandy Wilsonʷ/ᵐ *(Noel Gay)*. A fantasy about some very strange people. It was a hit in London but a two week flop in New York. Cover: assorted characters, birds, and trees.

2407 The Vamp (*see also* **Delilah**) (Broadway, 1955). Carol Channing, David Atkinson.

Have You Met Delilah? / I've Always Loved You / Ragtime Romeo / Why Does It Have to Be You — John Latoucheʷ & James Mundyᵐ *(Robbins-Wise)*. A quick failure with Channing as queen of the silver screen. It was called *Delilah* during preview. Cover: Carol Channing.

2408 The Vanderbilt Revue (Broadway, 1930). LuLu McConnell, Joe Penner.

Blue Again / Button Up Your Heart — Dorothy Fieldsʷ & Jimmy McHughᵐ *(Robbins)*; I Give Myself Away — Edward Eliscuʷ & Jacques Frayᵐ *(Robbins)*. A poor revue that lasted almost two weeks. Cover: Times Square and chorus girls.

2409 Vanessa (Opera, 1958). Eleanor Steber, Nicolai Gedda.

Must the Winter Come So Soon / Under the Willow Tree — Gian Carlo Menottiʷ & Samuel Barberᵐ *(Schirmer)*. This production was performed on a limited basis at the Metropolitan Opera. Cover: a costume sketch of Vanessa by Cecil Beaton.

2410 Velvet Lady (Broadway, 1919). Eddie Dowling, Fay Marbe.

Anytime New York Goes Dry / Bubbles / Come Be My Wife / Fair Honeymoon / I've Danced to Beat the Band / Life and Love / Little Boy and Girl / Logic / Spooky Ookum / There's Nothing Too Fine for the Finest / Velvet Lady — complete vocal score / What a Position for Me — Henry Blossomʷ & Victor Herbertᵐ *(Witmark)*. A musical about love letters and stolen jewels with an ordinary score and good dancing. It lasted four months. Cover: a lady in a large hat.

2411 Velvet Revue (Broadway, 1929). Stars unknown.

Hot-cha-cha / Lady of My Day Dreams — Rubey Cowan^w & Phil Boutelje^m *(Famous)*. A mini-stage show presented by Paramount-Publix in between showings of their new pictures at large movie theatres. Cover: flowers and designs.

2412 Venus in Silk (*see also* Beloved Rogue) (closed before Broadway, 1935). Harold Murray, Audrey Christie.

Baby, Play with Me / Eyes That Are Smiling / I Ask Not Who You Are / You Are the One — Lester O'Keefe^w & Robert Stolz^m *(Chappell)*. This romantic operetta type musical originated at the St. Louis Opera Co. and was called *Beloved Rogue*. It toured as *Venus in Silk* and folded on the road. Cover: girl in evening gown and *Venus de Milo* statue.

2413 Very Warm for May (Broadway, 1939). Eve Arden, Donald Brian.

All in Fun / All the Things You Are (first version) / All the Things You Are (second version) / Heaven in My Arms / In Other Words, Seventeen / In the Heart of the Dark / That Lucky Fellow — Oscar Hammerstein^w & Jerome Kern^m *(Harms)*. A musical with a summer theatre theme. It had a poor book and lasted for two months but produced the standard song *All the Things You Are*. Cover: masks, flowers, and designs.

2414 Via Galactica (Broadway, 1972). Irene Cara, Raul Julia.

All My Good Mornings [PC] / Children of the Sun [PC] / Dance the Dark Away [PC] / Home [PC] / New Jerusalem [PC] / Shall We Friend [PC] / Take Your Hat Off — "Up" [PC] / Via Galactica [PC] — Christopher Gore^w & Galt MacDermott^m *(Chappell)*. This was the first musical in the new Uris theatre. It lasted one week.

2415 The Victory Girl (closed before Broadway, 1919). Justine Johnston.

I Want to Be Good — Frank Fay^w & Dave Dreyer^m *(Von Tilzer)*. Cover: Justine Johnston.

2416 Virgin (closed before Broadway, 1972). Stars unknown.

Kyrie Eleison — John O'Reilly^w/m & J. Venneri^w/m & A. Delmonte^w/m *(Hansen)*. Cover: a cross.

2417 Virginia (Broadway, 1937). Gene Lockhart, Helen Carroll.

Good and Lucky / Goodbye Jonah / If You Were Someone Else / My Heart Is Dancing / Virginia — Albert Stillman^w & Arthur Schwartz^m *(Robbins)*; My Bridal Gown / An Old Flame Never Dies / You and I Know — Albert Stillman^w & Laurence Stallings^w & Arthur Schwartz^m *(Robbins)*. A colonial operetta commissioned for the huge Center Theatre. It folded in two months. Cover: an elegant couple before an elegant country home.

2418 Viva O'Brien (Broadway, 1941). Marie Nash, Hugh Diamond.

Broken Hearted Romeo / Carinito / Don Jose O'Brien / How Long / El Matador / Mood of the Moment / Mozambamba / Our Song / To Prove My Love / Wrap Me in Your Serape / Yucatana — Ray Leveen^w & Maria Grever^m *(Portilla)*. A musical about a tour in Mexico that lasted for two weeks. Cover: different girls, Mexican hat and serape.

2419 Vogues (Broadway, 1924). Fred Allen, Odette Myrtil.

Hee Bee / Land of Happiness — Jee Bees / When the Piper Plays — Clifford Gray^w & Herbert Stothart^m *(Harms)*; That's the Tune — Graham John^w/m & Nelson Keys^w/m & Max Darewski^w/m *(Harms)*; When Katinka Shakes Her Tambourine — Lloyd Fry^w & Rudolph Nelson^m *(Jack Mills)*; Why — J. Donovan^w & Roger Kahn^m *(Jack Mills)*. A minor revue that lasted for three months. Cover: Odette Myrtil; flowers and designs.

2420 The Voice of McConnell (Broadway, 1918). Edna Leslie, Chauncey Olcott.

Ireland, My Land of Dreams / When I Look in Your Eyes, Mavourneen / You Can't Deny You're Irish — George M. Cohan^w/m *(Witmark)*; That Tumble

Down Shack in Athlone — Richard Pascoe[w] & Monte Carlo[m] & Alma Saunders[m] *(Berlin)*. A play with music and an Irish story that lasted three weeks on Broadway. COVER: Chauncey Olcott and green flowers.

2421 Wait a Minim! (Broadway, 1966). Andrew Tracey, Paul Tracey.

Wait a Mimim — selections of seven folk songs — Andrew Tracey[w/m] & Paul Tracey[w/m] *(Frank)*. A revue of folk material from South Africa. It had inventive staging that kept it going over a year. COVER: a row of strange hats and letters.

2422 Waiting in the Wings (British, 1960). Sybil Thorndike, Graham Payn.

Come the Wild, Wild Weather [B] / Oh, Mister Kaiser [B] — Noel Coward[w/m] *(Chappell)*. A play — with music — about growing old. It ran for nine months in London and on tour. COVER: a blue and green cover with title only.

2423 Wake Up and Dream (British, 1929). Jessie Matthews, Sonny Hale.

Aqua Sincopada Tango [B] / I Dream of a Girl in a Shawl [B] — piano selections / I've Got a Crush on You [B] — piano selections — Cole Porter[m] *(Chappell)*; Banjo — That Man Joe Plays [B] / I Loved Him — But He Didn't Love Me [B] / I Want to Be Raided by You (not published) / Let's Do It — Let's Fall in Love [B] / Looking at You [B] / Wake Up and Dream [B] / What Is This Thing Called Love? [B] — Cole Porter[w/m] *(Chappell)*. A Cole Porter hit in London. It ran for almost nine months and later came to New York. COVER: red, white, and blue letters and designs.

2424 Wake Up and Dream (Broadway, 1929). Jessie Matthews, Jack Buchanan.

After All, I'm Only a Schoolgirl [VS] [CUT] — Cole Porter[w/m] *(Warner Bros.)*; Fancy Our Meeting — Douglas Furber[w] & Philip Charig[m] & Joseph Meyer[m] *(Harms)*; Gigolo / Looking at You / What Is This Thing Called Love / Which? — Cole Porter[w/m] *(Harms)*; She's

Such a Comfort to Me — Douglas Furber[w] & Donovan Parsons[w] & Max Lief[w] & Nathaniel Lief[w] & Arthur Schwartz[m] *(Harms)*; Why Wouldn't I Do? — Ivor Novello[w] & Desmond Carter[w] & Ivor Novello[m] *(Harms)*. This hit London revue brought to New York lasted only three months due to the stock market crash. COVER: red, white, and blue letters and designs.

2425 Walk a Little Faster (Broadway, 1932). Beatrice Lillie, Bobby Clark.

April in Paris / Off Again, On Again / A Penny for Your Thoughts / Speaking of Love / That's Life / Where Have We Met Before — E.Y. Harburg[w] & Vernon Duke[m] *(Harms)*; So Nonchalant — E.Y. Harburg[w] & Charles Tobias[w] & Vernon Duke[m] *(Harms)*. A musical revue with a talented cast and a fine score. It ran only four months but produced one hit song. COVER: a sketch of fish, snails, and water.

2426 Walking Happy (Broadway, 1966). Louise Troy, Norman Wisdom.

Circle This Day on the Calendar [PC] / How D'ya Talk to a Girl? / I Don't Think I'm in Love / If I Be Your Best Chance / I'll Make a Man of the Man / It Might as Well Be You [PC] / Love Will Find a Way — They Say [PC] / Such a Sociable Sort [VS] / Use Your Noggin' / Very Close to Wonderful [PC] / Walking Happy / What Makes It Happen? / Where Was I? [VS] — Sammy Cahn[w] & James Van Heusen[m] *(Shapiro, Bernstein)*. A dull musical about a shoemaker. It had one good song and Norman Wisdom and lasted five months. COVER: a bootmaker's sign.

2427 Walt Whitman Songs (Concert, 1942). Stars unknown.

Walt Whitman — three songs — Walt Whitman[w] & Kurt Weill[m] *(Chappell)*. A concert piece for baritone and full orchestra. COVER: black and white cover with title and designs.

2428 The War Song (Broadway, 1928). George Jessel, Shirley Booth.

Wait for Me—Sam Lewis[w] & Joe Young[w] & Harry Akst[m] *(Remick)*. A play about World War I that lasted only ten weeks. COVER: George Jessel.

2429 Watch Out, Angel! (closed before Broadway, 1945). Carol Haney, Lester Allen.

It's a Great Life If You Weaken / Watch Out, Angel—Eddie DeLange[w] & Jerry Seelen[w] & Josef Myrow[m] *(Morris)*. COVER: girl with wings and glass of champagne.

2430 The Water's Fine (closed before Broadway, 1919). May Irwin.

Boys Are Like Wonderful Toys / I'm in Love with You / In Ding Dong Land / In the Land of Go to Bed Early / Jazzin' the Alphabet / Minute They Say "I Do" They Don't / On Guard / Shadows Always Make Me Blue / The Way to Win a Girl / With a Little Bit of Cider Inside of Ida—Sam Lewis[w] & Joe Young[w] & Ted Snyder[m] *(Berlin)*. COVER: girl in bathing suit testing the water.

2431 We Take the Town (closed before Broadway, 1962). Robert Preston, Carmen Alvarez.

How Does the Wine Taste? / I Don't Know How to Talk to a Lady / I Marry You / I've Got a Girl / The Only Girl / Silverware / A Wedded Man / When?—Matt Dubey[w] & Harold Karr[m]*(Chappell)*. A musical based on the movie *Viva Villa!* It folded in Philadelphia after a month on the road. COVER: sketch of a bunch of Mexicans.

2432 Weber-Friedlander Vaudeville (Regional, 1922). Stars unknown.

Allez Up—William Friedlander[w/m] *(Marks)*. A vaudeville show that toured the circuit. COVER: beautiful Spanish senorita with musician.

2433 Wedding Bells (Broadway, 1919). Wallace Eddinger, Margaret Lawrence.

Wedding Bells—B.C. Hilliam[w/m] *(Witmark)*. A hit comedy about a couple about to be married. COVER: Eddinger and Lawrence.

2434 Welcome to the Club (Broad-

way, 1989). Avery Schreiber, Marilyn Sokol.

At My Side / Piece of Cake [VS] / Rio [VS] / Southern Comfort [VS]—Cy Coleman[w] & A.E. Hotchner[w] & Cy Coleman[m] *(Notable)*. A musical about divorce and alimony. It lasted 12 performances. COVER: a large mouth chewing up a man.

2435 The Well of Romance (Broadway, 1930). Howard Marsh, Norma Terris.

Fare Thee Well / Hail the King / I'll Never Complain / Melancholy Lady / The Moon's Shining Cool / My Dream of Dreams / Rhapsody of Love—Preston Sturges[w] & Maurice Jacquet[m] *(Witmark)*. A terrible operetta about a princess and king fairy tale. It featured the stars of *Show Boat* and lasted one week. COVER: a lady by a wishing well.

2436 Well Well Well (*see also* Pleasure Bound) (Broadway, 1929). Fred Lightner, Jack Pearl.

We'll Get Along / Why Do You Tease Me—Max Lief[w] & Nathaniel Lief[w] & Muriel Pollock[m] *(Shubert)*. This revue tried out as *Well Well Well*. With bad reviews, it was recast and revised and opened on Broadway as *Pleasure Bound*. It lasted only four months. COVER: man and woman in elegant clothes.

2437 West Side Story (Broadway, 1957). Larry Kert, Carol Lawrence.

A-me-ri-ca / America (show version) [VS] / Cool (show version) [VS] / Gee, Officer Krupkee / Gee, Officer Krupke (show version) [VS] / I Feel Pretty (show version) [VS] / Maria (show version) [VS] / One Hand (show version) [VS] / One Hand, One Heart / Something's Coming / Something's Coming (show version) [VS] / Somewhere / Somewhere (show version) [VS] / Tonight (show version) [VS] / West Side Story—complete vocal score—Stephen Sondheim[w] & Leonard Bernstein[m] *(Schirmer)*; Cool / I Feel Pretty / Maria / Tonight—Stephen Sondheim[w] & Leonard Bernstein[w] & Leonard Bernstein[m] *(Schirmer)*; West Side

Story—four movements (Jets, Cha Cha, Cool, Jump)—Leonard Bernstein[m] *(Schirmer)*. A musical version of the Romeo and Juliet story set in contemporary New York pitting native Americans against Puerto Ricans. It was not a major hit when it opened but has since become a classic. It had a dramatic book, wonderful score, and excellent dancing but ran only two years. Bernstein and Sondheim each helped on the music and lyrics but each relinquished his credits for sole credit as either composer or lyricist. Early sheet music shows Bernstein as co-lyricist but none show Sondheim as co-composer. COVER: Carol Lawrence and Larry Kert running down the street.

2438 West Side Story (Broadway, 1980). Debbie Allen, Ken Marshall.

West Side Story—vocal selections of eight songs (1980)—Stephen Sondheim[w] & Leonard Bernstein[m] *(Schirmer)*. A revival of the hit musical that ran for nine months. COVER: a silhouette of a group of dancers.

2439 Wet and Dry (closed before Broadway, 1920). Kolb and Dill.

Beautiful Garden of Day Dreams / Everybody in the Town Is Sober Since My Cellar Went Dry / I'm Glad He's Irish / Let's Pretend / Love's Bouquet / Pickaninny Sam—Jean Havez[w/m] *(Remick)*. COVER: flowers and designs.

2440 What a Day! (*see also* **Great to Be Alive!**) (Broadway, 1950). Vivienne Segal, Mark Dawson.

Blue Day / Call It Love / Dreams Ago / It's a Long Time Till Tomorrow / What a Day!—Walter Bullock[w] & Abraham Ellstein[m] *(Chappell)*. A hopeless musical about a haunted mansion that lasted for four weeks. It was called *What a Day!* during try-out. COVER: sketch of a house and dancing people.

2441 What Girls Do (Jewish, 1935). Molly Picon, Muni Serebrov.

Just Say When—Jacob Jacobs[w] & Alexander Olshanetsky[m] *(Metro)*. COVER: Molly Picon.

2442 What Makes Sammy Run? (Broadway, 1963). Steve Lawrence, Sally Ann Howes.

Bachelor Gal / The Friendliest Thing / Maybe Some Other Time / My Home Town / A New Pair of Shoes / Paint a Rainbow / A Room Without Windows / Some Days Everything Goes Wrong / Something to Live For / A Tender Spot / You're No Good—Ervin Drake[w/m] *(Harms)*. A musical about a ruthless movie producer that became a moderate hit because of Steve Lawrence and some hit songs. It ran for 15 months but closed when Lawrence started missing performances. COVER: man in dinner jacket with voluptuous showgirl.

2443 What Next (closed before Broadway, 1920). Stars unknown.

Jibber Jabber Jazz—Annelu Burns[w] & Madelyn Sheppard[m] *(Stern)*. A musical advertised for the Princess Theatre in N.Y. that never made it. COVER: beautiful show girl in showy gown with her suitors and roses.

2444 What's in a Name (Broadway, 1920). Allen Kearns, Frank Parker.

How Do They Get That Way?—Grace Doro[w/m] *(Remick)*; In Fair Japan / In the Year of Fifty-Fifty / The Jewels of Pandora / My Bridal Veil / Rap Tap, a Tap / Strike! / That Reminiscent Melody / Valley of Dreams / What's in a Name? / Without Kissing, Love Isn't Love / A Young Man's Fancy—John Murray Anderson[w] & Jack Yellen[w] & Milton Ager[m] *(Feist)*. An ordinary revue noted for its great sets and costumes. It ran only 11 weeks. COVER: girl in flowing gown and gentleman in top hat and tuxedo.

2445 What's the Odds (*see also* **Honey Girl**) (Broadway, 1920). Lynne Overman, Edna Bates.

Close to Your Heart / I Love to Fox Trot / I'm Losing My Heart to Someone Else / Rainbow of Love / You're Just the Boy for Me—Neville Fleeson[w] & Albert Von Tilzer[m] *(Art Music)*. A musical about horse racing that had everything going for it but lasted only four months. It was called *What's the Odds* during the try-out but opened as *Honey Girl*. COVER: Edna Bates in racing outfit.

2446 What's Up (Broadway, 1943). Jimmy Savo, Johnny Morgan.

Joshua / My Last Love / You Wash and I'll Dry / You've Got a Hold on Me — Alan Jay Lerner[w] & Frederick Loewe[m] *(Crawford)*. A musical about a foreign ruler visiting the U.S. This was the first collaboration of Lerner and Loewe and it lasted two months. COVER: two aviators and two girls strolling.

2447 When Summer Comes (closed before Broadway, 1925). James Barton, Luella Gear.

I Ain't Got Nothin' Now — Billy Baskette[w/m] *(Waterson)*; I'm Lonesome for Someone Like You / When Summer Comes — Jack Arnold[w] & A. Baldwin Sloane[m] *(Witmark)*. COVER: James Barton; sketch of Southern plantation.

2448 When You Smile (Broadway, 1925). Imogene Coca, Jack Whiting.

June / When You Smile / Wonderful Yesterday — Phil Cook[w] & Tom Johnstone[m] *(Harms)*. A musical dealing with publishing. The show was so dreadful that it ran only six weeks. COVER: flowers and designs.

2449 Where Poppies Bloom (Broadway, 1918). Marjorie Rambeau, Percival Knight.

Where Poppies Bloom — Alex Sullivan[w] & Lynn Cowan[m] *(Berlin)*. A melodrama dealing with the war that ran for three months. COVER: Marjorie Rambeau and soldier.

2450 Where's Charley (Broadway, 1958). Ray Bolger, Allyn Ann McLerie.

Lovelier Than Ever / Make a Miracle / New Ashmolean Marching Society and Students Conservatory Band / Once in Love with Amy / The Years Before Us (choral arrangement) / Where's Charley? — complete vocal score — Frank Loesser[w/m] *(Frank)*; My Darling, My Darling / Pernambuco / Where's Charley — Frank Loesser[w/m]

(Morris). A hit musical that ran for two years with several hit songs and Ray Bolger. COVER: Ray Bolger.

2451 Whirl of New York of 1921 (*see also* The Belle of New York of 1921) (Broadway, 1921). Harold Murray, Smith and Dale.

Cora Angelique / I Know That I'm in Love — Sidney Mitchell[w] & Lew Pollack[m] & Alfred Goodman[m] *(Remick)*; Gee, I Wish I Had a Girl Like You — Cliff Friend[w] & Lew Pollack[m] & Al Goodman[m] *(Remick)*; Molly on a Trolley — William Jerome[w] & Jean Schwartz[m] *(Witmark)*; One Last Good Time — Cyrus Wood[w] & Lew Pollack[m] & Alfred Goodman[m] *(Remick)*; They'll Be Whistling It All Over Town — Ray Goetz[w] & Jean Schwartz[m] *(Witmark)*. A girl's life alone in New York was the topic of this show. It had a run of three months and was called *Belle of New York* in tryout. COVER: Salvation Army girl.

2452 Whirl of the Town (closed before Broadway, 1921). Jack Strouse.

Anna in Indiana — Billy Gorman[w/m] & Eddie Gorman[w/m] & Harry Rose[w/m] *(Broadway)*; Any Night on Old Broadway — Harold Atteridge[w] & Jean Schwartz[m] *(Remick)*; C-H-I-C-A-G-O / You Tickle Me — Sidney Clare[w] & Lew Pollack[m] *(Remick)*; How'd You Like to Put Your Head Upon My Pillow — Alfred Bryan[w] & Jean Schwartz[m] *(Remick)*. COVER: a dancing ballerina with flowers.

2453 The Whirlwind (Broadway, 1919). Mimi Aguglia, Orrin Johnson.

When Night Comes Stealing — Carrier Worrell[w/m] & J.J. Scholl[w/m] *(Remick)*. A melodrama about a Mexican maid and an American soldier that had a short run. COVER: Mimi Aguglia.

2454 Whispers of 1924 (Regional, 1924). Mae Desmond.

In My Chateau of Love / Mae Dear / Make Love to Me / Polly / Tapestry Maid — Kenneth Burton[w/m] *(B and F)*. COVER: Mae Desmond.

2455 Whispers of 1926 (Regional, 1926).

In the Heart of My Garden / Land of Love / May Say Maybe / Same Old Moon — Kenneth Burton[w/m] *(B and F)*. COVER: Mae Desmond.

2456 White Eagle (Broadway, 1927). Marion Keeler, Allan Prior.

Alone / Gather the Rose / Give Me One Hour / A Home for You / Regimental Song / Silver Wing / Smile, Darn You, Smile! — Brian Hooker[w] & Rudolf Friml[m] *(Mills)*. A musical about a rancher and his Indian girlfriend. It had a terrible book and poor score and lasted six weeks. COVER: a large eagle.

2457 White Horse Inn (Broadway, 1936). Kitty Carlisle, William Gaxton.

Blue Eyes — Irving Caesar[w] & Robert Stolz[m] *(Harms)*; Goodbye — Irving Caesar[w] & Eric Coates[m] *(Chappell)*; I Cannot Live Without Your Love / The White Horse Inn — Irving Caesar[w] & Ralph Benatzky[m] *(Harms)*; I Would Love to Have You Love Me — Irving Caesar[w/m] & Sammy Lerner[w/m] & Gerard Marks[w/m] *(Chappell)*; In a Little Swiss Chalet — Norman Zeno[w] & Will Irwin[m] *(Chappell)*; Leave It to Katarina — Irving Caesar[w] & Jara Benes[m] *(Chappell)*; The Waltz of Love — Irving Caesar[w] & Richard Fall[m] *(Chappell)*; White Sails — Irving Caesar[w] & Vivian Ellis[m] *(Chappell)*. An operetta from Germany and England with a lavish production and a run of six months. COVER: the White Horse Inn.

2458 White Lights #1 *(see also* **Ritzie** *and* **White Lights #2**) (Broadway, 1927). Stars unknown.

Better Times Are Coming / Deceiving Bluebird / Carpet of Green / Quivering Step / Some Other Day / The Wine of Life Is Love — Dolph Singer[w] & Jimmie Steiger[m] *(Shapiro, Bernstein)*. This musical opened out of town as *White Lights* and folded. It was totally revised and recast and toured as *Ritzie*. For the Broadway opening, the title was again changed back to *White Lights*. It lasted four weeks. COVER: girl in gown surrounded by flowers.

2459 White Lights #2 *(see also* **White Lights #1** *and* **Ritzie**) (Broadway, 1927). Rosalie Claire, Sam Ash.

Don't Throw Me Down / Eyeful of You / Romany Rover / Show Girl / Sitting in the Sun / Tappin' the Toe / White Lights — Al Dubin[w] & Fred Coots[m] *(Marks)*; I'll Keep On Dreaming of You — Fred Coots[w/m] & Al Dubin[w/m] & Walter Rode[w/m] *(Marks)*. This musical started out as *White Lights*, changed to *Ritzie,* and then changed back to *White Lights*. It lasted four weeks on Broadway. COVER: playgirl with cigarette holder on playboy's shoulder.

2460 White Lilacs *(see also* **The Charmer** *and* **Chopin**) (Broadway, 1928). Odette Myrtil, Guy Robertson.

Adorable You — David Goldberg[w] & Maurie Rubens[m] *(Harms)*; Don't Go Too Far Girls / Far Away and Long Ago / I Love You and I Adore You — Harry B. Smith[w] & Karl Hajos[m] *(Harms)*; Lonely Heart / Our Little Castle of Love — J. Keirn Brennan[w] & Sam Timberg[m] *(Harms)*; Melodies Within My Heart / White Lilacs — J. Keirn Brennan[w] & Karl Hajos[m] *(Harms)*; My Dream Comes True — Harry B. Smith[w] & Karl Hajos[m] *(Harms)*. A musical about George Sand and Frederic Chopin that toured as *The Charmer* and as *Chopin* and opened as *White Lilacs* for a run of four months. COVER: a house, trees, and flowers.

2461 Who Is Guilty? (Jewish, 1944). Lillian Lux, Paul Burstein.

Got Hit Op Mein Bashertn — Louis Markowitz[w] & Ilia Trilling[m] *(Metro)*. COVER: Lillian Lux and Paul Burstein.

2462 Who Stole the Hat (Army, 1918). Soldiers.

All Aboard for Home Sweet Home — Addison Burkhart[w] & Al Piantadosi[m] & Jack Glogau[m] *(Piantadosi)*; My Salvation Army Girl — Jack Mason[w] & Al Piantadosi[m] *(Piantadosi)*; They Are the Stars in the Service Flag — Jack Mason[w] & Al Piantadosi[w] & Jack Glogau[m] *(Piantadosi)*. A show produced in Aberdeen, Maryland. COVER: a Salvation Army girl; military leaders.

2463 Whoop-Up (Broadway, 1958). Susan Johnson, Paul Ford.

The Best of What This Country's Got / Caress Me, Possess Me, Perfume / Chief Rocky Boy / Flattery / The Girl in Your Arms / Glenda's Place / I Wash My Hands / Love Eyes / Men / Montana / Never Before / Nobody Throw Those Bull / Quarrel-tet / Sorry for Myself / Till the Big Fat Moon Falls Down / What I Mean to Say / When the Tall Man Talks — Norman Gimbel[w] & Moose Charlap[m] *(Saunders)*. A musical set on an Indian reservation. Though panned by all the critics, it did, however, have some good songs and comedy and was not all that bad. COVER: fancy letters and Indian bonnet.

2464 Whoopee (Broadway, 1928). Eddie Cantor, Ruth Etting.

Big Hearted Baby — Raymond Egan[w] & Phil Philips[m] *(Finck)*; Come West, Little Girl, Come West / Gypsy Joe / Gypsy Song / Here's to the Girl of My Heart / I'm Bringing a Red Red Rose / Love Me or Leave Me / Makin' Whoopee! / The Song of the Setting Sun / Until You Get Somebody Else — Gus Kahn[w] & Walter Donaldson[m] *(Donaldson)*; Ever Since the Movies Learned to Talk — Walter O'Keefe[w/m] & Bob Dolan[w/m] & James Cavanaugh[w/m] *(Shapiro, Bernstein)*; Everything I Do, I Do for You — Al Sherman[w/m] & Abner Silver[w/m] & Al Lewis[w/m] *(Shapiro, Bernstein)*; Hungry Women — Jack Yellen[w] & Milton Ager[m] *(A Y and B)*; I Faw Down an' Go Boom — James Brockman[w/m] & Leonard Stevens[w/m] & B.B.B.[w/m] *(Donaldson)*; If I Give Up the Saxophone — Sammy Fain[w/m] & Irving Kahal[w/m] & Willie Raskin[w/m] *(D B and H)*; I'm on the Verge of a Merger — Eddie Cantor[w] & Ralph Rainger[m] *(Harms)*; Just a Little Bit o' Driftwood — Benny Davis[w/m] & Dohl Davis[w/m] & Abe Lyman[w/m] *(Robbins)*; Maybe! Who Knows? — Johnny Tucker[w/m] & Joe Schuster[w/m] & Ruth Etting[w/m] *(Witmark)*; My Blackbirds Are Bluebirds Now — Irving Caesar[w] & Cliff Friend[m] *(Feist)*; My Wife Is on a Diet — Charles Tobias[w/m] & George Bennett[w/m] *(Shapiro, Bernstein)*. A musical about a shy guy who elopes and goes to the West. Ziegfeld gave it a lavish production, plus it had a wonderful score with several hit songs and girls. It was still going strong after six months but Sam Goldwyn, who bought the rights, closed it to make the movie with Cantor. COVER: girl on horseback with a red rose.

2465 Whoopee (Broadway, 1979). Charles Repole, Beth Austin.

I'm Bringing a Red Red Rose [VS] / The Song of the Setting Sun [VS] / That Certain Party [VS] / Until You Get Somebody Else [VS] — Gus Kahn[w] & Walter Donaldson[m] *(Schirmer)*; Love Me or Leave Me / Makin' Whoopee! / My Baby Just Cares for Me / Yes Sir, That's My Baby — Gus Kahn[w] & Walter Donaldson[m] *(Donaldson)*; Out of the Dawn [VS] — Walter Donaldson[w/m] *(Schirmer)*; You — Harold Adamson[w] & Walter Donaldson[m] *(United Artists)*. A revival of the hit from the Goodspeed Opera Company that lasted for six months. COVER: a boy and girl on a horse.

2466 Who's Who (Broadway, 1938). Imogene Coca, Rags Ragland.

The Girl with the Paint on Her Face — Irvin Graham[w/m] *(Mills)*; I Dance Alone / I Must Have a Dinner Coat — James Shelton[w/m] *(Mills)*; It's You I Want — Paul McGrane[w/m] & Al Stillman[w/m] *(Mills)*; Let Your Hair Down with a Bang — June Sillman[w] & Baldwin Bergersen[m] *(Mills)*; Rinka Tinka Man — Lew Kessler[w/m] & June Sillman[w/m] *(Mills)*; Train Time / You're the Hit of the Season — June Sillman[w/m] & Baldwin Bergersen[w/m] *(Mills)*. A dreadful revue that lasted three weeks. COVER: sketches of goofy faces.

2467 Why Not of 1922 (closed be- ̄ ̄ Broadway, 1922). Stars unknown.

Let's Pretend — Jacquelyn Green[w] & Richard Myers[m] *(Green, Myers)*. COVER: girl in evening gown.

2468 Why Not of 1925 (closed before Broadway, 1925). Stars unknown.
Good-Bye — Jacquelyn Green[w] & Cooper Paul[m] *(Squires)*. COVER: designs and lettering.

2469 Wild Oats (British, 1938). Sydney Howard, Arthur Riscoe.
If I Can't Sing, I've Got to Dance — Harry Woods[w/m] *(Mills)*. A rags-to-riches musical that was a London hit for nine months and had songs published in the U.S. COVER: a sprig of wild oats.

2470 The Wild Rose (Broadway, 1926). Joseph Santley, Inez Courtney.
Brown Eyes / Love Me, Don't You? / One Golden Hour / We'll Have a Kingdom / Wild Rose — Otto Harbach[w] & Oscar Hammerstein[w] & Rudolf Friml[m] *(Hammerstein)*. A musical about a man who breaks the bank at Monte Carlo. The musical was very poor and ran only two months. COVER: buildings, flowers, and the sky.

2471 Wildcat (Broadway, 1960). Lucille Ball, Keith Andes.
Angelina / Give a Little Whistle / Hey, Look Me Over / One Day We Dance / El Sombrero [PC] / Tall Hope / What Takes My Fancy / Wildcat — complete vocal score / You're Far Away from Home / You've Come Home — Carolyn Leigh[w] & Cy Coleman[m] *(Morris)*. A musical set in the oil country with a pleasant score. After six months of going strong, Lucille Ball left for California and the show closed. COVER: Lucille Ball.

2472 The Wildflower (Broadway, 1923). Edith Day, Guy Robertson.
April Blossoms / Bambalina / Good Bye Little Rosebud / I Can Always Find Another Partner / I Love You, I Love You, I Love You! / If I Told You / Wild Flower / Wildflower — complete score / You Never Can Blame a Girl for Dreaming — Otto Harbach[w] & Oscar Hammerstein[w] & Herbert Stothart[m] & Vincent Youmans[m] *(Harms)*. An old fashioned operetta about a girl and her inheritance. With a good score and a poor book, it ran for over a year on Broadway. COVER: flowers and designs.

2473 Will Morrissey's Newcomers (Broadway, 1923). Al Fields, Frank Gaby.
Covered Wagon Days / Down on Panga Panga Bay / Peacock Strut / Washington Strut — Will Morrissey[w/m] & Joe Burrowes[w/m] *(Berlin)*. A revue of new talent that lasted two weeks. COVER: the stork delivering a baby surrounded by sketches of comedians.

2474 Will-o'-the-Whispers (British, 1928). Stars unknown.
I Never Dreamt You'd Fall in Love with Me — Donovan Parsons[w] & Vivian Ellis[m] *(Santly Bros.–Joy)*. A successful revue that had one song published in the U.S. COVER: Gladys Rice, singer.

2475 The Will Rogers Follies (Broadway, 1991). Keith Carradine, Dick Latessa.
The Big Time [VS] / Favorite Son [VS] / Give a Man Enough Rope [VS] / It's a Boy [VS] / Look Around / Marry Me Now [VS] / My Big Mistake [VS] / My Unknown Someone [VS] / Never Met a Man I Didn't Like / No Man Left for Me [VS] / Willamania [VS] — Betty Comden[w] & Adolph Green[w] & Cy Coleman[m] *(Warner Bros.)*. A musical about the life of Will Rogers that ran for over two years due to the staging of Tommy Tune. COVER: cartoon of cowboy hat with red lips inside.

2476 The Willow Plate (Broadway, 1924). Tony Sarg Marionettes.
The Willow Plate — five themes — Victor Herbert[m] *(Harms)*. A background score for a marionette play performed for a limited run. COVER: black and white cover with titles only.

2477 The Wind Blows Free (closed before Broadway, 1959). Stars unknown.
Douglas Mountain [VS] / Where Do You Go? [VS] — Arnold Sundgaard[w] & Alec Wilder[m] *(Hampshire)*. A musical

that tried out on the summer circuit. COVER: Alec Wilder.

2478 Windy City (closed before Broadway, 1946). Al Shean, Frances Williams.

As the Wind Bloweth / Don't Ever Run Away from Love / Where Do We Go from Here — Paul F. Webster[w] & Walter Jurman[m] *(Chappell)*. This musical involved a gambler and his problems in Chicago, wherein it also folded. COVER: the skyline of Chicago, with the elevated train and people below.

2479 Winged Victory (Military, 1943). Barry Nelson, Karl Malden.

My Dream Book of Memories / Winged Victory — David Rose[w/m] *(B V and C)*. An Army–Air Force show that toured the country raising money for war relief. COVER: airplanes and the Air Force insignia.

2480 Wings of War (Army, 1944). Soldiers.

Wings of War — James Herbert[w] & Ferde Grofe[m] *(Robbins)*. A song from a revue which toured the country during the 5th War Loan Drive. COVER: plain cover with titles only.

2481 The Winter's Tale (Regional, 1958). John Colicos, Inga Swenson.

Shepherd's Song [VS] / Vendor's Song [VS] — William Shakespeare[w] & Marc Blitzstein[m] *(Schirmer)*; Song of the Glove [VS] — Ben Jonson[w] & Marc Blitzstein[m] *(Schirmer)*. These songs were written for a summer production at the American Shakespeare Festival in Stratford, Conn. COVER: titles only.

2482 A Wise Child (closed before Broadway, 1921). Vivienne Segal.

Baby Blue / My Dear Old Daddie / Oh Joy / The Roses Say You Will — Rida Johnson Young[w] & William Schroeder[m] *(Harms)*. COVER: flowers and designs.

2483 Wish You Were Here (Broadway, 1952). Jack Cassidy, Florence Henderson.

Could Be / Don Jose of Far Rockaway / Everybody Love Everybody / Flattery / Glimpse of Love / Relax /

Shopping Around / Summer Afternoon / There's Nothing Nicer Than People / They Won't Know Me / Tripping the Light Fantastic / Where Did the Night Go? / Wish You Were Here / Wish You Were Here — complete vocal score — Harold Rome[w/m] *(Chappell)*. A musical about a summer camp with a pleasant score and talented people. Most of the reviews were unfavorable but the hit recording of the title song and the onstage swimming pool kept the show running for 18 months. COVER: boy and girl in bathing suits.

2484 The Wishing Well (closed before Broadway, 1929). Harriet Bennett, Reginald Dandy.

I Love You / Love of Mine / The Time for Dreams — Peter Gawthorne[w] & Harold Garstin[m] *(Harms)*. An import from England that folded in San Francisco. COVER: a wishing well and a tree.

2485 Without Rhyme or Reason (closed before Broadway, 1948). Stars unknown.

I Worry About You [PC] — Fred Hillebrand[w] & John Alton[m] *(Feist)*.

2486 The Wiz (Broadway, 1975). Stephanie Mills, Tiger Haynes.

Be a Lion / Don't Cry Girl / Don't Nobody Bring Me No Bad News [VS] / Ease On Down the Road / Everybody Rejoice / The Feeling We Once Had [VS] / He's the Wizard / Home / I Was Born on the Day Before Yesterday [VS] / If You Believe / I'm a Mean Old Lion [VS] / A Rested Body Is a Rested Mind / Slide Some Oil to Me [VS] / So You Wanted to See the Wizard / Soon as I Get Home [VS] / Tornado [VS] / What Would I Do If I Could Feel [VS] / Who, Who Do You Think You Are? [VS] / Y'All Got It [VS] — Charlie Smalls[w/m] *(Fox)*. A musical version of the *Wizard of Oz*. It was very ordinary and very overrated, but ran for four years. COVER: silhouette of a girl with flowing ribbons.

2487 Woman of the Year (Broadway, 1981). Lauren Bacall, Harry Guardino.

The Grass Is Always Greener [VS] / I Wrote the Book [VS] / One of the Girls / See You in the Funny Papers / Sometimes a Day Goes By / We're Gonna Work It Out / Woman of the Year [VS] — Fred Ebb[w] & John Kander[m] *(Fiddleback)*. A musical about career conflicts which was quite ordinary but kept on for two years by the stars. COVER: Lauren Bacall.

2488 The Wonder Bar (Broadway, 1931). Al Jolson, Patsy Kelly.

The Cantor — Traditional *(Harms)*; Elizabeth / Good Evening Friends / Something Seems to Tell Me — Irving Caesar[w] & Robert Katscher[m] *(Harms)*; Ev'ry Day Can't Be Sunday — Al Jolson[w/m] *(Remick)*; Lenox Avenue — Irving Caesar[w/m] & Al Jolson[w/m] & Joseph Meyer[w/m] *(Harms)*; Ma Mere — Al Jolson[w/m] & Irving Caesar[w/m] & Harry Warren[w/m] *(Harms)*; Oh, Donna Clara — Irving Caesar[w] & J. Petersburski[m] *(Harms)*; Trav'lin' All Alone — J.C. Johnson[w/m] *(Harms)*. A musical, set in a cabaret in Paris, that lasted only ten weeks. COVER: Al Jolson.

2489 Wonderful Girl (Broadway, 1928). Stars unknown.

Wonderful Girl — Joseph Santley[w] & Harry Ruskin[w] & Dave Stamper[m] *(Harms)*. A mini-musical presented by Paramount-Publix between showings of their movies in large theatres. COVER: silhouette of a lady in lace and jewels.

2490 A Wonderful Life (closed before Broadway, 1989). Stars unknown.

Christmas Gifts — Sheldon Harnick[w] & Joe Raposo[m] *(Warner Bros.)*. COVER: a gift wrapping.

2491 Wonderful Town (Broadway, 1953). Rosalind Russell, Edith Adams.

It's Love / It's Love (show version) [VS] / Little Bit in Love / Little Bit in Love (show version) [VS] / My Darlin' Eileen / My Darlin' Eileen (show version) [VS] / Ohio / Ohio (show version) [VS] / One Hundred Easy Ways (show version) [VS] / Pass That Football

(show version) [VS] / Quiet Girl / Quiet Girl (show version) [VS] / Swing / Swing (show version) [VS] / Wrong Note Rag / Wrong Note Rag (show version) [VS] — Betty Comden[w] & Adolph Green[w] & Leonard Bernstein[m] *(Chappell)*. *My Sister Eileen* set to music turned out to be a hit with a great production and score. It ran for 15 months. COVER: Rosalind Russell.

2492 Wonderworld (World's Fair, 1964). Chita Rivera, Gretchen Wyler.

Wonderworld — Stanley Styne[w] & Jule Styne[m] *(Chappell-Styne)*. A musical spectacle put on four times a day. COVER: a sketch of the Wonderworld set.

2493 Woof Woof (Broadway, 1929). Louise Brown, Eddie Nelson.

I Mean What I Say / Satanic Strut / That Certain Thing / Topple-Down / Why Didn't You Tell Me / Won't I Do — Edward Pola[w/m] & Eddie Brandt[w/m] *(Robbins)*. A musical about a girl seeking stardom. It was very bad and lasted only five weeks. COVER: four girls and a dog on a dog house.

2494 Words and Music (British, 1932). Graham Payn, John Mills.

Let's Say Goodbye [B] / Love and War [B] / Mad About the Boy [B] / Mad Dogs and Englishmen [B] / The Party's Over Now [B] / Something to Do with Spring [B] / Three White Feathers [B] / Words and Music — complete vocal score [B] / The Younger Generation [B] — Noel Coward[w/m] *(Chappell)*. A musical revue that became a hit in London and ran for six months. In New York it was called *Set to Music*. COVER: black and white cover with titles.

2495 Working (Broadway, 1978). Rex Everhart, Arny Freeman.

All the Livelong Day [VS] — Walt Whitman[w] & Stephen Schwartz[m] *(Valando)*; Brother Trucker [VS] / Millwork [VS] — James Taylor[w/m] *(Valando)*; Cleanin' Women [VS] / If I Could've Been [VS] / Lovin' Al [VS] — Micki Grant[w/m] *(Valando)*; Fathers and Sons [VS] / It's an Art [VS] / Neat to Be a Newsboy [VS] — Stephen Schwartz[w/m] *(Valando)*; Joe [VS] / Just a Housewife [VS] / Mason [VS] / Something to Point Out [VS] — Craig Carnelia[w/m] *(Valando)*; Nobody Tells Me How [VS] — Susan Birkenhead[w] & Mary Rodgers[m] *(Valando)*; Un Mejor Dia Lendra [VS] — Graciela Daniele[w] & Matt Landers[w] & James Taylor[m] *(Valando)*. A musical portrait of working people that lasted three weeks. COVER: a sketch of people working.

2496 The World of Charles Aznavour (Broadway, 1970). Charles Aznavour.

Yesterday, When I Was Young — Herbert Kretzmer[w] & Charles Aznavour[m] *(T R O)*. A limited three week engagement of French songs of Aznavour at the Music Box Theatre. COVER: Roy Clark, singer.

2497 The World of Jules Feiffer (closed before Broadway, 1962). Ronny Graham, Dorothy Loudon.

Truly Content [VS] — Stephen Sondheim[w/m] *(Revelation)*. A comedy revue that tried out on the summer circuit. COVER: Stephen Sondheim.

2498 World of Pleasure (closed before Broadway, 1925). Stars unknown.

Cinderella / Make Up Your Mind / Midsummer Night's Dream — Mack Gordon[w] & Anton Scibilia[w] & George Wiest[m] *(Marks)*. COVER: a globe surrounded by girls and clowns.

2499 The World of Suzie Wong (Broadway, 1958). William Shatner, France Nuyen.

How Can You Forget? — Lorenz Hart[w] & Richard Rodgers[m] *(Harms)*. A hit drama about an Oriental prostitute. COVER: Suzie Wong.

2500 World's Fair 1939 (Regional, 1939). Stars unknown.

For Peace and Freedom — Eugene La Barre[w/m] *(Worlds Fair Co.)*; Meet Me at the New York World's Fair — Bob Randolph[w] & Joseph Howard[m] *(Paull-Pioneer)*; Rising Tide — Al Stillman[w] & William Still[m] *(Fischer)*. These were the two theme songs of the 1939-1940 N.Y. World's Fair. COVER: the

perisphere and the trylon.

2501 World's Fair 1962 (Regional, 1962). Stars unknown.

The World of Tomorrow! — Edward Heyman[w] & Morton Gould[m] *(G and C)*. This was the theme song of the 1962 fair in Seattle. COVER: a high tower and a monorail.

2502 World's Fair 1964 (Regional, 1964). Stars unknown.

Fun at the Fair — theme / Pavilions of Industry — theme — Ferde Grofe[m] *(Robbins)*. COVER: an open globe with the world's countries.

2503 A Yankee at the Court of King Arthur (British, 1929). Stars unknown.

I Feel at Home with You [B] / On a Desert Island with You [B] / Thou Swell [B] — Lorenz Hart[w] & Richard Rodgers[m] *(Chappell)*. This musical, which was a hit in the U.S., was a failure in London lasting only five weeks. COVER: green and white lettering with titles only.

2504 Yankee Doodle (closed before Broadway, 1929). Arthur Geary, Olga Steck.

Ballydrockin [ABQ] / Dreams [ABQ] / Drum Song [ABQ] / I Believe in You / The Jolly Roger / Lady Fair [ABQ] / Souvenir / Teeny Weeny Bit / Yankee Doodle [ABQ] — Shafter Howard[w/m] *(Marks)*. This patriotic musical folded in Philadelphia. COVER: the Yankee-Doodle with fife and drums.

2505 Yankee Princess (Broadway, 1922). Vivienne Segal, John T. Murray.

Forbidden Fruit / I Still Can Dream / In the Starlight / My Bajadere / Roses, Lovely Roses / The Waltz Is Made for Love — B.G. DeSylva[w] & Emmerich Kalman[m] *(Harms)*. An American actress and an Indian Rajah were the subjects of this ten week failure. COVER: red, white, and blue shield and letters.

2506 The Yearling (Broadway, 1965). David Hartman, Carmen Alvarez.

Boy Thoughts [VS] / Everything in the World [VS] / Growing Up Is Learning to Say Goodbye [VS] / I'm All Smiles / Kind of Man a Woman Needs

[VS] / My Pa (My Love) [VS] / One Promise Come True [VS] / Someday I'm Gonna Fly [VS] / Spring Is a New Beginning [VS] / Why Did I Choose You? — Herbert Martin[w] & Michael Leonard[m] *(Morris)*. This was a musical about a boy and his fawn. Though it lasted only three days, it produced several hit songs. COVER: a fawn.

2507 The Yellow Mask (British, 1928). Bobby Howes, Phyllis Dare.

The Bacon and the Egg [B] / Deep Sea [B] / I Love You So [B] / I Still Believe in You [B] / I'm Wonderful [B] / You Do, I Don't [B] — Desmond Carter[w] & Vernon Duke[m] *(A H and C)*; Blowing the Blues Away [B] / Half a Kiss [B] — Eric Little[w] & Vernon Duke[m] *(A H and C)*; Chinese Ballet (B piano selections) [B] / Chinese March [B] / March [B] / Opening Chorus Act One [B] / Walking on Air (B piano selections) [B] / Yellow Mask [B] — Vernon Duke[m] *(A H and C)*; Mary [B] — Laddie Cliff[w] & Desmond Carter[w] & Harry Acres[m] *(A H and C)*. A musical about a Chinaman and a stolen jewel. With an average score, it ran for six months. COVER: a large yellow mask.

2508 Yes, Yes, Yvette (Broadway, 1927). Jeanette MacDonald, Jack Whiting.

Do You Love as I Love? — Irving Caesar[w] & Joseph Meyer[m] *(Harms)*; For Days and Days / Six O' Clock — Irving Caesar[w] & Philip Charig[m] *(Harms)*; Good Morning / I'm a Little Fonder of You / Sing, Dance and Smile / You, or Nobody — Irving Caesar[w/m] *(Harms)*; How'd You Like To? — Irving Caesar[w] & Stephen Jones[m] *(Harms)*; Maybe I Will — Irving Caesar[w] & Harold Orlob[m] *(Harms)*; My Lady — Frank Crummit[w/m] & Ben Jerome[w/m] *(Harms)*; Pack Up Your Blues and Smile — Jo Trent[w] & Peter DeRose[m] & Albert Von Tilzer[m] *(Harms)*; The Two of Us — Van Phillips[w/m] & Jimmy Campbell[w/m] & Reg Connelly[w/m] *(Harms)*. This musical involved a bet to tell the truth. It was a Chicago hit but a N.Y. failure

of five weeks. COVER: flowers and designs.

2509 Yesterday (closed before Broadway, 1919). Stars unknown.

Bebe / The Clown / It Isn't the Same in the Daylight / It's Paris Everywhere / A Man's Forever / The Montebanks March / My Yesterday / Phantom Rose — Glen MacDonough[w] & Reginald DeKoven[m] *(Witmark)*. COVER: a ballroom scene and a crowd before a church.

2510 Yip, Yip, Yahank (Army, 1918). Irving Berlin, Sammy Lee.

Bevo / Ding Dong / Dream On Little Soldier Boy / Ever Since I Put On a Uniform (not published) / I Can Always Find a Little Sunshine in the YMCA / Kitchen Police / Ladies of the Chorus [VS] / Mandy (Sterling Silver Moon) / Oh, How I Hate to Get Up in the Morning / Ragtime Razor Brigade / Send a Lot of Jazz Bands Over There / We're on Our Way to France — Irving Berlin[w/m] *(Berlin)*. A show with some classic Berlin songs. It had a limited run of four weeks before soldiers were shipped to France. COVER: soldiers.

2511 Yoicks! (British, 1924). Mary Leigh, Richard Dolman.

Forbidden Fruit (Every Little Peach) [B] — Noel Coward[w/m] *(Chappell)*. This was Noel Coward's first complete song with lyrics and music featured in a revue that lasted nine months. COVER: Noel Coward.

2512 Yokel Boy (Broadway, 1939). Buddy Ebsen, Judy Canova.

A Boy Named Lem / Comes Love / I Can't Afford to Dream / It's Me Again / Let's Make Memories Tonight / Uncle Sam's Lullaby — Lew Brown[w/m] & Charlie Tobias[w/m] & Sam Stept[w/m] *(Chappell)*; Time for Jukin' — Lew Brown[w/m] & Charlie Tobias[w/m] & Walter Kent[w/m] *(Chappell)*. A rise to stardom in Hollywood was the basis of this musical. It was quite ordinary but was kept alive for six months by its very talented cast and one hit song. COVER 1: states Jack Pearl, Buddy Ebsen, Judy Canova with a picture of Jack Pearl. COVER 2: states Buddy Ebsen, Judy Canova with no mention of Pearl or picture.

2513 Yo-San (closed before Broadway, 1920). Stars unknown.

Get In Your Overalls [ABQ] / I Shall Never Tell [ABQ] / Lantern Song / A Little Cup of Tea [ABQ] / Old Fashioned Sweetheart of Mine / Riding in a Ricksha / Sailors of Uncle Sam [ABQ / Stop Look and Listen [ABQ] / Tell Me Ouija [ABQ] / When You're Married [ABQ] / Yo-San [ABQ] — L.S. Bitner^w & R.L. Harlow^m *(B and H)*. COVER: Japanese lady with fan and cherry blossoms.

2514 Yo-San (*see also* **Cherry Blossoms**) (Broadway, 1927). Howard Marsh, Desiree Ellinger.

I've Waited for You / My Own Willow Tree / Someday / Tell Me Cigarette / Wait and See — Harry B. Smith^w & Sigmund Romberg^m *(Harms)*. An imitation of *Madama Butterfly* that folded fast. The try-out title was *Yo-San*. COVER: oriental designs and lettering.

2515 You Never Know (Broadway, 1938). Clifton Webb, Lupe Velez.

At Long Last Love / For No Rhyme or Reason / From Alpha to Omega / I'm Going In for Love [VS] [CUT] Maria / What Is That Tune? / What Shall I Do / You Never Know — Cole Porter^w/m *(Chappell)*; By Candelight — Rowland Leigh^w & Robert Katscher^m *(Chappell)*; No, You Can't Have My Heart — Dana Suesse^w/m *(Chappell)*. A dull musical with ordinary songs; it ran for ten weeks. COVER: lettering and designs. One set of covers is red and blue and one is pink and blue.

2516 You Said It (Broadway, 1931). Lyda Roberti, Benny Baker.

If He Really Loves Me / It's Different with Me / Learn to Croon / Sweet and Hot / What Do We Care? / While You Are Young / You Said It / You'll Do — Jack Yellen^w & Harold Arlen^m *(A Y and B)*. A college musical with Arlen's first full score. It was

nothing great, but it ran six months. COVER: a college girl with loudspeaker and boy in sweater.

2517 You'd Be Surprised (Broadway, 1920). Dorothy Fields, Phillip Leavitt.

A Breath of Springtime — Lorenz Hart^w & Richard Rodgers^m *(Harms)*; Princess of the Willow Tree / When We Are Married — Milton Bender^w & Richard Rodgers^m *(Harms)*. A musical that had a one performance run in the Plaza Hotel Grand Ballroom. COVER: black and white cover with title.

2518 You'll Like It (closed before Broadway, 1919). Stars unknown.

All Alone / There's a Reason / What Do You Mean? / When the First Girl You Love Says Goodbye — Joseph Burrowes^w/m & Al Brown^w/m *(Remick)*. COVER: a gentleman giving a lady a beautifully wrapped gift.

2519 You'll Never Know (College, 1921). Students of Columbia.

You'll Never Know — complete vocal score — Lorenz Hart^w & Richard Rodgers^m *(Harms)*. A college show for Columbia University for a limited run of four performances. COVER: black and white with titles only.

2520 Young Abe Lincoln (Broadway, 1961). Judy Foster, Dan Resin.

A Little Frog in a Little Pond / Someone You Know — Joan Javits^w & Victor Ziskin^m *(Fairway)*; Skip-Hop Dance — Arnold Sundgaard^w & Victor Ziskin^m *(Fairway)*. A musical about Abe Lincoln that had a moderate run. COVER: sketch of Abe Lincoln and crowd.

2521 Your Arms Too Short to Box with God (Broadway, 1976). Delores Hall, Salome Bey.

Your Arms Too Short to Box with God — vocal selections of 16 songs — Alex Bradford^w/m *(Blue Pearl)*. A black gospel musical that ran for several months. COVER: girl's face with hand up.

2522 Your Own Thing (Off Broadway, 1968). Leland Palmer, Russ Thacker.

Be Gentle [VS] / Come Away, Death

[VS] / Don't Leave Me [VS] / The Flowers [VS] / I'm Me [VS] / I'm Not Afraid [VS] / I'm on My Way to the Top [VS] / The Middle Years [VS] / The Now Generation [VS] / What Do I Know? / Young and in Love / Your Own Thing — Hal Hester^{w/m} & Danny Apolinar^{w/m} *(National General)*. Shakespeare's *Twelfth Night* set to music with a pleasant score and good book. Some talented people kept this musical running for two and one half years. COVER: sketch of a goofy looking character.

2523 You're a Good Man, Charlie Brown (Off Broadway, 1965). Gary Burghoff, Reva Rose.

Baseball Game [VS] / Book Report / The Doctor Is In [VS] / Happiness / The Kite [VS] / Little Known Facts [VS] / My Blanket and Me [VS] / Schroeder [VS] / Snoopy [VS] / Suppertime [VS] / You're a Good Man, Charlie Brown — Clark Gesner^{w/m} *(Jeremy)*. A musical based on the popular comic strip that ran for almost four years. COVER: Charlie Brown and Snoopy.

2524 You're Gonna Love Tomorrow (closed before Broadway, 1983). Stars unknown.

Isn't It [VS] — Stephen Sondheim^{w/m} *(Burthern)*. COVER: Stephen Sondheim.

2525 You're Some Girl (closed before Broadway, 1920). Stars unknown.

I Want the World to Know You're Mine — A. Seymour Brown^w & Alex Marr^m *(F-B and M)*. COVER: pretty girl.

2526 Yours Truly (Broadway, 1927). Irene Dunne, Leon Errol.

Don't Shake My Tree / Fearfully, Frightful Love / Jade / Look at the World and Smile / Lotus Flower / Somebody Else / Yours Truly — Anne Caldwell^w & Raymond Hubbell^m *(Harms)*. A musical about a rich girl and her father. Though not too good, it lasted three months due to the clowning of Leon Errol. COVER: colored designs.

2527 Yvonne (British, 1926). Ivy Tresmand, Hal Sherman.

Billing and Cooing [B] / Couceur de Rose [B] — Percy Greenbank^w & Jean Gilbert^m *(A H and C)*; Day Dreams [B] / It's Nicer to Be Naughty [B] / Lucky [B] / Magic of the Moon [B] / We Always Disagree [B] — Percy Greenbank^w & Vernon Duke^m *(A H and C)*; Tantalizing Toto [B] / Taxi for Two [B] / Teach Me to Dance [B] / What Does the Hot Water Say to the Cold? [B] — Percy Greenbank^w & Arthur Wood^m *(A H and C)*; Yvonne [B] — complete vocal score — Percy Greenbank^w & Vernon Duke^m & Jean Gilbert^m & Arthur Wood^m *(A H and C)*. A hit in London with a run of nine months. COVER: letters and designs.

2528 Zenda (closed before Broadway, 1963). Alfred Drake, Chita Rivera.

In This Life [VS] / Let Her Not Be Beautiful / The Night Is Filled with Wonderful Sounds — Martin Charnin^w & Vernon Duke^m *(Morris)*. A lavish production of the classic story produced by the San Francisco Civic Light Opera Company with an eye to Broadway. The show folded several months later in Pasadena. COVER: a flag with the name of Zenda.

2529 Ziegfeld Follies of 1918 (#12) (Broadway, 1918). Eddie Cantor, Marilyn Miller.

Any Old Time at All / In Old Versailles / Marriage of Convenience / The Ship Song / We Are the Follies / When I Hear a Syncopated Tune — Gene Buck^w & Louis Hirsch^m *(Witmark)*; Blue Devils of France / I'm Gonna Pin My Medal on the Girl I Left Behind / Oh! How I Hate to Get Up in the Morning — Irving Berlin^{w/m} *(Berlin)*; Broadway's Not a Bad Place After All — Harry Ruby^{w/m} & Eddie Cantor^{w/m} *(Berlin)*; But — After the Ball Was Over! / If She Means What I Think She Means — Arthur Jackson^{w/m} & B.G. DeSylva^{w/m} *(Remick)*; Come On Papa — Edgar Leslie^{w/m} & Harry Ruby^{w/m} *(Berlin)*; Frisco's Kitchen Stove Rag — Francis C. Reisner^w & Jimmie Morgan^m *(Fairman)*; Garden of My Dreams — Gene Buck^w & Louis

Hirsch^m & Dave Stamper^m *(Harms)*; I
Want to Learn to Jazz Dance /
Starlight / When I'm Looking at
You—Gene Buck^w & Dave Stamper^m
(Harms); Military Buck Dance—Jack
Blue^m *(Blue Co.)*; The Navy Will Bring
Them Back—Howard Johnson^w & Ira
Schuster^m *(Feist)*; Roaming Romeo—
Billy Duval^w & Jimmie Morgan^m
(Fairman); She Shook Her Head and
Said, Uh, Uh—Harold Orlob^w/m
(Plaza); Shine On Harvest Moon—
Jack Norworth^w/m & Nora Bayes^w/m
(Remick); Tackin' 'em Down—B.G.
DeSylva^w & Albert Gumble^m
(Remick); Would You Rather Be a
Chicken—Sidney Mitchell^w & Archie
Gottler^m *(Feist)*; You Can Tell That
He's an American—Howard Johnson^w
& Percy Wenrich^m *(Feist)*. A lavish
production that ran for five months.
The music was ordinary but the
talented cast kept it going. COVER: Ed-
die Cantor; beautiful girls; Frank
Carter; Lillian Lorraine.

2530 Ziegfeld Follies of 1919 (#13)
(Broadway, 1919). Eddie Cantor,
Marilyn Miller.

Bebe—Sam Coslow^w & Abner
Silver^m *(Witmark)*; Bevo / Harem Life
/ I'd Rather See a Minstrel Show / I'm
the Guy Who Guards the Harem /
Mandy / My Tambourine Girl / A
Pretty Girl Is Like a Melody / A Synco-
pated Cocktail / You Cannot Make
Your Shimmy Shake on Tea / You'd Be
Surprised—Irving Berlin^w/m *(Berlin)*;
The Dixie Volunteers—Edgar
Leslie^w/m & Harry Ruby^w/m *(Berlin)*;
Don't Take Advantage of My Good
Nature—Howard Rogers^w & James
Monaco^m *(Shapiro, Bernstein)*;
Johnny's in Town—Jack Yellen^w &
George Meyer^m & Abe Olman^m
(Feist); King Solomon—Maxwell
Sokolow^w/m & Dave Snell^w/m &
Chauncey Haines^w/m *(Hatch)*; Look
Out for the Bolsheviki Man—Irving
Berlin^w/m *(Harms)*; My Baby's
Arms—Joseph McCarthy^w & Harry
Tierney^m *(Feist)*; My Orchard of Girls
/ Shimmee Town / Sweet Sixteen /

Tulip Time—Gene Buck^w & Dave
Stamper^m *(Harms)*; Oh! The Last
Rose of Summer—Harry Ruby^w/m &
Eddie Cantor^w/m & Phil Ponce^w/m
(Berlin); Save Your Money, John—Les
Copeland^w/m & Alex Rogers^w/m *(Tri-
angle)*; Sweet Kisses—Lew Brown^w &
Eddie Buzzell^w & Albert Von Tilzer^m
(Broadway); They're All Sweeties—
Andrew Sterling^w & Harry Von
Tilzer^m *(Von Tilzer)*; When They're
Old Enough to Know Better—Sam
Lewis^w & Joe Young^w & Harry Ruby^m
(Berlin); You Don't Need the Wine to
Have a Wonderful Time—Howard
Rogers^w & Harry Akst^m *(M and F)*.
This edition of the Follies is regarded as
the finest edition in the series. The ur-
ban sets were outstanding, Marilyn
Miller, Eddie Cantor, and Bert
Williams were at their peak, and the
score was excellent with some hit songs.
It ran for over six months. COVER: Ed-
die Cantor; Van and Schenck;
beautiful girls.

2531 Ziegfeld Follies of 1920 (#14)
(Broadway, 1920). Fannie Brice, W.C.
Fields.

All She'd Say Was Umh-Hum—Mac
Emery^w/m & King Zany^w/m & Van and
Schenck^w/m *(Von Tilzer)*; Any Place
Would Be Wonderful with You / Mary
and Doug / Sunshine and Shadows—
Gene Buck^w/m & Dave Stamper^w/m
(Harms); Bells / Chinese Firecrackers /
Come Along / The Girls of My Dreams
/ I Live in Turkey / The Leg of Na-
tion's / The Syncopated Vamp / Tell
Me Little Gypsy—Irving Berlin^w/m
(Berlin); Desertland—Ethwell Han-
son^w/m *(Riviera)*; Every Blossom I See
Reminds Me of You—Eddie Can-
tor^w/m *(Harms)*; Everybody Tells It to
Sweeney—Sidney Mitchell^w & George
Fairman^m *(Berlin)*; Green River—
Eddie Cantor^w & Van and Schenck^m
(Van Schenck); Hold Me—Art
Hickman^w/m & Ben Black^w/m
(Remick); How'dja Like to Kiss Me
Goodnight, Baby—Edwin Gilbert^w &
John Shubert^w & Jean Schwartz^m
(Grobe); I Found a Baby on My Door

Step — Eddie Cantor^{w/m} *(Harms)*; I Saw You Last Night at the Sh...! / They're So Hard to Keep When They're Beautiful / When We Start a Family of Our Own / Where Do Mosquitos Go in the Wintertime — Joseph McCarthy^w & Harry Tierney^m *(Feist)*; I've Got the A-B-C-D Blues — George Kershaw^w & Harry Von Tilzer^m *(Von Tilzer)*; Love Boat / When the Right One Comes Along — Gene Buck^w & Victor Herbert^m *(Harms)*; Moon Shines on the Moonshine — Francis DeWitt^w & Robert Hood Bowers^m *(Shapiro, Bernstein)*; My Home Town Is a One Horse Town — Alex Gerber^w & Abner Silver^m *(Witmark)*; My Midnight Frolic Girl — Art Hickman^{w/m} & Ben Black^{w/m} *(Feist)*; Noah's Wife Lived a Wonderful Life — Jack Yellen^w & Roger Lewis^w & Ernie Erdman^m & Abe Olman^m *(Forster)*; O-H-I-O — Jack Yellen^w & Abe Olman^m *(Forster)*; Somebody Else — Ballard MacDonald^w & James Hanley^m *(Shapiro, Bernstein)*; Tia Juana — Joseph McCarthy^w & Jose Padilla^m & Harry Tierney^m *(Remick)*; Till I Met You — Ray Klages^{w/m} *(Graham)*. An entertaining if not outstanding edition of the Follies with its usual lavish sets and girls. It lasted three months with good comedy and pleasant songs. COVER: beautiful girls; John Steel; Bert Williams; Eddie Cantor; Van & Schenck; Delyle Alda.

2532 Ziegfeld Follies of 1921 (#15) (Broadway, 1921). Fanny Brice, Mary Eaton.

Ain't Nature Grand? / I Hold Her Hand and She Holds Mine — BillyRose^w & Ben Ryan^w & Irving Bibo^m *(Feist)*; Ain't You Coming Out Malinda? — Andrew Sterling^w & Edward Moran^w & Harry Von Tilzer^m *(Von Tilzer)*; Allay! Up! / I Know — Ballard MacDonald^w & James Hanley^m *(Shapiro, Bernstein)*; Anna in Indiana — Billy Gorman^{w/m} & Eddie Gorman^{w/m} & Harry Rose^{w/m} *(Broadway)*; Bring Back My Blushing Rose (two covers) / Everytime I Hear a Band Play (two covers) / Two Lovely Lying

Eyes (two covers) — Gene Buck^w & Rudolf Friml^m *(Harms)*; I Can't Resist Them (two covers) / Raggedy Rag (two covers) / Sally Won't You Come Back? (two covers) — Gene Buck^w & Dave Stamper^m *(Harms)*; In Khorassan (two covers) / Legend of the Golden Tree (two covers) / Princess of My Dreams (two covers) — Gene Buck^w & Victor Herbert^m *(Harms)*; In My Tippy Canoe — Fred Fisher^{w/m} *(Fisher)*; In That Little Irish Home Sweet Home — Billy Jerome^w & Harry Von Tilzer^m *(Von Tilzer)*; In the Old Town Hall — Harry Pease^{w/m} & Ed Nelson^{w/m} & Howard Johnson^{w/m} *(Feist)*; It Takes a Good Man to Do That — Jack Bayha^{w/m} & Chris Smith^{w/m} *(Stark, Cowan)*; My Man — Channing Pollock^w & Maurice Yvain^m *(Feist)*; O'Reilly — Elsie White^{w/m} & Harry Pease^{w/m} & Ed Nelson^{w/m} *(Feist)*; Our Home Town — Ballard MacDonald^w & Harry Carroll^m *(Shapiro, Bernstein)*; Plymouth Rock (two covers) — Channing Pollock^w & Dave Stamper^m *(Harms)*; Rosemary (two covers) / What a World This Would Be! (two covers) — B.G. DeSylva^w & Dave Stamper^m *(Harms)*; Roses and You — Gus Edwards^{w/m} & Will Cobb^{w/m} *(Shapiro, Bernstein)*; Roses in the Garden (two covers) — Brian Hooker^w & Rudolf Friml^m *(Harms)*; Second Hand Rose — Grant Clarke^w & James Hanley^m *(Shapiro, Bernstein)*; Strut Miss Lizzie — Henry Creamer^{w/m} & Turner Layton^{w/m} *(Jack Mills)*; Wang-Wang Blues — Leo Wood^w & Gus Mueller^m & Buster Johnson^m & Henry Busse^m *(Feist)*; While Miami Dreams — Raymond Egan^w & Richard Whiting^m *(Remick)*; You Must Come Over (two covers) — B.G. DeSylva^w & Jerome Kern^m *(Harms)*. This lavish production was the most expensive to date — $250,000. It still had great comedy and two hit songs and a run of three months. COVER: Van and Schenck; beautiful girls; Fanny Brice; girl with parrot.

2533 Ziegfeld Follies of 1922 (#16)

(Broadway, 1922). Gilda Gray, Will Rogers.

Come Along — Henry Creamer[w/m] & Turner Layton[w/m] *(Berlin)*; I Don't Know What I'll Do Without You / I Don't Want to Be in Dixie / It's Getting Dark on Old Broadway / List'ning on Some Radio / My Rambler Rose / 'Neath the South Sea Moon / Pep It Up / Sunny South — Louis Hirsch[w/m] & Gene Buck[w/m] & Dave Stamper[w/m] *(Harms)*; Oh, Mister Gallagher and Mister Shean (#1) / Oh, Mister Gallagher and Mister Shean (#2) — Ed Gallagher[w/m] & Al Shean[w/m] *(Jack Mills)*; Sing a Song of Swanee — Louis Breau[w/m] & Nat Sanders[w/m] *(Harms)*; Some Sweet Day — Dave Stamper[w/m] & Louis Hirsch[w/m] *(Harms)*; South Sea Eyes — Harry Akst[w/m] *(Richmond-Robbins)*; Throw Me a Kiss — Louis Hirsch[w/m] & Gene Buck[w/m] & Dave Stamper[w/m] & Maurice Yvain[w/m] *(Harms)*; Waiting for the Robert E. Lee — L. Wolfe Gilbert[w/m] & Lewis Muir[w/m] *(Gilbert)*; Weaving My Dreams — Gene Buck[w] & Victor Herbert[m] *(Harms)*. The last great edition of the Follies. It went downhill from then on. It was still a lavish spectacle with good comedy but the music was ordinary. This version ran for one year. COVER: beautiful girls; Gilda Gray; Al Shean and Ed Gallagher.

2534 Ziegfeld Follies of 1922 (summer edition) (#16) (Broadway, 1923). Evelyn Law, Gilda Gray.

If I Can't Get the Sweetie I Want — Joe Young[w] & Sam Lewis[w] & Jean Schwartz[m] *(Berlin)*; It's Getting Dark on Old Broadway / List'ning on Some Radio / My Rambler Rose / Neath the South Sea Moon / Nobody But You / Pep It Up / Some Sweet Day — Louis Hirsch[w/m] & Gene Buck[w/m] & Dave Stamper[w/m] *(Harms)*; Throw Me a Kiss — Maurice Yvain[w/m] & Louis Hirsch[w/m] & Gene Buck[w/m] & Dave Stamper[w/m] *(Harms)*; Weaving My Dreams — Gene Buck[w] & Victor Herbert[m] *(Harms)*. A slightly revised edition of the 1922 version. COVER: beautiful girls.

2535 Ziegfeld Follies of 1923 (#17) (Broadway, 1923). Fanny Brice, Brooke Johns.

As Long as He Loves Me / From Me to You / It Shouldn't Taste from Herring / Lonesome Cinderella / Russian Art — Lew Brown[w] & James Hanley[m] *(Shapiro, Bernstein)*; Chansonette — Dailey Paskman[w] & Sigmund Spaeth[w] & Irving Caesar[w] & Rudolf Friml[m] *(Harms)*; Dancing Mad — Blanche Merrill[w] & Leo Edwards[m] *(Shapiro, Bernstein)*; Eddie (steady) — Eddie Cantor[w/m] *(Bee-Tee)*; The Fool / Red Light Annie — Benton Ley[w] & Lee David[m] *(Witmark)*; Foolish Child — Jack Nelson[w] & Lindsay McPhail[m] & Roy Bargy[m] *(Curtis)*; I Must Go to Moscow — Mort Dixon[w] & Leon Flatow[m] & Ernest Breuer[m] *(Berlin)*; I Want 'em Wild, Weak, Warm and Willing — Eddie Cantor[w/m] & Sam Coslow[w/m] *(Stark, Cowan)*; I'd Love to Waltz Through Life with You / Lady of the Lantern / That Old Fashioned Garden of Mine — Gene Buck[w] & Victor Herbert[m] *(Harms)*; Little Brown Road — Frank Crumit[w/m] *(Harms)*; Maid of Gold — Gene Buck[w] & Rudolf Friml[m] *(Harms)*; Mary Rose — Gene Buck[w] & Maurice Yvain[m] *(Harms)*; My Girl Uses Mineralava — Eddie Cantor[w/m] *(Cantor)*; Oh! Gee, Oh! Gosh, Oh! Golly I'm in Love — Ole Olson[w] & Chic Johnson[w] & Ernest Breuer[m] *(Berlin)*; Russian Rose — John Winne[w/m] & Ferde Grofe[w/m] & Peter DeRose[w/m] *(Ricordi)*; Shake Your Feet / Swanee River Blues / That Broadway Indian of Mine / Your Eyes Have Told Me — Gene Buck[w] & Dave Stamper[m] *(Harms)*; So This Is Venice — Grant Clarke[w] & Edgar Leslie[w] & Ambrose Thomas[m] *(C and L)*; Sweet Alice — Frank Crumit[w/m] *(Harms)*; Take, Oh Take Those Lips Away — Joseph McCarthy[w] & Harry Tierney[m] *(Feist)*; When Nathan Was Married to Rose of Washington Square — James Kendis[w/m] *(Feist)*; Why Did I Buy That Morris Chair for Morris? — Harry Ruby[w/m] & Bert Kalmar[w/m] & M. Kissen[w/m]

(Berlin). With this edition, the Follies started to go downhill, beginning with all the stars leaving for the movies. This mediocre show was kept on Broadway for nine months because Ziegfeld was going broke and could not afford to mount a road company. COVER: beautiful girls; Brooke Johns; Eddie Cantor; Fannie Brice.

2536 Ziegfeld Follies of 1923 (#18) (second edition) (Broadway, 1923). Brooke Johns, Paul Whiteman.

Ever Lovin' Bee / Shake Your Feet / Swanee River Blues / That Broadway Indian of Mine / Your Eyes Have Told Me So — Gene Buck^w & Dave Stamper^m *(Harms)*; I'd Love to Waltz Through Life with You / That Old Fashioned Garden of Mine — Gene Buck^w & Victor Herbert^m *(Harms)*; Little Brown Road / Sweet Alice — Frank Crumit$^{w/m}$ *(Harms)*; Maid of Gold — Gene Buck^w & Rudolf Friml^m *(Harms)*; Mary Rose — Gene Buck^w & Maurice Yvain^m *(Harms)*. The 18th edition of the Follies was a slightly revised version of the 17th edition. COVER: beautiful girls.

2537 Ziegfeld Follies of 1924 (#18) (second edition) (Broadway, 1924). Brooke Johns, Ann Pennington.

Adoring You / All Pepped Up / In a Big Glass Case / The Key to the Land of the Free / The Old Town Band — Joseph McCarthy^w & Harry Tierney^m *(Feist)*; Biminy / I Believe You / Lonely Little Melody / Montmartre / Rose of My Heart — Gene Buck$^{w/m}$ & Dave Stamper$^{w/m}$ *(Harms)*; Everybody Loves My Baby — Spencer Williams$^{w/m}$ & Jack Palmer$^{w/m}$ *(Williams)*; Not Yet Suzette! — Sam Coslow$^{w/m}$ & Fred Coots$^{w/m}$ *(Remick)*; San — Lindsay McPhail$^{w/m}$ & Walter Michels$^{w/m}$ *(Curtis)*; A Sun-kist Cottage — J. Greer$^{w/m}$ & George Olsen$^{w/m}$ & Louis Hirsch$^{w/m}$ & A. Kilfeather$^{w/m}$ *(Harms)*; Tessie! Stop Teasin' Me — Brooke Johns$^{w/m}$ & Ray Perkins$^{w/m}$ *(Curtis)*. This edition ran for one year which was the longest run of any Follies. It was quite ordinary, however. COVER: Brooke

Johns; George Olsen; designs and lettering; Ann Pennington; a Vargas girl.

2538 Ziegfeld Follies of 1924 (#19) (Broadway, 1924). Brooke Johns, Ann Pennington.

Biminy / Ever Lovin' Bee / I Believe You / Lonely Little Melody / Montmartre / Rose of My Heart — Gene Buck$^{w/m}$ & Dave Stamper$^{w/m}$ *(Harms)*. Ziegfeld continued to reuse material and call his shows *New Editions* or *Summer Editions* to keep them running longer. This edition was called #18 in 1923 and #18 in 1924. COVER: a beautiful Vargas girl with a string of beads.

2539 Ziegfeld Follies of 1924-25 (#19) (second edition) (Broadway, 1924). Ann Pennington, W.C. Fields.

Biminy / Eddie Be Good / I'm Going to Wait Till the Right One Comes Along / In the Shade of the Alamo / Lonely Little Melody / Rose of My Heart — Gene Buck$^{w/m}$ & Dave Stamper$^{w/m}$ *(Harms)*; Settle Down in a Little Town — Gene Buck^w & Werner Janssen^m *(Harms)*; Someone Someday Somewhere — Gene Buck^w & Rudolf Friml^m *(Harms)*; Toddle Along — Gene Buck^w & Dave Stamper^m *(Harms)*. A revised version of the 1924 (#19) show. COVER: Vargas girl with beads.

2540 Ziegfeld Follies of 1925 (new summer edition) (#19) (Broadway, 1925). Ann Pennington, W.C. Fields.

Biminy / Eddie Be Good / Lonely Little Melody / Rose of My Heart / Syncopated Sadie — Gene Buck$^{w/m}$ & Dave Stamper$^{w/m}$ *(Harms)*; In the Shade of the Alamo — Gene Buck$^{w/m}$ & Raymond Hubbell$^{w/m}$ *(Harms)*; Tondeleo — Jack Osterman^w & Gene Buck^w & Dave Stamper^m *(Harms)*. Another revised edition which comes from the 1924-25 (#19) version. COVER: Vargas girl holding beads.

2541 Ziegfeld Follies of 1926 (Wintz) (#20) (Broadway, 1926). Stars unknown.

The Black Bottom Blues — George Wintz & Baldy Wetzel^m *(Wintz)*; Who's That Pretty Baby? — Bobby Heath$^{w/m}$ & Alex Marr$^{w/m}$ *(Joe Morris)*. Due to

Ziegfeld's legal and financial troubles, George Wintz acquired the title *Ziegfeld Follies*. He produced one edition in *Ziegfeld's Follies of 1926* (20th edition). This edition was a cheap imitation on the vaudeville-burlesque level and had a short life. COVER: a bunch of pretty faces.

2542 Ziegfeld Follies of 1926 (Ziegfeld) (#20) (Regional, 1926). James Barton, Ray Dooley.

Monkey Song—Fred Steele[w/m] & Billy Heagney[w/m] *(Steele)*; Nize Baby—Ballard MacDonald[w] & James Hanley[m] *(Shapiro, Bernstein)*. Ziegfeld won his legal battle and regained his title. He toured the Palm Beach Revue as *Ziegfeld Follies of 1926* with the original score plus a few new songs and stars. COVER: beautiful girl; the singing group Yacht Club Boys.

2543 Ziegfeld Follies of 1927 (#21) (Broadway, 1927). Eddie Cantor, Ruth Etting.

Everybody Loves My Girl—Sam Lewis[w] & Joe Young[w] & Maurice Abrahams[m] *(Shapiro, Bernstein)*; It All Belongs to Me / It's Up to the Band / Jimmy / Learn to Sing a Love Song / My New York / Ooh, Maybe It's You / Rainbow of Girls / Shaking the Blues Away—Irving Berlin[w/m] *(Berlin)*; It's Ray-Ray-Raining—Howard Johnson[w/m] & Al Sherman[w/m] & Charles Tobias[w/m] *(Shapiro, Bernstein)*; Let's Misbehave—Cole Porter[w/m] *(Harms)*; She Don't Wanna—Jack Yellen[w] & Milton Ager[m] *(A Y and B)*. This edition was very expensive and Ziegfeld was going broke. The show ran for 20 weeks and Cantor quit because he wanted more money. The show closed and Ziegfeld lost more money. COVER: Eddie Cantor; sketch of a beautiful girl; Cliff Edwards.

2544 Ziegfeld Follies of 1931 (#22) (Broadway, 1931). Ruth Etting, Harry Richman.

Broadway Reverie / Let's K'nock K'nees—Gene Buck[w] & Dave Stamper[m] *(Miller)*; Cigarettes, Cigars! / Your Sunny Southern Smile—Mack Gordon[w] & Harry Revel[m] *(Miller)*; Do the New York / Here We Are in Love / Wrapped Up in You—J.P. Murray[w/m] & Barry Trivers[w/m] & Ben Oakland[w/m] *(Miller)*; Ev'rything Must Have an Ending—Stanley Adams[w] & Nat Osborne[m] & Frank Stillwell[m] *(Marlo)*; Half Caste Woman—Noel Coward[w/m] *(Harms)*; Help Yourself to Happiness—Mack Gordon[w/m] & Harry Revel[w/m] & Harry Richman[w/m] *(Miller)*; I'm Good for Nothing But Love—Pat Ballard[w] & Bernard Maltin[m] *(Harms)*; I'm with You—Walter Donaldson[w/m] *(Donaldson)*; Mailu—E.Y. Harburg[w] & Jay Gorney[m] & Hugo Riesenfeld[m] *(Miller)*; The Picture Bride—Gene Buck[w] & Dave Stamper[m] & Hugo Riesenfeld[m] *(Miller)*; Two Loves—J.P. Murray[w] & Barry Trivers[w] & Vincent Scotto[m] *(Miller)*; Was I?—Chick Endor[w/m] & Charlie Farrell[w/m] *(Miller)*; You're in Ev'ry One's Arms—Al Hoffman[w/m] & Allen Taub[w/m] & Lou Herscher[w/m] *(Kornheiser Music)*. This was the last Follies produced by Ziegfeld and it ran for 20 weeks. It was an ordinary revue and revues were dying out. COVER: a Vargas girl; Helen Morgan; Ruth Etting; Harry Richman.

2545 Ziegfeld Follies of 1934 (#23) (Broadway, 1934). Fanny Brice, Jane Froman.

Careful with My Heart / Rain in My Heart / To the Beat of the Heart—E.Y. Harburg[w] & Samuel Pokrass[m] *(Harms)*; The House Is Haunted—Billy Rose[w] & Basil Adlam[m] *(Donaldson)*; I Can Sew a Button—Sammy Lerner[w] & Gerald Marks[m] *(Caesar)*; I Like the Likes of You / What Is There to Say—E.Y. Harburg[w] & Vernon Duke[m] *(Harms)*; The Last Round-up /Night on the Desert—Billy Hill[w/m] *(Shapiro, Bernstein)*; Moon About Town—E.Y. Harburg[w] & Dana Suesse[m] *(Harms)*; Suddenly—Billy Rose[w] & E.Y. Harburg[w] & Vernon Duke[m] *(Harms)*; This Is Not a Song—E.Y. Harburg[w] & E. Hartman[w] & Vernon Duke[m] *(Harms)*; Wagon Wheels /

Why Am I Blue? — Billy Hill[w] & Peter DeRose[m] *(Shapiro, Bernstein)*; Winter Wonderland — Dick Smith[w/m] & Felix Bernard[w/m] *(Donaldson)*. Ziegfeld's chief rival, the Shuberts, produced this edition after Ziegfeld's death. Though not as lavish as Ziegfeld, the show had some good songs and talent and ran for six months. COVER: Jane Froman; sketch of dancer in brief costume.

2546 Ziegfeld Follies of 1936 (#24) (Broadway, 1936). Eve Arden, Bob Hope.

Economic Situation (New War Situation) [VS] / Fancy, Fancy [VS] / She Hasn't a Thing Except Me! [VS] / Time Marches On [VS] / We Hope You'll Soon Be Dancing to Our Score / We Somehow Feel That You've Enjoyed Our Show [VS] — Ira Gershwin[w] & Vernon Duke[m] *(USO)*; The Gazooka / I Can't Get Started / Island in the West Indies / My Red Letter Day / That Moment of Moments / Words Without Music — Ira Gershwin[w] & Vernon Duke[m] *(Chappell)*; The Harlem Waltz — Richard Jerome[w/m] & Walter Kent[w/m] *(Chappell)*; Midnight Blue — Edgar Leslie[w] & Joe Burke[m] *(Robbins)*; Nice Goin' — Bob Rothberg[w] & Joseph Meyer[m] *(Chappell)*; Ridin' the Rails — Edward Heyman[w] & Harold Spina[m] *(Chappell)*; You Don't Love Right — Tot Seymour[w] & Vee Lawnhurst[m] *(Chappell)*. This edition of the Follies was again produced by the Shuberts. It had some great songs and talented people but closed early due to Fanny Brice's illness. It was recast and opened for a short run of three months. COVER: a silhouette of three dancers.

2547 Ziegfeld Follies of 1943 (#25) (Broadway, 1943). Milton Berle, Ilona Massey.

Come Up and Have a Cup of Coffee / Hold That Smile — Jack Yellen[w] & Ray Henderson[m] *(Harms)*. A mediocre imitation of the revues produced by the Shuberts that somehow ran a year and a half. COVER: Milton Berle; Ilona Massey; Arthur Treacher; and sketch

of dancer.

2548 Ziegfeld Follies of 1955 (Nightclub, 1944). Stars unknown.

Sailor Boys Have Talked to Me in English — Bob Hilliard[w] & Milton DeLugg[m] *(Morris)*. COVER: singer Rosemary Clooney.

2549 Ziegfeld Follies of 1956 (#26) (closed before Broadway, 1956). Tallulah Bankhead, David Burns.

The Lady Is Indisposed [PC] — Joseph McCarthy[w] & Cy Coleman[m] *(Valando)*; A Pretty Girl — Arnold Horwitt[w] & Richard Lewine[m] *(Chappell)*; Runaway [PC] — Floyd Huddleston[w] & Alton Rinker[m] *(Valando)*; Small Winner / What It Was, Was Love — Arnold Horwitt[w] & Albert Hague[m] *(Chappell)*. A dreadful production with lavish settings and nothing else. It folded in Philadelphia. COVER: sketch of show girl in full costume.

2550 Ziegfeld Follies of 1957 (#27) (Broadway, 1957). Beatrice Lillie, Billy DeWolfe.

Mangoes — Sid Wayne[w] & Dee Libbey[m] *(Redd Evans Music)*. Another poor edition of the Follies using the sets and costumes from the folded Tallulah Bankhead version. It ran three months. COVER: a row of show girls.

2551 Ziegfeld Girls of 1920, the New 9 O'Clock Revue (#14) (Broadway, 1920). Lillian Lorraine, W.C. Fields.

Algiers — Joe Meyer[w/m] *(Sherman Clay)*; Dance Dream / Departed Spirits / Emancipation Day / I'm Crazy About Somebody / My Man / Remember Me / Telephone Song / Wonderful Girl — Gene Buck[w/m] & Dave Stamper[w/m] *(Harms)*. A limited run special revue on the New Amsterdam roof. COVER: circular designs and letters.

2552 Ziegfeld Midnight Frolic (#12) (Broadway, 1918). Fannie Brice, Lillian Lorraine.

Baby — Gus Kahn[w] & Egbert Van Alstyne[m] *(Remick)*; Beautiful Girl / By Pigeon Post / Cane Song / Carmen / I Long to Linger Longer, Dearie / I'm Looking for Old Broadway / My Little

Belgian Maid / Ring Those Bells / Springtime / Sweetie Mine / They're Getting Shorter All the Time / Tipperary Mary / When I Hear That Jazz Band Play / When My Sweetie Comes Back to Me — Gene Buck^w & Dave Stamper^m *(Harms)*; One Gozinto Two — Phil Ponce^w/m *(Rock and White)*. A nightclub type entertainment on the roof of the New Amsterdam Theatre. COVER: a large clock with faces; Frances White; Lillian Lorraine; sketch of dancer.

2553 Ziegfeld Midnight Frolic of 1919 (#13) (Broadway, 1919). Fannie Brice, W.C. Fields.

Colonial Days / Shanghai / The World Has Gone Shimmee Mad / You're a Perfect Jewel to Me — Gene Buck^w & Dave Stamper^m *(Harms)*; I Want to Shimmee — Shelton Brooks^w/m & Gran Clarke^w/m *(Feist)*; I'll See You in C-U-B-A — Irving Berlin^w/m *(Berlin)*; It's Nobody's Business But My Own — Will Skidmore^w/m & Marshall Walker^w/m *(Stern)*; Mammy o' Mine — William Tracey^w & Maceo Pinkard^m *(Shapiro, Bernstein)*; You Know What I Mean — Al Dubin^w & Fred Rath^m *(Witmark)*; You'll Find Old Dixieland in France — Grant Clarke^w & George Meyer^m *(Feist)*. A seasonal revue on the New Amsterdam roof. COVER: Kathlene Martyn; Bee Palmer; Jane Greene; Bert Williams; red and black designs.

2554 Ziegfeld Midnight Frolic of 1920 (#14) (Broadway, 1920). Fannie Brice, W.C. Fields.

All the Boys Love Mary — Andrew Sterling^w & Van and Schenck^m *(Von Tilzer)*; Early to Bed and Early to Rise — Alex Gerber^w & Abner Silver^m *(Witmark)*; I Was a Florodora Baby — Ballard MacDonald^w & Harry Carroll^m *(Shapiro, Bernstein)*; In Madagascar Land — L. Wolfe Gilbert^w/m & James Conlin^w/m *(Gilbert)*; Lonesome Alimony Blues — William Tracey^w & James Hanley^m *(Shapiro, Bernstein)*; My Wonder Girl — Art Hickman^w/m & Marty Bloom^w/m & Ben Black^w/m *(Sherman Clay)*; Rockabye Baby — Ballard MacDonald^w & Harry

Piani^m & Sammy Stept^m *(Shapiro, Bernstein)*; Rose of My Heart — Weston Wilson^w & Neil Moret^m *(Feist)*; Rose of Washington Square — Ballard MacDonald^w & James Hanley^m *(Shapiro, Bernstein)*; When Alexander Blues the Blues — Max Freedman^w & Harry Squires^m *(Jack Mills)*; Whispering — Malvin Schonberger^w & John Schonberger^m *(Sherman Clay)*. A revue on the New Amsterdam roof. COVER: Fanny Brice; John Steel; Eddie Cantor; Frances White; Keegan and Edwards.

2555 Ziegfeld Midnight Frolic of 1921 (#15) (Broadway, 1921). Will Rogers, Leon Errol.

Come On, Let's Go! / Honey Bunch / Lovelight / Violet Ray — Gene Buck^w/m & Dave Stamper^w/m *(Harms)*; Day Dreams — Matthew Woodward^w & Robert King^m *(Shapiro, Bernstein)*; Get Hot — Al Siegel^w/m *(Jack Mills)*; Gondolier — Ballard MacDonald^w & Dave Stamper^m *(Harms)*; Sorry for Me — Ben Russell^w & George Bennett^m *(Stasny)*; Springtime / Swinging Along — Gene Buck^w & Dave Stamper^m *(Harms)*. Another annual revue on top of the New Amsterdam Theatre. COVER: beautiful girl; Bee Palmer; Art Hickman Orchestra.

2556 Ziegfeld Midnight Frolic of 1922 (#16) (Broadway, 1922). Ford Dabney Orchestra.

What Could Be Sweeter, Dear — James Murray^w/m & James White^w/m *(White)*. COVER: Margaret Hastings and young couple.

2557 Ziegfeld Midnight Frolic of 1929 (Broadway, 1929). Helen Morgan, Lillian Roth.

Days — Nathan Caress^w & Martin Freed^m & Milton Rosen^m *(Donaldson)*; Looking for Love / Raisin' the Roof / Squeaky Shoes — Dorothy Fields^w & Jimmy McHugh^m *(Mills)*; Maybe, Who Knows? — Johnny Tucker^w/m & Joe Schuster^w/m & Ruth Etting^w/m *(Witmark)*; Who Cares — What You Have Been? — L. Wolfe Gilbert^w & Martin Freed^m *(Feist)*. This revue is listed as a new show "atop the New Amsterdam Theatre." COVER:

Helen Morgan; stars, circles and designs.

2558 Ziegfeld Palm Beach Nights (also called Palm Beach Girl, American Revue and No Foolin') (#20) (Broadway, 1926). Charles King, James Barton.

Every Little Thing You Do / Honey Be Mine — Gene Buck[w] & James Hanley[m] *(Harms)*; Florida, the Moon and You — Gene Buck[w] & Rudolf Friml[m] *(Harms)*; No Foolin' — Gene Buck[w/m] & James Hanley[w/m] *(Harms)*; Wasn't It Nice — Irving Caesar[w] & Rudolf Friml[m] *(Harms)*. This musical was intended to be *Ziegfeld Follies of 1926*; however, Ziegfeld had financial and legal problems and could not use the word *Follies*. So he opened his show in Florida under two different titles. The show toured and became *Ziegfeld's American Revue*. Due to the success of the song *No Foolin'* it opened in New York under that title where it ran for only three months. COVER *(Palm Beach Nights)*: coconut trees and villa by the sea. COVER *(Palm Beach Girl)*: coconut trees and villa by the sea. COVER *(American Revue)*: two gentlemen holding platform with girl in evening gown and crown.

2559 Zip Goes a Million (closed before Broadway, 1919). Harry Fox.

A Business of Our Own / Forget-Me-Not / Give a Little Thought to Me / The Language of Love / Little Back Yard Band / A Man Around the House / Telephone Girls / Whip-Poor-Will / You Tell 'Em — B.G. DeSylva[w] & Jerome Kern[m] *(Harms)*. The last

Princess show; it folded on the road. COVER: black and white cover with titles only.

2560 Zorba (Broadway, 1968). Maria Karnilova, Herschel Bernardi.

The First Time [VS] / Happy Birthday to Me / I Am Free [VS] / No Boom Boom / Only Love / The Top of the Hill [VS] / Why Can't I Speak / Zorba Theme — Fred Ebb[w] & John Kander[m] *(Valando)*; Zorba — John Kander[m] *(Valando)*. A musical adaptation of the popular movie. Though the adaptation had nothing going for it, it ran nine months. COVER: sketch of Zorba standing on his head.

2561 Zorba (Broadway, 1983). Anthony Quinn, Lila Kedrova.

Woman — Fred Ebb[w] & John Kander[m] *(Fiddleback)*. A revival of the 1968 musical with the original movie stars. It toured the whole country and played Broadway for almost a year. COVER: Anthony Quinn.

2562 The Zulu and the Zayda (Broadway, 1965). Menasha Skulnik, Louis Gossett.

Crocodile Wife [VS] / How Cold, Cold, Cold an Empty Room [VS] / It's Good to Be Alive / Like the Breeze Blows / May Your Heart Stay Young [VS] / Out of This World / River of Tears / Some Things [VS] / Trambuza [VS] / The Water Wears Down the Stone [VS] / Zulu Love Song [VS] — Harold Rome[w/m] *(Chappell)*. A play with music dealing with prejudice in South Africa. It ran for almost six months. COVER: special lettering and designs.

Appendix:
Collectors' Groups

There are four collecting groups in the United States. Each group issues periodicals, with two of them holding monthly meetings. Members of these groups meet and correspond with the intention of buying, selling, and trading music in addition to giving and gaining knowledge on the subject.

Anyone who is searching for any of the songs listed in this book could contact any of these groups for information as to how to locate the songs.

Lois Cordrey
Remember That Song
5821 N. 67th Avenue.
Glendale, Arizona 85301
(Monthly Magazine)

Joseph Albertson
Sheet Music Exchange
P.O. Box 2114
Key West, Florida 33045
(Monthly Magazine)

New York Sheet Music Society
P.O. Box 1214
Great Neck, New York 11023
(Monthly newsletter and meetings)

National Sheet Music Society
1597 Fair Park Avenue
Los Angeles, California 90041
(Monthly newsletter and meetings)

Bibliography

Ardoin, John. *The Stage of Menotti*. New York: Doubleday, 1985.

Arnold, Elliott. *Deep in My Heart* (Sigmund Romberg). New York: Duell Sloan and Pearce, 1949.

Baral, Robert. *Revue: A Nostalgic Reprise of the Great Broadway Period*. New York: Fleet, 1962.

Bergreen, Laurence. *As Thousands Cheer* (Irving Berlin). New York: Viking, 1990.

Bloom, Ken. *American Song: The Complete Musical Theatre Companion*. New York: Facts on File, 1985.

Bordman, Gerald. *American Musical Theatre*. New York: Oxford, 1978.

_____. *Jerome Kern: His Life and Music*. New York: Oxford, 1980.

_____ and Vincent Youmans. *Days to Be Happy, Years to Be Sad*. New York: Oxford, 1982.

Burton, Jack. *Blue Book of Broadway Musicals*. New York: Century House, 1951.

Cahn, Sammy. *I Should Care*. New York: Arbor House, 1974.

Clarke, Norman. *The Mighty Hippodrome*. New York: Barnes, 1968.

Dietz, Howard. *Dancing in the Dark*. New York: New York Times Books, 1974.

Duke, Vernon. *Passport to Paris*. Boston: Little, Brown and Co., 1955.

Eells, George. *The Life That Late He Led* (Cole Porter). New York: Putnam, 1967.

Ewen, David. *Richard Rodgers*. New York: Henry Holt, 1957.

Farnsworth, Marjorie. *The Ziegfeld Follies*. London: Peter Davies, 1956.

Fordin, Hugh. *Getting to Know Him* (Oscar Hammerstein). New York: Random House, 1977.

Ganzl, Kurt. *British Musical Theatre*. New York: Oxford, 1986.

Gill, Brendon. *Cole*. New York: Holt Rinehart Winston, 1971.

Gordon, Eric. *Mark the Music* (Marc Blitzstein). New York: St. Martin's Press, 1989.

Green, Stanley. *The World of Musical Comedy*. New York: Ziff Davis, 1960.

Guernsey, Otis and Burns Mantle. *Best Plays* (75 volumes). New York: Dodd Mead and Applause, 1899–1991.

Hart, Dorothy. *Thou Swell, Thou Witty* (Lorenz Hart). New York: Harper, 1976.

_____ and Robert Kimball. *Complete Lyrics of Lorenz Hart*. New York: Knopf, 1986.

Higham, Charles. *Ziegfeld*. Chicago: Regnery, 1972.

Hummel, David. *Collector's Guide to the American Musical Theatre*. Metuchen, N.J.: Scarecrow, 1984.

Jablonski, Edward. *Happy with the Blues* (Harold Arlen). New York: Doubleday, 1961.

_____ and Lawrence Stewart. *The Gershwin Years*. New York: Doubleday, 1958.

Jasen, David. *The Theatre of P.G. Wodehouse*. London: Batsford, 1979.

Kaye, Joseph. *America's Greatest Romantic Composer* (Victor Herbert). New York: Crown, 1931.

Kimball, Robert and William Bolcom. *Reminiscing with Sissle and Blake*. New York: Viking, 1973.

_____ and Alfred Simon. *The Gershwins*. New York: Atheneum, 1973.

Kreuger, Miles. *Show Boat*. New York: Oxford, 1977.

Leonard, William. *Broadway Bound*. Metuchen, N.J.: Scarecrow, 1983.

Lesley, Cole. *Remembered Laughter* (Noel Coward). New York: Knopf, 1976.

Leslie, Peter. *A Hard Act to Follow*. New York: Paddington Press, 1978.

Lewine, Richard and Alfred Simon. *Encyclopedia of Theatre Music*. New York: Bonanza, 1961.

Lingg, Ann. *John Philip Sousa*. New York: Henry Holt, 1954.

McCabe, John. *The Man Who Owned Broadway* (George Cohan). New York: Doubleday, 1973.

McGuire, Patricia. *Lullaby of Broadway* (Al Dubin). Secaucus, N.J.: Citadel, 1983.

McKnight, Gerald. *Andrew Lloyd Webber*. New York: Granada, 1984.

Mander, Raymond and Joe Mitchenson. *Musical Comedy* (London). London: Davies, 1969.

_____ and _____. *Revue in Pictures* (London). New York: Taplinger, 1971.

_____ and _____. *Theatrical Companion to Noel Coward*. New York: Macmillan, 1957.

Marx, Samuel and Jan Clayton. *Bewitched Bothered and Bedeviled*. New York: Putnam, 1976.

Mercer, Ginger and Bob Bach. *Our Huckleberry Friend* (Johnny Mercer). Secaucus, N.J.: Stuart, 1982.

Rodgers, Richard. *Musical Stages*. New York: Random House, 1975.

Sampson, Henry. *Blacks in Blackface*. Metuchen, N.J.: Scarecrow, 1980.

Sanders, Ronald. *The Days Grow Short* (Kurt Weill). New York: Holt Rinehart Winston, 1980.

Schwartz, Charles. *Cole Porter: A Biography*. New York: Dial, 1977.

_____. *Life and Music of Gershwin*. New York: Bobbs Merrill, 1973.

Singer, Harry. *Black and Blue* (Andy Razaf). New York: Schirmer, 1992.

Sobel, Bernard. *Pictorial History of Vaudeville*. New York: Citadel, 1961.

Suskin, Steven. *Berlin, Kern, Rodgers, Hart, and Hammerstein*. Jefferson, N.C.: McFarland, 1990.

_____. *Show Tunes 1905 to 1991*. New York: Limelight, 1992.

Taylor, Theodore. *The Story of Jule Styne*. New York: Random House, 1979.

Thomas, Tony. *Harry Warren and the Hollywood Musical*. Secaucus, N.J.: Citadel, 1975.

Walsh, Michael. *His Life and Works, Andrew Lloyd Webber*. New York: Abrams, 1989.

Willis, John and Daniel Blum. *Theatre World: 48 volumes*. New York: Greenberg, Chilton, Crown, Applause, (1944–1991).

Woll, Allen. *Black Musical Theatre*. Baton Rouge: Louisiana State University, 1989.

Zadan, Craig. *Sondheim and Company*. New York: Macmillan, 1974.

Lyricists and Composers Index

333, 1540, 2454, 2455
Burton, Marion 1067
Burton, Val 1035, 1037
Burwell, Cliff 2186
Busse, Henry 2532
Butler, Ralph 1314, 1478
Butt, Billy 1899
Buzzell, Eddie 524, 2530
Byers, Hale 1792
Byrne, Andrew 1496

Cacoyannis, Michael 1397
Caddigan, Jack 886
Caesar, Irving 60, 178, 183, 276, 339, 376, 418, 524, 550, 597, 770, 781, 836, 879, 889, 890, 891, 992, 1014, 1018, 1013, 1122, 1147, 1235, 1236, 1255, 1257, 1345, 1359, 1367, 1418, 1490, 1495, 1577, 1631, 1634, 1644, 1648, 1651, 1653, 1654, 1812, 1841, 1840, 1857, 1863, 1954, 1974, 2103, 2172, 2238, 2258, 2275, 2332, 2364, 2382, 2457, 2464, 2488, 2508, 2535, 2558
Cahn, Sammy 440, 489, 703, 720, 812, 857, 859, 1002, 1053, 1055, 1161, 1353, 1945, 2119, 2386, 2426
Calahan, Will 896
Caldwell, Anne 304, 321, 333, 415, 418, 504, 745, 835, 943, 1016, 1120, 1255, 1412, 1444, 1620, 1636, 1689, 1806, 2005, 2006, 2066, 2200, 2257, 2317, 2344, 2526
Callahan, Will 1791

Calloway, Cab 476, 480, 2186
Calvi, Gerard 899
Camby, Leo 886
Camp, Shep 836, 914, 1978
Campbell, David 1050
Campbell, Elaine 77
Campbell, Jimmy 608, 2508
Campbell, Norman 77
Cantor, Eddie 1218, 1418, 1514, 1794, 2464, 2529, 2530, 2531
Cantor, Sam 1219, 1220
Capote, Truman 1063, 1064
Caress, Nathan 2557
Carhart, Jim 844
Carle, Richard 58
Carlo, Monte 316, 396, 604, 624, 1066, 1360, 1596, 1688, 1863, 1874, 2278, 2420
Carlton, Carle 1244, 1771, 1772, 2278
Carlton, Hector 2199
Carmelia, Craig 2495
Carmichael, Hoagy 23, 30, 720, 2086, 2186, 2316
Carmines, Al 1800, 1881
Carr, Leon 2037
Carr, Michael 1697
Carroll, Albert 853, 854, 856
Carroll, Carroll 390
Carroll, Earl 597, 598, 600, 601, 612, 1260
Carroll, Harry 225, 315, 539, 638, 665, 772, 894, 939, 1015, 1137, 1311, 1765, 1835, 2554, 2532
Carroll, June 1110, 1615, 1616, 1617, 1618, 1619
Carroll, Lewis 28

Carroll, Pauline 225
Carroll, R. 273
Carter, Desmond 256, 427, 502, 711, 871, 990, 1148, 1227, 1247, 1334, 1785, 1809, 1872, 2233, 2239, 2292, 2364, 2507
Carter, Lou 47
Carter, Sydney 117
Carvalho, Claire 1755
Caryll, Fred 1807
Caryll, Ivan 333, 794, 1061, 1236, 1324, 2344
Casey, Warren 865
Cavanaugh, James 2464
Caymmi, Corival 2184
Chakraband, A. 1512
Chamberlain, Ida 628
Chancer, Charles 64
Chaplin, Sid 251, 489, 703, 857, 859, 1053, 1055, 1945
Charig, Philip 45, 59, 109, 710, 891, 1200, 1647, 1690, 1761, 1857, 2025, 2033, 2075, 2250, 2301, 2330, 2508
Charlap, Moose 457, 1161, 1215, 1820, 1823, 2072, 2463
Charles, Milton 105, 1130
Charnin, Martin 79, 84, 137, 677, 1059, 1092, 2209, 1467, 1837, 2138, 2379, 2528
Cherniavsky, Joseph 2318
Chilton, Charles 1695
Chisholm, Hazel 1302
Chodosh, Richard 2214
Chopin, Frederic 381, 1861
Christine, H. 1601

Christy, Harold 1218, 1574
Church, Harden 363
Churchill, A. 825
Churchill, Frank 825, 2134
Clapson, A. 1939
Clare, Sidney 609, 772, 1514, 1793, 1853, 1978, 2304, 2452
Claret, Gaston 454
Clark, Cumberland 315
Clark, Dorothy 2344
Clark, Edward 415, 804, 1323, 1391, 1693, 1694
Clark, H. Knight 1079
Clarke, Grant 214, 249, 276, 565, 622, 1849, 2041, 2095, 2553, 2532, 2535
Clarke, Harry 333, 1146, 1436, 2290
Clarke, Urana 338
Cleary, Michael 119, 593, 606, 608, 995, 1038, 1039, 2032, 2075, 2283, 2310
Clements, Otis 1137
Cleveland, Del 2033
Cliff, Laddie 2507
Clifford, John 436
Clifford, William 1598
Clifton, John 1429
Coates, Eric 2457
Cobb, George 2344
Cobb, Will 539, 738, 901, 902, 2532
Cobey, Lou 1631
Coburn, Richard 353, 1033
Cocharane, Nick 12
Cochran, Dorcas 599
Coghill, Melville 337
Cohan, George M. 192, 768, 794, 1326, 1503, 1958, 1991, 2420
Cohan, Phil 595

Song Index

Jolly Roger 2504
Joseph and the
  Amazing Techni-
  color Dream-
  coat — Score 1179
Joseph's Dreams
  1179
Josephine 8, 1645,
  2094
Joshua 2446
Journey of a Life-
  time 114
Journey to the
  Heavy Side
  Layer 361
Journey's End 321,
  418, 1988, 2397
Joy 921
Joy Bells 161
Joy Out of Life
  2231
Joyful Noise 1182
Juarez and Lincoln
  1622
Juba 593
Jubilation T. Corn-
  pone 1304
Jubilee 1078
Jubilee Joe 1928
Jubilo 1620, 2066
Judgement of Paris
  961
Judy 1138
Judy, Who D'ya
  Love 1184
Jug of Wine 535
Juggling 669
Juke Box Saturday
  Night 2196
Julianne 628
Julie and Her
  Johnnies 333
Julie Is Mine 393
Julie's Lament 2080
Julie-Oolio-Oolio-
  Oo 14
Jump de Broom
  1064
Jump for Joy 1190
Jumpin' Jive 480
Jumping Jiminy
  2212
Jumping to the
  Jukebox 2116,
  2190
June 2448
June Days 1192
June Is Bustin' Out
  All Over 350
June Love 405,
  1193

June Moon 1194,
  1793
June, My Honey-
  moon Girl 963
Jungle Bungalow
  1841
Jungle Drums
  1195
Jungle Rose 1917
Jungletown Has
  Moved to Dix-
  ieland 565
Jungoland 1176
Jupiter Forbid 46,
  312, 313
Just a Bunch of
  Wild Flowers
  1598
Just a Cozy Hide-
  away 1431
Just a Crazy Song
  221, 289
Just a Friend of
  Mine 1875
Just a Girl Just a
  Boy 1971
Just a Housewife
  2495
Just a Kiss 1685
Just a Kiss Apart
  766
Just a Little After
  Taps 626
Just a Little Bit
  More 2191
Just a Little Bit of
  Driftwood 837,
  2464
Just a Little Blue
  for You 1208
Just a Little Joint
  with a Juke Box
  175
Just a Little
  Laughter 814
Just a Little Line
  2066
Just a Little Love
  855, 1725
Just a Little Love-
  song 258
Just a Little Smile
  from You 2091
Just a Little Thing
  Called Rhythm
  2238
Just a Little Touch
  of Paris 625
Just a Memory 1431
Just a Pretty Little
  Home 11

Just a Regular Girl
  243
Just a Sentimental
  Tune 2283
Just an Honest
  Mistake 1289
Just an Hour of
  Love 306
Just as Long as
  You Have
  Me 793, 1362
Just Ask for Joe
  330
Just Because 1199
Just Because I
  Looked at You
  1452
Just Between the
  Two of Us 1844
Just Beyond the
  Rainbow 99
Just Cross the
  River from
  Queens 318
Just for Once 1931
Just for the Bride
  and Groom 924
Just for the
  Moment 1070
Just for the Ride
  786
Just for Today 986
Just for Tonight
  370, 1861, 1205,
  2309
Just for You and
  You Alone 1991
Just Go to the
  Movies 536,
  1163
Just Hello 719
Just Imagine 837,
  838, 1197
Just in Love with
  Me 2357
Just in Time 166,
  1789
Just Like a Dia-
  mond 2355
Just Like a Doll
  2179
Just Like a Dream
  809
Just Like a Gipsy
  1245
Just Like a Man
  2251, 2386
Just Like a Rose
  840
Just Like That 536
Just Like the

House That Jack
  Built 414
Just Like the Sun-
  shine 2362
Just Like the Wild,
  Wild Rose 2272
Just Like You 2382
Just Listen to My
  Heartbeat 181
Just Married 1201
Just Mention Joe
  330
Just Met a Friend
  from My Home-
  town 291
Just My Luck 246,
  261, 1277, 1608
Just Once Around
  the Clock 1469
Just One Kiss 1363
Just One More
  Waltz with You
  1046, 1416
Just One of Those
  Things 1183, 1628
Just One Person
  2133
Just One Rose 396
Just One Way to
  Say I Love You
  1525
Just One You 435,
  529
Just Plant a Kiss
  1248
Just Round the
  Corner 1746
Just Say Goodbye
  800, 1611
Just Say the Word
  22, 1057, 1383,
  2009
Just Say When
  2441
Just Sit Around
  1800
Just Snap Your
  Fingers at Care
  887
Just Squeeze Me
  2166
Just Suppose 236,
  1853
Just Sweet Sixteen
  887
Just the Two of Us
  1245
Just the Way You
  Are 597
Just to Be a Little
  Boy Again 120